ERA OF EXCESS

ERA
OF EXCESS

A SOCIAL HISTORY OF THE
PROHIBITION MOVEMENT

By
ANDREW SINCLAIR

WITH A PREFACE BY RICHARD HOFSTADTER

Illustrated

HARPER COLOPHON BOOKS

**Harper & Row, Publishers
New York and Evanston**

This book was first published by Little, Brown & Company in 1962 under the title *Prohibition: The Era of Excess* and is here reprinted by arrangement.

First HARPER COLOPHON edition
published 1964 by Harper & Row, Publishers, Incorporated
New York, Evanston, and London

LIBRARY OF CONGRESS CATALOG CARD NUMBER: 62-8071

To My Mother

Preface

A GOOD HISTORIAN, set loose on a good subject, will trace out the pattern not only of his subject itself but also of the whole social fabric into which it is woven. It is so here with Andrew Sinclair. His foreground is the American experiment with prohibition — one of the most instructive episodes in our history — and he has given us not only the best account of this experiment but also one of the most illuminating commentaries on our society, for he deals with the ramifications of the alcohol problem on our politics and religion, our law and medicine, our city and country life, our guilts and fears, our manners and morals.

"The Era of Excess" is the characterization Mr. Sinclair gives to the unhappy episode with which he deals; and he has realized brilliantly the implications of the central term, "excess." He sees the incredibly naïve effort to fix a ban on drinking into the Constitution itself as a final assertion of the rural Protestant mind against the urban and polyglot culture that had emerged at the end of the nineteenth century and the beginning of the twentieth. This assertion, though it flew in the face of history and human nature, was temporarily successful because it was carried out by the drys with major organizing gifts and incredible zeal and because it was linked with a passion for reform that swept the country in the years before World War I.

Like others who have written on prohibition, Mr. Sinclair sees in it a kind of Protestant revival which led to a crusade against the saloon. But he sees also, as many have failed to see, that this crusade became a war of extermination partly because the churches and the saloons were rivals in the same business — the business of consolation. The cause of prohibition was pressed forward with the unbridled ruthlessness of those who are absolutely sure that their cause is just and that it can be carried to the point of total victory. The prohibitionists did not mean to limit or control the evils of alcohol: they meant to stamp them out altogether. Reformers who begin with the determination to stamp out sin usually end by stamping out sinners, and Mr. Sinclair is sensitive to the ironies, sometimes amusing but sometimes terrible, to which this effort at total reform could lead. Before prohibition became law, the prohibitionists decried alcohol as a form of deadly poison.

After prohibition was law, they approved the legal poisoning of industrial alcohol, knowing full well that men would die from drinking it. Excess had this way of turning things into their opposites: an amenity became a crime; the imposition of controls led to a loss of control; the churches created gangsters; reformers became reactionaries; purifiers became poisoners. Excess also made it impossible for the politicians to fulfill their customary function of compromising opposed interests and mediating between extremes. That some men may live by principle is possible only because others live by compromise. Excess destroyed this nice symbiosis: it converted the politician into a bogus man of principle, a breed of hypocrite who voted one way while he drank the other.

To me one of the freshest and most illuminating aspects of Mr. Sinclair's book is his study of the way in which the movement for prohibition mobilized popular guilts and fears — an aspect of the movement which other historians have hardly done more than touch upon. Prohibition could be made an outlet for the troubles of every cramped libido. In an earlier day, anti-Catholicism had served as the pornography of the puritan: the inhibited mind had wallowed in tales of errant priests and nuns. During the prohibition movement both prurience and fear were exploited by those who dwelt on the linkage of alcohol and sexual excess, or on the fear of insanity and racial degeneracy, even of the racial self-assertion of the Negro. Mr. Sinclair has given us a full and instructive exploration of the medical and sexual mythology of prohibitionism.

But Mr. Sinclair is a humane historian, and he has not written his book to ridicule or belittle prohibitionists or as an ex parte plea for the wets. He is far from blind to whatever there was of validity in the case of the drys. The old-time saloon — particularly, he believes, in the rural areas and the small towns — was often a filthy and repulsive place. He observes that the wets also responded to the era of excess by making claims for the benefits of repeal as absurd as the earlier promises of the drys. And, above all, he is careful to remind us that alcoholism today is a serious medical and social problem. The dry lobbies had saddled the country with a vicious and ineffective reform; Mr. Sinclair concludes that the wet lobbies performed a similar if less sweeping disservice to the country by insisting upon absolute repeal, and thus replacing overstrained and ineffective controls with no federal controls at all. Some readers may quarrel with this and other conclusions, but I doubt that informed students of Americana will quarrel with the judgment that he has given us the definitive study of prohibition for our generation.

RICHARD HOFSTADTER

Contents

Illustrations

xi

ERA OF EXCESS

Prologue

When deplorable excesses happen, I hear many cry, "Would there were no wine! O folly! O madness!" Is it the wine which causes this abuse? No. If you say, "Would there were no wine!" because of drunkards, then you must say, going on by degrees, "Would there were no night!" because of thieves, "Would there were no light!" because of informers, and "Would there were no women!" because of adultery.

St. John Chrysostom

The Saloon Bar

A bar to heaven, a door to hell —
Whoever named it, named it well!
A bar to manliness and wealth,
A door to want and broken health,
A bar to honor, pride and fame,
A door to sin and grief and shame;
A bar to hope, a bar to prayer,
A door to darkness and despair,
A bar to honored, useful life,
A door to brawling, senseless strife;
A bar to all that's true and brave,
A door to every drunkard's grave,
A bar to joy that home imparts,
A door to tears and aching hearts;
A bar to heaven, a door to hell —
Whoever named it, named it well!

Anonymous

THE SUCCESS of those who wanted to prohibit the liquor trade in the United States seems inexplicable now. As Jonathan Daniels wrote of his father, Josephus, Woodrow Wilson's Secretary of the Navy, "I doubt that any later generation will quite be able to understand the prohibitionists. I do not. I do know that my father . . . brought to the prohibition movement hope and sincerity."[1] Yet it is in

3

this capacity to inspire hope and sincerity in intelligent men that understanding of the prohibition movement lies. Many Victorians felt in all honesty that progress and science, reform and learning were on the side of prohibition. The new and fashionable science of eugenics, developed by Sir Francis Galton, seemed to point towards the elimination of alcohol in order to improve the race. The progressive movement sided with the prohibitionists in trying to get rid of the corrupt city machines and the vice areas based on the saloons. Most medical research seemed to be in favor of the banning of liquor for the sake of health and hygiene. The social work carried out by the settlements in the slums found drink as much an enemy as poverty and often pointed to the connection between the two evils. The rising tide of women's rights seemed to make prohibition certain; a woman's vote was presumed to be a vote against the saloon. Even before the Great War identified beer drinkers with Germans and the Kaiser, the consumer of alcohol appeared a reactionary. His selfish imbibing was a last protest against progress, a deliberate effort to weaken his children and deny the future.

The success of the prohibitionists is, in fact, easier to understand than their defeat would have been. For they had control of the best part of the communications of the time. They had organization, money, and a purpose. The leaders of opinion were often on their side. They had been indoctrinating the young for thirty years in the public schools and through their mothers. History, optimism, and improvement were their supporters. With hope and sincerity, the prohibitionists looked forward to a world free from alcohol and, by that magic panacea, free also from want and crime and sin, a sort of millennial Kansas afloat on a nirvana of pure water.

The prohibitionists had no doubt that they would win their battle against the demon drink. Not only was God behind them, but also history. By the time of the Civil War, thirteen states had tried prohibition laws. Although this number shrank to three after the war, five more states joined their ranks after 1880. Again the second wave of prohibition receded until only three states remained, but the third wave engulfed the nation. The foundation of the Woman's Christian Temperance Union and of the Anti-Saloon League before the close of the nineteenth century gave the prohibitionists a disciplined army, ready to exploit politics and the American people in the interests of their chosen reform. The refusal of the liquor trade to regulate the saloons of its own accord and the national psychology created by the First World War were sufficient to give victory to the prohibitionists. From January 16, 1920, until December 5, 1933, a period of nearly fourteen years, the American people were forbidden by the Eighteenth Amendment of their own Constitution to manufacture, sell, or transport any intoxicating liquor. Although no one was forbidden to buy or drink intoxicating liquor, the Volstead Act, passed by Congress to enforce the Eighteenth Amendment, tried to prevent the illegal trade in liquor. It failed, and national prohibition also failed. The origins, politics, lessons, and results of that failure are the matter of this book.

The questions which occupied the American people in the first three decades of this century were not the questions which occupied their Presidents. While the White House was concerned with trusts and taxation and tariffs and foreign affairs, the people worried over prohibition and Romanism and fundamentalism and immigration and the growing power of the cities of the United States. These worries lay under the surface of all political conflicts. For the old America of the villages and farms distrusted the new America of the urban masses. Prohibition was the final victory of the defenders of the American past. On the rock of the Eighteenth Amendment, village America made its last stand. As Walter Lippmann commented in 1927:

> The evil which the old-fashioned preachers ascribe to the Pope, to Babylon, to atheists, and to the devil, is simply the new urban civilization, with its irresistible scientific and economic and mass power. The Pope, the devil, jazz, the bootleggers, are a mythology which expresses symbolically the impact of a vast and dreaded social change. The change is real enough. . . . The defense of the Eighteenth Amendment has, therefore, become much more than a mere question of regulating the liquor traffic. It involves a test of strength between social orders, and when that test is concluded, and if, as seems probable, the Amendment breaks down, the fall will bring down with it the dominion of the older civilization. The Eighteenth Amendment is the rock on which the evangelical church militant is founded, and with it are involved a whole way of life and an ancient tradition. The overcoming of the Eighteenth Amendment would mean the emergence of the cities as the dominant force in America, dominant politically and socially as they are already dominant economically.[2]

The Eighteenth Amendment was repealed by the Twenty-first. The old order of the country gave way to the new order of the cities. Rural morality was replaced by urban morality, rural voices by urban voices, rural votes by urban votes. A novel culture of skyscrapers and suburbs grew up to oust the civilization of the general store and Main Street. A technological revolution broadcast a common culture over the various folkways of the land. It is only in context of this immense social change, the metamorphosis of Abraham Lincoln's America into the America of Franklin Roosevelt, that the phenomenon of national prohibition can be seen and understood. It was a part of the whole process, the last hope of the declining village. It was less of a farce than a tragedy, less of a mistake than a proof of changing times. The right of the new to their novelties is no more sacred than the right of the old to their nostalgias. The great error was, as H. G. Wells said, the "crowning silliness" of writing a liquor law into the national Constitution.

Note on Vocabulary

Prohibition seems so long past that even its vocabulary has largely disappeared. In this study, various terms are used which were once current. They are defined here.

Alky Cooker	A distiller of homemade alcohol
Ardent Spirits, John Barleycorn, Rum	Nineteenth-century terms for all hard liquor
Blind Pig, Blind Tiger	An unlicensed saloon
Bootleg, Booze, Canned Heat, Home-Brew, Hooch, Moonshine, Shine, Smoke	Various types of illegal liquor made before, during, and after national prohibition
Bootlegger	A maker and distributor of bootleg liquor
Dispensary System	The sale of liquor through state-owned retail liquor stores
Dry	A supporter of prohibition
High-License System	A policy of charging the owners of saloons a large annual tax in order to regulate the number of saloons
Hijacker	A robber of a bootlegger
Local Option	An election in which communities could vote to close up the saloons within their area
Modification	A change in the wording of the Volstead Act to allow the manufacture and sale of light wines and beer
Prohibition	The banning by statutory or constitutional law of the saloons and/or of the liquor trade and/or of all liquor; also a psychological attitude favoring legal coercion on moral grounds
Repeal	The repeal of the Eighteenth Amendment by another amendment to the Constitution
Rum Row	A line of liquor ships outside United States territorial waters
Saloon	A legal drinking place between the Civil War and the Volstead Act
Speak-easy	An illegal drinking place during the period of national prohibition
Wet	An opponent of prohibition

PART 1

The Roots of Prohibition

CHAPTER 1

God Made the Country

In the last fifty years a vast change has taken place in the lives of our people. A revolution has in fact taken place. The coming of industrialism, attended by all the roar and rattle of affairs, the shrill cries of millions of new voices that have come among us from over seas, the going and coming of trains, the growth of cities, the building of the interurban car lines that weave in and out of towns and past farmhouses, and now in these later days the coming of the automobiles has worked a tremendous change in the lives and in the habits of thought of our people of Mid-America. Books, badly imagined and written though they may be in the hurry of our times, are in every household, magazines circulate by the millions of copies, newspapers are everywhere. In our day a farmer standing by the stove in the store of his village has his mind filled to overflowing with the words of other men. The newspapers and the magazines have pumped him full. Much of the old brutal ignorance that had in it also a kind of beautiful childlike innocence is gone forever. The farmer by the stove is brother to the men of the cities, and if you listen you will find him talking as glibly and as senselessly as the best city man of us all.

SHERWOOD ANDERSON
Winesburg, Ohio, 1919

The vices of the cities have been the undoing of past empires and civilizations. It has been at the point where the urban population outnumbers the rural people that wrecked Republics have gone down. There the vices of luxury have centered and eaten out the heart of the patriotism of the people, making them the easy victims of every enemy. The peril of this Republic likewise is now clearly seen to be in her cities. There is no greater menace to democratic institutions than the great segregation of an element which gathers its ideas of patriotism and citizenship from the low grogshop and which has proved its enmity to organized civil government. Already some of our cities are well-nigh submerged with this unpatriotic element, which is manipulated by the still baser element engaged in the un-American drink traffic and by the kind of politician the saloon creates. The saloon stands for the worst in

9

political life. All who stand for the best must be aggressively against it. If our Republic is to be saved the liquor traffic must be destroyed.

PURLEY A. BAKER
The Anti-Saloon League Yearbook, 1914

THE FIRST American colonists brought over the doctrine that country and village life were good, while city life was wicked. The sturdy yeoman farmer was considered to be the backbone of England, the essential fodder of her army. The creeping enclosures which displaced the farmers from the earth of England were evil, as were the land speculators and absentee owners, corrupted by the luxuries of the Court and of the great wen, London. The city was the home of vice, and the royal palace hid covert Popery. It was to flee these persecuting enemies that the *Mayflower* crossed the first frontier, the Atlantic Ocean.

In the new colonies, however, the courts and cities grew again. They were the center of British government, garrisoned by British troops, filled with grogshops and brothels. The aristocrats of America lived there. But nine out of ten Americans lived on the farms, and their brief incursions into the cities only confirmed their prejudice against the urban Satan. When the American Revolution broke out, the battle lines quickly set themselves up along the division of piedmont and tidewater, except in New England, where there was a strong sense of community between town and country. The British could hold the ports and major cities. Tories who fled there would find protection. Meanwhile, the colonists held the back country, and could gain victories whenever the British ventured out of the cities. Even if the American colonists won the war because of the intervention of the French fleet, the surrender of Yorktown still seemed to be more the triumph of the farmer than of the seaman.

The new Constitution carefully protected the rights of the country. The composition of the Senate settled to this day the unfair representation of the country at the expense of the city. The new capitals of the state governments were founded far from urban mob and power, in isolated villages, such as Albany or Harrisburg. And American writers, politicians, and philosophers, secure in the comfort of urban life, created a eulogy of rural virtues which was accepted across the length and breadth of America as the truth, even when industrial might and agrarian depression had turned the flattery into a falsehood.

The first of the major revolutions of modern times was the agrarian.

It preceded the Industrial Revolution. The urban masses which manned the factories could not have been fed without improved methods of agriculture. Thus the radicals and intellectuals of the eighteenth century were interested in farming as the newest and most progressive of the sciences. Benjamin Franklin and the American Philosophical Society, George Washington and Thomas Jefferson all proselytized the farming discoveries of Arthur Young and Lord Townshend. Agricultural societies, fairs, and journals sprang up across America. To be a farmer at the time was to be in the forefront of science and progress. It was also to be better than the city dweller.

The French *philosophes* had made fashionable the doctrine that man's nature was good although the corruption of society had turned him evil. Therefore, the man closest to nature was the least corrupt. He was freer than the townsman because he was economically independent, and more important because his toil satisfied man's first need, the need for food. Jefferson put forward this creed clearly in his *Notes on Virginia*.

> Those who labor in the earth are the chosen people of God, if ever He had a chosen people, whose breasts He has made His peculiar deposit for substantial and genuine virtue. It is the focus in which He keeps alive that sacred fire, which otherwise might escape from the face of the earth. Corruption of morals in the mass of cultivators is a phenomenon of which no age nor nation has furnished an example.[1]

The radical intellectuals of nineteenth-century Europe turned to praise the machine rather than the plow. Karl Marx approved of the conquest of the country by the bourgeois cities, and the rescue of the villagers of Europe "from the seclusion and ignorance of rural life."[2] But America remained largely an agricultural nation. Politicians and novelists were quick to praise the majority of the American people. Nativity in a log cabin was considered to be part of the availability of Presidents. When a candidate for the White House did not have the necessary uncivilized background, such as General William Henry Harrison in 1840, his party manufactured a rude childhood for him. Meanwhile, a long line of writers from James Fenimore Cooper to William Dean Howells hymned the Eden of the wilderness and the Canaan of the village. Moreover, Mark Twain made fun of Hannibal, Missouri, only to show his love for the place. Not until the end of the century and the publication of Edgar Watson Howe's *The Story of a Country Town* and of Hamlin Garland's *Main-Travelled Roads* was there a serious effort to picture the bleakness and squalor of life on the farm and frontier. Indeed, these two books were viciously attacked by the literary critics, who were deceived by the Western myth into thinking that the farmer's life was a mixture of cornhusking, roast pork, and contented cows. Garland pointed out that farmers hated milking and hogs, and that their most common neighbors were army worms, flies, mosquitoes, heat, and the smell of manure. Those who actually lived in the prairies supported him. One woman wrote, "You are entirely right about the loneliness, the stagnation, the hardship. We are sick of lies. Give the world the truth."[3] Yet even Garland ended his life the victim of the lies which he had tried to correct, writing sugary flatteries of farm life for urban magazines.

As Sinclair Lewis said in his acceptance speech before the Nobel Prize committee, it was an "American tragedy that in our land of freedom, men like Garland, who first blast the roads to freedom, become themselves the most bound." It was another American tragedy that the cities, made by men, first fostered and then destroyed the myth that God had made the country.

THE WEST AND "THE ENEMY'S COUNTRY"

THE FRONTIER was the American dream. And dreams are not seen in their everyday dreariness and dullness. The frontiersmen themselves were too preoccupied with survival to report their disillusion. They needed, too, the justification of their own virtue to make their drudgery and hardship bearable. They believed that large profits and the good life were to be found in the country; and if they did not find these things in one piece of country, they must move their wagons to another, not back to the evil cities, which could only offer them jobs as unskilled workers. "A mighty spreading and shifting" went on all over the West.[4] Jefferson had forecast that the small farmer would take a thousand years to settle the land as far as the Pacific. A hundred years was too little for the restless frontiersman, searching endlessly for a perfection in nature that was never there, and for speculative profits in land which often he did not bother to cultivate properly. For the farmer was a businessman first and foremost, even if his toil was held to be particularly blessed by God.

The only news from the West that reached the cities was exciting. Circuses and Buffalo Bill Cody and the heroic tales of the Methodist and Baptist circuit riders who rode with the Gospel in their saddlebags — all these meant a land of adventure.[5] The picture was gilded by the reports of railroad companies and shipping lines, land speculators and small-town boomers, who advertised easy harvests and quick profits and free land. Agricultural journals and local newspapers frantically painted the Western skies into the colors of a peacock's tail to keep old settlers where they were and to attract fresh ones. For if a small town did not grow, it was abandoned; Iowa, in less than a hundred years, held more than two thousand deserted settlements. Thus the actual settlers of the West were forced to gild the country myth still more to attract the new peasant immigrants from Germany and Ireland and Scandinavia.[6] It was enough to lure immigrants out West. They usually came with too little money to be able to afford the return fare. In fact, colorful lying became so much a part of the frontier that it took on the trappings of virtue. In Texas to this day, exaggeration in the interest of the state is considered to be a truer version of the truth. A roving Texan is his country's ambassador, sent to lie abroad.

The West was peopled rapidly by a race of farmers and speculators and refugees. If the farmers' dream of the frontier turned sour, the fact of their flight from Europe and the Eastern cities still stayed with them. Their hope in Western land and easy money was often killed by the sufferings inflicted by nature, but their hatred of the past only grew. For the settlers were the disinherited of the cities, those disowned by urban civilization, displaced by industry. They fled to an agricultural myth which told them that their exclusion was a successful repudiation of wealth and aristocracy and luxury. Farmers were the only true democrats. They were the representatives of the best in the American tradition. The cities held the idle rich and the owners of mortgages and the dregs of Europe. When William Jennings Bryan denounced the East as "the enemy's country," he voiced a rural prejudice older than the Declaration of Independence.

Both the hardness of existence and the simple religion brought to the West by the Baptist and Methodist missionaries buttressed the fears of the settlers. The world around them was a world of simple divisions, a world of land and sky, stone and earth, drought and rain, hail and calm, night and day. The Manichaeanism of fundamental religion, with its clear-cut right and wrong, and good and evil, fitted into a landscape of hard and infinite definitions. In the midst of suffering and toil and frequent death, the pastoral religion and patriarchal law of the Old Testament peculiarly suited the pioneers. The ritualistic faiths of Episcopalianism and Judaism and Roman Catholicism, with their ceremonies and ranks, seemed only to confirm the Westerner's view of the oppressive cities. But the simple creeds of Methodism, Baptism, Presbyterianism, and Congregationalism, with their emphasis on individual toil and the Bible and hell and hope of heaven, seemed to be the rough and democratic faiths needed in the mountains and prairies of the West.

Willa Cather, in a series of novels, described the hard truth of the frontier. She spoke of that Nebraska which produced the great flatterer of the West and champion of prohibition, William Jennings Bryan. In her *O Pioneers!* she wrote of the sad wilderness and isolation which drove the settlers into harsh fundamentalism. A boy was leaving the small town of Hanover, Nebraska, with his family on a horse-drawn cart.

> The little town behind them had vanished as if it had never been, had fallen behind the swell of the prairie, and the stern frozen country received them into its bosom. The homesteads were few and far apart; here and there a windmill gaunt against the sky, a sod house crouching in a hollow. But the great fact was the land itself, which seemed to overwhelm the little beginnings of human society that struggled in its somber wastes. It was from facing this vast hardness that the boy's mouth had become so bitter; because he felt that men were too weak to make any mark here, that the land wanted to be let alone, to preserve its own fierce strength, its peculiar, savage kind of beauty, its uninterrupted mournfulness.[7]

Suffering bred political radicalism in the great plains of the West.[8] The discontent born of poverty and unending labor forged the farmers' organizations of protest, the Grange and the Farmers' Alliance, the Populist movement, the Farmers' Union and the Non-Partisan League.* The ideology of these movements was a peculiar mixture of reaction, xenophobia, and progressiveness. But above all, this ideology was set in terms of black and white. In the days of Jackson, it was the Bank of the United States which was held solely responsible for the slump in the West. Later the Jews, the Roman Catholics, Wall Street, gold, the immigrants, the railroads, the trusts, the Huns, and the Reds all became the necessary scapegoats for Western ills. The rural radicals rarely admitted the guilty truth, that their own plundering of the land and heavy borrowing from the banks of the East had caused many of the sufferings which they sought to blame on others.

There is a traditional theory of conspiracy at the grass roots of American politics.[9] It was at first the product of geography and hardship and religion. Later, when farming in the prairies became dependent on urban and international markets after 1850, the money power of the East grew into a real enemy, capable of ruining farmers surely and inexorably. Commercialization, specialization, business methods, new machinery, improved communications, the mail-order catalogues called "wishing books," all destroyed the self-sufficiency of farm and village and made them dependent on the wicked city. Bryan's campaign for free silver in the presidential election of 1896 was less an economic

---

* Strangely enough, the farm movements were led by city reformers. Not one of the seven founders of the Grange was a farmer by occupation for more than a short period of his life. Between 1892 and 1932, not a single farmer was elected to Congress. In fact, the leaders of rural reform movements often knew too little of rural reality to disbelieve the myths which inspired the movements.

matter than an expression of the rural hatred of Eastern financiers, who waxed fat under the mysterious protection of the devilish gold standard.

It was in this atmosphere of struggle against unyielding soil and of crusade against Eastern capital that the prohibition agitators flourished. For they presented the fight of God against the saloon in the simple terms of right and wrong. Drunkenness was a prevalent and dangerous vice of the frontier. Men who drank frequently lost ground in the battle against the elements. An isolated farmer who rode twenty miles to the nearest saloon might die of exposure if fatigue made him sleep during his return. The lumber camps and mining towns of the Far West were packed with saloons and brothels, crooks and whores, who kept the woodsmen and miners in a state of continual poverty and fleeced any stray countryman who came their way. Farmers' wives, who had to remain in isolation and terror on the farm with small children, grew to hate the saloons, which kept their husbands in the villages and took away their money. There was also envy in their hatred. For they had no relief from the endless chores of farm women: tailoring, sewing, cleaning, cooking, nursing, grinding, shifting to make a home where no homes were.[10] They envied their husbands' brief escape into alcohol and listened to the ministers who told them how to shut down the saloons, which took their men away.

The women on the farms also wanted decency. For an accepted standard of decency was their only protection against the rough male world. The brave efforts towards some style in living, the piano in the log cabin, the magazine illustrations on the shanty wall, the curtains of sacking — all these represented a fumbling for a civilized way of life that asks for understanding, not for derision. Moreover, there was a surplus of women on many farms. The males died off more quickly than the females. A prosperous farmer often found himself with too many daughters, whose smattering of education made it impossible for them to marry the illiterate and uncouth farm laborers. These spinsters became that American phenomenon, the "schoolmarms" of the frontier. In Europe, secondary education remained in the hands of men; in America, women took over the country schools and the minds of the children. The Census of 1900 showed that, even with the influence of the large city of Chicago, three out of every four teachers in Illinois were women. Other professions were closed to them.

Thus the education on the subject of alcohol that a respectable country child received was usually in favor of prohibition. His mother, his female schoolteacher, and his minister would warn him against the saloon. Even if the rural proletariat, the hired hands, the loafers, the livery stablemen, the barbers, and the drunkards encouraged an occasional tipple, no country lad could have a drink without feeling sinful.

The progressive Brand Whitlock noticed in his Ohio village that "if men of the more respectable sort took a drink, they did it with a sense of wrong-doing that gave it a spice of adventure, and an invitation to indulge was generally accompanied by a half-humorous, half-guilty kind of wink."[11] In fact, even horror could be instilled by careful indoctrination. James M. Cox, who was nominated for the presidency by the wets in the Democratic convention of 1920, wrote that he had never even dared to look into the village saloon. He was taught to believe that it was "a den of the devil." It remained so loathly in his mind that when he became Governor of Ohio, he had the building condemned as a fire menace and torn down by the state marshal.[12]

For the village saloons were terrible places. They were little better than shacks, containing a bar, a brass rail, liquor bottles, cigars, a few tables and chairs, a floor covered with sawdust and chewed tobacco, and an array of spittoons. They sold bad, cheap liquor, which was not protected by a brand name. Such local disorder and crime as there was usually began in the saloons. Fabian Franklin, no friend of prohibition, conceded that the village grogshop and the bar of the small-town hotel presented little but the gross and degraded aspect of drinking.[13] Farmers, who had not seen the superior saloons in large cities, would naturally support prohibition to rid themselves of these country cesspools.

In a village society, where everybody knew the business of everybody else and called it neighborliness, the saloon became the local devil. No one could drink there without being found out. No fight could start there without being reported. The chief "theater" of the year, the revival meeting, denounced the place as the entrance to a future life of fire and brimstone.[14] The saloonkeeper himself was the outcast of country society. Sherwood Anderson recorded of his boyhood that the saloonkeeper, who lived on his street in the Ohio village of Clyde, walked silently with bent head. His wife and child were seldom seen. They lived an isolated life. "Could it have been that the saloon keeper, his wife and child, were socially ostracized because of the business in which he was engaged? It was an age of temperance societies and there were two churches on our street. To sell liquor, to own a saloon, was to be, I am sure, the devil's servant."[15]

In this culture bound together by suspicion and hardship, labor and earth, the fundamentalist crusade against alcohol was highly successful. It suited the direct judgment of the faithful. The man who was not for abolition of the saloon must be "a despicable Minion of the Rum Power and a Tool of Satan."[16] Bryan spoke for a whole stereotype when he pleaded in 1910 for a law allowing rural counties in Nebraska to close their local saloons by vote. "County option is not only expedient, but it is right. This is a moral question. There is but one side to a

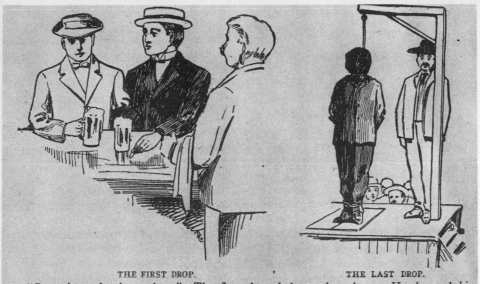

THE FIRST DROP.   THE LAST DROP.

"Come in and take a drop." The first drop led to other drops. He dropped his position, he dropped his respectability, he dropped his fortune, he dropped his friends, he dropped finally all his prospects in this life, and his hopes for eternity; and then came the last drop on the gallows. BEWARE OF THE FIRST DROP.—*The Watchman.*

Brown Brothers Photographers

DRY LOGIC

moral question. Which do you take?"[17] By this simplification, any man who opposed any dry measure necessarily supported drunkenness and vice. There was no room for the moderate in such a clear-cut world. Bryan took the argument to its apogee in opposition to a wet plank at the Democratic convention of 1920, when he asked his famous questions: "If you cannot get alcohol enough to make you drunk, why do you want alcohol at all? Why not cut it altogether and go on about your business?"[18] The questions were rhetorical. Like the jesting Pilate, Bryan did not stay for an answer.

Not all of those who lived in the West supported prohibition. In the early days of the frontier, whisky was the most portable form of grain and served as currency in many parts. The Kentucky distillers rebelled again the United States government in the eighteenth century because of the liquor tax and in the twentieth because of the Eighteenth Amendment. Whisky was their only source of income when crops failed or soil grew barren, as well as being necessary for health and "killing the bugs" in river water.[19] Social gatherings on the frontier traditionally demanded hard cider at the least; it was carefully exempted from the provisions of the Volstead Act. In the days of the famous flatboats on the Ohio River, an open keg of raw spirits and a dipper were left on each landing stage. Drunkenness was by far the most common cause for discipline in the frontier churches, for the abundance of liquor made a large section of pioneer society debauched and whisky-sodden in their land of "sinful liberty."[20] The later immigrants to the West, the Germans and the Irish, the Italians and Slavic peoples, saw no reason to give up their traditional drinking habits. In fact, the severity of prohibition sentiment in the West seems to have been the result of the widespread and continual drinking there. Moderation was never the habit of the pioneers. They either escaped from virtue through swinging doors or embraced it at the altar.

The extremity of their life forced the Westerners to extreme solutions. Whether an action was good or bad mattered less than that it should be certain and immediate. Justice, vice, liquor, virtue, all had to be taken straight and fast. Life was too violent for half measures. It had to be lived on the saddle, with the vigilantes, at the bar, urgently. During prohibition, when the rough and speedy lawlessness of the frontier had invaded the large cities, the great cowboy philosopher Will Rogers commented sadly on the psychology of a whole nation, "If we must sin, let's sin quick, and don't let it be a long, lingering sinning."[21]

SMALL TOWN AND LARGE CITY

THE FARMS were, however, too isolated to be of great help to the prohibitionists. Although the rich commercial farmers might support prohibition to get more work out of their hired hands, the political strength of the drys lay in the villages and small country towns, particularly among the wealthier people. For the small town was never the democratic and classless society which it claimed to be. It was usually divided into a dominant middle-class Protestant group given to religion and stern morality; an upper-class group of "respectable" people who did not see that pleasure and sin were necessarily in league together; Roman Catholics and foreigners; and a "lower" class, which ignored the morality of the dominant group except for a brief period after revival meetings.[22] This dominant village middle class provided religious fodder for pulpit politics and prohibition and gave the Ku Klux Klan the majority of its four million members during its revival after the Great War.

The prohibitionists were always conscious that their support lay in the country. They carefully attacked alcohol in its urban and foreign forms — beer and rum. They did not crusade with any vigor against country liquor — hard cider and corn whisky. They represented the cities as full of foreigners making evil profits out of poisonous drinks.

It was impossible to raise good Americans there. The International Reform Bureau warned the God-fearing:

> In this age of cities it is to be expected that conversions will decrease if we allow needless temptations about our youth to increase, such as foul pictures, corrupt literature, leprous shows, gambling slot machines, saloons, and Sabbath breaking. Instead of putting around our boys and girls a fence of favorable environment, we allow the devil to put about them a circle of fire; and then we wonder that they wither. *We are trying to raise saints in hell.*[23]

There was a quality of desperation in the country's fear of the city after 1896. When Bryan was defeated by McKinley, the country seemed to have lost its chance to govern the nation. The Census of 1900 showed that nearly two in every five Americans lived in the great cities. In 1860, it had been one in five, and the cities were now growing faster than ever, as European immigrants poured into the urban slums. Within twenty years, more people would live in the cities than in the country, and the old rural America of the small farmer, on which the Republic had been founded, would become impotent. It is small wonder that denunciations of the city rose to the pitch of hysteria on Chautauqua circuits and in dry periodicals. Alphonso Alva Hopkins, dry editor and Prohibition party supporter, wrote a typical harangue in 1908, calculated to appeal to every prejudice in the small-town mentality:

> Our boast has been that we are a Christian people, with Morality at the center of our civilization. Foreign control or conquest is rapidly making us un-Christian, with immorality throned in power.
> Besodden Europe, worse bescourged than by war, famine and pestilence, sends here her drink-makers, her drunkard-makers, and her drunkards, or her more temperate but habitual drinkers, with all their un-American and anti-American ideas of morality and government; they are absorbed into our national life, but not assimilated; with no liberty whence they came, they demand unrestricted liberty among us, even to license for the things we loathe; and through the ballot-box, flung wide open to them by foolish statesmanship that covets power, their foreign control or conquest has become largely an appalling fact; they dominate our Sabbath, over large areas of country; they have set up for us their own moral standards, which are grossly immoral; they govern our great cities, until even Reform candidates accept their authority and pledge themselves to obey it; the great cities govern the nation; and foreign control or conquest could gain little more, though secured by foreign armies and fleets.
> As one feature of this foreign conquest, foreign capital has come here, and to the extent of untold millions has invested itself in breweries, until we are told that their annual profits at one time

reached about $25,000,000 yearly, sent over seas to foreign stock-holders, who shared thus in their conquest of America, while to them, in their palaces and castles, American Labor paid tribute, and for their behoof American morals were debased, the American Sunday sur-rendered.[24]

These theories of conspiracy might be credible to small-town audi-ences. But they did not convince the great cities, nor their representa-tives in Congress. The prohibitionists might never have been able to gain the necessary vote in the Senate and House of Representatives to secure the passage of the Eighteenth Amendment if they had not had a murderous stroke of luck. Their chance was the Great War, and America's part in the slaughter. There is no room for moderation in war. Woodrow Wilson, agonized by doubt before he read his war message to Congress, said that what he feared most from the war was that the people would forget there was ever such a thing as tolerance. Wilson was correct. "The spirit of ruthless brutality" did enter into the very fiber of American life, until Harding restored normalcy.[25] Pabst and Busch were German; therefore beer was unpatriotic. Liquor stopped American soldiers from firing straight; therefore liquor was a total evil. Brewing used up eleven million loaves of barley bread a day, which could have fed the starving Allies; therefore the consumption of alcohol was treason. Pretzels were German in name; therefore, to de-fend Old Glory, they were banned from the saloons of Cincinnati. Seven years after the end of the war, a Pennsylvania doctor was still suggesting that the name of German measles be changed to victory or liberty measles.[26]

In this orgy of simplicity, this crusade for peace through war, this national bandwagon of unreason and false logic, the arguments of the drys seemed irrefutable. They were for God and for America, against the saloon and against Germany. The wets therefore must be for Satan and for Germany, against God and against America. Briefly, city and country thought alike. Clarence Darrow was wrong in 1924, when he said that "the vast centers of population, where all the feeling for liberty that still persists in this country is kept alive, the great centers of tolerance and independence and thought and culture – the cities – all of them were wet before prohibition, and since."[27] He had forgotten the Great War, when the cities were as intolerant and moralistic and patriotic as any Gopher Prairie.

The war, however, had its shocks for the boosters of the countryside. The drys discovered to their surprise that more country boys were rejected as unfit from the First Selective Draft than city boys. More than one in three of the draftees were rejected, mainly on account of feeble-mindedness. In addition, the draft boards found that city boys as a whole were much more fit than country boys. The drys countered these facts by saying that the fit city boys were merely intelligent immigrants from the country. As for the problem of feeble-mindedness, the drys gave the excuse that the idiot city girl caught venereal diseases, became sterile, and produced no sons for the Army. The pure but moronic country girl, sadly enough, had a great many illegitimate babies.[28]

The drys always maintained that the country was the reservoir of strong manhood for the city. In fact the reverse was the case. Although conditions in the cities were bad, they were not as bad as on many farms. Child labor laws increasingly protected the sons of factory workers; nothing saved the children of farmers from exploitation at the plow and cowshed. Hamlin Garland plowed all day at the age of ten.[29] He tells of prematurely aged boys of fourteen, with stooped shoulders from overwork. Disease, ignorance, poverty, filth, all took their toll in the countryside. Rural slums were, in many cases, worse than urban slums. If the small towns sent their fit and willing sons into the cities, they also sent their criminals, their diseased, and their drunkards. The history of the Jukes family, which contributed thousands of mental defectives and criminals to American society, says little for the pure Anglo-Saxon stock of the backwoods. The best sight for a Scotsman, in Dr. Johnson's opinion, was the high road to England. The highway to the city was often the same blessing for the farmer boy.

Inevitably, the country began to submit to the rescue operations of the cities. Culture often follows in the wake of economic exploitation. Although urban and international markets tied the farmer to the manipulation of world prices by financiers, the same Industrial Revolution that produced the stock exchange produced the improved communications that made piedmont into a suburb of tidewater. Mass-circulation newspapers pushed out local newspapers, chain stores destroyed country stores, cheap branded goods drove out expensive local products, better highways and automobiles punctured rural isolation, radio and cinema impregnated the minds of the young with city habits. Machines were invented to lighten the burden of field and kitchen on man, woman, and child. Hospitals, doctors, and hired nurses saved those country sufferers who were being slowly killed by home medicines. The declining influence of ignorant country preachers and biased textbooks allowed some relief to women crushed under incessant childbearing and child raising. Slowly, slowly, after the turn of the century, the American city began to take over the American country. Yet the country won battles in its defeat. Among these victories was national prohibition.

The contagion of war caught up the cities of America in the simple choices of the country mind. When victory was the aim of the nation, there was no time for fine distinctions between right and wrong. To win was to be moral, and any means used in winning were good means. But while the psychology of belligerence swept through the United States only in time of emergency, it was always part of the force behind the leaders and followers of prohibition. They were militant and aggressive, demanding present remedies for present evils. The Satan of the saloon was everywhere. It must be abolished so that the reign of God could begin on earth. Below their inheritance of rural beliefs, the drys had deeper wellsprings of action. In them, the battle against King Alcohol always continued; in them, there was a holy prejudice.

CHAPTER 2

The Psychology of Prohibition

> All we have to do is to think of the wrecks on either bank of the stream of death, of the suicides, of the insanity, of the ignorance, of the destitution, of the little children tugging at the faded and withered breast of weeping and despairing mothers, of wives asking for bread, of the men of genius it has wrecked, the men struggling with imaginary serpents, produced by this devilish thing; and when you think of the jails, of the almshouses, of the asylums, of the prisons, of the scaffolds upon either bank, I do not wonder that every thoughtful man is prejudiced against this damned stuff called alcohol.
>
> ROBERT G. INGERSOLL
> *The Commoner,* July 11, 1913

RECENT RESEARCH on the nature of prejudice has made a momentous discovery. The cognitive processes of prejudiced people are different in general from the cognitive processes of tolerant people. In fact, a person's prejudice is not usually a particular attitude to a particular question; it is more often a whole pattern of thinking about the world.[1] The prejudiced person is given to simple judgments in general, to assertions, to definite statements, to terms of black and white. Ambiguity is an evil to him because set truth is the good. He thinks in stereotypes, in rules, in truisms, in the traditional folkways of his environment. Such education as he receives merely gives him more reasons for his old beliefs. Indeed, he is the man who was found frequently in the dominant middle class of the small town, on the Western farms, and in the Southern shacks, where no complex clamor of urban life unsettled the mind and brain and eyes from the easy pairings of right and wrong. He is the man who was the backbone of the dry cause.

The Eighteenth Amendment could not have been passed without the support of the psychologically tolerant, made temporarily intolerant by the stress of war. But when the moderates deserted the drys in time of peace, the hard core of the movement was revealed. The main areas of prohibition sentiment were the areas where the Methodist and

Baptist churches had their greatest strength. These were the areas that fathered the bigot crusade of the Ku Klux Klan, which supported prohibition, among other moral reforms. Although many sincere drys were not bigots at the beginning of the campaign for the Eighteenth Amendment, they became bigots or left the cause by the time of repeal. Prohibition, an extreme measure, forced its extremes on its supporters and its enemies. Its study becomes a study of social excess.

Although there were reasonable moral and economic and medical reasons for supporting prohibition, the drys themselves exploited many irrational motives within themselves and their followers. Among the leaders of the cause, there was hysteria in their passion to wean the human race from alcohol. There was what one leader of the Anti-Saloon League found in another, "an almost revengeful hatred of the liquor traffic . . . a dogmatic and consecrated prejudice against organized wrong."[2] There was an element of sadism and undue persecution in the drys' legislative pursuit of the sinner, and in the flogging of prostitutes and bootleggers by the Ku Klux Klan. There was a thirst for power, which revealed itself in the savage struggles for position and prestige within the dry organizations, and in the sixteen-hour days worked year after year for no profit except self-satisfaction by such men as Wayne B. Wheeler, the great lobbyist of the dry cause. There was also a deliberate exploitation of prejudiced mentalities among their listeners by revivalist preachers such as Billy Sunday. Above all, until the failure of the World League Against Alcoholism, there was a feeling that prohibition was a winning global crusade, and that those first on the wagon would be first in the promised land of earth and heaven.

Among the followers of prohibition, there were other blind motives. There was the release from tension offered by the crusade against wrong. One "chastened crusader" confessed after the Women's Crusade against the saloons in Ohio in 1873, "The Crusade was a daily dissipation from which it seemed impossible to tear myself. In the intervals at home I felt, as I can fancy the drinker does at the breaking down of a long spree."[3] Allied with this release was an unreasoning fear of hard liquor, instilled by decades of revival sermons. As a female supporter of beer and wine wrote in 1929, "It is not love of whisky which makes real temperance impossible in this year of grace. It is the fear of it, the blinding, demoralizing terror felt by good people who have never tasted anything stronger than sweet communion wine."[4] This terror drove the extreme drys into a stupid and obnoxious pursuit of the drinker during prohibition, which made the whole dry cause stink in the nostrils of the moderate. The Durant and Hearst prize contests for a solution to the prohibition problem revealed its

WOMEN'S CRUSADE, 1873

distorted importance in the minds of certain drys and gave them wide publicity. One woman suggested that liquor law violators should be hung by the tongue beneath an airplane and carried over the United States. Another suggested that the government should distribute poison liquor through the bootleggers; she admitted that several hundred thousand Americans would die, but she thought that this cost was worth the proper enforcement of the dry law. Others wanted to deport all aliens, exclude wets from all churches, force bootleggers to go to church every Sunday, forbid drinkers to marry, torture or whip or brand or sterilize or tattoo drinkers, place offenders in bottle-shaped cages in public squares, make them swallow two ounces of castor oil, and even execute the consumers of alcohol and their posterity to the fourth generation.[5]

This extremism was only prevalent among a small group of the drys, but it was enough to damn all drys as fanatics. They were not so, although their spokesmen often were. Yet, living in a time before Freud and psychology were widely understood, they did not question their own motives. It was a time when "the figure of God was big in the hearts of men," and the drive of personal frustration was put down to divine guidance.[6] Men were not aware of the subconscious motives which made them prohibitionists; but these motives were none the less real. Behind the crusade against the saloon lurked the tormented spirits of many people.

Freud's masterpiece, *Civilization and Its Discontents*, suggests some of the unconscious forces that drove on the drys. The childish, the immature, those who had least recovered from the ignorant certainties of youth sought consolation in an authoritarian crusade, in the same way that those who cannot bear life without a father often make a father of God. Refuge from the ambiguities and difficulties of modern life was, for many of the drys, only to be found in total immersion in clear-cut moral reform. The saloon was a sufficient Satan to become the scapegoat of the devil in man. Abolition of the saloon was interpreted by the prohibitionists as a personal victory over doubt and sin in their own lives. With a terrible faith in equality, the prohibitionists often wanted to suppress in society the sins they found in themselves. G. K. Chesterton put the matter well:

> When the Puritan or the modern Christian finds that his right hand offends him he not only cuts it off but sends an executioner with a chopper all down the street, chopping off the hands of all the men, women and children in the town. Then he has a curious feeling of comradeship and of everybody being comfortable together. . . . He is after all in some queer way a democrat, because he is as much a despot to one man as to another.[7]

It was in this wish to extend their own repressions to all society that the drys felt themselves most free from their constant inward struggle. Indeed, they defended their attacks on the personal liberty of other men by stating that they were bringing these men personal liberty for the first time. According to one dry leader, personal liberty reached its highest expression where the strongest inhibitions were invoked and enforced.[8] Moreover, personal liberty was only possible once prohibition had freed the slaves of alcohol. Of course, in reality the drys were trying to bring personal liberty to themselves, by externalizing their anguished struggles against their own weaknesses in their battle to reform the weaknesses of others. The conflict between conscience and lust, between superego and id, was transferred by the drys from their own bodies to the body politic of all America; and, in the ecstasy of that paranoia which Freud saw in all of us, they would have involved the whole earth.

Freud, whose own life was hard, considered intoxicants a great blessing in the human struggle for happiness and in the warding off of misery.

> It is not merely the immediate gain in pleasure which one owes to them, but also a measure of that independence of the outer world which is so sorely craved. Men know that with the help they can get from "drowning their cares" they can at any time slip away from the oppression of reality and find a refuge in a world of their own where painful feelings do not enter.[9]

Freud saw that the moderate use of liquor was necessary for driven men, who could not find other interests or gratifications against the miseries of the world. The prohibitionists, however, presumed that a man who was denied the bottle would turn to the altar. They were wrong. They closed the saloons, but the churches did not fill. Luckily, drugs, radios, motion pictures, automobiles, proliferating societies, professional sports, paid holidays, and the relaxed sexual ethics of the flaming twenties provided new outlets for the libidos of deprived drinkers. Without these new outlets, the drys might have had to deal with a psychological explosion.

Yet extremism was not confined to the ranks of the drys. If the moderate drys were shamed by the excesses and motives of the extreme drys, so the moderate wets were damned by the millions of heavy drinkers and alcoholics on their side. If some prohibitionists were compulsive in their craving for water for everybody, some drinkers were even more compulsive in their craving for an excess of liquor for themselves. Alcoholics may suffer from many inadequacies — emotional immaturity, instability, infantilism, passivity, dependence, pathological jealousy, oral eroticism, latent homosexuality, isolation, narcissism, and masochism.[10] People who possess such defects are not to be deprived of their liquor by respect for the law of the land. They need understanding, not prohibition, which merely drives them into drinking any murderous substitute for liquor rather than no liquor at all. For the compulsive drinker drinks because he is compulsive by nature, as is the fanatical reformer. To deprive the compulsive drinker of his drink does not cure him. He is merely forced into the search for substitutes. Equally, the prohibition of a reform to a reformer would not make him give up all reforms. He would merely turn his neuroses onto another brand of reform.

The real tragedy of the prohibitionist ideology was that it left no room for temperance. The dry crusade slipped slowly from a moderate remedy for obvious evils into a total cure-all for society. The creed of the dedicated dry would not admit the existence of the moderate drinker. By definition, all drinkers were bound to become alcoholics. The moral of the famous propaganda piece *Ten Nights in a Bar-Room* was that the first sip of beer always and inevitably led to a drunkard's grave. So believing, the Anti-Saloon League could not attract moderate support by allowing the sale of light wines and beers. National prohibition had to be total. Yet if prohibition had been confined to prohibition of ardent spirits, as the early nineteenth-century temperance associations had recommended, the Anti-Saloon League might have had the support of the brewers, the winegrowers, and the majority of the American people to this day. A survey conducted in 1946 in America showed that fewer than two-fifths of the adult population ever drank spirits, either regularly or intermittently.[11]

In the early days of their counterattack, the brewers and distillers matched the hysteria of the drys in their denunciations. They accused the prohibitionists of being cranks and crackpots, "women with short hair and men with long hair." According to the wets, America was less threatened by the "gentlemanly vices" than by "perfidy and phariseeism in public and private life." Many men "marked the distinction between moderation and intemperance," and rich red blood, rather than ice water, flowed in their veins.[12] The drys were accused of being

> . . . more critical of each other, more self-conscious . . . harder, drabber in speech. Iced water, ice cream, icy eyes, icy words. Gone the mellowness, generosity, good humor, good nature of life. Enter the will-bound, calculating, material, frigid human machine. Strange that the removal of this thing, supposed to pander to the animal in us, makes one feel less a man and more an animal, above all, an ant. . . . Although — who knows? — ants may drink.[13]

The doctrine of prohibition appealed to the psychology of excess, both in its friends and in its foes. They could find only evil in each other. Extremes conjure up extremes. The fight against the devil carries another devil in its exaggerations. With a consecrated prejudice on the part of the drys opposed to an unenlightened self-interest on the part of the wets, there was little room left for compromise. Indeed, the drys were proud of their prejudice. It seemed to them a holy sentiment. With Robert Ingersoll, they did not believe that any person could contemplate the evils of drink "without being prejudiced against the liquor crime."[14]

THE SPECTER OF THE SOUTH

THE EXTREMES of dry psychology were well suited to white Southerners. They had a special use for prohibition. It offered them a moral refuge from their guilty fear of the Negro, as well as a method of controlling one of his means of self-assertion. Liquor sometimes gave the Negro the strength to repudiate his inferior status. It also encouraged him to loose his libido on white women, incited, so it was said, by the nudes on the labels of whisky bottles.[15] Thus the Negro should be prevented from drinking alcohol. To a lesser degree, the same rule should be applied to white men, although this reform was not so urgent. Congressman Hobson, from Alabama, made this clear in the House of Representatives in 1914, while speaking on his resolution for a prohibition amendment to the Constitution. "Liquor will actually make a brute out of a negro, causing him to commit unnatural crimes. The effect is the same on the white man, though the white man being further evolved it takes longer time to reduce him to the same level."

In the same debate, Congressman Pou, of North Carolina, although he opposed Hobson's resolution on account of the sacred doctrine of states' rights, did not question the need for racial control. He reminded Congress gently that the South had been forced to take away the ballot from the Negro "as the adult takes the pistol from the hand of a child."[16] * Since the ballot and alcohol were the two means of assertion given to the Negro, they must be denied to him. By the time of the Hobson resolution, all the Southern states had discriminated against the Negro voter and all but two had adopted prohibitory laws against liquor. The first measure had allowed the second. Congressman Quin, of Mississippi, stressed this in reference to the South. "Prohibition itself gained a foothold there and was made possible only after the

* As Mr. Dooley pointed out, the South did actually allow the Negro to vote, "only demandin' that he shall prove that his father an' mother were white."

restriction upon the suffrage of the negro."[17] To Northern drys, even if the South was in the rout of democracy at the polling booth, it was in the van of reform at the saloon. If it denied the Fifteenth Amendment, it was rabid in support of the Eighteenth.

This paternalism among the responsible Southern leaders and the denial of the principle of equality was not confined to the white race. Professor Councill, the principal of the Negro school in Huntsville, Alabama, spoke out for the abolition of the saloon as the first step in the emancipation of his own race. J. F. Clark agreed with him, although from a position of racial superiority:

> The saloon is a place of rendezvous for all classes of the low and vulgar, a resort for degraded whites and their more degraded negro associates, the lounging place for adulterers, lewd women, the favorite haunt of gamblers, drunkards and criminals. Both blacks and whites mix and mingle together as a mass of degraded humanity in this cesspool of iniquity. Here we have the worst form of social equality, but I am glad to know that it is altogether among the more worthless of both races.[18]

Booker T. Washington was of much the same opinion. Prohibition would be a blessing to the Negro people second only to the abolition of slavery. "Two-thirds of the mobs, lynchings, and burnings at the stake are the result of bad whisky drunk by bad black men and bad white men."[19] Negro and white leaders could join together in the crusade against the saloon, which often incited the racial fears of the South to the pitch of murder.

Two other forces drove the Southerners towards prohibition. The first was patriotism. The South was once again the moral leader of the nation in this reform, and in this reform lay the chance of revenge. If the North had abolished chattel slavery in the South, the South would retaliate by abolishing rum slavery in the North. The second force was the monolithic structure of the Democratic party in the South. Traditionally, the Negroes voted Republican and the whites Democratic. The elimination of Negro ballots at the polls left the Democratic party solidly in control of Southern patronage. The only chance for the Republicans to regain some form of political power lay in the proper enfranchisement of the Negroes, which was impossible, or in the wresting of the moral leadership of the South from the Democrats. To do so, they had to find a popular cause which was both moral and an instrument of racial control. Prohibition was such a cause. Fear that the Republicans might seize the leadership of the prohibition movement, or that the Prohibition party, founded in 1869, might split the Democratic vote and let in the Republicans, drove the Democrats into the dry column in the South.[20] Thus the anomaly of a party based on the wet cities of the North and the dry rural counties of the South was emphasized. The quarrel over prohibition brought into the open a deep fissure among the Democrats that made them ineffective as a party for a decade.

Other forces conspired to give alcohol a special position in the psyche of the South. Although white rural Southerners shared in the nationwide economic and moral drives towards prohibition, they also suffered from the peculiar compulsions given to them by their environment. In the Southern character, an overwhelming need to master the Negro was coupled with a split between Puritanism and hedonism. This split made the Southerner seek the forbidden as a necessary part of his greatest pleasure, while a sense of guilt drove him into dependence on the absolution of violence or of orgiastic religion.[21] The ambivalent attitude of the Southern country white toward the Negro, his emotional cocktail of fear shaken up with lust, was also his attitude toward liquor. It is no coincidence that Mississippi, the most deeply rural of all states, is the last state in the Union to keep to the Southern trinity of official prohibition, heavy liquor consumption, and an occasional lynching. When Will Rogers commented that Mississippi would vote dry as long as the voters could stagger to the polls, he was too kind to mention that they would also lynch Negroes as long as they could stagger to the rope.*

The drys deliberately exploited this darkness in the Southern mind. Fundamentalist religion often attracted large audiences by the very emphasis on vice and iniquity, violence and rape, which the mass media and the yellow press adopted in the twentieth century. An example can be taken from the work of the Reverend Wilbur Fisk Crafts. He was very influential, being president of the International Reform Bureau at Washington, a prolific writer and speaker, and a pastor at different times in the Methodist Episcopal, Congregational, and Presbyterian churches. His favorite sermon on prohibition began with a description of a man in seventeenth-century Bavaria who confessed on the rack that he had eaten thirteen children, after being changed into a wolf by the devil's girdle. The man was then sentenced to be put on the wheel and beheaded, once he had been pinched in twelve places on his body with red-hot irons. His dead body was burned, and his head was set for many years on a wooden wolf as a warning.

* There were 573 recorded lynchings in Mississippi between 1882 and 1944. During this period, Georgia came second with 521 lynchings and Texas third with 489. After the Second World War, the number of lynchings declined dramatically, since more severe legal action was taken against those who were responsible for the murders.

After this edifying start, the preacher continued,

> So runs the old chronicle. Has it any parallel in present-day life? The next time you open your newspaper and read the scare heads describing the latest lynching horror in the black belt of the United States, ask yourself what devil's girdle has changed so many negroes into sensual hyenas. Remember that during the four years of the Civil War the whole white womanhood of the South, in the absence of husband and brother, in the death grapple of battle, was at the mercy of the black population of the plantations.

Yet there was no rape at that time. What, then, had changed the Negroes? Was it emancipation or education, or the possession of the suffrage? Or was it the fact, "which for all rational men is a sufficient answer," that 75 per cent of all liquor sales in the South Carolina dispensaries were to Negroes? Naturally, it was liquor which was the devil's girdle and brought about the punishment reserved for those who wore the devil's girdle. "The souls of the black men are poisoned with alcohol and their bodies in due course drenched in petroleum and burned."[22]

Of course, lynching was only the extreme manifestation of the Southern urge to violence in the same way as hoggish drunkenness and ecstatic shakes were extreme reactions to the saloon and the revival meeting. There was a responsible and moderate leadership in the Deep South, composed of such people as Senator Oscar Underwood, of Alabama, who opposed prohibition and the excesses of his countrymen with conviction and dignity. But unfortunately, the very conditions which made the Western farms and small towns susceptible to the Manichaean doctrines of the drys were present in an exaggerated form in the South. There were few large cities. The hold of the primitive Methodist and Baptist churches and of the fundamentalist sects was widespread and powerful. Little industry existed below the Potomac. Conquest by the North and memories of Reconstruction lived on. And the cult of purity and white womanhood allied with the fact of miscegenation and Negro mistresses produced in the white Southerner a strange discrepancy between stressed morality and denied fact. In this interval between ideal and reality, the cant of the drinker who voted dry flourished like a magnolia tree.

INTERNATIONAL MISSION

THE SOUTH adopted prohibition to protect itself against its poor and its Negroes and its own sense of guilt. Those American missionaries who supported prohibition at home and abroad had like motives. The poor and the colored people of the earth were dangerous when drunk. Moreover, as the greed of Southern planters was held responsible for the existence of the Negro problem in the South, so the greed of white traders was usually held responsible for the corruption of the native races overseas. Early American imperialism imitated the European pattern of traders who corrupted the local people with rum and fire-arms and diseases, followed by clergymen who tried to save those people from that corruption. In America itself, the defeat of the red Indians had been made easy by their introduction to rum; once they had been defeated, they were immediately protected from the con-sequences of rum by the federal government.

A similar process took place in the Pacific islands. In 1901, Senator Henry Cabot Lodge had a resolution adopted by the Senate to forbid the sale by American traders of opium and alcohol to "aboriginal tribes and uncivilized races."[23] These provisions were later extended to cover "uncivilized" elements in America itself and in its territories, such as Indians, Alaskans, the inhabitants of Hawaii, railroad work-ers, and immigrants at ports of entry.

The evil which the American missionaries were trying to eradicate was real enough. As they said, Christian nations were making ten drunkards to one Christian among backward peoples.[24] Prohibition of rum traders was obviously a good thing in those areas controlled by the colonial powers. But when the same paternal attitude was applied within the home ground of the colonial powers to "handle the hun-dreds of thousands of God's weak children, who are being ruined and destroyed through the oppressions of the liquor traffic," the mission-aries ran into trouble.[25] They could say with truth, "Let no one think we are neglecting saloons on our own shores in this crusade for the defense of native races at a distance."[26] But the fact that the colonial power itself was often a democracy made this missionary attitude objectionable at home. No American workingman liked to be classified with those "uncivilized" peoples, whom he was taught to consider an inferior species. He also objected to the attitude of the missionary, who claimed to know what was good for labor better than labor knew itself. Moreover, there was a suspicious similiarity between the views of the employers, who said that prohibition was good for the efficiency of workingmen, and those men of God, who said that prohibition was necessary for the salvation of their souls.

The idea of world-wide prohibition was contemporaneous with the idea of America as the Messiah of mankind and the Savior of the degenerate world. The ideology of salvation, which was once applied by middle-class reformers only to backward races and the American poor, was applied to the whole globe, after the First World War seemed to prove to many Americans that their country was the last refuge of peace and virtue. In addition, the spate of prohibition legislation adopted by the belligerent powers seemed to herald a world-wide prohibition revolution. Canada and Russia forbade liquor during the war; Britain and France and Germany severely regulated liquor. The Moslem and Buddhist world was also officially under religious prohibition. In fact, over half the area of the earth seemed behind the dry banners, and that area was growing. It is small wonder that William Jennings Bryan could prophesy that "alcohol as a beverage has been indicted as a criminal, brought up to the bar of judgment, condemned, and executed. Our nation will be saloonless for evermore and will lead the world in the great crusade which will drive intoxicating liquor from the globe."[27]

The mentality of war and the fantastic hopes of a millennial peace encouraged the drys' sense of international mission. As the leader of the Anti-Saloon League said to its assembled delegates in 1919, "The President said to make the world safe for democracy. Now, it is your business and mine, it is the business of the church of God, to make a democracy that is safe for the world, by making it intelligent and sober everywhere."[28] The reason for converting the world was simple. It was the same reason, incidentally, that the Bolsheviks gave for insisting on the world-wide Communist revolution. As long as a dry America was surrounded by wet nations, or a Communist Russia by capitalist nations, neither prohibition nor Communism would be safe. How, in the opinion of the drys, could prohibition be enforced when the United States was bounded "on the north by hard liquor, on the south by liquor, on the west by rum and on the east by no limit"?[29] The best hope of prohibition, like the best hope of communism, lay in the conquest of the world.

Of course, the drys saw themselves as the sworn enemies of the Bolsheviks and of communism. They said that they were the defenders of the law and the Constitution, where the Eighteenth Amendment was enshrined. But they did not mention their revolutionary destruction of the vast property interests of the liquor trade without compensation. There were further curious similarities between the Anti-Saloon League and the Bolshevik party. Both organizations were founded at much the same time. Both were small, successful, well-organized minority groups who knew what they wanted. Both exploited a condition of war to put themselves in power. Although the drys used propaganda while the Bolsheviks used revolutionary warfare, both used the methods most likely to succeed in their societies. Both groups expected through historical necessity to be the leaders of a global revolution in the habits of human society. The expectations of both groups were quickly disappointed. While Russia settled down under Stalin to "Socialism in one country," the United States settled down to prohibition in one country. Both revolutions failed in their immediate social objectives, although the names and the language of the Russian revolution lingered on.

But the analogy can be taken too far. The fact that the drys relied on the Christian churches and on democratic procedures limited their success. The methods of the World League Against Alcoholism could not be the methods of international subversion of the Comintern.[30] When Bishop Cannon demanded of the Anti-Saloon League, "Shall It Live or Die?" and came to the conclusion that it should live to lead in the international crusade against alcohol, his suggested methods of conquest were the usual propaganda methods of the League. "It must carry to every nation its testimony for Prohibition, by printed page, by cartoon, poster, in every language, and by trained workers and speakers who will be veritable apostles of Prohibition truth."[31] That such a crusade was hardly likely to be effective in Mediterranean countries, long used to drinking wine, did not deter the leaders of the League. For, as long as the crusade against liquor lasted at home and abroad, they kept their power and their jobs and their hopes and their satisfaction in the good fight well fought. It is the habit of revolutionaries never to be content with the limits of their gains, and of moral reformers rarely to accept less than the conversion of the human race.

The hidden urges behind dry leaders and white Southerners and foreign missionaries made them adopt prohibition as a panacea for themselves and for their fellow men. The dry cause brought them peace from their inner struggles and fears and guilts. They sought to extend this peace to races and classes which they considered inferior and eventually to the whole earth. The freedom of the globe from the evil of liquor would bring the condition of liberty for the first time to all mankind. In this battle for the good of all, the drys would use any means to win. For the liquor enemy was evil and could only be fought by evil. In their exploitation of the fears and weaknesses of their fellow Americans, the drys were guilty of many questionable methods, which could hardly be justified by the purity of their intentions.

CHAPTER 3

The Exploited Terror

Ye mouldering victims, wipe the crumbling grave-dust
from your brow; stalk forth in your tattered shrouds and
bony whiteness to testify against the drink! Come, come
from the gallows, you spirit-maddened man-slayer, grip
your bloody knife, and stalk forth to testify against it! Crawl
from the slimy ooze, ye drowned drunkards, and with
suffocation's blue and livid lips speak out against the drink.
Snap your burning chains, ye denizens of the pit, and come
up, sheeted in fire, dripping with the flames of hell, and
with your trumpet tongues testifying against the deep
"damnation of the drink."

JOHN B. GOUGH
Platform Echoes, 1885

The human species, with all its immense advantages, has
made many conspicuous missteps. Its eating habits are such
as to have induced a wide assortment of wholly unnecessary
diseases; its drinking habits are glaringly injurious; and its
excessive indulgence in sex-waste has imperiled the life of
the race.

CHARLOTTE PERKINS GILMAN, 1924

THE POPULAR belief that liquor did a man good was older than the
American colonies. The first colonists brought over from Europe a
taste for ardent spirits and a faith in the healing power of *aqua vitae.*
Rum was drunk everywhere in the colonies, at weddings and funerals,
at the founding of churches and during the swindling of red Indians.
Childish ills were quieted, if not cured, by small doses of spirits.
Housebuilding, harvesting, husking, quilting, bundling, logrolling — all
the particular festivities of pioneer life were incomplete without huge
quantities of hard cider and corn whisky. Alcohol was thought to be
a necessity for heavy work with the hands. In 1927, after sixty years
of medical testimony to the contrary, the truckmen in the old Chelsea
district in New York still thought that they had to start their days with
a nip, while the hatters of Danbury could not work without enough

alcohol to control their "hatter's shakes."[1] Even now, the brandy bottle is still in the medicine cupboard, and beer is sometimes prescribed as a remedy for old age.

The War of Independence was fought partially on Dutch courage and American liquor. The official ration for each soldier at Valley Forge was a daily gill or a half pint of whisky, depending on the quartermaster's supplies. James Thacher, while visiting the troops there, heard their continual complaints, "No pay, no clothes, no provisions, no rum."[2] The shortage of liquor became so great that General Gates, president of the Board of War, threatened to seize all the supplies of spirits that were being held back by profiteers. Only the unheeded voice of the physician-general of the Middle Department of the Continental Army, Dr. Benjamin Rush, cautioned against the use of spirits. He had noticed that the consumption of alcohol seemed to increase fatigue and lower resistance to disease. The war, however, was won despite his pleading.

In 1784, Dr. Rush published his famous pamphlet, *An Inquiry into the Effects of Spirituous Liquors on the Human Body and Mind.*[3] He advocated complete abstinence from ardent spirits. In an appendix called "A Moral and Physical Thermometer," he made the case that rum paved the way to the debtor's cell and the gallows, while small beer and occasional cups of wine or cider led to strength of body and length of life. His writings were the basis of the temperance sermons of the great preacher, Lyman Beecher, who later became an advocate of total prohibition and helped to spread the war against rum across the whole of the United States. Beecher appealed to God's law as well as to medical knowledge in his *Six Sermons on the Nature, Occasions, Signs, Evils and Remedy of Intemperance.*[4] The wandering missionaries of the West echoed his words everywhere. By 1834, some million Americans were enrolled in temperance societies. They signed the pledge after appeals to their reason and morality by the respected leaders of their communities.

In 1840, however, a new method of spreading the dry gospel was discovered. The Washingtonians, a society of reformed drunkards, found out that hundreds of thousands could be made to sign the pledge after hearing the confessions of saved alcoholics. The techniques of persuasion of the Washingtonians appealed to the heart rather than to the head. Mass meetings, processions of thousands of small girls and boys in Cold Water Armies, torchlight rallies, titillation by descriptions of the life of sin followed by redemption through repentence — these were the weapons of the new advocates of temperance.

Although the Washingtonian movement declined rapidly, its techniques and speakers remained behind. John H. W. Hawkins, John B.

Gough, and their imitators spoke to millions in the cities and small towns.[5] Their coming was the highlight of the dreary year in country villages. The most lurid of Brand Whitlock's memories of his little Ohio town was that of the "dashing and romantic fellow," who recounted the fascinating adventures of the life of sin on the temperance platform.

> It was as thrilling as anything in *Night Life in New York*, a book of shocking revelations showing just how wicked a place New York was; it was sold by subscription only, and was not at all Fit for the Young. But the Reformed Drunkard was even better than the book; he had been there and had seen it all himself, and that made it more real.[6]

Indeed, the chief worry of the local small boys on signing the pledge was that they themselves could not become Reformed Drunkards.

The original drives behind the temperance movement in America are clear. There was a sentiment of nationalism, a feeling that self-control was necessary to the working of American democracy. There was an urge towards social reform, a campaign against drunkenness and prostitution and crime. There was the need to protect the home, the wife, and the children of the drunkard against disease and want. There was the power of evangelical Protestantism, which condemned liquor as the Devil's own drink. There was thriftiness, the knowledge that alcohol makes men work less and play more. And there was, finally, the success of the movement. In 1851, Neal Dow secured the passage of the Maine Law, which banned the sale of liquor throughout the state.[7] Twelve states followed the lead of Maine in the next four years. After using moral suasion and emotional appeal, the prohibitionists found their most effective method of influence in legal coercion. The Civil War, however, brought about a slump in all reform, dry or otherwise.

THE HIPPOCRATIC LIE

AFTER THE Civil War, the prohibitionists found new weapons. Medical research into the effects of alcohol was flourishing, particularly in Germany, Scandinavia, and Great Britain. The early findings of scientists were usually against the use of liquor. Veneration for science was increasing in America itself. The temperance societies set out to diffuse the results of medical research through pamphlet and pulpit. But they were careful to diffuse only that scientific data which was in line with their beliefs. The research which supported God's ban against drink was good; the research which found for the moderate use of liquor was faulty, biased, bought, or downright evil. The drys perfected techniques for misrepresenting scientific experiments, for quoting out of context, for making final dogmas out of interim reports, and for manufacturing literary water bottles out of laboratory test tubes.[8]

Instances of the misuse of medicine by the prohibitionists are legion. Dr. Thomas Sewall made six drawings of the stomachs of corpses. These drawings were labeled "Healthful," "Moderate Drinking," "Drunkard's," "Ulcerous," "After a Long Debauch," and "Death by Delirium Tremens." Reproductions of these were made for seventy years by the drys. The violent pigments of Grand Guignol were used to terrify the simple into teetotalism.[9] Another favorite trick of temperance lecturers was to drop the contents of an egg into a glass of pure alcohol and to tell their audiences that the curdled mess was similar to the effect of liquor on the lining of the human stomach. A similar horror technique was the threat of spontaneous combustion. The medical journals of the 1830's and Charles Dickens, in *Bleak House,* testified that drunkards might suddenly catch fire and burn to death, breathing out blue flame. The idea that children conceived in drunkenness would be born defective was stressed and documented.[10]

Widespread use was made of medical statistics to win over the intelligent. The dry propagandists were among the first to discover the modern device of bemusing the opposition with facts and figures, while forgetting to mention any contrary evidence. Laitinen's studies of twenty thousand Finnish children were widely touted to show, to two places of decimals, that drinkers lost more of their children than abstainers.[11] Contemporary studies of three thousand English children were ignored because they seemed to prove that drinking parents did not lose more of their children.[12] The drys wanted to show that parents who used liquor were murderers of unborn babies. Their selected statistics merely buttressed their preconceptions. It was unfortunate that their devotion to their cause exceeded their devotion to scientific truth.

Another fault of the drys was argument by false inference. For instance, in the same year that Stockard was writing, on the basis of his experiments, that "it is highly improbable that the quality of human stock has been at all injured or adversely modified by the long use of alcohol,"[13] the eighteenth edition of a phenomenally successful dry textbook on hygiene, *How to Live: Rules for Healthful Living Based on Modern Science,* still stated that "Dr. Stockard has also shown in mice, on which he has experimented, the effect of alcohol on the germ-plasm is distinctly injurious. It is a fair inference that the use of alcohol by parents tends to damage the offspring."[14] The same textbook quoted evidence by an obscure doctor in Battle Creek that nicotine sometimes produced degeneration and sterility among rats.

Defective Children
Increased With
ALCOHOLIZATION
of FATHERS

Among the Defects were Epilepsy, Feeble-mindedness and St. Vitus Dance

219 Children of Occasional Drinkers

2.3% *DEFECTIVE*

130 Children of Regular Moderate Drinkers

4.6% *DEFECTIVE*

67 Children of Regular Heavy Drinkers

9% *DEFECTIVE*

53 Children of Drunkards

19% *DEFECTIVE*

Alcoholism and Defects of Brain and Nerves Go Hand in Hand

Regular "Moderate" Drinkers Drank daily less than the equivalent of 2 qts. of Beer; Heavy Drinkers more than this amount.

Bunge: Graphische Labellen Zur Alkolfrage, 1907, p. 169.

ANTI-SALOON LEAGUE POSTER

"This fact should at least give the human parent pause."[15]

Argument by analogy was another favorite method of the prohibitionists. Contemporary scientists frequently experimented with the effects of alcohol on small animals. Although they were careful to say that the results of their experiments could not be applied to the human species, the drys repeated time and time again that human babies would suffer from drunken parents as badly as the litters of intoxicated dogs, fowls, guinea pigs, mice, frogs, rabbits, and albino rats.[16] What hurt a rat would hurt a man. Were not both living creatures? Yet the same people who argued that a man who drank a cocktail a day might harm his children as much as an alcoholic rat his posterity were the leaders of the fundamentalist crusade against evolution. When William Jennings Bryan rose to defend the Bible against Darwin in Tennessee, his dry supporters could see no correspondence between men and monkeys.

ALCOHOLISM
AND DEGENERACY

61 Children in 10 Very Temperate Families

5 Died in Infancy

2 Had St. Vitus Dance

2 Were Backward, not Idiotic

2 were Deformed

50 were Normal

57 Children in 10 Intemperate Families

25 Died in Infancy

1 Had St. Vitus Dance — Idiotic

6 Were Idiotic

5 Were Deformed

5 Were Dwarfed

5 Were Epileptic

10 Were Normal

Temperate Parents Had | Defective Children 18% / Normal Children 82 %   Alcoholic Parents Had | Defective Children 82.5% / Normal Children 17.5%

Demme: The Influence of Alcohol on the Child. Investigations in Berne, Switzerland, 1878-1889. Families lived in same section and were similarly situated except as regards intemperance.

ANTI-SALOON LEAGUE POSTER

Often the drys wrote straight lies about medical research. Experiments on thirty thousand white mice showed that alcoholized parents did not produce defective progeny.[17] Although the fertility of the mice was decreased, this selective process strengthened the species. Yet the *Scientific Temperance Journal,* the compendium of medical knowledge for the drys, continued to quote the results of these experiments as proof of their belief that alcohol caused "a persistent transmissible injury to the males."[18] Up to the present day, alcohol is still miscalled a poison in temperance publications, although it is no more than a mild sedative if taken in small quantities.

The brewers and distillers also distorted and suppressed medical evidence, although they were less efficient than the prohibitionists. They insisted on calling beer "liquid bread"; the drys retorted by calling apples "God's bottles" and by saying that the wets might as well call a chaw of tobacco "liquid milk."[19] The United States Brewers' Association tried to influence students in its favor by putting out a bibliography entitled *Five Feet of Information for Impartial Students of the Liquor Problem*. But the impartiality of the recommended reading was questionable. Highly praised was Dr. Robert Park's *The Case for Alcohol, or the Action of Alcohol on Body and Soul*. This treatise stated that "man is made for Alcohol, or Alcohol is made for man, which comes to the same thing. On the meat side, Alcohol is a sort of broth prepared specially with loving care and evident skill. . . . Alcohol is an aliment superior to sugar; the reason for that being that for the same weight it contains more aliment."[20] Similar claims for the food value of liquor were made until the brewers realized in the thirties that they were depriving themselves of half their market.[21] Women would not drink liquor which might make them fatter. Since that time, advertisements for beer and spirits have stressed the refreshing qualities or snob value of a particular brand of drink.

But until the passing of prohibition and the reversal of their roles, the drys were always on the attack and the wets on the defense. The drys chose their battleground, and the wets had to meet them there. Eugenics was the fashionable science, and the wets could not deny its claims. Percy Andreae, the chief publicity expert of the brewers, had to confess to the New Jersey State Chamber of Commerce in 1915 that "race-betterment has become the dominant — well, I will not say fad, because the subject is too sacred — but let me say the dominant trend of our age."[22] His only reply to the dry arguments for purifying the racial stock by prohibition of liquor was a plea for happiness, which involved the claim that men could not be happy without alcohol. Even the more determined counterattacks of other writers, subsidized by the brewers, were curiously ineffective. They merely maintained that the drys were materialists and often ate too much, which was equally bad for their health. As for wet degeneracy,

> . . . people should understand that, far from indicating a superior moral status, the aversion to alcohol is a symptom of physical, moral or mental defectiveness, or inferior, sub-normal nature, not so far out of the normal as to be classed as decidedly diseased, or degenerate, but nevertheless far enough out of the road of health to be called morbid.[23]

Until the coming of national prohibition, the whole history of dry and wet medical propaganda was a history of misrepresentation unworthy of the declared aims of its writers.

THE TEXTBOOK CRUSADE

ANOTHER DIFFERENCE in the dry campaign after 1870 was its emphasis on education. The minds of children had been influenced in churches and Sunday schools. But they were taught little about the evils of liquor in the public schools, except by the ubiquitous McGuffey Readers. Dr. McGuffey was a friend of John B. Gough and an advocate of temperance. His textbooks and readers, of which 122,000,000 copies were sold between 1836 and 1920, formed the minds of country Protestant America. Many farmhouses, such as Ed Howe's childhood home in Missouri, possessed a library only of religious books, the *Christian Advocate,* and McGuffey Readers.[24] The texts taught the virtues of thrift, labor, obedience, duty to God, and temperance. They helped to create the climate of decency and informed prejudice which made the passing of prohibition legislation possible.

Temperance teaching was incidental, however, to McGuffey's purpose. It was only one method among others to produce the restrained and dutiful child who was admired in nineteenth-century America. A lesson such as "The Whisky Boy," which traced the decline of John from early drinking of whisky to death in the poorhouse, was more concerned with showing liquor as the enemy of industry than as sinful in itself. Another lesson, "Don't Take Strong Drink," did make the point that "No drunkard shall inherit the kingdom of heaven," but its main emphasis was on the evil which liquor brought to this life. "Whisky makes the happy miserable and it causes the rich to be poor."[25]

McGuffey was more interested in stressing the social rewards of temperance than in frightening his readers into virtue. He wanted to bring some form of civilization to the frontier through the schoolhouse. His attacks on drunkenness and gambling were more the attacks on specific evils than on the trade in alcohol. In fact, the extreme prohibitionists thought that too little was being done to win the children to the dry banner. They decided to increase the amount of temperance teaching in the public schools.

Six years after its founding in 1873, the Woman's Christian Temperance Union adopted Mrs. Mary Hannah Hunt's plan for introducing compulsory temperance education. Mrs. Hunt was put in charge of a Department of Scientific Temperance Instruction, which cajoled and bullied Congress and the state legislatures into passing laws requiring temperance teaching in the public schools. By 1902, every state and territory except Arizona had such a law. That day seemed near which Mrs. Hunt had predicted was "surely coming when from the school houses all over the land will come trained haters of alcohol to pour a whole Niagara of ballots upon the saloon."

But laws were not enough. The temperance textbooks had to be rewritten to include the selected medical knowledge approved by the dry leaders. There can be no indoctrination without misrepresentation. Mrs. Hunt set about changing the teaching of a nation. In 1887, she circulated to all publishers of textbooks on hygiene and physiology a petition signed by two hundred leading prohibitionists. This petition requested that all textbooks should teach that "alcohol is a dangerous and seductive poison"; that fermentation turns beer and wine and cider from a food into poison; that a little liquor creates by its nature the appetite for more; and that degradation and crime result from alcohol. The textbooks on hygiene should contain at least one-quarter of temperance teaching and should be suited to the minds of the children in each grade. If these conditions were observed, a board of professors, clergymen, reformers, and doctors picked by the Woman's Christian Temperance Union would endorse the books.[26] As the prohibitionists were influential on most of the school boards in the country and had the power to buy textbooks, the publishers soon fell into line. Before her death in 1906, Mrs. Hunt could point to more than forty endorsed texts in use all over the country in public schools, of which the numbers doubled between the turn of the century and the Great War.

Mrs. Hunt saw the struggle for the children's minds as more than a matter of pressure politics or economics. Her obituary said that "the fundamental and motivating power of her intense and fruitful activity was the belief in the divine plan for mankind which alcohol must not be allowed to mar, coupled with the conviction that through the children the race would be saved."[27] Her belief in destiny and her concern for the Anglo-Saxon race was sufficient to make her rate her job as a revolutionary crusade. "Childhood saved today from the saloon, and the nation thus saved tomorrow, is the stake played for in this desperate game," she wrote in 1887. "All that is holiest in mother-love, all that is purest in the patriotism that would save the country from the saloon, for God and humanity, enters into our opposition, or our support of these books."[28] In her terms, there was no room for any scientific defense of the moderate use of alcohol. The only medical evidence deemed "scientific" was that which supported the prohibition of liquor.

The moderates and the wets realized too late that the drys had spread the idea of their infallibility on the subject of alcohol. After nearly a century of rarely disputed teaching, backed by a majority of the Protestant churches and by Congress, the prohibitionists seemed to have authority and tradition behind their statements. Alcohol research was their preserve. Until the passing of the Eighteenth Amendment, the only strong challenge to the dry dogmas came from the findings of the Committee of Fifty, a group of scholars and businessmen interested in temperance, who sponsored research studies at the turn of the century. Their physiological subcommittee examined the dry misuse of methods of education. The subcommittee deplored the rewriting of the textbooks on hygiene by Mrs. Hunt and her helpers. It noted the false statements in the endorsed textbooks and the careful flattery paid to their obscure authors, who were introduced as "the greatest living authority" or "the foremost scientist" or "an eminent scholar."

The members of the subcommittee examined carefully twenty-three of the endorsed textbooks from seven publishers. They noted that publishers found it difficult at times to sell textbooks which were not endorsed. They found many misleading statements and deliberate attempts to frighten young children in the dry texts. Some of the more horrific statements read:

> A cat or dog may be killed by causing it to drink a small quantity of alcohol. A boy once drank whisky from a flask he had found, and died in a few hours. . . .
> Alcohol sometimes causes the coats of the blood vessels to grow thin. They are then liable at any time to cause death by bursting. . . .
> It often happens that the children of those who drink have weak minds or become crazy as they grow older. . . .
> Worse than all, when alcohol is constantly used, it may slowly change the muscles of the heart into fat. Such a heart cannot be so strong as if it were all muscle. It is sometimes so soft that a finger could easily be pushed through its walls. You can think what would happen if it is made to work a little harder than usual. It is liable to stretch and stop beating and this would cause sudden death.[29]

In their final summary, the subcommittee called for a "prolonged struggle . . . to free our public school system from the incubus which rests upon it."[30] Mary Hunt immediately retaliated by having a resolution passed by the United States Senate. The Committee of Fifty was wrong in its allegations that the textbooks were unscientific and imposed on the public schools. It was ridiculous to suppose that an unaided woman could have caused all the states to pass laws for the teaching of temperance without wide popular support and much rational discussion. "The American public," the resolution stated, "is too intelligent, too patriotic, and too conscientious to have adopted this movement hastily or to retire from it in the face of the good it is doing."[31] That the good was questionable was shown by the answers of Massachusetts schoolchildren to questions on alcohol, after they had been taught from dry texts. One answer stated that alcohol would "pickel the inside of the body," while another affirmed that the stomach of a drinker became "black and covered with cancers."[32]

In the eighty years before the passing of the Eighteenth Amendment, the drys had a near monopoly of the means by which the results of research on alcohol reached the voters. The minds of a whole generation had been conditioned to feel guilty every time that they took a drink of liquor. They had been told time and time again, in school and at church and on the science pages of the newspapers, that alcohol harmed them and their children. However much a man wanted liquor, he might vote to deprive himself of the temptation, as did Thomas Wolfe's drunken Oliver Gant, pressured by his wife until he "piously contributed his vote for purity."[33] A secret shame made many a drinker support the drys. He had been taught to fear his own weakness and the bad opinion of his teetotal betters. Like Babbitt, the respectable voter disliked being known as a Drinker even more than he liked a drink.

THE SPOILED SEED

THE DRYS used other potent weapons in the second wave of prohibition. What appeared to be their greatest threat, the Prohibition party, founded in 1869, was the least. Party political action helped their cause far less than psychological conditioning. Until a large enough group of people had been guided toward their policies, the Prohibitionists would lose at the polls. And so, partly consciously and partly subconsciously, the temperance forces worked on those hidden urges in America and Americans which might help them. The emotion which they exploited was fear: the fear of sin and God; the fear of race against race and skin against skin; the fear of venereal diseases; the fear of idiot children; the fear of violence suppressed by conscience and loosed by liquor; and the dark sexual fears of civilization. Francis Bacon may have found nothing terrible except fear itself. But the fear of others was the hope of the drys.

The prohibitionists claimed that the drinking of alcohol was more than a crime against God. It was a crime against society, self, and race. According to them, the findings of medicine and science proved absolutely that alcohol turned even the moderate drinker into the bad citizen, who infected his innocent children with the diseases of liquor. Wise men from the time of Plato had warned parents against drinking before procreation. Degenerate offspring was the result of abuse of the bottle. "The history of heredity conducts us to alcoholism, and these two should be considered the principal causes of degeneration."[34] As the consumption of alcohol rose, so the quality of the racial stock declined. There was only one way to give "posterity a square deal": that was to keep a father from "faulty habits" and to prevent him from passing on to his child a feeble constitution.[35] The drys echoed the words of Dr. J. W. Ballantyne, of Edinburgh, "Alcohol is a danger from one conception, from one procreation, to another; there is no time under the sun when it is suitable or safe to court intoxication."[36]

Evolution, heredity, and eugenics were the chief scientific concerns of the laymen between the Civil War and the Great Depression.[37] The ideas of the survival of the fittest and of the danger posed to American ideals by the inferior immigrant masses were popular everywhere. This widespread concern was the most powerful ideological club of the drys. They trumpeted abroad that prohibition would strengthen the American stock, already degenerating fast under immigration and the attacks of the Siamese twins, alcohol and venereal disease. As late as 1927, a Frenchman in the United States was still warning visitors from Europe to take a treatise on eugenics with them as well as a Bible. Armed with these two talismans, he assured them that they would never get beyond their depth.[38]

The drys set out to prove that alcohol was a race poison. They were helped by the early scientific experiments with alcohol on animals, by the belief of most of the eugenic experts, and by the current folklore that a taste for liquor could even be inherited through the nipple of a drunken nurse.* According to such influential British eugenicists as Caleb W. Saleeby, all theories of heredity, those of Lamarck and Weismann and Mendel and Darwin's pangenesis, made out that the drunkard must not have children. Alcohol, as well as destroying degenerates, made degenerates. Alcoholism was both a cause and a symptom of degeneracy. The main source of the supply of drunkards was the drunkard himself. Parents might ignore the fact that spirits were a racial poison, but their selfishness ruined the unborn. There was an urgent need to save first women and children from alcohol, then fathers and possible fathers. Otherwise, the noblest races in the world, the English and the Scotch and the French, would be conquered by alcoholic imperialism. Those who defended the alcoholic poisoning of the race were easily classified. Some few stood honestly for liberty. They would rather see their country free than sober, not asking in what sense a drunken country could be called free. Some were merely

---

* In *Munsey's*, September, 1917, Professor Reginald Daly, of Harvard, accused the Germans of giving their children a brutal streak by introducing them to alcohol too young. "If the [German] baby has not been already prenatally damaged because of beer drunk by his mother, he still runs the risk of poisoning from the alcohol-bearing milk of a drinking mother or wet nurse."

irritated by the temperance fanatic. Many feared that their personal comfort might be interfered with.

> But probably the overwhelming majority are concerned with their pockets. They live by this cannibal trade; by selling death and the slaughter of babies, feeble-mindedness and insanity, consumption and worse diseases, crime and pauperism, degradation of body and mind in a thousand forms, to the present generation and therefore to the future, the unconsulted party to the bargain. Their motto is "your money and your life."[39]

Professor Saleeby was mild in his denunciation of alcohol as a racial poison compared with his American contemporaries. One Kentucky horse breeder demanded in 1917 the right of all Americans to be well-born. Anyone who had studied eugenics could "discover if a child comes from a parent or parents addicted to drink, just as well as from parents that have syphilis. . . . Every drink taken by young people is a menace to the nation. Children conceived of parents, who, at the moment of conception, are under the effect of liquor, often are stupid or brainless and inherit the taste for liquor." Drinking by young married people was a conspiracy to destroy half of their children. "It would be less cruel to dispose of children at birth than to allow the indiscriminate use of liquor by men and women who are to become parents."[40]

But the most popular of all the writers or speakers on the subject of race degeneracy through alcohol was the great orator Richmond Pearson Hobson. The hero of the sinking of the *Merrimac* in Santiago harbor in the war in Cuba, Captain Hobson was held by George Jean Nathan to be the most dashing figure of romance for American women until the coming of Valentino. He turned his talents to lecturing and representing Alabama in Congress. In December, 1914, he introduced in the House of Representatives an early version of the Eighteenth Amendment to the Constitution. During the following nine years, he lectured for forty or fifty weeks a year for the Anti-Saloon League, earning the incredible total of $171,250 in that time.[41]

One of his speeches was endlessly repeated before audiences on the Chautauqua circuit and in Congress. It was called "The Great Destroyer." Hobson saw the history of the world as the history of alcohol. Civilizations rose with prohibition and temperance, only to decline with luxury and liquor. In the past 2300 years of civilized history, war had killed off five times fewer people among the white races than alcohol killed each year in modern times. Furthermore, 125,000,-000 living people with white skins were presently harmed by liquor. Alcohol destroyed yearly over half of America's wealth and tainted half her people. A man had to be selfish to oppose prohibition. "A man may take chances with himself, but if he has a spark of nobility in his soul, he will take care how he tampers with a deadly poison that will cause the helpless little children that he brings into the world to be deformed, idiotic, epileptic, insane." Moreover, the decay of civilizations showed that a nation only survived while the good country life ruled over the evil cities.

> As young as our Nation is, the deadly work of alcohol has already blighted liberty in our greatest cities. At the present rate of the growth of cities over country life, if no check is put upon the spread of alcoholic degeneracy, the day cannot be far distant when liberty in great States must go under. It will then be but a question of time when the average standard of character of the Nation's electorate will fall below that inexorable minimum, and liberty will take her flight from America, as she did from Greece and Rome.

The death grapple of the races was already imminent. If the United States became degenerate under the influence of the great destroyer, alcohol, the yellow man would take over the world.

> In America the star of empire moving westward finishes the circle of the world. In America we are making the last stand of the great white race, and substantially of the human race. If this destroyer can not be conquered in young America, it can not in any of the old and more degenerate nations. If America fails, the world will be undone and the human race will be doomed to go down from degeneracy into degeneracy till the Almighty in wrath wipes the accursed thing out.[42]

This complex of racism and nationalism based on sexual fears of disease was repeated over and over again by the advocates of prohibition. The Census figures of 1910 which showed that the wicked city-dwellers and the foreign-born and their children were nearly half of the population of the United States drove the drys wild with the sense of urgency. National prohibition had to come. It would save the inferior hordes of Eastern Europe from themselves and preserve the strength of the Anglo-Saxon stock. In 1913, the same year that the Anti-Saloon League adopted its policy of seeking national prohibition, an extreme dry was writing, "By continuing the alcoholization of the immigrant we are bringing ourselves dangerously near to the time when the question will not be what America will do for the immigrant but what the immigrant will do for America."[43] The old America of the country was being threatened; the ideals of the Republic were being attacked. Something had to be done.

THE FEAR OF THE UNMENTIONABLE

THERE IS an important and unwritten history of the Western world. Its subject is the influence of venereal diseases on the culture and morals of societies. The records of such a history would be hard to discover. And it would be harder to calculate the exact influence of the fear of the diseases. How much repression, how much unhappiness, how much moral legislation has been caused by dread of the pox? No one can tell; because few, except the prohibitionists, have declared their real motives and terrors. It has been said with some truth that the brothel is the bricks of the church. It is more certain that syphilis was the cement of the drys.

In the nineteenth century, the words "syphilis" and "gonorrhea" were taboo, except among doctors or among ministers attending meetings of The National Christian League for the Promotion of Purity. The use of the precise words describing these widespread diseases was as difficult as the use now of the legal term "buggery." Although everyone knew of the two diseases by some sort of whispering grapevine, no one called them by their true names. The consequences of sleeping with infected prostitutes were referred to as "the dread disease," "the fruits of sin," "the infant's blight," "the social horror," and "the awful harvest." Venereal diseases were usually lumped together with the concept of alcohol as a racial poison. For instance, the *National Temperance Almanac,* in its *Second Declaration of Independence* in 1876, attacked King Alcohol in general for his rule:

> He has occasioned more than three-fourths of the pauperism, three-fourths of the crime, and more than one-half of the insanity in the community, and thereby filled our prisons, our alms-houses and lunatic asylums, and erected the gibbet before our eyes.
> He has destroyed the lives of tens of thousands of our citizens annually in the most merciless manner.
> He has turned aside hundreds of thousands more of our free and independent citizens to idleness and vice, infused into them the spirit of demons, and degraded them below the level of brutes.
> He has made thousands of widows and orphans, and destroyed the fondest hopes and blasted the brightest prospects.
> He has introduced among us hereditary diseases, both physical and mental, thereby tending to deteriorate the human race.[44]

This indictment of liquor did not, however, state the actual diseases which alcohol was supposed to cause. The shocking detail of these plagues was left to hearsay and the imagination.

By the turn of the century, social reformers were more ready to call venereal disease "venereal." The first reliable statistics were too horrifying to ignore. The secretary of the Illinois Vigilance Committee estimated that there were eighty thousand known cases of venereal disease in Chicago in 1910. In Syracuse, New York, the known cases were over three people in every hundred.[45] And these were only the known cases. Estimates of the unknown were huge. In 1913, a leading dry claimed to show "three-fifths of the rising generation mentally and physically diseased."[46] Richmond Pearson Hobson supported this claim, saying, "Probably, certainly, more than fifty per cent of adult males are tainted with some form of terrible vice disease, the whelp of liquor." The solution was simple: "If we make the world sober, we solve the vice disease, the vice problem. If we win our great reform, we eliminate racial poison."[47] In actual fact, it is unlikely that many more than one in ten Americans suffered from venereal diseases at that time. The reasonable estimate of the dry Josephus Daniels made out that 8 per cent of the American population suffered from syphilis, while more fell victim to gonorrhea.[48]

The prohibitionists used venereal disease as they used other medical facts, as a weapon of distortion and terror. They wanted to scare people into chastity and purity and temperance. To point out the advantages of these states was not enough. One of the posters issued by the press of the Anti-Saloon League in 1913 advertised THE EFFECT OF ALCOHOL ON SEX LIFE. It declared in bold black type that sex life was dominated by a compelling instinct as natural as eating and drinking. The laws of custom and modern civilization demanded that sex life be under the control of reason, judgment, and will. Alcohol made all natural instincts stronger, and weakened judgment and will, through which control acted. Alcohol and all drinks of which alcohol formed even a small part were harmful and dangerous to sex life for four reasons:

I. ALCOHOL INFLAMES THE PASSIONS, thus making the temptation to sex-sin unusually strong.

II. ALCOHOL DECREASES THE POWER OF CONTROL, thus making the resisting of temptation especially difficult.

III. ALCOHOL DECREASES THE RESISTANCE OF THE BODY TO DISEASE, thus causing the person who is under the influence of alcohol more likely to catch disease.

IV. ALCOHOL DECREASES THE POWER OF THE BODY TO RECOVER FROM DISEASE, thus making the result of disease more serious.

The influence of alcohol upon sex-life could hardly be worse.

AVOID ALL ALCOHOLIC DRINK ABSOLUTELY.

The control of sex impulses will then be easy and disease, dishonor, disgrace and degradation will be avoided.[49]

Again medical science was on the side of the drys. Various studies at the beginning of the century claimed to show that up to four out of five men and two out of three women caught syphilis when they were in a drunken condition. According to these results, too much liquor would make men and women more likely to catch venereal diseases, by lowering their self-restraint and their resistance to infection. Actually, alcohol does not make a man more susceptible to disease, although it does increase his sexual desire and weaken his self-control. It is also a convenient excuse for yielding to temptation. An article in the *Lancet* of 1922 found that many people who confessed that they had caught a venereal infection because of liquor were merely applying a convenient drug to their consciences.

But alcohol does delay the curing of syphilis through certain types of treatment. Some of the new arsenical remedies against syphilis proved dangerous in the case of alcoholics.[50] Therefore, the prohibitionists could and did claim that alcohol increased the incidence of syphilis

SPEAKING OF VICE –

DRY TERROR, 1911

and gonorrhea and prevented their cure. If only prohibition could be enforced, fewer people would contract venereal disease.

Dr. Howard A. Kelley put forward to the delegates of the Anti-Saloon League the vital connection between medicine and morals.

He said that doctors as a group were interested in prohibition more than any other because they met the effects of alcohol wherever they went. They were interested in moral questions because many diseases were wholly due to the infringement of moral laws. To say that a man was interested in the causes and cure of diseases, and then to say that moral questions did not concern him, was to blow hot and cold in the same breath. Three diseases above all others were due "to violations of God's moral code." They were syphilis, gonorrhea, and alcoholism. The Christian minister was interested in these diseases because "they corrupt character, and are associated with a breakdown of the whole moral nature, and absolutely preclude a Christian life." The statesman was interested because "they disrupt the family unit, or poison the fountains of paternity, without which no nation can long exist." And the doctor as a citizen took both of these views, although he was also interested in "the degenerative changes wrought in the brain and the other organs of the body." The alcoholic strained his heart and was prone to arteriosclerosis, chronic gastritis, fibrous liver, and tuberculosis; pneumonia was particularly fatal to beer drinkers. The alcohol habit led easily to other drug habits. Alcohol caused poverty, diminished patriotism, and killed people on the roads. And time and time again, the doctor heard the cry of the wretched victims of syphilis, "Why, doctor, I would never have entered such a house if I had not been drinking."[51]

WOMEN AND CHILDREN FIRST

THE METHODS of terror of the drys worked particularly well on women and children. Men might be expected to be scofflaws, but women were presumed to be the moral guardians of the nation. Female education in the nineteenth century, both in school and through popular magazines and almanacs, emphasized the importance of purity, health, hygiene, and the rigid control of sexual desire. Walter Lippmann pointed out in 1929 that until quite recently the conventions of respectable society had demanded that a woman must not appear amorous unless her suitor promised marriage and must submit to his embraces only because the Lord had somehow failed to contrive a less vile method of perpetuating the species. Even in marriage, procreation was woman's only sanction for sexual intercourse.[52]

According to the conventions of the Victorian middle classes, adultery was possible inside marriage. The sexual instinct should not be gratified too often. Desire was a male preserve. A wife should yield to her husband not more than once or twice a month in case overindulgence might weaken his seed. During pregnancy and nursing and menstruation, a husband should keep away from his wife. The generative powers of the male were thought to be "much greater and better if the organs never had more than a monthly use."[53] The Mormon men had become degenerate and heretical because of too much intercourse. Women must use reason and gentleness to control the lusts of the male. Anything that made a man forget his consideration for his wife was evil. And alcohol was the chief enemy of self-restraint and conscience. If sex was to be kept within the woman's control, liquor must be banned.

This middle-class concept of the differing sexual roles of men and women led to the rise of the "double standard," which held that women represented the good and men the base. Although some women were held to be lewd, they were only the small minority of the sex. "Let us save that greater per cent," urged a Southern Congressman, "the unwilling deflowered."[54] Alcohol was the means by which women were persuaded to give way to their own hidden lusts. It was the very instrument of sin. Although these beliefs were middle-class in origin and practice, they were the dominant beliefs and affected the behavior of working-class women through the popular literature of the time. There was, indeed, another "double standard" between the behavior of the middle classes and that of the rural and urban proletariat. For the hired hands on the farms, a girl "was the most desired thing in the world, a prize to be worked for, sought for and enjoyed without remorse. She had no soul. The maid who yielded to temptation deserved no pity, no consideration, no aid. Her sufferings were amusing, her diseases a joke, her future of no account."[55] But the fact that the reform movements were usually middle-class movements, and that the sexual taboos of the middle classes were often adopted by women lower down the social scale, made the bourgeois concept of sexual repression and reserve a potent drive behind the dry cause.

Carry A. Nation, who broke up rumshops in Kansas with a hatchet at the turn of the century, wrote a revealing autobiography. Unconsciously and clearly, she showed how sin and frustrated desire turned her into a dragon of temperance. Born in 1846 in Kentucky, she was brought up in the idealized position of a Southern maiden. Her father was a zealous churchgoer and gave her a fear of going to the "Bad Place." Her family later moved to Missouri. She was converted to the Christian, or Disciples', Church, after total immersion in an icy stream. She then suffered from "consumption of the bowels" for five years. During the Civil War, she nursed the wounded. After the war, she became a teacher and hoped for a husband.

Her own comments on her amatory nature show up her times. "I was a great lover," she wrote, yet "my native modesty prevented me

from ever dancing a round dance with a gentleman. I cannot think
this hugging school compatible with a true woman." In 1865, a young
physician who was boarding with her family kissed her for the first
time in her life. "I had never had a gentleman to take such a privilege
and felt shocked, threw up my hands to my face, saying several times;
'I am ruined.'" Two years later, Carry married the young doctor. He
immediately took to the bottle and tobacco, and neglected his wife's
loving care. She became jealous, accusing the Masons of making her
husband into a drunkard. A daughter Charlien was born. Of this
event, Carry wrote, "Oh, the curse that comes through heredity, and
this liquor evil, a disease that entails more depravity on children unborn, than all else, unless it be tobacco." Her mother made her leave
her husband to protect the child, although he begged her to stay.
"I did not know then that drinking men were drugged men, diseased
men." Six months later, her husband was dead, as he had forecast
when she left him.

Soon Carry married again; her new husband was the Reverend
David Nation, a Union Army veteran, a lawyer, a newspaper editor,
and minister. The marriage was not a happy one. Carry thought her
husband deceitful. Her combative nature was developed by living
with him, for she had to fight for everything she kept. After a while,
they separated. Carry ran a boarding house and looked after her
daughter Charlien. The child developed typhoid fever; her right cheek
rotted away; she was unable to open her teeth for eight years. Carry
knew that her sin in marrying her first husband and in conceiving a
child had brought its retribution.

> This my only child was peculiar. She was the result of a drunken
> father and a distracted mother. The curse of heredity is one of the
> most heart-breaking results of the saloon. Poor little children are
> brought into the world with the curse of drink and disease entailed
> upon them. . . . If girls were taught that a drunkard's curse will in
> the nature of things include his children and also that if either parents
> allowed bad thoughts or actions to come into their lives, that their
> offspring will be a reproduction of their own sins, they would avoid
> these men, and men will give up their vice before they will give up
> women.

Luckily, Carry's daughter recovered and eventually married. Carry
moved to Kansas, which was then under state-wide prohibition.
Pushed by her sense of guilt and religion, she naturally joined the
local Woman's Christian Temperance Union and became a Jail Evan-
gelist. She stood outside the shops of the illegal "druggists" who sold
liquor, singing with other women:

Who hath sorrow? Who hath woe?
They who dare not answer no;
They whose feet to sin incline,
While they tarry at the wine.

At last she found her vocation in life, after many years of unhappiness and drudgery. Her explanations of this new happiness are particularly revealing:

> The man I loved and married brought to me bitter grief. The child I loved so well became afflicted and never seemed to want my love. The man I married, hoping to serve God, I found to be opposed to all I did, as a Christian. I used to wonder why this was. I saw others with their loving children and husbands and I would wish their condition was mine. I now see why God saw in me a great lover, and in order to have me use that love for Him, and others, He did not let me have those that would have narrowed my life down to my own selfish wishes. Oh! the grief He has sent me! Oh! the fiery trials! Oh! the shattered hopes! How I love Him for this! "Whom the Lord loveth He chasteneth and scourgeth every son whom He receiveth."

From this time on, Carry became a little mad. She saw demons who threatened to tear her up. She seemed to suffer from a sort of delirium tremens of virtue. Her fellow temperance workers became so frightened by her aggressiveness that they tried to disown her. She made plans to wreck saloons with rocks and a hatchet. Again the drive behind her crusade against alcohol seems to have been sexual. On December 27, 1900, she strode into the Carey Hotel in Wichita.

> The first thing that struck me was the life-size picture of a naked woman, opposite the mirror. This was an oil painting with a glass over it, and was a very fine painting hired from the artist who painted it, to be put in that place for a vile purpose. I called to the bartender; told him he was insulting his own mother by having her form stripped naked and hung up in a place where it was not even decent for a woman to be in when she had her clothes on. . . . It is very significant that the pictures of naked women are in saloons. Women are stripped of everything by them. Her husband is torn from her, she is robbed of her sons, her home, her food and her virtue, and then they strip her clothes off and hang her up bare in these dens of robbery and murder. Truly does a saloon make a woman bare of all things! The motive for doing this is to suggest vice, animating the animal in man and degrading the respect he should have for the sex to whom he owes his being, yes, his Savior also!

During her raid, Carry was attacked by saloonkeepers' wives, mistresses, and prostitutes. She spent some time in jail. She then capitalized on her national renown, and went on Chautauqua tours and on the vaudeville circuits, selling little souvenir hatchets wherever she went. Her second husband divorced her after twenty-four years of marriage on the grounds of cruelty and desertion. Carry took this action as another of God's decisions to confirm her in her cause. When he died in 1907, she had a headstone and footstone put on his grave and declared that she was glad God was the judge between them. "God never used or blessed any man or woman that was not a prohibitionist." She warned Yale and Harvard that only teetotalers ever reached heaven. Whenever she met a young man alone with a young woman, she told them of the terrible consequences of sin and sent them fleeing in terror. She died of paresis in June, 1911, after doing much to publicize both the evils of the saloon and the excesses of the drys.[56]

Carry Nation is worth examining at length because she embodied in an extreme form nearly all the sexual fears and contradictions which dry propaganda exploited. She was brought up among the "downright gyneolatry" of the South in a nation where women were widely flattered in words, only to be exploited in work.[57] She was taught an acute sense of sin and a belief in sexual restraint, although her nature was passionate and ready to love; her frustration was easily turned to moral crusading. She was indoctrinated with the myth that the Devil and disease lurked in strong drink; thus any illness which afflicted her child was attributed to the known evils of liquor rather than to the attacks of an unknown virus. Once her child had left her and her second husband was estranged, she could find no outlet for her urge to do political work except in the Woman's Christian Temperance Union. Above all, her suppressed sexual desire was perverted into an itching curiosity about vice, an aggressive prurience which found its outlet in violence, exhibitionism, and self-imposed martyrdom. Significantly, the first two rocks she threw at the Carey Hotel in Wichita were at the painting of the naked woman; the third stone demolished the mirror behind the bar. Only then did Carry destroy the contents of the sideboard with an iron rod.

Respectable women of this time not only feared that their husbands would pick up venereal diseases from prostitutes in the saloons or taint their children with the poison of alcohol. They were also afraid that they could not control the lusts of drinking men. A dry social worker wrote that, even if prostitution were to be eliminated, an evil hardly less "was the sex abuses committed within the bonds of wedlock by men returning home after an evening of alcoholism accented by sex suggestion. This, to the discerning, has been one of the final arguments against the saloon as an intolerable canker on the body politic."[58] Purity before marriage and decency afterwards were not possible

GOING INTO CAPTIVITY

when liquor might turn the subservient Negro into the drink-crazed raper or the docile husband into the insistent Casanova.

Since not all women were demonstrably either pure or virtuous, alcohol was made the scapegoat for their fall. In dry literature the consequence of a boy's first beer was always death by delirium tremens, while a girl who drank liquor inevitably met with seduction, prostitution, or worse. The inevitable horror-monger, Richmond Pearson Hobson, accused alcohol of more than destroying the race; it was unquestionably "the primary cause of the condition of feeble-minded, unbalanced female sex-perverts, and of those women and girls who, though of sound mind, were taken advantage of through the temporary suspension of their higher faculties as the result of drink."[59] The Anti-Saloon League widely publicized Jane Addams's conclusion that alcohol was the indispensable tool of the white-slave traders.[60] In areas of the country where Jews were not accused of buying up the virtue of Gentile virgins or Roman Catholic priests of seducing Protestant girls in nunneries, the denunciation of alcohol and vice provided a desired titillation for church audiences.

But the drys appealed to women's rights as well as to their phobias. Their appeal was called an appeal to freedom. How could drinkers claim that their personal liberty was being attacked when their wives were slaves? Did not freedom to drink for men mean mere freedom for women to drudge, to scrape, and to starve? Could any woman be called free who did not have a decent income and husband? Did not women have the right to ensure the health of their children? Was not the real slave the drink slave? Jack London was so persuaded by this propaganda that he voted for female suffrage in California in 1911 so that the women in turn could vote to deprive him of liquor. "The moment women get the vote in any community, the first thing they proceed to do, or try to do, is to close the saloons. In a thousand generations to come men of themselves will not close the saloons. As well as expect the morphine victims to legislate the sale of morphine out of existence."[61] True freedom for men lay in allowing their womenfolk to purify the race by depriving weak male nature of all opportunities for sin in the saloons.

THE DOCTORS AND THE PROFITS

THE AMERICAN Medical Association is a formidable organization. As far back as 1907, it was called the "most powerful trained lobby in the country."[62] It had an agent in each of the 2830 counties of the United States. Its list of approachable political leaders numbered sixteen thousand. It was backed by the life insurance companies and Standard Oil.

Only the influence of the Anti-Saloon League and the veterans compared with its power among lobbies which were not obviously dedicated to big-business interests.

Doctors in America have continually fought the tradition of folk medicine. Their fight has sometimes been difficult, since folk medicine is much cheaper than a physician. At the end of the nineteenth century, patent medicines heavily laced with alcohol were enjoying a great vogue in dry areas, as well as such home remedies as cider vinegar and honey. Medical practitioners often found that patients relied on quack nostrums bought at county fairs, or on remedies advertised in farmers' almanacs, such as Healey's Bitters and Allen's Cherry Pectoral "to purify the blood." The rise of Christian Science, faith healers, osteopaths, chiropractors, and dietitians made further inroads into the incomes of physicians licensed by the Medical Association. Official pharmacists also found themselves menaced by unqualified druggists, who dealt in powders and herbs and dilute alcohol. Before the passage of the Pure Food and Drug Act of 1906, an annual business worth seventy-five million dollars a year was done by makers of patent medicines, which "eradicated" asthma with sugar and water, "soothed" babies with deadly opiates, "relieved" headaches with dangerous coal-tar drugs, "dispelled" catarrh with cocaine, and "cured" tuberculosis, cancer, and Bright's disease with disguised alcohol.[63] * Even after the Act, the patent-medicine trade continued to flourish.

A new menace to the profits of the doctors arose at the beginning of the century. Chemotherapy was developed to compete with serum therapy. The doctors had a monopoly of treatment by serums; but when research seemed to make possible in the near future direct treatment by tonics and pills, physicians became frightened for their livelihood. The discovery by Ehrlich in 1909 of Salvarsan, the first nontoxic germicide, appeared to be an attack on doctors' fees; an improved germicide was on the market by 1916. Those who suffered from venereal and other diseases could now be cured quicker and much more simply. Other chemical preparations would be discovered to take the place of prolonged and expensive courses of medical treatment. Drug manufacturers would thrive, while doctors and pharmacists grew poor.

This fear for the future of their professions is an explanation for the strange behavior of the pharmacists and the American Medical Asso-

* R. and H. Lynd, in their seminal Middletown, found that advertisements for patent medecines filled up a great deal of the advertising space in newspapers as late as 1925. Most of these advertisements offered some form of quick and suspicious treatment for disease. Among these were Musterole ("Usually gives prompt relief from [nineteen ailments] — it may prevent pneumonia"); Lydia E. Pinkham's Vegetable Compound ("An operation avoided"); and Baume Bengué ("When in pain").

ciation. In 1916, *The Pharmacopoeia of the United States* dropped whisky and brandy from its list of standard drugs. On June 6, 1917, the President of the American Medical Association delivered a speech in favor of prohibition. The House of Delegates then passed one resolution, which asked the United States Senate to control the spread of syphilis by ending the German patents on the manufacture of Salvarsan, and another resolution condemning the use of alcohol. This second resolution stated:

> WHEREAS, We believe that the use of alcohol as a beverage is detrimental to the human economy, and
>
> WHEREAS, Its use in therapeutics, as a tonic or a stimulant or as a food has no scientific basis, therefore be it
>
> *Resolved*, That the American Medical Association opposes the use of alcohol as a beverage; and be it further
>
> *Resolved*, That the use of alcohol as a therapeutic agent should be discouraged.[64]

This resolution was extremely useful to the drys in their campaign for national prohibition. Senator Sterling, of South Dakota, referred to it in the debate on the Eighteenth Amendment as "one of the most valuable pieces of evidence we can find in support of the submission of this amendment to the several States of the Union."[65] Wayne B. Wheeler quoted it as definitive evidence, while defending the dry definition of "intoxicating" in the courts. The resolution was also very profitable to the doctors. After the passage of the Eighteenth Amendment and the Volstead Act, they were the only people who could legally issue to their patients whisky, brandy, and other strong drinks. Moreover, no patent medicine containing alcohol could be officially sold without a doctor's prescription. By constitutional amendment, the doctors controlled all supplies of beverage alcohol in the United States, except for the hard cider of the farmers and the sacramental wine of the priests.

If the American Medical Association had really believed that alcohol was detrimental to the human economy, its condemnation would have been just. But alcohol was still being widely prescribed as a medicine in 1917. It was recommended by many doctors in cases of fainting, shock, heart failure, exposure, and exhaustion. It was believed to be an antidote to snake bite, pneumonia, influenza, diphtheria, and anemia. It was used as a method of feeding carbohydrates to sufferers from diabetes. It was given to cheer and build up the aged. Insufficient research had been done to state definitely that alcoholic drinks possessed no food value. Nothing was said in the resolution about the fact that small quantities of alcohol taken with meals might aid the digestion and relax the mind. The wording of the resolution did not mention the use of alcohol as a narcotic and depressant, nor as a necessary solvent in many chemical preparations. The American Medical Association had laid itself open to the charge that it was trying to control the competition of patent medicines and chemotherapy through its alcohol monopoly.

The prohibitionists exploited the medical and sexual terrors of the people of America in order to further their cause. In the course of this indoctrination, they were helped by the findings of research and the dicta of doctors. They used every means of propaganda to abolish the saloons. For the conflict between the Protestant evangelical churches of the United States and the saloons was unceasing and bitter. The saloons were held to be the enemies both of God and of the Protestant faith. They were embroiled in a religious quarrel between rival churches, and a social quarrel between clericals and anticlericals. They also competed with the pulpits in their attraction to all and sundry. The conflict of country and city and the aggressive psychology of the drys demanded that the struggle between the churches and the saloons be fought to a finish.

The Churches against the Saloons

The saloon is an infidel. It has no faith in God; has no religion. It would close every church in the land. It would hang its beer signs on the abandoned altars. It would close every public school. It respects the thief and it esteems the blasphemer; it fills the prisons and the penitentiaries.

It cocks the highwayman's pistol. It puts the rope in the hands of the mob. It is the anarchist of the world, and its red flag is dyed with the blood of women and children; it sent the bullet through the body of Lincoln; it nerved the arm that sent the bullets through Garfield and William McKinley. Yes, it is a murderer.

I tell you that the curse of God Almighty is on the saloon.

BILLY SUNDAY

Undoubtedly the church and the saloon originated in pre-historic times — probably simultaneously. And they have been rivals ever since. Man first began to pray to his idols. The priest gathered around him under his sacred tree or in his sanctified cave those whom he could induce to believe in the "gods" while the preparer of the *real* joys of life required no argument to induce people to trade with him. So the saloon man had the advantage from the start.

BREWER'S JOURNAL, 1910

Somehow or another, Hinnissy, it don't seem just right that there shud be a union iv church an' saloon. These two gr-reat institutions ar-re best kept apart. They kind iv offset each other, like th' Supreem Coort an' Congress. Dhrink is a nicissry evil, nicissry to th' clargy. If they iver admit it's nicissry to th' consumers they might as well close up th' churches.

FINLEY PETER DUNNE

My objection to the saloon-keeper is the same that I have to the louse — he makes his living off the head of a family.

SAM P. JONES

THE CHURCHES AT CANA

GREAT CITIES were the enemies of the evangelical Protestant churches of America. They fostered liberals and agnostics, saloons and Roman Catholics. Nothing seemed more dangerous to the fundamental beliefs of primitive American Protestantism than the urban millions.

The Roman Catholic Church in America, except for the areas which were once under Spanish rule and the border districts settled by French Canadians, was based on the large cities. Immigration to America from the middle of the nineteenth century until the Great War favored the Roman Catholic faith. The immigrants tended to remain as cheap labor in the large cities, displacing the old population which moved out West. From being a small minority group, communicants of the Church of Rome grew to a total of more than one-third of all church members between 1890 and 1916.

In the latter year, the Roman Catholic Church had over half the church members of fifteen states, and was first in number in thirty-three states. Its main strength lay in the East, with pockets on the Pacific and in Louisiana and Texas. Over one-half of the Catholics were concentrated in five great states with large votes in the electoral college: New York, Pennsylvania, Massachusetts, Illinois, and Ohio. Over 5,000,000 Catholics lived in cities with a population of 300,000 or more; they constituted two out of three church members in those cities. Nearly 4,000,000 Catholics lived in cities with a population of between 25,000 and 300,000; they made up one out of two church members in those smaller cities. Although over 6,500,000 Catholics lived outside these urban districts, they lived among more than 26,000,000 Protestants. In rural areas, only one out of five church members were Catholics. Yet, by 1916, over four-fifths of the land of America was nominally dry, although less than half of the population lived in these counties. The saloons were concentrated in the large cities. The Protestant charge that the cities were the home of rum and Rome was true.*

The main supporters of prohibition were the Methodist, the Baptist, the Presbyterian, and the Congregational churches, aided by the smaller Disciples of Christ, Christian Science, and Mormon religious groups.[1] Four out of five of the members of these churches lived in small towns or in the countryside, for their converts had been made chiefly by mis-

---

* This has remained true. The election of President Kennedy in 1960 was largely due to the heavy Roman Catholic vote for him in the Eastern cities. The ratio of Catholics to Protestants in America has remained roughly one to two ever since 1890, although the proportion of nominal church members has grown from 40 to 60 per cent of the whole population.

sionary circuit riders. The Methodist churches were the most militant of the seven. In 1914, the secretary of the Liquor Dealers' Association said that it was necessary only to read the list of those preachers who were active in the propaganda for prohibition to realize that the Methodist Church was obsessed with the ambition to gain control of the government.[2] Although the statement was exaggerated, there was truth in it. The Methodist churches were the largest Protestant body in the country, and they worked closely with the Anti-Saloon League.

The Anti-Saloon League, founded in 1893, claimed to be the political machine of the Protestant churches in the matter of prohibition.[3] It called itself "the Protestant church in action" and relied on the various churches for its recruits and finances, although it was careful not to employ those clergymen unwanted by their own churches, "ministerial misfits and clerical flotsam and jetsam."[4] Spokesmen of the League would approach individual pastors and ask their permission to speak at a Sunday service to the congregation. After the sermon, a collection of cash and signed pledges for monthly subscriptions to the League would be collected. The League made it a policy never to send out its speakers unless a collection for the League was taken afterwards. Moreover, each League spokesman had to be an expert fund-raiser. As one League leader put the matter, "If he does not know how, or cannot learn how to present the work in such a way as to secure a hearty response financially, he may as well hand in his resignation."[5]

The League's use of the churches as a milch cow for campaign funds led to much unpleasantness. In the early days of the League, many pastors would refuse the League the opportunity of speaking to their congregations. There was little enough money in the pockets of the faithful for other causes. Moreover, national church councils would not order their ministers to give the League free run of their facilities. They would endorse the League, but fail to help it by particular recommendations. Finally, many churches, jealous of the large harvests reaped from congregations by the League speakers, put their income on a budget basis, allocating a percentage of the yearly take to the League. This system crippled the finances of the League, although it provided more money for other good causes.

The League was officially only a political and educational organization, and thus did not break overtly the American tradition of separation between church and state. Between 1911 and 1925, the average number of churches affiliated to the League was some 30,000, rising to a maximum of 60,000 at the zenith of the League's influence. Through these churches, the League collected up to two million dollars a year in revenue and called out dry votes against wet candidates in political elections. In 1908, Superintendent Nicholson, of Pennsylvania, stated

THE ATTITUDES

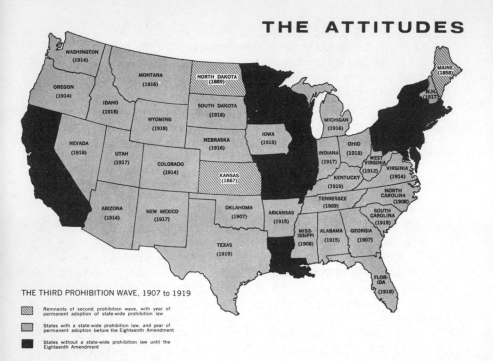

THE THIRD PROHIBITION WAVE, 1907 to 1919

Remnants of second prohibition wave, with year of permanent adoption of state-wide prohibition law

States with a state-wide prohibition law, and year of permanent adoption before the Eighteenth Amendment

States without a state-wide prohibition law until the Eighteenth Amendment

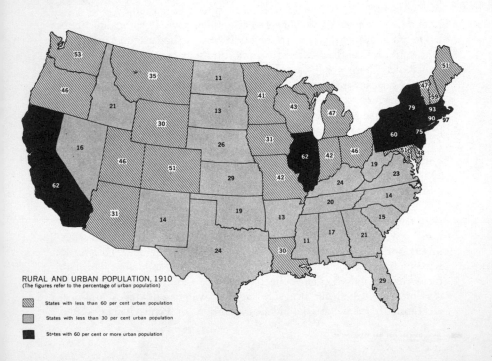

RURAL AND URBAN POPULATION, 1910
(The figures refer to the percentage of urban population)

States with less than 60 per cent urban population

States with less than 30 per cent urban population

States with 60 per cent or more urban population

OF GEOGRAPHY

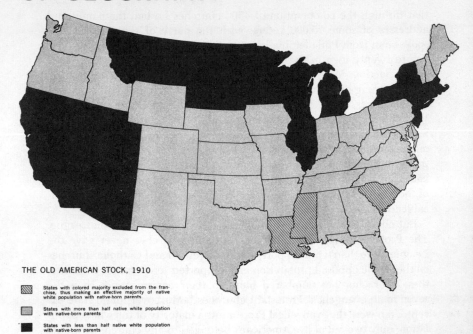

THE OLD AMERICAN STOCK, 1910

░░ States with colored majority excluded from the franchise, thus making an effective majority of native white population with native-born parents

▒▒ States with more than half native white population with native-born parents

██ States with less than half native white population with native-born parents

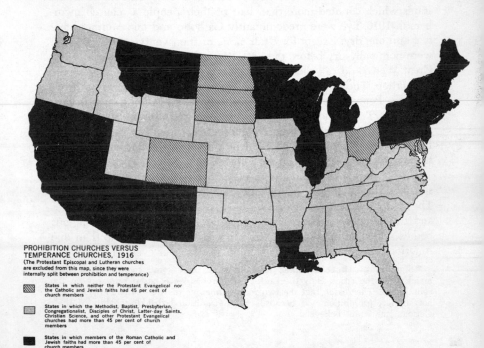

PROHIBITION CHURCHES VERSUS TEMPERANCE CHURCHES, 1916
(The Protestant Episcopal and Lutheran churches are excluded from this map, since they were internally split between prohibition and temperance)

░░ States in which neither the Protestant Evangelical nor the Catholic and Jewish faiths had 45 per cent of church members

▒▒ States in which the Methodist, Baptist, Presbyterian, Congregationalist, Disciples of Christ, Latter-day Saints, Christian Science, and other Protestant Evangelical churches had more than 45 per cent of church members

██ States in which members of the Roman Catholic and Jewish faiths had more than 45 per cent of church members

that through the co-operation of 4500 churches he had the names and addresses of some 75,000 voters, with the party of their choice. His spokesman from Philadelphia boasted that he could dictate twenty letters to twenty men in twenty parts of the city and thereby set 50,000 men in action. With such a political weapon, the Protestant crusade against strong drink had a good chance of conquering even the corrupt city machines, backed by the liquor trade. The first League lobbyist in Washington spoke the truth when he said, "The graves of many state legislators and members of Congress can be seen along our line of march, and there are other graves waiting." He was unconsciously paraphrasing the words of a church politician who had opposed Abraham Lincoln sixty years before: "If there is any thing dear to the hearts of the Know Nothings, it is to write the epitaphs of certain noted political leaders."[6]

But not all of the churches co-operated with the Anti-Saloon League. The Protestant Episcopal and the Lutheran churches never gave the League more than tepid support, while the Jewish and Catholic churches on the whole opposed prohibition and supported temperance. Together, these four churches numbered more in their congregations than the seven main evangelical Protestant churches.* Moreover, in no state except Utah were the evangelical Protestants a majority of the whole population; only two out of five Americans belonged to any church. Of the six states which counted more than half of their people as church members in 1916, five were predominantly Catholic and one Mormon, five wet and one dry. Except for Utah, none of the twenty-six states which were nominally dry before the patriotic and repressive hysteria of the Great War could call their church members a majority of their whole population. The twelve large states of New York, New Jersey, Massachusetts, Pennsylvania, Ohio, Illinois, Wisconsin, Minnesota, Missouri, Louisiana, Texas, and California had no state prohibition law, and contained more than half the church members of America. They also possessed a larger population, more electoral votes, wealth, factories, and schools than all the other thirty-six states.

Thus, national prohibition appeared to be persecution of the large states by the small ones, of the city churches by the country churches. The claim of the Anti-Saloon League that it represented the churches and the majority of Americans was false. The seven major religious bodies which supported prohibition could not muster more than one American out of five behind their banners. Also, for every church mem-

* Significantly, three of these four churches had some two-thirds of their members in the cities. Only the Lutheran churches were based primarily on the countryside. The reason that the two most numerous of the Lutheran synods did not support prohibition was because of the traditional drinking habits of their German immigrant believers.

ber who was a dry, there was another church member who was a wet.

Yet the fact is that national prohibition did become the law of the land. This was partly due to the brilliant political methods of the drys. But it was above all due to their conquerors' air. They had said so repeatedly and so insistently that prohibition would come to the nation that few were surprised when it did, and fewer would speak out openly against it. No one wanted to seem to oppose the inevitable success of "The Prohibition Band-Wagon":

> O, it won't be long, is the burden of our song,
>   Till we get our wagon started on the way,
> And our friends who vote for gin will all scramble to jump in,
>   When we get our big band-wagon, some sweet day.

Indeed, the drys pushed the problem of liquor so much into the forefront of political affairs that it overshadowed more important matters. The Jesuit weekly *America* acknowledged this in an editorial:

> The decalogue is no longer up to date. "Thou shalt not kill," in certain contingencies, is of less moment than "Thou shalt not drink wine"; "Thou shalt not commit adultery" is on a par with "Thou shalt not use tobacco"; whereas, "Thou shalt not steal," appears to be of less consequence to a class of reformers than "Thou shalt not play Sunday baseball."[7]

The fantastic disproportion which the question of alcohol and the Puritan reformers assumed in the minds of clergy and laity was the measure of the success and of the shame of the drys. When a moral movement hailed a Great War because of the huge wave of prohibition legislation passed by the combatants, it ran the risk of being accused of supporting mass murder to gain the doubtful benefits of universal pure water.

The drys, who relied heavily on the authority of the Bible and the bad examples of the drunken Noah and Belshazzar, had one great problem. Clarence Darrow put the matter nastily when he wrote:

> The orthodox Christian cannot consistently be a prohibitionist or a total abstainer. If God, or the Son of God, put alcohol into his system, then alcohol cannot be a poison that has no place in that system. God, or the Son of God, would hardly set so vicious and criminal an example to the race he is supposed to have come to save.[8]

Moreover, there was the more unpleasant fact that Jesus Christ Himself turned water into wine at Cana and drank that wine. He also recommended that His followers should drink wine in memory of Him. Both biology and the Bible seemed to make the position of the religious prohibitionist untenable. He could not answer John Erskine's question to his dry friend: Was the Eighteenth Amendment an amendment to the Constitution or to the New Testament?[9]

There was a classical argument between church scholars on this point. To the drys, the Bible sanctioned the total prohibition of liquor. The process of distillation had not been invented until seven centuries after Christ, nor was there any proof that the Jews knew how to make beer. Therefore, prohibition of spirits and ale was perfectly in accordance with the Bible. Although wine was mentioned in the Bible over two hundred times and approved by God Himself, it was only a slightly fermented substance mixed with honey. The wine of the Hebrews was not adulterated, nor did the local liquor traders have an organized power for evil. The Jewish race was never as much addicted to intemperance as the Anglo-Saxon because of the mild climate of Palestine and of the easygoing way of life there. Moreover, the Jewish peasant was too poor to buy much liquor. Therefore, the drink problem was insignificant among the Hebrews compared with the Anglo-Saxon communities. Wine was indeed a staple article of food in the ancient world like grain, oil, and milk; but it was so only because of the plenteous vineyards, the impossibility of storing grapes, and the illusion that wine was a tonic or medicine. Although the Bible could be quoted by the Pharisees of the drink trade to prove that God had blessed wine, there was no doubt that a reborn Christ would blast the saloon and back total abstinence.[10]

To wet clergymen, the dry cause and the fanaticism of fundamentalist reformers denied the liberal principles of Christianity. Alcohol was expressly sanctioned by the Bible. The Hebrew word *yayin* and the Greek word *oinos* both referred to fermented grape juice. Jehovah and Jesus Christ blessed its use in moderation. *Yayin* was certainly used at the Passover feast, and Jesus definitely made wine of the finest quality at the feast of Cana. It was to save the world from the harsh doctrines of John the Baptist and his immersion of the faithful in cold water that Christ instituted a wine feast in His memory. The very bondage from which mankind was saved by Christ's death was being imposed again by the prohibitionists. Legalism had crucified Jesus. The new legalists would crucify Him afresh and put Him to open shame by blaspheming the liberty He won for men. According to one Episcopalian, the Christ-spirit only tended one way. It freed men from the Sabbatarianism and teetotalism which the prohibitionists were trying to impose anew. The typical and symbolic miracle of modern Pharisees would be the turning of wine into water.[11]

Freud says that judgments of value are attempts to prop up illusions by arguments.[12] Whatever the truth of this judgment of value, the matter of sacramental wine did seem to split the churches more on the lines of their attitudes toward prohibition than toward biblical research.

The seven major evangelical Protestant churches served only unfermented grape juice at religious ceremonies. Their brothers, the Roman Catholic and the Jewish and the Episcopalian churches, continued to use altar wine with an alcoholic content throughout prohibition. Religious conviction, ill health, and a taste for fermented apple juice were the three conditions of body and soul allowed legal liquor throughout the twenties.

During the whole of its career, the Anti-Saloon League depended on the evangelical churches. When the League was attacked, those churches were also attacked. Before the passage of the Eighteenth Amendment, proposals were made that since the churches had engaged in politics through the medium of the League, their property should be taxed. In 1876, President Grant had recommended a constitutional amendment to this effect, which had passed the House and had only failed in the Senate by two votes. Should not his proposal be revived? A bill was actually introduced in the New York state legislature for this purpose. The answer to clerical interference in politics was to be political interference in the church. But the passage of the Eighteenth Amendment changed the direction of the wet counterattack to the repeal of existing constitutional errors, not to the addition of more.

During the years after 1913, Congress became increasingly bitter about the political influence of the church reformers and the Anti-Saloon League. Representative Barchfeld, of Pennsylvania, in the debate on the Hobson resolution, voiced this discontent when he said that prohibition had been an instrument of despotism since the world began, the first and the last resource of those who would compel where they could not lead. He then accused the Anti-Saloon League of adopting the methods of the Caesars by proscribing Senators, of being the heir of the old Know-Nothings, and of setting itself up falsely as "the real representative of the moral, sober, industrious, and God-fearing people of the land to dictate to the Congress and employ weapons that belong to the old age of absolutism."[13] Louis Seibold stated in a group of articles in the New York *World* of May, 1919, that the average member of Congress was more afraid of the League than he was of the President of the United States. On all temperance matters, this statement was true.

The entry of the Protestant evangelical churches into politics was a dangerous precedent. Although the church congregations could form the basis of an effective political machine, the traditional separation between church and state in America opened an avenue for a counterattack by politicians on the privileges of religious bodies. And the churches, too, by engaging in political actions, could offend their own members. The church militant can lose as much support as the church dormant.

From *Outlook and Independent*

DRIVEN OUT OF THE CHURCH

THE SALOONS AT SODOM

THE SALOON was the church of the poor. While the churches supplied a meeting place for the respectable, the saloons were the rendezvous of the workers. If religious services provided many of the consolations of the well-to-do, the brass rail provided an equal footing with the rest of humanity for the down-at-heel. While the minister advised and aided his flock, the bartender performed the same service for his regular patrons. Both took in money and dispensed comfort. Both provided an escape from the world. But the virtue of the churchgoers put them at odds with the assumed vice of the refugees of the swinging doors. For the sin of the saloon was that it sold alcohol. And alcohol was dangerous, once it escaped from the control of the virtuous. It is a fact that the only three groups who were allowed by law to make, prescribe, or sell beverage alcohol after the passing of the Volstead Act were the three groups who had been the most active in condemning it: the ministers, the farmers, and the doctors and druggists.

The paternalism and uplift of the reformers were psychologically opposed to the saloon. When the members of the Committee of Fifty at the turn of the century looked for substitutes for the saloon, they recognized the needs which it filled:

> The saloon is the most democratic of institutions. It appeals at once to the common humanity of a man. There is nothing to repel. No questions are asked. Respectability is not a countersign. The doors swing open before any man who chooses to enter. Once within he finds the atmosphere one in which he can allow his social nature freely to expand. The welcome from the keeper is a personal one. The environment is congenial. It may be that the appeal is to what is base in him. He may find his satisfaction because he can give vent to those lower desires which seek expression. The place may be attractive just because it is so little elevating. Man is taken as he is, and is given what he wants, be that want good or bad. The only standard is the demand.

The members of the committee recognized that the saloon was the competitor of the home; but they maintained that the answer was not to close the saloons but to make the homes more welcoming. Once slums were turned into garden suburbs, then a man would drink at his own fireside. "When a man sees outside of the saloon what is more attractive than what he finds in it, he will cease to be its patron."[14]

One reformer thought the church could learn many things from the saloon. There was human fellowship and equality in the saloon, little in the charity home. The saloon had no doorstep; the church hall had. The saloon had glitter; the chapel was drab. The saloon was easy to enter; the religious hall was locked. The saloon was active one hundred

THE OLD-TIME CITY SALOON

and forty hours a week, the church four. No one bothered about a man's business at the saloon. No one asked about his worries or his home troubles. Ragged clothes were not a mark of shame. Free lunches were given for a five-cent glass of beer; if the saloons of New York were closed, twenty-five thousand men would declare that the food had been taken out of their mouths. The saloon provided newspapers, billiards, card tables, bowling alleys, toilets, and washing facilities. And, above all, the saloon provided information and company. The bartender could direct and advise salesmen, pass the time of day with trucksters, enlighten strangers about the habits of the town. "For many the saloon is the most precious thing in life — why destroy it?"[15]

Exclusive of its psychological benefits, the saloon did great service, as well as great harm, to workingmen. It was, in particular, the friend of the immigrant, his only contact with the outer world. It is easy to forget how small and friendless the world of the immigrant was. In Henry Roth's brilliant novel about Jewish immigrant culture in New

York City, *Call It Sleep,* a Jewish mother is made to describe the constriction of her life, after several years spent in America:

> But here I am. I know there is a church on a certain street to my left, the vegetable market is to my right, behind me are the railroad tracks and the broken rocks, and before me, a few blocks away is a certain store window that has a kind of white-wash on it — and faces in the white-wash, the kind children draw. Within this pale is my America, and if I ventured further I should be lost.[16]

For many new Americans, the local saloon was the arbiter of their small world.

The saloon provided immigrant votes to the city boss and corrupt politics to America; but it could only do so by providing jobs and help to the immigrants in return. The ward heelers and barkeepers were the first welfare workers of the slums. The saloons were the first labor exchanges and union halls. They had names such as the "Poor Man's Retreat," "Everybody's Exchange," "The Milkman's Exchange," "The Social," "The Fred," and "The Italian Headquarters." The saloonkeepers had a near monopoly on small halls which could be used for labor meetings and lodges. They would charge no rent for these places in return for the privilege of selling liquor at the meetings. A dry labor leader confessed that he felt a "sensation akin to shame" when he did not buy a glass of beer in the free hall provided by a saloon.[17] In one sense, the attack on the saloons was the attack of capital on the haunts of labor.

The East Side of New York, which produced Al Smith, showed the huge influence of the saloon on the lives and careers of the city communities. Happy memories of Smith's early days were set among lager beer drinkers in the Atlantic Garden; for, in the words of an East Side reformer, the New York drinking places had "the monopoly up to date of all the cheer in the tenements."[18] Even the prohibition clergyman from the Bowery, Charles Stelzle, praised certain features of the old-time saloon, pointing out that most drys had no conception of what it meant to workingmen.

> It was in the saloon that the working men in those days held their christening parties, their weddings, their dances, their rehearsals for their singing societies, and all other social functions. . . . Undoubtedly the chief element of attraction was the saloon-keeper himself. . . . He was a social force in the community. His greeting was cordial, his appearance neat, and his acquaintance large. He had access to sources of information which were decidedly beneficial to the men who patronized his saloon. Often he secured work for both the working man and his children.[19]

In industrial cities, the saloon was often what the church was in a village. It was a center of faith and tradition, political rather than religious. It was a place of recreation and joy. Membership in the right saloon brought social prestige and good jobs, as did membership in the right church. Al Smith's political career began in Tom Foley's saloon, which Smith was careful to call a "café" in his memoirs.[20] The saloon-keeper had in his gift jobs in the police force, the fire department, and City Hall for those who would vote the right ticket. Tammany chowders on the scale of Tim Sullivan's outshone in warmth and charity any of the monotonous overfeeding that took place at Methodist country picnics. Al Smith loved both his saloon and his church, allowing both a place in his life. His Protestant enemies forgave him neither.

Yet there were saloons and saloons. For every decent saloon that filled a need in the community, there were five that increased poverty and crime among working people. Immigration, artificial refrigeration to preserve beer indefinitely, and the incursion of the English liquor syndicate into the American market led to the phenomenon of too many saloons chasing too few drinkers. By 1909, there was one saloon for every three hundred people in the cities.[21] Where the saloonkeeper's job depended on his sales, he was forced to go out on the streets, blandish customers into his bar, and deprive the wives of workingmen of their husband's pay envelopes. If sales were unsatisfactory, he was evicted by the breweries, which owned seven out of ten saloons in America. A description of Beer Town, the home of Hamm, where "the very beery breath of God" filled the air, spoke of the saloonkeeper Tony waylaying the brewery workers on their way home:

> "Glazabeer, boys?" Tony would say, blocking their way on the road, in his hale way suggesting that good fellowship was as good as good beer. "Begates, Glazabeer, boys?" Begates, slap on the shoulder, warm meeting, the bar glistening within, no shrewish women, no brats, no trouble, glistening warmly of forgetfulness and pleasure. "A schnit of beer, boys?"[22]

Two of the most effective propaganda weapons used by the drys were a wet appeal to the Liquor Dealers' Association of Ohio to "create the appetite for liquor in the growing boys," and an offer by the Kentucky Distillers Company to supply the Keeley Institutes for inebriates with a mailing list of their regular customers at the cost of four hundred dollars for every fifty thousand names.[23]

Moreover, the free lunch was vastly overrated as a means of feeding the poor. The saloonkeeper was in business to make money. No free lunches were provided in Southern saloons, since Negroes ate too much and even poor whites would not eat out of the same dish as

Negroes. In large cities, bouncers threw out of saloons any man who ate more than his money's worth of drink. Moreover, the barkeepers provided only dry or salty food. Rye bread, crackers, cheese, sausage, wienerwurst, sauerkraut, salt meat, potato salad, dill pickles, pretzels, salt fish, dried herring, and baked beans provided the staple dishes. The object of the free lunch was not to provide nourishment but merely to excite an undying thirst. Only in the Far West, where food was abundant and cheap, were the free lunches enough to put all the expensive restaurants out of business — so much so, that a lady temperance leader complained that her sons could only afford to eat in the saloons of San Francisco. The free lunch was, however, both the cause and effect of an American custom. The frontier habit of bolting snacks while standing at a bar or counter traveled from the saloon through the drugstore to the quick-lunch dispensaries of modern times.

Competition among themselves drove the brewers and distillers into folly. Although many of the saloons were vile in the nineteenth century, the poor quarters of the cities and the rural slums were viler. The filthy bar seemed a paradise of cleanliness to the tenement dweller. But, at the moment when the progressive wave of reform was pressing for better conditions of life, the old city saloon was becoming worse.

> Very often it stood on a corner so as to have two street entrances and wave a gilded beer sign at pedestrians drifting along from any point of the compass. The entrance was through swinging doors which were shuttered so that any one standing on the outside could not see what was happening on the inside. The windows were masked by grille work, potted ferns, one-sheet posters and a fly-specked array of fancy-shaped bottles which were merely symbols and not merchandise. The bar counter ran lengthwise at one side of the dim interior and always had a brass foot-rail in front of it. Saw-dust on the floor was supposed to absorb the drippings. Behind the bar was a mirror and below the mirror a tasteful medley of lemons, assorted glasses and containers brightly labeled to advertise champagne, muscatel, port, sweet Catawba, sauterne and that sovereign remedy for bad colds, Rock and Rye. Most of these ornamental trimmings were aging in glass and there was no demand for them whatsoever.[24]

Such proliferating drinking places in industrial cities occupied most street corners and some of the block in between. In 1908, there were some 3000 breweries and distilleries in the United States, and more than 100,000 legal saloons.[25] There were, in addition, some 50,000 blind pigs and tigers. Over half of the population of Boston and Chicago paid a daily visit to the saloon. Chicago under Capone was a paradise compared with Chicago at this time. "When a drink parlor was opened

FREE LUNCH

anywhere in the Loop, the proprietor went over and threw the key into the lake."[26] The Chicago Vice Commission of 1910 found that there were, at a conservative estimate, 5000 regular prostitutes and 10,000 occasional ones in the city. Their chief hangouts were the saloons, the brothels, and the dance halls, all of which sold liquor. Similar red-light districts fouled all the major cities. Under the pressure of the reformers, frequent and ineffective raids were made by the police on these areas of vice. But the raids did no more than levy a small fine on the saloonkeepers, pimps, and madams, who returned to their trade when the hue and cry was stilled.

Vice statistics were collected, however, which provided fuel for the fire of the drys against the saloon. With their simplifying techniques, the spokesman of the prohibitionists equated the worst type of Chicago saloon with all saloons, and the worst sort of poisonous liquor with all liquor. Because the evidence of the brute in men was the evidence they needed, the drys gathered their facts from only the most brutal places. And they did seem to offer some form of counterattack on social evils. If the saloons could be restricted or closed down for good by law, prostitution and vice would be hard hit. Moreover, the fashionable doctrines of environmentalism seemed to promise a dramatic decrease in crime and poverty and evil if only the breeding places of these ills, the saloons and the brothels, could be eliminated.[27]

A muckraker in 1908 wrote in approval of the wave of dry legislation in the South:

> Everywhere the saloons have disobeyed in the most flagrant fashion all rules made for their government and regulation; and when put under pressure to reform they have fought back through their characteristic American alliance with bad politics. So insolent has been the attitude not only of the saloon-keepers but also of the brewers, distillers, and wholesale liquor men, that many communities have gone dry simply because of the disgust which this attitude has bred in good citizens. Men who do not object to the moderate use of liquor, men who use it themselves, have held the balance of power in these prohibition elections; the result shows how they have voted.[28]

It was the failure of the liquor trade to reform itself that brought the wrath of the moderates and progressives on its head. The smelly crew of old soaks and regulars was taken out of the bar to the polling booth once too often. "They had never been told they stood for liberty; they stood rubily, stubbornly, with the strong brown smell of shame in their nostrils, for the bloodshot, malt-mouthed, red-nosed, loose-pursed Demon Rum."[29]

In England, prohibition was unsuccessful because the brewers put their own public houses in order. In the United States, the brewers and distillers would not clean up the saloons, despite the repeated warnings of their own spokesmen, Hugh Fox and Percy Andreae. For instance, Andreae advised the International Brewers' Congress of 1911 to support temperance reformers. If the brewers would only license respectable saloonkeepers, close the saloons in red-light districts, and agree to the suppression of saloons in dry areas with proper compensation, then they would defeat the drys. For the decent saloon was the most powerful enemy of the prohibitionists. The brewers applauded Andreae but followed their nose for quick profits rather than his suggestions. In the cut-throat struggle against each other to survive at all, profits were more important to liquor traders than public relations. Although the area of their operation grew smaller each year, 177,790 legal saloons were still open on the eve of national prohibition.[30]

There is truth in the wet excuse that the increasing efforts of the drys to suppress the saloons increased the degeneracy of the saloons. No sensible businessman was going to invest money in properties that might be closed up without compensation within a year. The fact that the prohibitionists were winning made the drinkers drink more frantically and the saloonkeepers try to gouge out a maximum profit while they could. Despite dry successes in winning state and county prohibition measures between 1906 and 1917, the consumption of liquor in gallons reached an all-time high in those years, while the very year that the Eighteenth Amendment was passed saw the consumption of spirits reach the highest total for thirty-seven years. The threat and the passage of prohibition put its opponents on as long a spree as they could afford. Although it may be salutary for a man to live each day as if it were his last, it is not advisable for him to drink each drink as if it were so.

Once the countryside of America had largely rid itself of its saloons, it might have been expected to leave the city saloons in peace. But the drys claimed that the city saloons forced the country back into the drink evils from which it was trying to escape. The saloons at the city's edge helped to nullify country prohibition and to put up the costs of law enforcement in dry districts. The city saloon sent back country immigrants as penniless drunks to their villages and threw them onto local support; these drunks were the very people whom rural voters had aimed to protect against the saloon. Moreover, the city was constantly renewing its vital strength from the sons and daughters of the country, and their parents had the right to protect their children against the temptations of their new environment. Finally, according to the Census of 1910, a majority of the population of America still lived in the country, and that majority was entitled to protect itself against the vice and corruption of the minority which patronized the city saloon.[31] For these reasons, the drys could never accept a Dry Curtain situation, a partition in which the sober country left the city saloons in peace.

Yet the drys, in seeking to close all saloons, did not admit the need to provide compensations for the facilities which the saloons had provided. Their point of view was that until the saloons had been closed nothing should be done to replace them. The competition of cinema and music hall, of public parks and libraries, of church halls and temperance bars, had not lessened the quantity of drinking before the Great War. While the saloons still existed, the drinker could not begin his redemption. The drys made the added mistake of believing that those who supported the prohibition of the saloons also supported the prohibition of the liquor trade. While the drys used the word "prohibition" loosely to attract both the foes of the saloon and the foes of all liquor to their banner, their gloss over their own extreme definition of prohibition made many of their early supporters feel later that they had been tricked into the banning of the whole liquor trade. Moreover, even the drys fell victim to their own lack of clarity. They tended to believe that the saloon and the drink habit were one and the same thing. Remove the first and the second would also disappear.

This confusion of dry thought was expressed by one of their writers on the eve of national prohibition. According to him, the saloon had been proved by 1919 to be in no sense a social necessity. Men went to the saloon primarily for a drink. The drink habit itself was abnormal and artificial. Therefore, the saloon had created an abnormal demand for its services. The great success of the teetotal canteens in Army camps during the Great War proved that young men did not really want liquor. It was only the false lure of the saloon that gave them the habit. Once prohibition was established, the home and the church would soon fill all the wants once filled by the cancer of the saloon, and the artificial taste for liquor would perish utterly.[32]

The drys could not logically provide substitutes for the saloon. They were the victims of their own propaganda. They had condemned the saloon for so long as the ultimate vice that they could not admit its small virtues. Moreover, they wanted to spend all their funds on the campaign against the liquor trade rather than on refuges for displaced drinkers. The future must look after itself. Only those small sections of the dry movement which were more concerned with saving men than shutting down their drinking haunts tried to find alternative meeting places for drinkers. General Evangeline Booth declared that the Salvation Army would take over a string of saloons, coast to coast, and serve soft drinks over the old bars. For it was important to preserve "the psychology of the brass rail. There is something about the shining bar which brings all men to a common footing. The easy and relaxed attitude of those who lean against the mahogany or cherry suggests solid comfort. Because wine and beer are to go, shall not a man take his ease in his own inn?"[33]

The refusal of most of the drys to provide substitutes for the saloon created a vacuum. And drinking abhors a vacuum. If there were no saloon, another drinking place would be found. The drys, by failing to compensate for the needs of those who drank in the saloons, drove them to drink in worse haunts. The prohibition of an abuse too often denies the preservation of a good.

The struggle between the Protestant evangelical churches and the saloons was based on different views of the role of God and man in society. It was also bound up with nativist fears of the Roman Catholic Church and of the corruption which the liquor trade had brought to politics and life in the large cities. The problem of the drys was to translate this struggle into political terms. If the drys wanted a law against the saloons, they would have to obtain it through the democratic process. The first temperance wave had used political pressure to secure dry laws; but it was not opposed by an organized liquor

WORKERS' SALOON

trade. The entry of the liquor trade into politics after the Civil War
made the drys follow them there. The huge influence of the brewers
and distillers within both the Republican and Democratic parties made
the prohibitionists set up a party of their own. Its failure led the drys
to find other methods of political pressure. By the manipulation of
electorates and legislators, the drys sought the legal victory of the
churches over the saloons. As a leader of the Anti-Saloon League
wrote in 1908, "It was already recognized that if the church was right,
the saloon was wrong, and that the church must overcome the saloon
or eventually be overcome by it."[34]

CHAPTER 5

The Politics of Reform

> The typical American man had his hand on a lever and his eye on a curve in his road; his living depended on keeping up an average speed of forty miles an hour, tending always to become sixty, eighty, or a hundred, and he could not admit emotions or anxieties or subconscious distractions, more than he could admit whisky or drugs, without breaking his neck.
>
> HENRY ADAMS
> *The Education of Henry Adams*, 1919

> Jay Gould once said that in Republican districts he was a Republican, in Democratic districts a Democrat, but first, last, and all the time he was for the Erie Railroad. That is precisely our policy.
>
> REVEREND HOWARD HYDE RUSSELL
> Founder of the Anti-Saloon League

PROHIBITION was the joker in major party politics. It straddled the tenuous line between the Republicans and Democrats, and it made blatant the secret conflicts which hid under party unity. In 1884, the issue of prohibition helped to take the White House from the Republicans, although it helped to restore the presidency to the Grand Old Party later by setting the Democrats at each other's throats. In nation and in state, in county and in town, in election and in conversation, prohibition took over from wine as the mocker and causer of dissension.

The Prohibition party was formed in 1869. With chattel slavery abolished through Civil War and presidential action, certain reformers wanted to abolish rum slavery by similar means. As Gerrit Smith, twice radical Abolitionist candidate for President and associate of John Brown, put the matter:

> Our involuntary slaves are set free, but our millions of voluntary slaves still clang their chains. The lot of the literal slave, of him whom others have enslaved, is indeed a hard one; nevertheless it is a paradise

compared with the lot of him who has enslaved himself — especially of him who has enslaved himself to alcohol.[1]

Since neither the Republican nor the Democratic party would take a stand against the saloon, those who believed in prohibition had to find another party. And this they did. In 1872, a Prohibition party ran its candidates in the presidential election on a platform of universal suffrage, business regulation, public education, encouragement of immigration, and constitutional prohibition. The ticket received a little more than five thousand votes out of a total of more than six million.

The major political parties could afford to ignore a puny and ineffective competitor, until the second prohibition wave and the election of 1884 gave them pause. In that election, the Republican presidential candidate, James G. Blaine, lost narrowly to the Democrat, Grover Cleveland. The Republicans lost New York state by 1047 votes as well as the election; the Prohibition party candidate, the dry Governor of Kansas, John P. St. John, polled 24,999 dry votes in that state. Most of these votes would have been Republican. The unfortunate remark of Dr. Burchard that the Democrats were the party of Rum, Romanism, and Rebellion had given the wet, immigrant vote to Cleveland, even if it had rallied the drys to Blaine. Thus, for the first time, the Prohibition party and the dry issue had tipped the balance in a national election by taking important votes from a major party candidate. Prohibition had played its first trick on American national politics.

The Republican party paid the drys the compliment of mentioning their cause in their platform of 1888. For the Prohibition party promised to become a dangerous third party in those rural areas where the Grand Old Party was strong. At the Republican convention, the Boutelle resolution was adopted as an annex to the party platform. It ran, "The first concern of all good government is the virtue and sobriety of the people and the purity of the home. The Republican party cordially sympathizes with all wise and well-directed efforts for the promotion of Temperance and morality." The wet Republican *Commercial Gazette* of Cincinnati commented nastily that if the plank had meant anything it would not have been passed. And *Bonfort's Wine and Spirit Circular* went so far as to praise the resolution, stating on behalf of the wine and spirit trade that they accorded the declaration their unreserved approval.[2]

At the election, the Republican presidential candidate, Benjamin Harrison, barely defeated Cleveland; he secured only a minority of the popular vote. Had the greater part of the quarter of a million Prohibition party votes gone to Harrison, he would have won a popular majority. Again the Prohibition party seemed to hold the balance of power in national elections. The rise of the Populists as the most aggressive third party in 1892 and the increasing majorities of successful presidential candidates after four successive narrow elections, however, made the Prohibition party lose all the precarious power which it had once exercised. The Socialist candidate, Eugene V. Debs, polled more votes than the Prohibitionist candidate after the turn of the century, while the Progressive party attracted those voters who were interested in general reform outside the major parties, not in the particular reform of constitutional prohibition. It was useless for the Prohibitionists to say of the Republicans and Democrats, "like Herod and Pilate, they make common cause to crucify the Christ in politics in every election."[3] Few voters heeded the accusation.

Yet the chief contender of the Prohibition party rose from the dry ranks. In 1893, the Anti-Saloon League was founded. It gradually took over the leadership of the dry cause. Indeed, the reason for its foundation was the very failure of the Prohibition party. Oberlin, Ohio, where the League began, had been a center of the abolition movement and was a staunchly Republican town in honor of the party which had overcome slavery. Prohibition party speakers were refused the use of the pulpits there. Although the Oberlin Anti-Saloon League was founded to work with drys in both parties, it amalgamated with such groups as the Anti-Saloon Republicans and helped to choose as the first president of the National Anti-Saloon League, Hiram Price, who had been five times a Republican Congressman from Ohio and who had tried to block the nomination of a Prohibition party ticket in 1884 in the interests of the Grand Old Party.[4] The Prohibition party leaders were justified in thinking that the League was hostile to them, although they were less justified in accusing it of being an annex of the Republican party. Although many of the League leaders were personally Republicans, they never supported a wet Republican candidate for office against a dry Democrat who had a better chance of election. It is, however, true that when the League was dominant in Midwestern politics during the congressional elections of 1916, the number of dry Republican Midwesterners in the House of Representatives rose from a total of twenty-six to sixty-five, while the number of dry Democrats declined. Outside the South the League preferred to work for dry candidates within the Republican party, especially when the Republicans became the majority party in charge of law enforcement after 1920.

As a result of this policy of infiltration within and pressure upon the major parties, the Anti-Saloon League fell out with the Prohibition party. The Prohibition party found the League policy of supporting "good men" in both major parties immoral. Its spokesmen said that it was useless to elect "the angel Gabriel himself, if his party relied on the support and funds of the liquor trade."[5] The Prohibitionists had spent forty years in the wilderness, stirring up sentiment for prohibition, and now another organization threatened to reap the fruits of its labors. As Eugene Chafin, Prohibition party candidate for President in 1908, declared, "We have got to kill the Anti-Saloon League and then lick the Republican and Democratic parties."[6] To those who cared for good government and political morality as well as prohibition, some of the League's methods smacked of the devil. The League was prepared to support men of questionable morality and habits who would vote dry against men of honesty and integrity whose election was improbable. One statement in the League's *Catechism* admitted this concern with success rather than morality. To the question, "May the League properly favor the election of candidates who are not wholly in faith and practice acceptable to friends of temperance reform?" the answer ran, "While it is desirable that candidates for office should be in all respects acceptable, it may be necessary at times, in order to secure some desired end, to vote for candidates committed to the object, though not wholly committed to the plan and purpose of the League."[7] Such Jesuitical reasoning in support of drunken Republican and Democratic hacks who could be scared into voting dry brought down the wrath of moral Prohibitionists on the heads of the League.

Yet, whatever the virtues of the League's political methods, its legislative success was undoubted. The policy of the League worked in terms of passing dry laws through state legislatures and Congress. But it did not work at getting those laws enforced. As the Prohibition party rightly pointed out, there was "just as much sense in voting for a horse-thief to enforce the law against stealing horses" as in voting for the major parties to enforce the law against the liquor traffic.[8] Professional politicians were quick to discover that lax enforcement would not make the drys bolt their party, while firm enforcement would offend the wets. Thus the formula of dry law and little enforcement gave the Republicans and Democrats the excuse to obey the League with respect to means and disappoint it with respect to ends. The devious methods of the League made for devious returns. And the uncompromising Prohibition party, although it could never have taken over the White House, could play Cassandra on the edge of the battle and prophesy the ills which the League would and did bring upon the dry cause through its success.

Perhaps the fairest estimate of the role played by the Prohibition party and the Anti-Saloon League in the dry victories was made by a man who defected from the first to the second. John G. Woolley, a reformed drunkard, became Prohibition party candidate for President in 1900. He was a great orator with a "God-given power to stir the hearts, awaken the consciences, and compel conviction in the minds of his hearers."[9] It was he who, with his keynote speech at the national convention of the Anti-Saloon League in 1913, brought the audience of four thousand to their feet, "yelling like a regiment of Louisiana tigers making a charge" for the new cause of nationwide prohibition. His text was "Make a chain; for the land is full of bloody crimes and the city is full of violence."[10] He wanted to reconcile all drys together in the struggle. And if he could not bring about this reconciliation and preferred to work with the successful League, he did not forget the Prohibition party. In his words, "The Prohibition Party was like a fire bell. It awoke the people. They are up and doing. In such a case there are two things to do, ring the bell more or put out the fire. I am for putting out the fire, whatever becomes of the bell."[11]

The decline of the Prohibition party from a progressive organization into one which sought support from the racist and fundamentalist crusades of the twenties parallels the decline of the rural radical movements from the Populists to the Ku Klux Klan. For the first time in 1924, the party had a plank on the Bible and a plank on the Americanization of aliens. The first plank stated that the Bible was "the Magna Carta of human liberty and national safety" and should have a large place in the public schools. The second stated that large numbers of unassimilated aliens were a present menace to American institutions and should be Americanized by a constructive program. These planks were a far cry from planks in the first platform of the Prohibition party — planks which supported "the imperishable principles of civil and religious liberty" in the Constitution and "a liberal and just policy" to promote foreign immigration to the United States.

THE LEAGUE IN OHIO

THE ACTIVITIES of the Anti-Saloon League in its home state of Ohio give a fair microcosm of its activities throughout the nation. Ohio was a state precariously split between allegiance to the Democrats and loyalty to the Republicans, between industrial towns and country villages and farms. In such urban centers as Cleveland and Cincinnati, the large "foreign element" of the state population, estimated at one-third of the whole in the Wickersham report, was clustered behind the wet machines.[12] In the dry rural areas, the voters were directed by the pulpits and the Anti-Saloon League to cast their ballots in support of the dry cause. Through this conflict between factory and farm, prohibition and liquor, Ohio became a litmus paper to party politics. Indeed, since the founding of the Republic, Democrats and Republicans have considered Ohio so pivotal that they have selected more Presidents from that state than from any other. In 1920, both major parties went so far as to nominate an Ohioan to be their leader and sway the state to their side.

Ohio was a hotbed of the abolitionists, the prohibitionists, and the suffragettes. These three reform groups seemed to flourish in a state whose hinterlands were studded with the pulpits of the Methodist and Baptist churches. Prohibition sentiment was strong in the state before the Anti-Saloon League was ever founded. In 1851, an antilicense clause was put in the state constitution, although this clause was by-passed through a law providing for a liquor tax rather than a liquor fee. In 1883, a prohibition amendment to the state constitution was passed by a majority of those voting on the issue, although it failed because a majority of all the votes cast in the election were not cast for the amendment.

But industry came to Ohio along with the Anti-Saloon League, and the German brewers of Cincinnati began to organize the new wet city masses against the pressure of the dry congregations in the country. The League had to adopt a policy of conquering the state step by step. First by local option elections, then by county option elections after 1908, the state was dried up.[13] Meanwhile, pressure was put on the state legislature to help the drys in every way. Within ten years of its first victory in defeating State Senator Locke in 1894, the League defeated over seventy wet candidates who were entitled by party custom to renomination.[14] Its triumphs culminated in the election of a Democrat, J. M. Pattison, as Governor of Ohio against the incumbent Republican Governor, Myron T. Herrick, in 1905. The League had vainly asked the Republican party in Ohio to nominate a dry candidate; instead, the Republican boss of Cincinnati, George B. Cox, had seen to the second nomination of the wet Herrick. In a campaign of unprecedented vigor, the League workers turned their pulpits "into a battery of Krupp guns, from which to hurl the bursting shells and solid shot against the saloon and its defenders."[15] Pattison was elected by a majority of some 42,000 votes. The influence of the League was dramatically shown by the fact that the entire Republican ticket was elected in the rest of the state.

The major parties heeded their lesson in Ohio. They trod warily with the drys. And the "Ohio Idea" of political action by the churches and the drys through the Anti-Saloon League spread. The "Ohio Idea" consisted of the use of paid professional officials and workers who gave their entire time to League activity, a financial system based upon monthly subscriptions, political agitation directed toward the defeat of wet candidates and the election of dry candidates, and concentration upon the liquor question to the exclusion of all other issues.[16] The

League's methods of agitation, legislation, and enforcement were also broadcast. The materials for dry agitation could be secured from the Westerville printing plant of the League, which was producing forty tons of temperance literature each month by 1912. Advice on methods of legislative pressure were contained in *Anti-Saloon League Yearbooks* or were available in the flesh by experts sent from the national headquarters in Ohio. As for enforcement, detectives were supplied to dry communities to denounce liquor law violators. By their success in Ohio, the Anti-Saloon League became the model of reform pressure groups throughout the nation.

The industrialism of Ohio itself, however, made total victory there very difficult. It was easier for the Anti-Saloon League to win battles in rural Southern and Western states. Although the drys controlled the Ohio legislature where the countryside was overrepresented, the large wet votes of Cincinnati and Cleveland kept Ohio wet in the state-wide referendums of 1914, 1915, and 1917. In 1918, a week before Armistice Day, a state prohibition amendment which allowed the manufacture and importation of liquor for home use did finally pass by a small majority. Nevertheless, by another referendum in 1919, the people of Ohio narrowly disapproved of the ratification of the Eighteenth Amendment by their state legislature, which duly ignored this slap in the face. The following passage of the Nineteenth Amendment and the extension of the suffrage to women in Ohio did something to ease the dry situation in the state. For the first time in 1920, the League could guarantee a popular majority for dry measures in Ohio, after twenty-seven years of agitation.

The care which politicians took of the League and of the brewers in Ohio was exquisite. Both major parties did their best to alienate neither wet nor dry. There was a real fear in both parties that the nomination of a politician honestly committed to either side of the prohibition issue would throw the election to the opposing party. The Ohio dry Republicans even put out a pamphlet in 1917 which quoted General Critchfield's statement that "the Republican party never lost an election in Ohio except as a result of passing some measure looking to the regulation or curtailment of the evils of the liquor traffic." The pamphlet went on to declare that, as a consequence, the Republicans in Ohio had compromised too much with the wets. The Democrats, seeing the growing dry sentiment, were preparing to lead it. With their control of an efficient political machine, this would give them control of the state for many years. Therefore, the saloon should be eliminated from Republican and state politics by prohibition of the liquor trade. Only then would the Republicans enjoy their natural hold on all offices in Ohio.[17]

Prohibition in Ohio complicated an already complicated situation. The League's fanaticism changed the natural position of an Ohio politician from a slap on the back to a straddle. Yet, in the all-important years of the Great War, when the Eighteenth Amendment was passed in Congress and ratified by the states, the state politicians were sufficiently weathercock to swing with the dry wind. A letter from Senator Warren Harding's political manager in 1917 clearly brings out the temporary factors which made politicians in Ohio go dry. He wrote, "If conventions were to be held in Ohio this year, no political party would dare to refuse to endorse prohibition. There is only one side to the moral, economic, political or patriot phase of the question."[18] It was in answer to this temper of the times, as read by canny politicians, that Harding switched from wet to dry and took Ohio with him. His action wrung a doubtful compliment from the leader of the Anti-Saloon League, Purley A. Baker. He said, "Senator Harding, you can talk wetter and vote dryer than any man I have ever known."[19]

The passage of the Eighteenth Amendment and the success of Harding in the presidential election of 1920 gave the Republican and Anti-Saloon League leaders of Ohio great power. At last, the League's dream of a national prohibition law and a sympathetic administration seemed to have come true. Ohio had bred great men in politics and in prohibition. Now they would co-operate to realize the leader of the League's intention, "the making air tight, water tight, beer tight, wine tight, whisky tight, for all time, firmly imbedded and buttressed in the constitution of the United States, the eighteenth amendment."[20] This was the "Ohio Idea" writ large.

A further idea of the havoc which prohibition wrought in state politics can be gleaned from a survey of the states in 1913, the year that prohibition began to play a part through the Anti-Saloon League in national elections. In California, Nevada, Illinois, New Hampshire, New Jersey, New York, Rhode Island, and Wisconsin, both parties opposed prohibition; in the states of the Deep South, however, both parties supported prohibition. In Colorado, the Republicans were dry and the Democrats wet, while in Oklahoma, the Democrats were dry and the Republicans wet. In Indiana, the Republicans supported county option, while the Democrats supported local option; in Pennsylvania, both parties supported license.

Indeed, sense can be made of party attitudes towards the prohibition issue only in terms of the split between city and country, for the states were divided in themselves. In Missouri, Republican St. Louis was more friendly with Democratic Kansas City over prohibition than either was with the rural Democratic majority; the part of Kansas

City in Kansas itself was opposed likewise to the dominant Republican majority upstate. The refusal of Congress after the Census of 1910 to give the cities more seats in the House of Representatives was a frank confession by the country members that they wished to continue ruling the cities. Reapportionment of seats in the House was postponed until after the Census of 1930, in defiance of the Constitution. The oversight was partially due to the pressure of the dry lobby, which otherwise made so much of the need to obey the Constitution and its Eighteenth Amendment.

TRINITY OF REFORM

THREE MOVEMENTS helped each other to assault certain American laws and customs at the beginning of the twentieth century. These movements were the progressive crusade, the dry crusade, and the crusade for female suffrage. After growing from similar roots and seeking similar goals, they realized their differences and abandoned each other. Each movement would not have succeeded so well without the support of the others; but, in success, each found itself alone.

The progressive movement was the heir of a long line of reforms and reactions. American reform movements have usually combined within their creeds a love of certain remedies for social ills, allied with a hatred of the presumed makers of those ills. The search for the good of society usually fed off a loathing of the chosen scapegoats of the reformists. Moreover, the nativist movements, such as the Know-Nothing party, the American Protective Association, and the Ku Klux Klan appealed to those who wished to fight for God by a call for an immediate attack on a named devil. This militant persecution of the bad for the sake of the good was also an element of other rural reform movements: the Grange, the Populists, the country progressives, and the Non-Partisan League. The very ideology of crusade was sympathetic to the rural mind.

The same ideology suited the temperance reformers and the woman-suffrage party. The temperance supporters hated the saloon and the liquor trade; "they did not pray to God so much as at the saloon-keeper"[21] The feminists hated the unequal position of women and those legislators who kept it so. To these scapegoats, the Know-Nothing party added immigrants and Roman Catholics, while the Grange and the Populists damned the trusts and the money power of the East. In general, the evil and corruption of Washington and the great cities was a common grievance to all these reformers. And the most obvious symbol of that evil and corruption was the urban saloon, where immigrants and Roman Catholics drank and provided the bought votes that supported the unholy Congresses in Washington. Since all major reform movements believed that they would gain the votes of the majority of the God-fearing American people if only elections were direct and clean, the assault on the saloon and the restoration of democracy to American politics seemed to Know-Nothing and dry and suffragette to be the first step towards their ultimate victory.

Early elections in America were bloody and drunken affairs. William Dean Howells described the elections of 1840 and 1844 in Hamilton, Ohio, in lurid terms: "The fighting must have come from the drinking, which began as soon as the polls were opened, and went on all day and night with a devotion to principle which is now rarely seen."[22] The drunken mobs in the urban and village saloons were the dupes of any political shyster who could pay for their support. An election by such means offended the democratic morality of all reformers, particularly those of old American stock, who had been brought up to believe in democratic practice, as well as in the virtues of temperance and the Anglo-Saxon race. Thus, the drys tended to support political reformers, and political reformers tended to support the drys. For the success of one against corrupt practices or saloons seemed to help the success of all, especially as the supporters of the Know-Nothings and of the early temperance reformers and the feminists were found principally among the same Protestant Americans in rural areas. Thus the Know-Nothing party convention in 1855 in California passed a resolution approving of the temperance reforms in the state and promising to nominate "none for office but men of high character and known habits of temperance." The Know-Nothing domination of the state legislature also resulted in the passage of a prohibition referendum bill.[23] The supporters of one crusade could frequently be induced to support another.

Similarly, the early feminists bid for dry support. Elizabeth Cady Stanton, Susan B. Anthony, Lucretia Mott, and Abby Kelly all spoke out for temperance as well as for women's rights. Since the dry movement was led by clergymen and religious work was "the only activity outside the home in which married women might take part without violating the proprieties," the femininists pressed to be included among the dry ranks in higher positions than those of the kneeling women, who closed down many Midwestern saloons in the 1870's by the humility of their example.[24] As Mrs. Stanton confessed:

> Whenever we saw an annual convention of men, quietly meeting year after year, filled with brotherly love, we bethought ourselves how we could throw a bombshell into their midst, in the form of a resolution to open the doors to the sisters outside. . . . In this way, we

assailed in turn, the temperance, educational, and church conventions, agricultural fairs, and halls of legislation.[25]

But although the first temperance wave of the 1850's aided and was aided by the Know-Nothings and the feminists, the fourth reform movement of the time, the abolition movement, worked against the dry cause. For the Northern drys supported the abolition of slavery, while the Southern drys did not. Equally, the feminists, by equating their own condition with those of the Negro slaves, lost support in the South. Only the Know-Nothings knew enough to keep silent over abolition, as over most other affairs. But the combination of temperance, slavery, and female-suffrage agitation split the reformers among themselves. By concentrating on many reforms, the reformers tended to lose that one reform which they desired above all others. In the future, they would have to adopt a policy of selfish co-operation, making use of other reform organizations only to further their own separate cause. As Susan B. Anthony later wrote to a friend, after an unfortunate attempt to popularize "bloomers": "To be successful a program must attempt but one reform."[26] She ended by refusing the support of the Woman's Christian Temperance Union for fear of alienating those wets who supported women's rights.

The Civil War put reform at a discount. Although the victory of the North ended the divisions of the reformers over the question of abolition, the Know-Nothing movement had subsided even more quickly than it had grown, while the temperance movement and the feminists lost support in the lassitude of postwar times. The 1870's, however, saw the beginning of a second temperance and general reform wave, for the evil saloons had multiplied until there was one for every two hundred Americans. The Prohibition party offered many progressive measures in its platform and endorsed female suffrage. The Woman's Christian Temperance Union also joined the dry cause to further female emancipation; in the words of its leader, Frances Willard, the white ribbon aimed to promote "prohibition, purity, philanthropy, prosperity, and peace."[27] Both organizations sponsored broad programs of social reform to attract supporters to their fight against the saloon. And they did attract additional support. The Grangers and the Populists inspired new victories for temperance in their bids for power. In California, the Granger triumph of 1873 and the Populist success in 1894 both coincided with peaks of temperance agitation and legislation in the state.[28] The labor movement of the time, the Knights of Labor, under its leader Terence V. Powderly, brought more help to the dry cause, although this help was less in gratitude for Frances Willard's backing of labor legislation than in fear of the immigrant menace, marshaled by the corrupt city bosses through the saloons. "Every reformatory movement of the day," declared the *Journal of the Knights of Labor* in 1890, "finds here its most persistent and indefatigable foe."[29]

Thus, at the beginning of the twentieth century, those reformers who wished to end certain evils of government and of the liquor trade and of discrimination against women could agree on many of their objectives. Corrupt politics and the saloon vote was the enemy of all reform; clean politics and a sober vote was the friend of all reform. Female suffrage was thought to mean more votes for the dry cause and the cause of good government. The "superior moral force of women" would save America from the saloon and from the plutocrats, who were ruining American institutions.[30] The staid *North American Review* gave progressive reasons for endorsing female suffrage in 1906 as a "paramount necessity"; the rise of both socialism and the trusts had made the voting of women necessary, as a means "of purifying the ballot, of establishing and maintaining lofty standards as to qualifications required of candidates for public office, of effecting an evener distribution of earnings, of providing a heavier balance of disinterestedness and conservatism against greed and radicalism."[31] Dry clergymen also bid for progressive support of prohibition measures. "The bartender poses as the dictator of American destiny. . . . His royal scepter is a beer faucet."[32] Since the liquor trade had corrupted American politics to such a great extent, it was the job of all good progressives to give the women the vote so that they could help the drys to abolish the cursed trade that corrupted all government. The question was simple.

> *Whisky spiders, great and greedy,*
> *Weave their webs from sea to sea;*
> *They grow fat and men grow needy;*
> *Shall our robbers rulers be?*[33]

The feminists had special reasons for helping the drys. The Prohibition party was the first major party to endorse female suffrage. In return, the Woman's Christian Temperance Union had endorsed the Prohibition party in 1884, after supporting female suffrage four years earlier.* It was due to the Union that those women with a political bent first learned to organize the members of their sex and apply pressure upon politicians. The Union had both invented and perfected many of the dry lobbying techniques while pushing through its tem-

---

* After the death of Frances Willard, the Woman's Christian Temperance Union adopted the nonpartisan policy of the Anti-Saloon League and refused to endorse the Prohibition party, except in the election of 1916 when both major party candidates were thought unsatisfactory.

perance education bills. Moreover, the eleven states which adopted female suffrage before 1917 were all in the West; seven of these were prohibition states, and the other four had large areas under local option. The liquor trade was held to be the particular foe of womankind; as the Wisconsin Vice Committee declared, "the chief direct cause of the downfall of women and girls is the close connection between alcoholic drink and commercialized vice."[34] A woman's vote was thought to be a dry vote, and for that reason, the liquor trade was condemned for opposing the suffragettes; a feminist pamphlet, *The Secret Enemy*, reprinted a circular sent out by the Brewers' and Wholesale Liquor Dealers' Association of Oregon to every retail liquor dealer in the state, asking him to get out twenty-five votes against the state woman-suffrage amendment. The German-American Alliance, the chief foe of the drys, also opposed the feminists. And finally, woman suffrage was intended to bring about many of the same benefits as prohibition. It would rid the cities of vice and crime by supporting reform governments and would herald an era of peace and prosperity. Even if Mrs. Carrie Chapman Catt thought that women would have been enfranchised two generations earlier had there been no prohibition movement, the success of the suffragettes increasingly became dependent on the help and fortunes of the drys.

Many progressives were also supporters of prohibition. The rural progressives were the heirs of the Populists and their forerunners; to them, the whisky trust was even more devilish than the railroad, the steel, and the oil trusts. And the novelty of the progressive movement, its appeal to the urban middle classes as well as to the rural middle classes, gave the crusade against the saloon an immediate meaning to city dwellers, who had suffered too much from the corrupt saloon vote. Moreover, the strengthening of the federal government through the promise of national prohibition pleased those supporters of Theodore Roosevelt and the Progressive party who demanded a more highly centralized power in the United States. The dry arguments for increased efficiency of administration and business through prohibition were equally seductive to progressives. Although the Prohibition party justly claimed its members were the "original Progressives," its eclipse by the nonpartisan Anti-Saloon League made the Progressive party increasingly bid for dry support after its good showing in the presidential election of 1912, when Theodore Roosevelt, coming in second to Woodrow Wilson, pushed Taft and the Republican party into third place. In 1914, thirteen state Progressive party conventions backed state prohibition, and seventeen Progressives out of the twenty in Congress voted for the Hobson resolution for national prohibition.[35] Both the general sentiment of progressivism and the Progressive party itself were sympathetic to the dry cause.

Yet the one factor which distinguished the progressives and the Progressive party from other American reform and third-party movements was the alliance between city and country within their ranks. The prohibition movement, however, was held to be the assault of the country upon the city. For this reason, the Progressive party convention of 1916 did not endorse national prohibition, although it had endorsed female suffrage four years before. The split among the progressives on the question of prohibition was already evident in rural and urban areas. For instance, in California, Hiram Johnson and the Progressive party rose to power in the state with the help of the Anti-Saloon League and the vote of dry Los Angeles; but although the progressives could combine to fight the power of the Southern Pacific Railroad, they split along urban-rural lines over the vote in 1911 on a county option measure. It was also significant that the thirteen state conventions of the Progressive party which endorsed state prohibition in 1914 were all in rural or semirural states; not one Progressive party convention in an industrial state came out for prohibition. In the last resort, the Progressive party would only support the closing of the saloons when it helped their fight for clean government, but not when it threatened the uneasy alliance within the party between city and country. The Northeastern urban progressives would never support total prohibition of the liquor trade, even if they might support certain measures against the saloons.

Similarly, the South presented problems to the combination of progressivism, prohibition, and women's rights. White Southerners were enthusiastic over prohibition for economic and racial and moral reasons. Progressivism, too, appealed to them as a method of ending the chronic Southern economic depression through increased efficiency. But Southern progressives also equated clean government with the abolition of the Negro franchise as well as the saloons. In addition, their veneration for Southern womanhood made them deny the female sex any political rights. The Negro's place in the South was thought to be outside the polling booth and the woman's inside the home. Thus, although prohibition and a form of progressivism was prevalent below the Potomac, it excluded all hopes of increasing the franchise.

In the election of 1916, however, the Progressive party returned to the Republican fold, and many progressives voted for Woodrow Wilson in disgust. The majority of the drys supported the nonpartisan policy of the Anti-Saloon League, voting for those major party candidates who had the backing of the League. The Woman's party, under the leadership of Alice Paul, refused to back the Prohibition party, although it had declared for female suffrage. Alice Paul tried to organize a protest vote against President Wilson and the Democrats in those Western states where women had the suffrage. For the Woman's party was held to be "not pro-Republican, pro-Socialist, pro-Prohibition," but "simply pro-woman."[36] But the Western campaign against the Democrats failed. Wilson swept the Western progressive states. As William Allen White pointed out, the Republican candidate for President, Charles Evans Hughes, by refusing to take a bold progressive stand on woman suffrage, prohibition, the initiative and referendum and recall, seemed to the right of Wilson and lost the votes of the reformers.[37] Wilson also held out the promise of peace, which attracted Western reformers with their isolationist tendencies and domestic preoccupations.

One reform movement illustrated particularly well the common goals of the reform trinity of progressives and drys and feminists. This was the sterilization movement, which was backed by the eugenic and nativist and paternalist cast of mind that belonged to all three groups. The confluence of these attitudes was expressed by Frances Willard in England. "I am first a Christian, then I am a Saxon, then I am an American, and when I get home to heaven I expect to register from Evanston."[38]* To her and to other reformers, the reasons for all reform were the duties owed to God and race and nation in that order, while the place of the reformer's activity gave him his particular opportunities. The Anglo-Saxon race was held to have a divine and national mission to preserve the purity of the old American stock, which would support progressive reforms and abolish the racial degeneracy caused by alcohol. "We are going to have purer blood as the poison of alcohol becomes eliminated," said William Jennings Bryan. "We are going to have a stronger race because of prohibition."[39] This concern with the future of their children was a strong incentive for the Woman's party to give support to the drys. The legend on the banner of a suffragette procession in Chicago put the matter clearly:

> For the safety of the nation, let the women have the vote,
> For the hand that rocks the cradle will never rock the boat.[40]

Eugenics and the sterilization of the defective and the degenerate provided a good common ground for reformers for additional reasons. Sterilization promised to abolish the criminal type in society before he was corrupted further by urban slums or saloons. It also offered a method of controlled breeding which would favor the reproduction of the Anglo-Saxon race and prevent the reproduction of its rivals. The

---

* The home of Frances Willard in Evanston, Illinois, is the present headquarters of the Woman's Christian Temperance Union.

biological laws of necessity, upon which the position of the eugenic reformers rested, also justified the position of the rich and the middle classes of America; for, by their very position in society, they had proved that they were the fittest to survive. Moreover, eugenic sterilization promised to reduce taxation on the wealthy by diminishing the number of hereditary criminals in the prisons and poorhouses of the United States. It was not surprising that sterilization, along with progressivism and prohibition and feminism, was supported by those whom a Wisconsin clergyman called "our best people."[41]

By 1922, fifteen states in America had sterilization laws. Of these states, ten had passed state prohibition laws before the ratification of the Eighteenth Amendment, and eight had allowed woman suffrage before the ratification of the Nineteenth Amendment. Twelve of these states were Western or Midwestern, and three were Northeastern; none were Southern. This geographical proportion of support for sterilization gives a fair idea of the geographical support for the Progressive party and the Woman's party, even if the Southern support of prohibition excluded support of its allied causes. Although the motives for passing sterilization laws varied from a "purely punitive" motive in Nevada to a "purely eugenic" motive in Washington, the reasons for the eugenic crusade appealed to the vast majority of American-born Protestants, whatever their geographical location. The rural progressive, the prohibitionist, and the feminist seemed to hear their own voices in the accusation of Chief Justice Harry Olson, of the Chicago Municipal Court. European governments had made of the United States "an asylum and dumping ground for their own vagabond, drunken, degenerate, feebleminded, dementia praecox, epileptic, and criminalistic classes."[42] By sterilization and prohibition and political reform and women's rights, a beginning might be made in preserving the old virtues of the American race from the corrupt immigrant flood that deluged the cities of the United States. Indeed, the Eighteenth Amendment seemed the final legacy of twenty years of struggle, the last testament of such reformers as Harry Carey Goodhue, of Spoon River.

> Do you remember when I fought
> The bank and the courthouse ring,
> For pocketing the interest on public funds?
> And when I fought our leading citizens
> For making the poor the pack-horses of the taxes?
> And when I fought the water works
> For stealing streets and raising rates?
> And when I fought the business men
> Who fought me in these fights?

Then do you remember:
That staggering up from the wreck of defeat,
And the wreck of a ruined career,
I slipped from my cloak my last ideal,
Hidden from all eyes until then,
Like the cherished jawbone of an ass,
And smote the bank and the water works,
And the business men with prohibition,
And made Spoon River pay the cost
Of the fights that I had lost?[43]

DRY GOODS

FREDERICK JACKSON TURNER, in his famous essay on the American frontier, saw his society as a democracy of expectant capitalists. The American dream was liberty for all to live as they would and get what they could. He did not foresee that the getting of billions of dollars by the few might prevent the getting of hundreds of dollars by the many, and that the living in luxury by the few could ensure the living in poverty of the many. The great industrial fortunes of America were built on the sweated labor of the men and women and children of the immigrant masses in the cities. The twelve-hour day, seven days a week, which was usual in the American steel industry until the twenties, built vast corporations on the early deaths of many men. It also drove the laborers to drink and to the saloons, for the shortest way out of Pittsburgh or Birmingham was a bottle of booze.

Much of the heavy drinking in the industrial slums was caused by the long hours and foul conditions of mills and factories. Yet, in turn, the heavy drinking increased the foulness of the conditions of existence for workingmen. It led to more industrial accidents and less output from the factories. Therefore, the employers and manufacturers, after creating a slum hell from which alcohol was the only release, tried to block up the sole means of escape in the interests of efficiency and output. Only they did not talk of efficiency and output except among themselves. To the workingmen, they talked of morality and concern for the welfare of the poor.

The saloons threatened the manufacturers of America in many ways. Drunkards at work and inefficient labor on Blue Mondays cut down production. As one employer testified before a committee of the North Carolina legislature, "Gentlemen, there is a liquor shop, a dispensary, two miles from Selma, and you must shut up that place or I must shut up my cotton mill. It is for you to say which you will encourage in North Carolina, liquor mills or cotton mills — the two cannot go together."[44] Another industrialist, Lewis Edwin Theiss, wrote, "Until

booze is banished we can never have really efficient workmen. We are
not much interested in the moral side of the matter as such. It is purely
a question of dollars and cents."[45] It was also the concern of the
manufacturers to eliminate the saloon in order to secure more of the
workers' pay for the purchase of their manufactured goods. As a
Californian businessman wrote, "Leaving aside any moral or social
aspect, the question of commercial benefits . . . makes it mighty good
business to put the saloons on the toboggan."[46] Prohibition would
replace the demand for liquor with a demand for dry goods. "Canny,
shrewd, business-like America knew that it would be a good financial
bargain."[47]

There was also hostility to the labor movement in the employers'
support of prohibition. The suppression of the saloons would hurt the
labor unions, which often used the saloons to organize workingmen.
Moreover, if the liquor bill of the worker were eliminated, then he
would have a greater spending power without a rise in wages. As
Frances Willard said in 1886, the aim of labor should not be to get
higher wages, but to turn present wages to better account.[48] In addition, there was a real fear on the part of respectable people in the
nineteenth century that they would be insulted and injured by drunken
individuals or mobs. Liquor encouraged crimes of violence in those
who had criminal tendencies. There was even the possibility of a social revolution, if demogogues or radicals exploited the "drink-sodden,
muddled and fuddled proletariat."[49]

The new technology further helped the drys. The excitement of
invention and machinery created its own rationale. The industrial leap
forward demanded the continuous sobriety and concentration of the
workers. Many industries, particularly the railroad and steel companies, forbade their workers to drink. A typical poster in a plant
read, THE LAST MAN HIRED, THE FIRST MAN FIRED—THE
MAN WHO DRINKS. The powerful railroad brotherhoods supported
the employers in the matter of prohibition. One observer exulted,
"John Barleycorn has been caught in the fast revolving machinery of
American industry. There is no hope for him!"[50] Prohibition had become a necessity for the life of the nation. "This dry thing which has
overtaken the United States is by no means suddener than the steam-
boat, the telegraph, and the automobile. Because they are, it is; it is
their logical and essential consequence and condition."[51]

There was the further matter of taxes. Dry propaganda stressed over
and over again that the middle classes of America were paying high
rates and taxes for the upkeep of the jails, almshouses, asylums, and
charity organizations, where the victims of drink ended their unhappy
lives. If the liquor evil were to be prohibited, there would be no need

for any more penal institutions. The result would be a lowering of taxes. America would be a land of silk and money for all. The drys did not mention, however, the sore point of the federal and state liquor tax, which provided a large part of the income of the government. The tax was, in a leading prohibitionist's words,

> . . . perhaps the most far-reaching and calamitous in its ultimate effect of any action ever taken by Congress. It made the Government financially interested in the perpetuation of the liquor traffic. It stimulated the organization and growth of the traffic and thereafter made it impossible to deal with the liquor question upon its merits, disassociated from the question of revenue. It served to entrench the liquor traffic in politics and government from which it proved impossible to dislodge it for over half a century.[52]

The tax was first levied in the Civil War; but its duties were lowered after the war, owing to the pressure of the liquor trade. The rates were soon raised, however, and raised again and again, to pay for the war in Cuba and the First World War. Between 1870 and 1915, the liquor tax provided between one-half and two-thirds of the whole internal revenue of the United States, providing some two hundred million dollars annually after the turn of the century. But with the introduction of the federal income tax by the Sixteenth Amendment, the Eighteenth Amendment became possible. Income and excess-profits taxes provided the vast bulk of the federal revenue in the five years before 1920, two-thirds of a total swollen by the demands of war to eight times the total needed in the previous five years. The new size of the federal budget had made the liquor tax less important to the government, although the wealthy people of America began to realize for the first time that the loss of the liquor tax would be made up by higher taxes on themselves.

Yet the question of the liquor tax seemed trifling when the drys promised such huge economic gains to industry and incomes with the coming of national prohibition. To the drys, the economics of the matter were simple. The consumers of drink and the liquor trade were a dead loss. "It would be a saving to the Nation," wrote one prohibitionist in 1908, "if we could kill off all its hard drinkers tomorrow. There are two and one-half millions of these, and their first cost, at twenty-one years of age, was at least FIVE BILLIONS OF DOLLARS — as much as the estimated value of all the slaves in this country before the war." According to this dry, it was a "natural law" in the human world that every man should pay his way through life. He should put back into society by steady toil the amount of money invested in his upbringing.[53] Liquor was a stumbling block in the way of honoring this debt of existence. Each drink taken by each man was another fetter on the feet of the progress of all. Both the making of liquor and its consumption chalked up deficits in the national economy. The great liberal economist Adam Smith had himself written:

> All the labour expended producing strong drink is utterly unproductive; it adds nothing to the wealth of the community. A wise man works and earns wages, and spends his wages so that he may work again. Employers, taken all around, do not pay more wages to total abstainers, but the latter contribute more to their own and fellow workers' wages fund than do the drinkers.[54]

This traditional view of economics, which equated the service trades and pleasures of society with waste, and which thought in terms of a limited "wages fund" only benefited by "productive" labor, could see only virtue in prohibition. If the laboring poor were prevented from buying liquor, they would purchase more dry goods. The Committee of Fifty quoted the statistics of charity organizations to show that one in four cases of destitution was directly or indirectly due to liquor.[55] Although, as the Buffalo Charity Organization pointed out, "Innocent poverty with a long working day and insufficient food leads to drink just as much as drink causes poverty," prohibition was one way of breaking out of this "vicious circle."[56] The increased consumer market in a dry America would lead to increased production, which would lead in turn to higher wages and more jobs. The whole concept was one of an ascending spiral to perfection on earth, with poverty, jails, almshouses, pauper hospitals and taxes on the middle classes abolished forever. Moreover, for the first time, prohibition would bring real liberty to all Americans by bringing them prosperity. For, as a dry apologist stressed, real liberty lay in the creation and distribution of wealth. "A poor man never can be free. And hence that which may be labeled liberty is not worth anything if it makes for poverty."[57]

There was much truth in the claims of the drys. Judged in terms of pure economics, the efficient prohibition of liquor would bring benefits to a society. Unfortunately, liquor cannot be efficiently prohibited in a democracy, and man, whatever the liberal economists may have believed, is not an economic animal. Thus, the theory of economics favored the dry position, while the facts of enforcement and of the nature of mankind favored the wets. Yet neither side would concede victory to the other on any ground.

These economic reasons for prohibition made many of the manufacturers of the United States support the drys, who wanted prohibition for moral reasons. The *Villager* commented, "It was the industrial movement which made use of the moral movement, and so achieved the Eighteenth Amendment."⁵⁸ The employers had two advantages to gain from their alliance with the drys. The first was the diversion of the reform element in society into an attack on the saloons rather than the trusts. The era of the muckrakers, which had attacked political bosses and corporations and stock manipulation and capitalism itself, was superseded by the prohibition era, in which the energies of reformers were devoted to remedies for the liquor evil rather than for economic evils. Prohibition became a sort of moral mask for big business.

The support of the drys was helpful to big business in a second way. In 1909, Purley A. Baker called the labor movement "fundamentally a Holy crusade . . . a struggle toward light and justice and a square deal." It sought to "correct a great wrong."⁵⁹ This possible coalition between the prohibition and the labor movements might be dangerous to capital. But once the drys saw clearly that they had the widespread support of business and the widespread opposition of labor over light wines and beer, then they were quick to sing the virtues of their backers. The business ethic of the virtues of work and efficiency and wealth was, anyway, similar to the dry ethic; it stemmed from the same Puritan roots. Indeed, before national prohibition became the law of the land, many drys supported the manufacturers in keeping down the wages of their workers, for they thought that higher wages would only be spent on more drink. As the *National Temperance Almanac* declared, "If this body and soul destroying malady is not arrested in its progress, it is but a small thing to say that the increased wages and increased leisure of the working-classes would be a curse and not a blessing."⁶⁰

There was an additional moral reason for the support of the drys by the large industrialists. Prohibition was a partial salve to the conscience of the rich. The wealthy people of the United States could never justify themselves by European pleas of good birth or the divine right of inheritance. The American Dives had to find a better excuse. Thus he usually claimed that his riches had been acquired through the will of God, whose methods of distribution were inscrutable. But with these riches God had also conferred on him the duty of looking after the poor. Although the fittest rightly ruled by the sanction of Darwin and the Almighty, they should be conscious of their obligations towards the less fortunate.

Prohibition was a marvelous cause in its appeal to the paternalism of the rich and the powerful. While the suppression of the saloon made little difference to the recreations of the rulers, it did seem to them to remove temptation from the poor and needy. The governors of society knew enough to work and drink; the governed only knew enough to work. This attitude offended the workers, for "the laboring man, like other men, objects to being treated like a child or a machine."[61] It also seemed paradoxical that the government should apply *laissez-faire* principles to business and paternalism to individual habits. The paradox would be more acceptable if reversed, so that there was "a little more regulation of business and a little less regulation of personal habits."[62]

The labor movement itself was divided in its attitude toward prohibition. Traditionally, workingmen were drinkers. In the nineteenth century, up to one-third of their wages had been paid in whisky, while their dinner pails were more often full of beer than soup. But the increasing demands of the industrial revolution on labor, coupled with the urgent need to organize strong unions and improve working conditions, made many of the labor leaders openly or secretly support the prohibition of liquor. The *Seamen's Journal* stated bluntly: "Whisky is a most valuable friend of capitalism." Those who drank it were enemies of their class.[63] But this was only whisky. For the workers themselves demanded their beer and wine as a right, and thus their leaders had to support their demand. Therefore, while a majority of the labor leaders opposed the saloon, they also backed the sale of beer and light wines. It was in the failure of the drys to differentiate between these two attitudes, and the failure of the labor leaders themselves to make their position clear, that the misunderstanding about the backing of labor for prohibition arose.

In the days before the Eighteenth Amendment, the union leaders were swayed by many of the eugenic arguments that also swayed the middle-class reformers. They listened to the savage speeches of such men as Father Cassidy, who maintained that "the saloon lusteth against Labor and Labor lusteth against the saloon 'and these are contrary one to the other.'" Father Cassidy denounced the wet votes of the workers as a deliberate attack on the future hopes of their young ones by making them victims to "this cursed thing which has stunted more growing intellects, robbed more children of their birthright, sent stupid through the world, tied to the warper, the spooler and the spinning-frame more half-grown, half-developed little ones than unionism can ever count."[64] A poll of more than five hundred labor leaders taken by the *Literary Digest* in 1920 discovered that two out of three privately thought that prohibition was a benefit to the workingman, whether he liked it or not.

There was also a genuine co-operation between the moderate drys, who were interested in social reform in general, and the leaders of labor. Such reformers as Frances Willard and Jane Addams recognized that poverty caused alcoholism as much as alcoholism caused poverty.

The answer to the saloon was to shorten hours of work and raise wages, for, as Charles Stelzle pointed out, the best-paid workers with the most leisure time spent least in the saloons.[65] The leader of the social gospel movement, Walter Rauschenbusch, thought that liquor was an instrument of the Mammon of Big Business and urged the labor unions to break away from the liquor trade if they wanted strength and higher wages.[66] Drink and low wages were inseparably connected. As one dry social worker said, "low wages played directly into the hands of the saloon-keeper. The lower the wage the hungrier the man or girl, and more certainly the saloon with its stimulants called."[67] Her view was confirmed by another convinced prohibitionist. "Terrible heat, inhumanly long hours and night work gave controlling power to the craving for stimulants."[68] Industrial drinking among the workers was the direct consequence of their beastly living conditions.

The misery caused by drinking in the urban slums was a blatant fact. The prohibition of the saloon seemed one way to combat this evil. The manufacturers and the middle classes had many selfish financial and social reasons for supporting the campaign against the saloons. The labor movement itself had reason to dislike the influence of the liquor trade, although it stressed the fact that bad conditions forced the workmen of America to drink. The reformers of the time pressed both for better conditions and for the abolition of the saloons. If the supporters of the dry movement were more concerned with attacking King Alcohol than Mammon, it was because their energies could only be turned in one direction, and because Mammon backed their cause.

Although the Anti-Saloon League had powerful backing among reform and economic groups in the United States at the beginning of the century, it had to translate this support into blocks of votes for its political friends on election day. Without an organized voting group behind it, the League would not have been able to apply political pressure on the legislatures of the states and on Congress. With the menace of thousands of votes cast at the next election against any legislator who dared to vote against a dry measure, the League could make the representatives of the people vote against their personal wet convictions. The job of the organized drys was to perfect their means of persuasion. To this end, they invented new political techniques and also used the methods of the brewers and distillers but "deodorized and disinfected them and turned them back on the liquor traffic."[69]

CHAPTER **6**

Creeping Barrage

The mind has shown itself at times
Too much the baked and labeled dough
Divided by accepted multitudes.

HART CRANE

Many a bum show is saved by the American flag.

Impresario GEORGE M. COHAN

PROPAGANDA IS concerned with belief rather than truth, with distortion rather than presentation, with influence rather than argument. The matter of propaganda is less important than its methods and its foes. If a group is alone in its field and presents its objectives with persuasion and without contradiction, it will usually gain those objectives. But if its propaganda is denied by a hostile group with opposite goals, its success will largely depend on its control of the available means of communication. The drys, at the beginning of prohibition, had the better of the struggle for the communications system of the United States. A world war briefly gave them absolute power over likely methods of influencing others; but an economic and technological and moral revolution, allied with a boom followed by a depression, put the mass media in the hands of their enemies. The birth of prohibition was in the days of local news and self-contained areas; the flowering of prohibition took place when a national war effort put a centralized control over America for the first time; the dying of prohibition lay in the new machines which carried the presumed manners of the urban rich into every backwater and sharecropper's shack. Propaganda was the Frankenstein of the drys. At first, it was their power and glory; but, at the last, it murdered its maker.

The drys held a monopoly of the good side in the fields of science, education, medicine, evangelical religion, progressivism, and economics. But they made further claims for prohibition in terms of history, tradition, and patriotism. While their claims were little disputed in the beginning, a growing body of wet protests and counter-

106

claims, equally biased and injudicious, grew up and eventually swamped the prohibitionists under a deluge of answers. The myth of dry virtues was countered by the myth of wet rights, and only the believers in temperance suffered. As Mencken moaned, "To one side, the professional gladiators of Prohibition; to the other side, the agents of the brewers and distillers." He then asked himself why all neutral and clear-headed men avoided the liquor question, and came to the conclusion that "no genuinely intelligent man believes the thing is soluble at all."[1] He was right. Once the liquor question was seen in terms of a choice between the prohibitionists and the liquor trade, few reasonable men wished to choose at all.

LOBBY FOR THE LORD

BIG BUSINESS began the practice of lobbying in America, but the Anti-Saloon League perfected the techniques. While the corporations used the greed of legislators, the League used their fear of losing elections. Bribery may have been an effective instrument for controlling some representatives of the people, but loss of a majority of the popular vote was a sufficient threat to control all. It is a flaw in democracy that it can allow those pressures which, by influencing the democratic process unduly, pervert democracy.[2]

The Woman's Christian Temperance Union developed most of the methods of legislative pressure later used by the Anti-Saloon League. The methods were discovered by the formidable lobbyist of temperance teaching, Mrs. Mary H. Hunt. In an address in 1897, she outlined the means which she had used in the preceding years:

> The people are the real source of power. They must be the lobby. There the first step for compulsory temperance education should be taken before the primary meetings are held for the nomination of legislators, by agitating through pulpit, platform, press and prayer-meeting for the choice of temperance men as legislators. After these are elected, before the legislature convenes, appeal to their constituents in like manner to instruct these law-makers to vote for temperance education in public schools. This should be so universally and systematically done that every legislator will feel this pressure before he leaves his constituents.[3]

An example of Mrs. Hunt's practice has been preserved in an account of the passing of a temperance education bill through the Pennsylvania legislature in 1885. For the previous eighteen months, Mrs. Hunt had been preparing the way by buttonholing representatives, addressing meetings, preparing material for newspapers, and organizing petitions. At the opening of the legislative session, the galleries were packed with members of the Woman's Christian Temperance Union.

> Almost before the amen to the opening prayer had been uttered, a dozen members were on their feet offering the petitions sent in from their various districts, on behalf of the bill for scientific temperance education. The dozen swelled to scores, and the scores multiplied all in a moment until so many boy messengers were flying down the aisles with the papers, and so many arms were waving in the air, that from every seat there seemed suddenly to have sprung a great fluttering white blossom of petition.

And the women did not stop with petitions, "but they bombarded the hearts and heads of their representatives with letters; letters admonitory and beseeching, letters solemn and warning, letters proper and patronizing, letters of all sorts, shapes, sizes and degrees of eloquence, but all pregnant with one mighty purpose, the ultimate passage of the bill."[4]

The dry women also made use of another great weapon, the children. Newborn infants had a white ribbon tied around their wrists and a prayer said over them; they were then official members of the dry Cradle Roll. Loyal Temperance and Lincoln-Lee Legions of children, more powerful than the massed youth of the Children's Crusade, were set to march and sing about the polling booths when local or county option elections were held. As the known wets approached the polling booths,

> . . . the church women of the town, bent like huntresses above the straining leash, gave the word to the eager children of the Sunday schools. Dressed all in white, and clutching firmly in their small hands the tiny stems of American flags, the pigmies, monstrous as only children can be when they become the witless mouths of slogans and crusades, charged hungrily, uttering their shrill cries, upon their Gulliver.
>
> "There he is, children. Go get him."
>
> Swirling around the marked man in a wild elves' dance, they sang with piping empty violence:

> *We are some fond mother's treasure*
> *Men and women of tomorrow,*
> *For a moment's empty pleasure*
> *Would you give us lifelong sorrow?*
>
> *Think of sisters, wives, and mothers,*
> *Of helpless babes in some low slum,*
> *Think not of yourself, but others,*
> *Vote against the Demon Rum.*[5]

William Jennings Bryan noticed the effectiveness of this form of pressure during his own speaking tours.

> At county seats all the children in the county would be in line, thousands of them, the girls in white with gay sashes, each child carrying a flag, and marching proudly with their banners. "When we can vote, the saloon will go." "Aren't we worth protecting?" etc. A most impressive sight and the work of women. Women are largely responsible for national prohibition, which was secured without equal suffrage.[6]

Moreover, the women knew that the children would exert a more devastating pressure in the future than in the present. In 1920, Anna Gordon, who became President of the Woman's Christian Temperance Union after the death of Frances Willard, claimed that the Union's work among the children should bear much of the credit for the passage of the Eighteenth Amendment.

> "'Tremble, King Alcohol, we shall grow up," shouted the children, and in spirited fashion they sang, "We'll purify the ballot box, we'll consecrate the ballot box, we'll elevate the ballot box when we are twenty-one." In State and National Prohibition campaigns, as Young Campaigners for Prohibition, in patriotic regalia, with pennants flying and appealing, significant banners held aloft, the boys and girls prophesied the downfall of the trade that with its cruel heel dared "stifle down the beating of a child's heart." The cry of the children has been heeded by this great nation. Educated by the facts of science, by the precepts of the Bible, and by the joy of temperance service, the children have grown to manhood and womanhood and have helped vote out of existence the traffic in alcoholic beverages.[7]

The Anti-Saloon League quickly learned the political methods of the Woman's Christian Temperance Union.[8] And it added certain refinements and techniques of its own. In reaching the lobby of the people, the real source of power, it used the existing organization of the evangelical churches. Ernest Cherrington, the head of the League's educational and propaganda work, admitted this when he wrote, "The church voters' lists . . . constituted the real key to the situation." Although it took "many years of difficult and persistent endeavor" to line up the churches on the side of the League, in the end many of the churches co-operated. Then, "the information as to men and measures sent to the Christian voters was bound to receive attention and secure results." To disseminate still further this information about the friends and foes of prohibition, the League arranged for two-way contacts between the League lobbyist in Washington and those at each state legislature, who in turn passed their information on to the church voters. As Dinwiddie, the first League lobbyist at the national capital, put the matter, if those drys in Congress knew who their friends were in the states and those drys in the states knew who their friends were in Congress, "between the upper and nether millstones" something would happen.[9]

As well as keeping the drys informed about the voting habits of their representatives, the League arranged for those representatives to be swamped with appeals and with threats of defection at the polls before they voted on each important measure. The invention of the telephone led to the addition of the telegram to the great fluttering white blossom of petition. The founder of the League, Howard Hyde Russell, played an interesting part in the passage of the Eighteenth Amendment itself. He testified that, with the aid of the financial angel of the League, S. S. Kresge, he had compiled a list of thirteen thousand businessmen favorable to national prohibition. They were told what to do. Russell's testimony continued:

> We blocked the telegraph wires in Washington for three days. One of our friends sent seventy-five telegrams, each signed differently with the name of one of his subordinates. The campaign was successful. Congress surrendered. The first to bear the white flag was Senator Warren Harding of Ohio. He told us frankly he was opposed to the amendment, but since it was apparent from the telegrams that the business world was demanding it he would submerge his own opinion and vote for submission.[10]

Fear of the power of the League was so great and blatant among Congressmen that, according to the Washington *Times*, the Eighteenth Amendment would not have passed if a secret ballot had made it impossible for the League to punish the disobedient at the next election.[11]

Wayne B. Wheeler, in a series of articles in the New York *Times* in 1926, gave more details of the League's methods of pressure. He said that the Washington headquarters of the League corresponded with every possible friend in Congress and went to see each personally. All fifty thousand field workers of the League in the states were kept advised of the attitude of their members in Congress. They were also advised on methods of winning over new converts in the states.[12] It was in this excellent contact between Washington and the states, and in the channeling of information from the Capitol through the church leaders to the church voters that the League had its influence. Even when the "decent vote" was in a minority in a state, the Democrats and Republicans were usually so evenly divided that a switch of that vote from one side to the other would decide the election. The League held the balance of power in many areas and thus exerted pressure out of proportion to its following. Moreover, it consciously tried to attract those people who were influential in their communities. Mrs. Elizabeth Tilton made this clear at the National League convention of 1919. She said that prohibition was put through by getting the 500,000 "opinion-makers" on the dry side, for the other 99,000,000 people of America were apathetic and unimportant. She continued, "As we hold these 500,000 so we shall hold the law; as we let them become apathetic we shall lose the law."[13] She was correct.

Against such efficient dry pressure politics, the brewers and distillers did both too little and too much, but invariably too late. Again and again, their paid publicists warned the liquor traders that they would be doomed unless they cleaned up their business and organized against the drys. Percy Andreae pointed out to the Brewers' Association in 1913, the year that the League decided upon its national drive, that the greatest irony about the liquor trade was to be accused of meddling in politics when it did little or nothing of the sort. In all of the 435 congressional districts of the United States, the League had an organization. The brewers had none. Their only hope was to organize the "millions and millions of falsely described foreign citizens" to hold the drys at bay. By a quick subsidy of the foreign-language press and use of the saloonkeepers and their friends, the wets might save the day. Otherwise, they would be destroyed.[14]

The trouble with the wet movement in its inception was that it was directed by those who were financially interested in the liquor business. These men relied on the traditional practices of bribery and corruption, which had served the trusts well in the nineteenth century. Only the times had changed. When a contagion of progressive reform was sweeping the country, the brewers and distillers were among the few who did not catch the disease. Thus they died of it, refusing to pay for the few inoculations of house cleaning which would have split the temperance reformers from the extreme prohibitionists.

Moreover, the dry lobbies were angels of agreement compared with the disharmonious wet interests. Although in the nineteenth century the grape growers and brewers and distillers had clung together to fight prohibition by "skulking behind the grape" and preaching the virtues of light wines and beer to hide the horrors of ardent spirits, they soon split apart as the drys grew more successful. In California particularly, where the wine industry had great local support, the grape growers would support the drys in their attacks on the saloons, which chiefly sold beer and spirits. The brewers, in their turn, tried to save themselves by referring to beer as the temperance drink and supporting the prohibition of spirits. They ran large advertisements in 1917, claiming that the true relationship of beer was "with light wines and soft drinks — not with hard liquor." Meanwhile, the distillers accused the brewers of debauching America in the saloons, which were chiefly owned and controlled by the breweries. The brewers even fought among themselves. "Domestic" brewers supported the Anti-Saloon League against "shipping" brewers when the League wanted to prohibit or tax heavily the shipment of beer across state borders. "Shipping" brewers would then support the drys in neighboring states, for a dry state meant greater profits for the liquor traders in the wet states nearby. Indeed, in the economic war between the various liquor groups, each saw the dry cause as a possible ally in the suppression of its competitors. Only when the dry cause became too strong and the hour was already too late did the winegrowers and brewers and distillers make common cause. Even so, in the same year that Congress passed the Eighteenth Amendment, the drys in California were delighted by the sight of large posters, bought by wet organizations, which read, "There is no place in America for the saloon. This not an economic question, but it is a moral one."[15]

Of course, the brewers were further unlucky in that they were strongly pro-German by birth and preferred to use as propaganda units such groups as the "unpatriotic" German-American Alliance. Their known sympathies made them appear to be tainted by the militarism and alleged atrocities of their country of origin. But if they were unfortunate to be branded as traitors by the Great War, they were stupid to be caught in 1917 in the act of buying up newspapers and elections. The revelations of the last-minute efforts of the liquor trade to bribe itself out of trouble seemed to confirm all the allegations of the drys. If the brewers were proved to be disloyal and corrupt, so was the substance which they made. Perhaps it really was the beer which tainted both the maker and the drinker. If it was abolished, then America could become truly patriotic and democratic at last.

The actual methods of disseminating their propaganda differed from drys to wets. The Anti-Saloon League and the Woman's Christian Temperance Union poured out a volume of pamphlets, clipsheets, and posters to church voters and the unregenerate. By 1912, the eight Westerville presses of the League were turning out approximately 250,000,000 book pages of literature a month. These included thirty-one state editions of the *American Issue*, the *American Patriot*, the *New Republic*, and the *Scientific Temperance Journal*. Two more papers, the *Worker* and the *National Daily* were begun in 1915. By 1920, although some of the smaller papers of the League had been discontinued, the printing of the *American Issue* rose to a yearly total of eighteen million copies.[16] The Woman's Christian Temperance Union was hardly outdone. Its presses at Evanston, Illinois, produced in the year of crisis, 1928, ten million copies of a pamphlet listing the wet record of Al Smith.[17]

But even more numerous were the pamphlets printed by the League. In the fourteen years after 1909, the League printed over one hundred million pamphlets and leaflets. These were distributed through churches, corporations, and labor unions. Propaganda fell thicker than hailstones on the heads of the people. Few escaped the ubiquitous slogans of the drys, which filled the billboards and hoardings and newspapers of the time.

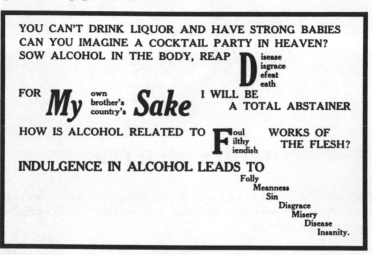

YOU CAN'T DRINK LIQUOR AND HAVE STRONG BABIES
CAN YOU IMAGINE A COCKTAIL PARTY IN HEAVEN?
SOW ALCOHOL IN THE BODY, REAP **D**isease / isgrace / efeat / eath

FOR ***My*** own / brother's / country's ***Sake*** I WILL BE A TOTAL ABSTAINER

HOW IS ALCOHOL RELATED TO **F**oul / ilthy / iendish WORKS OF THE FLESH?

INDULGENCE IN ALCOHOL LEADS TO Folly / Meanness / Sin / Disgrace / Misery / Disease / Insanity.

The drys also used another method of propaganda, which had once been credited with bringing about the Reformation. That was the hymn, or religious marching song. The melodies were often familiar evangelical tunes with new words set to them. The most popular of all the songs was, perhaps, "The Saloon Must Go":

> *I stand for prohibition*
> *The utter demolition*
> *Of all this curse of misery and woe;*
> *Complete extermination*
> *Entire annihilation*
> *The Saloon must go.*

In a more patriotic vein, the tune of the "Marseillaise" was given new words:

> *Arise, arise, ye brave*
> *The world, the world to save*
> *O, break, O, break Rum's mighty pow'r,*
> *The world, the world to save. . . .*

He Can't Put It Out

The democratic method of bringing down the saloon was also urged musically at dry song fests. All that was necessary for victory was "Only a Ballot, Brother":

> Then slight not the ballot, my brother,
> Be mindful to vote as you pray;
> For God is as just as gracious,
> Then choose for the right today.

Another propaganda device of the prohibitionists was the use of authorities, lifted out of context, to justify their cause. Amen-em-an, an Egyptian priest from 2000 B.C. was credited with the first temperance statements; and after him came a motley collection of patriarchs, prophets, politicians, and poets, including such notorious drys as Solomon and Homer. To prove the prohibitionist sympathies of Homer, Hector's retort to his mother was quoted:

> "Far hence be Bacchus' gifts!" Hector rejoined.
> "Inflaming wine, pernicious to mankind,
> Unnerves the limbs and dulls the noble mind."

The frequent drinking feats of the Greek heroes went unmentioned. They were forgotten, while the warnings of Isaiah, Habakkuk, Anacharsis the Scythian, Buddha, the anonymous author of the Chinese classic *She-King*, St. Paul, Pliny the Elder, Plutarch, St. Augustine, Mohammed, the author of the Eddas, Luther, and even Shakespeare were brought into line behind the drys. Shakespeare's real sympathies were held to lie in the line from *Othello*, "Oh, thou invisible spirit of wine, if thou hast no name to be known by, let us call thee devil." The roll of the dry forerunners continued through Bacon, writing under his own name, and Milton.

> *Some by violent stroke shall die*
> *By fire, flood, famine; by intemperance more.* . . .

The list of the prophets approached modern times with Prior, Kant, Young, Chesterfield, Rowland Hill, Fielding, Wesley, John Adams, Goldsmith, Cowper, Goethe, Moltke, Bismarck, and, until the Great War, Kaiser Wilhelm.[18]

The propaganda reply of the wets was initially in the hands of the brewers and distillers. They employed some of the methods of the drys, but, instead of the organization of the churches, they used the organization of the saloons and of the foreign-language associations and newspapers. After the beginning of this century, the brewers were spending some seventy thousand dollars a year on advertising in foreign-language newspapers. By 1915, they estimated that their distribution of wet literature was about 450,000,000 pieces a year, including a magazine and a weekly newsletter to some 5300 small-town newspapers.[19] This propaganda, however, so blatantly displayed self-interest that it was ineffective. Moreover, the fact that the brewers were largely responsible for the immense expansion of the German-American Alliance as their chief pressure group involved them in its downfall.

Against the songs of the drys, the wets had a tradition of drinking songs which reached back into the feasts of antiquity. But somehow these songs seemed to express pathos and roister rather than sincere feeling. A wet apologist conceded:

> The representative of the Anti-Saloon League could play on a thousand chords of memory and of sentiment that touched the emotions. The Liquor Dealers' Association had no such unfailing resource; they could have offered nothing more moving in the sentimental line than the memory of "My Bonnie Lies Over the Ocean," bawled at midnight with beery emotion by a casual quartette, dwelling long and lovingly on the chord of the diminished fifth.[20]

Even the most sentimental of all the saloon songs, "The Face on the Barroom Floor," ended with the awful warning of the drunkard's death:

Another drink, and with a chalk in hand,
the vagabond began
To sketch a face that might well buy
the soul of any man.
Then, as he placed another lock
upon the shapely head,
With a fearful shriek, he leaped and fell
across the picture — dead.[21]

As for the authorities of history, the wets had an endless source of politicians to justify the running over of the flowing bowl. These wet champions included Oliver Cromwell, George Washington, Thomas Jefferson, Jefferson Davis, Theodore Roosevelt, Woodrow Wilson, and Samuel Gompers. The wets also claimed the sympathies of the most popular hero of the time, Abraham Lincoln. It was a proved fact that Lincoln had run a grocery store which sold liquor, and that he was President of the United States when the federal government had put a tax on liquor for the first time. On the other hand, he had praised the cause of temperance; and, according to the unsubstantiated word of a contemporary United States commissioner, had said to him, "Don't drink, my boy; great armies of men are killed each year by alcohol."[22] But Lincoln's real position seems to have been one of moderation, in which he chided the dramsellers for the wrongs they did and defended them against the "thundering tones of anathema and denunciation" of the militant drys.[23] The Anti-Saloon League, however, was less interested in his true feelings than his myth. It called its Total Abstinence Union the Lincoln-Lee Legion, thus making one at last the two heroes whom the Civil War had separated.

THE DRYS WIN THE WAR

EVEN IF patriotism is not always the last refuge of a scoundrel, it was certainly the final barrage of the prohibitionists. It was the ideal which put the Eighteenth Amendment "over the top." Prohibition was presented as "first and foremost a patriotic program of 'win the war.' "[24] An incessant volley of dry propaganda preached that all patriots must be prohibitionists to save food for the starving Allies; that German-Americans were guilty of spying and treason and drinking beer; that the German armies had committed their atrocities under the influence of alcohol; that the worst Kaiser of all was the liquor Kaiser; and that peace without victory and a land fit for heroes were only possible in an earth free from the jack boots of Hun brewers. Indeed, not only would the war bring about national and international prohibition, but lack of the ideology of prohibition had brought about the world war. Purley A. Baker made this quite clear.

The junker, the Kaiser, the murderer of the Arch-Duke Ferdinand and his wife, in fact the very house of the Hohenzollern, are but the merest incidents in bringing on this world holocaust. The primary and secondary and all-compelling cause is that a race of people have arisen who eat like gluttons and drink like swine — a race whose "God is their belly," and whose inevitable end is destruction. Their sodden habits of life have driven them constantly toward brutality and cruelty until they were prepared to strike for universal conquest, though millions of lives and oceans of blood was to be the price of reaching that unholy ambition. Beer will do for a nation exactly what it will do for an individual. . . . We seek a saloonless and drunkless world.[25]

The interest of the Anti-Saloon League and of the drys in military and naval preparedness was nothing new. In both the American Revolution and the Civil War, Congress had passed ineffective measures designed to keep troops from hard liquor. But what lawgivers could not do, reform groups did. Their first point of attack was the sale of liquor to troops through Army canteens. This had been forbidden in 1832 and again in 1882, but the canteens were still flourishing at the end of the nineteenth century, although they were restricted to selling light wines and beer to the troops. In 1901, Congress, under dry pressure, passed a law forbidding the sale of alcohol from Army canteens. Although military efficiency was the plea of the drys for this measure, they were perhaps more interested in protecting the morals of the defenders of the nation. For, to them, "prostitution, alcohol, and venereal diseases have been, and are, an inseparable trio, and to successfully combat one, means a concerted attack on all three."[26]

Woodrow Wilson gave the drys both a supporter as Secretary of the Navy, Josephus Daniels, and the exploitable condition of war. Daniels had been brought up on a farm and was the editor of a small Southern newspaper; his upbringing and convictions had made him a confirmed prohibitionist. On April 5, 1914, he issued an order forbidding the use of alcoholic liquor in the Navy. This caused a burst of protest; no event in the first half of that year was so lampooned or cartooned.[27] As the New York *World* protested, America was sending splendid fleets to sea with their officers tutored like schoolboys and chaperoned like schoolgirls.[28]

War hysteria made Daniels's later measures more acceptable, however, for efficiency rather than liberty had become the symbol of the nation. The American Medical Association passed a resolution in 1917 which came to the startling conclusion that "sexual continence is compatible with health and is the best prevention of venereal infections" and that one of the methods for controlling syphilis was the control of

alcohol.²⁹ As a result, Daniels stopped the practice of the distribution
of contraceptives to sailors bound on shore leave, and Congress passed
laws setting up dry and decent zones around military camps.* The object was to give America "the soberest, cleanest, and healthiest fighting
men the world has known."³⁰ But the prohibitionists also used the
five-mile dry area around military bases as a weapon to close the
saloons of large cities. In California, the drys even tried for a fifteen-
mile limit around camps, which would have closed all the saloons in
San Francisco.³¹ In wet Hoboken, the brewers lost a battle with the
military authorities to keep the swinging saloon doors open after ten
o'clock at night.³² Many barkeepers were fined for selling liquor to men
in uniform. Only at Coney Island could soldiers and sailors change
into the grateful anonymity of bathing suits and drink without molesta-
tion from a patriotic passer-by.³³

The prohibitionists were not, however, content with protecting the
soldiers in the United States. They also demanded that the Army
should be protected overseas. An order of General Pershing that American troops in France should be allowed light wines and beer was
bitterly attacked in Congress by the sole Prohibition party Congressman, Randall, of California, who asked the President to rebuke Pershing for disobeying Army regulations. Pershing replied that he was
merely bringing the American Army into line with French regulations.
Moreover, it was a standard practice to issue liquor to front-line troops
in the British and French armies.³⁴ Pershing did not tell the real truth
of conditions in Europe behind the lines. These were noted by an
American intelligence officer who was keeping up his diary in a French
city in September, 1918. "Place full of newcomers, trying to dry up
France in one evening. Also full of tarts, with Yanks falling *en
masse*."³⁵

The people of America were not protected from the drys as was the
Army overseas. They were subject to all the rumors and fears of
civilians at war. And these rumors and fears were exploited and directed by the activity of the propaganda experts of the time, George
Creel, his notorious Committee on Public Information, and the prohibitionists. For, in time of war, "all the specific means of conquering
the Evil One are, and should be, glorified. The cult of battle requires
that every form of common exertion (enlistment, food-saving, munition making, killing the enemy) should have the blessing of all the holy
sentiments."³⁶ As the Secretary of War said, the government aimed at

---

* The Woman's Christian Temperance Union was jubilant over this measure
by Daniels. It thought that the armed forces would be forced into continence,
thus ending the "double standard," and beginning, for both the man and the
woman, "the white life for two."

"the whole business of mobilizing the mind of the world."[37] This was also the whole business of the drys. A huge majority of Americans were swept up in the fervor of patriotism, and this same fervor could be used for the dry cause if only the people were convinced that "prohibition spells patriotism."[38] Even such a bitter foe of prohibition as Mencken admitted that prohibition did have substantial popular support during the war.

> *Homo boobiens* was scientifically roweled and run amok with the news that all the German brewers of the country were against the [eighteenth] amendment; he observed himself that all German sympathizers, whether actual Germans or not, were bitter opponents of it. His nights made dreadful by dreams of German spies, he was willing to do anything to put them down, and one of the things he was willing to do was to swallow Prohibition.[39]

The extent of war hysteria between 1917 and 1919 is difficult to imagine. Never have so many behaved so stupidly at the manipulation of so few. George Creel, whose genius at misrepresentation and exaggeration was hardly exceeded by that of Gargantua, could call on the propaganda services of most of the artists and intellectuals of the nation, whose peacetime sanity was deranged by the excesses perpetrated in the name of country. Spies were thought to be everywhere, lurking in each foreign accent and behind each puff of smoke without fire. Voluntary societies of a quarter of a million zealous informers channeled gossip to the Department of Justice. "There was no community in the country so small that it did not produce a complaint because of failure to intern or execute at least one alleged German spy." Terror gave every suspicious occurrence the color of conspiracy.

> A phantom ship sailed into our harbors with gold from the Bolsheviki with which to corrupt the country; another phantom ship was found carrying ammunition from one of our harbors to Germany; submarine captains landed on our coasts, went to the theater and spread influenza germs; a new species of pigeon, thought to be German, was shot in Michigan; mysterious aeroplanes floated over Kansas at night. . . .[40]

There were not policemen enough to track down every denunciation, and the volunteer committees of citizens merely added to the general terror. An invisible enemy plotted an unseen conspiracy throughout the land, and fear and the drys profited.

But the brewers played into the hands of the Anti-Saloon League. They had decided that their only hope of survival was to organize support among the largest and most respectable group of beer drinkers in the nation, the German-Americans. In 1901, a Dr. Charles John Hexamer had organized a National German-American Alliance, whose object was ostensibly the teaching of German culture and, in reality, the formation of an antiprohibition organization. In 1914, the Alliance claimed a membership of two million and was certainly the most formidable foe of the drys. In the areas of its greatest strength — Pennsylvania, New York, Ohio, Wisconsin, Indiana, Illinois, and Iowa — state-wide prohibition could not be passed. The Alliance considered that prohibition was directed primarily against "German manners and customs, and the joviality of the German people," in the same way as the drys considered that the saloon was primarily an attack on the old American virtues.[41] As an article in the Alliance monthly magazine said, "In order to gain for the Germans of America that place in the sun which has hitherto always been denied them, it is absolutely necessary that they enjoy personal liberty, and that this shall not be whittled away by the attacks of the prohibitionists and the persecutors of the foreign-born." In fact, the Alliance was quite correct in considering prohibition as an attack on the more recent immigrants to America, although it was foolish to place the main emphasis of its defense of the saloons on its Germanism rather than on the promise of America to all immigrants.

After 1913, through the medium of the brewers' publicist, Percy Andreae, the Alliance received heavy subsidies from the beer companies. A "lobbying committee" of the Alliance was set up in Washington to combat the influence of the Anti-Saloon League. After the outbreak of the war in 1914, this lobby was also concerned with trying to keep the United States strictly neutral. Indeed, as the Anti-Saloon League linked patriotism with prohibition and preparedness against Germany, so the German-American Alliance linked prohibition with the enmity of German-Americans against England and with loyalty to the fatherland. John Schwaab, of the Ohio Alliance, made this clear in 1915. "The drink question is forced upon us by the same hypocritical Puritans as over there are endeavoring to exterminate the German nation."

In 1918, the German-American Alliance was investigated by the Senate and made to disband. It was discovered that the leaders of the Alliance had said some arrogant and stupid things which could be construed as disloyalty to the United States. The Alliance had displayed the German flag and sung "Deutschland über Alles." Moreover, it had become associated with political deals of questionable honesty with the brewers in the fight against prohibition.[42] This concatenation of evidence was enough, in the zealous mood of war, to damn both the Alliance and the brewers. And the material was perfect for exploitation by the speakers and pamphleteers of the Anti-Saloon League. One League pamphlet, reviewing the findings, said of Hexamer's statement that the only correct form of government was a constitutional monarchy:

> No loyal citizen would compare his country in this way with Germany. Who would trade freedom for slavery, or democracy for autocracy? Lives there a man in America with soul so dead, that he has never said with pride, this is my native or chosen land, the best country in the world? If there be such let him ask for a passport at once. America is good enough for Americans.

The time had come, the pamphlet went on, for a division between those who were for German beer drinkers and those were for the loyal drys, for a split between "unquestioned and undiluted American patriots, and slackers and enemy sympathizers." Since this was the year of the ratification of the Eighteenth Amendment, the most patriotic act of any legislature or citizen was "to abolish the un-American, pro-German, crime-producing, food-wasting, youth-corrupting, home-wrecking, treasonable liquor traffic."[43]

Their connection with the German-American Alliance was not the end of the folly of the American brewers. Later on in the same year, they were proved to have interfered with elections and bought newspapers, including the Washington *Times* for a sum of half a million dollars. In the indictment brought against them by the spy-hunting Attorney General A. Mitchell Palmer, they were accused of conduct worthy of a corporate Benedict Arnold. "The organized liquor traffic of the country is a vicious interest because it has been unpatriotic, because it has been pro-German in its sympathies and its conduct." According to Palmer, the breweries were owned by rich men of German sympathies, and they deliberately founded organizations "to keep young German immigrants from becoming real American citizens." It was "around the sangerfests and sangerbunds and organizations of that kind, generally financed by the rich brewers, that the young Germans who come to America are taught to remember, first, the fatherland, and second, America."[44] In the atmosphere of the day, such a jumbled accusation was tantamount to proof, and the contention of the drys seemed evident, that beer corrupts and powerful brewers corrupt powerfully.

Two more tendencies in the state of war worked for the dry cause. The first was the tendency towards centralization. With the federal government taking over railroads and shipping, putting through conscription and the requisition of factories, the friends of states' rights and personal liberty were powerless. The current argument was one of human efficiency, whether in the production of munitions or in the killing of Huns. Obviously, alcohol was helpful neither to men who worked long hours at machines nor to those who aimed at the enemy through rifle sights. As a popular dry stereopticon slide said, above a reproduction of American soldiers shooting at Germans, beer drinkers showed three times as many "errors of precision," and "good shooting demands good eyesight." Moreover, the rise in federal power through wartime prohibition seemed trifling compared with the huge new powers of the government over the lives and goods of Americans. Yet no other war measures of the Wilson government were written into the Constitution. They were repealed immediately upon the close of demobilization. Only national prohibition was preserved in the Constitution like "an unpleasant fly in imperishable amber."[45]

The second passing trend that the prohibitionists utilized was the pressure towards food conservation. Herbert Hoover had dramatized the need of the Belgians for food. The submarine blockade of England and France emphasized this need. One dry economist claimed that the grain used in liquor manufacture would produce eleven million loaves of bread a day for the starving Allies. Another said that these foodstuffs would meet the energy requirements of seven million men for a year. According to Maud Radford Warren, "Every man who works on the land to produce drink instead of bread is a loss in winning the war; and worse, he may mean a dead soldier."[46] Moreover, it was claimed that the liquor trade was "the Kaiser's mightiest ally" in using up space in the American communications system.

> Brewery products fill refrigerator cars, while potatoes rot for lack of transportation, bankrupting farmers and starving cities. The coal that they consume would keep the railroads open and the factories running. Pro-Germanism is only the froth from the German beer-saloon. Our German Socialist party and the German-American Alliance are the spawn of the saloon. Kaiser kultur was raised on beer. Prohibition is the infallible submarine chaser we must launch by thousands. The water-wagon is the tank that can level every Prussian trench. Total abstinence is the impassable curtain barrage which we must lay before every trench. Sobriety is the bomb that will blow kaiserism to kingdom come. We must all become munition-makers.[47]

Such irrational and emotional slogans were effective, where all was appeal and slogan and glory and "The Star-Spangled Banner." The wets, indeed, retaliated less effectively, but in kind. They threw back the charges of treason in the faces of the drys. Sergeant Arthur Guy Empey, war hero and author of the best-selling *Over the Top,* declared that front-line troops needed a rum ration to put them in fighting trim. "Many of the extremists, on the dry side, think they are patriotic. All

THE FOE IN THE REAR

they are doing is playing into the hands of the Hohenzollern gang."[48]
Accusations were made that the dry effort to prohibit the manufacture
of alcohol was a German plot to stop supplies of the vital alcohol
used for making smokeless gunpowder. Another line of wet attack was
that the loss of revenue from the liquor tax would cripple America's
war effort. The *National Bulletin* of the brewers and distillers went so

far as to say that the antidraft uprisings in the prohibition states of Arizona, Oklahoma, Idaho, Washington, and Oregon showed the "great lack of patriotism" in dry areas. Even worse, there were "many close students of conditions and events who believe that the Anti-Saloon League did all it could to encourage war with Germany, in the hope that the upheaval incident to strife would enable them to push their special propaganda." The *Bulletin* rightly pointed out that the League's effort to tack wartime prohibition onto the Food Control Bill was holding up Wilson's program for victory, but came to the unfair conclusion that the drys were "Anti-Saloon Leaguers and Prohibitionists first and American citizens afterwards." This statement, the *Bulletin* righteously observed, did not surprise anyone who had intimate knowledge of the personal and mental traits of the drys. "The Kaiser has no better friends."[49]

Yet if the condition of war was necessary for the drys to secure the passage of the Eighteenth Amendment through Congress and the state legislatures, the fact that the amendment was passed in time of war left a bitter taste in the mouth of the wets, which was not solely their disappointed thirst. The *North American Review* accused the drys of "taking advantage of the Nation's peril." The Eighteenth Amendment was the work of "the incorrigible bigots, the hired lobbyists and the pusillanimous Congressmen who place Prohibition above Patriotism."[50] Lieutenant-Colonel Theodore Roosevelt, Jr., expressed a similar feeling when he said, "Over in France and in the occupied parts of Germany the doughboys feel very much peeved that prohibition should have been enacted in their absence. They feel that something has been put over on them."[51] This resentment, whether true or false in theory, was real enough in its psychological effects. And, on demobilization, this feeling of disillusion and of being cheated by their country persisted within that highly influential group of Americans, the veterans, so strongly that their organization was among the first supporters of modification and repeal. William Faulkner gave a brilliant description of a bunch of demobilized soldiers sitting about a dance floor in a small Southern town, feeling that the postwar world of 1919 had taken advantage of their absence to exclude them. They were "the hang-over of warfare in a society tired of warfare. Puzzled and lost, poor devils. Once Society drank war, brought them into manhood with a cultivated taste for war; but now Society seemed to have found something else for a beverage, while they were not yet accustomed to two and seventy-five per cent."[52]*

The drys denied that the Eighteenth Amendment was put over on the American people while the Army was away in France. They

---

* Faulkner is referring to the weak beer legalized under wartime prohibition.

pointed out that Congress and the legislatures which passed the amendment were elected in 1916, before America entered the war.[53] This is correct, and it is true that the drys gained many victories in the elections of 1916. But they could not have secured the two-thirds majority which they needed in both houses of Congress without the switched votes of such people as Senator Harding, who were ready to change sides because of the changed feeling of America at war. A reading of the House debate on the Eighteenth Amendment confirms this conclusion. Patriotism was the bugle call sounded by the drys to switch the wavering over to their camp. Congressman Cooper, of Ohio, quoted Lloyd George's words that the liquor traffic was a greater enemy to England than Germany and Austria were. According to him, the sacrifice by American mothers of their sons to the Army gave the government the plain duty of returning each soldier boy "as pure and morally clean" as on the day he left home. Lunn, of New York, resented the wet slur on American workingmen, that they could only uphold the President with their right hand if they were allowed a bottle of whisky in their left. Campbell, of Kansas, said that munitions workers should not be permitted liquor, since they might send defective armaments to the soldiers in France. Kelly, of Pennsylvania, said that everything which helped Prussian might was hurtful to America, and liquor was the chief ally of the Kaiser. He continued darkly:

> There is coming a new political alignment in this country, with Americans on one side and anti-Americans on the other. All those who fight under the black banner of corruption and the yellow flag of treason must be lined up so that Americans may know their enemies. That division will be made. That battle will come. The elimination of the liquor traffic in American will mean assured victory to the forces of Americanism.

There were still more appeals to the war psychology of the House. Congressman Smith, of Idaho, accused Busch, the brewer, of trying to introduce the German saloon system into America, by his proposal to serve in his saloons only light wines, beer, and temperance drinks. Good Americans would no more take his advice than the Kaiser's on how to run the war. Tillman, of Arkansas, found that "the most arrogant, the least polite, the coldest mannered, the most disdainful citizen, is that haughty plutocrat, the American brewer, usually tainted with Teuton sympathies and damned by a German conscience." Tillman thought "home" was the dearest word in the language save the word "mother," and both had to be protected. This could be done by abolishing the "tainted O.K." of the government tax on liquor. Americans must be mobilized in the dry cause as the Scots clans had been rallied to war, with all carrying "the burning cross of this crusade to every home in our great Republic."[54] In such a charged atmosphere of cries to the heart and the flag, it was hardly surprising that more than two-thirds of Congress voted dry.

Another reason for supposing that the Anti-Saloon League waited for the war to launch its campaign for the Eighteenth Amendment is its timing. If the League had been sure of a majority before war was declared, it would have pressed for the amendment at the beginning of 1917 rather than at the close of the year. Indeed, the drys made many damaging admissions that they had cleverly exploited the war to bring about prohibition. And whether national prohibition would have come without the war or not, the fact that the drys praised their own smartness in using the war damned them out of their own mouths as guilty of employing abnormal times to secure their own ends. In the words of the *American Issue* of May 14, 1919, "The spirit of service and self-sacrifice exemplified in an efficient and loyal staff made it possible to take advantage of the war situation, and of the confusion which He whom we serve has wrought among our enemies."[55] A sense of destiny, rarely absent from the minds of revolutionaries, touched the League leaders with the conviction that the League had been created to save America from a pacifist, German conspiracy by aiding it to plunge into the militant Christianity of a just war. Purley A. Baker thought there was no doubt that, without the Anti-Saloon League, "America would have been sufficiently Germanized to have kept her out of the war." Baker continued, "The hand of a good Providence may be as distinctly seen in the origin of the Anti-Saloon League a quarter of a century ago, as it was in the delivery of the children of Israel from their forty years of wandering."[56]

The hysteria of war cast its false and persecuting simplicity across the land until the Red Scare of 1919 died from lack of evidence and from ridicule. In this period, the Volstead Act was passed. Again, the drys made use of the militant spirit of the times to accuse their opponents of treason. An Anti-Saloon League official declared that the man who sent a bomb to Palmer's home "was inspired by Germans with wet tendencies."[57] Senator Arthur Capper, of Kansas, attributed his home state's decency and progress to prohibition, which had kept anarchists, the Bolsheviki, and strikers out of the state.[58] * Congressman Alben

---

* A current folk song ridiculed the eternal claims of Kansas to arid virtue:

> Oh they say that drink's a sin
> In Kansas
> Oh they say that drink's a sin
> In Kansas
> Oh they say that drink's a sin
> So they guzzle all they kin
> And they throw it up agin
> In Kansas.

Barkley, of Kentucky, knew of nothing else in the country which contributed so much to Bolshevism as the pernicious doctrine of the wets.[59] Indeed, the pending "industrial war" in the United States was given as a reason in the Senate for hurrying through the Volstead Act.[60] Over and over again, the drys took the stand that law and obedience to the Eighteenth Amendment was the only way to preserve American liberties from the new scapegoat of the nation, the Bolsheviki, whose ideology had, in William Howard Taft's opinion, a "curious affinity" to autocratic German mentality.[61]

But the mood of national militancy declined when the Palmer raids proved that the seven thousand most dangerous radicals in America were guilty of nothing at all, and that the police power of the federal government could be more subversive of personal liberty than any chimera of Red revolution. The Anti-Saloon League tried to preserve its belligerent spirit and its concept of itself as the shock troop of the Lord, but the appeals which brought out dry voters in wartime were answered by catcalls in time of peace. The drys were left with a sense of nostalgia for the years when their voice seemed to be the voice of all true Americans and patriots. The national feeling then had not been "manufactured sentiment"; all the Anti-Saloon League had done "was simply to direct it where and in the manner in which it would do the most good."[62]

The drys thought that, even if prohibition had been passed because of the psychology of war, this was a good state of mind.

> The truth is that the tension of war lifted the general American mind to a rare elevation of unselfishness and moral courage; the thought of a society organized for everybody's welfare and for nobody's anti-social profit cast over the people's imagination a spell that promised a far better post-war than pre-war America.

And if, in the twenties, many of the high colors of that promise had faded, "the sensible reaction for sensible men" was "not a sneer at disappointed hopes but an honest resolve to recover and retain the aims that then stirred the national heart."[63] But what the drys forgot is that, although war breeds its own sacrifice, it is a sacrifice of lives as well as personal habits; and, although peace breeds its own laxity of morals, it also allows the voice of reason and tolerance to be heard. Such a convinced wet as G. K. Chesterton could admit in 1922 that prohibition had been passed "in a sort of fervour or fever of self-sacrifice, which was a part of the passionate patriotism of America in the war." But he continued shewdly that men could not remain standing stiffly in such symbolic attitudes; nor could a permanent policy be founded on "something analogous to flinging a gauntlet or uttering a battle cry."[64]

The dry mastery of the techniques of pressure and propaganda exerted influence on Americans from the cradle to the grave. The politicians of America were particularly susceptible to this influence. Those who had political ambitions were forced to take up a stand on the prohibition issue. Yet if they announced their support of either wets or drys, they would alienate powerful groups of voters, and that would be the end of their political ambitions. Thus the nature of the prohibition problem forced the trimmers of mankind, the politicians, to trim still more. They could not declare themselves on the issue; yet if they did not declare themselves, they might still be defeated at the polls. They sought a middle road, but that road was hard to find. Thus they progressed, shifting back and forth, along the delicate path of representatives of the people.

Each politician met the prohibition issue in his own particular way. His attitude was a compound of upbringing and circumstance, geography and party line. He demonstrated both his own feelings and the feelings of those whom he sought to represent. His evasions were a mirror and a reflection of the evasions of a complete country over the matter of prohibition. If politicians were forced to equivocate over the dry dilemma, their fault lay originally in the divided feelings of the people.

Those who were, or sought to be, President of the United States were particularly troubled by the issue. They had to appeal to a national majority and could not afford to offend large groups. In their attempts to reach the White House, they had no relief from the liquor problem. Their personal histories provide examples of the choices and pressures which prohibition forced upon all politicians and upon all men who were dependent for their jobs on the will of the people. In the story of these individuals, who sought to represent a whole nation, lies a microcosm of the tragedy which overtook the whole nation. All these men tried to avoid the prohibition issue, or to be moderate in their solutions. But the extremism of the dry reform, the urging of political ambition, or the exigency of office drove them to the same excess that they deplored in the friends and foes of prohibition. He who would be President is the least able to avoid the problems of his time.

CHAPTER 7

Trimming for the White House

> I am not a politician, and my other habits are good.
>
> ARTEMUS WARD

WILLIAM JENNINGS BRYAN: APOSTLE OF PROHIBITION

WILLIAM JENNINGS BRYAN was frequently called the Great Commoner. Much of his greatness lay in his mastery of the great commonplace. For rural America, he was the apostle of the average, the evangel of everyman, the *doyen* of the drys. He thought that he believed in what his father had believed, and his father's father: in the virtue of the female country virtues and the value of the male country values. Those were good who had a white skin, a farm, or a small business; who went to a Protestant church and believed that the Bible was wholly true; and who preached peace and prohibition.[1] Those were bad who were not Anglo-Saxon, had large businesses, and lived in large cities; who went to mass or even worse did not believe in the Bible at all; and who preached war and wetness. If Bryan talked isolationism and practiced imperialism as Secretary of State, talked poverty and died with an estate worth over a million dollars, and talked peace only to be buried at his own request with full military honors in Arlington Cemetery, he was defeated by the same vices that were to defeat his village America. For he embodied the prejudices of the old Middle West and the South. He spoke with a silver tongue of the things that his countrymen already knew and could not say. He went down with them before mass communications and the masses in the cities. Loved and jeered at, he died, after outliving his time. The savior of one day is the snigger of the next.

Bryan's parents were dry and quickly made him a total abstainer. He once said that he did not know the day he first signed the pledge, but that he guessed it was the day he first signed his name. He signed the pledge many times afterwards, not because he had broken it, but to encourage college students to do the same; his wife called the students he thus improved "stars in his diadem."[2] When he was a student himself at Illinois College, he defended in debate the resolution that intemperance was more destructive than war; indeed, his own death was partially the result of his gluttony. Leaving college, he became an unsuccessful lawyer. He earned his first money by collecting the debts of a saloonkeeper; he satisfied his conscience on the point by stating that, although those who drank alcohol were sinners, those who drank and did not pay for it were worse ones.[3]

But Bryan, for the first eighteen years of his political career, did not allow his private habits to obtrude upon his public life. In 1890, he was elected to a seat in Congress with the help of the business and liquor interests in Omaha. As he became more and more powerful in the Democratic party, he became less and less outspoken on the liquor question. The Democrats depended for some of their money and much of their vote on the brewers and the drinking cities.

When Bryan, then the leader of the Nebraska Democrats, came to the party convention of 1896 as a young man of thirty-six, he came, in the opinion of Clarence Darrow, expecting to be nominated for the presidency, although no one else thought of him as such a possibility. Darrow, later to turn the aged Bryan's eloquence to ridicule at the Scopes trial, went on to explain why Bryan's well-rehearsed cross-of-gold speech had the fantastic effect of making him the presidential candidate that year, after men and women had cheered and laughed and cried to listen to him.

> Platforms are not the proper forums for spreading doubts. The miscellaneous audience wants to listen to a man who *knows*. How he knows is of no concern to them. Such an audience wishes to be told, and especially wants to be told what it already believes. Mr. Bryan told the Democratic convention of 1896 in Chicago what he believed. Not only did he tell them that, but he told them what they believed, and what they wanted to believe, and wished to have come true.[4]

Bryan had the gift of expressing uncommonly well the common yearnings of the rural mind.

Bryan ran for President in 1896, 1900, and 1908; he lost each time by an increasing number of votes. On the 1896 campaign train, he used to rub himself with gin to remove his sweat so that he frequently appeared, smelling like a wrecked distillery; but the reporters never accused him of drinking his rub, since he spent the long journeys trying to convert them to abstinence. He campaigned for free silver and various progressive measures; but he never mentioned prohibition. As his wife rather naïvely stated in his memoirs, he was slow to take up the cause of national prohibition, since "he did not want to confuse the mind of the voter with too many issues and was unwilling to approve this reform until it was ripe for action."[5]

Prohibition was the bugaboo of would-be Presidents; it lost wet votes without gaining enough compensatory dry ones. William Jennings Bryan did not adopt the cause of national prohibition until he was fairly certain he would never be able to run for President again, and until he needed a victorious new crusade to restore his political power and reputation. In 1920, he was to have an unpleasant row with William H. Anderson, the superintendent of the New York Anti-Saloon League, who accused him of jumping on the dry wagon only when it was sure to roll home.

Bryan's wife wrote that he started his campaign for county option in a hired hall in Omaha in 1908. He had reason to be annoyed with the liquor interests. Missouri, which had voted for him in 1896 and 1900, voted for Taft in 1908. Bryan explained the switch and his losses in the large cities by blaming the influence of the brewers, who opposed all potential Presidents who were personal teetotalers. Moreover, although Bryan had supported the progressive reforms of the initiative and the referendum in Nebraska, they had been blocked by Democratic Senators in the pay of the wets, who feared that the drys would force through measures to close the saloons by means of a referendum.

Bryan brought up the matter at a state party convention in 1910 and split the Democrats over the issue. He was heavily defeated in the voting by the wets and lost control of the Democratic state machine. He had his revenge by turning against the Democratic and wet nominee for Governor, and by securing his defeat. Bryan's reasons for disloyalty to his party were moral:

> The liquor business is on the defensive; its representatives are for the most part lawless themselves and in league with lawlessness. They are in partnership with the gambling hell and the brothel. They are the most corrupt and corrupting influence in politics, and I shall not by voice or vote aid them in establishing a Reign of Terror in this state.[6]

Despite the bitter opposition of the Nebraska wets, Bryan was elected as a delegate to the Democratic convention of 1912. Because of his help in Woodrow Wilson's nomination and because of his party services in the campaigns of sixteen years, Bryan was appointed Secretary of State by Wilson. His only aid to the dry cause was to ban liquor from his official dinners. American policy in the Caribbean remained as aggressive as ever, provoking in Theodore Roosevelt the remark, "Well! grape juice diplomacy under Wilson does not bid fair to be much better than dollar diplomacy under Taft."[7]

The adoption of the policy of national prohibition by the Anti-Saloon League in 1913 put pressure on all politicians to declare themselves on the issue. The pressure was particularly hard on Bryan. He was the leading teetotaler among politicians, and he depended for his political power on the dry Middle West. Yet his behavior shows that he put his party before his personal convictions until his personal convictions could become a weapon to keep his power within his party. In the elections of 1914, he was careful to equivocate on the prohibition issue, since Wilson wanted no wet votes lost in the election of a Democratic majority in Congress. It was only at the safe end of the campaign that Bryan's magazine, the *Commoner,* announced that he would in future support state-wide prohibition, although he would not support national prohibition.

Bryan was unhappy in Washington. His home was on the Chautauqua circuits, delivering his golden platitudes on the subject of "The Prince of Peace" or "The Price of a Soul." Moreover, his political power lay in the West. After failing in three presidential campaigns, his only hope of retaining his influence in his party was to lead a new crusade, which would capture both party and country. That crusade was prohibition. In 1915, Bryan looked at the increasing victories of the drys in the country areas which loved him, and found them good. While he was still Secretary of State, in defiance of the policy of his party and his President, Bryan began campaigning for state prohibition. In 1915, he made sixty speeches in forty counties to some quarter of a million people. He accepted payment for some of these speeches, although his wife declared that he made a dozen free prohibition speeches for each hired one. Bryan declared shockingly that he could not live within his income as Secretary of State, and justified his dry lectures as a means of keeping in touch with the American people as well as making a living.[8]

Indeed, Bryan was right. His last hope of leading the Democrats was to capture the party for the dry cause. After his resignation from his cabinet post in 1915, this became even more true. Bryan resigned as a protest again Wilson's policy towards Germany, which he thought was leading towards war. By his resignation, Bryan put himself at the head of what he knew to be a majority of his countrymen, those who wanted to preserve the peace and to abolish the saloon. Although, out of deference to Wilson in the elections of 1916, he spoke softly on the topic of national prohibition, he declared for it less than one month after the elections were over. His reasons for doing so were curiously outspoken for a moral leader. He said that he had not expected to see prohibition become an "acute national question" until 1920. But "owing to causes which no one could foresee," the issue had been precipitated upon the nation. "The Democratic Party, having won without the aid of the wet cities, and having received the support of nearly all the Prohibition States and the States where women vote, is released from any obligation to the liquor traffic."[9] Therefore, he implied, for the best political reasons, he must now lead the Democrats publicly in the way in which his own private morality had always led him.

Yet, once war was declared against Germany, Bryan's behavior mirrored that curious aggressive nationalism at the basis of American pacifism, that strange violence at the core of the Christian drys. Bryan volunteered to serve in the Army as he had done in the war in Cuba, as colonel of his own Nebraska volunteers. He wrote to Wilson that he would fill in his time before he was called to the colors by assisting the Young Men's Christian Association in safeguarding the morals of the soldiers in their camps. He would preserve the Army from liquor and loose women so that the soldiers could die pure and sober. He was not called to the colors, nor was that other famous veteran from Cuba, Theodore Roosevelt. Bryan's mission in winning the war was confined to propaganda. He traveled widely in the West and South, speaking in Kentucky, Ohio, Illinois, Indiana, Wisconsin, Tennessee, and Louisiana, at "mostly peace and prohibition meetings."[10] * But this time, his message was of the virtues of peace with victory, and of prohibition as patriotism.

As Bryan lost his political influence, he tried to increase his moral influence. His example and practice taught clergymen how to lobby for peace, prohibition, and the Bible.[11] He had the happiness of seeing his old state, Nebraska, ratify the Eighteenth Amendment; suitably, it was the thirty-sixth state to ratify, making the amendment legal. He also received a touching message from the leaders of the Anti-Saloon League, thanking him for his propagandist and political support of the Eighteenth Amendment. He had done "so much to put the cause of temperance and prohibition 'over the top.'"[12] And he was in the select company that met at Washington to herald the first day of regenerated America under the Volstead Act on January 16, 1920. The audience greeted the great change with the doxology. At one minute to midnight, Bryan preached a sermon on the text, "They are dead that sought the young child's life." He explained that the text was peculiarly appropriate, as King Alcohol had slain a million times as many children as Herod.

Bryan's lectures on temperance were enormously effective. He made abstinence the supreme self-sacrifice and liquor the ultimate sin. He linked prohibition with every virtue and with the cause of peace. He was the very voice and soul of that great American movement for self-education, the Chautauqua. In fact, Bryan's rise paralleled the rise of the Chautauqua in the closing years of the nineteenth century, and his

* Mrs. Bryan significantly recorded in her diary, "I had some glimpses of what a national campaign on the subject would be — a veritable religious crusade."

death in 1925 was also reflected in the decline of Chautauqua, after its apogee in the previous year, when thirty million Americans had heard its message.

Historians of the Chautauqua movement have brought out its huge influence on country and small-town life.[13] They point out that Bryan's virtues — his sweetness of temper, his magnificent appearance, his teetotalism, his simplicity, and his bell-like voice — were exactly what the Chautauquas demanded. His power in rural America was very real. His tragedy was that the clear-cut values of the village could not be translated into the complex political action demanded by national affairs.

Bryan was, in fact, most at home in front of that tented audience, which adored him, delivering "passages of serious beauty and haunting logic" on the good things of life, such as peace and prohibition, love and water. His encomium of water is worth quoting, as an example of that style which impressed the rural crowds as the revealed truth.

> Water, the daily need of every living thing. It ascends from the seas, obedient to the summons of the sun, and, descending, showers blessing upon the earth; it gives of its sparkling beauty to the fragrant flower; its alchemy transmutes base clay into golden grain; it is the canvas upon which the finger of the Infinite traces the radiant bow of promise. It is the drink that refreshes and adds no sorrow with it — Jehovah looked upon it at creation's dawn and said — "It is good."[14]

Bryan embodied and voiced rural faith and rural prejudice. He ran for President when this creed could put up a fair fight for victory. In his closing years, he was jeered by the urban masses, which would overthrow these beliefs. Although he successfully kept wet planks out of the Democratic party platforms in the conventions of 1920 and 1924, he was hooted and booed at the second convention by galleries of New Yorkers for his defense of the Ku Klux Klan.[15] Still more tragic was the international ridicule of the aging Bryan defending his holy Bible at the Scopes trial against the sniping of the city lawyer, Clarence Darrow. Truly, the urban intellectuals made a monkey out of the pathetic old man.

Bryan's death seventeen days after the Scopes trial was merciful. He did not live to see the destruction by depression of the country America in which he believed. He did not live to find his chief method of influence, his hold over the rural Chautauqua audiences, destroyed with the financial failure of the circuits. For Bryan's power and weakness lay in his voice. It was his tongue which persuaded others of the virtues of prohibition and himself. He expressed exactly what country America wished to hear, but only what country America wished to hear. His success with a minority of the people meant his failure with the majority. Moreover, the competing voices of civilization, of radio and movies, of entertainers and advertisers, diminished the attraction of the golden tones of the Great Commoner. When technology could make a fireside chat audible throughout a nation, of what value was a single voice which could be heard without artificial aid from a distance of a quarter of a mile?

The phenomenon that was Bryan was a danger as well as a tragedy. This aspect of him was well brought out in the vicious epitaph on him printed in the New York *World.*

> He professed himself a Democrat and a Christian, but at bottom he was always a man looking for a point of conflict where his talent for factionalism could find free play. Thus as a Democrat he spent his chief energies quarreling with Democrats, and as a Christian he ended his life quarreling angrily with other Christians. . . . It was his conviction that you could solve great questions cheaply, on hunches and by a phrase, that made his influence and his example a dangerous one. The harm he did to his party by committing it against its own tradition to the centralized coercion of prohibition, the harm he did to pacifism by associating it with empty phrases, the harm he did to Protestantism by associating it with ignorance and legalized intolerance — above all, the great and unforgivable harm he did to his country by introducing a religious feud into politics — were all part and parcel of a life lived without respect for or loyalty to the laborious search for truth.[16]

THEODORE ROOSEVELT: KAISER OF DEMOCRACY

WHILE BRYAN was popular only in the country, Theodore Roosevelt was popular everywhere. Scholar and boxer, historian and Western sheriff, intellectual and cavalry leader, his appeal cut across lines of party and geography. Yet, moral and forthright though his statements were, his attitude toward prohibition declared the calculating and paternalist streak at the back of all his political doings. He was not concerned with the rights and wrongs of the dry cause any more than he was concerned with the rights and wrongs of the trusts. His arguments against both were the same, that they made the body politic corrupt. Thus he believed in their strict regulation according to the law. As George Bernard Shaw said, Roosevelt was the nearest thing to a Hohenzollern that the American Constitution would allow him to be. He did not mind about the effect of spirits on the soul, but he was anxious about their effect on the health of the people. He was brought up too graciously to think that beer drinking was a sin except for soldiers and sailors when they were fighting for their country. Liquor was a mere police and economic problem, only a menace when it was unlicensed and uncontrolled. In reality, the liquor seller was often far less of a problem in politics than the dedicated prohibitionist.

Roosevelt first expressed his views on prohibition in public to the state legislature of New York in 1884. He opposed a resolution asking for a referendum on a state prohibition amendment. He pointed out that it was idle to hope to enforce a law when nineteen-twentieths of the people did not believe in its justice. The resolution was lost. But later Roosevelt found himself ironically in the opposite position. He was made one of the New York Police Commissioners in 1895, with orders to close down all New York saloons on Sundays. His urge for efficiency and authority as usual got the better of his sympathies for the freedom of the Sunday drinker. He persecuted violators of the Sabbath law with vim and vigor. As he told the Catholic Total Abstinence Union, the people of America, although they were united in striving to do away with the evils of the liquor traffic, did not have morals as their primary concern. "We recognize as the first and most vital element in Americanism the orderly love of liberty. I put two words together, 'Orderly-Liberty'; and we recognize that we feel that absolutely without regard to race, or origin, or different creeds."[17] In Theodore Roosevelt's version of Americanism, orderliness came before liberty.

Roosevelt's views on prohibition are shown most clearly in a manuscript which he was too cautious to publish. It is called *On the Needs of Commonplace Virtues* and was written in 1897, after his unfortunate experiences as a policeman. It is an interesting document, in view of his later prohibitionist statements. It shows that, above all, he was a politician and a pragmatic prophet, concerned with the possible rather than the good. To him, reformers who were extremists become "at best useless members of the world's surface, and at worst, able allies of the vicious and disorderly classes." The temperance people were a good example. "Few things would more benefit the community as a whole than the widespread growth of a healthy temperance movement. Among poorer people especially there is probably no other one evil which is such a curse as excessive drinking." But, Roosevelt continued, while he grew more and more to realize the damage done by intemperance, he also grew more and more to realize the damage done by "the intemperate friends of temperance. When temperance people were willing to act wisely, and with appreciation of the limitations of human nature, and therefore of human effort, they could do much good. When they were not willing to act wisely they merely did harm; sometimes only a little harm, and sometimes very much."

Roosevelt particularly objected to the dry habit of running prohibition candidates in an election between a reform and a machine politician; this stupidity often split the progressive vote and led to the victory of corruption. Politics was more than the art of the possible; it was the need for the possible.

> The effort to get the impossible is always bound to be feeble. . . . No liquor law at all, or the worst liquor law which the wit of a Tammany alderman could devise, would work better in New York than absolute prohibition, for the very excellent reason that nobody would pay the slightest heed to such absolute prohibition, and so, in addition to having free liquor, we should have the demoralizing spectacle of open and contemptuous disregard of the law of the land.[18]

Vote splitting was the chief nuisance of prohibition for all politicians. It cut across the usual party loyalties. Moreover, when the prohibitionists had not got what they wanted in state or nation, they tended to blame the party in power. The minority party was obviously innocent since it had no legislative means of suppressing the saloons. Therefore it could afford to make vague promises to the drys in return for electoral support. Only the dominant party could be damned by the drys, until it enacted prohibition. Then the drys switched to its support. For now they wanted executive law enforcement, not law change. They wanted conservation, not revolution. They wanted a strong federal and state power, not freedom for small communities. And here Roosevelt agreed with them.

If Roosevelt disliked the attack on personal liberty which was the ideology of prohibition, he also liked the order of a land free of saloons — especially in time of war. He made the same equation of prohibition and patriotism as did the drys. A measure of Roosevelt's change of attitude is shown by a letter written to William Allen White, the Kansas editor, in 1914 in time of peace. White had asked Roosevelt to support national prohibition and government-controlled railways. Roosevelt replied:

> As for prohibition nationally, it would merely mean free rum and utter lawlessness in our big cities. Worthy people sometimes say that liquor is responsible for nine tenths of all crime. As a matter of fact foreigners of the races that furnish most crime in New York at the present time do not drink at all. . . . I do not believe that the American people can be dragooned into being good by any outside influence, whether it is a king or the majority in some other locality.[19]

Yet, with the declaration of war in 1917, Roosevelt supported both the federal control of the railroads and the forcible conservation of food through prohibition. National efficiency and preparedness, irrespective of morality, demanded prohibition. Patriotism in time of war meant the dragooning of people into being sober, if not into being good. He wrote a much-misused letter to Clarence True Wilson, the author of *Dry or Die: the Anglo-Saxon Dilemma*. The letter stated that one of Roosevelt's sons had become a permanent prohibitionist after seeing the effect of alcohol on the soldiers in Pershing's Army, and that Roosevelt himself wished the drys every success in their effort to stop the waste of food, men, labor, and brainpower during these days.[20] Roosevelt died a public supporter of the Eighteenth Amendment.

Yet there was more than patriotism to the ex-President's change of front. There was a shrewd political calculation. Roosevelt was a past master at swimming the way the tide was running, and speaking as if he were swimming the only way that his morality and his God could let him swim. A study of his letters to his political associates on the liquor problem shows the careful expediency at the back of his moral protestations.

In the presidential campaign of 1908, he was continually sending the Republican candidate, William Howard Taft, letters of advice. On July 16, he wrote that he approved of Taft's stand on prohibition; it was the same as Roosevelt's own. The matter was not a national issue; it was a state or local issue. Indeed, the fanatical drys had a wicked attitude, but they must be dealt with carefully.

> As a mere matter of precaution I would be careful to put in your hearty sympathy with every effort to do away with the drink evil. You will hardly suspect me of being a prohibitionist crank. . . . My experience with prohibitionists, however, is that the best way to deal with them is to ignore them. I would not get drawn into any discussion with them under any circumstances.[21]

Roosevelt's arguments on prohibition are clear at this point: to avoid the subject if one can, and to straddle if one must. He himself was so discreet in public on the subject that both sides claimed him as a supporter in 1914. The drys said that he had declared for state-wide prohibition and the dry vote in Ohio, the wets that he was against state-wide prohibition on principle. Roosevelt tried to get the best of both worlds, writing on October 2 that he only spoke on the matter when he knew about the local conditions involved.[22] If he failed to be convincing it was because it was difficult to seem a friend of temperance in intemperate times.

By 1915, however, every politician could see that the prohibitionists were gaining dry ground. National prohibition, especially if war was declared, seemed likely to win. And Roosevelt liked to be on the winning side, even if there was hardly an enemy to defeat, as at San Juan Hill. Thus he wrote to Raymond Robbins on June 3 in a far more sober mood. Robbins had made out that no President could be elected in

1916 who was not sound on the issues of Rum and Romanism. Roosevelt took exception to the imputation that an attack on Romanism should be an issue in a presidential campaign; he was dead by the time Al Smith ran in 1928. But he was very wary over the question of alcohol and forecast a dry victory.

> I do not believe that Prohibition at the moment would prohibit in the United States; but I am heartily in favor of the vigorous control and ultimate suppression of the open saloon for private profit; and I would make the Federal Government at once take active action in support of the local authorities of every district in which Prohibition has been voted by the people themselves. I do not want to go in advance of the people on this issue, for I do not believe you can do any good on an issue of this kind by getting too far in advance of them; but I believe they will ultimately come to the national suppression of the liquor traffic and *I am heartily with them when they do so come to it.*[23]

Patriotism and political *expertise* made Theodore Roosevelt a prohibitionist. He became so confirmed a dry that he brought a libel action against a small-town editor who claimed that Roosevelt was a heavy drinker. He was careful to explain that if he had ever said that he was a heavy drinker he had said it as a joke, and that listening fools had taken the jest too seriously.[24] He was even ready to refuse the chance of running for Governor of New York State in 1918, on the grounds that he supported the drys. This actually did him no political harm, since Boss Barnes, when he was told, said with much force: "I don't care a damn whether he is for prohibition or against prohibition. The people will vote for him because he is Theodore Roosevelt!"[25]

This was the truth. "Teddy's" views on prohibition did not matter, because he was "Teddy." He was dear to the heart of every urban American who dreamed of an outdoor life spent in the massacre of the larger animals, and of every country American who liked the paradox of the clean-living politician. He was rough, tough, and efficient, the friend of the cowboy and the boxer and the nation. His speeches about liquor did not matter too much; he had drunk sufficient in his time. Whatever his devious political utterances might be, it was more or less understood that he really wanted every virile, manly American to have his small amount of beer and war. But war before beer. If his beloved Germany was the enemy, then the German brewers must go.

President Wilson continued to deny Roosevelt his two dearest wishes, the Congressional Medal of Honor for his Cuban charge and command of his own division in the war of France, despite pleas in the House to recruit this "kaiser of democracy."[26] In return, Roosevelt was plotting with Senator Henry Cabot Lodge how best to wreck Wilson's peace when he died. He had remained true to his prejudices concerning the necessity for power politics and war among competing nations, even if the sentiment of the majority may well have supported the League of Nations in 1919. He was false, however, to his beliefs about temperance, in order to accommodate himself with the apparent majority. He might have died more honestly if he had held to his opinions of 1907 on both peace and prohibition:

> With the sole exception of temperance, I think that more nonsense is talked about peace than about any other really good cause with which I am acquainted. Everybody ought to believe in peace and everybody ought to believe in temperance; but the professional advocates of both tend towards a peculiarly annoying form of egoistic lunacy.[27]

WILLIAM HOWARD TAFT AND CHARLES EVANS HUGHES: FROM TEMPERANCE TO JUSTICE

IF POLITICS pushed William Jennings Bryan and Theodore Roosevelt into declaring themselves for prohibition, the administration of justice did the same service for William Howard Taft and Charles Evans Hughes. There were, indeed, many other similarities between these two physically dissimilar men. Both had fathers who objected to the use of strong liquor and tobacco; both reacted from these early prohibitions of their youth. Both became Chief Justice of the Supreme Court after running unsuccessfully for President. Taft had been President for four years from 1908 owing to his nomination within the Republican party by Theodore Roosevelt; he lost the office to Woodrow Wilson when Roosevelt came forward as a Progressive in 1912 and split the Republican vote. Had Hughes avoided a split between the Progressives and Republicans in 1916 by shaking Hiram Johnson's hand in California, he might have been President in 1916; but California voted for Wilson, and he returned to the White House. Both Taft and Hughes opposed national prohibition and found themselves in the position of heading the Supreme Court, which upheld the Eighteenth Amendment. But, while Taft's experience as Chief Justice made him change his opinion from wet to dry, Hughes remained a wet in all but interpretation of the law, and became one of the greatest champions of civil rights ever to sit on the Supreme Court.

In the presidential campaign of 1908, Taft took Theodore Roosevelt's political advice and followed his own inclinations. He was a temperate man himself; in his own opinion, he was "as temperate a man as there is anywhere."[28] He applied his personal wariness of liquor to his political opinions and declared that he supported the moderate position of local option. Even the visit of the amazon Mrs. Carry Nation did not shake his position. Taft would not say to her that he supported the temperance crusade. Luckily, she had left her hatchet at home, and could only denounce him vocally as a wet and an infidel, since he was Unitarian by faith and thus believed Christ to be a bastard.

Taft was President before the Anti-Saloon League decided on their campaign for national prohibition. Thus he was not unduly bothered by the dry problem while he was in the White House. He had all the lawyer's veneration for the holiness of the Constitution and did not want the sacred document altered. After runing third in the presidential campaign of 1912, behind Wilson and Roosevelt, he continued his opposition to the Eighteenth Amendment from private life. He conceded that a great deal of evil resulted from the drinking of too much alcohol; but his impression was that there was less drinking among the intelligentsia than ever before, and that the failure of state prohibition had provided a warning against national prohibition.[29] He was glad of the failure of the Hobson resolution in 1914, since he was too much of an individualist and a Republican to welcome the vast increase in the number of federal officials needed to enforce such a law. He forecast correctly that prohibition would make politics in the big cities even more corrupt than the saloons did.[30]

Indeed, by 1919, *The Yearbook of the United States Brewers' Association* was gleefully reprinting the ex-President's denunciation of the Eighteenth Amendment. Taft stated bluntly:

> I am opposed to national prohibition. I am opposed to it because I think it is a mixing of the national government in a matter that should be one of local settlement. I think sumptuary laws are matters for parochial adjustment. I think it will vest in the national government, and those who administer it, so great a power as to be dangerous in political matters. I would be in favor of state prohibition if I thought prohibition prohibited, but I think in the long run, except in local communities where the majority of the citizens are in favor of the law, it will be violated. I am opposed to the presence of laws on the statute book that cannot be enforced and as such demoralize the enforcement of all laws. . . . I think it is most unwise to fasten upon the United States a prohibitory system under the excitement of the war, which I do not hesitate to say, every sensible supporter of prohibition in the end will regret. . . . I don't drink myself at all, and I don't oppose prohibition on the ground that it limits the liberties of the people.

Taft's views were similar to those of Theodore Roosevelt; he opposed national prohibition on practical grounds, not in support of any nonsense about the sacred liberty of the subject. As he declared later:

A national prohibition amendment to the federal Constitution will be adopted against the views and practices of a majority of the people in many of the large cities, and in one-fourth or less of the states. The business of manufacturing alcohol liquor and beer will go out of the hands of law-abiding members of the community, and will be transferred to the quasi-criminal class. In the communities where the majority will not sympathize with a federal law's restrictions, large numbers of federal officers will be needed for its enforcement. The central government now has very wide war powers. When peace comes, these must end, if the republic is to be preserved.

Taft continued to say that, although wartime prohibition might be temporarily desirable, the nation must "summer and winter" such a measure for years. People must learn to adjust themselves to soft drinks in time of peace. The Eighteenth Amendment would be a strain on the bonds of the Union. It would produce variety in the enforcement of the law. The matter of light or heavy enforcement would corrupt and confuse elections. Individual self-restraint, improved social standards, and strong employers were better ways of bringing about temperance. Taft opposed both the corrupt saloons and the moral crusade of the "minority" drys. He deplored the fact that the Anti-Saloon League backed dry candidates for political office, however useless their public service was, and that weak politicians knuckled under to the prohibitionists for fear of losing the dry vote.[31]

Taft's opinions at this time are worth quoting at length because they set out admirably the conservative's and lawyer's objections to national prohibition. Extension of the power of the federal government, fear of increased opportunities for graft and crime, dislike of moral legislation, knowledge of the impossibility of effective enforcement, anger at the methods of the drys and their use of war psychology to get their business through, stress on the need for prolonged testing of such a vast reform, belief in individualism and education — these were the reasons Taft gave for opposing the Eighteenth Amendment. They were the same reasons that were given by the conservative Association Against the Prohibition Amendment, which pressed for repeal throughout the twenties.

But politics made Taft deny himself in the interests of justice. President Harding appointed him to head the Supreme Court in June, 1921. His new job was to make the Constitution work, with all its amendments and additions. Taft venerated the document as the basis of American law and liberty. He believed in it whole and indivisible, as he believed in his Unitarian God. So he changed his mind and his convictions over prohibition and became the most arid of the drys, even quarreling with his wife in the only running row they had in all their long marriage. Later he wonderingly said, in the naïve belief that his old world, not himself, had changed its mind: "It used to be that all the nuts were drys. But now it seems all the nuts are wets."[32]

Charles Evans Hughes was already an Associate Justice on the Supreme Court when he decided to accept the Republican nomination for President in 1916. It was the first time a major party had taken its candidate from the Supreme Court; but the Republicans were hard pressed to find someone of like mental and moral stature to President Wilson, running for office for a second time on a peace policy. Both Hughes and Wilson were progressive intellectuals, sons of clergymen, internationalists, sometime university professors, and reform state Governors. In fact, Theodore Roosevelt once said Hughes was merely Wilson with whiskers.

Prohibition was not a major issue in the campaign of 1916. Peace or preparedness was the battleground. Theodore Roosevelt's belligerent bellowings effectively branded the Republicans as the war party, despite Hughes's protestations. The known Anglophile Wilson even received the majority of the German votes, only to declare war on the Kaiser, soon after winning the election. The Anti-Saloon League continued its policy of endorsing dry candidates of both parties; but the drys do not seem to have backed war and the Republican presidential candidate overmuch, even though lining up with the Allies might have given national prohibition its best chance of enactment. Yet care for the dry vote made both candidates cautious of their public relations. Mrs. Hughes served only grape juice to the thirsty pressmen on board the Republican campaign train, the *Constitution*.[33]

Hughes was a moderate drinker himself, but his record as Associate Justice on the matter of prohibition was unexceptionable. In December, 1912, he had upheld the right of the state of Mississippi to ban the manufacture of all malt liquors, whether intoxicating or not. There was a widespread opinion that the sale of nonintoxicating malt liquors led to surprising intoxication in those who drank them; therefore, it was certainly reasonable for states to legislate on such matters.[34] When Hughes later became Chief Justice of the Supreme Court on Taft's resignation in February, 1930, he was to continue to enforce the existing laws fairly; but he did not change his personal beliefs or habits in the matter of the propriety of an occasional drink.

Yet Hughes, who had returned to private law practice after his defeat in 1916, refused a brief worth an enormous sum to argue on the side of the wets in the famous National Prohibition Cases. Rhode Island had challenged the validity of the Eighteenth Amendment and had refused to ratify it. The state's case was that Congress had no right to put "basic changes" or "alterations" into the Constitution;

moreover, the state legislatures, not the people, had accepted the amendment. The case was too absurd for Hughes to defend, even though he thought national prohibition was unwise and impracticable.[35] In fact, Hughes filed a brief, on behalf of twenty-one attorneys general, supporting the legality of the Eighteenth Amendment. Article 5 of the Constitution expressly provided for further changes, which experience might make necessary. The Constitution was a flexible, not a rigid, document; this prevented it from becoming the instrument of reaction or revolution. Even if the Eighteenth Amendment was an unwise addition to the Constitution, it was more important to preserve Article 5 than to oppose any amendment. The Supreme Court agreed with Hughes.[36]

Taft, as Chief Justice throughout the twenties, argued the case for the letter of the Constitution even more than Hughes did. He saw himself as the last ditch where all inroads into the American laws should end. Although he was at first discouraged about the liquor situation, he decided that the remedy for bootlegging and evasion of the Volstead Act was more and better enforcement, not repeal. By the end of 1923, he had fallen into the extreme dry error of saying that even moderate drinkers were wrong and that the use of alcohol for pleasure at parties was wicked. Those who wanted modification of the Volstead Act and the sale of light wines and beer really wanted to deny the Eighteenth Amendment altogether. "They say they are opposed to saloons, but that they want a moderate limitation. What they really want is an opportunity to drink and to entertain others with drink, and all these suggestions are their conscious or unconscious outgrowth of that desire."[37]

No other issue during his nine years in the Supreme Court caused Taft as much worry as prohibition. His wife and members of his family were convinced wets. There were wets among the Supreme Court judges. Twice he had to cast his vote to break a deadlock over an unpleasant issue dealing with prohibition. He consistently voted on the dry side, even voting to uphold such reactionary decisions as those in favor of double jeopardy and wire tapping by prohibition agents. His zeal in opposing national prohibition before it was enacted was matched by his zeal in supporting the Volstead Act after he joined the Supreme Court. His death in March, 1930, was timely. He did not live to read the report of the Wickersham Commission, which proved that the laws he had once thought unenforceable were truly unenforceable.

Hughes also accepted office from President Harding. He became Secretary of State and was likewise embarrassed by prohibition. It caused stupid international problems. Great Britain strongly objected to any attempt to push back the bootlegging fleet of Rum Row by extending territorial waters beyond the three-mile limit. London also objected to prohibition agents searching and seizing rumrunners which flew the British flag more than three miles off the American coast. In addition, all the fleets in the world objected to the clause in the Volstead Act forbidding foreign ships to carry intoxicating drinks into American ports. But by bullying and by persuading the drys and Lord Curzon, Harry Daugherty and the Supreme Court, Hughes eventually worked out a compromise. Foreign ships would be allowed to bring liquor under seal into American ports, if the United States Coast Guard was allowed to seize rumrunners within an hour's steaming distance from the shore. Treaties with seven countries, including Great Britain, were signed to this effect.[38] To do so, Hughes made the enforcement agents restore five seized bootlegging craft to their British owners, banged the table and shouted in front of reporters on the subject of the pigheaded Lord Curzon, spoke sharply to the easy-riding Daugherty in Cabinet meetings, and called the Supreme Court "unnecessarily rigid" over its interpretation of the Eighteenth Amendment. Thus he achieved a sensible compromise. He always opposed all extremes and tried to find a working solution. Hughes was a clever and upright politician and a temperate man.

Hughes eventually became a respected judge on the World Court at the Hague. President Herbert Hoover failed to persuade him in 1929 to head the proposed National Commission on Law Observance and Enforcement. Although Hoover wrote to him on March 25, saying that only he and Justice Stone could head the commission and Stone was not available, Hughes refused the thankless job. So did Owen J. Roberts, although Hoover, in tempting Hughes with the job, had referred to the commission as "the oustanding necessity of the next four years."[39] Thus the task landed on Hoover's fourth choice, George W. Wickersham, who had been Attorney General in Taft's Cabinet.

Hughes, however, did accept the vacant chief justiceship in 1930, after Taft had resigned just before his death. The insurgent fury in the Senate at his nomination was directed more against the depression President who appointed him than against his own liberal character. Yet, as Chief Justice, he found himself in the position of upholding the most savage of the prohibition statutes, the Jones Law. For three years, until repeal took the bitter duty from him, Hughes had to interpret the law of the land in favor of the strict enforcement of prohibition. Only after 1933 could he become a great defender of the liberty of the individual and of civil rights. The Supreme Court, which, under Taft and prohibition, had tended towards the defense of social privileges and reactions, under Hughes and repeal tended towards the defense of personal liberties and opportunities.

Taft, a liberal by temperament, was unlucky to be Chief Justice during the period of prohibition. He was compelled by the political situation to administer the dry law with reactionary severity. The political situation was kinder to Hughes. Repeal and depression made it easier for him to judge with justice and mercy.

WOODROW WILSON: THE TEMPERATE MESSIAH

THE DRY extremism, which political ambition or the duty of the law forced on Bryan and Roosevelt and Taft and Hughes, came finally to Woodrow Wilson through political disappointment. The coercion of prohibition appealed to frustrated minds. Moreover, Wilson was conditioned in favor of the drys by his heredity, if not by his intellect. His father and maternal grandfather were Presbyterian ministers; he came of Scotch-Irish stock and was born in Virginia. He remained a lover of tradition and paternalism until he died. Even his progressive reforms were conservative, intended to restore the good of the past by tidying up the present. Like many Southerners and Presidents, he tended to speak in public as his Messiah did, but to compromise sometimes in private as his world did. When he did not compromise on the question of America joining the League of Nations, he fell and his policy with him. His disappointment made him turn from support of wine and beer to support of total national prohibition.

Woodrow Wilson himself was free from a bone-dry upbringing. He had seen in his boyhood his beloved grandfather smoking and drinking toddy in the Presbyterian manse.[40] He agreed with the more liberal Southern aristocrats that drinking and smoking were no sins, so long as alcohol and cigarettes were kept in the righteous white hands of the right sex. The later Mrs. Woodrow Wilson herself disapproved of women smoking; she was rather embarrassed when mistaken for a divorcée, Mrs. Wilson Woodrow, who advocated this feminine sin in a magazine article.[41] Wilson himself thought that drinking and smoking habits should be settled by the democratic decision of the small communities he had known when he was young.

When Boss Smith, of New Jersey, was looking for a "progressive" state Governor as a front in 1910, he sent an attorney for the State Liquor Dealers' Association to sound out the President of Princeton's views on prohibition. He warned his messenger, "Unless we can get the liquor interests behind the Doctor, we can't elect him." For the Democratic machine in New Jersey was openly supported by the brewers, and they expected Democratic candidates to support them with equally openness. But Woodrow Wilson replied to Smith's envoy, "I am not a prohibitionist. I believe that the question is outside of politics. I believe in home rule, and that the issue should be settled by local option in each community." When it was pointed out that the brewers had been fighting local option in New Jersey for years and that it was the Democratic party's bête noire, Wilson merely said, "Well, that is my attitude and my conviction. I cannot change it."[42]

Wilson's stubbornness on the issue was far more astute than Boss Smith thought when he threatened to "smoke out" Wilson later in the campaign. By removing the loaded question of prohibition from state politics to the sphere of local politics, as he tried to do with the other dangerous question of woman suffrage, Wilson could hold Democratic support together behind him, without introducing any divisive issues. If possible, he would have liked to remove the liquor question from politics altogether.

Later he tried to act in the same way on a national scale in the presidential election of 1912, but with less success. He had carefully stated his position in a letter to the head of the Anti-Saloon League of New Jersey in the previous year.

> I am in favor of local option. I am a thorough believer in local self-government and believe that every self-governing community which constitutes a social unit should have the right to control the matter of the regulation or of the withholding of licenses. But the questions involved are social and moral and are not susceptible of being made parts of a party program. Whenever they have been made the subject matter of party contests, they have cut the lines of party organization and party action athwart to the utter confusion of political action in every other field. They have thrown every other question, however important, into the background and have made constructive party action impossible for long years together. So far as I am myself concerned, therefore, I can never consent to have the question of local option made an issue between political parties in this State.[43]

But Wilson did not leave the matter there. He played a dangerous game in trying to make political capital in a state where the Democrats were predominantly dry. The same year, he wrote to a prohibitionist in Texas, denying that he was always a supporter of local option.

> I believe that for some states, state wide prohibition is possible and desirable, because of their relative homogeneity, while for others, I think that state wide prohibition is not practicable. I have no reason to doubt from what I know of the circumstances, that state wide prohibition is both practicable and desirable in Texas.[44]

Unfortunately, this letter was used against him by wet Republican newspapers in the North. His first political manager, William F. Mc-

Combs, had to try to disown the letter as a trick of Wall Street. He was unsuccessful. The wets claimed loudly that Wilson supported local option, the drys that he was for state-wide prohibition. The controversy became so unpleasant that Wilson's second political manager, Joseph E. Tumulty, had to set up a special interview in 1915 with a wet reporter from the Louisville *Times*. In this interview, Wilson wearily said to Tumulty that he did not know how he came to write the Texan letter. Tumulty assured the reporter that Wilson would be able to explain it away somehow; there was very little he could not do with the English language.

And explain it away Wilson did, in an open letter to the Louisville *Times*. Wilson wrote that the first letter represented his real convictions. He had only meant by the second letter that he was not self-confident or self-opinionated enough to say what the proper course of action was, either in Texas or in any other state where he did not know the conditions.[45] Wilson's gloss had the opposite meaning to his original text; but the truth of the matter was that Wilson had returned to his original convictions. No additional dry votes were worth the fact that the President and minister's son seemed to be ready to fit his convictions to his political advantage.

During Wilson's first term as President, the prohibition issue was little bother to him. In 1914, the Hobson constitutional amendment failed to get the necessary two-thirds vote in the House of Representatives. The issue was then ingeniously linked with that of a woman-suffrage amendment in the House Judiciary Committee. This tactic of the wets hamstrung the Southern drys, who opposed votes for women as fanatically as they supported national prohibition. Wilson remained neutral during this time and did not use his influence to separate the two amendments. The separation was not effected until 1916.

During Wilson's second term as President, the Webb-Kenyon Act, which restricted the import of liquor into dry states, was strengthened by the passage of the Reed Bone-dry Amendment. But this legislation represented the limit of prohibition legislation tolerable to Wilson's mentality. Indeed, after war was declared on the Central European Powers, Wilson opposed any further concessions to the drys, since he believed that they were using the war emergency to dry up the country through Congress. In his opinion, wartime prohibition was not intended to save for men's bodies the boasted eleven million loaves of bread a day wasted in beer production;[46] it was intended to save their souls, which were not the concern of the federal government.

Under pressure from the Anti-Saloon League and the dry majority in Congress, Wilson approved the assorted wartime prohibition measures. But he was put in a quandary by the growth of agitation against wartime prohibition after the Armistice, particularly on the part of the American Federation of Labor. On May 20, 1919, Wilson cabled a message back from Paris to Congress, recommending that the ban on the making of beer and light wines be lifted until the Volstead Act came into force in January, 1920. He was disobeyed. Tumulty later warned the President that if the ban was not lifted, the wets might not only drink up all the bonded whisky in the United States but also turn against him. Pennsylvania had already voted to legalize weak beer and light wines. In Tumulty's opinion, Wilson should legalize light wines and beer by presidential proclamation.

But Wilson could not do this. If he did, he would finally brand the Democrats as the party of the wets. They would suffer for this at the polls in 1920, and a Democratic defeat would bring down all Wilson's plans for peace. Thus he took refuge in the legally sound position that wartime prohibition must remain in force until the Army was demobilized. Once again, Tumulty claims, Wilson thought of devolving his responsibility by asking Congress to legalize light wines and beer, but he gave up the idea since Congress was hostile and dry.[47] Tumulty also states that Wilson gave an unnamed and trusted friend a copy of a proposed wet plank, favoring the repeal of the Volstead Act, to be presented at the Democratic convention in 1920; but again the dry temper of the delegates caused the dropping of the plan.[48] The dry Senator Carter Glass, chairman of the Committee on Resolutions, had already told Wilson that it would be impossible to present the plank. And Wilson was always too politic to press any controversy beyond the bounds of compromise, except for the matter of the League of Nations. When reporter Seibold, of the New York *World*, tried to pump him on the three explosive topics of prohibition, women, and William Jennings Bryan, Wilson said the same words about each, that he had great confidence in the sober judgment of the leaders of the Democratic party at San Francisco.

James M. Cox was nominated by the Democrats as presidential timber. He fought the campaign of 1920 as the heir of Woodrow Wilson. Out of admiration for Wilson's courage, Cox supported the League of Nations. It was an act of admirable loyalty, but of stupid politics. Cox's only hope was to disassociate himself from the President, who was unfairly blamed with driving America into war and national prohibition. Cox was badly beaten by the charming and affable Warren Harding, whose "big, bow-wow style of oratory" was well described by the dry Democrat McAdoo as "an army of pompous phrases moving over the landscape in search of an idea."[49]

Wilson settled down to die; his League of Nations was dying too.

He became more autocratic, more conscious that he was alone and right. For the 1924 Democratic convention, he hardened his position on prohibition, circulating a plank among his friends which stated categorically, "The Eighteenth Amendment should remain unchanged. And the Volstead Act should remain unchanged."[50] He wanted the federal government, however, to be merely responsible for preventing interstate commerce in liquor. This had been the limit of their responsibility in 1917, and could be justified by reference to the Constitution. What had been given to the federal government under his own rule was well given. More was evil. Moreover, he had been brought up in the South, where states' rights were jealously guarded in domestic affairs. Of course, Wilson's solution left the main burden of enforcement on the state governments, and would have meant practical nullification in wet states. But, at least, under this plan the evils of prohibition enforcement would have been restricted. The plank was, however, considered dangerous and was never presented.

Wilson, a temperate man, miscalculated badly on the one thing which he wanted above all. He might have compromised with Senator Lodge and preached the United States into the League of Nations if he had given his enemies a few concessions. But, against the advice of Colonel House and other friends of the League, he categorically refused to accept the Senate's fourteen reservations concerning the Versailles Treaty, even though he had allowed his Fourteen Points to be whittled away at Versailles itself. He had become as die-hard as a professed prohibitionist. On the question of the League of Nations, Wilson was more inflexible than the most dedicated leader of the Anti-Saloon League.

Wilson became the victim of that moral rigidity which he deplored in the dry extremists and which he increasingly came to share with them over the matter of prohibition.[51] Like Plato, he became more authoritarian as he aged. Like Plato, he ended by approving of severe moral legislation enacted in the laws of states. Like Plato, he died disappointed, with his scheme for the ordered government of society defeated, and his visionary Republic only a vision.

Whatever the temperament and background of prominent politicians in the opening years of this century, they were forced into an extreme position by the extreme measure of the national prohibition of the liquor trade. There was no escape for the wary political animal. Silence on the issue was taken to be antagonism to the views of the questioner, whether he was wet or dry. Bryan's country background or Taft's city background might put them on opposite sides of the dry question in their personal sympathies. But they were political beings first and reformers second. Their political ambition and office dictated their parallel silence, equivocation, moderate support, and eventual wholehearted backing of the prohibitionists.

The Anti-Saloon League relied on the necessary malleability of the politician to push its measures through both houses of Congress and through the legislatures of forty-six states. The weathercock tendencies which the Presidents and presidential aspirants had shown individually were shown collectively by the legislative representatives of the people. Indeed, the people themselves shifted back and forth on the issue, under the propaganda and prodding of the drys. But it is in their pressure on the lawmakers of America that the drys showed their full genius for political manipulation. For only from the lawmakers of America could they secure national prohibition by the Eighteenth Amendment to the Constitution and by the Volstead Act.

CHAPTER **8**

The Turncoat Congress

> No caterpillar ever crawled into its cocoon and came out
> so changed as came this drink question out of Congress. It
> went in temperance and came out prohibition. It went in
> license and came out enforcement. It went in personal
> choice and came out a national mandate. It went in an
> individual right and came out a social responsibility. It
> went in a brewer and barkeeper and came out a bootlegger
> and a kitchen still. It went in local option and came out the
> Eighteenth Amendment.
>
> DALLAS LORE SHARP

> Booze an' iloquence has both passed out iv our public
> life. . . . A statesman wud no more be seen goin' into a
> saloon thin he wud into a meetin' iv th' Anti-Semitic
> league. Th' imprissyon he thries to give is that th' sight iv
> a bock beer sign makes him faint with horror, an' that he's
> stopped atin' bread because there's a certain amount iv
> alcohol concealed in it. He wishes to brand as a calumny
> th' statement that his wife uses an alcohol lamp to heat her
> curlin' irns. Ivry statesman in this broad land is in danger
> iv gettin' wather-logged because whiniver he sees a possible
> vote in sight he yells f'r a pitcher iv ice wather an' dumps
> into himsilf a basin iv that noble flooid that in th' more
> rugged days iv th' republic was on'y used to put out fires
> an' sprinkle th' lawn.
>
> FINLEY PETER DUNNE

L IQUOR WAS a power in Congress before prohibition was. The
fondness of Washington legislators for the bottle was supplemented
by the lobby of the liquor trade. The Internal Revenue Act of 1862
put a license fee of twenty dollars on retail liquor dealers and a tax
of one dollar a barrel on beer and twenty cents a gallon on spirits. The
drys always accused this act, signed by Abraham Lincoln himself, of
making an evil traffic legitimate and of corrupting politics for half a
century. However true this accusation, it is undeniable that the United
States Brewers' Association was formed in the same year. The object

152

of the association was to prosecute its interests "vigorously and energetically" before the legislative and executive branches of the nation and to defeat the maneuvers of the temperance party.[1] After less than a year of pressure, the Association managed to secure a cut in the beer tax to sixty cents a barrel. By 1866, a permanent committee had been set up at Washington, on such cordial terms with the Commissioner of Internal Revenue that it helped to revise the Federal Excise Tax Law of that year.

Other organizations were also set up to exert pressure at Washington on behalf of the liquor trade. There was the National Wholesale Liquor Dealers' Association, the National Retail Liquor Dealers' Association, the National Association of Wine and Spirit Representatives, the United States Manufacturers' and Merchants' Association, and various other pressure groups, often misnamed civic or liberty leagues. These associations, although they were mainly concerned with influencing Congress, also aimed to secure the elections of sympathetic Congressmen. A resolution of the National Brewers' and Distillers' Association stated in 1882 that it was pledged to work harmoniously and assiduously at the ballot box against any party which favored a prohibition amendment to the Constitution.[2] In New York the following year, the local brewers employed a technique which would have defeated the drys in perpetuity, if it had been properly exploited; they asked all political candidates where they stood on temperance matters and fought the silent along with the drys at the polls.[3]

The scandals caused by the connection of the liquor trade and the politicians were nasty and frequent. As Mr. Dooley knew, the friendship of the great was worse than their enmity.[4] The exposure of the Whisky Ring under President Grant, of the Whisky Trust in 1887, and of the conspiracies of the brewers in Texas elections showed the political skulduggery of the liquor trade. The aim of the trade to control Congress, even if it lost the support of the majority of Americans, was manifest. A final damning indictment of the brewers was reported to the Senate in 1919. The report disclosed that the brewers had bought large sections of the press, had influenced campaigns, had exacted pledges from candidates prior to election, had boycotted the goods of their enemies, had formed their own secret political organization, had subsidized the banned German-American Alliance, "many of the membership of which were disloyal and unpatriotic," had formed a secret agreement with the distillers to split political expenses, and had done their utmost to subvert the processes of democracy.[5] This disclosure coincided with the passage of the Volstead Act through the Senate, and was the final nail in the coffin of the liquor trade.

With such powerful opponents behind the scenes in Washington, the drys had to organize a strong lobby of their own. Although the first Congressional Temperance Society was begun by the Reverend Justin Edwards in 1833, and eight abortive attempts to pass a national prohibition amendment were made by Senators Blair and Plumb between 1876 and 1885, no strong political pressure was exerted by the drys in the national capital until 1899. In that year, the first legislative superintendent of the Anti-Saloon League, Edwin C. Dinwiddie, arrived in Washington. After a period of trial and error, the political power and *expertise* of the League grew, and Congress leaped to do its bidding.[6] For twenty years after 1913, the League lobby under Dinwiddie and his successor, Wayne B. Wheeler, was the most powerful and successful reform lobby in Washington.

The first major triumph of the Anti-Saloon League was the passage of the Webb-Kenyon Law in 1913. The law used the federal power in interstate commerce to prevent liquor dealers from sending liquor in packages into dry states. Before the passage of the law, a mail-order liquor business had flourished in dry states, using such advertising slogans as "Uncle Sam Is Our Partner."[7] Although the bill was bitterly denounced in Congress as the work of "a few rabid, misguided, professional prohibitionists," it was passed over Taft's veto by a vote of 63 to 21 in the Senate and 246 to 95 in the House of Representatives.[8] All but two Senators of the dry majority came from the South and West, where the dry cause was strong. Although the wets hoped that the Supreme Court would declare the measure unconstitutional, they were forced to concede that the drys had won a great victory. It was "the impressive fact that in the face of the united effort of all branches of the alcoholic liquor trade, the National Congress voted for the bill."[9] Four years later, the Supreme Court upheld the law.[10]

The first classic debate on the subject of national prohibition came with the vote on the Hobson resolution in the House on December 22, 1914. The resolution called for a national prohibition amendment to the Constitution. Kelly, of Pennsylvania, opened the dry case. He said that the drys were the real friends of liberty — not the false personal liberty which meant license to do wrong. They would grant every liberty save that of injuring the rights of others. Congress should pass the Hobson resolution because of the very forces against it:

> . . . the allied powers that prey, the vultures of vice, the corrupt combinations of politics, the grafters and gangsters, the parasites that clothe themselves in the proceeds of woman's shame, the inhuman ones that bathe themselves in the tears of little children, the wastrels who wreck and ruin material things while they contaminate childhood, debauch youth, and crush manhood; the plunder-laden ones who fatten themselves upon the misery and want and woe that their own

greed has created, the Hessians in the black-bannered troop whose line of march is over wrecked homes and broken hearts and ruined lives.

Hobson himself followed up by condemning the alcohol poison which attacked "the tender tissues associated with reproduction both in male and female." Hulings, of Pennsylvania, and Tribble, of Georgia, said that the resolution was not an attack on states' rights but a confirmation of them; for the constitutional amendment would be referred to the legislatures of the various states. Garrett, of Texas, regretted the inevitable progress of boys from high-class beer gardens to the doggery. Lindquist, of Michigan, called for the support of patriots; zeppelins, submarines, bombs, and siege guns were not the only things that could destroy a nation; the treasonable conspiracy of the liquor trade had already captured the great cities of America, and was devastating the land and robbing it of its manhood. And Hobson concluded with his famous speech on "Alcohol, the Great Destroyer."

Cantrill, of Kentucky, began the defense of the wets. He denied the capacity of national prohibition to prohibit. The Hobson resolution should really be called "a resolution legalizing the unlimited manufacture of intoxicating liquor without taxation." Underwood, of Alabama, spoke up for the fundamental beliefs of the Republic, for individual liberty, states' rights, and the rights of property. He denied that the drys represented the forces of temperance, because all men believed in temperance; they were a mere faction "that would tear down the very fabric of the Government itself and destroy the foundation stones on which it rests." Kahn, of California, also pointed out that temperance applied to all things in life, not only to liquor. Prohibition generally resulted in making men liars, sneaks, and hypocrites. If men wanted liquor, they could invariably get it. "We are trying to regulate all human conduct by laws, laws, laws. Efforts of that character are as old as the world. And they have invariably resulted in failure."

Vollmer, of Iowa, scoffed at the great American superstition, "belief in the miraculous potency of the magical formulae: Be it resolved, and Be it enacted." He stood beside George Washington, the brewer; Thomas Jefferson, the distiller; Abraham Lincoln, the saloonkeeper; and Jesus Christ of Nazareth, who had turned water into wine. For him, the policeman's club was not a moral agent; morality which was not self-imposed was not morality. Vicious propensities that could not find an outlet in liquor would find another; they would not be prohibited. Johnson, of Kentucky, said that he was not concerned with the merits of prohibition, but with its economic effects. The measure would destroy property worth billions of dollars, while the wets would have to pay increased taxes to make up the lost revenue. Moreover, the sacred American principle of home rule would be attacked. Finally, Morrison, of Indiana, objected that the House was being stampeded by the Anti-Saloon League and was being forced to reform under fire. Prohibition, even if put into the Constitution, could never be enforced, when Sears, Roebuck catalogues were advertising home distilling kits for less than five dollars an outfit.[11]

At the close of the debate, the vote was taken. The Hobson resolution was passed by 197 votes to 190. Since a two-thirds majority was necessary for the passage of a constitutional amendment, the resolution failed. The drys, however, had given a further demonstration of their growing power. And, significantly, the word "saloon" was never mentioned in the debate except in a derogatory sense. Indeed, Colonel Gilmore admitted in *Bonfort's Wine and Spirit Circular* that the saloon was now doomed.[12]

The widespread prohibition legislation of the powers engaged in the Great War and the certainty that America would enter that war gave the drys a strong lever. When Europe was starving, how could America in God's name turn its grain into sinful drink? In 1917, under the pressure of patriotism, Congress passed the Eighteenth Amendment to the Constitution. It also passed other laws giving prohibition to Alaska and Puerto Rico, setting up dry zones around Army camps and Naval bases, and banning soldiers and sailors from all liquor.[13] In addition, three further laws were passed, which showed the political trafficking of both wets and drys at their worst.

The first of these three laws was the Reed Bone-dry Amendment to a bill to exclude liquor advertisements from the mails. Senator Reed, of Missouri, was a dripping wet; but he decided to confound the cautious Anti-Saloon League lobby by making it an offense to use imported liquor in dry territory, as well as to transport or sell it. The use of imported liquor had not been forbidden by the Webb-Kenyon Law. The League was caught napping. Its chief lobbyist, Dinwiddie, advised against voting for Reed's amendment; but Congress, voting freely for the first time for some years, passed the amendment, as much to show their independence of the League as to demonstrate their belief in the tricks of Senator Reed. The League then claimed credit for the measure. Indeed, the position of Reed and the wets was worsened by such a stringent law, especially as its provisions caused no revulsion of moderate support away from the dry cause.

The second law was the District of Columbia Prohibition Law, which banned the legal liquor trade in the capital. The drys refused to hold a referendum on this matter for fear of the popular vote going against them. Moreover, despite the Reed Bone-dry Amendment, the law only prohibited the traffic in liquor, not its use by members of Congress and others.[14]

The third law passed in 1917 was a prohibition clause in the Food Control Bill. The drys were holding up this vital war measure in Congress by threatening to tack onto it various clauses forbidding food to be made into alcohol for drinking purposes. In fact, the drys were so insistent that prohibition was necessary to win the war that Woodrow Wilson was forced to write a letter to Bishop James Cannon, Jr., who was head of the legislative committee of the Anti-Saloon League. He appealed to the Bishop's patriotism: "I regard the immediate passage of the [Food] bill as of vital consequence to the safety and defense of the nation. Time is of the essence." Cannon replied the next day that the League would compromise. If the manufacture of distilled spirits should be forbidden, the President could stop the supply of food to the brewers and winemakers at his own discretion. Wilson replied that he appreciated the Anti-Saloon League's attitude, which was "a very admirable proof of their patriotic motives."[15]

Wilson, however, failed to use his discretionary powers, and received a rebuke from the Anti-Saloon League. Its legislative committee wrote to him on April 1, 1918, pointing out that:

> . . . the people have been requested to have heatless days, meatless days, wheatless days and to eliminate waste in every possible way, and yet the breweries and saloons of the country continue to waste food-stuffs, fuel and man-power and to impair the efficiency of labor in the mines, factories and even in munition plants near which saloons are located.[16]

After hearing nothing from Wilson and getting nowhere with him in a conference at the White House, the League used the same device and tacked total wartime prohibition onto the Agricultural Appropriation Bill. All use of foods in the making of spirits, beer, and wine was banned. One report said that Wilson felt so strongly about the matter that he would have vetoed the prohibition measure, if he could have got the rest of the bill through in any other way.[17] But he could not. Wartime prohibition was passed by Congress. The manufacture of liquor in the United States was legally prohibited after June 30, 1919, unless demobilization were to be completed before that date.

A majority in Congress seemed to be inspired by the same false logic that made Senator Myers, of Montana, declare, "There is nothing to understand except one thing, and that is that bread will help us win this war more than whisky. That is the only thing that it is necessary to understand."[18] In face of such implacable reasoning, Wilson had to act. Dry pressure was too great. On Colonel House's advice, he did not veto the Agricultural Appropriation Bill. On September 16, he issued a proclamation that forbade the use of food in making beer. But he did not exercise the authority given him by the Agricultural Appropriation Bill to declare "dry zones" at once in strategical mining and industrial areas. He still supported the flow of such strong drink as could be got for the factory workers. Like any good democrat, he was conscious of the need not to offend too much or too many. This meant the simultaneous gift of sops to the wets and sponges to the drys.

THE EIGHTEENTH AMENDMENT

THE WILSON administration was often blamed for the passage through Congress of the Eighteenth Amendment and the Volstead Act. Actually, Wilson had nothing to do with these measures. They were put through, despite the urgency of the war, by the power of the dry lobby in Congress. At the same time that the Anti-Saloon League was helping to defeat the Kaiser by sobering up America, it was also preparing to win the peace by making a land fit for heroes to live in. Its remedy for demobilization and the future was national prohibition.

Professor Irving Fisher, of Yale, a notable dry apologist and statistician, revealed that the Anti-Saloon League knew some of the wet Senators were psychologically prepared to accept national prohibition after the preliminary failure of the war prohibition measure in the Food Control Bill. It is even possible that the League made a deal with them.[19] However that was, Fisher wrote that the League "very astutely took advantage of the situation to propose the act submitting the Eighteenth Amendment. . . . It was easy even for wet Senators to let this act pass, on the theory that it did not really enact Prohibition, but merely submitted it to the States." Then, once the Eighteenth Amendment was safely through Congress, wartime prohibition was reintroduced and passed, "as a means of filling in the gap between the adoption of Constitutional Prohibition and its taking effect. This was pretty hard on the brewers."[20] In other words, by playing on the urge of Congress to escape responsibility for national prohibition, and by yielding ground on wartime prohibition only to revive it again once peacetime prohibition had passed Congress, the dry lobby showed itself guilty of political genius and bad faith.

During the debate on the Eighteenth Amendment in the Senate and the House, various deals were made between the wets and the drys. As Wheeler put it, "we traded jackknives with them."[21] The willing and mindless Senator Harding, of Ohio, was the go-between. In return for a year's grace for the liquor trade to wind up its affairs after possible ratification of the amendment by the states, the wets agreed to put a time limit of six, and then seven, years on ratification. With this limit, the wets in Congress were lulled into a sense of false security. Thirty-six states had to ratify the amendment for it to become part of the Constitution. The wets counted on holding at least thirteen state legislatures. Only twenty-seven states had passed state prohibition laws. The drys would have to gain nine more for their side, as well as convincing the legislatures of the twenty-seven that national prohibition was necessary. The Eighteenth Amendment appeared as a heaven-sent opportunity for wet Senators to wash their hands of the whole affair and to be left in peace at the polls by the Anti-Saloon League.

In the debate on the amendment in the Senate, Harding summed up in his heartfelt and confused way the sentiments of many middle-of-the-road Senators. He said that he was not a prohibitionist and had never pretended to be, although he did claim to be a temperance man. He did not see prohibition as a great moral question, but he did see its ethical and economic side. The need for concord in wartime and the fact prohibition would never be effective made him think that the timing of the proposed Eighteenth Amendment was "unwise, imprudent, and inconsiderate"; but he would vote for it, since he was fed up with seeing every politician measured by the wet and dry yardstick. It was high time for the question to be settled. In this way, the people, through their state legislatures, would settle the issue. Although he preferred that compensation be paid to the breweries, he would not insist on this clause.[22] And yet Harding, after declaring himself for the drys, was one of only four Senators who voted for Hardwick's attempt to wreck the passage of the amendment by making it illegal to purchase and use liquor, as well as to manufacture, sell, or transport it.

The Anti-Saloon League lobby, which did much to write the Eighteenth Amendment, was careful to pussyfoot on the question of the use of liquor, as they had done with the Webb-Kenyon Law and with the District of Columbia Prohibition Act. They wanted to punish makers and sellers of liquor, not respectable drinkers. Moreover, they could not afford to alienate the majority of the Senators, who were drinkers. They had to represent the measure as an economic and patriotic necessity. It was no reflection on the personal habits of the legislators of the nation. It was the liquor trade that did evil, not those decent people who supported the trade. In this way, the League could and did gain moderate support in both Senate and House, especially as the blackmail of the open ballot threatened retribution at the polls for the foes of the Eighteenth Amendment.

The extreme drys in the Senate ignored the careful approach of the

League and the objections of moderates such as Norris to "this ill-advised attempt."[23] Sheppard, of Texas, set the tone of the Senate debate on the amendment with a full-blooded denunciation of alcohol as the cause of venereal disease, blighted babies, fallen women, and waste to the toiling millions. Kenyon, of Iowa, shook blood out of the flag with his unanswered queries, "If liquor is a bad thing for the boys in the trenches, why is it a good thing for those at home? When they are willing to die for us, should we not be willing to go dry for them?" Jones, of Washington, denied the brewers' charges that prohibition would produce anger, resentment, and disaffection among millions as "a base libel on American workers," who were "as loyal and patriotic a class as we have." Intelligent labor knew that prohibition was being passed for its benefit. Moreover, those opposed to prohibition would live to bless prohibition. Ashurst, of Arizona, saw the amendment as a great referendum to the states. Sherman, of Illinois, remembered his many liberal friends of thirty years past who had been killed off by the saloons and had died "with strange complaints, seeing strange things in the air and hearing strange voices." Kirby, of Arkansas, did not doubt that through the ages one increasing purpose ran. And Myers, of Montana, rounded off the dry case with his declaration that the world was steadily becoming better. He suggested that the momentous day when the Senate passed the amendment should be observed as another Fourth of July, a second Declaration of Independence.

The drys could afford rhetoric, for they were certain that their cause was won. But the wets were forced to appeal to reason, for they knew that they had lost. Underwood, of Alabama, warned the Senate that the tyranny of corruption could be replaced by the subtler, less tangible, more enduring tyranny of reform. Moreover, the propaganda of the drys that Congress should pass its responsibility on to the states was subversive of the spirit of republican government. Lodge, of Massachusetts, gave a prophetic denunciation of the impossibility of enforcing national prohibition. Without a prepared public sentiment, all prohibition could hope to effect was the destruction of every control on the liquor traffic. People would resent the dry law as a gross and tyrannical interference with personal liberty. Respect for justice would vanish. "Where large masses of the people would consider it even meritorious — at least quite venial — to evade and break the law, the law would inevitably be broken constantly and in a large and effective way." Lodge doubted that there could be an army large enough to enforce absolute prohibition. The measure was "the worst thing that could be done to advance temperance and total abstinence among the people." But the wet protests were unavailing. The amendment passed the Senate by a vote of 65 to 20.[24]

One new idea came out of the House debate on the Eighteenth Amendment, and a legion of old ideas. While the Senate's version of the amendment had provided for the prohibition of the manufacture, sale, or transportation of intoxicating liquors, Congressman Webb introduced the phrase, "the Congress and the several States shall have concurrent power to enforce this article by appropriate legislation." By his term "concurrent power," Webb meant to protect states' rights, for "nobody desires that the Federal Congress shall take away from the various States the right to enforce the prohibition laws of those States." He also intended that the states should take much of the burden off the federal government in law enforcement. "We do not want 10,000 Federal officers, with all the expense of salaries, going over the country enforcing these laws when the States have their own officers to do so and are willing to do so." In answer to questions, Webb denied that there would be a conflict of jurisdiction between state and federal courts. A man ought not to be tried twice for the same offense. "One punishment ought to be sufficient." He said that he was not afraid to trust the states to enforce the amendment. "I never saw one that went counter to the United States Constitution, or whose law officers failed to enforce the law." Yet, whatever Webb's reasons, the inclusion of the term "concurrent power" in the amendment led to a myriad of later legal complications.

Webb also referred to the letter which Samuel Gompers, head of the American Federation of Labor, had written to the newspapers that morning, December 17, 1917. Gompers had complained that prohibition would throw two million people out of work; it was also a class law against the beer of the workingman. Webb replied that the jobs of only about sixty thousand people directly connected with the liquor trade would be affected. He quoted William Jennings Bryan, that it was a slander to intimate that the great laboring classes of America measured their patriotism by the quart or by the schooner.

After many other loyal dry appeals, Robbins, of Pennsylvania, reminded the House that there were three constitutional amendments pending, those of prohibition and woman suffrage and writing the name of God into the Constitution. All three should be referred to the states, for vox populi vox Dei. Little, of Kansas, raised laughter when he referred to a gentleman from "some semi-civilized foreign colony in New York City" who damned prohibition as a mere reform from "the outlying settlements." According to Little, the outlying settlements provided all the reforms that New York City would ever get. Norton, of North Dakota, would have gone so far as to send all the wet spokesmen to the front, for their arguments showed them to be "marvelously great camouflage artists."

In face of these patriotic and rural appeals, the wets in the House countered with some reason and some wit. Gard, of Ohio, said that the Eighteenth Amendment would substitute "controversy for sure settlement." The President had it in his power to forbid the use of food in making liquor by proclamation. Congress should not waste time debating the amendment, but should help the President in winning the war. Magee, of New York, made the good point that the question was "not temperance versus intemperance, but whether we are willing to use the condition of war as the chief instrument in attempting to bring about Nation-wide prohibition at this particular time." In fact, no grain would be conserved by the passage of the amendment, since it probably would not go into effect until the war was over. As for himself, he had no brief for wets or drys, but a brief for "his country first, last, and all the time."

Walsh, of Massachusetts, observed that temperance in thought and speech was sometimes as wise as temperance in the use of food and drink. Small, of North Carolina, said that the dry effort to get the House to pass responsibility for the measure on to the states was pernicious, for "we are not mere automatons to register the will of the Anti-Saloon League or any other organization of reformers." Slayden, of Texas, warned that a constitutional amendment would perpetuate the tyranny of a temporary majority in the country. McArthur, of Oregon, said that the League would be better off spending its money on educating people against liquor, while Gordon, of Ohio, resented the attack of rural morality on the large cities. The vote on the amendment would, anyway, not be an honest one, as Gallagher, of New York, pointed out. A secret ballot would show the drys that their majorities came from fear.[25]

When the vote was taken, the Eighteenth Amendment passed the House by 282 votes to 128. It was then referred to the states for ratification. Lengthy extracts from the speeches in Congress on the issue have been included to demonstrate the charged atmosphere in which the measure was passed, and the arguments which were repeated ad nauseam by both wets and drys in the years preceding and following the amendment. The extracts also show that boredom played some part in the passage of the amendment.[26] The members of Congress were sick of being badgered by the Anti-Saloon League and their dry constituents. They ignored Heflin, of Alabama, who said that no member of the House could dispose of the question simply by saying he was tired of being bothered with it.[27] It was unfortunate for

Congress that the Eighteenth Amendment was only the beginning of dry fuss about the liquor issue.

A comparative analysis of the vote on the Hobson resolution and the Eighteenth Amendment in the House shows how and where the drys gained support between 1914 and 1917, and how the speeches of Congressmen were motivated less by party consideration than by geography. The drys gained 85 votes in this period. Their largest gain was a block of 39 Republican votes from Midwestern states, where the Anti-Saloon League had its most powerful political organization and where the Democratic party was associated with the liquor interests. During these three years, with the help of the League, the Republican party in the Midwest doubled its strength, while the Democrats, despite Woodrow Wilson's victory of 1916 against Hughes, lost 37 seats in the House of Representatives.

Yet the League was a nonpartisan organization. It supported drys in both parties. The votes on the Hobson resolution and the Eighteenth Amendment were not party matters. In the first case, 120 Democrats and 73 Republicans voted for the measure, 141 Democrats and 47 Republicans against. In the second case, 140 Democrats and 138 Republicans voted for the measure, 64 Democrats and 62 Republicans against. The vote proved correct both the Anti-Saloon League's assertion that the only way to obtain national prohibition was to support drys in both of the major parties, and also the Prohibition party's objection that both of the major parties were too divided on the issue to enforce national prohibition wholeheartedly. Prohibition was a party matter only on a sectional basis. Northern Democrats, whose support was based on the wet cities, were opposed by the Anti-Saloon League and the Republican party, while Southern Democrats in the dry and one-party South were helped by the League. The nonpartisan approach of that powerful dry organization helped to build the irreparable split in the Democratic party on the prohibition issue. Meanwhile, the Republican party, freed of the garrulous conscience of the South, was able to straddle the issue more circumspectly during conventions and elections.

The vote on the Hobson resolution shows clearly on what a rock the dry congressional group was founded. Of the 197 members of the House who voted for the Hobson resolution, 129 were from cities of less than 10,000 people, while 64 of them were from country villages of less than 2500 people. Only 13 were from cities containing a population of more than 100,000. Of the 190 opponents to the resolution, 109 were from cities of more than 25,000 people, and only 25 from villages with less than 2500 inhabitants. In fact, national prohibition was a measure passed by village America against urban America. This conclusion is confirmed by the fact that San Francisco, St. Louis, St. Paul, Chicago, Cincinnati, Cleveland, Detroit, and Boston all rejected prohibitory laws during the period when the Eighteenth Amendment was being considered by Congress and the states.[28]

An analysis of the Senate vote on the amendment also proves the rural support of the measure. Of course, both in the United States Senate and in the various state senates the country was overrepresented at the expense of the cities, as Senator Calder pointed out.[29] This was the reason why the drys wanted prohibition to be passed by the legislatures as an amendment to the Constitution, rather than by state referendum. For the populous cities often upset dry majorities in country areas during state referendums. Ohio itself, the headquarters and home state of the Anti-Saloon League leaders, did not pass statewide prohibition until 1918, owing to the opposition of Cincinnati and other wet cities. But if the League could only cow the lower houses of the various states into passing a constitutional amendment, they could rely on the country majorities in the senates to support them.

While the vote in the House of Representatives on the Eighteenth Amendment gave the measure a bare two-thirds majority, in the Senate the measure passed by a majority of more than three to one. Of the twenty Senators who opposed the measure, nine came from the populous Atlantic states, seven from the South, ever eager to protect the doctrine of states' rights, and the remaining four from states whose beer or wine interests would suffer from the amendment. A similar disproportion is shown when the votes of the senates and lower houses of the ratifying states are compared. While the combined senates of the forty-six ratifying states voted 1310 to 237 to carry the amendment, the combined lower houses voted 3782 to 1035.[30] Where the country was more heavily represented than the cities, the drys could count on more support for dry measures.

The drys reversed their tactics to secure the ratification of the Eighteenth Amendment by the states. While they had told Congress that the amendment was a democratic measure because the question of national prohibition had to be referred to the states, they told the state legislatures that their duty was to ratify the Eighteenth Amendment, since it had been approved by a two-thirds majority of both houses of Congress. Moreover, it was easier for the drys to get the states to ratify, for they needed only a straight majority in each house of three-quarters of the states. The necessary thirty-six states ratified within fourteen months, forty-five within sixteen months. New Jersey ratified in 1922, but Connecticut and Rhode Island never ratified.

The terms of the Eighteenth Amendment show the great care of the dry lobby not to push legislators too far too fast. The amendment read:

SECTION 1. After one year from the ratification of this article the manufacture, sale, or transportation of intoxicating liquors within, the importation thereof into, or the exportation thereof from the United States and all territory subject to the jurisdiction thereof for beverage purposes is hereby prohibited.

SECTION 2. The Congress and the several States shall have concurrent power to enforce this article by appropriate legislation.

SECTION 3. This article shall be inoperative unless it shall have been ratified as an amendment to the Constitution by the legislatures of the several States, as provided in the Constitution, within seven years from the date of the submission hereof to the States by the Congress.

If the prohibitionists had insisted on total prohibition of liquor in America, they would not have allowed the Eighteenth Amendment to be presented in this form. But the Anti-Saloon League was more concerned with enshrining the practice of prohibition in the Constitution than with enacting a stringent and unequivocal measure. The first step was to pass the amendment in any form; the second was to pass a severe law to enforce it. The League was always occupied with the possible in politics, although it favored the eternal in propaganda.

There were many flaws in the wording of the Eighteenth Amendment. As in the Webb-Kenyon Law, the amendment did not forbid the purchase or use of liquor — only four Senators could be found to support Hardwick's motion to this effect. Therefore, any man who could afford to fill his cellars before the amendment became legal could serve liquor to his guests perfectly legitimately until his stocks were exhausted. Also, the fact that the amendment gave the liquor trade a year to wind up its business destroyed the dry argument that the liquor trade was criminal. No criminal organization would be guaranteed by Congress a year to put its affairs in order. Moreover, instruments for manufacturing liquor in the home were not banned, and the bootlegger was given ample time to prepare for his future profession. Again, the amendment served to increase class hatred, for it was only the poor who could not afford to stock up liquor. In Samuel Gompers's words, "The workers who have no cellars and have not the opportunity of gratifying a normal even though temporary rational desire learn to hate their more fortunate fellow citizens more bitterly and uncompromisingly."[31]

The failure of the Eighteenth Amendment to include a purchase clause was a further weakness. Since there was no penalty attached to buying liquor, people were prepared to buy. The threat of putting bootleggers in jail hardly deterred their respectable patrons, who ran no risk at all. Thus the amendment allowed a safe demand for liquor to exist, and only persecuted the suppliers of that demand. The consciences of many good citizens was salved by the consideration that they were not legally breaking the letter of the Constitution themselves, nor even aiding and abetting others to break it. When only the trade in liquor was criminal and liquor itself not so, legal reasons for abstaining did not exist.

There were additional flaws in the amendment. The words "concurrent power" were ambiguous and set the stage for a long legal battle between the states and the federal government. Furthermore, the omission of the word "alcoholic" from the amendment in favor of the word "intoxicating," despite the protests of the Prohibition party, allowed many cases in the law courts to be dismissed. Proof that liquor was "intoxicating" was harder to demonstrate than proof that liquor was "alcoholic" and had been sold. Although the Volstead Act later defined "intoxicating" as one-half of 1 per cent of alcohol by volume, an amendment to the Volstead Act, such as the Cullen Bill of 1933, could allow the sale of beer before the Eighteenth Amendment had been repealed.

In the debate on the Eighteenth Amendment in the House, Congressman Graham, of Pennsylvania, had said that the wet argument of the unconstitutionality of the amendment was a bugaboo. The Supreme Court later upheld his wisdom in the National Prohibition Cases.[32] But Graham was even wiser in his succeeding remarks, when he detailed his reasons for voting against the measure. For him, the Eighteenth Amendment destroyed the purpose of the Constitution. That fundamental law was only a declaration of principles, never of policy.[33]

THE VOLSTEAD ACT

IN 1930, a journalist unkindly suggested that the whole history of the United States could be told in eleven words: Columbus, Washington, Lincoln, Volstead, Two flights up and ask for Gus.[34] In a sense, his cheap wit was truer than he knew. For if the speak-easy and the bootlegger were aided by the loopholes of the Volstead Act, those loopholes were only in the act because of the whole tradition of American history.

Although the prohibitionists had written prohibition into the fundamental law of America, that fundamental law prevented them from enforcing it. The Constitution guaranteed Americans certain rights. The Volstead Act and other means of enforcing the Eighteenth Amendment seemed to deny Americans their heritage. The Fourth Amendment gave people the right to be secure in their persons, houses, papers, and effects against unreasonable searches and seizures. The

Fifth Amendment prevented people from being forced to be witnesses against themselves or from being tried twice for the same offense. The Sixth Amendment guaranteed "a speedy and public trial by an impartial jury." Yet these individual rights were attacked by the Volstead Act and its successors. Moreover, those states that by tradition or conviction opposed the increasing power of the federal government, were never persuaded that the Eighteenth Amendment did not violate the Tenth, which reserved all powers not delegated to the United States by the Constitution to the states or to the people.

Yet Congress, once the Eighteenth Amendment had been ratified by the states, had to provide for its token enforcement. The amendment could not be properly enforced without a bill, which would invade American liberties intolerably. The American people and Congress were not prepared for this. Thus the drys had to put through a measure which would deter without terrifying too much, and compromise without excusing everything. The principal author of this unhappy mish-mash of the possible and the desirable was the Anti-Saloon League Washington attorney, Wayne B. Wheeler. Despite the jealous opposition of Bishop Cannon, he drafted such a complex measure that he gave himself great power for the nine years before his death.[35] He was the only man who could understand and interpret the code of enforcement. Like Moses, he interpreted the commandments of his law to the faithful. The sponsor of his law was Representative Andrew Volstead, of Minnesota. Volstead lost his seat in Congress four years later for his pains.[36]

The original Volstead Bill was considerably more severe than the amended act of sixty-seven sections, later supplemented by another six sections, which evolved out of the debates on the measure in Congress. First, the House Judiciary Committee weakened the clauses of the bill that dealt with search and seizure, with the soliciting of orders for liquor, and with the report of arrests for drunkenness by local officers. House amendments, although partially restoring the search and seizure clauses, provided for severe penalties against the wrongful issue of search warrants, and allowed the possession of liquor in private homes and the sale of sacramental wine. The amended bill was passed in the House by a vote of 287 to 100, a loss to the wets of 28 votes since the division in the Eighteenth Amendment owing to dry and Republican victories in the elections of 1918.

The bill was then referred to a Senate Judiciary Subcommittee and the Senate Judiciary Committee. Further amendments were passed. Dwellings where people could possess liquor without fear of reprisals were defined as including residences, apartments, hotels, or similar places of abode. Individuals were still allowed to store and consume liquor and, in addition, to manufacture light wine and cider at home. Although the provision defining "intoxicating" at such a trivial volume of alcohol was upheld, the Senate insisted that the government must bear "the burden of proof" in the prosecution of liquor violations. The Senate then passed the bill without roll call and returned it to the House, which refused to accept the Senate's amendments. A conference was set up between the houses to reach an agreement. At the conference, the Senate won virtually every one of its liberal provisions, even in minor matters, such as striking out the clause penalizing drunkards on public vehicles, allowing alcoholics to be given liquor while under hospital treatment, and legalizing the manufacture of beer before it was made into near-beer.

The Volstead Act, as passed by Congress, was a curious document. Although the Armistice had been signed for eight months, the Act provided for the enforcement of wartime prohibition. The drys maintained that the period of demobilization was so difficult that it should be considered as part of the war; the wets said that the clause was a dishonest attempt by the drys to go back on their promise to give the liquor trade a year to wind up its business. For, by the device of prolonging wartime prohibition, the Volstead Act closed up the gap between its passage in 1919 and the start of national prohibition under the Eighteenth Amendment on January 16, 1920. However this was, Woodrow Wilson used the anomaly of the clauses relating to wartime prohibition to veto the Volstead Act on October 27, 1919. In his message to Congress, he added the cryptic warning that in all matters having to do with the personal habits and customs of large numbers of people, the established processes of legal change had to be followed.[37] But he did not express specifically in his veto message either approval or disapproval of the Eighteenth Amendment or of the main body of the Volstead Act. The House and the Senate immediately reacted by passing the act over Wilson's veto.

In brief, the amended Volstead Act provided for the manufacture of industrial alcohol by permits, and its denaturing to render it unfit for human consumption. The use of beverage alcohol was restricted to the patients of doctors, communicants at religious services, and makers of vinegar and cider. The Commissioner of Internal Revenue was charged with administering the enforcement of the act. The Commissioner and his assistants were given powers to investigate offenders and report them to United States attorneys, who would prosecute them before the federal courts. Penalties for bootleggers were set at a maximum fine of $1000 and six months in jail for first offenders, and $10,000 and five years in jail for second offenders. Places selling liquor illegally could be padlocked by court injunction for one year. Personal property used for the transportation of liquor, such as automobiles, boats, and airplanes, could be seized and sold by public auction to help defray the costs of enforcement. The purchase of liquor, however, did not make the purchaser liable for prosecution under the law of conspiracy.[38]

The Volstead Act was full of flaws. It was the result of compromises in the House and the Senate between the determined dry lobbyists and a majority of the members of Congress who did not desire that the Eighteenth Amendment should be rigidly enforced. Even the drys in Congress did not want to jeopardize the amendment by making the Volstead Act too severe and by causing a public revulsion against national prohibition. Only three members of the House voted for an amendment to the Volstead Act on July 21 to make the home possession of liquor unlawful; both drys and wets opposed such a stringent provision. The aim of the act was to secure as much enforcement as the country would endure, not total enforcement.

The faults in the framing of the Volstead Act were quickly revealed, once national prohibition was put into effect. Yet these shortcomings were no reflection on the sincerity of the drys. They wanted prohibition to be enforced as efficiently as possible; but they knew that Congress and the wet cities would not allow them to get all they wanted. Even so, by the compromise of the Volstead Act, they did the dry cause great damage. They did not secure the blessings of good law enforcement for their supporters, and they gave great cause for resentment to their opponents. The provision that allowed the making of home cider and light wines seemed a monstrous discrimination in favor of the farm against the town. As Congressman Barkley pointed out, if fermented apple juice and grape juice were legal, "how about corn juice?" Congressman McKiniry further saw in the legislation the "malicious joy" of the rural districts of America in "inflicting this sumptuary prohibition legislation upon the great cities. It preserves their cider and destroys the city workers' beer."[39]

But perhaps Congressman Crago, of Pennsylvania, best put the objections of those old-fashioned Americans whom the Volstead Act was designed to protect. He feared that the law would breed "a discontent and disrespect for law in this country beyond anything we have ever witnessed before." The act refused trial by jury in some cases; it confiscated personal property; it extended the power of the judiciary beyond anything since the shameful days of Judge Jeffreys in England; it invaded the sanctity of the home; and it made "crimes of the ordinary harmless housekeeping acts of nearly every family in our country."[40]

In this way, the Eighteenth Amendment and the Volstead Act became the law of the land. Through the many roots of prohibition — rural mythology, the psychology of excess, the exploited fears of the mass of the people, the findings of science and medicine, the temper of reform, the efficiency of the dry pressure groups, their mastery of propaganda, the stupidity and self-interest of the brewers and distillers, the necessary trimming of politicians, and the weakness of the elected representatives of the people — through all these channels the sap of the dry tree rose until the legal prohibition of the liquor trade burst out new and green in the first month of 1920. The roots had been separate; yet they were all part of a common American seed. They combined and contributed to the strength of the whole. The Anti-Saloon League, bent on its particular reform, was the heir and beneficiary of many interactions in American life. As the drys stood on the threshold of victory at the opening of the twenties, they could see manifest destiny in the success of their cause. They seemed to be the darling army of the Lord. Behind them appeared to lie one mighty pattern and purpose. Before them hung the sweet fruits of victory.

PART **2**

The Dry Tree

CHAPTER 9

Prelude to Deluge

> Oh, fatal Friday!
> Monumental Dry Day!
> Ah, dreadful Sixteenth Day of January
> That expurgates the Nation's commissary,
>   For all the years to come,
> Of whisky, brandy, gin and beer and rum,
> The sparkling flow of Veuve Cliquot and Mumm
> And all the wines — I cannot speak the worst;
> Drought leaves me glum and dumb,
>   O Day accurst
>   Of Thirst!
>
> Arthur Guiterman

> the season 'tis, my lovely lambs,
>
> of Sumner Volstead Christ and Co.
> the epoch of Mann's righteousness
> the age of dollars and no sense.*
>
> e. e. cummings

NATIONAL PROHIBITION began silently, and with little resistance. The creeping campaign of the drys and wartime restrictions had inured all travelers in the United States to the sanctions of the liquor laws. Moreover, the end of alcoholic drink had already been celebrated or mourned three times before the actual sixteenth of January, 1920. The first funeral orgy had taken place with the opening of wartime prohibition on July 1, 1919. From that date onwards, the people of America were reduced to drinking up the remaining stocks of liquor, for its manufacture was now forbidden. Most of these stocks were bought up by the wealthy and by institutions, in order to make the approaching desert years more tolerable with a well-stocked cellar. The Yale Club, with prophetic insight, laid down enough bottles to last out fourteen years; other moneyed groups did the same. The re-

---

* From *Poems 1923-1954*, copyright, 1954, by E. E. Cummings. Reprinted by permission of Harcourt, Brace & World, Inc.

maining stocks of matured liquor were drunk up in October, when all drinkers held a wake at the passing of the Volstead Act. The final spree took place over Christmas. Liquor was already scarce enough by this time to cause the deaths of more than one hundred people who celebrated the New Year by drinking adulterated whisky made from wood alcohol. Sixteen suspected bootleggers were charged with murder in Massachusetts for selling this poison.[1] It was not a happy augury for the Eighteenth Amendment.

Only the rich and the farsighted laid away enough bottles to stand the siege of the dry decade. A curious fatalism seemed to grip the rest of the drinkers of the land. This was compounded partly of a false hope that something would happen which would stop prohibition; it was impossible to conceive of such a monstrous reality. "Like Noah's neighbors," the *Outlook* said, "the wets up to the last apparently did not believe that the flood was coming."[2] There was also a guilty conviction among many drinkers that perhaps the drys were right; prohibition might well be an excellent thing for the nation. This conviction was allied with a spirit of defeatism, because of the continued victories of the drys. As a citizen of Charlotte, North Carolina, acknowledged, "When the women, the churches, and business are united in any fight, as they are in this one, nothing can stand against them."[3] Moreover, there was a real indifference to the matter. The country was in the grip of the Red Scare, demobilization, and the quarrel over the League of Nations. Articles on Starving Austria, the triumphs of the Red Armies, Bolshevism in America, the need for "delousing" the United States by getting rid of all undesirables "regardless of race, color, creed, money, position and whether citizens or aliens" — these urgent topics pushed prohibition to the back pages of newspapers and magazines.[4] The long wait for the dry law had made men believe that it would never come, and yet accept it when it did.

In contrast to the previous and later cascades of talk about prohibition, a strange moratorium of controversy was widespread in 1919. One observer wrote on the dry law:

> Few people really want it. But nobody cares to say so. Politicians wait in vain for the sign that is not given. Judges on the bench hand out reluctant sentences, wondering what they will do when the stock of wine in their own cellars is exhausted. Lawyers, doctors, professors and merchants sit tamely by awaiting the extinction of their private comfort. The working man watches the vanishing of his glass of beer and wishes that he was a man of influence with power to protest. The man of influence wishes that he were but a plain working man and might utter a protest without fear of injury of his interests.[5]

Only the drys were content with this situation, although they mistook this expectant apathy for popular sympathy.

Much of the lack of resistance was due to the success of dry propaganda. People believed the Anti-Saloon League spokesmen when they said that they would enforce the law quickly and cheaply. The Commissioner of Internal Revenue in Wilson's administration sent out a circular letter to all the clergymen of America, asking them to set up local committees on law enforcement. These committees were to receive complaints about the violations of the liquor laws. They were to channel all relevant evidence to the local police or prohibition authorities. Granted this active support, the Commissioner promised, "We will have little difficulty in the work of enforcement."[6] An efficient force of agents, 1500 strong, had been prepared by John F. Kramer, the first Prohibition Commissioner. With the prospect of such a strong fist of the law ready to strike, the drinkers were prepared to throw aside their bottles. After three weeks of enforcement, the wet *Nation* was lamenting that never had such an army of officials been gathered to apply any law or constitutional amendment. "A small army of Federal officials is busily engaged in searching buildings, trains, vessels, express wagons, and private conveyances, and in spying upon individuals."[7] With such terror rampant among the wets, the supervising revenue officer in New York could confidently say, "There will not be any violations to speak of."[8]

In Orange County, North Carolina, the county which the Treasury agents at Washington called "the banner county" of the United States for illegal whisky stills, the traditional distillers themselves lay low for a while to see whether the government was going to interfere formidably with their living.[9] Although the whole Appalachian mountain system from West Virginia down to Georgia was "literally honeycombed with homemade stills for the illicit manufacture of the beverage known familiarly as Moonshine, Blue John, and Mountain Dew," business was slack in the first weeks of the Volstead Act.[10] For the drys seemed to be still in the saddle. Newspapers now vied with each other, priggishly telling their readers how to obey the law with long lists of bewares. And the Anti-Saloon League had issued a formal warning that it would "stay in politics" until the wets had given up all attempts to nullify the law. A campaign for a fighting fund of $25,000,000 to enforce the law was begun by League leaders in the Southern states.[11]

On the day before the Volstead Act came into force, the drys had won another great victory. A judge in a United States District Court in New York had ruled that private liquor kept in warehouses, safe-deposit boxes, or lockers could be seized by prohibition agents. This disastrous ruling had galvanized the wets out of their lethargy. On

January 16, despite the bitter weather, everything on wheels was commandeered to carry bottles. Nothing was spared, not even perambulators. Never was so much liquor carried by so many in so few hours. When midnight struck and the land went officially dry, millions of dollars' worth of liquor was lying on the dockside, waiting to be shipped out of the United States, or was being rushed in automobiles and express trains to the safety of private homes. Saloonkeepers were shutting up their saloons quietly forever, as they thought, and were looking for buyers, who would convert such desirable corner sites into drugstores or candy counters. One of the most notorious saloons in Hell's Kitchen, New York, was serving soup and coffee and quick lunches within a week, with glass food cases set on top of the cherrywood bar. And a brewer, closing down, offered all his stockholders two barrels of beer instead of a last dividend.[12]

The farewell parties to legal liquor were lugubrious affairs. There were mock funerals at Maxim's and the Golden Glades and the Roman Gardens in New York; at Reisenweber's, all ladies at the grave of drink were given compacts in the shape of coffins. But the most joyous funeral was held by the revivalist Billy Sunday, who ceremoniously dealt with the twenty-foot corpse of John Barleycorn at Norfolk, Virginia. His example was followed by thousands of church and white-ribbon meetings all over the land, which celebrated the end of the Demon Rum. Their rejoicings were premature. Already the first drops of the deluge had fallen.

In the three months before the Eighteenth Amendment became effective, liquor worth half a million dollars was stolen from government warehouses. Although the guards at the warehouses were augmented, bonded liquor continued to disappear. When a fifth of whisky was fetching between ten and twenty dollars in large Eastern cities, and a gallon of corn liquor was selling in the hills for twenty dollars without allowing for the costs of distribution, many were tempted into the bootleg trade. Moreover, some states were openly nullifying the law. The Governor of New Jersey in his campaign for re-election promised to make the state wetter than the Atlantic Ocean. Lawyers there were trying to make legal drinks containing up to one-quarter of pure alcohol, by claiming that they were "nonintoxicating." The Anti-Saloon League's enforcement fund was abandoned owing to lack of support. The President, Woodrow Wilson, had had a stroke, and was setting the pace of inaction over prohibition for his successors. The appointees of the Prohibition Bureau were of low caliber, and were anxiously awaiting a change of administration. And the Customs and Coast Guard agents, try as they might, could only intercept a small amount of the liquor, which was being smuggled into the country to meet the huge demand.

In the first six months of prohibition, the later problems of the reform show themselves. On February 19, two prohibition agents were indicted in Baltimore on charges of corruption.[13] By June 17, the federal courts in Chicago were hopelessly congested with prohibition cases — there were some six hundred liquor trials pending. In western Pennsylvania, the local police restored liquor to its owners, after it had been seized by federal officials. Examples of the diversion of industrial alcohol, of the refusal of state legislatures to appropriate money for enforcement, of the huge rise in the number of illicit stills, of the rich and middle classes drinking openly, of the old saloons reopening as speak-easies under police protection, and of the flagrant drunkenness of many of the delegates at both the Republican and the Democratic nominating conventions — these examples showed that the future dry road of America would be subject to storms.[14]

Yet, in 1920, these were mere gusts of the storm. They were not serious. For the bootleggers were not yet organized on a national scale. Wealthy private citizens were still using up their private stocks of liquor and were not in the market for more. Many people were willing to give the law a fair trial. Although there was moonshine available in the hills, smuggled liquor near the borders and coasts, diverted industrial alcohol in the cities, hard cider in the country, and hair tonics everywhere, brewing and wine making and gin mixing in the home were still undiscovered arts. If the drys had been able to push through a vigorous campaign of deterrence at the outset, they might have had a longer period of triumph. But instead, the dry leaders, sensing a cheap victory at home, looked out for a world to conquer. And some wets encouraged them in the passage "from confidence and power to arrogance and political coercion." For they put the drys in the place of Greek tragic heroes, when "arrogance was the step just before madness and after madness came destruction."[15]

Meanwhile, the drys only foresaw some minor mopping-up operations before America turned bone-dry. And the country waited for a change of Presidents and for proof of the practical wisdom of the Volstead Act. And a doctor recommended to the International Congress Against Alcoholism and to the nation, "Of all the blessings in the world, probably water taken inside and outside is the best."[16]

CHAPTER 10

The Toothless Law

> With what chance of success, for example, would a legislator go about to extirpate drunkenness and fornication by dint of legal punishment? Not all the tortures which ingenuity could invent would compass it: and, before he had made any progress worth regarding, such a mass of evil would be produced by the punishment, as would exceed, a thousand-fold, the utmost possible mischief for the offence. The great difficulty would be in procuring evidence; an object which could not be attempted, with any probability of success, without spreading dismay through every family, tearing the bonds of sympathy asunder, and rooting out the influence of all the social motives.
>
> JEREMY BENTHAM

> Law is whatever is boldly asserted and plausibly maintained.
>
> AARON BURR

> Now let him enforce it.
>
> ANDREW JACKSON
> (of John Marshall, Chief Justice
> of the Supreme Court)

MORALITY AND LAW

"**N**OTHING CAN be more certain," wrote Oliver Goldsmith, "than that numerous written laws are a sign of a degenerate community, and are frequently not the consequences of vicious morals in a state, but the causes."[1] His Puritan contemporaries in America held the opposite opinion. To them, numerous written laws were a sign of a godly community and were the curb of vicious morals in a state, not the causes. The laws of the community should reflect the ideal morality of the community, not its practice. As in the Ten Commandments, the ethics of society should be directed by a series of prohibitions of all the possible sins of mankind. The doing of good was to be a process of banning the bad. The way of the Lord on earth was to be found in fear of the law. It was this attitude to legislation which resulted in the writing of the famous Blue Laws of New England. The Blue Laws regulated swearing, blasphemy, Sabbath observance, sex, gambling, and drunkenness. The Laws of the Saints in Massachusetts were, indeed, an incentive to Western immigration. For, in the frontier wildernesses, sinners could indulge themselves in peace. Beyond the confines of civilization, law was largely a rough and ready personal justice. The way of the free man in the West was to be found in the absence of the law.

Thus, on the continent of North America, two different traditions of law and morals developed. The first, which was developed by the Puritans, regarded morals as a fit branch of legislation. The second, which was the result of frontier conditions, considered morality as a private matter, and moral reformers as representatives of the very tyranny of civilization and church from which America had revolted. The first attitude became the logical argument of the drys, the second of the wets. To the drys, "the ultimate source of all progress" was "in the words, law and its penalty."[2] To the wets, "no man was ever made good by force"; it was impossible to take a man "by the scruff of the neck and lift him up into heaven."[3] Both arguments could quote tradition and history as their justification.

A third attitude toward law and morals grew up at the close of the nineteenth century. This was an attitude compounded of pragmatism, cynicism, Darwinism, and Marxism. Its argument was that the laws of society were the laws of the strongest members of that society. This was also true of the morals of society. Therefore, the connection between law and morals followed the interests of the ruling group. Henry Adams wrote of himself that from early childhood his moral principles had struggled blindly with his interests; but he had become certain of "one law that ruled all others — masses of men invariably follow interests in deciding morals."[4] This attitude towards law and morality initially helped the drys, and then worked against them. While eugenics and progressivism were the dominant intellectual forces, the drys could and did plead that their opponents were trying to retard the inevitable march of history and the majority. Prohibition of liquor should be enacted because it was the popular will. But when economics superseded eugenics as the main interest of the intellectuals, and the revolt against moral reforms seemed to be the contribution of the twenties to the progress of human liberty, the drys were the victims of their own past reasoning. Now the repeal of prohibition was represented as something which should be enacted because it was the popular will. An appeal to the right of the majority and of the strongest and of the fittest only suits those who feel themselves temporarily to be part of the fit and the strong and the many.

The drys were misled by their wide backing at the beginning of the century by the middle-class progressives of America. They were also deluded into thinking that those who helped them in the attack on the saloon would also help them in the attack on all liquor. In their eyes, the aroused millions of the American *bourgeoisie*, particularly the female of the species, would inform on any transgressor of the prohibition laws. Thus the work of enforcement officers would be a mere matter of arresting the guilty few with the approval of the righteous many. The passing of the Volstead Act was to prove the opposite, that the many were guilty and that the arrested few were judged by the many to be righteous. It was a formidable miscalculation on the part of the drys, who were more conscious of the desirability of their reform than its possibility.

Moreover, the success of the drys went to their heads. If they had succeeded in prohibiting liquor, why should they not succeed in banning other pernicious habits? More and more, the drys forgot the practical limits of the law and remembered only their view of the good of society. And in seeking beyond the practical and the possible they made themselves ridiculous. The history of the reform crusades against the cigarette and jazz are examples of the lengths to which the moral reformers would go in courting failure and jeers. Even when they were successful, as in the passage of the Mann Act, which used the federal power in interstate commerce to attack the white-slave trade and fornication across state borders, they were open to the sneers of their enemies that, while they pretended to regulate the commerce between the states, in fact they sought "to regulate commerce between the sexes."[5]

The anticigarette crusade went hand in hand with the fight against the saloon. As the *Century* said, "The relation of tobacco, especially in the form of cigarettes, and alcohol and opium is a very close one. . . . Morphine is the legitimate consequence of alcohol, and alcohol is the legitimate consequence of tobacco. Cigarettes, drink, opium, is the logical and regular series."[6] In the words of Dr. Frank Gunsaulus, there was no "energy more destructive of soul, mind and body, or more subversive of good morals, than the cigarette. The fight against the cigarette is a fight for civilization."[7] Medical fears, similar to those exploited by the drys, were used as deterrents to possible smokers. As late as November, 1930, the *National Advocate* printed the opinion of a doctor that "sixty per cent of all babies born of mothers who are habitual cigarette smokers die before they are two years old." The opponents of the cigarette used a strategy parallel to that of the drys — they were often the same people — to secure by 1913 the passage of anticigarette laws in nine states, all in the South or in the West. The tide in favor of the prohibition of cigarettes, however, receded even faster than the dry tide. By 1929, no state forbade the smoking of cigarettes by adults.

The crusade against the new styles of dancing and jazz was another exercise in futility. In 1914, the General Federation of Women's Clubs put under a ban the tango and hesitation waltz.[8] A clergyman added to the proscribed list the bunny hug, turkey trot, Texas Tommy, hug-me-tight, fox trot, shimmy dance, sea-gull swoop, camel walk, and skunk waltz. The Methodist Church would not even approve of a decorous dance step which was hopefully called the Wesleyan waltz.[9] But worse was to come with the black bottom and the Charleston. The sexual desires of the young seemed to reign on the dance floor. And as for the growing influence of jazz on dance music, the superintendent of schools in Kansas City, Missouri, warned a thousand teachers, "This nation has been fighting booze for a long time. I am just wondering whether jazz isn't going to have to be legislated against as well." For the intoxicating influence of jazz music was held to be as dangerous as that of alcohol. "Does Jazz Put the Sin in Syncopation?" asked Anne Shaw Faulkner in the *Ladies' Home Journal* in 1921; she thought it did, and she quoted a musical supervisor of a large urban high school that only forty out of two thousand best-selling songs were fit for boys and girls to sing together. Jazz was held to cause a mental drunkenness or, as Dr. Henry Van Dyke complained, "a sensual teasing of the strings of physical passion."[10] It loosed all those moral restraints which the drys held desirable, and therefore, like alcohol, it should be prohibited. But the advent of the radio and talking picture spread the influence of jazz all over the United States and gave the Negro his first victory in America.

The excesses of the moral reformers in these losing causes did harm to the drys. For moderates were alienated from all moral reformers. Moreover, the campaign for the prohibition of liquor seemed to many to be the thin end of the wedge, the prelude to a reign of terror by moral zealots over the habits of America. When the Anti-Saloon League had presented its first petition for national prohibition as far back as 1913, the New York *World* had voiced this fear: "Tomorrow it is likely to be the Anti-Cigarette League that is clamoring for a constitutional amendment to prohibit smoking, or the Anti-Profanity League that insists on a constitutional amendment to prevent swearing, or a Eugenics Society that advocates a constitutional amendment to stop the birth of imperfect babies."[11] The progress of the reform crusades against the cigarette and the jazzy dance merely seemed to confirm this suspicion. The field of moral reform seemed to have been taken over by fanatics. Thus all moral reform suffered. Few people tried to press for a limited good any more, a temperate betterment of a bad situation. It had to be all or nothing, either an excess or a nullification of moral legislation.

During the dominance of these concepts of law and morality, which dated from the views of the Puritans and of the pioneers, moderation and reason and respect for all law suffered. Those who were terrified by the selected laws of their chosen God tried to impose their own holy terror on their fellow citizens through the law of men. It was a hopeless task and led to scoffing at government and churches. When Clarence True Wilson advocated that buyers of bootleg liquor should be sentenced to a maximum of five years in prison in order to put "the fear of God in the minds of those who fear neither God nor man," he was shaming his God by representing Him in this light and slandering his fellow men who thought it no sin to drink.[12] It was the drys who had originally held liquor to be a sin, and who claimed that the dry law "brought sin" to all drinkers.[13] If they failed to convince the majority of their countrymen that this was so, the fault lay in their teaching, not in the unconverted.

THE UNWANTED ENFORCERS

"THE WILLINGNESS to exclude the saloon is largely conditioned by the opportunity to secure liquor for private use."[14] This was the basic principle of the popular support of prohibition. Indeed, the leaders of the drys knew that they could never get a majority of the American people to give up drinking immediately. They hoped that a new generation of teetotalers would grow up from the ranks of the young, and that the protected drys would win converts among the shamed wets.

The supporters of the Eighteenth Amendment wanted primarily to outlaw the liquor trade, not to prevent dedicated wets from drinking.[15] National prohibition was meant to stop the wet cities from swamping the dry country; only then could there be a counterattack by the rural moralists on the cities. In fact, even these limited hopes of the drys were doomed to disappointment. There was never any serious effort to enforce national prohibition until the early thirties, and by that time it was too late. After less than four years under the Volstead Act, it was clear that "three tremendous popular passions" were being satisfied, "the passion of the prohibitionists for law, the passion of the drinking classes for drink, and the passion of the largest and best-organized smuggling trade that has ever existed for money."[16] Once legalism had turned the possession of alcohol into a popular obsession and the sale of alcohol into a new Gold Rush, enforcement of the liquor laws had no chance.

The failure of the enforcement of the Volstead Act was due to administrative stupidity, political graft, the federal structure of the United States, an antiquated legal system, and the flaws in the act itself. These interlocking and corrigible causes for failure were overshadowed by one overriding consideration, that the prohibition law could not be adequately enforced in the America of that time. Indeed, it is doubtful that national prohibition can ever be enforced, even under a dictatorship. Alcoholic drinks have been made in every civilized society in history. The Wickersham Commission itself sadly conceded, "Few things are more easily made than alcohol."[17] The job of the Prohibition Bureau was to enforce the impossible. But it could have made a better job of this impossible task. The chase of bootleg liquor by prohibition agents too often resembled the chase of foxes by Oscar Wilde's hunters, a case of the unspeakable in full pursuit of the undrinkable.

The Prohibition Bureau was always the tool of national and state politics. In evidence given before the Wickersham Commission, it was said that the pressure exerted on the Washington headquarters of the Bureau was "greater at times than any group of men could be expected wholly to withstand." Congressmen had insisted upon the appointment or transfer of men within the service. Political organizations had tried to accelerate or retard enforcement in given areas in accord with the dictates of political expediency. Large and powerful trade associations had tried to force the Bureau to look after their particular needs.[18] Moreover, the Prohibition Bureau itself was continually kept short of men, money, and supplies by a cheeseparing Congress. If Americans got the political representatives they deserved, they also got the prohibition agents they deserved.

While the Volstead Act was pending in Congress, the Commissioner of Internal Revenue protested against being given the responsibility for enforcing such a thankless measure. He said that there could be no sort of adequate enforcement unless the Prohibition Bureau had the fullest co-operation from state policemen, churches, civic organizations, educational societies, charitable and philanthropic societies, and all the law-abiding citizens of the United States. The Commissioner stressed hopefully that it was "the right of the Government officers charged with the enforcement of this law to expect the assistance and moral support of every citizen, in upholding the law, regardless of personal conviction."[19] Unfortunately, the majority of American citizens conceived of other rights — the right to patronize the bootlegger or speakeasy of their choice, and the right to keep mum about the drinking habits of their neighbors. Where the duty to inform on bootleggers was widely considered to be a wrong, prohibition agents could expect little support.

The very organization and methods of the Prohibition Bureau were hopelessly inadequate. The Bureau was not under Civil Service rules. The salaries of prohibition agents compared unfavorably with those of garbage collectors. This low pay made the agents easy victims to corruption. The total number of agents and investigators employed in prohibition enforcement varied between 1500 and 2300 men for the whole of the United States, and the entire staff of the Bureau never exceeded 4500 men. The normal rate of pay for agents was between $1200 and $2000 a year in 1920, and $2300 a year in 1930.[20] For this inadequate wage, they were expected to work long hours and put their lives in danger from the attacks of armed bootleggers. When the bribes offered for a month's co-operation in winking at the actions of large bootlegging rings might total over one million dollars, prohibition agents were sorely tempted not to clip the wings of the goose which laid the golden eggs.[21] In the first eleven years of the Prohibition Bureau, there were 17,972 appointments to the service, 11,982 separations from the service without prejudice, and 1604 dismissals for cause.* The grounds of these dismissals included "bribery, extortion, theft, violation of the National Prohibition Act, falsification of records, conspiracy, forgery, perjury and other causes." And these were not all the cases of corruption, for, in the words of the Wickersham Commission, "bribery and similar offenses are from their nature extremely difficult of discovery and proof."[22]

The rapid turnover in the prohibition service, and the notoriety of some of its agents, gave it a bad name. One disgruntled prohibition administrator called the Bureau "a training school for bootleggers," because of the frequency with which agents left the service to sell their expert knowledge to their old enemies.[23] The reasons for having such poorly qualified agents in the Bureau are hardly surprising, since the Bureau was run for eight years on the spoils system, and since there was no effort to give even the key men in the Bureau special training for their jobs until 1927. The bootleggers had more than a hundred times the appropriation of the Bureau at their disposal, and were far better organized. The inadequate were forced by their country to pursue the prepared. When drastic attempts were made to reform the Bureau by President Hoover after 1929, it was already too late. Too many urban Americans had become disgusted with the petty thieveries of the whole service. They shared the opinion of Stanley Walker, the city editor of the New York *Herald Tribune,* that, although there were always some good prohibition agents such as Izzy Einstein and Moe Smith, "as a class, however, they made themselves offensive beyond words, and their multifarious doings made them the pariahs of New York."[24] .

An efficient enforcement agency demands three things: continuity of

---

* Roughly, one in twelve agents was dismissed for cause. The explanation of one of the dry Senators from Oklahoma was that, after all, "One out of twelve of the disciples went wrong."

personnel, large enough salaries to make graft unnecessary, and public and federal co-operation. The Prohibition Bureau had none of these three essentials. The first Prohibition Commissioner, an Ohio lawyer, John F. Kramer, served for a year and a half. His promise that he would see that liquor was not manufactured, "nor sold, nor given away, nor hauled in anything on the surface of the earth nor under the sea nor in the air" was not put to the test in his short term.[25] His successor, Roy A. Haynes, was endorsed by dry Congressman Upshaw as a man of "amazing genius and energy in organization."[26] His four years' tenure of office did not demonstrate these qualities. His personal press releases preached the imminent collapse of bootlegging, while his political appointees made the Prohibition Bureau a center of graft and corruption. All that could be said of his term was that the scandals which took place in the Prohibition Bureau were nothing, compared with the scandals which took place in the Department of Justice, under the benevolent gutting of Harry Daugherty and the Ohio Gang. During the regime of President Harding, the Volstead Act merely provided a fertile field for the private profit of certain members of the government. The Ohio Gang dealt in protection to bootleggers, illegal withdrawals of bonded liquor, pardons and paroles for ready cash, prosecutions dropped for a price, and even in federal offices for sale. Law enforcement became open robbery.*

The failure of Haynes to achieve anything more than a confident manner and a few spectacular raids on New York hotels made Coolidge appoint a new head of the Prohibition Bureau, a retired General, Lincoln C. Andrews. Although Haynes kept his official position, Andrews was given all real authority. He immediately attempted to reorganize the Prohibition Bureau on military lines and to drive all political influence from the service. Senator "Sunny Jim" Watson commented cynically, "It can't be done," and he was right. General Andrews could not drive the political spoilsmen out of the Bureau. For, in the words of a contemporary reporter, "the venerable pie counter is firmly fastened and the ancient plum tree is indeed deeply rooted."[27] The General's reorganization was largely a paper job; America was divided up into twenty-four districts, and some retired officers from the Army and

---

* The Volstead Act was used by the Ohio Gang as a protection racket. A file from the Department of Justice listed convicted bootleggers, who could be sold pardons. Special agent Gaston B. Means testified that he collected some $7,000,000 from bootleggers in a goldfish bowl to square the Department of Justice. George Remus, the so-called King of the Bootleggers, who was estimated to have made a gross profit of $40,000,000 from bootlegging, testified that he paid more than $250,-000 to a member of the Ohio Gang. Even so, he was prosecuted and sent to jail. He commented sourly, "I tried to corner the graft market, only to find that there is not enough money in the world to buy up all the public officials who demand a share in the graft."

Navy joined the prohibition service. General Andrews resigned in March, 1927, after offending the politicians and the drys by his forthright statements, including one admission before a Senate subcommittee in 1926 that his task would be greatly simplified by the modification of the Volstead Act to permit the sale of light wines and beer. Major Chester P. Mills, one of General Andrew's officers in New York, estimated that three-quarters of the Prohibition Bureau at the time were "ward heelers and sycophants named by the politicians."[28]

The successors of General Andrews were the Assistant Secretary of the Treasury, Seymour Lowman, and the chief chemist of the Prohibition Bureau, James M. Doran. The whole service was made to take the Civil Service examination, for "there were scores of prohibition agents no more fit to be trusted with a commission to enforce the laws of the United States and to carry a gun than the notorious bandit Jesse James."[29] The result of the examination, which was the standard test, was shocking. Only two-fifths of those in the Prohibition Bureau could pass the test after two attempts. Most of the remainder were dismissed and replaced. Not until 1930 was a beginning made in setting up a stable body of men prepared to enforce prohibition. When the average length of tenure in the most difficult of the top administrative posts of the service was six months, and the prohibition commissioners themselves were not continued long in office, there was no hope of enforcing the unpopular dry laws.[30] By 1929, the state of New Jersey had vanquished fourteen prohibition administrators, and had gained an accolade from a poet in the New York *Times:*

> One by one they interfere
> With those Jersey tides of beer;
> Manfully they face the flood,
> Then, alas! their name is mud.
> Heroes for a little day,
> One by one they pass away.[31]

But if there were replacements and conflicts within the Prohibition Bureau, there were still more conflicts with other law enforcement agencies of the federal government. The Customs Service and the Coast Guard had a long and proud tradition of policing the American borders, and they were unwilling to share their knowledge with the upstart Prohibition Bureau. The border patrols of the Bureau of Immigration, formed in 1925, were also unco-operative, except when bootleggers also happened to be aliens. Rivalry between the services and the "wholesome disgust" of the other services for the despised Prohibition Bureau added to the difficulties of the enforcers of the dry laws.[32]

Courtesy of the St. Louis *Post-Dispatch* by Fitzpatrick

VOLSTEAD RULES THE WAVES

Certain methods of the Prohibition Bureau gave it still more disrepute. The disguises of Izzy and Moe as undertakers or baseball players were treated as good fun; but when dry agents escorting young women posed as legitimate diners in search of a drink, they were accused of corrupting the very sex which prohibition was meant to save. Other methods of collecting information such as bribery and wire tapping did not make the American people think better of the Bureau. The fact that the chemists of the Bureau approved of putting poisonous denaturants in industrial alcohol, which might easily be diverted into the bootleg market, made them seem accomplices in murder. And the final folly of the prohibition service was to run a speak-easy of its own at the taxpayers' expense, the Bridge Whist Club at 14 East Forty-fourth Street, New York; the club sold liquor to all comers for six months and trapped a few bootleggers. But the spectacle of the Prohibition Bureau spreading the bad habits which it was charged to prevent was too much for the country. The Bridge Whist Club was closed down, and the expense accounts for the undercover agents' drinking were lopped.

But worst of all was the direct murder of innocent citizens by prohibition agents. In the opening days of the Volstead Act, there were shooting affrays between agents and bootleggers. By 1923, thirty prohibition agents had already been killed; Roy Haynes called them "our little band of martyrs."[33] Yet the gunplay was confined, more or less, to the agents and violators of the liquor law. Unfortunately, mistakes of prohibition agents resulted in the killing of women and children, and the serious wounding of Senator Greene, of Vermont, in Washington itself. The innocent deaths of Mrs. Lillian DeKing, whose small son retaliated by shooting the responsible dry agent in the leg, of Henry Virkula, shot down while driving his family in Minnesota, and of Mildred Lee and Sheridan Bradshaw, a girl of eleven years and a boy of eight, made dry agents loathed everywhere. In a popular pamphlet, the Association Against the Prohibition Amendment claimed that more than a thousand people in ten years had been killed outright in the prohibition war between the law enforcers and the violators. Official records admitted the deaths of 286 federal officers and private citizens during this period; the officers had killed the civilians at a ratio of one officer to every three citizens.[34]

The government showed its feelings by sending federal attorneys to defend prohibition agents accused of murder. The officers of the law were rarely convicted, even in the most flagrant cases of slaughter. The Association Against the Prohibition Amendment investigated 184 killings of citizens by prohibition agents; only six of the agents were convicted of any crime, and only one of murder in the second degree. The government seemed to be sanctioning indiscriminate killing by its officers. Although various directives were sent out ordering agents to be careful before shooting, the whole service seemed to be too quick on the draw. "What the prohibition situation needs," wrote Jane Addams, "first of all, is disarmament."[35] Only after the Prohibition Bureau had been transferred to the Department of Justice, and the reasonable rule of Dr. A. W. W. Woodcock, was there any cessation in the shooting.[36]

But it was already too late. Too many dry leaders had made unfortunate remarks similar to that of Senator Brookhart, of Iowa, that the protests against the killings were simply "gush stuff about murders by men who make mistakes once in a while."[37] [*] Cartoons, editorials, and sneering poems reflected widespread public disgust. Perhaps the wittiest of these protests was "The Patriot's Prayer," written by Arthur Lippman:

> *Now I lay me down to sleep —*
> *My life and limb may Hoover keep,*
> *And may no coast guard cutter shell*
> *This little home I love so well.*
> *May no dry agent, shooting wild,*
> *Molest mine wife and infant child,*
> *Or, searching out some secret still,*
> *Bombard my home to maim and kill.*
> *When dawn succeeds the gleaming stars,*
> *May we, devoid of wounds and scars,*
> *Give thanks we didn't fall before*
> *The shots in Prohibition's War.*

The drys always maintained that national prohibition had never had a fair trial, because there was no real attempt at enforcement until ten years of bungled efforts had exhausted the tolerance of the public. To Senator Neely, of West Virginia, "a thought, a hope, or a dream of satisfactory enforcement of prohibition" with Andrew Mellon holding the position of Secretary of the Treasury was "as idle as a painted ship upon a painted ocean." Since Mellon had had millions of dollars invested in the liquor trade before prohibition, it was useless to expect him to enforce the dry law. "Obviously, a thief will never enforce the law against larceny; a pyromaniac will never enforce the law against arson; a distiller or brewer will never enforce the Volstead Act."[38] With the wets powerful in every Republican Cabinet, what hope was there of a zealous prosecution of the dry law?

The drys did not mention, however, the role of the Anti-Saloon League in exempting the Prohibition Bureau from Civil Service rules, in backing its inclusion in the Treasury rather than in the Department of Justice, and in appointing fellow citizens from Ohio to top posts in the Bureau. The fairest comment on the matter was made in the *Wickersham Report*, that the Eighteenth Amendment and the National Prohibition Act came into existence "at the time best suited for their adoption and at the worst time for their enforcement."[39] The political tri-

[*] Mrs. Ella Boole, president of the Woman's Christian Temperance Union, was reported as the author of an even more unfortunate remark about the murdered Mrs. DeKing, "Well, she was evading the law, wasn't she?"

umph of the drys was not, and could not be, translated into a social victory. In fact, if an army of federal agents had been raised to insist on the observance of the Volstead Act in the wet cities, it is probable that repeal would have come about even sooner. When Hoover began to enforce prohibition with some efficiency, he dried up its support as well as supplies of bootleg liquor.

The statistics of prohibition enforcement show the increasing efficiency of the Prohibition Bureau and the increasing volume of the bootleg trade. In 1921, a total of 95,933 illicit distilleries, stills, still worms, and fermenters were seized; this total rose to 172,537 by 1925 and to 282,122 by 1930. In the latter year, some forty million gallons of distilled spirits, malt liquor, wine, cider, mash, and pomace were also seized. The number of convictions for liquor offenses in federal courts, which had averaged about 35,000 a year after 1922, showed a startling jump under the Hoover administration to a maximum of 61,383 in 1932. Jail sentences, which reached a total of only 11,818 by 1927, rocketed to 44,678 in 1932, finally demonstrating, as President Hoover himself wrote, "the futility of the whole business."[40]

President Hoover reckoned later that the federal government could not have come anywhere near enforcing prohibition with a police force of less than a quarter of a million men. Yet even his small efforts at enforcement were enough to write the death warrant of the Eighteenth Amendment. Prohibition had developed from a joke into a threat to all and sundry. While the situation in large cities was "not enforcement but a sort of safe regulation of the liquor-selling traffic" through the co-operation of criminals and policemen against interlopers and price cutters, the drinkers were not worried.[41] But the moment that efficient federal agents began to put respectable citizens in jail, the situation became intolerable. Although bad enforcement disgusted America with prohibition, it was good enforcement which helped to cause the revolt of repeal.

THE DEFECTIVE ACT

THE FLAWS in the Volstead Act were quickly revealed by the methods used by bootleggers to circumvent it. The clause relating to industrial alcohol allowed fake denaturing plants to divert the alcohol into bootleg channels by permitting the establishment of denaturing plants anywhere in the United States, once a bond had been filed and a permit issued. In 1929, Major Mills testified that the major part of bootleg liquor in circulation came from diverted industrial alcohol. His testimony is accurate for the middle years of prohibition, although home-brew was the major source of supply by the end. And the home-brewing of wine and beer was itself legal under the Volstead Act, although the regulations of the prohibition unit proscribed the making of "nonintoxicating cider and fruit-juices" from dried fruits, dandelions, and rhubarb. Moreover, the legal manufacture of real beer, before its alcohol was removed and it was turned into near-beer, allowed the makers to divert large quantities of genuine ale into the ever-thirsty market.

The clauses dealing with medicinal and sacramental alcohol in the act provided more illicit liquor in America. In the House debate, Congressmen had voiced their fears of scalawag and jackleg physicians, although no one foresaw the possibility of bootlegging ministers.[42] The testimony of Dr. Bevan that doctors made roughly $40,000,000 in 1928 by writing medical prescriptions for whisky, the opposition of the National Association of Retail Druggists to the vast profits of the speakeasy drugstores, and proof that even sacramental wine often reached the dinner table rather than the communion cup provided damning evidence against these loopholes in the Volstead Act.[43]

Moreover, the transfer of the duties of enforcement to the Treasury Department rather than to the Department of Justice was ill-advised. Wayne B. Wheeler had originally insisted upon this for various reasons. "The Internal Revenue Commissioner is obviously the choice for the chief law enforcement official. The reason for this is that this department has dealt with the liquor traffic through many years. The machinery is already built."[44] There was a further motive behind Wheeler's insistence. While the Volstead Act was pending, the Commissioner had complained that his department was already overburdened with the fiscal and revenue problems of the government. Thus Wheeler could volunteer unofficially to relieve the Treasury of the burden of its duties relating to prohibition enforcement. He could, then, personally organize, check, and staff the Prohibition Bureau. And this he largely did. During the administration of President Harding (a fellow citizen from Ohio, who was beholden to the Anti-Saloon League for many political services) and during the administration of President Coolidge, Wheeler was the clearinghouse for most appointments to the Prohibition Bureau through the agency of his contact, Roy A. Haynes, the Prohibition Commissioner. Unsuccessful petitions were made in 1921 and 1924 to transfer prohibition enforcement to the Department of Justice. But these recommendations were resisted by Wheeler through his influence in Congress. He feared he would lose his power over appointments. Not until the death of Wheeler and the preliminary report of the Wickersham Commission in 1929 was the Department of Justice given the duty of enforcing the Eighteenth Amendment. But it was already the evening of prohibition

Other deficiencies in the Volstead Act were evident in the prosecution of offenders. There was bad liaison between the Prohibition Bureau and the United States attorneys, and between the United States attorneys and the federal judges. The old tradition that indictment in a federal court was tantamount to conviction and proper punishment did not apply to prohibition cases. Many cases were dismissed because the Prohibition Bureau was held to have exceeded its legal powers while collecting evidence. Other cases were voided on technicalities. Some federal judges were obviously out of sympathy with the Volstead Act and used its complex and verbose phrasing to acquit offenders. The penalties for breaking the law were not sufficient to deter large-scale bootleggers and first offenders. Not until the passage of the Jones Act in 1929, which supplemented the Volstead Act by providing for a maximum penalty of five years in jail and a fine of $10,000 for first offenders, did the law acquire teeth enough to deter those in search of easy money from bootlegging.

This was not the end of the catalogue of errors in the Volstead Act. Although court injunctions to padlock for one year any place discovered selling liquor were the most helpful tool of the Prohibition Bureau, their use was blunted by the provisions of the act. Judges were not required to issue injunctions, but recommended to issue them. Also, the injunctions had to be served on the owners of the property which was being used as a speak-easy or bootleg factory, and these owners were often absent. Moreover, the act prevented prohibition agents from confiscating the cars of bootleggers if the license of the car was made out in the name of a company which could plead ignorance of the illegal use of its property. And, above all, enforcement was well-nigh impossible when purchasers of bootleg liquor could not be held for conspiracy.

The Volstead Act was a hodgepodge of cunning and compromise, and it produced a hodgepodge of enforcement and evasion of national prohibition.

THE UNWILLING STATES

THE PROBLEM of law enforcement in the United States also lay in the divisions between and within the states. The states had many more police officers than the federal government had — a total of some 175,000 officers of the law in 1930. But these officers were badly paid and overworked, in the interest of low taxes. The states also had different opinions, laws, and judicial practices from those of the federal government. In these discrepancies, evasion of the consequences of the law, particularly of the prohibition law, flourished. National prohibition needed central control if there was to be any efficient enforcement. This central control was impossible when a major part of enforcement was left to the individual states.

Most of the states passed laws to supplement the Volstead Act, by making evasion of the dry law a state crime as well as a federal crime. Sixteen states defined the word "intoxicating" even more stringently than did the Volstead Act. Other states forbade the possession of liquor. Some gave the state police greater powers of search and seizure. In Indiana, jewelers were forbidden to display cocktail shakers or pocket flasks in their windows. In Michigan, the savage Baumes Law made violation of the liquor laws for the fourth time punishable by life imprisonment; a mother of ten children was so sentenced for possessing one quart of gin. But, in general, there was an unmistakable hiatus in the states between the law and its enforcement.[45] A drastic law was all very well; but the fact that the states never appropriated more than a pittance for enforcement or for policemen or for additional courts of judgment drew the teeth from these drastic laws.

The Mullan-Gage Law is a good example. The New York legislature passed this law to supplement the Volstead Act in 1921, and failed to appropriate any money to enforce its provisions. Within a week, the courts of the state were clogged up with liquor cases. Nearly 90 per cent of the accused were dismissed by the courts; 7 per cent pleaded guilty; only 20 cases out of nearly 7000 resulted in a trial by jury, conviction, and jail sentence.[46] When Alfred E. Smith signed the repeal of the law in 1923, making New York the first state to confess to the utter failure of state prohibition enforcement, the impossibility of the job had already been demonstrated. Prohibition could not be enforced in large urban areas unless vast sums were set aside by the legislatures for the purpose, and no legislature in the United States would do this.

Not only did the states fail to enforce their own prohibition laws, but often they prevented the federal prohibition agents from doing their duty. Over and over again, zealous prohibition officers found themselves transferred or removed from their jobs because state politicians were annoyed by their efficiency. In Massachusetts, the chief prohibition officer raided a Republican party banquet where liquor was being served; his own superior officer in the Prohibition Bureau was there, and the zealous subordinate was removed for his pains.[47] In New Jersey, a new dry officer, who pictured himself as the "prohibition St. Patrick," found himself in a "whirlpool of disloyalty, intrigue, espionage within and without the service, graft, lack of support from Washington, lack of sympathy of the public, double-crossing everywhere, and cut-throat tactics"; after months of the most strenuous effort, the new officer found that he had only accomplished one thing — he had raised the price of liquor and reduced its quality.[48] In Philadelphia, the formidable General Smedley D. Butler made a valiant attempt to dry up the city. But he left his post before his two years were ended, since he found that the job was impossible. He had arrested more than 6000 people, but only 212 had been convicted in the courts. In his opinion, enforcement had not "amounted to a row of pins after the arrests were made."[49]

The federal prosecuting attorney in Philadelphia wrote a sad chronicle of how national prohibition destroyed the morale of the law in city and state. To him, the law had been respected and moderately efficient before the Volstead Act. Afterwards it became corrupt and unworkable. The ingenious provisions of the dry laws "simply added infinite variety to the means of crookedness. It wasn't only the law that was broken, it was every rule of ordinary decency among men." The whole of the legal system of Philadelphia became demoralized within a year. Political leaders fought for the office of the state director of prohibition, who "could control numerous highly desirable appointments, could afford protection to favored persons and provide permits in payment of political debts, and, what was still more important, could collect unlimited sums of money for campaign purposes." So many respectable people became involved in the graft of prohibition enforcement in Pennsylvania that it seemed that "the community was in a vast conspiracy against itself."[50]

With a honeycomb of graft sweetening the integrity of whole states, with prohibition enforcement allied to the political needs of party machines, with state policemen demoralized by the billions of dollars in the bootleg business, it was vain to expect too much from local officers of the law. If the federal government wanted to enforce prohibition, it would have to go it alone. Wayne Wheeler might appeal to the states to co-operate with the Prohibition Bureau in the matter, but the states were deaf to his appeal. Indeed, the doctrine of states' rights was antagonistic to federal interference in any of the affairs of the states. Wheeler could say with some truth that "only when some hoary and lucrative evil custom is attacked do the champions of organized vice or crime arise and call high heaven to witness that the sacred rights of the states are being violated if the white slave traffic, the drug evil, gambling or booze are placed outside the pale of the law."[51] But the fact was that the states would not help federal agents over prohibition, unless they wanted to do so. There could be no compulsion of an unwilling state, short of Civil War.

In the voluminous pages of the *Wickersham Report,* the efficacy of law enforcement in the various states is related. Many of the testimonies from the states are disappointing, merely reflecting the wish fulfillments of the officers of the law. Other testimonies show the despair of those set to enforce the Volstead Act. Above all, a picture of the *local* nature of prohibition enforcement comes out of the document. Obedience to the law and the actions of its officers varied from town to town, from one officer to another. In Florida, for instance, enforcement was very poor in Miami and Tampa, but good wherever the Customs Service had jurisdiction. In Colorado, twenty-five out of twenty-six grand jurors of high character admitted that they drank liquor. In Georgia, the state superintendent of the Anti-Saloon League could testify that the state was rapidly becoming dry, while speak-easies and brothels were run openly in Macon. In the dry Senator Borah's home state of Idaho, enforcement was spotty, with a United States marshal complaining about the laws that Borah had helped to pass, "The more laws we have, the easier it is for the bootlegger to escape. We need simple laws like the Commandments, and then enforce them." In large wet cities such as St. Louis, the frank admission was that "no officer in St. Louis could be elected unless he declares he is opposed to the Volstead Act," while "outside of four or five counties Missouri is dry, and to be elected to any important State office one must be on the dry ticket." In North Dakota, dry sentiment was so strong that the state Supreme Court judged that liquor crimes involved "moral turpitude"; but a pamphlet for compulsory Temperance Day teaching could include Will Rogers's remark, "If you think this country ain't dry, just watch 'em vote; if you think this country ain't wet, just watch 'em drink. You see, when they vote, it's counted, but when they drink, it ain't." Yet, in the depths of dry Texas, conditions were so bad in towns such as Galveston, with open bawdy and gambling houses and saloons, that a prominent law officer had to shrug off the town as "outside the United States."[52]

The Volstead Act was enforced in the United States wherever the population sympathized with it. In the rural areas of the South and West, there was effective prohibition, as there still is in certain counties. In the large cities, however, there was little or no attempt at enforcement. The police merely aimed at regulating the worst excesses of the speak-easies. In the ports of America, as the president of the International Seamen's Union said, there was no such thing as enforcement or prohibition for the seaman. "He can get all the drink that he can possibly swill or buy, and it is strong drink."[53] Along the main highways of the land, roadhouses offered hard liquor to passing travelers. In addition, no tourist resort would ever dry up its means of attracting patrons. Wherever urban conglomerations or modern communications spread, liquor spread too. The South and West were protected by their isolation for a long time, but even dry Kansas could not keep its citizens from catching jake paralysis in the western part of Kansas City. Enforcement was only effective where it relied on political and religious sanctions. Where political and religious tradition sanctioned liquor, enforcement was a farce.

The quarrel between the drys and the wets about the rights and wrongs of the state attitude toward law enforcement was a quarrel in Cloud-Cuckoo-Land. When Borah urged the states to pick up their share of the burden under the "concurrent" clause of the Eighteenth Amendment, he was heard and ignored. When Governor Ritchie, of Maryland, insisted that the "concurrent" clause merely reserved the right of their own police power to the states without imposing a duty upon them to help the federal government, the wet states applauded him and the dry ones cursed him.[54] But the argument made no difference to the facts of enforcement. When the state legislatures would appropriate even less than a niggardly Congress to enforce an unpopular law, any argument about the rights and wrongs of state enforcement was a mere exercise in legal casuistry.

The states themselves showed increasing opposition to the Volstead Act. After New York had repealed its prohibition law, it was followed in the twenties by Nevada, Montana, and Wisconsin. In 1930, Massachusetts, Illinois, and Rhode Island all voted by referendum to repeal their state prohibition laws. Although the drys had won six out of ten popular referendums before 1928 on the question of keeping the state enforcement codes in operation, they lost ground steadily after the election of Herbert Hoover to the White House.[55]* Their margin of victory in referendums had always been narrow, and the growing unpopularity of prohibition during the depression turned their slight majorities into minorities. The drys ended by opposing state referendums as a means of expressing popular opinion, and tried to rally the legislatures alone behind the dry law. But as state after state gave up its enforcement law, until even California with its dry stronghold of Los Angeles went wet in 1932, the drys could no longer hold back the tide of popular discontent.†

* Out of further referendums in nine states before 1928, however, asking for modification or repeal of the national prohibition laws, the wets won seven and the drys only two.

† Los Angeles, with its immigrant Midwestern population, was the only major dry city outside the South in the United States.

The Wickersham Commission, in looking through the record of the states on prohibition, could only commend Kansas and Virginia as truly zealous prohibition states. Even in these two areas of virtue, there was a failure of enforcement in the cities. And a failure of enforcement in the cities meant a "failure in the major part of the land in population and influence."[56] In fact, the commission recognized that the failure of the states to enforce the dry laws was really a reasonable response to the failure of the people within those states to uphold those laws. The states were united in the prosecution of other laws, such as the narcotics law. Perhaps, the fault was more in the Eighteenth Amendment itself than in the states which held together in agreement about most of the Constitution. As Heywood Broun commented on Herbert Hoover's dry messages to Congress, he found it difficult to see how a man could say in one breath that he loved the Constitution and also the amendment which had brought it into such disrepute and peril. "One might as well maintain that he is for both the heroine and the villain who threatens her, Red Riding Hood and the wolf, Nancy Sikes and also Bill."[57]

THE BOOTLEG SPRINGS

THERE WERE five main sources of illegal liquor: imported liquor, diverted industrial alcohol, moonshine, illicit beer, and illicit wine.* The first two sources supplied most of the decent liquor available in the early twenties. If this condition had continued into the late twenties, there might have been some hope of adequate enforcement of the prohibition laws. But the production of moonshine and beer and wine in the home decentralized the making of bootleg liquor to such an extent that enforcement became impossible. Where the springs of bootleg liquor rose in half the homes of America, there was no stopping of the flood.

American prohibition was very profitable to its geographical neighbors. The migration of thirsty Americans into Canada sensibly helped the Canadian economy. Hotels, bars, roads, and steamboats were built

* There were two other minor sources of beverage alcohol. The first was legal: the supplies of liquor provided through doctors' and druggists' prescriptions, and through sacramental wine. The small extent of this supply made it relatively unimportant. The second source was the mysterious disappearance of spirits held in government warehouses under bond during prohibition. In 1920, there were 50,-550,498 gallons of whisky under bond; this amount had shrunk to 18,442,955 gallons by 1933. Even allowing for the legitimate prescription of medical alcohol, at least 20,000,000 gallons of whisky must have been diverted somewhere or other.

for the new tourist trade. The financial attractions of the new demand proved too much for the prohibition laws of the Canadian provinces, and they were mostly repealed. The number of Canadians visiting America was only half the number of Americans visiting Canada, while, on the average, each American spent twice as much money as his Canadian counterpart. Indeed, Canada profited very much from prohibition in America.[58] The liquor monopolies in the Canadian provinces reaped huge benefits from the sale of liquor and from taxes on "export houses," which smuggled liquor into the United States. After seven years of American prohibition, Canada was exporting officially more than one million gallons of spirits each year to its neighbor. Not until 1930 did the Canadian government make a real effort to stop the flow of whisky into America.

Roy Haynes referred sadly to the remark that it was impossible to keep liquor from dripping through a dotted line.[59] The Canadian-American border was some thousands of miles long, and hardly patrolled. The Mexican border was similarly easy to cross, although it was never a major source of bootleg supply. Through these undefended frontiers, a deluge of liquor descended. Between 1918 and 1922, imports of British liquor into Canada increased six times and into Mexico eight times. Although it is impossible to calculate how much liquor was actually smuggled into America, the liquor revenues of the Canadian government increased four times during prohibition, while the consumption of spirits by the Canadian population almost halved.[60] In the busiest smuggling area, Detroit, graft averaging two million dollars a week bought immunity for liquor traders. General Andrews calculated that the law enforcement agencies caught only one-twentieth of the liquor smuggled into America.[61] If his estimate was accurate, the flow of liquor into America can be calculated at between five and ten million gallons a year. The Department of Commerce gave the worth of smuggled liquor at the "low estimate" of $40,000,000 a year.[62]

Smuggled liquor was brought into the United States by sea as well as by land. Prohibition saved the economy of many poor islands off Canada and in the West Indies. Imports of liquor into St. Pierre and Miquelon, the Bahamas, and other islands would have been sufficient to keep the local population dead-drunk for hundreds of years.[63] The liquor was exported again, however, to the fleets of rumrunners which lurked outside American territorial waters and sold their cargo to the owners of fast speedboats to run in past the Coast Guard cutters. One contemporary account by a rumrunner brings out the monotony and dullness of life on the waiting ships of Rum Row.[64] Sensational accounts of Rum Row and Bill McCoy, whose liquor was guaranteed to

Courtesy of the *Evening World*, by Clive Weed

KING CANUTE!

be the "real McCoy" and no fake brand, cast a glamorous light on the sea-smuggling business, which was hardly felt by the smugglers themselves.[65] After the first four years of easy profits and quick sales, over-competition, murders by hijackers, the harrying of the Coast Guard, and long months at sea with too much liquor on board reduced the ships on Rum Row to a desolate line of vessels which barely paid their way. Only the islanders and owners of the goods at the home ports of the rumrunners made safe profits. Perhaps the real gainer from Rum Row was the United States Navy, which was training its future sailors in gunnery and navigation without any government expense.[66]

The second spring of bootleg liquor flowed from the business of industrial alcohol. Little industrial alcohol was used in America until the beginning of this century. By 1906, however, the demand had become sufficient to secure its exemption from the excise tax on distilled liquors, once special denaturants had been added to the alcohol to render it unfit for human consumption. Between 1920 and 1930, legitimate production of industrial alcohol increased nearly four times to just over 180,-000,000 proof gallons a year, although beverage alcohol was prohibited at this time. The Volstead Act carefully exempted industrial alcohol from its provisions, and set up complex rules for its supervision by the Prohibition Bureau.

The huge increase in the business of industrial alcohol was partly due to the boom in industry and partly due to bootlegging. In 1926, General Andrews referred sourly to the special denaturing plants which manufactured industrial alcohol as "nothing more or less than bootlegging organizations."[67] He estimated that some 15,000,000 gallons of alcohol a year were diverted into bootleg channels; the United States Attorney for the Southern District of New York lifted this figure to between 50,000,000 and 60,000,000 gallons.[68] Since each gallon of industrial alcohol, when doctored and watered and colored by bootleggers, produced three gallons of so-called whisky or gin, the amount of booze available from this source was large. But the heyday of the diversion of industrial alcohol passed in the middle twenties, and, through better regulation, the total quantity of bootlegged alcohol from this loophole had sunk to less than 15,000,000 gallons a year by 1930.[69]

The Prohibition Bureau tried to make industrial alcohol undrinkable by insisting on the addition of one of seventy-six denaturants, made up from different formulas. Some of these denaturants were harmless, such as lavender and soft soap; others were poisonous, such as iodine, sulphuric acid, and wood alcohol. The bootleggers, once they had laid their hands on the denatured alcohol, tried to recover it for drinking purposes. The Wickersham Commission conceded that a skilled chemist, given adequate resources, could recover drinking alcohol from almost any mixture which contained it.[70] But the trouble was that too many bootleggers in search of quick profits did not bother to set up and pay for the expensive processes of recovery. With little more than a token effort at removing the denaturants, the bootleggers mixed industrial alcohol with glycerine and oil of juniper and called the product gin. Scotch whisky was made by adding caramel and prune juice and creosote to the industrial alcohol. Then forged labels and bottles, resembling those of high-grade liquor firms in England or Canada, were used to peddle the mixture into the throats of the unsuspecting.[71] The world was suddenly full of people "putting new gin into old bottles."

The number of deaths due to poisonous drink in the United States gives a fair picture of the height of the influence of doctored industrial alcohol. The peak of these deaths was during the period 1925-1929, when some forty people in every million were dying from bad liquor each year. Most of the slaughter was caused in the New York area by the sale of bootleg containing wood alcohol, a denaturing substance which could blind and kill. The wet press accused the Prohibition Bureau of conspiring to poison American citizens, because the Bureau knew that at least one gallon of industrial alcohol in ten would be diverted into the human stomach. "A skull and cross-bones becomes the badge of the enforcement service," screamed the New York *World*. The Borgias had poisoned only individuals, while the government of the United States proposed "collective slaughter." Even the Venetian prisoners, according to the *World*, "never could be accused of preparing venomous doses for purposes of reform."[72] The publicity not only caused consumers to be more careful about what they drank, but made the Prohibition Bureau, despite the protests of the drys, research into the possibility of finding nontoxic, but more revolting, denaturants to put into industrial alcohol. Wayne Wheeler might say that those who drank industrial alcohol were deliberate suicides.[73] But it was a nasty truth that the very same reformers who had supported the Hepburn Pure Food and Drug Bill twenty years before now wanted to put poisons into alcohol which they knew would be drunk by human beings.[74]

The third spring of the bootleg liquor, and its chief source by the close of the twenties, was moonshine — illegal spirits distilled in America for local consumption. Moonshine had been distilled in the Appalachian Mountains since the eighteenth century, and, even before prohibition, up to two thousand illicit stills a year were seized by revenue officers. But national prohibition developed the moonshining industry from small business into big business. In 1929, twelve times as many illicit stills were seized as had been seized in 1913. Methods of making high-quality liquor by speedy aging processes had made obsolete the means of both the legitimate and the illegitimate distillers of the days before the Volstead Act. By the early thirties, the huge circulation and low price of moonshine of moderate quality was a tribute to the scientific ingenuity and legal immunity of its makers. In fact, moonshining has continued to this day to be a profitable industry, with an output of up to 100,000,000 gallons of liquor a year.

In the early days of prohibition, too many small operators with too little knowledge went into the business of operating stills. Poisonous salts of copper and lead and zinc found their way into the moonshine from defective worms and coils used in the process of distillation. The greed of amateur moonshiners made them include the "heads" of the

A MOONSHINE STILL

distillation, high in aldehydes, and the "tails," shot through with fusel oil, in the final mixture. These should have been thrown away, and only the "middle run" taken. Moreover, the addition of dead rats and pieces of rotten meat to the mixture to give it a kick did not make the drink better for the health of the drinkers. The composition of the original mash, from which moonshine was distilled, was described by a Massachusetts prohibition administrator as a blend of sugar, water, yeast, and garbage. His dictum was: "The more juicy the garbage, the better the mash, and the better the 'shine.' "[75] Only when the production of moonshine became based on the growing corn-sugar industry did its basic elements become clean enough to avoid too much contamination of the drinker's stomach. The corn-sugar industry expanded from a production of 152,000,000 pounds in 1921 to 960,000,000 pounds in 1929, making the Prohibition Bureau calculate sadly that there were at least seven or eight gallons of high-proof moonshine alcohol in circulation for every gallon of diverted industrial alcohol.[76] This estimate put the production of moonshine made from corn sugar alone at a minimum of 70,000,000 gallons a year, with an absolute alcohol content of some 23,000,000 gallons.[77]

The small moonshiners were gradually taken over or pushed out by the large criminal distributors of moonshine. These distributors either ran large distilleries of their own (more than three thousand distilleries costing up to $50,000 each were captured in 1929) or else farmed out their corn sugar to hordes of home "alky cookers" in the tenements of the large cities. Corn sugar and yeast would be supplied to the alky cooker in Chicago at a cost of fifty cents a gallon. He would sell his distilled moonshine to the distributor at two dollars a gallon. The distributor would bottle it, and retail it to the speak-easy owner at six dollars a gallon.* The speak-easy owner would then charge twenty-five cents for each drink, making some forty dollars on the original gallon.[78] Local brands of moonshine had names that testified to their kick — Panther and Goat Whisky, Jackass Brandy, White Mule, White and Jersey Lightning, Yack Yack Bourbon, Soda Pop Moon, Straightsville Stuff. The extent of the moonshine industry was so great that the Wickersham Commission had to confess:

> . . . the improved methods, the perfection of organization, the ease of production, the cheapness and easy accessibility of materials, the abundance of localities where such plants can be operated with a minimum risk of discovery, the ease with which they may be concealed, and the huge profits involved, have enabled this business to become established to an extent which makes it very difficult to put to an end.[79]

Ten years of prohibition were calculated to have increased the consumption of spirits from all sources in America by one-tenth, when compared to the legal drinking days before the Great War.[80]

Not all drinkers of moonshine bought the final product directly from the bootleggers. A sophisticated and economical group of Americans preferred to "mix their own poison." They bought raw alcohol directly from the alky cookers or bootleggers or druggists. They then mixed the alcohol in their own bathtubs with quantities of glycerine and oil of juniper, according to individual taste. It was this mixture, which was known as "bathtub gin," that did much to ruin the digestion of the American middle classes. The mixture was served with quantities of ginger ale to hide the flavor, although nothing could disguise the crawling horrors of the aftereffects.

The moment that the Prohibition Bureau admitted that a major source of supply was homemade moonshine in some form or another, it

---

* Dr. Bundesen, Public Health Commissioner of Chicago, gave an exciting description of the alky cooker and his customer. For them, speed was everything. "Their apparatus is makeshift. Their surroundings are filthy. Their processes are hurried. Their materials are the cheapest. They themselves are usually novices. They constantly face the danger of detection and that fact alone would render them desperate if they were not by nature desperate men."

BATHTUB GIN, CAGNEY STYLE

was an admission that prohibition could never be enforced. Thus the spokesmen of the drys blinded their eyes to the truth for a decade. In 1923, Roy Haynes wrote, "Home-brew, the last source of supply, is out of fashion. . . . Synthetic gin is following the same course."[81] By 1929, Mabel Walker Willebrandt was repeating, "The still problem is a comparatively unimportant phase of lawlessness at the present time."[82] This was not the truth. For the truth was that, if the truth were admitted, the Prohibition Bureau could do nothing about it. Moonshine was the source with which the Prohibition Bureau was least equipped to deal.[83] Indeed, the Bureau did not attempt to deal with it. When a hundred pounds of corn sugar cost five dollars and a portable one-gallon still cost seven dollars, when the libraries of America kept a special shelf of dog-eared books on how to make liquor in the home, when the government itself issued *Farmers' Bulletins* on the methods of making alcohol, when Senator Reed could circulate in print his own recipes for making pumpkin gin and applejack, when constitutional amendments prevented the search of private homes, the attempt to stop people from making their own liquor and selling it on a small scale was impossible. The only just comment was a verse by John Judge, Jr., in his *Noble Experiments:*

There's gold in them there mountains,
There's gold in them there hills;
The natives there are getting it
By operating stills.[84]

The fourth major spring of booze was beer. The manufacture of legal near-beer involved the manufacture of real beer, which was then deprived of most of its alcoholic content. Many breweries were bought up by gangsters and run openly in defiance of the law. Other breweries fulfilled the letter of the law in making near-beer, and then sent supplies of the alcohol removed in the manufacturing process along with the product, so that the seller could "spike" the liquid back to its previous condition. Nearly one billion gallons of near-beer were manufactured during the first five years of prohibition, although the production of near-beer by 1925 was less than one-tenth of the production of beer in 1914. The problem of the Prohibition Bureau was to see that this output of near-beer was free from alcohol and was the only approximation to beer on the market. It failed in both tasks. By 1921, the first hopeful advertisements of near-beers, such as Kreuger's Special — "brewed and aged and fermented in the famous Kreuger way, to give it all the old-time tang, snap and incomparable flavor" — and Feigenspan's Private Seal — "mellow and tasty as ever" — had given way to a protest by Anheuser-Busch, called *The Penalty of Law Obedience.* The big brewing company pointed out that prohibition had made valueless a plant worth $40,000,000; the company had spent another $18,000,000 in converting the plant to make a near-beer called Bevo; and now they could not sell their near-beer because of the huge and unchecked competition of bootleggers selling real beer. The pamphlet complained, "Those who are obeying the law are being ground to pieces by its very operation, while those who are violating the law are reaping unheard-of rewards. Every rule of justice has been reversed. Every tradition and principle of our Government has been overturned."[85] But the protest was of no use. In the main, the production of legal near-beer from the old breweries reached a maximum of one-third of its former volume, and a minimum of one-fiftieth. Only two major breweries managed to equal or increase their production of near-beer over their past output of beer.[86]

As the increased production of corn sugar was evidence of the amount of moonshining in America, so the increased production of wort and malt syrup showed up the popular practice of illicit brewing. Wort is cooled, boiled mash from which beer is made. With the mere addition of yeast, beer can be manufactured from wort. The process of making beer from malt syrup is a little more complicated, and involves boiling. Nevertheless, the legal production of both of these non-alcoholic substances, whose chief use was in the manufacture of beer, sprang up to unrivaled heights during prohibition, increasing over six times during the space of seven years.[87] The production of hops in the United States also continued to flourish; 15,000,000 pounds of hops were sold in 1928, enough to produce some 20,000,000 barrels of beer, according to the estimate of the Association Against the Prohibition Amendment.[88] The suggested figures for the manufacture of home-brew in 1929, given by the Prohibition Bureau, are just under 700,000,-000 gallons of beer, or about a third of the quantity consumed in 1914.[89] These estimates are confirmed by other reliable figures.[90]

The final major spring of bootleg was the making of wine and cider in the home. In 1920, many owners of vineyards in California had pulled up their vines, expecting financial ruin; one of them had even committed suicide. But the first six years of national prohibition brought unparalleled prosperity to the California grape growers. Shipments of grapes, wine and table and raisin, to all parts of America more than doubled. The salvation of the California grape industry was in the notorious Section 29 of the Volstead Act, which permitted the making in the home of fermented fruit juices. The section was inserted, origi-nally, to save the vinegar industry and the hard cider of the American farmers; it was now used to save the wine of the immigrants. The Cali-fornia grape growers, who had often supported the drys against the local brewers and distillers and saloons in a vain effort to enlist dry support for their native industry, now found themselves saved by the dry law. They even produced a processed "grape jelly" called Vine-Glo for those who were too lazy to make their own wine. When water was added to Vine-Glo, it would make a potent wine within sixty days. It was remarkable that both Mabel Walker Willebrandt, after she had given up her job as Assistant Attorney General, and the Anti-Saloon League state superintendent supported this product, until the United States government threatened to prosecute its makers. Mrs. Wille-brandt even persuaded the government to advance $20,000,000 to the grape growers who had ruined themselves by planting too many grapes for the prohibition market. And the legal production of "wine tonics" of high alcoholic content and low medical value continued un-til repeal.[91] As a wet colonel remarked, "Andrew Volstead should be regarded as one of the patron saints of the San Joaquin Valley."[92]

Most of the California wine-grapes went to the immigrant popula-tions in New York City, Chicago, Boston, Philadelphia, and Pittsburgh. The Bureau of Prohibition calculated that, by 1930, more than a hun-dred million gallons of wine were being made in private homes each year.[93] The consumption of wine in America probably rose by two-thirds in the ten years of prohibition.[94] No figure was ever given for the production of hard cider on the farms, since rural virtue was not capable of being assessed by statistics, nor even by guesses. But the home production of wine and cider reached a huge volume and was the one branch of the bootleg trade which remained in the hands of small businessmen. Roy Haynes might characterize the big or little bootlegger as "a man constantly haunted with fear of apprehension and with a veritable Damoclean sword hanging by a thread over his head"; but, in fact, small makers of wine were rarely prosecuted.[95] The production of wine for friends and neighbors and occasional buyers was considered a respectable way of adding to the family income.

A typical case of the small bootlegger was Jennie Justo, the "queen of bootleggers" in Madison, Wisconsin.[96] She paid her way through the university there by bootlegging wine from the local Italian quarter. She drifted into the profession casually, after two journalists had asked her if she could sell them a gallon of wine each week end from her uncle's drugstore. In the end, she set up a speak-easy herself for the university students; she now claims that it was as safe and easy to run as her present tavern in Madison. She did spend six months in the Milwaukee House of Correction for bootlegging, but it was a "nice rest anyways." To her, the whole episode was a respectable way of making a living and of fulfilling a community need. The only villains in the piece were the federal officials, who trapped her by claiming to be friends of her brother.[97]

There were many such cases among the small peddlers of bootleg and small makers of wine. And there were few means of proceeding against them. "We never would get anywhere by arresting distributors," General Andrews conceded, "because the brother or uncle of the man that is arrested takes it up and goes right on."[98] Although the spectacle of immigrants making and selling and drinking their wine drove the drys to paroxysms of fury, so that they recommended the deportation of alien violators of the Volstead Act, nothing much could be done to stop the practice.[99] Too many people were making too much liquor at home in a society which resented police invasion of privacy. The Wickersham Commission conceded as much:

> Necessity seems to compel the virtual abandonment of efforts for effective enforcement at this point, but it must be recognized that this is done at the price of nullification to that extent. Law here bows to actualities, and the purpose of the law needs must be accomplished by less direct means. An enlightened and vigorous, but now long neglected, campaign of education must constitute those means.[100]

But it was too late to start the campaign of education. In the opinion of Senator Reed, brewing and wine making had returned to their place in the home as domestic arts. "The rathskeller is merged with the family coal-celler. The secrets of the hofbrau have been handed over to the hausfrau."[101] Once a wide knowledge of how to make passable hard liquor and beer and wine was widely disseminated across America, and once a depression had made all sources of income desirable, nothing could stop the flood of homemade alcohol from swamping the nation.

Even the virtuous countryside pushed itself onto the side of the bootleggers, since its income from agricultural products had halved in the decade. A man who paddled a canoe from the headwaters of the Mississippi River to its mouth wrote that the scent of mash had assailed his nostrils from Lake Itaska to the dock at New Orleans.[102] The making of alcohol flourished everywhere because it was easy to make. As the executive secretary of the Boston Trade Union Club testified, the process was simple:

> You can take ordinary prunes, raisins, or grapes. You do not have to have hops or malt. You can take ordinary chicken corn, ordinary wheat, ordinary barley, and simplify that with a certain process of cooking and fermentation, and within 24 hours you can have a fair concoction that will give you a kick. That is all there is in alcohol, is a kick.[103]

The making and consumption of alcohol in all its various forms led to some tragedies. Admissions to hospitals showed that alcoholics drank corn whisky mixed with Veronal or aspirin, bad home-brew, various sorts of industrial alcohol including radiator and rubbing alcohol, bay rum, hair tonics, varnish mixtures, and canned heat or smoke.[104] Some of these mixtures had been drunk by poor men before prohibition, but more were drunk afterwards, because the price of good liquor was beyond the means of low-paid workers. In 1928, a doctor claimed that the net dividend of national prohibition was a casualty list in that year which would "outstrip the toll of the War."[105] This statement was an exaggeration; but it was true that the rates of death from alcoholism approached the rates of the days before the First World War, and that some of the deaths, caused by wood alcohol or Jamaica ginger, took horrible forms.

A plague of wood alcohol killed off twenty-five men in three days in October, 1928, in New York City. Even more horrible was the plague of jakitis, jakefoot, jake paralysis, or ginger-foot that swept the Southwestern states in 1930. This disease was caught by drinking Jamaica ginger with its high alcoholic content. Its victims were easily recognizable. "They lumber along clumsily, because crutches are new to them; they bend far forwards on their crutches as they walk, because they do not dare to trust their weight on paralyzed toes and insteps."[106] The Prohibition Bureau estimated that there were 8000 cases of jakitis in Mississippi, 1000 each in Kentucky and Louisiana, 800 in Tennessee, 400 in Georgia, and several hundred more in Kansas, Massachusetts, Rhode Island, and Connecticut. In all, Dr. Doran estimated there were 15,000 cases of jake paralysis in the country, particularly in the slum areas of dry states, such as Kansas, and in the South, where efficient law enforcement made rotten liquor the only available source of alcohol for poor people.

The springs of bootleg could not be dried up while alcohol was so easy and so profitable to make. The New York *World* expressed this point of view in a charming parody of a popular song, which summed up the situation of millions of seekers after solace and income in the depression:

> *Mother makes brandy from cherries;*
> *Pop distills whisky and gin;*
> *Sister sells wine from the grapes on our vine —*
> *Good grief, how the money rolls in!*[107]

THE LEGAL GAP

BETWEEN THE arrest of the suspected bootlegger and his conviction, there were many ways of escape. The first loophole was the United States Commissioner. He issued search warrants and dismissed evidence obtained through improper search and seizure. Arrested bootleggers were brought before him for a preliminary hearing, and it was up to him to decide whether the case warranted a grand jury trial or not. He could put off trial of a particular case for month after month, while the bootlegger continued with his operations. He could refuse to believe the testimony of the prohibition agents, and dismiss the case. One United States Attorney in New York testified that the Commissioner there dismissed nine liquor cases out of ten, or fifty thousand cases a year, to keep the courts moderately free.[108] Many commissioners were appointees of state political machines and treated their cases in the interests of their local machine. In the most flagrant instances, the commissioners would warn a small clique of attorneys when search warrants were issued; these attorneys would, in turn, warn the bootleggers, so that the prohibition agents would find on their raids "only soft drinks and church music."[109] Mrs. Willebrandt wrote that a great part of her time as Assistant Attorney General was spent in prosecuting prosecutors, rather than the men they should have prosecuted.[110]

The second weak link in the chain of prosecution was the United

States District Attorney. His role was all-important in securing a conviction. As the Wickersham Commission was told, "The opportunities of a district attorney to affect the outcome of criminal cases is so great that the assumption of that responsibility without sympathy with the law to be enforced becomes a dangerous and doubtful public service." Even where the district attorneys were on the side of the dry law, the flood of prohibition cases in the federal courts forced them to allow many bad practices just to clear away the congestion. Often the offenders were persuaded to plead guilty and forego a jury trial in return for the promise of a small fine or sentence from the judge. Sometimes cases were dismissed outright for this purpose, or because of political pressure. During the preparation of cases, corrupt attorneys might make slips, which would result in the quashing of the case by the judge. Moreover, they could usually find legal grounds for securing the continuance of a case. The *Wickersham Report,* although discovering "a substantial number of thoroughly competent and wholly sincere United States district attorneys," deplored the fact that some of them showed "a marked want of a sincere spirit of public service." It regretted that the office was appointive and thus in the hands of politicians. It was also sad that the office carried a low salary. Both of these facts made the integrity of district attorneys open to temptation. For these reasons, the commission concluded, "The typical United States district attorney, the focal point and keystone of the entire Federal criminal law-enforcement structure, too often falls short of the demands and opportunities of his office."[111]

The third weak link was the jury. Complaints of the wet sympathies of juries in liquor cases were legion. Where a prohibition case was of such importance that it did reach trial by jury, the jury often returned a verdict of "not guilty," despite overwhelming proofs of guilt. J. J. Britt, on the legal staff of the Prohibition Bureau, said that it was very difficult in New York or Pennsylvania "to get a verdict of any great consequence in either civil or criminal cases relating to prohibition matters."[112] In one trial in Virginia, a member of the jury dropped a half pint of liquor in court; no action was taken, and the jury as a whole found the defendant, a bootlegging Negress, guilty.[113] On another occasion, a jury in San Francisco was itself put on trial for drinking up the evidence in a liquor case.[114] Indeed, the notorious difficulty of getting dry verdicts from urban juries gave wet defendants a strong bargaining position with the district attorney; their pleas of "guilty" in return for the promise of a small fine were as much a favor to him as to them. The jury trial, instituted to protect justice, ended by becoming a method of bypassing justice.

The fourth door of escape was the judge himself. There were certain famed judges in America whose sentences on bootleggers were so light that they approached invisibility. The leniency of some judges to violators of the dry law provoked a famous outburst from Clarence True Wilson. According to him, the worst anarchists in America were not bootleggers — they were judges. He even claimed that he could call a roll of judges, "whose names would look like a criminals' list."[115] Although he exaggerated, it is true that the American bench beneath the Supreme Court showed a surprising leniency to offenders against the Volstead Act, until the Hoover regime. Hoover retired eighteen district attorneys and two federal judges, and made good appointments. Only then was a determined and hopeless attempt made to enforce the dry laws.

The condition of the American judiciary in the twenties was such that there was no hope of enforcing the Volstead Act. "We do not begin to arrest all that are guilty, Mr. Senator," General Andrews said to Reed, of Missouri, in 1926; "we can not."[116] The fault was in the courts and the prisons as much as in the police. Since the beginning of the century, the number of cases tried in federal courts had been rapidly increasing. With the passage of the Mann and the National Motor Vehicle Theft and the Narcotics Acts, bringing increased legal responsibilities to the federal authorities, the number of cases terminated in the federal courts increased from 15,371 in 1910 to 34,230 in 1920, of which 5095 were prohibition cases.[117] But then the prohibition cases increased phenomenally, and with them increased the load on the already burdened courts. By 1928, there were 58,429 prohibition cases concluded in the federal courts; two cases out of every three were terminated there. By 1932, the number of prohibition cases had risen to a maximum of 70,252.[118] The machinery of justice was inadequate to cope with this volume of business, especially as insufficient new judgeships were created to share the load.[119]

Faced with an impossible situation, the federal courts fell back on the expedient of "bargain days." On these days, a vast proportion of the backlog of prohibition cases was cleared off the records by quick pleas of "guilty" from the defendants, in return for low fines or short jail sentences. Nine out of ten convictions under the Volstead Act were obtained in "bargain days." Until 1930, not more than one out of three convictions in federal courts resulted in any form of jail sentence, and the average fine was low, between $100 and $150.[120] This method of dispensing justice destroyed the high reputation which the federal courts had enjoyed before prohibition. As the Wickersham Commission reported:

Formerly these tribunals were of exceptional dignity, and the efficiency and dispatch of their criminal business commanded wholesome fear and respect. The professional criminal, who sometimes had scanty respect for the state tribunals, was careful so to conduct himself as not to come within the jurisdiction of the federal courts. The effect of the huge volume of liquor prosecutions, which has come to these courts under prohibition, has injured their dignity, impaired their efficiency, and endangered the wholesome respect for them which once obtained. Instead of being impressive tribunals of superior jurisdiction, they have had to do the work of police courts and that work has been chiefly in the public eye.

The commission continued its indictment of the bad effects of prohibition on the federal courts. Prosecutors, state and federal, had been appointed and judged for their conduct in prohibition cases alone. Judges, too, had been considered in this light. The civil business of the courts had been delayed, while even "bargain days" could not clear up the backlog of all the prosecutions under the dry law. Sometimes, cases lingered on beyond the three years allowed for their prosecution under the statute of limitations. Moreover, the Jones Act of 1929 had allowed "gross inequalities of sentence." The very cases prosecuted in the courts included far too many small violators of the dry law, and far too few large ones.[121] Although the Wickersham Commission disagreed on much, it did agree on one thing, that the effects of prohibition on the actual workings of the law were deplorable.

But if the Volstead Act placed a severe strain on the courts of America, it nearly burst the federal prisons. In 1916, there were five federal prisons and penitentiaries; there were still five in 1929, although President Hoover began to build more jails to accommodate the convicted. In 1920, those prisoners who were serving long-term sentences in federal prisons numbered just over five thousand; by 1930, they numbered more than twelve thousand, of whom more than four thousand had been sentenced for violating the liquor laws.[122] The five prisons and penitentiaries were desperately overcrowded, since they had been built to accommodate a maximum of seven thousand prisoners. Indeed, the federal authorities were forced to board out most of their prisoners in state and county jails, for they could not accommodate them in their institutions.

In his Inaugural address, President Herbert Hoover promised the reform, the reorganization, and the strengthening of the whole judicial and enforcement system in the United States. For, in his opinion, "rigid and expeditious justice is the first safeguard of freedom, the basis of all ordered liberty, the vital force of progress."[123] And Hoover did what he said he would do. He reformed judicial procedure, the

From New York *Evening World*

STILL PACKING THEM IN

bankruptcy laws, the Federal Bureau of Investigation, and the kidnap-
ing laws, and started to build Alcatraz and five other prisons. He re-
organized, consolidated, and increased the efficiency of the Prohibition
Bureau. He appointed the Wickersham Commission, which, despite its
sloth and evasiveness, produced a mass of absorbing information about
law enforcement in America and dealt the deathblow to prohibition. In
fact, in the legal sense, Hoover was probably one of the best Presi-

dents ever to sit in the White House. It was unfortunate that the mouths and the pockets of the American people were becoming empty while Hoover was filling their jails.

The drys insisted on a prohibition law which could not be enforced by their policemen and prosecutors and judges. The failure of this enforcement was, to the wets, a proof of the failure of the law. In fact, such a revolutionary theory as national prohibition could never have been enforced without a revolution in criminal procedure. Yet this second revolution was not supported by the drys, for they saw themselves as the defenders of the ancient customs and liberties of America. Their revolution was to restore the myth of the good old days, with its emphasis on the American virtues of law and order.

But a law can only be enforced in a democracy when the majority of the people support that law. And the majority of the people did not support the Volstead Act. When an attempt at enforcement was made by Hoover, it was already too late. No general legal reform could satisfy a people angered by a particular law. James J. Forrester, who investigated the coal-mining regions of Pennsylvania for the Wickersham Commission, found everywhere a "strong and bitter resentment" against national prohibition among workingmen and their leaders.

> Very few of them believe in, or have any respect for, the prohibition laws and do not hesitate to say so. They consider these laws discriminatory against and unjust to them and therefore have no compunction in violating them. If their attention is called to the fact that these acts are the laws of the country and just as binding on the people as any other laws and that violation of them is criminal, they almost invariably come back with the assertion that they do not believe in the laws; that they are harmful to themselves and their families; that they are discriminatory against the working people and the so-called middle classes, and that they, therefore, resent being classed as criminals. But they do admit that their violation has a tendency to teach the older and growing children a disrespect for other laws and is breeding conditions of crime.[124]

The price that the drys paid for the partial prohibition of liquor was the cheapening of all the laws of the land, and of all the procedures of justice.

THE DEFENDERS OF THE LAW

THE EIGHTEENTH Amendment brought new legal problems to the judges of America. For it made great changes in legal precedent.

> It withdrew power from the states and from the people. It did not merely grant power but attempted to fix an implacable policy. It vastly

increased the hitherto limited police power of Congress. It vastly curtailed the police power of the states. Unlike most other constitutional prohibitions it was directed not to the national or the state governments but to individuals. It was a sumptuary fiat quite different from anything else found in the constitution.[125]

It also put judges in the difficult position of trying to dovetail a constitutional amendment with other contradictory and previous amendments. If the Eighteenth Amendment strained the enforcement and judicial machinery of the United States, it tested to the breaking point the very interpretation of the law itself.

The Supreme Court was the ultimate judge of the most controversial prohibition cases. After its famous decisions which upheld the legality of the Webb-Kenyon Act, the Eighteenth Amendment, and the Volstead Act, it was committed to make workable in law the enforcement of an unpopular measure. Although the majority of the Supreme Court Judges were dry in their sympathies, there were ticklish problems in aligning dry laws with the liberties guaranteed to citizens under the Constitution. The chief problems arose over search and seizure, trial by jury, forfeiture of property, double jeopardy, and methods of enforcement.

The Fourth Amendment to the Constitution protected American citizens against unreasonable search and seizure of their persons, papers, houses, and possessions. In the first six months of national prohibition, more than seven hundred cases involving search and seizure procedures were reported in the *American Law Digest;* nearly six hundred of these cases involved violations of the Volstead Act. Although several states allowed search and seizure on the merest suspicion or sense of smell of officers of the law, there was doubt about the extent to which the Supreme Court of the United States would allow questionable practices in collecting evidence. Yet, obviously, the prohibition agents could not obtain a search warrant to investigate every car suspected of carrying bootleg liquor. In 1924, the Supreme Court laid down in the case of *Carroll v. United States* that vehicles of transportation might be searched when "the seizing officer shall have reasonable or probable cause."[126] Although this ruling was difficult to interpret, it did make the business of enforcement easier. Even so, dry officers without a search warrant were still excluded from private homes, though they could see through the windows a distillery running at full blast.[127]

The lengthy process of trial by jury would have made the enforcement of prohibition impossible, for there were too many offenders. On the other hand, American citizens were assured of trial by jury for federal offenses, if they so wished. Although the convinced prohibitionist wanted to see the abolition of trial by jury in liquor cases, he did not get what he wanted by law, although he was largely successful by judicial practice. The new institution of "bargain days" in prohibition cases meant that the accused person was glad to escape the publicity of a jury trial and the possibility of a jail sentence in return for a plea of guilty and a small fine. Moreover, the practice of padlocking for one year by legal injunction any place where intoxicating liquor was "manufactured, sold, kept or bartered" had the effect of depriving the owners of these places of a jury trial. Although prohibition agents secured a padlocking injunction in only one out of three cases, the method proved so speedy and effective that agents padlocked 4471 places in 1925, including a California redwood tree which was concealing a still.[128] Padlocking could result in great financial loss to property owners, if the padlocked premises were restaurants or hotels, and could penalize innocent people who did not know that their tenants were using their property illegally. Although padlocking was one of the most effective deterrents in the armory of the drys, it did seem to conflict with the legal rights of American citizens. As one legal expert wrote, "Like Rome, and Sparta and Carthage, America in liquor cases is becoming in large measure a 'stranger to the trial by jury.' "[129]

Although the claims of the brewers and distillers to compensation for the effective forfeiture of their property under the National Prohibition Act were not upheld, the owners of the pre-Volstead liquor and of rumrunning automobiles could claim the restoration of their seized property.[130] Ownership of liquor bought before 1920 for private consumption was legal throughout prohibition. This liquor could not be seized under federal law. Moreover, even though an automobile was discovered by prohibition agents to be carrying bootleg liquor, it could not be seized under the terms of the Volstead Act if the owner did not know of its illegal use. Dry agents bypassed this difficulty, however, by securing forfeiture of seized vehicles under the revenue law before proceeding against the driver of the car by criminal prosecution. In addition, under some state laws, rumrunning automobiles and pre-Volstead liquor could be seized without benefit of trial by jury.[131] Prohibition caused many surprising lapses in the habitual respect of Americans for property rights.

Another anomaly in American law publicized by the Eighteenth Amendment was the decision of the Supreme Court in favor of double jeopardy. The Fifth Amendment contained a clause, "nor shall any person be subject for the same offence to be twice put in jeopardy of life or limb." Yet, in 1922, the Supreme Court, in the case of *United States v. Lanza*, ruled that a man could be tried and convicted twice

DE FACTO ENFORCEMENT

for the same crime — once by the state government and once by the federal government. Since prohibition cases involved two sovereignties, "an act denounced as a crime by both national and state sovereignties is an offense against the peace and dignity of both and may be punished by each."[132] Although this decision was justified in terms of past decisions of the Supreme Court, occasions for double jeopardy had been few and were now, under national prohibition, made many. Even if this new opportunity to prosecute people twice for the same offense was little used, it was employed in special cases.[133] And these special cases added to the notoriety of prohibition.

But the most famous of the prohibition cases was, perhaps, *Olmstead v. United States*. Roy Olmstead, a former police lieutenant in Seattle, Washington, ran a large liquor-smuggling ring, which did business worth some two million dollars a year. He and his fellow conspirators were indicted upon evidence obtained by tapping their telephone wires. Although the Supreme Court upheld the government, it was by a majority of five to four. In dissenting, Justice Brandeis wrote a famous decision, saying that "discovery and invention have made it possible for the Government, by means far more effective than stretching upon the rack, to obtain disclosure in court of what is whispered in the closet." Justice Holmes sadly referred to the whole thing as "such a dirty business." Ten years later, the Supreme Court reversed the decision under the Federal Communications Act of 1934. It feared the increased control of the government over the lives of private citizens through the mass media, and honored the eloquent plea of Brandeis for "the right to be let alone — the most comprehensive of rights and the right most valued by civilized men."[134]

There were many international cases fought in the courts over the search and seizure of rumrunners in international waters. The most celebrated of these was the sinking of the Canadian ship *I'm Alone* by an American Coast Guard cutter. The cutter had pursued the *I'm Alone* from American territorial waters to a distance of some two hundred miles off the American coast, before it finally sunk the smuggler. The American case rested on the fact that the cutter had remained continuously in hot pursuit of the *I'm Alone;* the Canadian owners demanded compensation since their vessel was far outside territorial waters. The whole incident caused bad blood between the United States and Canada. Eventually, the United States paid compensation, and the matter was settled to the satisfaction of Canadian pride.

Prohibition caused the judges of the law to strain their interpretations of that law in an effort to reconcile the irreconcilable. The inclusion of the Eighteenth Amendment in the Constitution seemed to many to put "a hideous wart on its nose."[135] Although the judges of America were charged with mediating between new laws and old precedents, there was a limit to their powers of arbitration. The difficulties brought to the courts by prohibition stretched those powers of arbitration to their limit. And the prohibition law itself made unpopular those who had to interpret it, the supreme courts of the land. The organizers, the makers, the policemen, and the judges of the dry laws lost repute, for the law created a hatred of those whose duty was its enforcement. As the notable lawyer Elihu Root wrote after the New York Repeal Convention of 1933, "It will take a long time for our country to recover from the injury done by that great and stupid error in government."[136] It did. Many years of tradition are needed to build up respect for the law, and once the tradition is broken, it is not easily put together again.

The fact of national prohibition presented insoluble problems to the machinery of the law in the United States. Judges and prisons and policemen were few; stills and home-brewers and bootleggers were many. Yet this excess of law and lack of possible enforcement was, as Walter Lippmann noticed in 1932, endemic to the national scene. The idea of moral perfection made the American people enshrine in their Constitution ideals which they could not fulfill, and made them outlaw habits in which they rather generally indulged. By their moral fervor as lawmakers, they made a large part of the people the allies and clients of lawbreakers. And, at the same time, they insisted that the federal government which executed the laws should remain weak. The very same voters and lawmakers who made laws which would defeat the powers of a despotism were jealous to the point of absurdity about giving their own executive and judiciary any power at all. Thus the United States had "the strongest laws and the weakest government of any highly civilized people."[137] It also had the strongest criminal classes and weakest public sentiment against them of any highly civilized people.

CHAPTER **11**

The Respectable Crime

> I make my money by supplying a public demand. If I break the law, my customers, who number hundreds of the best people in Chicago, are as guilty as I am. The only difference between us is that I sell and they buy. Everybody calls me a racketeer. I call myself a business man. When I sell liquor, it's bootlegging. When my patrons serve it on a silver tray on Lake Shore Drive, it's hospitality.
>
> AL CAPONE

> O, to hell with them Sicilians.
>
> DEAN O'BANION

> Once you're in with us you're in for life.
>
> HYMIE WEISS

> The country club people will probably go on boozing until the end of time. The best prohibition can hope to accomplish is to save the poor man. It saves him by making drink too expensive for him.
>
> COLONEL PATRICK H. CALLAHAN

THE PROHIBITIONISTS thought that the sale of liquor was a social crime, that the drinking of liquor was a racial crime, and that the results of liquor were criminal actions. They quoted Havelock Ellis for their hereditary and environmental ammunition. "Alcoholism in either of the parents is one of the most fruitful causes of crime in the child."[1] They quoted Lombroso and nineteenth-century criminologists to prove that liquor was responsible for most criminal acts. The extensive researches of the Committee of Fifty on the case histories of more than thirteen thousand convicts found that liquor was a cause in 50 per cent of all crimes, the first cause in 31 per cent, and the sole cause in 16 per cent. Although these figures were exaggerated, they were the only ones available until the close of national prohibition. The reason for that exaggeration was the fact that criminals usually put the blame for their actions on liquor rather than themselves, hoping that the judge would treat them more leniently. Prohibition made such an excuse unfashionable, and a Freudian or social plea for mitigation took its place. Criminals pleaded that they had been deprived in some way by nature or by society. And the crimes once charged against liquor were now charged against the prohibitionists, who were accused of causing the rise of the national syndicates of crooks and murder gangs by making over to them all the profits of the illegal liquor trade. In the judgment of the famous criminologist, John Landesco, prohibition had enormously increased the personnel and power of organized crime. It had "opened up a new criminal occupation, with less risk of punishment, with more certainty of gain, and with less social stigma than the usual forms of crime like robbery, burglary, and larceny."[2]

Gangs and crime syndicates did not begin with prohibition. They rose to power through the saloons, gambling houses, and brothels of the nineteenth century, and through the murderous wars of labor and capital in the days of the robber barons. Al Capone inherited his empire on the South Side of Chicago as the heir of a line of vice bosses, such as Big Jim Colosimo and John Torrio. If this criminal estate was and is bequeathed frequently because of jail or sudden death or loss of nerve, it has endured longer than many American bequests.

The simultaneous coming of automobiles, Thompson machine guns, and telephones allowed successful local gangsters to extend their control over whole cities and states. To do this, they needed a steady income. This income was provided by national prohibition. In the early days of the Volstead Act, gangsters were merely the "fronts" of ordinary businessmen who owned the breweries and distilleries. They provided protection and ensured delivery of the liquor, while the businessmen had the necessary political influence to prevent interference. In the first four years of prohibition in Chicago, under the corrupt administration of William Hale Thompson, John Torrio was in partnership with a well-known brewer, Joseph Stenson, who put the stamp of Gold Coast respectability on the Torrio gang. As the Chicago *Tribune* said, Stenson was "the silk hat for the crowd." He had contacts in the federal building. He raised the money, bought the discontinued breweries, and made "the connections necessary to undisturbed brewing." He then installed a board of directors in the brewery, who would "take the fall" when there was trouble; they would even go to jail while Stenson escaped scot-free. In 1924, the profits of the Torrio-Stenson combine were estimated at fifty million dollars in four years, of which Stenson's share was twelve million dollars.[3]

A reform mayor, William Dever, however, succeeded Thompson. His policy was to prosecute the large bootleggers, not their stooges. His new chief of police raided the Sieben brewery on May 19, 1924,

and found enough evidence to indict most of the leading gangsters
and pre-Volstead brewers of Chicago. The brewers, however, had
enough influence to vanish from the indictment. Torrio and two of his
aides were convicted. He lost prestige as a result, was shot down by
rival gangsters, recovered, and emigrated to Italy, leaving his empire
in the hands of Al Capone. The old-time brewers were also scared
and left the beer business to their previous employees, the hoodlums
and killers. Only the public suffered from paying enough to satisfy
both businessmen and criminals for their liquor.

The profits of prohibition were so enormous that a pattern developed for the manufacture and sale of illicit liquor. From 1920 to 1923,
there were a host of small bootleggers and rumrunners competing for
the profits of the trade. Only those criminal gangs which were already
organized in the large cities, such as the Torrio gang in Chicago and
the Unione Siciliano, could keep an enormous slice of the cake for
themselves. The bootleg situation was similar to the American business
situation in the middle of the nineteenth century. The rise of the big
bootleggers paralleled the rise of the robber barons and trusts, with
the elimination, through terror or murder or price cutting, of all
rivals. During the five years after 1924, the big-city gang wars flourished, and the remnants of the respectable brewers and distillers, who
were still in the illegal trade, fled for their lives. In the time of the
consolidation of Capone's power in Chicago, there were between 350
and 400 murders annually in Cook County, Illinois, and an average
of 100 bombings each year. By 1929, however, a convention of major
racketeers could meet at Atlantic City, New Jersey, each with his defined territory, in which he held monopolistic power. The *condottieri*
of New York — Frank Costello, Frankie Yale, Larry Fay, Dutch
Schultz, and Owney Madden — knew their place, and relinquished
Philadelphia to Maxie Hoff, Detroit to the Purple Gang, Cincinnati
and St. Louis to the old Remus mob, Kansas City to Solly Weissman,
and the major part of Chicago to Capone. Indeed, a case could be
made for the good results of organized gangdom. The menace of the
unattached hoodlum had almost disappeared, for the police and regular gangs co-operated to eliminate him.[4] In the suppression of competition, the big gangs were a positive benefit to society.

But, on the whole, the gangs made more rotten the rotten situation
which had existed in the days of the red-light districts and old-time
saloons. In its practical effects, national prohibition transferred two
billion dollars a year from the hands of brewers, distillers, and shareholders to the hands of murderers, crooks, and illiterates. However
badly the liquor traders and shareholders misused their wealth, their
middle-class sympathies prevented their money power from spreading

From *Outlook and Independent*

UNCLE SAM'S HOME-BREW

a slimy trail of racketeering and corruption everywhere. In politics and in business, in labor unions and employers' associations, in public services and private industries, prohibition was the golden grease through which organized crime insinuated itself into a position of incredible power in the nation.

The Reed Committee of 1926 divulged some of the influence of gangsters in politics. Worse evidence was to come. In the primary elections in Chicago two years later, "pineapple" bombs were exploded at the polls, and hordes of gangsters openly intimidated voters. Although such an unwise display of force caused a public reaction and revulsion, it showed the sorry state into which the citizens of Chicago had allowed themselves to fall. They were caught between the mutual services rendered to each other by the political bosses and the gang leaders. The politicians would prevent the police force from proceeding against gamblers, panders, bootleg kings, and racketeers in return for large campaign contributions and blocks of votes on election day.[5] The *Illinois Crime Survey* of 1929 discovered that chain voters, colonized voters, and crooked election boards were recruited regularly from the ranks of organized crime.[6] Only the mass vote of the aroused middle classes of Chicago could make occasional forays of reform against the eternal tie-up between crime and politics and liquor, which was bad before and after, and at its worst during, prohibition.

There were connections between the class struggle in America and the rise of the gangsters.[7] Employers first used criminals against strikers. Hundreds of gunmen were hired through detective agencies to protect machines and scabs against armed strikers, and to assault and murder union organizers among the workers. Later, in the same way that the drys had copied the tactics of the wets and were in turn copied by them, the labor unions hired professional gangsters to attack scabs and foremen, and dynamite mills and factories. This retaliation led to the hiring of permanent private armies by large industrialists and farmers, such as the notorious coal and iron police of Pennsylvania and the thugs of the California grape growers, described in *The Grapes of Wrath.*[8]

Perhaps the most flagrant connection of big business and the prohibition gangsters was through Harry Bennett's "Ford Service Department," the largest private army in America. The ringleader of Detroit's underworld, Chester LaMare, whose bootlegging empire was estimated by federal agents to be grossing $215,000,000 a year in 1928, was a partner in a Ford sales agency and owned the fruit concession at the Ford plant at River Rouge.[9] While technically employed by the Ford Service, LaMare spent his time developing his enormous racketeering industry until he was shot down by rivals. Joe Adonis, the Brooklyn bootlegger and racketeer, was also on the Ford payroll as the exclusive trucker of Ford cars to markets on the Eastern seaboard. There were, in addition, up to eight thousand men with prison sentences in the Ford factories, whom Harry Bennett claimed, in Ford's name, to be "rehabilitating." Throughout the twenties and thirties the Ford plants remained outside the labor unions, while strikers and organizers were killed, beaten up, and threatened by Ford Service men and criminals.[10] This alliance between the biggest of businessmen and the underworld gave immunity to gangsters from prosecution for their bootlegging and immunity to businessmen in their defiance of labor unions. Both were guaranteed the profits which they set for themselves, and were insured against assault by each other. Again, only American democracy and the American people suffered.

Yet if big business was flagrantly guilty of encouraging the entry of gangsters into the business world and of protecting gangsters against legal penalties in return for their help against workingmen, the labor unions were also guilty of calling in gangsters to aid them, and of losing control of the unions themselves to the gangsters. For instance, in the war between the garment workers and garment manufacturers in New York in 1926, the unions employed Augie Orgen's gang of thugs to use against the hired mercenaries of the employers, Legs Diamond and his gang. A simultaneous plea to the underworld boss of the time, Arnold Rothstein, made him call off both gangs, for they were both under his control.[11] But his price was a cut in the profits of the industry. Similarly, in other great cities, gangsters were called in to protect labor from the gorillas hired by capital. The result was that some labor unions fell into the hands of the gangsters. Indeed, they were often forced to hire gunmen to proctect their own strikers against the local police force. The "Strong-Arm Squad" of the New York City police was particularly brutal towards strikers; in the furriers' strike, they were paid some $30,000 to beat up strikers and protect strikebreakers.[12] The president of the Cigarmakers' International Union told the Wickersham Commission that this sad state of affairs was due to prohibition.

> The police departments throughout the country where we have to conduct our work have been completely demoralized; the police departments are charging so much to permit a barrel of beer to come into a speak-easy and so much for a case of whisky. Now, when we have a strike on in some of the important cities we get the worst of it unless we pay the police officer; so he has become so accustomed to closing his eyes to the violation of the law.[13]

The gangsters, however, as they grew in numbers and power on the profits of prohibition, did not always wait to be asked to intervene by labor or management. Often, they merely "muscled in" on any trade which would pay them money for protection against themselves. This method of blackmail was called a "racket," a word which was used widely after 1927. It was defined as "any scheme by which human parasites graft themselves upon and live by the industry of others, maintaining their hold by intimidation, force, and terrorism."[14] Its methods were simple. First the gang leader chose his line of exploitation. Then he threatened all traders in his line that if they did not pay him a monthly bribe he would destroy them and their businesses. In return, he would protect the traders from any competition by other traders in the same line who were not paying the bribe. In Chicago, in the heyday of Capone, there were at least sixty active rackets flourishing in the city. For a long time, every man in Chicago who wanted his trousers pressed paid fifty cents to the racket, since gangsters controlled the cleaners' and dyers' trade. Crooks also controlled the Chicago bakers, barbers, electrical workers, garage men, shoe repairers, plumbers, garbage haulers, window cleaners, milk salesmen, confectionary dealers, and undertakers. The cost of these sixty rackets to the people of Chicago was estimated at $136,000,000 a year, while gangsters from all their illegal activities were thought to be earning $6,000,000 weekly. It was a high price to pay to murderers and petty thieves.[15]

The entry of gangsters into legitimate business was made easy by archaic restraint-of-trade laws against price fixing and labor unions. Moreover, the actual sentiments of the class struggle supported the gangster who achieved results by violence. As Landesco found out in his study of the "42" gang in Chicago, young men in the poor quarters of Chicago knew that crime, on the whole, did not pay, but "from experience they have also learned that it is the only avenue available to them."[16] The wealthy racketeer and bootlegger was, in the eyes of the Italian or the Slavic community, the American dream come true. The recent immigrants had come to America in pursuit of a golden mirage, and those among them who made fortunes by violating antipathetic laws were their first heroes and helpers. They were the "successes of the neighborhood."[17] The prestige and power of the Unione Siciliano gave all poverty-stricken Sicilians a hope in the future and a certain national pride against an America which discriminated against them. Only those few Sicilians who had respectable jobs in middle-class professions hated the reputation which the Unione gave to the Sicilian people. The plea of such priests as Father Louis Giambastiani against the internecine slaughter of the Sicilian gangs was rare in a community which associated wealth and power with criminal action.

The chief sources of bootleg liquor in all major cities by the close of prohibition were to be found in the tenements, in the Little Italys and Little Bohemias of the slums. There, the tenement dwellers were organized by the gangsters into an army of alky cookers and booze-runners. The accusation of the drys that most of the large bootleggers were of foreign extraction was correct; but the contention of the wets that most of the hard-liquor drinkers, who kept the bootleggers in business, were of old American stock was also correct. Indeed, the patronage of the new America by the old was one of the first efforts made by the old America to look after the welfare of the new. Although the prohibition laws only proceeded against the sellers and manufacturers of bootleg, not the buyers, with the consequence that the foreign-born landed in jail more frequently than their patrons, Americans of an older vintage were responsible for keeping the bootleg trade in such a healthy financial state. And even though a higher percentage of foreign-born Americans were sentenced for drunkenness and violation of liquor laws and neglect of their families, the virtue of the native-born could hardly be maintained on the basis of crime figures. For a higher percentage of native white Americans violated narcotic laws, and the laws against fraud, forgery, robbery, adultery, and rape.[18]

If the sympathy of the poor was on the side of the bootlegger and criminal, for traditional Mediterranean reasons as well as for reasons of poverty, so was much of the sympathy of the rich. The underside of the café society which grew up in the twenties was simply a service trade in vice.[19] In the sense that respectable people patronized criminals, America had the criminals it deserved.[20] Matthew Woll spoke for a host of law-abiding people before the Wickersham Commission, when he said of the racketeers:

> Today there is not any feeling of resentment against them, because they are looked upon as being part of a trade to satisfy a social want. There is not a feeling of prosecution on behalf of the law even for the most vicious crime committed. It is all a reflection on the social mind. We seek by law to tell the people you can not do so and so, when the people are not in that frame of mind. . . . They want their liquor. They do not care what chances the other fellow takes so long as they don't take the chance.[21]

The concept of the honest bootlegger, making a living out of a trade just as other people did, was a common rationalization of respectable men to excuse their patronage of criminals. This attitude even extended to their children, who voted in one survey that the bootlegger took first place in community activities.[22]

The fact of making a living was more sacred to many Americans than life itself.[23] The whole of American society was too close to the violence of the frontier and the city jungle to worry unduly over the vendettas of gangsters. Where the law was inefficient and graft-ridden

Brown Brothers Photographers
AL CAPONE

(no legal punishment was given for even one of the 130 gang murders in Chicago between 1926 and 1927), respectable people were content to let criminals slay their own. In the belief in rough justice rather than the rotten enforcement of the law, in the dislike of informing on men who were fulfilling a public service in the eyes of most city dwellers, the prohibition racketeers flourished unchecked, until they began to be damned by bad publicity.

The criminals themselves were encouraged by the patronage of the respectable to think that they were equally good members of society. Al Capone himself asked, "What's Al Capone done, then? He's supplied a legitimate demand. Some call it bootlegging. Some call it racketeering. I call it a business. They say I violate the prohibition law. Who doesn't?"[24] The fact that he ordered murders seemed to him merely a method of business organization in criminal circles; it was certainly true that the magnates of early American big business had also condoned murders by their private police. In fact, Capone suffered under a delusion of conspiracy against him as severe as that of the drys. He protested:

> I don't interfere with big business. None of the big business guys can say I ever took a dollar from 'em. Why, I done a favor for one of

the big newspapers in the country when they was up against it. Broke a strike for 'em. And what do I get for doing 'em a favor? Here they've been ever since, clamped on my back. I only want to do business, you understand, with my own class. Why can't they let me alone? I don't interfere with them any. Get me? I don't interfere with their racket. They should let my racket be.

In Capone's terms, he dealt as fairly with the poor and the drinkers as big business dealt with the rich and the consumers. Indeed, Capone even had the gall to say, "Prohibition has made nothing but trouble — trouble for all of us. Worst thing ever hit the country. Why, I tried to get into legitimate business two or three times, but they won't stand for it."[25] At the time of this remark, Capone was making between $60,000,000 and $100,000,000 a year from the sale of beer alone.

But there was a reaction in Chicago and in the nation against the excesses of the gangsters, as there was a reaction against the excesses of the drys. The famous killing of Dean O'Banion in his flower shop might be forgiven as a feud between rival *condottieri*. But the murders of Assistant State Attorney William H. McSwiggin, in Capone's headquarters at Cicero, and of a crime reporter four years later aroused public opinion. Groups of citizens and lawyers were formed to arm themselves against gangsters and secure federal action; previously, the only vigilante group in Chicago had been a band of wealthy men who had organized themselves in 1919 to defend their liquor cellars against thieves.[26] The final killing of seven hoodlums in a garage on St. Valentine's Day, 1929, was the end of Chicago's easy acceptance of gang rule. The massacre was, in the famous apocryphal remark, "lousy public relations." Capone himself was committed to jail for eleven years in 1931 for income tax evasion. His attorneys offered the Bureau of Internal Revenue a bribe of $4,000,000, which was refused.[27] The *New Republic* noted that Bishop James Cannon, Jr., was on trial at the same time. "Justice, in clutching at these two culprits at once, has not shown itself wanting in the sense of the fitness of things." For "the one makes blue laws; the other arises to undo them."[28]

The prominence of gangsters in American life did nothing to help the dry cause. The only defense of the drys was that gangsters were powerful long before prohibition, on the profits of the saloons and brothels. The wets countered by pointing out that prohibition had fattened the profits of gangsters to an unparalleled extent. Moreover, their new money power purchased them immunity from all forms of legal punishment for any crime which they committed. The *Illinois Crime Survey* showed that criminals engaged in bootlegging did not give up other forms of crime. They continued to practice their pre-

Volstead lines of knavery, but, on account of the new prestige and power of the gang, members of gangs tended to secure immunity from punishment not only for bootlegging, but for these other crimes as well.[29] The immunity of the gangsters from prosecution and the contemporary killing of certain innocents by employees of the Prohibition Bureau gave the wets a strong propaganda case. In the words of Senator Edwards, of New Jersey, "It is noticeable that two kinds of people have been killed by the Prohibition agents: the poor and the innocent. The Chicago gunmen who not only broke the Eighteenth Amendment but who have killed right and left have scarcely been molested. They were guilty *and* rich."[30]

The history of prohibition and crime shows how the tolerance exercised towards criminals by respectable citizens, labor, and capital allowed gangsters to take over local governments, as Capone did the government of the small town of Cicero, and even state governments. The loot of prohibition was sufficient to buy judges, state attorneys, and whole police forces. It enabled the gangsters to spread their influence into new areas of legitimate business. They were allowed to terrorize citizens so much that no Chicago jury would return a verdict of murder against a gunman, because of fear. Hymie Weiss, after he was gunned down by the Capone gang, was found to be carrying the full lists of the jury and the witnesses for the prosecution in the proposed murder trial of his fellow criminal, Joe Saltis. In the words of John Stege, deputy commissioner of the Chicago police, a man could "figure out gangdom's murders and attempted murders with a pencil and paper, but never with a judge and jury."[31] It was tragic that the fantastic opportunities for corruption and intimidation in the prohibition era made a mockery of all the laws of America, which had been designed to protect the liberty of the individual and were perverted to license the anarchy of gangsters.

SPEAK-EASY AND WORSE

As PROHIBITION brought respectability to the criminal, so the speakeasy brought respectability to the saloon. The heyday of the speakeasy was during the twenties, when it flourished like the hydra. Chop off one of its heads, and two grew in its place. It displaced the old restaurants and cabaret entertainments, and offered in their place night-club acts, liquor, and indifferent food at huge prices. In 1929, the police commissioner of New York City estimated that there were 32,000 speak-easies in the metropolis, double the number of saloons and blind pigs of the old days.[32] The Police Department dropped this figure to 9000 speak-easies in 1933, the worst year of the depression

Brown Brothers Photographers

WET EXCHANGE

and the last year of national prohibition.[33] A moderate calculation of the whole number of speak-easies in the United States at this time put the number at 219,000, a little less than the number of saloons and blind pigs on the eve of the Eighteenth Amendment.[34] If the speak-easy was spawned by prohibition and the boom, it was doomed by repeal and the slump. Texas Guinan, the night-club queen of the twenties, used to give three cheers for prohibition and demand, "Where the hell would I be without prohibition?" And the sucker was right who replied, "Nowhere."

The usual speak-easy was a very different place from the old saloon. For a corner location, the speak-easy substituted a back room, a basement, or a "first-floor flat."[35] Swinging doors were replaced by locked doors containing a peephole. Carpets or bare boards took the floor from sawdust. The mirror behind the bar, the barkeeper's third eye, remained in place; but there was no free lunch. Drink prices went up from two to ten times, depending on supplies and law enforcement. The quality of spirits in the expensive speak-easies reached the pre-Volstead level after the first two years of adulterated hell. Beer, however, declined in quality and wine even more so.

The speak-easy brought some benefits, once it had become a national institution. It discouraged the patronage of down-and-outs, who might talk to honest policemen but could not pay enough to help

bribe dishonest policemen. It put an end to the saloon custom of treating to drinks; Jack London, in *John Barleycorn,* tells of the fatal effects
of this custom on nineteen sailors who were made the drunken victims
of land sharks by treating their friends and being treated in return
before they could in honor leave for their homes.[36] Also, the custom
of allowing drinkers to pour their own whisky out of the traditional
black bottle was superseded by the measured amount served in a glass.
Bootleg liquor was too expensive to allow barflies to administer their
own quantity of poison.

But, equally, the speak-easy brought more evils in its train than the
saloon had. A poll of speak-easy proprietors in New York in 1930 discovered that they opposed prohibition in a ratio of twenty to one.
This result was contrary to the popular belief that the owners of the
speak-easies and the drys co-operated to keep the Volstead Act in
force for their mutual benefit. The proprietors complained that they
always lived in fear of federal raids, of holdups by gangsters, and of
padlocking and the total loss of their investment. Moreover, landlords
charged double rents for fear of padlocking, while business in the
speak-easy itself was casual and uncertain. Too many policemen and
their friends did not pay and drank up the profits. The proprietors
disliked the social ostracism of the speak-easy owner and his family,
and resented the loss of their high-class patrons to the increasing
competition of large and small bootleggers, who delivered liquor at
the homes of the wealthy without risk to them. All in all, the proprietors thought that the speak-easy was far inferior to the legal saloon.[37]

Perhaps the worst effect of the speak-easies was indirect. The volume of complaints about their open operation resulted in spectacular
raids on all the best restaurants in New York. As the president of the
Anti-Saloon League exulted in 1924:

> Ask the big hotels and restaurants which laughed at the law,
> whether enforcement is a fizzle. Then hear the doleful chorus. Let
> the Paradise restaurant on 58th Street, New York, sing bass; let Shan-
> ley's, Murray's, and the Little Club sing tenor; let Cushman's and the
> Monte Carlo sing alto; let Delmonico's sing soprano, and the words of
> the music are "We have been padlocked, padlocked, padlocked." The
> famous Knickerbocker Grill sings "Amen, padlocked, amen and
> amen."[38]

Although these raids were no more successful in putting down public
drinking in New York than an attempt to dry up the Hudson River
with a sponge, they did serve the purpose of closing most of the
places where good food could be bought. Fine cooking was not
provided in the speak-easies until the last years of the "experiment,
noble in motive."

The costs of running a speak-easy in New York were estimated by one proprietor at $1370 a month. This included $400 of protection money to law-enforcement agencies, such as the Prohibition Bureau, the Police Department, and the district attorneys. The "lowly cop" collected another $40 each time that beer was delivered. A blackmail system of anonymous complaints might net the police a further income. Occasional raids were made for law-enforcement records — although the fines of the courts were remitted by a temporary decrease in the necessary protection money paid to the police.[39] Altogether, with the costs involved, the speak-easy could not survive the depression as an economic unit.

The speak-easy did not survive the depression as an economic unit. It shared the same fate that overtook the saloon. There were too many sources of drink chasing too few drinkers. Many of the regular speak-easies closed for lack of middle-class customers. Their place was taken by degenerate institutions, hole-in-the-corner bars, cordial shops, hooch stands in the streets which sold spiked fruit juice, and hordes of desperate amateur bootleggers competing for the remaining trade. It was cheaper to drink in the house, either home-brew or bootleg liquor brought to the door. There were myriads of makers and sellers of liquor among the jobless and hungry, who bypassed the speak-easy and supplied liquor direct to the customer. *Judge* commented that there was not a saloon on every corner now, but there were a couple of apple sellers.[40] There were also a couple of peddlers of home-brew.

The speak-easy was primarily for the middle classes. Prohibition gave the possession and consumption of alcohol in public all the glamour of social prestige. Scott Fitzgerald brings out in *The Beautiful and Damned* how the carrying of liquor was almost a badge of respectability. And even worse, the display of drunkenness became more than a mark "of the superior status of those who are able to afford the indulgence."[41] It became the very uniform of valor rather than folly. Although a drunken Chinaman at any time is thought guilty of a bad solecism, a drunken American under prohibition was considered the champion of liberty against tyrannical government. A visit to a cocktail party or a speak-easy became a sign of emancipation, a Purple Heart of individuality in a cowardly and conforming world. Perhaps one of the greatest crimes of prohibition against the middle classes was to make public drunkenness a virtue, signifying manliness, rather than a vice, signifying stupidity.

Public drinking became so fashionable that both decent and indecent women went to the speak-easy, even though the old-time saloon had been a male preserve, only spotted by the occasional prostitute. For women, too, liquor became a flag of their new freedom.

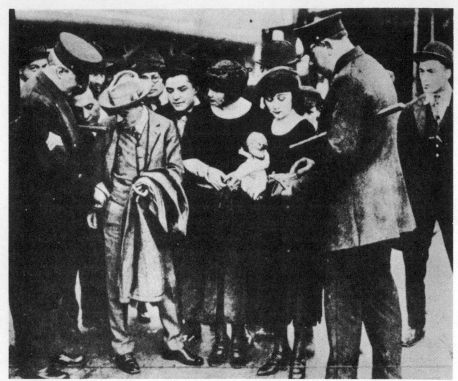

SEARCHING FOR HIP FLASKS

Although not many women copied the heroines of John O'Hara in calculating the distances in New York by the taxi fares between speak-easies, there were enough of them to set a standard of defiance for a whole sex. Like Michael Arlen's girl with the blind blue eyes, they were bored with boredom, and sought entertainment in the risky security of cafés and clubs. Once the old religious restraints against alcohol were dissolved and the social stigma against liquor was reversed to bless it, once laws like the New Orleans law banning females from saloons had become dead letters, then women took to drink and speak-easies in large numbers. As Heywood Broun complained, however bad the old saloons were, at least the male drinker did not have to fight his way through crowds of schoolgirls to the bar. Women remained, nevertheless, more sober as a sex than men.°

The drinking places of the poor, on the other hand, were worse than

° In 1946, while only one-quarter of American men were abstainers, nearly one-half of American women were. Moreover, three times as many men as women were regular drinkers.

the vilest saloon had been, and during the depression were even more numerous. They served liquor which could blind, paralyze, and kill. Once the saloon was gone, the laborer who wanted a drink was thrown onto the tender mercies of suspicious home-brew, drugstore concoctions, and alley-joint alcohol that might make him dead before he was drunk. The testimony of the labor leaders and investigators before the Wickersham Commission is nearly unanimous on this point. Workingmen switched from beer to hard and bad liquor under prohibition, and resented the fact that they were forced to do so. "The discussion of prohibition and its clever and cute violation is the general topic of conversation among workers." A workingman "has to buy a drunk to get a drink . . . he buys a half pint of liquor and he is afraid he is going to lose it, or be arrested or it will leak out of his pocket and he drinks it all at one drink."[42] One slug of the white mule current in the slums made a man crazy. And the majority sentiment among the workingmen had shifted. By the time of the *Wickersham Report*, union leaders put the number of their men who opposed the Volstead Act at more than nine out of ten, compared with some six out of ten in 1920. As among the wealthy, the drinker was now praised rather than condemned. The treasurer of the Plumbers' and Steamfitters' Union commented that in his social set before prohibition, "if a young man had a smell on him he was ostracized completely. Today, in the same social set, if he comes in lit up like a cathedral they want to know if he has something on his hip."[43]

For the abolition of the saloon created the "peripatetic bar," the hip flask, along with the illegal bar, the speak-easy. Restaurant proprietors so much expected their guests to bring their alcohol along with them that highball glasses filled with ice cubes were automatically put on dining tables. Ginger ale was served with a spoon in the tumbler even though the label on the bottle stated that the ginger ale was not to be used with alcoholic beverages. A spokesman of the American Hotel Association testified that corkscrews and bottle openers had to be left in every room to save the hotel furniture. According to him, this was the only relief from the disasters of the Eighteenth Amendment which hotel keepers enjoyed.[44]

Moreover, although the saloon was destroyed in order to preserve the home, the home "turned like a rattle snake an' desthroyed th' saloon — th' home an' th' home brew." According to Mr. Dooley, even if the old customers of the saloon did stay in their houses during prohibition, their families saw little of them. They were down in the cellars stewing hops. And if there was less drunkenness under the Volstead Act, what there was, was "a much more finished product."[45] The effect of taking away the serpent from outside the family circle was to loose him within. Many people who had been abstainers for fear of the rowdy saloon became drinkers within the sociable and respectable home. In rich houses, the ubiquitous cocktail shaker, imported with its contents from the West Indies, set an example of law defiance which parents could not blame children for using against themselves. In poor houses, the evils of making liquor were worse. There is a poignant testimony of a Croatian small merchant in 1927 about conditions in the slum areas of Cleveland:

> Now wine and whisky sold in homes. No good for woman to stay and sell liquor to mens all day. They get drunk and say bad things before children and she forget husband and children. Saloons was better; no children could go there and no women. Men who got drunk before prohibition get drunk now, but it costs them more. We want to have wine to drink, but dare not buy it for fear of being raided. Men used to go to a saloon maybe once a week and get a drink. Now go one or two months without a drink. Then meet a friend, go to private home, take one drink, then two, then another because they know it will be long before they can have more, and end by spending their whole pay and then getting very sick.[46]

Prohibition did turn many poor homes into the worst type of blind pigs, without even the space and exclusion once afforded there. Although the prohibitionists said that only aliens and foreigners made liquor in their own homes, they were wrong. Many wealthy Americans mixed their own gin for the hell of it, even when they could afford the prices of a good bootlegger. The spice of sin had come back into liquor for those who were too sophisticated to believe in the bogy of the demon rum, which the drys waved in the faces of the rest of the country. Also, the license to drink too fast and too much had been given to those who merely wanted to drink.

Edmund Wilson noted in 1927 how the vocabulary of drinking was changed by the abolition of the saloon. He remarked upon the disappearance of various terms; people no longer went on "sprees, toots, tears, jags, brannigans or benders." But Wilson's possible reason for the disappearance of these words was the fact that this fierce protracted drinking had now become universal, "an accepted feature of social life instead of a disreputable escapade." He then made a partial list of 155 words and phrases signifying drunkenness in common use during prohibition. A selection from Wilson's list rolls out like a hymn of praise to the virtues of bootleg gin. On such a drink a man might become blind, blotto, bloated, buried, canned, cock-eyed, crocked, embalmed, fried, high, lit, loaded, lushed, oiled, organized, ossified, owled, paralyzed, pickled, piffed, pie-eyed, plastered, potted, polluted, scrooched, shicker, sloppy, soused, spifflicated, squiffy, stewed, stiff, stinko, wapsed down, woozy, or zozzled.[47]

Prohibition revived the American frontier addiction to gulping down spirits, which the German immigrant brewers had threatened to drown with floods of ale. Heywood Broun called the Volstead Act a bill to discourage the drinking of good beer in favor of indifferent gin. Although New Jersey through tradition and Illinois through the organizational efficiency of Al Capone remained beer areas, wine and spirits became the habitual drink of the rest of America. This change was really a matter of self-help economics and communications. Reasonable home-brewed beer was harder to make than fermented grape juice or a passable gin, which could serve as a base for cocktails. Beer was more expensive to buy from a bootlegger than spirits were, if the only consideration of the consumer was to obtain the maximum quantity of beverage alcohol. Moreover, beer was too bulky and dangerous to transport for long distances; thus its addicts were forced to move to a district such as Hoboken, where the breweries were openly operating at full flood. A careful estimate of the amount of liquor drunk during the periods from 1911 to 1914 and from 1927 to 1930 concluded that, under national prohibition, beer consumption had declined by seven-tenths, while wine consumption had increased by two-thirds and spirits by about one-tenth. Three-quarters of the wine was manufactured at home, but only half of the beer and one-quarter of the spirits.[48] Thus the chief function of the bootlegger and the speak-easy was to supply spirits to the consumer, while the job of the head of the drinking home was to make wine or beer.

Prohibition popularized a drink that had only been served in the smartest of the saloons. While a habitué of the old Waldorf bar might list some three hundred varieties of cocktail which had been served there before the Eighteenth Amendment, the average saloon served only straight drinks, since the swallowing of diluted or mixed liquors was considered effeminate. Indeed, the usual apology of the gin drinker in a low saloon was that he was drinking the weak stuff for the health of his and his wife's kidneys.[49] But prohibition popularized the cocktail to an extraordinary degree. Perhaps drinks were mixed and their taste disguised because the basic alcohol in the cocktail was so foul upon the palate, somewhat as curry was first used to disguise the stink of rotten meat. Perhaps the cocktail fulfilled a basic American need, to get drunk in as short a time as possible. Perhaps it was a test of skill on the part of the server, a sort of guessing game in which the subtlety of the blend militated against the identification of the ingredients. Or perhaps the cocktail was really an eccentric expression of Puritanism, essentially a mixture of the incongruous and the incompatible, something intended to numb rather than stimulate, to do harm rather than please the taste.[50]

IF THE closing of the saloons changed the quality and type of liquor that Americans drank, it also changed the quality and type of the drinkers. While writing about the New Morality in 1927, George Jean Nathan noted one revolutionary fact. The American middle class had become the richest middle class in the world. Thus, they had the money and leisure to imitate upper-class behavior as soon as the fashion was set. Although Nathan was referring to the middle classes of the larger cities, he pointed out that the whole middle class would follow suit in due time, "as the hinterland, however independent of the cities it may be politically and alcoholically, is ever a vassal to the cities' dictate and prejudice in the matter of everything from radio music and moving pictures to store clothes and the philosophy of prophylactic sprays."[51] Although Nathan discounted the influence of the wet cities on the hinterland, it fell victim also to their bibulous influence.

It was the rapid spread of the drinking habits of rich Americans to the leisured middle classes and the young after the Great War that made prohibition a mockery. Even the class structure of the small towns was assailed eventually by the identification of the dominant middle class with the social and free habits of the wealthy. Novels, films, the radio, magazines, newspapers, all propagated the creed that drinking was considered to be smart in the best society. A long tradition of snobbery and conviviality backed this assertion, while a short tradition of temperance and self-restraint supported the drys. In addition, the very psychology of prosperity was responsible for a general relaxation and pursuit of pleasure. The effort of the drys to use the old American hatred of the rich as a weapon for prohibition was useless in a society where the new rich were the new gods. The time had not yet come when, as Scott Fitzgerald noticed in 1933, the rich could only be happy alone together.[52] It was a time when nearly everybody wanted to be in the company of the rich and happy.

Babbitt, when he was served a whisky toddy by the aristocratic banker, of Zenith, was taken aback. Since prohibition, he had not known anyone to be casual about drinking. "It was extraordinary merely to sip his toddy and not cry, 'Oh, maaaaan, this hits me right where I live.' "[53] The diffusion of the insouciant attitude of the rich first to the young, who were ready for anything that smacked of elegant bravado, and then to their respectable parents sounded the knell of the drys. For the prohibitionists depended on middle-class support. Once the middle class began to disobey flagrantly the law which had been passed for their protection against the drunken worker and millionaire liquor trader, the drys had little support left. For the working classes, as a whole, rightly regarded the practice of prohibition as a piece of class legislation, which deprived them of their beer while allowing other classes full freedom of the cocktail shaker. A social worker who asked a chauffeur in California if Santa Barbara was dry received a true answer: "That depends upon whether you sit inside or outside the limousine."[54] The rich rarely supported prohibition for themselves, although they thought it a good thing for workers and Negroes. Another social worker commented sourly that he had been asked time and again to sit on committees to consider the sin of the Bowery, but that he had yet to be asked to sit on a committee to consider the sin of Fifth Avenue. "If we must have laws to regulate the poor, in God's name let us have curbs to restrain the rich!"[55] Senator Brookhart, of Iowa, sneered that it was the wealthy "Wall Street gang," who denounced everybody as a Bolshevik that stood for economic equality with labor and the common people.[56]

But those who drank during prohibition did so for reasons of tradition and temperament as much as for reasons of social class. The regular drinkers of the time came from those groups of people who considered drinking a necessary part of entertaining, from the drunkards and the Bohemian set, and from the first and second generation of European immigrants. These people formed sections of the upper, middle, and lower classes. And there was, in addition, the age group of the young, which drank out of daredeviltry and imitation.[57] It was this last group that publicized the shortcomings and inefficiency of law enforcement and caused many of the scandals of the age.

Reports of drinking among young people during prohibition were legion and contradictory. But the truth is that children and young people copy their parents more than they react against them. The detailed studies recently made of the drinking habits of high-school students have revealed one common factor, that the children of drinkers usually drink and the children of abstainers usually abstain.[58] Habit is the hang-over of succeeding generations. Thus the frequency of drinking among the young during prohibition was a reflection of the manners of their parents; and if they drank spirits rather than beer, it was because spirits were more available. In face of the widespread contempt for the Volstead Act, the young saw no reason why they alone should obey the law. But the fact that the young did drink and get drunk was infinitely shocking to a generation of parents who had never had to deal with the problem of drunk adolescents. The very failure of law enforcement in the twenties was paralleled by a simultaneous failure of parental authority. Fathers could no longer use the whip of economics to keep their children in line when boom jobs made it easy for young people to leave home. It is depression which keeps the family together.

Wherever a man rose to say that prohibition was ruining the morals of the young, a dry spokesman quoted the authority of a hundred selected schoolteachers to deny the charge. When the report of the Federal Council of Churches mentioned alarming conditions in colleges due to the automobile and the hip flask, Wayne B. Wheeler immediately countered by saying that even if drinking was prevalent among youth, it was occasional, not regular, drinking. "The cost and quality of post-Volsteadian drinks does not create a habit as did the licensed intoxicants. The American youth problem is less serious than that in other countries."[59] This argument of the drys, that matters were worse elsewhere and would be worse in America if there were no prohibition, was irrefutable, as was their argument that speak-easies were better than revived saloons. Until repeal came, no one could tell whether conditions for all would improve with legal liquor or without. Meanwhile, the drys claimed all the triumphs of the boom as a proof of the benefits of prohibition to the nation.

The psychology of prosperity was both the strength and weakness of the drys. A national attitude of *laisser-aller* made it impossible both for the drys to enforce the law and for the wets to repeal it. In Ring Lardner's words, prohibition was one better than no liquor. The rich and the middle classes had enough clubs and speak-easies to find the "institutionalized spontaneity" which they wanted without agitating for repeal.[60]* The poor had little power in the matter, and were occupied in becoming richer. With the whole nation echoing Guizot's cry, *"Enrichissez-vous,"* neither reform nor the repeal of reform seemed important. When the gilded bubble burst and the market crashed and the bread lines grew and riches were a mark of betrayal and shame, then was the time to right wrongs. The rich men who drank in the depression were refugees rather than leaders. For the young, it was more important to work than to drink. The moral radicalism of the young was replaced by an economic radicalism.[61] And prohibition was replaced by repeal.

Drinking is primarily an economic matter. Men drink liquor when they can afford it. Mr. Dooley put prohibition in perspective. He

---

* George Jean Nathan noted in 1927 that prohibition could be got rid of with a hundred million dollars; but he also noted that, unfortunately or otherwise, the hundred million dollars was in the pants of men who knew of prohibition only by hearsay.

noticed that when liquor is "hard to get an' costly th' poor won't have so much iv it, an' what they'll have will be worse f'r thim. But it's makin' sad inroads on th' rich."[62] Even after repeal, it was still the rich and the educated who drank more than the poor and the ignorant.[63] For they had more opportunity to drink. The drys were right when they said that the abolition of the saloon would remove temptation from workingmen. But they were wrong in thinking that the rich and the middle classes would stop drinking out of a sense of fair play and responsibility. They had lost the 500,000 "opinion-makers" who had made possible the dry law.

Paternalism is not a popular doctrine in a democracy. The abolition of the saloon did discriminate against the working classes, for it was the middle classes that patronized the speak-easy. The drys were put in the position of appearing to support one law for the rich and another for the poor. Their appeals to the rich to observe the laws which protected their privileges brought little response. In fact, prohibition spread the habit of drinking among the Haves while partially depriving the Have-nots of one of their few pleasures.

If the workingman is considered as an economic unit, prohibition helped him. But he also demands to be considered as a man. The saloon thought him so, as did the church for its believers. But when the church rose up against the saloon and destroyed it in the name of giving the poor richer lives, it condemned the workingman to an existence bare of refuges from the consciousness of his inequalities. Yet the propaganda of the drys continued to trumpet that prohibition had made for the workingman an existence full of increased wealth and its possibilities.

CHAPTER **12**

Dry Defense

Prohibition is the nation's greatest Santa Claus.
F. SCOTT McBRIDE

I don't believe in Santa Claus.
ANONYMOUS CHILD, with probable wet tendencies

THE COMING of the Eighteenth Amendment and of the Volstead Act reversed the positions of wets and drys. The drys were no longer the attackers, but the defenders. All the crimes which were once attributed to the saloon were now fastened upon the speak-easy. Moreover, the new tone of business solidity and respectability of the wets made their propaganda more convincing. The reports of an organization such as the Association Against the Prohibition Amendment, whose 103 directors served on the boards of businesses, with 2,000,000 employees and assets of $40,000,000,000, could not be dismissed as mere propaganda.[1] These reports had all the weight of sound business behind them. Besides, the new pressure groups of the wets were, for the first time, not connected with the liquor trade. They were groups of wealthy private citizens who disliked national prohibition.[2] Thus their sayings seemed free from the taint of self-interest.

The exchange of propaganda between the drys and the wets during the twenties was incredible. In 1928, a visitor declared, "If there is less liquor consumed in the United States than elsewhere, in no country does liquor fill so large a place in the thought and talk of the average citizen."[3] The drys had successfully cast their spell over the minds of everybody. Other social reforms died for lack of interest. The social legislation of the twenties is a ghastly lacuna between progressive and New Deal measures. People had little time for improving the distribution of wealth, pursuing corruption, curbing Big Business, or making democracy possible in an age of mass voting. They talked only of prohibition, until the monstrous delusion of the reform hung like a miasma over the mind of the nation.

242

The propaganda of wets and drys was extreme and calculated to deceive. It made the people disgusted with "do-gooders." The harm of prohibition was less in its immediate effects on those who wished to drink, for these effects were small. It lay in the weariness and cynicism with which the nation began to look at all reforms and reformers. The excesses of the drys damned all other would-be changers of society and its habits. As a critic observed in 1930, at the end of a decade of boom and bonanza and social sloth:

> The liquor controversy is a conflict between two hardened and self-contained dogmatic systems. The official Dry position differs from the official Wet position on questions of organic chemistry, dietetics, pharmacy, biology, religion, psychology, jurisprudence and political philosophy, as well as on the interpretation of statistics on economic conditions. The rivalry between these two systems, each of which is seeking with evangelical zeal to indoctrinate the people, now threatens to paralyze our most promising political enterprises and to handicap with the dead weight of popular indifference the most necessary movements of social reform.[4]

Not until the reformers had got rid of the problem of prohibition could they concentrate on other urgent social problems of the time.

INSOLUBLE CONTROVERSY

THE FIRST argument of the drys was based upon their history. They pointed to the three prohibition waves which had arisen in the United States. Although the first two waves had receded, the third wave had swept onwards, state by state, until there were twenty-seven prohibition states by the time of the passage of the Eighteenth Amendment in Congress and thirty-three by the time that the Volstead Act came into force.[5] And, once the Eighteenth Amendment bound the whole nation, prohibition had reached a final point of no return.

The wets agreed with this argument, except for its last deduction. They said that if the history of temperance reform in America were truly cyclical, then the third wave would recede as had the first two. An interesting article claimed to show that every boom and slump in American history had changed the popular attitude towards liquor.[6] The wets accused the drys of insisting upon a constitutional amendment for this very reason, as a method of coercing the nation into prohibition indefinitely even when the people might react against their dry masters.

The drys countered by saying that a constitutional amendment was necessary to make the criminal elements among the wets respect the law of prohibition. Moreover, it showed that prohibition had come to stay. No constitutional amendment had ever been repealed in the whole history of the United States. What was done was done, and could not be undone. Those Americans who did not like prohibition must lump it and obey it, for it was written into the holy document of the United States which all Americans were sworn to uphold. The wets answered in their turn that the Eighteenth Amendment differed from all other parts of the Constitution. It was a piece of sumptuary legislation which had no right to be there and which conflicted with other rights guaranteed by the Constitution. Veneration for a document was no adequate substitute for a physical appetite.[7] And no amount of propaganda could make it so.

The reply of the drys was to urge obedience to the Constitution, whole and indivisible. "There is only one Constitution and no part of that Constitution is less sacred than any other part."[8] No other amendment had received so many votes from states or state legislatures. Only ten out of thirteen states had ratified the first eleven constitutional amendments; the others had failed to be ratified by at least four and at most twelve of the states. The Eighteenth Amendment had been ratified by the legislatures of all the states except two, which made it the most popular amendment in the Constitution. Against this, the wets declared that the method of ratification, although legal, was not directly democratic. The legislatures of the nation were packed in favor of the rural areas. A national referendum would have brought out a majority against prohibition, especially since women did not yet have the vote in all states. The Eighteenth Amendment was a modern Blue Law, foisted on the unwilling American people.

The drys denied this. They pointed out that, of the twenty-seven states which had adopted some form of state-wide prohibition before the passage of the Eighteenth Amendment, seventeen had done so by referendum, and in only seven of these referendums had women had the vote. Moreover, by 1917, more than four-fifths of the area and nearly two-thirds of the population of the United States lived under one dry law or another. National prohibition was merely the expression of the will of the majority. The minority wets should obey the democratic decision. If they did not, "It spells Bolshevism and Bolshevism spells nationalization of the women of our country and that spells hell and damnation."[9] Even the judicious William Howard Taft supported this point of view, saying that those who put their personal liberty above their duty to the Constitution were guilty of "practical Bolshevism."[10]

The wets said that this view was nonsense. If any people were Bolsheviks and Socialists, the drys were. National prohibition had confiscated without compensation property worth billions of dollars, and had put a federal force of secret police over the land. The very law of prohibition was an attack on individual freedom. "To undermine the foundations of Liberty is to open the way to Socialism."[11] In addition, although much of the area of the United States was indeed dry in 1917, it was "little but area" and not as dry as the Volstead Act wished to make the whole of America.[12] If the total of those who had voted against state-wide prohibition amendments had been added to those who lived in the wet cities and to the soldiers away in France, a large majority would have been produced against the Eighteenth Amendment.

The truth of the matter lay on both sides. If there was a long tradition of temperance work in America, there was a longer tradition of drinking. Although the liquor trade was an evil, the answer to its evils was not total prohibition but government regulation. The Constitution was certainly no place to write a law such as the Eighteenth Amendment; but, on the other hand, there was little hope of drinkers and bootleggers making an effort to obey such a law unless it was in the Constitution. Moreover, a long series of precedents in the states had made traditional the placing of such laws in constitutions. And the very fact that the most rabid wet considered repeal of the Eighteenth Amendment impossible as late as 1931 did, perhaps, make for more law observance among those who were not prepared "to barter their Constitution for a cocktail."[13] There was certainly no question that the amendment had been legally passed, although it is true that it was passed in a time of militancy and exaggerated patriotism, under a form of moral and political blackmail which made cool thought difficult for legislators. If prohibition was put over on the country, it was done so with all due formality.

The second line of propaganda of the drys was based on their idea of civilization. According to them, freedom was a positive concept. There was no question of a man being free to drink liquor. It was only when the liquor slave was free from his craving that he was free to act like a man and fulfill the better part of his nature. "Freedom from the narcotic force of alcohol permits one to function more, to enjoy more, to be more than he otherwise could be."[14] It was only with prohibition that every child and woman could be given the opportunity for the life of liberty which was the American dream. "For it is wholly impossible for the drinker, moderate or excessive, to keep the unfortunate consequences of alcohol to himself."[15] The drinker must deny himself for the sake of his own good and the good of others. "The immorality of the 'real temperance' drinker lies in the fact that, for the sake of a sensual gratification, he injures his body and imperils his soul."[16] In the interests of society, citizens must be prepared to give up their vices.

"Personal liberty ends where public injury begins. There is a higher personal liberty, and that is civil liberty."[17]

The wets countered by saying that if personal liberty meant anything, it meant freedom to drink. They said that there was such a man as the moderate drinker. Many men, after working all day, had the right to drink their glass or two of beer or wine. Alcohol was a depressant which aided the digestion and relieved the tensions of the day. It was a substance used freely in all societies at all times. Moreover, although men might be better machines if they did not touch alcohol, not all men wanted to be machines. They wanted to be men, and men wanted the opportunity to relax in peace. Human efficiency was a great thing; but there was a greater, human happiness.[18] If, in Huxley's words, civilization was a conspiracy against nature, then alcohol was the policeman trailing the conspirator.[19]

The technological revolution of the times provided the drys with both a theory and a seeming proof. Their theory was that increased industrial and mechanical demands on the worker made drink positively dangerous for him. The quick tempo of modern life necessarily meant the elimination of those agents which slowed men down, such as beverage alcohol. The proof of the efficacy of prohibition lay in the huge increase in productivity. The destined march of America onwards and upwards demanded the sacrifice of the selfish few who put their gullets before their country.

> The hoarse cry for license and anarchy, under the guise of so-called personal liberty, is merely the demand of the modern bureaucrat against the institutions of democracy. It represents the attitude of the modern road hog toward others who travel the highway of liberty protected by government. It is the cry of the moral and social savage against the advance of civilization.[20]

The fact that prohibition was a democratic law passed in a free society damned its opponents as both bureaucrats and savages at the same moment.

The wets denied that prohibition had anything to do with increased productivity. Technological change had brought about its own improvement. No causal connection could be proved between prohibition and economic growth. Moreover, the demands of the machine age made the relaxation of strong drink still more necessary to the worker. Indeed, the inefficiency of prohibition enforcement increased the danger of industrial accidents, for beer was harder to get than bad hard liquor. Workers who drank light wines and beer before prohibition had switched to "a much heavier beer and wine and mixtures which they call homemade whisky, mule, hootch, rattlesnake."[21] And there was a widespread feeling, true or false, that national prohibition was not a democratic law. In the words of an Indianapolis labor leader, "We did not get prohibition from the people as a whole. We really got it from a hand-picked jury."[22]

The drys, in their turn, said that those who drank bootleg liquor under prohibition were a small minority whose doings were much exaggerated by the press. Furthermore, that small minority was composed of people who had no reason to feel proud of themselves. Those who drank bootleg liquor to be social or smart were guilty of snobbery and of setting a bad example. Those who were old soaks and liquor addicts would die; their number would not be renewed from among the young. Even those young people who drank did so out of mere bravado, which maturity would cure. The only other types of drinkers were the aristocrats, who wrongly thought themselves above the law, the foreigners, who should become Americanized, and the members of the illegal liquor trade, who should be in jail. This "Dreibund of Defiance" was doomed to failure.[23] However bad things were under prohibition, they had been worse under the saloons. Bootleg liquor was prevalent and poisonous before the Volstead Act. Prohibition had made better the bad, even if it had not eliminated the liquor evil. As General Evangeline Booth said in 1930, "The wettest of wet areas is less wet to-day than it was when the saloon, usually accompanied by the speak-easy, were wide open."[24]

The wets repeated *ad nauseam* that conditions were worse under prohibition. And certainly the newspapers made it seem so. According to their testimony and the testimony of the trade union leaders before the Wickersham Commission, a greater number of young people and women drank under prohibition, and the same number of men. Not only were there more speak-easies by 1930 than there had been saloons, but liquor had come into every workingman's home. An official of the metal trades reported that "every molder's wife seemed to take as much pride in the home brew as she formerly did in her cooking." Other labor officials and observers confirmed his judgment. Strong drink could be found in nearly all homes and hotels, and people drank more of it. "Almost invariably when a bottle is put on the table nobody leaves until there is nothing left but the glass." And every year wet sentiment was growing in face of the universal contempt for the dry law. "The children are growing up and as they are making more atheists in Russia they are making more antiprohibitionists in the United States every day."[25]

Again, both drys and wets told the half truth, the half truth, and nothing but the half truth. While it is necessary for civilized men to accept certain restraints on their behavior, even restraints against making themselves too drunk too often, it is not necessary for the progress of civilization that all men should give up drinking alcohol. Equally, while the efficient prohibition of liquor would bring about economic benefits and increased productivity, it is true that, in Western democracies, society is thought to be made for man and not man for society. The insistence of the drys that the drinker must sacrifice his drink for the sake of the community was as extreme as the wet insistence that the drys must put up with the debauchery and corruption of the saloons for the sake of liberty. And, as for the prevalence of drinking under prohibition, no final answer can ever be given. Where a traffic is illegal, it cannot be regulated or counted. Authorities were quoted eternally on both sides to prove opposite cases. Statistics were collected and invented to demonstrate contradictory evidence. But nothing was finally shown false or true, although certain reasonable estimates were made just before repeal. As Mr. Dooley said, "Do I think pro-hybition is makin' pro-gress? Me boy, I'm no stasticyan. I hope to die without havin' that to do pinance f'r that."[26]

The drys also made more lavish claims. Before prohibition was actually put to the test, its effects were hoped to exceed credulity and approach paradise. In the hyperboles of Billy Sunday, "The reign of tears is over. The slums will soon be only a memory. We will turn our prisons into factories and our jails into storehouses and corncribs. Men will walk upright now, women will smile, and the children will laugh. Hell will be forever for rent."[27] Roy Haynes, the Prohibition Commissioner, claimed in 1923 that prohibition was the "most dominating and determining force" in "waning drunkenness, vice, and crime; emptying hospitals, asylums, and jails; rapidly accumulating savings, overflowing schools, sturdier, happier children, better, more prosperous homes, increasing and more wholesome recreation, healthier social life, and increased fruits of human labor." And Haynes found even more dry benefits than these in the flaming twenties, including "the sensational reductions in the death rate, the increase in longevity, the elimination of the brothel, the rapid disappearance of crimes against chastity," and "the startling decrease in major crimes."[28] It was unfortunate that Haynes seemed to see more what he wished to see than things as they were.

The wets pointed to the true facts of the increased crime and immorality of the twenties, and exaggerated them. With the zeal of muckrakers in a continent of garbage, they raked up and turned over a steaming mess of corruption and crime in politics and business. They aped the methods of the drys in attributing the whole rotten, stinking heap to the sole cause of prohibition. Every drunkard, every racketeer, and every bribed judge or policeman was the consequence of the unholy Volstead Act. National prohibition became the wet scapegoat for the sins of the United States, as the saloon had been the whipping boy of the drys.

But the chief quarrel of the wet and the dry propagandists was over the great god of boom times, business, and its connection with prohibition. To the drys, the prosperity of the twenties in America was the living proof of the good of their reform. They held the Eighteenth Amendment to be the main factor during the decade in the tripling of building and loan assets, in the doubling of pupils in educational institutions, in the increase of wages by just under one-half, in the sale of more than twenty million automobiles, in the rise in consumption of food and dairy products and fruit, and in the general benefits of the boom.

A judicious article called "Things Are in the Saddle" summed up the dry reasons for the over-all economic virtue of prohibition. "Drink cuts down general consumptive power. Drink takes from the nation's ability to use up goods; drink takes from a man's efficiency to consume; drink lessens the desire for things. Drink, to be sure, limits its own consumption; when it has its man under the table, that is the end; there is a limit to the amount a man can drink." But what was intolerable was that drink made inroads into the consumption of luxuries. The pleasure of drink took the place of the pleasure in things. The more things men had, the more they needed; but the more drink men had, the less things they needed. Therefore, the gain of prohibition was clear. "There are more law-breakers in the nation because of prohibition. But because of prohibition there are both more consumers and better consumers."[29] In all, the dry economists estimated that at least fifteen billion dollars had been diverted in the twenties from the buying of drink to the buying of goods, which was "the actual cause" of America's "wonderful prosperity."[30] This saving represented a net gain, in the much-quoted estimate of the British economist Sir Josiah Stamp, of between 8 and 15 per cent of the gross national product of an industrial society, such as the United States or Great Britain.[31]

Prohibition, according to the drys, had become necessary for the very continuance of boom times. Another dry article, "Prohibition as Seen by a Business Man," pointed out that families were able to pay their current bills and meet their installments only because the liquor bill was gone. The huge increase of the installment system in the twenties meant that business would collapse if drink again competed with goods for the wages of the workers. "Any credit man knows that a sober man is a better risk than a drinker. A sober man, too, will want things the drinker will not demand. A nation has to walk very steady to carry the lofty structure of general credit it has erected. It would not take much drink to bring that whole structure down in ruins."[32] It was unfortunate for the drys that the whole structure did come down in ruins in 1929, while the nation was still enjoying all the theoretical economic benefits of prohibition. In fact, by 1931, the drys were claiming that prohibition had prevented the depression from being a catastrophe. "Our present effort to control John Barleycorn has provided a cushioning of vast proportions against the impact of current unemployment."[33]

The wets considered that the claims of the drys were so much hot air. First, there was no connection between prohibition and prosperity. The boom of the twenties had taken place in the large cities, where liquor flowed continually and enforcement of the dry law was a farce. The country areas, where prohibition was a reality, suffered from declining income throughout the twenties. Moreover, prohibition itself was the most trivial of all the causes of the boom. The increased productivity of America, as the Hoover report on *Recent Economic Changes* showed, was due to the increased use of power, improved machinery, mass production, personnel management, and industrial research.[34] Even statistics contradicted the claims of the drys. If the average income of Americans was adjusted to the cost-of-living index, the total rose from $480 a year in 1900 to $620 in 1919 during the period of the saloons, while the rate of increase remained constant under prohibition to a total of $681 in 1929. The same was true of savings deposits; the increase between 1910 and 1919 averaged about 7 per cent a year, the same rate as in the twenties. In fact, the boom had begun under legal liquor and had continued despite prohibition. The rising sales of new goods were due to the phenomenal advance in advertising and in new consumer needs, rather than to the money saved from liquor sales. Indeed, the wets said that there had been no money saved on liquor sales, except during the first three years of prohibition. By 1929, the amount spent on bootleg liquor was equal to the buying power of the amount spent in 1914 on legal liquor. The only difference was that slightly less liquor was drunk in 1929 at a greater cost.[35]

A fair estimate of the economics of prohibition put the consumption of beverage alcohol in the period between 1927 and 1930 at two-thirds of the consumption between 1911 and 1914. The amount of money spent on bootleg liquor in this period, however, was between four and five billion dollars a year, exactly equivalent to the amount which would have been spent if legal liquor had been sold at the volume of the period between 1911 and 1914 and had been taxed at the wartime rate of 1917. Although the national liquor bill had been reduced by about two billion dollars a year during the first three years of prohibition, it had settled at its old level by the end of the twenties. Prohibition had not been a significant factor in the purchase of automobiles, consumer goods, or homes. Even the rise in the consumption of food and dairy products was partially due to increased knowledge about human health. Prohibition was a minor factor in the rise of industrial productivity, while the decentralized bootleg trade, which employed more people than the old liquor industry, wasted a great deal of productive resources and labor. The only real gainers from prohibition were the workingmen of America. They did drink half the amount which they had before, and probably spent a billion dollars a year less on liquor. On the other hand, the business and salaried classes drank the same amount as they had before prohibition, and annually spent a billion dollars more on liquor, as prices were higher.[36] After all the fuss and bother, prohibition made for small change.

The economic claims and statistics of wets and drys were as multitudinous as they were inaccurate. Their volume was only exceeded by their lack of worth. They surpassed fantasy and approached divine inspiration. Yet, at two important times, these claims and statistics were believed. The first time was in the few years before the passage of the Eighteenth Amendment. The second time was in the few years before repeal. During the first time, the drys were credited; during the second, the wets. The despicable exaggerations of the prohibitionists were imitated by their foes. The excited condition of the American people during the First World War made them relinquish their common sense for long enough to heed those dry voices, who promised them the millennium in terms of numbers and figures and dollars if the nation would only go dry. Equally, the fearful temper of America in the depression led most of the nation to believe in the ridiculous remedies of the wet "beer-for-taxes" crusade, which turned the repeal movement from "fine moral soil to the arid ground of economics, precisely where the Prohibitionists had planted their ignoble banner."[37]

CHAPTER 13

Masters of Inaction

> I am not a prohibitionist, Mr. President, and never have
> pretended to be. I do claim to be a temperance man. I do
> not approach this question from a moral viewpoint, because
> I am unable to see it as a great moral question.
>
> WARREN G. HARDING

> Never go out to meet trouble. If you will just sit still, nine
> cases out of ten someone will intercept it before it reaches
> you.
>
> CALVIN COOLIDGE

THE DRYS were not fortunate in the two men who were in the
White House for the first eight years of national prohibition. It was
a period of Republican ascendancy, a time when the nominees of the
Grand Old Party were insignificant men whose inability or inaction
gave free rein to the forces of Big Business. Warren Harding was a
small-town newspaper editor from Ohio, Calvin Coolidge a limited
lawyer from Vermont. Neither had the wish or the capacity to enforce
the dry law by a strong show of federal power. Although the heads
of the Anti-Saloon League acquired much influence in Washington
through their close contact with these men, the lack of leadership from
the White House meant a lack of leadership in the nation. Who would
obey the Eighteenth Amendment under a President who drank whisky
regularly? Who would exert himself to enforce the Volstead Act under
another President, whose idea of good government was economy, and
whose way of dealing with trouble was to ignore it?

WARREN GAMALIEL HARDING: JUST FOLKS

WILLIAM ALLEN WHITE called Harding a he-harlot.[1] Alice Roosevelt
Longworth called him just a slob.[2] Mencken, with prophetic sarcasm,
called him a numskull and an oil refinery.[3] Yet they all recognized
that he was a lovable and generous man. When he died suddenly in

1923 as he was returning from Alaska, some three million people gathered by the railroad tracks to see his body brought back to the East. He had declared that if he could not be the best President of the United States, he would like to be the best-loved. His timely death made him briefly so. He was more mourned immediately than any save Abraham Lincoln.

If, within five years, his name was only mentioned to be sneered at and forgotten, if Calvin Coolidge was too embarrassed to deliver a funeral oration at his memorial and Herbert Hoover had to attack his old Cabinet colleagues in his eulogy at the final burial, the fault was not Harding's. For his virtues were his vices. He was too faithful to his friends, too trusting of the untrustworthy, too easy with the hard. He shook hands with problems and was surprised that they were still impolite. He smiled at difficulties and was wounded by their permanent scowl. When he was worried over a tax bill, he complained to his secretary Jud Welliver that there must be a man who knew the answer, though Harding didn't know his whereabouts, and that there must be a book which solved the matter, though Harding couldn't read it if there was.⁴ His answer to Charles W. Forbes's peculations in the Veterans' Bureau was to try personally to choke him; he did not appoint a commission to investigate him.⁵

Harding died from the stabbings of his friends, like a small-town Julius Caesar. And his ordinary likabilities were sufficient to be an Anthony and bring the crowds weeping about his corpse. The collection of 121 obituary editorials called *He Was "Just Folks,"* which came out in the year of his death, showed the grief felt by small men at the end of a small man made great. Some of the titles of the editorials were: "An Ideal American," "The Greatest Commoner Since Lincoln," "A Man of the People," "His Opportunity Is Every Boy's," and "He Lives! He Lives!"⁶ The normal never dies.

Harding treated prohibition during the course of his political career with the same sloppy amiability and smiling lack of moral judgment with which he treated all his acquaintances. As a boy in Marion, Ohio, he had drunk and gambled and played pool with the rest of the town boys, and had "pursued the casual lecheries of the unattached."⁷ He bought a defunct newspaper, the Marion *Star*, and began to build up its circulation by putting out the correct and corrupt state Republican line, which included support of the drink interests and ridicule of the prohibitionists. He was married to a domineering woman five years his senior, whose first husband had left her and had died of drink. Florence Kling Harding believed in her own destiny and forced her husband into a fate that he did not intend. She made Warren Harding a financial success and a well-known political figure, aided by Harry M.

Daugherty, who had decided that a man who looked like a President should become one.

Harding was elected to the state senate in 1901, with the blessing and backing of the notorious George B. Cox machine, from its saloon-based headquarters in Cincinnati. There he was duly liked and duly dutiful. The only time he is known to have been against the party line was over a bill supported by the wets and the Republicans to extend the area of local option. On this occasion, the public galleries were full of the cohorts of the Woman's Christian Temperance Union. They had threatened to swing the next election against anyone who dared favor the bill. Warren Harding, never a man to resist the appeal of women, voted dry. If he drank himself and owned brewery stock, he had been advised often enough by Harry Daugherty to keep in with the prohibitionists. The Republican machine might and did overlook his one act of disobedience, while the Ohio Anti-Saloon League, the most powerful in the country, was often too militantly Christian to forgive its enemies.

When Harding ran for the office of Governor in 1910 against the progressive Democrat Judson Harmon, he emulated his opponent's straddle on liquor, if not his victory. Both candidates favored enforcing the law and putting prohibition in its proper place. Harding said obscurely:

> The temperance question is legislative rather than executive, and is not to transcend all other important issues in this campaign. My legislative record is written in the journals of two general assemblies. I couldn't change that record if I would. I stand for enforcement of the law and would not be worthy of your suffrages if I did not.[8]

The Ohio drys, distrusting both candidates, did not influence the election overmuch; but when Harding ran for the Senate in 1914, the drys supported him. One of their favorite candidates, Frank B. Willis, was running on the same ticket for Governor. Harding had their support both in his defeat of the slippery ex-Senator Foraker in the Republican primaries and in his victorious campaign, since he was running against a Roman Catholic. Wayne B. Wheeler went so far as to issue a statement approving of Harding's ownership of brewery stock as a method of accepting payment for beer advertisements in the Marion Star.[9] Moreover, the Cincinnati wets came out for Harding, as they were disgruntled with the "wet" Democratic Governor of Ohio, James M. Cox, who had actually closed the saloons on Sundays. With both extremes behind him, wets and drys, opposed only by the progressives and traditional Democrats, Harding won easily by nearly 75,000 votes. He was sent to drink whisky and play poker, to make many friends and influence few, in the most exclusive club in the world in Washington.

Harding spent the six happiest years of his life in the Senate, in a hail of respectable fellows well met.[10] He served on many committees, since he was known to know little about their work and to support the opinions of their senior members. He served on the committees for Naval Affairs, Public Health and National Quarantine, Standard Weights and Measures, Commerce, Claims, Expenditures in the Treasury Department, Foreign Relations, Territories, the Pacific Islands, the Philippines, Puerto Rico, and the Virgin Islands. His attendance at these committees was little better than his voting record, which was infrequent. Out of thirty-two calls on the matter of prohibition, he voted wet thirty times, mostly opposing unimportant prohibition riders to other measures. And yet the Anti-Saloon League backed him. For he stated to them charmingly that he believed in doing what the people told him to do; he would vote on prohibition as his state voted. Thus, when the Anti-Saloon League dried up Ohio, they would also dry up Ohio's mouthpiece, Senator Harding.

In fact, Harding voted to submit the Eighteenth Amendment to the states before Ohio had voted for constitutional prohibition. It was a nice and exactly calculated evasion of responsibility. In 1916, most of the wet Senators who sought re-election had lost their seats. In 1917, the third attempt to dry up Ohio was defeated by just over a thousand votes out of a total of one million; at each attempt, the drys had cut the majority against them and were bound to be successful in 1918. Harding acted as the go-between of wet Senators and the Anti-Saloon League in the negotiations for the time limit of seven years given for ratification of the Eighteenth Amendment. But when the vital votes on the Eighteenth Amendment and the Volstead Act veto were counted, Harding's vote was cast on the dry and winning side.

In the 1920 Republican convention, oil men and the senatorial soviet pulled the wires, not the advocates of abstinence. The Committee of the National Temperance Council did send a letter to urge a strong plank in favor of the Eighteenth Amendment; but the framers of the party platform were too canny to say anything on the subject. Harding's unsuitable nomination was fixed by the Old Guard of the Senate in a smoke-filled room as forecast by Harry Daugherty. The prospective candidate communed with himself for ten minutes and, ignoring the fact of his illegitimate child and the rumors of his Negro blood, announced that there were no obstacles to his running for President. The convention agreed with the choice of their leaders. The man who would win the election needed to be the antithesis of the academic, strong, idealistic Wilson. The country further concurred. And what had been a conspiracy by a powerful cabal to foist an inadequate figurehead on their party became a popular victory of huge proportions. A landslide majority of some seven million votes showed that after a time of war, restrictions, foreign commitments, and introspection, the country was for peace, plenty, isolation, and no questions. As Senator Johnson, of California, said correctly, "Rum was not the issue of this campaign."[11]

Harding conducted most of his campaign from his front porch at Marion. The party leaders sent him out to speak as little as possible, since they were afraid of his affable indiscretions. His polysyllabic and meaningless prose suitably spread an impenetrable miasma around his views on the League of Nations and prohibition and everything else. His later speeches reminded Mencken of a string of wet sponges, tattered washing on the line, stale bean-soup, college yells, and dogs barking idiotically through endless nights. They were so bad that a sort of grandeur crept into them.[12] While the election headquarters at Marion flowed with all sorts of liquor, Harding showed his handsome face and mouthed superfluities about the Eighteenth Amendment, that it was impossible to ignore the Constitution and unthinkable to evade the law.

Harding was opposed in the election by the Democratic candidate James M. Cox. Cox also came from Ohio, where he had been three times Governor. He was not liked by the leaders of the Anti-Saloon League, who had bitterly opposed him in many state campaigns. At the Democratic convention, copies of Cox's wet record in Ohio were circulated among the delegates by William Jennings Bryan in an effort to block Cox's nomination in favor of that of the dry A. Mitchell Palmer or William Gibbs McAdoo. Two officials of the Anti-Saloon League warned the Democrats against nominating a wet candidate: William H. Anderson said that Harding would be beaten if the Democrats nominated a dry, and "Pussyfoot" Johnson declared that any wet seeker after the White House would have as much chance of being elected as a "tallow-legged cat in hell."[13] Wayne B. Wheeler himself wrote to Bryan, telling him that Cox "must be defeated if there is any way possible to do it."[14]

Cox was nominated, however, with the support of the wets and Tammany and the business interests. The Anti-Saloon League refused to support either candidate officially, although their support went in secret to Warren Harding. Although both candidates came out for enforcement of the dry law, the League had previously supported Harding in Ohio and had opposed Cox. Moreover, the leaders of the League thought that they could exert more pressure on the malleable Harding

in Washington than they could on the efficient Cox. Thus Clarence
True Wilson came out with the statement that Harding was 90 per
cent dry, while Cox was accused of being the candidate of the wets.[15]
It was useless for Cox to denounce Wayne B. Wheeler as the tool of
the Republican party; for his own party in Ohio and the North was
associated with the wet city machines.[16] The campaign was slanderous
and unpleasant in general. Rumors circulated that Harding was a
Negro, while Cox was accused of heavy drinking and of secret sympathies with Rome.[17] Nevertheless, Harding's victory was assured, for
it was a Republican year.

Once Harding was installed in the White House, he found himself
incompetent, overworked, and in jail. He discovered that he had to
make up his own mind since the best minds of his party disagreed. He
was hounded for his drinking habits and his inefficiencies by Wheeler
and members of the Anti-Saloon League, who had only supported his
weak candidacy because he was weak while they were strong. They
treated him in Washington as they had done in Ohio, as a ninny to be
bullied and cajoled and led. Through their power in the President's
home state and through the appointment of a Buckeye Prohibition
Commissioner, Roy A. Haynes, Wheeler and the League transferred
their influence within a state to influence over a nation.

But other and more dangerous men from Ohio followed Harding to
Washington. These were his personal friends, who became the Ohio
Gang. He needed their poker games and highballs and backslapping
joviality to escape from the rigors of the unknown into the relaxation
of the known. He was unhappy without his cronies. He thought personal acquaintanceship more sure a basis for trust than past record or
party loyalty. Thus, physically and mentally unfit for his own high
office, he gave his friends high offices too. Washington received the
doubtful benefit of the most efficient gang of looters ever to gut the
capital city since the days of General Grant.

In fairness to Warren Harding, he knew little of the extortions of his
friends. He knew them only as charming boon companions. Alice
Roosevelt Longworth's description of the scene in the study at the
White House above the official reception on the main floor was all that
Harding wanted and expected of his chosen circle.

> No rumor could have exceeded the reality; the study was filled
> with cronies, Daugherty, Jess Smith, Alec Moore, and others, the air
> heavy with tobacco smoke, trays with bottles containing every imagi-
> nable brand of whisky stood about, cards and poker chips ready at
> hand — a general atmosphere of waistcoat unbuttoned, feet on the
> desk, and the spittoon alongside.[18]

It is not established, however, that Harding ever went to the notorious parties at 1625 K Street, where the Ohio Gang took up their headquarters and began their system of what Senator Brookhart, of Iowa, called "government by blackmail." With Harry Daugherty as Attorney General and the unscrupulous William J. Burns running the Department of Justice as a private police force for the gang's benefit, pickings were large and easy. Indeed, one of the main reasons that the Anti-Saloon League did not want the Prohibition Bureau transferred from the Treasury to the Department of Justice was that it would merely be a transfer from inefficiency to corruption.

Meanwhile, the unknowing Harding was making moral appeals for good citizens to obey the Eighteenth Amendment. At his home town, Marion, in 1922, he said that the amendment was the will of America and must be sustained by government and public opinion.[19] In his message to Congress in December of that year, he repeated his statement, although the corruption of the Prohibition Bureau had now become too notorious to be ignored. Harding darkly referred to the Volstead Act and "conditions relating to its enforcement which savor of nation-wide scandal." Yet his remedy was not the reorganization of the Prohibition Bureau but an exhortation for individuals to refuse to drink bootleg liquor and for larger appropriations by the states.[20]

Harding himself, at last grown aware of the treachery of his friends and the need of the President to set an example, even began to give up his own drinking habits. He moved his liquor stock up to the secrecy of his bedroom and, under pressure from Wayne B. Wheeler, announced to reporters in January, 1923, that he had become a total abstainer. No alcohol was put on the presidential train during his last trip to Alaska, and if a kind reporter slipped him a bottle of whisky on the sea voyage, it was his only known backsliding.[21] For Harding believed what he said, even if his words were incoherent. The job of being President became, by the end of his term, greater than the man. He seemed genuinely shocked by New York's repeal of its state enforcement law in May, and said, in an oblique attack on Governor Alfred E. Smith, that both national executives and state executives were equally sworn to enforce the Constitution.[22] He even claimed that the Prohibition Bureau was doing a good job in his foreword to Commissioner Roy A. Haynes's book, *Prohibition Inside Out*. "The Prohibition Department has made, and is making, substantial progress. It deserves the support of all our people in its great work."[23]

Harding spoke for the last time on prohibition at Denver, Colorado, during his fatal trip to Alaska. He stated that neither party was ever likely to urge repeal of the Eighteenth Amendment. He claimed, to the derision of the cartoonists, that the wets were a very small part of the population. And he puffed out the usual cloudy confusions of the dry propagandists, who tried to maintain that an occasional drink was equivalent to a full-scale assault on the American way of life. Harding's speech mirrored the intellectual inadequacy of the drys; it was a masterpiece of sonorous fallacies, lifting a difference of opinion to the level of an attack on order and government.

> The issue is fast coming to be recognized, not as one between wets and drys, not as a question between those who believe in prohibition and those who do not, not as a contention between those who want to drink and those who do not — it is fast being raised above all that — but as one involving the great question whether the laws of this country can and will be enforced.[24]

Harding died, probably of heart failure, on his return from Alaska. Had he lived, he might have been impeached for agreeing to sign away the oil lands put aside for the Navy. Within a few years, his wife, his doctor, and most of the Ohio Gang were dead or in prison. Allegations that his decease was not natural seem to be unfounded, although the suicides and sudden deaths of some of his Ohio associates were suspiciously convenient for the survivors. Whatever the reason for his end, Harding's burial was timely. Dying was the greatest service he could have performed for his party. For he was regarded in the succeeding presidential election as a martyr, killed by overwork and disloyal friends. His omissions over prohibition and greater matters were forgiven with his death.

CALVIN COOLIDGE: THE RESPONSIBILITY OF INACTION

"IN PUBLIC life it is sometimes necessary in order to appear really natural to be actually artificial," wrote Calvin Coolidge.[25] His own nature was always considered to have been formed by the nature of his native Vermont. He improved upon that inheritance merely to seem more like the product of the place. If the people of Vermont were thrifty and hard-working and ambitious, believers in God and local government and the worth of business and the Republican party, then Calvin Coolidge was ostentatiously so, in the clipped manner of his ancestors. He was parsimonious, even saving part of his presidential salary. He was industrious, cutting short his honeymoon to return to his law office. He was very ambitious, rising to be President through a planned series of electoral victories, which he called fate and his opponents called good management. As President, he left as much as he could in the hands of God and did as little as possible, in order to economize on the federal budget and to allow local authorities the luxury of effecting their own improvements. He trusted businessmen so faithfully that he even appointed them to staff the federal boards set up to regulate their businesses. And he was always a convinced Republican, although his sense that he was "but an instrument in the hands of God" made him think he was called to be above party, when he was being efficiently exploited by his own.[26]

Prohibition was no private problem to Coolidge, merely a political bore. He was a teetotaler, who drank rarely on certain social occasions. He practiced throughout his life his family's virtues of self-restraint and saving, even to the extent of refusing to allow himself to become a great President. He wrote, "It is a great advantage to a President, and a major source of safety to the country, for him to know that he is not a great man."[27] Thinking himself inferior, Calvin Coolidge made no effort to act like a great man. His fear of greatness was so strong that he let the various forces in American life operate unchecked except by Providence and the misunderstood principles of economy. He thought that the integrity of the President's own example was a better instrument of government than the use of federal power.

Calvin Coolidge's personal honesty was another quality he had inherited from his early society. Yet this virtue applied only to his private life. His political use of his personal honesty was the worst form of intellectual self-deceit. He took refuge in his own sense of incorruptibility to allow the powers which backed him, business and political, to corrupt whomsoever they wished. An honest man may be a dishonest politician by ignoring the interests of those he represents in the contemplation of his rectitude. Had Coolidge remained in Vermont, cultivating the forty acres left to him by his grandfather, his personal doctrine of work and save would have made him rightfully respected. But when his ambition drove him to the White House, he thought that his good fortune was the living proof of his doctrine of self-help, not the greatest opportunity given to a single man to help others.

Calvin Coolidge, become great in office, did as little as possible. He made few mistakes, but he did nothing to prevent the speculative boom that was to destroy in the slump of 1929 the image of business as Mammon, the friend of God. He himself personally saved his salary, put some hundred thousand dollars into safe gilt-edged stock, and was not affected by the Great Crash in his private life, although he was partially responsible for the depression by failing to use the federal power to control the stock market. Prohibition was another issue on which Coolidge, by doing little, was responsible for much.

When Calvin Coolidge left Amherst College, he went to Northampton, Massachusetts, to learn and practice law. More interested in the acquisition of political office than of money, Coolidge served in many municipal posts until he finally ran for Mayor of Northampton in 1910. In this campaign, prohibition first came to his aid. Although Coolidge was the attorney for a powerful brewery, the drys supported him, since his Democratic opponent had once, out of academic interest, taken the wet side in a debate in the Congregational Church. In the campaign, Coolidge followed his lifelong policy of saying nothing on prohibition at all, in order to appear the friend of all, a private tee-totaler and a public brewer's lawyer. He won the election, despite an accusation in the Northampton *Daily Herald* that his victory was due to Rum and Religion. As usual, he defended himself from this attack by a reference to his personal habits, not to his political helpers. He wrote to his father, "I did not have to reply to the *Herald* attack, for everybody knew it was not true. Folks know I do not go into saloons, and I never bought a drink during the campaign."[28]

Yet his political equivocation was evident on the morning of the election when he drove down to vote with a dry Methodist minister on his left and a wet politician on his right. An old friend pointed out that Calvin Coolidge was holding the communion cup in one hand and a glass of beer in the other and spilling neither.[29] By refusing to belong officially to any church until he became President or to any prohibition organization, Coolidge could attract the negative support of all who were offended by particular churches and liquor laws.

Coolidge's success in Northampton was due to his appeal both to the church and to the saloon vote. There were eighteen churches and eighteen saloons for a town population of 18,000, which was almost exactly split between the old American stock and the immigrants, between Protestants and Roman Catholics. This religious and racial split was a microcosm of the whole situation in Massachusetts and in the nation. Throughout his political career, Coolidge had to appeal to a certain number of wet, Roman Catholic, immigrant voters, although he was personally a dry, nondenominational, traditional Vermonter. Thus he had to be silent on racial and religious issues. This silence he built up into a myth of political honesty, not of political acumen.

The steady progress of Coolidge from the post of Mayor of North-ampton into the state House of Representatives and into the state Senate demonstrated that his shyness, economy of language, and discretion were great assets in the elections. For western Massachusetts was mainly Congregationalist and Republican and dry, the home of old American stock and small industries; while eastern Massachusetts was chiefly Roman Catholic and Democratic and wet, the home of Irishmen and large industries. Senator Murray Crane, the sophisticated Republican boss of his time in the areas where Senator Lodge had not carved out his own preserves, helped the prudently silent Coolidge into the leadership of the state Senate and eventually into the lieutenant governorship and governorship. A man like Coolidge, who had been progressive when Theodore Roosevelt was progressive within his party, and who was conservative when big business was accused of self-interest rather than public interest, was always useful to any Republican machine. Moreover, both Crane and Coolidge knew that, except in times of war or crusade, a shut mouth was better than a fiery tongue.[30]

Coolidge took refuge from the danger of opposing the drys on the good democratic grounds that local government was the best form of government. In Northampton, he had supported the license system by saying that total prohibition would be impossible to enforce on a town surrounded by wet areas. Besides, he refused to mention the liquor problem at all during his political campaigns, since he maintained that it distracted voters from more important issues. In his campaign for Lieutenant Governor, he was actually opposed by the drys and the progressives. But his own abstinence, allied with the support of the brewers and the conservatives, secured him a majority of over 100,000 votes.

But more and more states were going dry. Therefore, the careful Coolidge was discreet in his campaign for Governor in 1918. The Republican candidate for the Senate, John W. Weeks, was opposed by the suffragettes, labor, and the prohibitionists. Coolidge knew this and avoided any mention of Weeks during his campaign. Weeks lost; Coolidge won. He was helped by the fact that Frank W. Stearns, his self-appointed and selfless publicity manager, was actively working for the adoption of the Eighteenth Amendment by the Massachusetts legislature. Moreover, Senator Crane was backing ratification by Massachusetts, "first, because it's right, and secondly, because Massachusetts will lose its influence in the counsels of the Nation if it does not join in this movement of national conviction."[31] Crane may not have had a real change of heart in accepting the morality of prohibition, but he would certainly never be left off a successful bandwagon. Coolidge, always the lawyer and the friend of Crane, went dry after the election and after ratification by Massachusetts — an important victory which swung the immigrant and industrial Northern states behind the drys. In 1919, as Governor of Massachusetts, Coolidge vetoed a bill passed by the wets in the state legislature, which allowed the sale of weak beer. Coolidge's reason was that the bill was in violation of the Constitution that he had sworn to defend.

Prohibition was a strange factor in the incident which made Coolidge nationally known and led to his nomination as Vice President and later as President. The Boston police went on strike in 1919, because their commissioner refused to allow their union to become affiliated with the American Federation of Labor. The policemen were badly paid and depended on bribes from saloonkeepers to supplement their incomes.[32] But in the first two years of prohibition in Boston, some attempt was made to enforce the law. The old saloons were closed down, and the new bootleggers were not yet operating on a sufficiently wide scale to take their place as employers of the police. Thus, by efficient service, the policemen found themselves with too little money to support themselves. They went on strike. After some looting and a riot in Scollay Square, where two were killed and nine injured by the State Guard, Governor Coolidge intervened with messages and force, although the whole matter had already been settled by the Mayor of Boston. Coolidge always believed in gaining the credit for successful actions without running the risk of performing unpleasant ones. His message to Samuel Gompers that there was "no right to strike against the public safety by any body, any time, any where" had all the qualities of strength and brevity needed to impress a people scared of Reds and revolution. It was widely and carefully publicized.

Therefore, Calvin Coolidge had some hopes of nomination as a dark horse at the Republican convention of 1920. As always, there was little to be said against him, even if there was little to be said for him. He was, in fact, available, especially as he had won many elections in the key state of Massachusetts. Stearns, conscious of the power of the Anti-Saloon League, had taken care to have fifty thousand copies of Coolidge's veto of the beer bill sent around to a carefully selected list of prominent party members. The veto message had been commended by Wayne B. Wheeler as "characteristically epigrammatic, faultless in logic, American to the core and in harmony with the fundamental principles of law and order for which Governor Coolidge has made himself famous."[33] The stampede of the convention for Coolidge as Vice President may have had something to do with his dry reputation, but it was more a protest against the attempted foisting of Senator Lenroot on the delegates by the same senatorial soviet that had nominated Harding.

At this period, the office of Vice President was chiefly a time of waiting for a dead man's shoes. Coolidge duly waited, and was rewarded. President Harding died on August 3, 1923. Calvin Coolidge's father administered the presidential oath to his son at a carefully simple ceremony at his home in Plymouth Notch. Coolidge continued the Harding policy and Cabinet, only dismissing Daugherty with the greatest reluctance when prohibition scandals became too notorious.

The appointment of Harlan F. Stone to the position of Attorney General put a stop to the "government by blackmail" of the Department of Justice, and to official protection of bootleggers by the enforcement agencies.

Coolidge, however, was no more prepared than Harding to see that the Volstead Act was properly enforced. He merely did not collect official protection from the bootleggers. He was willing, as Harding was, to make speeches about the need to obey the law. At the Governors' Conference of 1923, Coolidge spoke of the necessity for state co-operation in enforcement and the duty of the citizen to obey the Constitution. The main problem arose from those who wanted to make money from bootlegging; if this could be eliminated, the rest would be easy.[34] In his message to Congress of that year, he again exhorted the private citizen to abstinence from liquor, asked for large appropriations from the states for enforcement, and demanded an increase in the efficiency of the Coast Guard by the use of fast speedboats.[35] Congress reduced the appropriation for the Prohibition Bureau from $8,500,000 to $8,250,000, listening to Coolidge's pleas for national economy rather than for good government.[36]

Coolidge was not prepared to challenge Congress to enforce its own legislation. He did not point out that the Volstead Act could never be put into effect by an ill-paid and minute force of agents. He thought it sufficient to set a good example in personal prohibition, not to force others to be as good as himself. Alice Roosevelt Longworth found the atmosphere in the White House under Coolidge "as different as a New England front parlor is from a back room in a speakeasy."[37] Coolidge used his own example to cover up his political evasion. Even the Republican William Allen White complained that, while the President believed in a fair trial at strict enforcement, he refused to evangelize or make sentiment for the Volstead Act — the one thing it needed.[38] White further complained that Coolidge was silent about the heavy drinking of the upper classes, when "prohibition was pretty badly up against it in the East."[39] But Coolidge ignored the moralists, sat tight, and did little except talk about the duties of the good citizen.

His prudent silence served Coolidge well in the election of 1924. He was the automatic, if unwilling, nominee of his party in 1924. The Progressive Senator from Wisconsin, Robert M. La Follette, bolted his party to oppose him. And the Democrats nominated a Wall Street lawyer from West Virginia, John W. Davis. Prohibition was one of the reasons for Davis's nomination in New York, after seventeen days and 103 ballots, and the longest and most unpleasant convention in a party history of long and unpleasant conventions.

There, the issues that split the Democrats until the depression came out violently and vulgarly into the open. William G. McAdoo, backed by the Solid South and the drys and the Protestants and the Ku Klux Klan, was deadlocked with Alfred E. Smith, the reform Governor of New York, backed by Tammany Hall and the wets and the Roman Catholics and the Northern urban immigrants. Neither would give way to the other, and neither could reach the required two-thirds majority for victory. Cox was also running as Ohio's favorite son, but he had merely had himself nominated to keep the votes of the state from McAdoo, whom he disliked. The galleries were full of Al Smith's supporters. They gave Bryan a dreadful drubbing when he rose to ask forgiveness for the Ku Klux Klan. He was booed and hissed and humiliated, and a motion to censure the Klan was lost by only one vote in over a thousand. Bryan did keep a wet plank out of the party platform and help to scotch Al Smith's nomination. But his pet abomination, a lawyer who had taken cases for J. P. Morgan, was eventually picked out by the tired delegates. Not even the nomination of Bryan's younger brother Charles as candidate for Vice President could mollify the aging Great Commoner to approve of Davis as the Democratic choice for President.

It might have been better strategy for Davis to declare himself in favor of modification of the Volstead Act, instead of shifting uneasily from dry foot to wet foot and ending on his knees. For, unless a Roman Catholic ran as the Democratic candidate for President, the Solid South would still probably vote solid, and a great many wet votes might be gained in the Northern cities. Mencken savagely attacked Davis for his evasiveness on the prohibition issue.[40] All Davis would say was what he said in his acceptance speech, that he held in contempt any public official who took an oath to uphold the Constitution and made a mental reservation to exclude any word of that great document. Silent Calvin Coolidge did far better by saying nothing about prohibition, or much else.

The continual speeches of Davis insisting that he would enforce the law properly lost wet votes without gaining dry ones. Wheeler even accused him of deviating from his party platform and having secret alcoholic leanings, because he constantly repeated such wet catch phrases as "personal liberty is the doctrine of self-restraint" and "home rule."[41] Davis, in trying to please both sides, pleased neither; he polled even fewer votes than Cox. At the end of the campaign, he wryly told a joke against himself, explaining how he had lost both wets and drys. He had received a letter from a habitual Democrat and prohibitionist who was sorry that he had had to vote for a Republican for the first time, but he could not vote for a Democrat who had been President of the New York Bar Association.[42]

Mencken, who was normally proud of being a reactionary, voted in the end for La Follette, since he was that impossible phenomenon, an honest politician. Yet La Follette, too, was a trimmer on prohibition. The Wisconsin Progressive and Senator had sometimes drunk too much in his youth, but he had paid for his sins by joining the Good Templars.[43] He had made Wisconsin a model state with a reform government and had led the progressive wing of the Republicans for many years. With six others in the Senate, he had voted against America's entry into the First World War. Even when Theodore Roosevelt had recommended that he should be hanged as a traitor, he had stuck firm, more for his principles than for the German vote in Wisconsin. He had supported the Eighteenth Amendment, as the articles in the *Nation* backing his candidacy pointed out; but he had voted against the Volstead Act. His decision to run for President at the age of sixty-nine was only taken when he found the nominees of both parties to be the friends of big business.

La Follette campaigned on his usual Progressive platform. He was inevitably and frequently accused of being a Red by Charles Dawes, Coolidge's Vice President. In addition, he was attacked by Clarence True Wilson as the only wet candidate for the presidency, although he had taken up the same position over prohibition as his two opponents, writing that while the Volstead Act was still law "it should be enforced for rich and poor alike, without hypocrisy or favoritism."[44] Perhaps this was the statement Clarence True Wilson disliked; the drys had attracted big business to their side by agreeing that prohibition should be enforced on the poor, with a blind eye turned on the rich. Wheeler's opposition to La Follette was more political. He shared in the fear that a large vote for a third party might throw the presidential election into the House of Representatives; and a deadlock there would mean the election by the Senate of one of the two Vice Presidents to the presidency, a man who probably would not be so amenable to Wheeler's dictates as Coolidge.

The danger of La Follette's candidacy was exaggerated. He secured only one vote out of six, and thirteen votes from Wisconsin in the Electoral College, although he ran ahead of Davis in twelve Western states. Coolidge won by a landslide, even though it was La Follette who had come from the genuine log cabin. Davis lost by a greater margin than Cox, since he had the further disadvantage of representing nothing except the traditional Democratic party between the candidate of the Haves and the candidate of the Have-nots.

Calvin Coolidge, elected to the White House in his own right by an overwhelming majority, presumed that his huge mandate was a public expression of gratitude for his policy of federal inaction. During the next four years, he continued to do little, and never did little when less would do. The enforcement of prohibition hardly improved, although Coolidge did sign a bill in 1927 to make the Prohibition Bureau an independent body. After his reorganization of the 144 departments in the Massachusetts government into a mere 20, he thought that good government was the result of the shuffling about of responsibilities and memoranda, not of increased taxes and increased efficiency.

Coolidge, during the five years he was President, was the curious negative image of boom times. He was the reverse of the society he led. He did not seek to end corruption and exaggerated profits and vast speculation. He did not try to stamp out bootleggers and speak-easies and bad prohibition agents. He merely was not corrupt himself and did not drink. He expected the rest of the United States to follow his good example, without even exhorting them by political speeches. He had won the election of 1924 by saying nothing about prohibition or the scandals of the Harding regime; he merely collected votes as he had done in the Northampton election for Mayor in 1910 by attracting through silence. La Follette was a Red, Charles Bryan was a radical Westerner like his brother William Jennings, John Davis was a rich corporation lawyer, while Coolidge was his thrifty and honest and negative self. Thus he amassed, as he amassed in all his campaigns, the votes that were annoyed by some characteristic in the other candidates and could find nothing positive enough in Coolidge to dislike.

As Walter Lippmann pointed out, Coolidge, with an exquisite subtlety that amounted to genius, used dullness and boredom as political devices; under him America attained a Puritanism de luxe, in which it was possible to praise the classic virtues while continuing to enjoy all the modern conveniences.[45] Coolidge was the figurehead of his people. They felt that, while he denied himself, his abstinence would excuse their own indulgence, and his narrow sense of his own duties would allow that indulgence. They were right. Coolidge, incorruptible to the end, allowed Wall Street and prohibition to plunge the country into speculative and moral disaster.[46]

On the fourth anniversary of his Inauguration, Coolidge announced that he did not choose to run for President in 1928. This formula was one of Coolidge's cleverest evasions, where an honest statement of abdication hid a dishonest attempt to allow his party to renominate him for a third term. He did not *choose* to run, but he did not refuse to run if his party chose him. This was the interpretation put on his statement by his intimate friends like Stearns and Chief Justice Taft. And if Herbert Hoover gained control of the Republican convention machinery so effectively that he was nominated on the first ballot, Coolidge's disappointment was real enough, although his *Autobiog-*

raphy states that he never intended to run again, as he did not want to be thought selfish.[47]

Coolidge was always cryptic in order to have an escape route ready against failure. He was always personally honest in order to defend himself against the use of corrupt friends. He was a teetotaler so that he could plead personal abstinence when he was accused of having the support of the liquor interests, or of failing to enforce prohibition. He was a small man who pushed himself into great offices by preaching his small virtues and allowing others their large vices. While tens of millions suffered in the great depression, Calvin Coolidge lived well and thriftily on the money he had saved from his salary, until he died suddenly in January, 1933, from coronary thrombosis. He was true to the grave, doctoring himself with indigestion powders rather than wasting money by consulting a heart specialist.

The drys were unfortunate and the drinkers fortunate that men of such little stature as Warren Harding and Calvin Coolidge filled the White House during the first eight years of national prohibition. But the men who were President were not the only men to blame for the supine enforcement of the dry law. The two great parties in the land, and the houses of Congress, were equally guilty of doing little about prohibition, and not doing it very well.

CHAPTER 14

The Amphibious Congress

> Congress is the one place in the whole United States in which a mouth is above the law; the heavens may fall, the earth be consumed, but the right of a Congressman to lie and defame remains inviolate.
>
> GEORGE CREEL

> The Constitution is a document by which Congress can make its mistakes permanent.
>
> *Life*

> Politicians, in general, are not fastidious, and most of those from the interior, especially the drys, are ready to drink anything that burns, at the same time giving thanks to God.
>
> H. L. MENCKEN

THE DRY POLITICS OF PARTY

THE MAJOR American parties are uneasy coalitions of areas. These areas have their own faiths and traditions and wants. Indeed, the conflict of areas within the parties is often more bitter than the conflict between the two parties themselves. Yet, for one party to defeat another, an appearance of harmony must be presented during elections. Although party conventions may be the place for what Carry Nation called "hatchetation," the hatchet must be buried to woo the voters. For this reason, both parties try to avoid those wounding issues which even party expediency cannot heal. Such an issue was prohibition.

The straddles of the dry issue by the major parties were remarkable. Although prohibition was a national problem between 1916 and 1932, only in that final year did the platform of either party make more than a passing reference to the need for honest law enforcement. For the bosses of both parties did not want the subject raised at all. The Republicans were successful at suppressing debate at the conventions on the matter until Hoover's second nomination, and the Democrats were unsuccessful. In this matter, the nature and differences of both of the major parties were revealed.

The tactics of the Anti-Saloon League played into the hands of the evasive strategy of the party bosses. For the League did not want either party to write a prohibition plank into its platform. Such an action might make prohibition a partisan issue, and the League was committed to a nonpartisan policy. As Bishop Cannon wrote in 1920, "While I would have been pleased had both conventions adopted short law enforcement planks, yet after it failed of passage by the Republican convention, it was better for the prohibition cause that it should not be adopted by the Democratic convention."[1] Thus at the Democratic convention in San Francisco the strange sight was seen of a Democratic League leader speaking against a plank for the enforcement of the prohibition law, in opposition to a Republican League leader, Wayne B. Wheeler, and other dry spokesmen. Cannon was successful in preventing the Democrats from passing the dry plank in 1920, at the cost of being denounced by William Jennings Bryan as a real, if not intentional, enemy of prohibition.[2]

As Mencken pointed out on the subject of national party conventions, "Of the platform only one thing may be predicted: that it will please nobody. And of the candidate only one thing also: that he will be suspected by all."[3] He went on to comment that a single factor broke all the rules in American politics. That factor was prohibition. It caused the delegates to buck their normal subservience to the party bosses and the masterminds, and defeated all attempts to bury its discussion, especially among the Democrats. Moreover, it brought out a fundamental difference between the personal habits of the delegates to the conventions. "The Republicans commonly carry their liquor better than the Democrats, just as they commonly wear their clothes better. One seldom sees one of them actively sick in the convention hall, or dead drunk in a hotel lobby." This individual behavior emphasized the party difference. "Republicans have a natural talent for compromise, but to Democrats it is almost impossible."[4]

Until 1932, the history of prohibition in major party politics is a history of the Democratic party. The discreet Republicans swept the affair under the carpet and concentrated on the business of Business. But the Democrats battled the issue up gallery and down hall. It was a mirror to them, an inescapable revelation of the aged wrinkles that marred the fair face of their party. In that glass, the uneasy coalition of Northern cities and Southern states saw its flawed donkey face, and brayed its self-hate to the ears of the nation. It was not until the South bolted from the dry cause to the wet Franklin D. Roosevelt that the Democrats trotted together to victory, pulling in the same harness.

The Democrats had the bad luck of losing their great leader William Jennings Bryan to the cause of prohibition. Bryan's way at conventions was not the way of hidden negotiation but the way of moral stampede. As an unknown, he had won the presidential nomination in 1896 by his oratory of righteousness, and his methods did not alter. In 1912, his resolution against the influence of the big businessmen, Morgan and Belmont and Ryan, and his switch to the support of Woodrow Wilson, changed the course of a convention which seemed bound to nominate Champ Clark, of Missouri. In 1916, Wilson did not need Bryan's help and used his loyalty to prevent him from forcing the issue over prohibition. But in 1920, Bryan was not so hampered. He went there, not in the interests of any candidate, but to combat the wet element of the East, which clamored for modification of the Volstead Act to allow the sale of light wines and beer.[5] He also went there, bullheaded and bright-armored, to secure an outright prohibition plank in the party platform. Rather than Wheeler's wish of a plank favoring law enforcement or Cannon's wish of no plank at all, Bryan wanted a plank favoring prohibition as the permanent policy of the country, and favoring the enforcement of the Volstead Law "in letter and in spirit."[6]

But the delegates at the convention were seduced not by the golden voice of morality, but by the sly whisper of expediency. Cannon's policy of silence prevailed. The convention voted down Bryan's dry plank by 929½ votes to 155½, and Bourke Cochran's wet plank by 726½ to 356. The platform, which made no mention of prohibition or of law enforcement, was accepted by acclamation. In the following struggle for the nomination, Bryan tried to block the nomination of Cox, who was the moist candidate of the wets, by circulating among the delegates lengthy statements of Cox's wet record in Ohio during his three terms as Governor. But the nominee of the drys, William G. McAdoo, had too many enemies to triumph over Cox, and Bryan's heart went "in the grave" with his defeat. There is truth in Cannon's nasty comment that Bryan was despondent because he had hoped to make prohibition a political asset and realized that possibly his last chance for the presidency went into the grave with the dry plank.[7]

The defeated McAdoo went after the presidential nomination at the next convention with all his thoroughness and pertinacity. He corralled behind him the vote of South and West, and the unspoken support of the Ku Klux Klan, which approved of such a dry representative of old American ideals and stock. He would have almost certainly won the nomination but for two factors. The first was the casual revelation of the corrupt oil millionaire, Edward L. Doheny, in the Elk Hills and Teapot Dome scandal, that he had employed McAdoo as his attorney at a retainer of fifty thousand dollars a year. And the second was the opposition of the Eastern cities, led by the wet Irish Governor of New York, Alfred E. Smith.

The Democratic convention in 1924 was the bitterest and bloodiest in party history. The packed galleries howled so savagely for Smith that a fearful Southern dry delegate ran to the press box for a stiff drink and protection. Nothing since the slavery issue had so broken apart the Democrats, and now three implacable divisions had arisen, those of prohibition and of religion and of the Ku Klux Klan. After seventeen days of balloting, the deadlock between McAdoo and Smith was resolved by the election of John W. Davis. But the divisions of the party, broadcast throughout the nation by radio for the first time, were neither solved, forgiven, nor forgotten. A resolution to condemn the Klan failed by one vote; luckily, the Klan itself failed within a few years. The religious issue would plague the Democrats until Smith was finally nominated and defeated in 1928. And prohibition remained the Democratic curse and muckrake.

The effort of the Democrats to sidestep the prohibition issue by trying to make the Republicans wholly responsible for the evils of enforcement met with no success. The wets knew already what the Democratic platform charged, that "the Republican administration has failed to enforce the prohibition law, is guilty of trafficking in liquor permits, and has become the protector of violators of this law." They did not want to vote for a party pledged "to respect and enforce the Constitution and all laws," but for a party pledged to outright modification or repeal. The wets were even disappointed by the radical Progressive, La Follette, who was so equivocal over prohibition that the Association Against the Prohibition Amendment refused to endorse him for the presidency.[8]

Yet, if the Anti-Saloon League played hell with the politics of the major parties, so did the major parties cause rifts in the united front of the League. After the death in 1924 of Purley A. Baker, the national superintendent of the League, a compromise candidate, F. Scott McBride, was put in his place. Wayne B. Wheeler and Bishop James Cannon then settled down to a bitter struggle for control of the political power and image of the League. Cannon relinquished the Republican party to the tender care of Wheeler, but he resented Wheeler's forays into his own sphere of influence, the Democratic party. He maintained that Wheeler's Republican bias and his backing of Coolidge for re-election in 1928 made him unfit to influence the choice of the Democratic candidate. Cannon allowed that it was fair enough for Wheeler to do his work among the Democrats through Bryan, who was a close friend of his; but he bitterly resented Wheeler's attempt to take credit for defeating a wet Democratic candidate in the convention of 1924. He issued a statement of his own on behalf of the Anti-Saloon League which merely read, "The wets have been defeated in their efforts to secure a wet plank or a wet candidate at the Democratic convention. There is no smell of beer or wine in the Democratic platform, and the candidate is a strong advocate of law enforcement."[9]

But although the League was split on its attitude toward the major parties, it was united on its attitude to Congress. In Washington, Wayne B. Wheeler had full control. He sat smiling in the Visitors' Gallery, counting the number of the drys and keeping them true to the cause by threats of retribution at the polls. As Senator Bruce, of Maryland, scornfully declared, "Wayne B. Wheeler had taken snuff, and the Senate, as usual, sneezed. Wayne B. Wheeler had cracked his whip, and the Senate, as usual, crouched."[10]

THE AMPHIBIOUS CONGRESS

AN ARTICLE in 1923 described the Volstead Act as neither wet nor dry. There was only one word to describe it. It was "amphibious."[11] This was also the public and private position of Congress during the course of national prohibition.

The mood of Congress after the passage of the Volstead Act was one of relief. They appropriated $2,000,000 for its enforcement, and hoped to be left by the triumphant drys in a decent peace. They should concentrate on more important matters, such as America's part in the League of Nations and the "nation-wide industrial war" threatening the United States.[12] During the first six months of national prohibition, the subject of liquor was mentioned in Congress only six times. Although the newspapers and law-enforcement agencies showed how wet the cities still were and how liquor smuggling was making a nonsense of the border, Congress remained in willed ignorance. The only serious contribution to the problems of prohibition was made by Senator Warren, of Wyoming, who pointed out that a proper attempt to enforce the Volstead Act might cost $50,000,000 a year. Senator Sheppard read in reply a letter from Wayne B. Wheeler which stated that, even if Senator Warren's figure was true, it would not be "an inexcusable expenditure," considering the waste of a billion dollars a year for liquor and in view of the lawlessness of the liquor traffic. In Wheeler's opinion, however, $5,000,000 a year was ample to enforce the Volstead Act, and this sum might even be reduced if the liquor dealers suddenly became law-abiding.[13]

The second year of prohibition was also quiet for Congress. It was true, there were complaints about the difficulties of enforcement from the Commissioner of Internal Revenue and the Attorney General. An increased total of $6,350,000 had to be voted to pay for enforcement in 1921. But the Anti-Saloon League was happy with the state of affairs, boasting that a billion dollars had been saved by the country in 1920.[14] Wayne B. Wheeler even predicted that prohibition enforcement would pay for itself in 1921, since its costs would be less than the money received from the sale of confiscated goods.[15] Only Attorney General Palmer's ruling in favor of the medical prescription of beer and wine disturbed the honeymoon of Congress and the dry lobbies. Nevertheless, the passage of the Willis-Campbell Act, to restrict the medical prescription of liquor, rebuffed the medical profession and overruled the Attorney General.

During these two years of congressional inaction, liquor entered America in an increasing flood. This was fully reported in the newspapers. Yet the dry lobbies made no protest. For they were in a difficult position. They were no longer revolutionaries seeking change, but conservatives defending the changes made. They could not admit that bootleg liquor was easy to get in America without seeming to confess to the failure of national prohibition. They could not agree that law enforcement was inadequate without seeming to preach increased taxes in a Republican age interested in public economy. And above all, they could not confess that the Volstead Act was a bad act, for they had written it themselves. They had to ignore their critics and cry complacency. For they were no longer the accusers, but the accused.

In one aspect of prohibition enforcement, however, the Anti-Saloon League and Congress were blatantly guilty. That aspect was the clause in the Volstead Act which exempted prohibition agents from Civil Service examinations. The National Civil Service Reform League opposed the clause in 1919, but Congress ignored their opposition. The secretary of the Reform League, finding Congressman Volstead unsympathetic, went to see Wheeler to plead his cause. Wheeler admitted the desirability of putting the Prohibition Bureau under Civil Service rules, "but he believed it would be impossible to obtain the passage of a bill in the House unless the places were exempted from the civil service law."[16] In other words, Wheeler and the Anti-Saloon League were prepared to let "the slimy trail of the spoils serpent" issue from Congress in return for the passage of the Volstead Act.[17] Wheeler wanted, in the words of Senator Bruce, of Maryland, "to trade the offices to be held by [prohibition] agents for congressional votes."[18]

Later, when corruption in the Prohibition Bureau became a national scandal, Wheeler admitted his mistake. But while appointments to the

Bureau remained in his hands and those of Congress, he would not relinquish such a fertile field for negotiations and pressure, even though several political appointments were made to the Bureau over his veto. Wheeler would never give up any area of his personal power even for his cause. For he had identified the cause of the Anti-Saloon League wholly with himself. Bishop Cannon later wrote that Wheeler's policy of political interference and personal aggrandizement undermined the real power of the Anti-Saloon League and brought it into discredit in later years.[19] It is certainly true that President Coolidge did not sign a bill to put the Prohibition Bureau under Civil Service rules until the year of Wheeler's death.

During the twenties, the Anti-Saloon League increased its power within Congress, and Wheeler increased his power within the Anti-Saloon League. The new national superintendent of the League, F. Scott McBride, gave Wheeler a free hand in Washington. Meanwhile, in the elections of 1922, Wheeler had provoked the wets into declaring a list of the candidates whom they were supporting. Such a deluge of letters poured upon the endorsed wet candidates that many of them swore to Wheeler that they were dry, and repudiated wet support. Although Volstead lost his seat in Minnesota, the drys increased their count in the House to 296, and won twenty-five out of thirty-five contests for the Senate.[20]

During the next two years, Congress still pussyfooted over the issue of prohibition. While the newspapers reported that the law-enforcement situation was steadily growing worse, Congress did little to increase the appropriations of the Prohibition Bureau. $6,750,000 was voted for 1923 and $8,500,000 for 1924. This provided for a field force of just over 1500 agents and investigators to dry up a nation whose coast line and border were 18,700 miles long, whose total area was more than 3,000,000 square miles, and whose population was over 105,000,000.[21] The statistics made each prohibition agent responsible for 12 miles of border, 2000 square miles of interior, and 70,000 people. Of course, if the states had been prepared to bear their share of enforcement, matters would have been easier for the Prohibition Bureau. But the states took their responsibility under the phrase "concurrent power" to mean that they should and did spend one-quarter of the amount on enforcing national prohibition that they spent on the upkeep of their monuments and parks.[22]

Proposals were made in 1924 for an investigation into the problems of law enforcement, but these were voted down by the dry majority. Senator Sheppard characterized an investigation as worse than useless, "a waste of funds and energy and time." The Prohibition Bureau should not be investigated but given a vote of thanks.[23] The drys in

Congress feared that an impartial investigation under the auspices of Congress would confirm what the wet press trumpeted, that prohibition was not and could not be enforced. Until there was such an impartial investigation, the drys could dismiss the allegations of reporters as biased balderdash. Meanwhile, they pursued a popular policy of government economy, moral protestations, and lax enforcement, which satisfied both the ears of the drys and the throats of the wets. Above all, Congress did not want a searching examination of the Prohibition Bureau, since it might reveal how political appointments had made the Bureau into a corrupt and inefficient institution.

In the elections of 1924, with the Democratic party crippled over its internecine struggle over prohibition and with the Republican party bound for an easy victory, the drys increased their three-to-one majority in both houses of Congress. This time, the wets published a list, not of those they supported, but of those they opposed. Five out of six candidates for the House opposed by the wets were elected. Of the thirteen new Senators in Congress, eleven favored prohibition legislation. Wheeler estimated that the Senate was dry by 72 to 24, and the house by 319 to 105.[24] He counted the defeat of Senator Stanley, of Kentucky, as a personal victory. The Senator had attacked the Anti-Saloon League on the floor of the Senate, and Wheeler's personal assistant had spent seven weeks organizing his overthrow.[25] "Each year," Wheeler testified complacently, "the Congress that has been elected has been drier than its predecessor."[26] Unfortunately, each year the country was growing wetter.

Increasingly, the wet minority in Congress became vocal and militant. Outside Congress, wealthy wet organizations such as the Association Against the Prohibition Amendment were offering statistics and political aid to champions of their cause. Fifty-nine identical bills to provide for the sale of light wines and beer were introduced in Congress; all came to grief in the dry House Committee on the Judiciary. Although the wets were powerless in Congress, their complaints became more and more publicized. Moreover, the dry majority in the House continued its policy of letting sleeping bootleggers lie by failing to increase appropriations for law enforcement to any great degree. The sums appropriated for the years between 1924 and 1926 averaged $9,310,000 a year. The lack of proper prohibition enforcement was blamed on the Prohibition Bureau, which was reorganized time and time again. But little was done to improve the poor quality of its agents, whose appointment was largely in the hands of that very same dry majority in Congress.

Congress showed its temper by its treatment of the program of the new head of the Prohibition Bureau, General Lincoln C. Andrews.

Wheeler had not been consulted about Andrews's appointment in April, 1925, and he disliked his exclusion. The efforts of Andrews to replace political appointees in the Bureau with retired Army and Navy officers brought a rebuke from Secretary of the Treasury Mellon, requiring Andrews to consult members of Congress before making new appointments to the Bureau. In his report to the executive committee of the Anti-Saloon League, Wheeler wrote, "Political leaders in the various states will resent the idea that their directors should be removed. It will interfere with political patronage."[27] Andrews antagonized the government, Congress, and Wheeler by his sincere efforts to get effective enforcement.

In 1926, Andrews proposed to Congress that the Prohibition Bureau should come under Civil Service rules, and should be given an increased appropriation of $3,000,000 a year. It should also have more control over medicinal liquor, industrial alcohol, and breweries which ostensibly manufactured near-beer. It should be given authority to board ships outside the twelve-mile limit, to confiscate captured vessels, and to search private homes on suspicion of commercial manufacture.[28] None of these recommendations was passed by Congress until Andrews had been forced to resign by Mellon because of growing disaffection with that law enforcement which he was not allowed to reform.

But Congressional rebellion against Wheeler and the dry lobbies had already begun in 1926, the very year that Wheeler's superhuman labors made him a sick man and kept him sick until his death two years later. This rebellion suddenly became public, although it had always smoldered in private. The appointment of the wet leader Senator James Reed, of Missouri, to a subcommittee of the Senate Committee on the Judiciary was the beginning of the congressional counterattack on the Anti-Saloon League. Congress had been humiliated too often by the League to treat its enemy lightly.

The private rebellion of Congress against prohibition was the private rebellion of drinkers all over the nation. In this way, the rebellion at Washington can be excused. For, although it was unconstitutional, it was truly representative. Like the public, members of both houses of Congress voted dry and drank wet. If there was no hypocrisy in their attitude, there was a fine distinction drawn between public and private belief. Some drys even defended such behavior as a sign of the good practical politician. It demonstrated, according to them, the strength of prohibition.[29]

And they were right. When a private habit cannot be made public by politicians, it is because they are truly afraid to speak. Fear of the Anti-Saloon League made a monstrous conspiracy of silence descend upon the national capital. An article in the Washington *Post* of 1928, quoted by Senator Blease, of Arkansas, claimed that there were nearly a thousand speak-easies in the city.[30] A new art had been discovered there, "the art of sotto voce in little back rooms." These speak-easies were not molested, as the powers-that-be wished for them to let alone.[31]

Yet, however discreet the politicians were, they provided evidence enough of their defiance of the law which they were sworn to uphold. Conditions in Washington under the presidency of Harding were notorious. The Ohio Gang openly peddled bootleg liquor from 1625 K Street. The liquor was brought there in plain view by agents of the Department of Justice; it was liquor which had been confiscated by the Prohibition Bureau. Coolidge's succession on Harding's death did something, however, to clean up the blatant scandals in the capital. The President's personal abstinence made the congressional drinkers less loud about their practices. Even those who made a profession of their wet beliefs, such as George Tinkham and Nicholas Longworth, did their drinking privately, although Tinkham kept on the walls of his office a collection of wild beasts' heads named after the dry leaders. It was perhaps unfortunate that the most convinced dry of all the Presidents, Herbert Hoover, was in power during the chief exposé of high life in Washington.

Mabel Walker Willebrandt, Assistant Attorney General in 1929, wrote about the *Inside of Prohibition*. According to her, many Congressmen and Senators who voted dry were persistent violators of the Volstead Act. Senators and Representatives had appeared drunk on the floor of the Senate and House. A waiter had dropped a bottle of whisky on the floor of the Capitol Restaurant. Nothing had done more to disgust honest men and women against prohibition. Why, Mrs. Willebrandt demanded, had no search warrants ever been issued to rout bootleggers out of government buildings? One agent had applied for such a warrant, and been refused it. This was, surely, bad law and bad policy.

Mrs. Willebrandt discovered a curious state of mind among members of Congress and other government officials. They believed that they were "above and beyond the inhibitions of the prohibition law."[32] One Congressman had been sentenced for conspiring to sell and transport liquor on fraudulent permits.[33] Another had been found "not guilty" by a jury, although he had in his possession "nonintoxicating" wine containing 12 per cent of alcohol.[34] Other Congressmen requested "freedom of the port" from the Treasury Department, and they landed their luggage unchecked by Customs. On one famous occasion, the baggage of a dry Congressman from Illinois went astray and was found to contain a keg of rum and twelve bottles of liqueurs. On another occasion, a Congressman from Ohio was discovered with booze in his baggage on a return trip from Panama. Although juries were lenient to these two offenders, who swore that the contrabrand was not theirs but another's, Mrs. Willebrandt and the grand jury of the Southern District of New York thought that "public officials should be the first to set the example of scrupulous acceptance and observance of the burdens of the law."[35]

The final denouement, which would have shattered the last pretensions of dry Washington, was fortunately suppressed. When the Senate Lobby Investigation Committee seized the complete secret files of the Association Against the Prohibition Amendment in 1930, they found a confidential report of the private drinking habits of members of Congress.[36] The report was never made public. As the *Outlook* commented, "Dry members of the Senate Lobby Committee welched very prettily when it came to a genuine showdown."[37]

The record of the behavior of members of Congress during prohibition is a nasty one. Many of them were dry in public speech and wet in private life. Many of them were whipped onto the prohibitionist side solely from fear of the influence of the Anti-Saloon League at the polls. Many of them were content to appropriate too little money for law enforcement, and then to denounce the evils of that inadequate enforcement. Many hoped that if they glossed over the problems of prohibition the problems would somehow disappear of themselves. Many wanted the appearance of morality, not the fact. Many echoed the personal habits of a Harding and the political quiescence of a Coolidge.

THE REED COMMITTEE

IF PROHIBITION made difficult the congressional and private lives of the representatives of the people, it also caused havoc to their electoral machinations. In 1926, Senator Reed, of Missouri, and four other Senators were directed by the Senate to investigate abuses in certain primary campaigns during the senatorial elections. This subcommittee turned up an extraordinary brew of corruption and crookery. As a consequence of its findings, William Vare, of Pennsylvania, and Frank L. Smith, of Illinois, were unseated by the Senate. Further evidence showed that the Ku Klux Klan had partially taken over the government of Indiana, and that copper companies were trying to take over the administration of Arizona. Only in Washington, where the dry Senator Wesley Jones had alleged that his Democratic opponent was using a slush fund of $150,000 donated by bootleggers, did the investigation discover that the charges were smears. The findings of the subcommittee are the most damning indictment of American democracy ever produced, and are also a searchlight on the corrupt politics which the dry and the wet lobbies encouraged in their struggle over prohibition.

Reed strained his powers as chairman of the subcommittee to seize the secret files of the Anti-Saloon League. He tried to prove that the League had interfered with the processes of democracy in Pennsylvania. But all he revealed was that the League had little real power in Pennsylvania at all. The Republicans were in such control of the state that victory in the primary there meant election to the Senate. Unfortunately, the Republican machine had fallen out with itself, and a three-cornered fight for the senatorial nomination had developed. Vare, the boss of Philadelphia, ran on a wet ticket calling for legal light wines and beer. The incumbent Senator Pepper, backed by the powerful Mellon interests, ran on a middle-of-the-road ticket, appealing to both wets and drys. And the state Governor, Gifford Pinchot, ran on an extreme dry ticket, backed by neither city machines nor billions of dollars.

The result of the election was that the Mellons elected their candidate for Governor and Vare elected himself as Senator. Pinchot ran well behind Vare and Pepper in the primary. He could not even get all the dry "decent vote" behind him, for both Anti-Saloon League and Woman's Christian Temperance Union were split between voting for him and voting for Pepper, whom Vare's manager called "dry in the east and wet in the west . . . wobbling from one side to the other, trying to dip in and get a little from both sides."[38] Although all the speak-easies and brothels in Pittsburgh displayed prominent signs asking their patrons to vote for Pepper, the dry lobbies did not condemn him.[39] Wayne B. Wheeler testified that the League had been split between Pepper, who "voted right," and Pinchot, who was "very aggressive on prohibition and its enforcement." In the end, the League put out a statement asking "all friends of good government to concentrate their vote on that one of the two satisfactory candidates who has the best chance to defeat Mr. Vare." This split dry vote was the reason that the drys, in Wheeler's words, "got licked."[40]

In fact, the leading organization of the wets, the Association Against the Prohibition Amendment, came out of the election far worse than the Anti-Saloon League, whose equivocal and unilateral methods of endorsing candidates it had adopted. A letter was sent to the 30,000 members of the Pennsylvania Association asking them to support Vare. The letter said that Pinchot, who was an honest and good reformer, had "intellectual affinities that did not justify anybody in supporting him for a dignified office"; that Pepper, although a good citizen, lacked "moral courage" and voted dry; and that Vare, although associated with a corrupt machine in Philadelphia, did possess "moral courage" and should be supported.[41] It was a choice among evils for the wets, but Vare was the least of the three evils. Like the dry lobbies, the wet lobbies would vote for any supporter, however bad, against any opponent, however good. Prohibition was the sole judge of their "moral courage" and fitness to represent their fellows.

In the Illinois election, however, the League came out of the investigation in a worse light than the Association. The League had successfully supported the nomination of Frank L. Smith in the Republican primary. After the primary, Smith was proved to have accepted a sum of at least $125,000 from the public utilities magnate of the Midwest, Samuel Insull. His Democratic opponent, George E. Brennan, was a Chicago boss and a wet. Thus the contest appeared to be one between business corruption and the corruption of prohibition. But at the last moment, a dry Independent candidate, Hugh S. Magill, announced his candidacy in the name of good government and honest law enforcement. He asked for the support of the Anti-Saloon League and its mailing list of 125,000 voters. Yet the League stuck to Smith. As the state superintendent of the League, George Safford, testified, the League felt forced to choose between the two major party candidates, since the Independent Magill did not have a chance of winning. The League's attitude was that of the Reverend John Williams of the Methodist Episcopal Church, "I will hold my nose and vote for Smith."[42] Indeed, the League tried to persuade Magill to withdraw and accused his supporters of wanting a wet victory, for his candidacy would split the dry vote and let Brennan win. This attitude provoked from Magill the declaration that he would "never take dictation from Wayne Wheeler or Scott McBride or George Safford, because by their actions in this case they have demonstrated to the Nation that they are absolutely unfit to advise, much less, dictate to the decent people of Illinois and the Nation."[43]

The scandals in Pennsylvania and Illinois did harm to the League and the Association Against the Prohibition Amendment. It showed that both put their cause above the cause of reform and good government. In addition, it showed that their support was often ineffective. For neither in Pennsylvania nor in Illinois did the League and the Association mean much. It was money and machine support that counted. The two radical drys, Pinchot and Magill, both came last in the polls by a large margin. A labor leader testified in Pennsylvania, "When the two extremely rich men got into a fuss, then it was a choice of the two evils."[44] In estimating the real source of each candidate's strength, the dry and wet factor sank into insignificance.[45] In fact, the true manipulator of elections was the hidden hand of big business and criminal interests, which often worked together. As an oil and mining operator told the state superintendent of the Anti-Saloon League in Arizona, "You can't do anything out here; this is a campaign for the big boys . . . Little tiddle-de-winks folks like the Anti-Saloon League couldn't buck that sort of game."[46]

The conditions prevalent under prohibition made it easier for big business men and criminals to co-operate and interfere in elections. A general tolerance of the bootlegger and a disrespect for federal law were translated into a widespread contempt for the processes and duties of democracy. This played into the hands of those who wished to elect their own agents to positions of power. A vice president of the American Federation of Labor told the Wickersham Commission, "There is a feeling of corruption, of everything being corrupt, and it is bringing itself into the trade-unions. They feel if a judge can be bought for liquor, he can be bought for anything else; if a police officer can be quieted by a little money for liquor, he can be quieted for something else."[47] It was the profits and power derived from protection rackets and bootlegging that gave the gangsters the gall to interfere flagrantly at elections. The Reed Committee discovered that gunmen had openly run the polls at the election of 1924 in Cicero, Illinois, the headquarters of Al Capone. They found out that the Chicago election judges and clerks were, in the testimony of one witness, "ex-convicts, confirmed criminals, disreputable men."[48] Meanwhile, in Indiana, the backers of the moist Senator Watson were bootleggers who were "forced at the point of a gun" by the police to contribute to his campaign. In addition, in Lake County, Indiana, there were "a large number of sluggers . . . from Chicago, who went from one polling booth to another, intimidating voters. They had at every polling place . . . polling officers favorable to the Watson organization."[49]

Indeed, if the dry lobbies put through prohibition under the theory that they were saving good government in America from the monstrous conspiracies of the liquor trade, they did not realize that they were delivering politics into the far worse hands of the bootleggers, fraudulent businessmen, and criminals. The use of sub-machine guns and bombs in elections was a result of the impudence of small-time crooks and big-time politicians, who thought themselves great from the profits of prohibition. It was the unlimited opportunities for graft as well as prosperity that made the America of the twenties seem such a rich and careless place. Clive Weed drew rightly in *Judge* the hand behind the back, waiting for the bribe as "The National Gesture." But few cared. The scandals of the Harding regime were not enough to

CLERK
PETTY OFFICIAL
MAGISTRATE
POLITICIAN
POLICE OFFICER
PROHIBITION AGENT
Weed

By Clive Weed in *Judge*

THE NATIONAL GESTURE

bring down the Republican party; they only served to confirm the Grand Old Party in power. Mass unemployment was the shock that made bribery and dirty business seem a shameful way of depriving the needy of the money and the jobs which were their due.

The last service of the Reed Committee was to reveal the most sinister element of all in American politics, the Ku Klux Klan, which had appointed itself in many American states as an unofficial dry enforcement agency as well as a political pressure group. Because of a split in the Klan in Indiana, many disgruntled Klansmen were prepared to break their horrific oath of secrecy and to reveal the workings of the organization there. The split was caused by the use of the Klan as an out-and-out political agency rather than as a "Christian, benevolent, fraternal organization — principles that the Klan stood for."* The leader of the political Klan machine, as a prohibition agent testified, was guilty of throwing drunken orgies in his own home, while some of the local Klan leaders had been convicted of preserving the purity of American women by trying to rape them. Indeed, the reputation of the Klan in Indiana had become so noisome that its membership had dropped to one-quarter of its former numbers. However stupid the Klansmen were, they had joined the Klan for a moral purpose, however mistaken, and would not tolerate the misbehavior of their leaders. As an evangelical minister said, "We have had some good men in the Klan. They are not staying by it now."[50]

Prohibition added lobbies to legislatures, corruption to corrupt politics, and conspiracies to democratic practice. The drys became, often enough, the unwitting whitewash on a rotting sepulcher. Indeed, the rackets which their moral legislation encouraged made that very moral legislation seem a racket in itself. Some of the chiefs of the gangs contributed to the dry movement and employed as fronts "Bible-backed" citizens. These employees were referred to as "amen racketeers."[51]

If great parties are fearful of offending, if Congresses care overmuch for economy and the electorate, if elections are often corrupt and nasty affairs, then prohibition increased the fear and the care and the nastiness of politics in its time. The Anti-Saloon League and the Eighteenth Amendment appeared to be permanent and implacable features in American life. Under their banner, the country took heart, and rallied in the presidential election of 1928, when the farm boy from Iowa beat the slum child from New York.

* The ignorance and social class upon which the Klan thrived is shown by some revealing remarks in the testimony of an Exalted Grand Cyclops of the Order. He said that the Grand Wizard of the Klan, Doctor Evans, "could almost convince the average Klansman that we had in the State of Indiana that Jesus Christ was not a Jew." Doctor Evans had also been asked why the Klansmen did not parade with their hoods raised; he had replied, "The morale of the Klan would kill itself."

CHAPTER 15

Last Victory

> I'd rather see a saloon on every corner in the South than see the foreigners elect Al Smith President.
>
> REVEREND BOB JONES

> God is still greater than Tammany. For if Al Smith is elected in November the Democratic Party with its heritage of glorious principles becomes the party of Rome and Rum for the next hundred years.
>
> REVEREND BOB SCHULER

THE INTERACTING roots of prohibition, the psychology of country and rural reform, the progressive temper of the times, the support of the middle classes and women, the social influence of the Protestant evangelical churches, and the particularism of the South were beginning to wither and separate in the twenties. But the presidential election of 1928 brought them together again briefly and powerfully. The threat of Alfred E. Smith in the White House combined against him many of those nativist, reform, and reactionary elements which had opposed the saloon as the home of rum and Rome.

By the end of the Great War, more people earned their living in a factory than on the land. In 1919, farmers had only 16 per cent of the national income; by 1929, only 9 per cent. Yet they were increasingly conditioned by advertising to desire the cash goods of the city, electrical appliances, automobiles, radios, smart clothes. Meanwhile, the howl of derision from the cities at the country's expense grew and grew. The attacks of Edgar Lee Masters on small-town life in *Spoon River Anthology*, of Sherwood Anderson in *Winesburg, Ohio*, and of Sinclair Lewis in *Main Street* were nothing to the persecution and baiting of H. L. Mencken and his hounds. As Walter Lippmann wrote in 1926, Mencken was "the pope of popes," the most powerful personal influence on his whole generation of educated people.[1] His chief target was country prejudices, which he answered with six volumes of his own. To him, the South was the Sahara of the Bozart, the small town the home of the boobery and the booboisie, and country Methodism a theology degraded almost to the level of voodooism. Prohibition was the result of the spite of envious yokels who wanted to force the city dwellers to drink the revolting mixtures of the farm. In a nation where Mencken was considered an intellectual leader, the country and small town were held beneath contempt.

The rural crusades of the twenties did much to increase the city's ridicule of the rube and the hick. Prohibition, the Ku Klux Klan, and the campaign against the teaching of evolution were unfortunate and tragic causes. They were the sad remnants of what had once been a fine frenzy for a republic of small farmers, a New World of husbandmen to redress the balance of the Old World of dwellers in Sodom. When the witty apostles of urban life, Clarence Darrow and H. L. Mencken, mocked the balding and corpulent old countryman, William Jennings Bryan, at the Scopes trial of 1925, they showed a pride and complacency and vindictiveness as mean as the bias of a dry fundamentalist. If the declining country had a paranoiac fear of the growing city, the city replied, despite its boasted superiority, with an equally vicious counterattack on the beliefs of the small town. Thus the farm belt of America was pressured into an even greater fear of urban power, which made it find a suitable hero and villain in the contest between Hoover and Smith.

Moreover, the country drys found themselves abandoned by some of their early supporters. The progressives became weak in the twenties, and lost much of their appeal. They suffered from the nationwide disgust which the antics of the drys gave to the name of reform. The drys themselves, by being successful with their legal victory, were damned with the curse of trying to enforce the unenforceable and the unpopular. And when the women of America received the vote with the Nineteenth Amendment, they proceeded to put their new privilege to little significant use. The millennium promised by woman suffrage was no more real than the millenniums of the referendum and the recall and national prohibition. When the three movements had come to their apogee, the sins of society remained much the same. The revolution in America was mechanical rather than spiritual, a metamorphosis of organization and mass rather than a return to the myth of America's rural youth. "The founder of the oil trust may give us back our money," a dry progressive had lamented, "but not if he send among us a hundred Wesleys can he give us back the lost ideals."[2] In this disillusion, the reformers blamed each other and split apart.

Not only did the reformers split apart, but they became openly hostile to each other. The progressives were disillusioned about their procedures for increased democracy, which only seemed to place political power more firmly in the hands of the party bosses, and about the increased power of the federal government, which was used by conservative Republican Presidents to buttress the power of the trusts rather than to regulate them. In the reaction from the misused powers of centralization, the old progressives tended to become the new liberals, more concerned with protecting the rights of individuals against federal coercion than with protecting human rights through the intervention of the government. Moreover, the determinism implicit in the current doctrines of Darwinism and Marxism and Freudianism made the reformers look upon their own motives for reform with suspicion. When Ben Hecht said, "To hell with Sigmund, he's corrupted immorality," he should have added that Freud had also corrupted morality.[3] The fine crusading drive of the progressives gave way to that moral relativism which swept through the United States in the twenties. The attack on the evils of society was turned into an attack on those men who saw the evils of others without looking into their own.

Moreover, many American women took their emancipation literally. They thought that freedom meant liberty to do what men did. As a woman writer had warned in 1917, "Women will drink, smoke, bet, swear, gamble, just as men do. Whether they like it or not, does not matter: men do these things, therefore women must, to show that they are as good as men."[4] The old concept of the drys, that a woman's vote would be a dry vote, was shattered. Women took to the speak-easy like ducks to water. They set up a rival image to the sober example of the Woman's Christian Temperance Union, an image under which women were supposed to drink and make drink to prove their equality with men. The muckraking feminist, Ida M. Tarbell, was forced to admit, "Where fashion points, women follow. They set up bars in their homes, boast of their bootleggers and their brews, tolerate and practice a looseness of tongue and manner once familiar only in saloons and brothels."[5] Under prohibition, the sight of women drinking in public became normal and respectable in large cities. Prohibition even provided a means for the economic emancipation of the female sex. The story was told, in the *Wickersham Report,* of a widow whose neighbors took up a collection to buy her a still and set her up in business.[6]

The prohibitionists, by their success, turned themselves from radicals into reactionaries. "We had to give America prohibition so the people could see exactly what it was," said one dry leader. "Now we will make them like it."[7] By concentrating on their one particular reform, as Susan B. Anthony had recommended to the suffragettes, the drys had largely disassociated themselves from other reformers. The Anti-Saloon League had always sought after a single object, the abolition of the liquor trade; the Woman's Christian Temperance Union had followed its example after the turn of the century, dropping its general reform program to concentrate utterly upon prohibition. The decline of the progressives and of the Progressive party in the twenties, and the dissolution of the Woman's party after the Nineteenth Amendment, left the prohibitionists and the Ku Klux Klan as the sole representatives of a great rural and urban reform wave that had changed the Constitution and the laws of a nation. The drys and the Klansmen were the hideous ghosts of a noble past, squatting in the new Eldorado of the twenties that had forgotten the morality which had once given the ghosts flesh. Indeed, the victory of the drys throughout the twenties seemed to be a proof of the lasting malice of the early reformers, rather than of their good intentions.

The monstrous dry bones of their past crusades led the progressives to deny the excesses of the leaders of prohibition. Although the old progressives in the Senate under La Follette supported prohibition on the whole, their support was all for the theory rather than the practice. They deplored the fanaticism which the issue of prohibition had brought to public life. The endorsement of political hacks by wets and drys exclusive of any considerations of good government, and the use of the Prohibition Bureau as a political pork barrel, deeply offended the old progressives. National prohibition, as administered by the Republican government and the Anti-Saloon League, was a national disgrace. When the progressive George W. Norris wrote his autobiography in 1925, he called it *Fighting Liberal.* His judgment on prohibition reflected the alienation of progressives and moderates from the dry leaders:

> I have been an abstainer throughout my life. I believe that temperance is the only rule of life. Yet on both sides of this issue are prohibitionists supporting a prohibitionist, regardless of how he may stand on any other governmental question, and wet bigots, narrow-minded enough to support a man opposed to prohibition regardless of how he may stand on other questions. I am sorry that these things exist.[8]

The South and the West remained true to the drys, but in such a way as to damn their cause by bad publicity. The crusade of the Ku Klux Klan and the fundamentalists in the twenties brought out the worst in rural manners.[9] The Ku Klux Klan had been, in some ways, a respectable resistance movement against the carpetbaggers after the Civil War; in its revived form, it was a pitiful expression of the prejudices and assumptions that underlay the usual attitudes of the country. The Klan satisfied the small-town urge towards regalia and secret societies; the hooded Kleagle or Klaliff of the Great Forest could easily believe that the Jews of Wall Street or the Knights of Columbus were engaged on a similar political conspiracy. A plot creates its own counterplot in its imagination. The prejudices of the small town against liquor, prostitutes, divorce, Roman Catholics, aliens, Reds, Jews, Negroes, Darwinism, modernism, and liberalism were excellent ground for commercial exploiters of hate. For an initiation fee of ten dollars, these salesmen of unreason gave the bigoted members of the majority group the organized luxury of hating the monstrous subversion of the minority groups around them.[10]

Harry Herschel has defined a majority group as a minority group careless with its membership. It was lucky that the Klan and the fundamentalists never became more than minority groups, although they claimed that they were the moral champions of the majority of white, Protestant, native-born Americans. The fear of their success was sufficient to destroy the unity of the Democratic party at its convention in 1924 and to bring out the defenders of liberalism in hordes to the Scopes trial one year later. Although the flagrant immorality of its leaders killed the Klan, and the overeating of Bryan, the champion of temperance and the Bible, killed him and the fundamentalist movement, their temporary threat was real enough. But while men in white sheets whipped bootleggers and prostitutes, smothered labor organizers and Negroes with tar and feathers, and forbade schoolmasters to teach that human beings were descended from the lecherous ape, the red lights of the sprawling cities cast their glow ever more brightly from New Orleans to Chicago, from Hollywood to New York.

Prohibition brought some prosperity to the backwoods. Sharecroppers, tenant farmers, fishermen of the bayous, dwellers on the mud banks of the Mississippi, all found the tending of stills or the sailing of rumrunners more profitable than the cultivation of the overworked soil. Corn whisky averaged five dollars a pint between 1920 and 1925. West Indian rum fetched more. The illicit liquor trade became almost decent as well as profitable. A student put himself through a Southern theological seminary by selling bootleg liquor to Congressmen. Federal enforcement of the liquor laws by a Republican government was resisted in the South in the name of Confederate pride and the Democratic party. Even the poor Negroes benefited, from the owners of the "speak-easy cabins" to the winking bellboys and porters at Southern hotels. Indeed, the simultaneous prohibition of prostitution and liquor below the Mason-Dixon line for the purpose of curbing the Negroes had the perverse effect of increasing their contempt for the white man's hypocrisy. For they became the procurers of alcohol and whores for their white masters, with all the accompanying privileges of pimps and middlemen.[11] Prohibition, instead of keeping Negroes from vice, put them in control of it.

The Protestant evangelical churches also suffered a relative decline in the twenties. As Harry Emerson Fosdick admitted, science had become "religion's overwhelmingly successful competitor in showing men how to get what they want."[12] Public schools and high schools and colleges began to take over the function of the churches as educators. Moreover, the automobile, the radio, motion pictures, and outdoor sports proved more attractive than the pulpit on a Sunday. Welfare agencies pushed the minister out of his role as counselor and guide. Although congregations nominally increased, the influence of religion declined. In rich city churches, the minister became increasingly a mere preacher to comfortable souls, a businessman of God among other businessmen. In poor city churches, the congregation was drawn chiefly from country immigrants, who sought the consolation of the old-time religion which they had left behind them.

Prohibition itself caused some unpleasant scandals in the churches. Those churches which used alcoholic sacramental wine found that not all of the wine reached the altar. Roy Haynes discovered hundreds of false rabbis manufacturing wine for fictitious congregations, while bootleggers were apt to hijack wine on its way to the sanctuary.[13] A report of the Federal Council of the Churches of Christ in America showed that nearly three million gallons of sacramental wine were withdrawn in 1924 from government warehouses. The report estimated that not more than one-quarter of this amount was used for the sacraments — the rest was used sacrilegiously.[14] Holy wine, however, was a mere drop in the ocean of the bootleg liquor which was swamping America.

The split ideology of the churches concerning prohibition was revealed while the "experiment, noble in motive" ran its course. The fundamentalist wing of the churches, those who backed the crusade against evolution and the sagging morals of the times, helped the enforcement officers and the Ku Klux Klan to persecute bootleggers. For their nativist followers, Billy Sunday preached his new "Booze Sermon," entitled "Crooks, Corkscrews, Bootleggers, and Whisky Politicians . . . Thoy Shall Not Pass," with its savage calls for deportation of foreign bootleggers and radicals and dissenters who would not kiss and obey the American flag.[15] The moderate group in the churches straddled the issue, preached obedience to the law, and kept mum. The liberal wing, however, supported the actions of the social gospel movement and of the Federal Council of Churches, even when these actions seemed to condemn the dry cause. The actual report of the

Federal Council which revealed the facts about sacramental wine was hailed by the wet propagandist Hugh Fox as a "searching criticism of prohibition conditions," although it was condemned by the dry Clarence True Wilson as a paid document of the Association Against the Prohibition Amendment.[16]

The report contained many damning facts about prohibition. Its publication with the apparent endorsement of the Federal Council of Churches was a telling blow to the claim of the Anti-Saloon League to represent the Protestant churches in action. Moreover, the report contradicted flatly many of the dry assertions that prohibition was becoming increasingly successful. The report stated the truth, that, although it had not yet been proved that prohibition could not be enforced, no adequate attempt at enforcement had so far been made. The fundamental fact was that a large part of the American people opposed the Eighteenth Amendment. The trouble was with the people rather than their government, which had tried to administer inadequately an impossible reform. The bootleg traffic had caused political corruption as well as being affected by existing corruption. The favorable trend toward temperance before 1920 had been reversed, at least temporarily, by 1925. In the matter of temperance education, the delinquency of the churches was greater than that of the federal government. Even the inferior type of religious temperance education, which was common before the Eighteenth Amendment, had been largely stopped. Prohibition was doomed unless religion and education changed the minds of the people about the virtues of the reform.

The Anti-Saloon League put such pressure on the Executive Committee of the Federal Council of Churches that steps were taken to brand the report as the sole work of the head of the Research Department. Furthermore, the Executive Committee issued a second report affirming its unequivocal support of national prohibition. But the damage was already done. The division of the churches over the matter of prohibition had been widely publicized across America. Criticism from inside the Protestant churches, widely touted by the drys as solid for the cause of prohibition, had at last become overt.[17] Bishop Cannon admitted that, in the judgment of men and women who had led the prohibition fight for very many years, "no document had ever been printed which had been productive of more real harm to the cause of prohibition."[18]

In face of their growing loss of public sympathy, the drys insisted on the ultimate success of their cause. As their power declined, their voices rose. As their difficulties increased, their confidence kept pace. As law enforcement became more impossible, the drys demanded more of it. In 1926, Wayne B. Wheeler declared, "The very fact that the law is difficult to enforce is the clearest proof of the need of its existence."[19] Setbacks did not dismay the militant prohibitionists, but drove them on to greater efforts. The climax of the crusade of the Protestant evangelical churches was reached in the presidential campaign of 1928. They treated the battle between the dry Hoover and the wet Smith as a national referendum on prohibition. And if much of the opposition of fundamentalist clergymen to Smith was on the grounds of his Catholicism and immigrant city birth rather than his habit of drinking cocktails, the liquor issue provided a genuine and convenient mask for religious and ethnic bigotry. Moreover, to the prejudiced mind, Smith's sins were the same. Liquor and the Pope, cities and immigration, were linked evils, an unholy unity which was the cause of all Protestant ills.

THE BATTLE OF THE BACKGROUNDS

THE CONFLICT between Herbert Hoover and Alfred Emanuel Smith for the presidency in 1928 was an excellent example of the divergent upbringings of those Americans who lived in the country and those who lived in the cities. Hoover was brought up on an Iowa farm. Rugged individualism and self-sufficiency were the facts of country life which Hoover later elevated to a philosophy. The farm produced its own foodstuffs, made its own soap, stored up against time of winter or slump full bins and jars and barrels, which were "social security itself." Hard times were to be helped, not by handouts in the Tammany fashion, but by hard work and trips to the private stores which every decent man put aside for bad days. Life on the homestead was thrifty and self-disciplined, especially among Quaker families like the Hoovers. His parents' view on education was as narrow as the limitations of their lives; they were "unwilling in those days to have youth corrupted with stronger reading than the Bible, the encyclopedia, or those great novels where the hero overcomes the demon rum." Hoover's mother, better educated than most of her contemporaries, spoke frequently at Quaker and prohibition meetings. On one occasion, the child Herbert was "parked for the day at the polls, where the women were massed in an effort to make the men vote themselves dry." But, by the age of eight, Hoover was orphaned of both parents, to be brought up among the virtues of toil and Inner Light on his uncle's farm. Long hours spent in the Quaker meetinghouse waiting for the spirit to move someone were an "intense repression" on the boy, who learned patience at the price of play.[20]

Hoover began his career as a mining engineer and consultant. He called himself "an industrial doctor."[21] He traveled continually over the world, introducing modern engineering methods to Australia and China and Russia. But, after a time, he found the promotion of companies in London more profitable than the sinking of mine shafts. He was concerned in a number of speculations. Accounts of these transactions were used against him in the campaigns of 1928 and 1932 by smear biographers.[22] Most of the transactions, however, are masked in a decent obscurity. Hoover's fortune at the outbreak of the First World War was some four million dollars. During the next fourteen years, he used up three million dollars in his political career, and in philanthropy.

During the War, Hoover made his reputation as the Great Engineer. He carried out two efficient jobs. The first was the repatriation of Americans stranded in Europe at the outbreak of the fighting; the second was his handling of the United States Food Administration to conserve supplies in America and feed starving Europe under and after the German occupation. Prohibition was one of the methods of conserving grain. Hoover was against stopping the production of beer, since he thought that saving four million bushels of grain monthly was not worth the likely substitution of whisky and gin for beer in the mouths of the munition workers. Al Smith, in a speech at Philadelphia in 1928, tellingly quoted Hoover's views of ten years before, that 2.75 per cent beer was "mighty difficult to get drunk on" and that "any true advocate of temperance and national efficiency" would shrink from stopping the making of beer altogether.[23]

Hoover was as practiced at promoting his own reputation as his companies'. The legend of the Great Engineer was so potent in 1920 that both parties approached him as a presidential possibility. He declared himself a Republican, and, although he did not secure many votes at the nominating convention, he made a good enough showing to make sure of a post in the Cabinet. For eight years he was Secretary of Commerce and "Undersecretary of all other departments."[24] He took the credit for the boom as though it were his own personal doing. His Department's press releases came "like flakes of snow in a heavy storm"; a small-town California editor declared that he had received a piece of Hoover publicity every day for several years.[25] Hoover used his undoubted efficiency in government as an instrument of advertisement. His Inner Light was not kept under a bushel.

While this image of Hoover the Master Builder was to help him against Smith, it was to damn him against Roosevelt. If he was the architect of prosperity, he was presumably also the architect of depression. When Will Rogers commented in 1927 that Herbert Hoover was "just waiting around between calamities" in his role of "America's family physician," he was describing the image that the Hoover publicists had put into the mind of many Americans.[26] Thus, after calamity came and Hoover was incompetent to deal with it, he was disbelieved when he said that the slump was not his fault. He had cried too often that the wolf of poverty was always shut out by the door of Republican prosperity. As Elmer Davis wrote, "Hoover said what he correctly judged the majority of voters thought, and promised what the majority wanted. Adult Americans elected him for the same reason that would have led Americans under the age of ten to elect Santa Claus."[27]

Alfred E. Smith represented the antithesis of Hoover. His tradition was the tradition of the American urban immigrant. He was the son of poor Irish parents. His mother brought up his sister and him with decent devoutness in a slum. When his truckman father died, Smith went out to work in the Fulton Fish Market at the age of twelve to support his family. He was an altar boy at the Roman Catholic Church of St. James, a frequent performer in amateur theatricals as long as he did not have to play the part of the villain, and an ambitious political supporter of Tammany. When he was twenty-six, he married an Irish girl, by whom he was to have five children. His loyalty, respectability, and dramatic talents recommended him to the Tammany organization. He rose steadily to prominence in the city and then in the state through the offices of subpoena server, assemblyman, majority leader in the Assembly, member of the State Constitutional Convention, and sheriff. Although he had the reputation of being a safe machine politician and of regularly voting the Tammany ticket, he was also known as a supporter of industrial and social legislation after the tragic Triangle Waist fire of 1911. If he always supported the liquor interests because they supported Tammany, he was still aware that unless they put their own house in order, the drys might do so for them.[28] But wherever the sale of liquor was prohibited he said that hypocrisy reigned.[29]

The Anti-Saloon League lobby at Albany depended largely on the Republican party in the state. Both organizations were based on the country districts. Yet the Republicans could not be too overtly dry, for they needed wet city support to elect their candidates for Governor. Although the League exploited the division between upstate and New York City, the urban areas were too powerful to give the prohibitionists the stranglehold over legislation that they had in Southern and Western states. Throughout his life, Smith courageously attacked the Anti-Saloon League. He accused it of influencing legislators against their better judgment and of being almost identical with the Ku Klux Klan.[30] The League suffered the mortification of seeing Governor Smith's majority increase election after election, although it had its revenge when he ran for President.

Smith was a Democrat in belief as well as in party. He thought that the cure for the ills of democracy was more democracy.[31] Thus he based his opposition to the Eighteenth Amendment on the grounds that it was not ratified by the people, denied the states' rights principle in the Constitution, and deliberately avoided definition of the word "intoxicating" in order to be passed without fear of failure.[32] He thought the definition by the Volstead Act of "intoxicating" was hypocritical and deceitful. He claimed that Wayne B. Wheeler had been unable to defend this definition, and had excused the drys by saying, "Well, we were in the saddle and we drove through."[33] For Smith, much of the hatred of the saloon by the prohibitionists was a covert attack on the immigrants who liked beer and wine more than cider. It was also an attack on the Irish control of city politics and on the Catholic religion, which was more concerned with salvation through temperance and faith than through legislation and repression. Moreover, prohibition was a Republican weapon in the state, and Smith was a Tammany Democrat.

In his successful campaign for Governor in 1918, Smith first met the anti-Catholic and prohibitionist sentiment that was to aid his defeat ten years later in his campaign for President. But New York was numerically powerful enough to cancel out the ill effects of the dry and Republican attempts at slander. Moveover, as Smith noted, the religious issue reacted in his favor in such places as the city of Albany, out of resentment that religion should be an issue at all.[34]

When the Eighteenth Amendment came up before the two houses of the state for ratification in 1919, Governor Smith sent his first message to the legislature, asking them for a referendum on the matter. He wrote, "I believe it is our duty to ascertain the will of the people directly upon this subject."[35] But a caucus of the Republican party, which was in a majority in both houses, insisted on ratification. The Republicans feared that a vote against the amendment would turn the dry rural areas against their traditional representatives. The Anti-Saloon League encouraged this belief. Smith was amused when the same Republican majorities, in an effort to placate the wet cities, passed a light-wines and beer bill, allowing the manufacture of beverages containing 2.75 per cent of alcohol. This bill was declared unconstitutional by the state Supreme Court. The Republicans had tried unsuccessfully, in Smith's later words, to carry water on both shoulders, dry among the drys and wet among the wets.[36]

For eight of the ten years after 1918, Smith was Governor of New York. His only losing campaign was in the Republican landslide of 1920, although he polled a million more votes than the Democratic candidate for President. He regularly polled more votes as Governor than his party's nominee in presidential years owing to his huge popularity and to the separate ballot system of voting in New York.[37] A regular Republican majority in the Assembly blocked his reform program during his first three years as Governor; but, by 1927, he had put through a large schedule of better housing, better highways, and better administration. He made New York an example of efficient government, and himself both a genius at the practical details of state politics and the leading candidate for his party's choice as President.

In the Democratic convention of 1920, Smith's position as favorite son of New York was only a maneuver on the part of Boss Murphy to keep the delegates from voting for the dry McAdoo. The move was successful, and the moist Cox was nominated. But after his second election as Governor in 1922, Smith knew that his presidential chances were greater. Few Presidents had been elected without carrying New York State, and Smith seemed capable of doing so. From this date, a significant and interesting change in Smith's attitude towards prohibition showed his increasing awareness of his presidential possibilities. His behavior over the repeal of the Mullan-Gage Law, which had been passed in 1920 to provide for the strict state enforcement of the terms of the Volstead Act, demonstrated his increasing caution to do nothing on the liquor issue which might prejudice his chances at a national convention of his party.

Although the Democratic state platform of 1922 had discreetly contained no condemnation of the Mullan-Gage Law, the suffering wets of New York had presumed that Al Smith would be more ready than his opponents to call off the state police from pursuit of the speakeasies. He was elected by a large majority and then proceeded to say and do nothing about the Mullan-Gage Law. But the Republican party was unlikely to let slip such a perfect chance for the political embarrassment of their enemies. They repealed the state enforcement law and sent the repeal bill to the Democratic Governor to approve.

Various pressures were put on Smith during the thirty days' grace he had in which to sign the bill. His presidential advisers warned him that his approval of the bill would make him the acknowledged leader of the wets and confirm the antagonism of the dry South and West within the Democratic party. His state advisers, Boss Murphy and Tammany, insisted that he sign the bill, for the state Democratic party depended on the wet vote. In addition, Al Smith had a personal conviction of his own honesty and courage, upon which he often acted. He himself drank and considered prohibition an intolerable affront to personal liberty. Yet he spent the full thirty days coming to a decision. The alternatives were clear. If he vetoed the repeal bill, he might lose his state at the next election, and thus lose all chances of the presidential nomination. If he signed the bill, he would retain the governorship of New York and his chances of nomination for President, but he would probably lose the following campaign. He signed the bill. An Albany in the hand was worth a White House in the bush.

Smith was conscious enough of the future, however, to send back with his approval a long memorandum to the legislature. The document was as specious and evasive as the best straddles of his Republican enemies. He pointed out that the repeal of the Mullan-Gage Law eliminated the possibility of double jeopardy by prosecution for the same crime in both state and federal courts. He denied that the word "concurrent" in the Eighteenth Amendment imposed a duty on the forty-eight states to enforce the Amendment. He stood up for the Jeffersonian and Southern doctrine of states' rights. He stated the obvious in saying that drinking was still illegal; but he became hypocritical in stating that repeal did not "in the slightest degree lessen the obligation of police officers of the state to enforce in its strictest letter the Volstead Act." By confining prosecution of prohibition cases to the already overflowing federal courts and by making the aid of the state police to the federal agents a mere obligation rather than a law, Smith ensured that New York would surpass even Chicago in its crusade to be the wet Jerusalem. His memorandum did him no good among the drys, and was immediately denounced by William Jennings Bryan and by representative Andrew Volstead, of Minnesota and notorious name.[38]

Smith tried to restore his position among the prohibitionists by making huge claims for the efficiency of enforcement in New York at the Governors' Conference in October, 1923, under the leadership of President Coolidge. He sought to prove by various figures that the value of liquor seized and the number of arrests in the state had doubled in the six months after the repeal of the Mullan-Gage Law, when compared with the six months before.[39] Half a million more dollars had been appropriated to policing the Canadian and interstate borders, since Smith maintained that smuggling was the chief source of liquor in New York. Thus he sought to allow home-brew to flourish and attract wet votes within the state, while the example of seized liquor from outside might attract dry votes from without the state.

The Democratic convention of 1924 in New York was a microcosm of the feuds, phobias, and hatreds that were to split the traditional alignments of the party wide open four years later. If the galleries were not packed in favor of the Governor from New York, at least they saw in him one of themselves, and hallooed for their likeness. Although the terrible struggle over the vote condemning the Klan pushed the prohibition issue into the background, the attitude of the Klan itself, with its declared prejudices against Catholicism and immigrants and saloons and the immorality of cities, reflected overtly the actual opposition to Smith that was to hide in 1928 under the name of prohibition. Here was the first hero of the new blood and iron of modern industrial civilization.[40] Against him stood the last dry nominee of the Democrats, William Gibbs McAdoo, backed by the Klan and the Anti-Saloon League. It was not surprising that the convention took 102 deadlocked ballots before nominating John W. Davis, who would call a brief truce in the death struggle of city against country and put off the fight until the next election.

Of course, by seeking an armistice in the vital battle, the Democrats ensured their defeat and an election of apathy, where all relied on the tepid support of their friends and sought to make no enemies. Less than half of the electorate bothered to vote. In New York State, however, Al Smith, running for the third time as Governor, polled over a million more votes than Davis and was the Democrats' only consolation in the worst defeat in their history.

But Smith's inadequate speech at the convention had shown that he was as much hampered by the narrow provincialism of the city as his enemies were by that of the village. He spoke of little else than his achievements in governing New York well. He seemed to know of nothing outside his own state, and confirmed the suspicions of the South and the West that he was too urbanized to want to understand their particular problems. But in the next four years Al Smith was groomed for a larger role by his clever advisers, the Moskowitzes and Judge Proskauer. Smith often picked his aides from among the New York Jews, knowing that they felt that he was their representative as much as did the Irish and the other American groups who found themselves unfairly considered as aliens.

So Al Smith from the East Side learned something of farm problems, international affairs, and national economics. He took up the challenge of his religion after an open letter in the *Atlantic Monthly* had voiced the fears of the Protestants that the Pope might have an undue influence on a Roman Catholic in the White House.[41] Smith wrote a dignified and brilliant reply. He stated that he would be a poor American and a poor Catholic alike if he injected religious discussion into a political campaign. He denied the possibility of any conflict between his religion and his duty as President. And he took up an extreme Protestant position in preferring to consult in difficult matters the dictates of his conscience rather than any ecclesiastical tribunal.[42] He appealed to the common brotherhood of man under the common fatherhood of God. If Protestant prejudice could have been allayed by anything Smith said, this letter should have done the miracle. Instead, it forced those of Smith's religious enemies who did not relish the name of bigots to concentrate on his wetness rather than his faith.

A discreet silence on the subject of prohibition except in terms of law enforcement shows Smith's wariness of further compromising situations, although he did sign the bill providing for a wet referendum in New York in 1926. By more than a million votes, New York asked for modification of the Volstead Act to allow the states to define their own criterion of what the Eighteenth Amendment meant by "intoxicating." Al Smith could point to his home state in his request for states' rights on the matter of prohibition. And if he said nothing on the subject of his wetness in 1927, much to the annoyance of Mencken, he was presumed to be on the side of the angels of alcohol.[43] His occasional demands for strict enforcement of the Volstead Act were presumed to be the result of politic advice and presidential ambition.

The glaring availability of Al Smith made the dry forces uneasy. The wet Chicago *Tribune* reported that the Anti-Saloon League was raising a special fund of $600,000 in 1927 to defeat any candidate for President who was not dry.[44] Wayne B. Wheeler issued a statement which was disavowed by more discreet officers in the League; he wrote that "if Governor Smith is nominated and the drys in the South would rather vote for an independent dry candidate for President than for a dry Republican, this would give them a chance to register their protest."[45] Bishop James Cannon, casting around for a dry candidate, was even ready to support McAdoo's nominee, Senator Walsh, of Montana, although he was another Roman Catholic.[46] Walsh would be, after all, the answer to those who accused the drys of fearing Smith more for his religion than his wetness. In fact, the drys knew that Walsh could never beat Hoover after eight years of prosperity, while they feared that Smith might win.

Thus Hoover and Smith approached the Republican and the Democratic nominating conventions in 1928. Each was the most available candidate of his party. Each represented a fundamental and antagonistic principle in American life. Each would symbolize in his victory more than the victory of a party, and in his defeat more than the defeat of a man.

VICTORY IN DEFEAT

AFTER CALVIN COOLIDGE's announcement that he did not choose to run, the Hoover managers arranged that the next Republican convention would be in their candidate's pocket. He was nominated on the first ballot. The party platform on prohibition matched the evasive stand of their nominee on the question. Senator Carter Glass, of Virginia, offered to pay a thousand dollars to anyone who could produce a single categorical dry declaration by Hoover; the money was never claimed. The Republican plank favored strict enforcement and observance of the Eighteenth Amendment; it did not say that the Grand Old Party approved of the principle of national prohibition. Hoover took the same line as his party, promising strict enforcement of the dry law as it stood, and calling prohibition "a great social and economic experiment, noble in motive and far-reaching in purpose." Although Hoover was not responsible for the popular paraphrase of his words as a "noble experiment," he did admit later that his words had unfortunate repercussions. He stated, "To regard the prohibition law as an 'experiment' did not please the extreme drys, and to say it was 'noble in motive' did not please the extreme wets."[47] It was unfortunate that Hoover's straddle ended in a muddle.

The Smith forces were equally in full control of the Democratic national convention at Houston, Texas. The Platform Committee was overwhelmingly wet. But because Smith's partisans wanted a "harmony" convention and the nomination of their candidate by a united party, they accepted a plank written by the dry Senator Glass and approved by Josephus Daniels. The plank pledged enforcement of the Eighteenth Amendment, although it was not as extreme as the Anti-Saloon League would have wished. This tactical victory by the Smith forces was a strategical error in the long run. For it allowed the anti-Smith prohibitionists to claim with some justice that Smith's telegram of acceptance denied his party's platform.[48] Smith was nominated on a revised first ballot with a dry Southerner, Senator Joseph Robinson, of Arkansas, as his running mate. The delegates ignored the prohibitionist sermons of the preachers outside the hall on the text that God would block Al Smith's nomination.[49] Certainly, sections of the Methodist and Baptist churches were to ensure that their version of God's will blocked Al Smith's election.

Smith sent a telegram of acceptance to the convention. He stated his old position on prohibition, which had only been played down for the purpose of having him nominated with Southern support. He said that he was well known to support fundamental changes in the provisions for national prohibition, based on the principles of Jeffersonian democracy. Although he appreciated that these changes could only be made by the people themselves or their elected representatives, he felt it the duty of the chosen leader of the people to point the way. Bishop Cannon immediately called an anti-Smith meeting at Asheville, North Carolina, declaring himself stunned by Smith's shameless proposition of political double-dealing and his action of brazen political effrontery.[50] In fact, Cannon could only have been surprised at Smith's sincerity in declaring himself a wet. His position on prohibition had remained consistent, though tacit.

The *Nation* called the following election the dirtiest political campaign ever, although one of its editors had spread the dirt with an article on Smith which stated that he drank four to eight highballs a day.[51] It was widely believed that Smith was a drunkard and had to be supported while he made his speeches in order to keep upright. The fact of the matter was that he drank beer when he was young, a little hard liquor when beer became difficult to procure under prohibition, and champagne with repeal and riches.

The religious campaign against Smith is impossible to distinguish from the dry campaign against him. They were part and parcel of the same attitude. The pretense of the drys that prohibition had everything to do with Smith's defeat and religion little is untrue. Cannon may have accused Smith of dragging the religious issue into the campaign to bring out the Catholic vote for the Democrats; but he cannot be excused from distributing 380,000 copies of his virulent anti-Catholic pamphlet *Is Southern Protestantism More Intolerant than Romanism?* The pamphlet was paid for by the money of a Republican financier; the greater part of its contents were called by *Current History* "completely untrue or gravely misleading."[52] Cannon's own freedom from religious bigotry was not shown by his judgment of Al Smith, that Smith was "of the intolerant, bigoted type, characteristic of the Irish Roman Catholic hierarchy of New York City."[53]

While Cannon still maintained that the bolt of the Southern Democrats to the side of Hoover was over prohibition, his helper at Asheville was more outspoken.[54] Dr. Arthur J. Barton, of the Anti-Saloon League, said openly in his address at Birmingham, Alabama, that religion was more important than prohibition; if Al Smith were to be elected, America would come under the domination of a "foreign religious sect"; in fact, Herbert Hoover was the real Democratic candidate for President.[55] Mabel Walker Willebrandt was sent by the National Republican Committee to exhort the Ohio Conference of the Methodist Episcopal Church; she begged the Methodist leaders to defend prohibition against Al Smith, who had dragged the issue into the campaign; the Republicans did not put an end to her speaking tour until the "moral" aspects of prohibition were significantly exploited.[56] Mencken, subscribing to all the Methodist and Baptist newspapers below the Potomac, found that two-thirds of them devoted half their space to bawling that anyone who was against prohibition was against God, and the other half of their space to damning the Pope.[57] As fair-minded a religious leader as the great Reinhold Niebuhr said that the real issues in the campaign were hid under the decent veil of loyalty to a moral ideal — prohibition.[58] Smith himself, his campaign supporters and biographers, most Roman Catholics, Senator Norris, Harold Ickes, the Socialist candidate Norman Thomas, James M. Cox, and those acute commentators on the South, Gunnar Myrdal and Wilbur J. Cash, all considered religion to be the real reason for Smith's defeat.

Smith, however, was stung to the limits of his courage by the viciousness of the attacks upon him. He chose to defend himself on the charge of religion in the Klan country of Oklahoma City, against the advice of his entourage, who feared that the prejudiced crowd might attack him. He reminded the audience that religious toleration was written into the American Constitution. To his way of thinking, he said, anyone who voted against him because of his religion was not a good citizen.[59] In New York, he called the Anti-Saloon League the twin brother of the Ku Klux Klan, and accused the Republicans of conniving at a campaign based "on religious bigotry and religious intolerance." Senator Moses, the Eastern manager of the Hoover campaign, had been discovered mailing to Kentucky scurrilous literature which attacked Smith from the point of view of his faith.[60] Smith's courage in his campaign even won over his opponent, William Allen White; White wrote that he had wound up his campaign against Smith with the pity that is akin to love for his opponent, a hero of tragedy.[61] Of course, White voted Republican as did many traditional Democrats, protesting their religious tolerance and casting a ballot for their bigotry.

Smith spoke out more against those who attacked him for his faith than for his wetness. He even denied in Omaha that prohibition was a great issue in the election,[62] while Senator Robinson was discreetly sent to the South to pacify the drys there. But Smith did speak out on prohibition in the wet cities, swinging them towards the Democrats. In Milwaukee, he called prohibition "the great political pork barrel for the Republican party." He quoted Senator Gore, who had stated that the Republican policy was to give liquor to the wets and law to the drys. Smith promised he would enforce the law as he found it, but he would work for the repeal of the Volstead Act to give the states control over their own liquor policy and police power.[63] He spoke similarly during his campaign in Nashville, emphasizing states' rights;[64] in Chicago, stressing the need to put an end to crime;[65] in Philadelphia, ridiculing former Governor Hughes for saying that prohibition was unimportant in order to disguise Hoover's evasiveness over the issue.[66] In Baltimore, he attacked Republican "wiggling and wobbling" over prohibition; he denounced the "cold-blooded threat" of the Anti-Saloon League; and he pointed out that no one could "make a new sin by law."[67]

The stand of Hoover and the Republicans on prohibition was indeed unsatisfactory. All that could be safely said of them was that they were more dry than their opponents. Senator Borah was sent through the South and West to represent that each vote for Smith was a vote for wetness; he had correctly predicted in Hoover's case that everyone would be talking about prohibition except the deaf, the dumb, and the candidates.[68] Meanwhile, F. M. Huntingdon-Wilson declared that the wets had their best chance of legal wine and beer under Hoover, while Charles Evans Hughes called Smith's plan for liquor control "State Socialism."[69] In general, the Republicans tried to bring out the rural vote in large quantities by calling the prohibition issue in the country "a city issue," while they quieted the cities by calling prohibition "a sham battle."[70] But perhaps no statement of the campaign approached the silliness of a declaration of J. W. Walker, when he termed Alfred E. Smith "America's greatest prohibitionist."[71]

Mencken put one problem of the election succinctly on the eve of polling. "If Al wins tomorrow, it will be because the American people have decided at last to vote as they drink, and because a majority of them believe that the Methodist bishops are worse than the Pope. If he loses, it will be because those who fear the Pope outnumber those who are tired of the Anti-Saloon League."[72] In fact, Al Smith lost by some six million votes mainly because of what he called "the false and misleading issue of prosperity." In his opinion, the Republicans had claimed so often to be the architects of good times that the Democrats were associated with bad times.[73] Yet, if no Democrat could have won against Hoover in 1928, it is surely true that no Protestant Democrat could have lost five Southern states. The South had stood firm in the Democratic *débâcles* of 1920 and 1924. It was religion and the Southern churches that broke the Solid South in 1928.

Yet the victory of the evangelical churches and the drys in 1928 put their cause in peril. By taking a presidential election to be a referendum on prohibition, they put the Eighteenth Amendment in jeopardy on the day when the presidential election should go against them. Moreover, this major incursion by the Protestant churches into politics brought to a head the old American resentment against clerical meddling in lay affairs. How could the Protestants maintain that they were attacking Smith to keep the Pope from dictating American policy when they themselves were denying the separation of church and state?

The candidacy of Smith had forced the Anti-Saloon League into a policy of what appeared to be religious bigotry and partisan politics. The League had always had tenuous relations with the Roman Catholic Church through the Catholic Total Abstinence Union, and some

Catholic drys voted for Hoover. But the foulness of the religious campaign against Smith seemed part and parcel of the virulence of the dry campaign against him. Although Senator Simmons could accuse the Democrats of hiding behind a "smoke-screen of intolerance" to disguise the real fault of Smith's wetness, although Clarence True Wilson and Scott McBride could call for a dry vote against Smith rather than a bigot vote, the fact was that prohibition and bigotry were associated in the public mind.[74] Moreover, once the election was ended, the drys claimed that the result was a referendum in favor of the drys, despite the opposite claim of Dr. Nicholas Murray Butler.[75] As Ernest Cherrington wrote, the election was "a referendum not only on prohibition but also upon the right of a President to use his office to secure practical nullification of the Constitution and the right of a state to interpret a provision of the Constitution to suit itself."[76]

The election of 1928 seemed to prove that the progressives and the women still supported prohibition, but they voted more for Hoover and against Smith than for the dry cause. The rural progressive counties which voted for La Follette in 1924 and Hoover in 1928 were voting for the Great Engineer and against the East Side Irishman from New York. Although Mrs. H. W. Peabody might call prohibition "women's only issue" and Mrs. Ella Boole might claim that women won the election for Hoover because he was a dry, the large women's vote for Hoover was, in part, a protest against the nasty manners of Al Smith.[77] The election of 1928 was not a popular referendum on prohibition, though it was held to be so. Conservatives voted for the conservative candidate, radicals for the radical candidate, and traditional Republicans and Democrats stuck to the parties of their prejudice.

Wet to the wets and dry to the drys, Hoover was swept to victory by a majority of over six million votes. The acute comic writer of the *New Republic*, Felix Ray, had his newsdealer Elmer Durkin comment on the three different fights going on at the same time.

> Hoover was telling the come-ons about how the Republican party had invented prosperity, bank accounts, good crops, radios and benzine buggies. Smith was shooting the works on prohibition, water power, wasteful government and farm relief. The rest of the population was talking about Al — where he went to church, what kind of a lid he wore, what liquids he took with his meals, how he was born and brought up in Tammany Hall and the way he pronounced "foist."

In Ray's opinion, it did Al Smith no good that he was the Happy Warrior, for he could not get the enemy to "trade wallops."[78]

The campaign of 1928 was the last great campaign fought by the drys. They took Hoover's victory as a referendum in favor of the

HOSANNA !

From New York *World*

Eighteenth Amendment, and an approval of the methods of the Anti-Saloon League. Kin Hubbard's bootlegger Ike Lark might construe the result "as simply a vote of confidence";[79] but the general feeling was that the Great Engineer would now enforce efficiently a law that had been famous only for the amount of crime and alcoholism that it had produced. Hoover would bring relief and good administration to dry America as he had done to starving Belgium. His propaganda had assured men so.

Although Smith lost the election, he totaled the largest number of Democratic votes ever cast. Many of these ballots were cast by new voters, children of immigrant families, whose numbers were to provide the Democrats with majorities for twenty years. Moreover, it was not a Democratic election. As Will Rogers commented, "Women, Liquor, Tammany Hall — all had their minor little contributing factors one way or another in the total, but the whole answer was: We just didn't have any Merchandise to offer the Boys that would make 'em come over on our side of the Street."[80] Depression would provide for that lack of merchandise.

The last major victory of the country over the city, of the old America over the new, was in the presidential election of 1928, when the dry Quaker from Iowa defeated the wet Roman Catholic from New York. But Smith, in his defeat, pulled the Northern cities into the Democratic column, where they stayed. Lippmann noted that the objections of the drys and the Protestants to New York and Tammany were perfectly sincere. They helped to make up an opposition to Smith which was as authentic and poignant as his support by the immigrant urban masses. The opposition was inspired by the feeling that the clamorous life of the city should not be acknowledged as the American ideal.[81] A man with an East Side accent and a brown derby, who spat frequently and publicly, should not be elected to represent all America. And he was not.

PART **3**

The Blight of Repeal

CHAPTER 16

The Spreading Change

> The liquor traffic may have been possible in the age of
> the ox-cart, but it is not possible in the age of the auto-
> - mobile.
>
> ERNEST CHERRINGTON
> *The Anti-Saloon League Yearbook,* 1922

A T THE VERY time that the country defeated the city by the pas
sage of the Eighteenth Amendment and by the election of Herbert
Hoover, the city had finally overcome the country through technology
and economics. The city newspapers largely displaced the country
newspapers. Automobiles and movies and radios brought the imagined
manners of the urban rich to every village. Again, the assault of metropolitan habits on rural habits increased the desperation of those who
loved the old country ways. But they could not keep back the new carriers of change, which helped to destroy prohibition along with the
isolation of the small town.

THE POPULAR PRESS

FOR MORE than forty years before the passage of the Eighteenth
Amendment, the press of the United States was flooded with articles
and editorials alleging that alcohol was the chief cause of poverty,
crime, disease, and insanity. Paid advertisements were the only means
of representing the wet point of view. Yet, by 1930, the position was
exactly the reverse.[1] The change of the popular press both led and
reflected the change of the American people in their attitude toward
prohibition.

In a series of studies made at the close of national prohibition, this
change was carefully calculated through samplings taken from middle-
class magazines. In 1905, out of 175 articles on prohibition taken from
the *Atlantic,* the *Arena,* the *Independent,* the *Review of Reviews,* the
Survey, and the *World Today,* not one article was unfavorable to the
dry cause. Out of a larger sampling taken in 1915, which also included

the *Ladies' Home Journal,* the *Living Age,* the *Nation,* the *New Republic,* the *North American Review,* and the *Outlook,* articles approved of prohibition in a ratio of nearly twenty to one. By 1920, the ratio had shrunk to less than four to three on the dry side. By 1930, with the addition of *Harper's, Collier's,* the *Commonweal,* and *World's Work,* the articles favoring prohibition had decreased until they compared with wet articles in a ratio of less than one dry article to two wet pieces. A parallel sampling showed a less dramatic shift from a dry to a wet attitude in these magazines; but if the two studies are taken together it can be said that opposition to prohibition in American bourgeois magazines increased five times between 1914 and 1931, while attitudes towards drinking also reversed themselves to a lesser degree. Similar magazine studies showed a switch from religious sanctions to scientific sanctions in this period, whereas the years from 1925 to 1928 were the peak of articles against religion and in favor of sexual freedom.[2]

A like process took place in the newspapers of the country. The dry monopoly of favorable comment at the beginning of the century gave way to an increasing wet attack throughout the twenties. While Purley A. Baker could claim justly that more than half of the nation's secular press supported the drys in 1907, twenty years later hardly a major newspaper praised them.[3] This change was partially due to the changing organization and techniques of the popular press of the day, but it was also due to the methods used to influence the press by wets and drys.

The drys had early set up methods of swinging newspapers to their side. They pioneered the clipsheet, which gave newspaper editors a cheap source of news, although the news itself was biased. They circularized a large number of "boiler-plate" articles, ready for printing, which cut down costs in small-town newspapers. They would send, free of charge, information and statistics and "fill-ins" to sympathetic dry editors. They would encourage dry manufacturers to advertise only in dry newspapers; indeed, half the newspapers of the country, including the New York *Tribune,* the Chicago *Herald,* and the Boston *Record,* would not accept liquor advertisements in 1912 out of conviction and fear of losing dry customers.[4] Moreover, the drys would buy full-page advertisements before elections to make converts for their cause. Charles Stelzle ran a "Strengthen America Campaign" to put across the Eighteenth Amendment, which used full-page advertisements in the *Saturday Evening Post,* the *Literary Digest,* the *Independent,* the *Outlook,* and the labor press, while a mass of articles was supplied without fee to those editors who would print such propaganda. The campaign was budgeted at a cost of a million dollars.[5]

The brewers and distillers probably spent more than the drys on subsidizing the popular press and on buying advertising space and editors. But their money was not placed wisely. Too much money was spent on the converted, on the foreign-language press. Too little money went into the popular magazines and uncommitted newspapers, except into ill-judged attempts to buy control of them.[6] But once national prohibition went into effect, the Association Against the Prohibition Amendment increasingly adopted the methods of press influence of the drys. Articles were written and placed by writers who were ostensibly impartial but who were in reality supporting repeal for a fee paid by the Association. Statistics, clipsheets, pamphlets, and free copy were supplied to any newspaper on demand. Similar means of exerting pressure on editors through advertisements were employed. There was a significant letter from Pierre S. Du Pont, the head of the Association, to a leader of the wets in Philadelphia, which asked him to point out to the officials of the *Saturday Evening Post* that the magazine was "intimately related to both the General Motors Corporation and the Du Pont Company," and that, as the aim of the paper was "to promote the welfare of the people of the United States," the Du Ponts hoped the paper would join them "in a move toward better things with respect to the manufacture and sale of alcoholic beverages."[7] By such indirect pressure, large sections of the press were swung over to the wet cause, although a few newspapers, such as those of Frank Gannett, remained dry to the end. A dry survey in 1931 found that the circulation of wet newspapers outnumbered that of dry newspapers by two to one.[8]

The propaganda techniques and economic pressures used to win over the press were developed by the drys and used against them by the wets. For most of the moneyed men changed in their attitude toward prohibition and took many of the newspapers and magazines with them. It was a case of the persuaders persuaded. Also the change of the progressives and men of science in their attitude toward alcohol, and the realization that the evils of prohibition were as great or greater than those of the saloon, were mirrored in the popular articles of the time. While, in 1917, the *American Magazine* would reprint an article of Booth Tarkington's on how he gave up liquor, and Cleveland Moffat in *McClure's* would warn girls not to give themselves even to moderate drinkers because their procreative powers were seriously impaired, by 1920 the articles had already begun to switch to the "Collapse of Prohibition," and by 1930, to sophisticated and witty pieces like "Have a Little Drinkie."[9] The warnings of the muckrakers about the evils of the saloons gave way to the accusing farragoes of a Mencken and the spiky witticisms of the *New Yorker* or *Vanity Fair*, whose solution to the problem of policing the Canadian border was not to erect a barbed-wire fence there, but to erect a brass rail.[10]

The metamorphosis of the American press itself did not help the dry cause. It was an age of the growing chain newspapers, competing savagely with each other and pushing local newspapers to the wall. In the war for increased circulation, quality and truth suffered and sensationalism and "human interest" stories gained, until some newspapers all but excluded legitimate news. The success of the tabloid New York *Daily News* in the twenties led to many imitations of its exploitation of melodrama and photographs; the success of *True Story* and *True Confessions* in the magazine field forced similar changes. Prohibition was marvelous copy for such presentation, in the large headlines and scare lettering developed by the war. Rumrunners and speak-easy proprietors and gangsters were interesting people and sensational stuff. Socialites caught in a raid made for good pictures and exposés. And the small man tried for brewing his own beer or carrying a hip flask always brought out mass sympathy for the underdog.[11] Moreover, the contemporary crimes of Leopold and Loeb, of Hall and Mills, and of Ruth Snyder, the sex dramas of Fatty Arbuckle and "Daddy" Browning, the gay escapades of Mayor Jimmy Walker and Big Bill Thompson — all this "series of tremendous trifles" provided that mixture of lawlessness and gaity, sex and crime, which cast the artificial glamour of the "jazz age" over an era in which many evils were excused on the grounds of a false, but glittering, scale of values. When Elinor Glyn was asked which way Hollywood would go after the notorious scandals of the early twenties, she answered for a whole national ethos which was to endure until the depression, "Whatever will bring in the most money will happen."[12]

With such a vogue for glamour and sensation, the dry cause was bound to suffer. The patriots of the war became the patsys of the peace. They had won the Eighteenth Amendment at a time when news of war crowded interest in prohibition to the back pages. But, as Mabel Walker Willebrandt wrote, the moment that prohibition went into effect, the subject became, for the first time, "big news" for the city press.[13] And the city press was becoming more and more the press of all America. Between 1925 and 1930, rural subscriptions to city newspapers doubled.[14] And the city press grew wetter and wetter. In New York, the *Times* and the *Herald* and the *World* were always opposed to prohibition, although the *World* died in the depression before the repeal came which it had advocated. The Hearst chain switched to support of modification of the law to allow the sale of light wines and beer, although it ran a competition in 1929 for plans to tighten up enforcement. In Chicago, four of the five newspapers, including the influential *Tribune*, were wet in 1930. This wetness of the city press represented its wish to appeal to the new market of the semiliterate workers as well as its exploitation of the color stories of the time. For the popular newspapers were little better or little worse than the tastes and opinions of the mass of their readers. If the drys attacked the wet press as a conspiracy against the people, they were really attacking the city majority as a conspiracy against the country minority.

Still, wet propaganda could be dismissed as mere lies, as could dry propaganda. What was difficult to dismiss was the evidence collected by the polls of the *Literary Digest*. In three sensational polls, which were copied by small polls conducted by other papers, the *Digest* showed the slipping of prohibition sentiment. A poll in 1922 showed that, of nine hundred thousand owners of telephones who answered the pollsters, two-fifths supported modification and one-fifth repeal. In 1930, five million owners of automobiles and telephones gave a majority for repeal or modification in every state in America except for five. In the poll of 1932, all the states except Kansas and North Carolina gave a majority for outright repeal. An exhaustive analysis of the *Literary Digest* polling techniques revealed a bias in favor of the wets.[15] But, even if the margin of wet sentiment was exaggerated, it nevertheless had received the accolade of the great American creed that a fact is always true as long as it is supported by figures. Moreover, the prestige of the *Literary Digest* was extremely high throughout the country until it dug its own grave by predicting the victory in 1936 of Alfred Landon over President Franklin D. Roosevelt.

The dry leaders became so incensed by the attitude of the press that they proposed to establish a chain of daily newspapers which would, in Bishop Cannon's words, "place the truth and the moral betterment of the people above the cash box." Cannon wanted a "stream of clean, properly filtered news" to be substituted for the "sewage which pours into our homes almost daily from the columns of many of the present-day secular dailies, weeklies and monthlies." The chain was to preach the great benefits of prohibition in place of the misrepresentation of the popular press, which preferred "to picture all the boys and girls with hip flasks, daring bootleggers outwitting enforcement officers, or tyrannical officers murdering innocent law violators."[16] The newspaper chain was never set up, and its success would have been doubtful. For the formula of success at that time was sensationalism, and the press was not responsible for the evils of prohibition which it exploited in its reports.

Indeed, there was much good in the publicity which the newspapers gave to the gangsters of the time. As John Landesco said in his study of crime in Chicago, "If it were not for the newspapers, gangdom and its political henchmen and protectors would have stolen this town."[17] James O'Donnell Bennett's exposure of the local gangsters in the Chicago *Tribune* was so salutary that it was reprinted in full in the *Wickersham Report*.[18] Indeed, the massive publicity given to Al Capone was really the reason for his downfall. He became too much of a threat to be ignored by the Department of Justice. Herbert Hoover made himself personally responsible for his imprisonment.[19] * Other and wiser gangsters, such as the New York racketeer Owney Madden, had an unholy fear of the attention of newsmen. As the city editor of the New York *Herald Tribune* wrote, it was a sure sign of doom to the Maddens of the world when they began to get too much publicity. All publicity, to them, was bad publicity.[20] Rackets did not flourish in the open.

The fact that much of the city press dramatized the evils of enforcement did not prevent them from dramatizing the heroes of the enforcement service. Izzy Einstein and Moe Smith, who made over four thousand arrests and confiscated more than fifteen million dollars' worth of liquor in their brief careers, probably made the front pages more often than any other personages of their time except for the President and the Prince of Wales.[21] Indeed, their dismissal in November, 1925, seems to have been due to the offended dignity of the heads of the Prohibition Bureau, who thought that Izzy and Moe corralled too much of the good publicity which should have gone to the rest of the Bureau. Moreover, even a wet newspaper such as the New York *Times* was scrupulously fair in printing the dry point of view, running for months the writings of Roy Haynes and Wayne Wheeler and Mabel Willebrandt.[22] Indeed, there was so much favorable dry publicity in the wet press that Mencken was put into a rage in 1927, writing that, although every reporter in America knew of the failure of prohibition enforcement, it was rare that an American newspaper came out "without a gaudy story on its first page, rehearsing all the old lies under new and blacker headlines."[23]

The popular press of America had much to do with the passage and repeal of prohibition. In doing so, it both mirrored and directed the thoughts of the majority of Americans, as well as of the dry and wet pressure groups. The extending influence of the city press over the country areas of America broke down that isolation in which rural prejudice and faith could support prohibition without doubt or contrary argument. If the drys profited from the trend in America towards

* Hoover, while writing of Al Capone, thought that "it was ironic that a man guilty of inciting hundreds of murders, in some of which he took a personal hand, had to be punished merely for failure to pay taxes on the money he had made by murder."

The Hydra-Headed Monster

MURDER · BLACKMAIL · VICE · BOOTLEG · CORRUPTION · RACKETS · UNDERWORLD · DOPE · GRAFT · AMERICAN CITIES

ENRIGHT

Washington, D.C., *Herald*

the national control of social problems, they were attacked by the instruments of that control, the improved communications of their land.
The prohibitionists wished to make the United States into a large
Kansas. But, as the Boston *Transcript* commented, to do so, they would
have to imitate Kansas and abolish all cities of more than fifty thousand people.[24] Instead, the large cities engulfed the small towns.

THE CARRIERS OF CHANGE

AT THE close of the twenties, Robert Binkley pointed out that the sex
morals of America had withstood centuries of liquor, but had broken
down with two decades of motoring. The car was the chief cause of
strife between children and parents, between husband and wife. It
had increased crime and wasteful spending. It had killed tens of thousands of people. It had taken away the American "birthright of health,"
for driving was both intoxicating and habit-forming. Millions of healthy
men would hardly walk again. Why, then, had the drys not prohibited
automobiles? The answer was that cars were useful, and that they
were kept under control by the responsibility of drivers, by compul-

sory insurance, by licenses and by laws. Could not the same be done for liquor?[25]

The same was not done for liquor. Imperfectly regulated, it deluged America again after 1933. But the automobiles rolled on, wheel after wheel, despite the efforts made to control them. They were the carriers of change, along with the motion pictures and the radios. They broke into the old rural isolation and the pockets of prohibition which spotted the land. They brought the manners of the cities into the hamlets of America. They spread wet propaganda throughout the villages. If prohibition put more money in the hands of a workingman so that he could afford to buy a car, that car gave him the means to go where liquor was to be found and to bring that liquor back to his own home. Without the carriers of change, the dry argument that a sober nation was necessary to meet the demands of a technological revolution would have been futile. But with the carriers of change, the enforcement of prohibition became impossible. The new devices helped to bring about the boom, which was claimed as a dry triumph; but they also took bootleg liquor or its tidings wherever they moved. Prosperity and booze seemed to be the new Siamese twins. There was a wry truth in the *New Yorker*'s comment on Henry Ford's declaration that he would stop making cars if prohibition was repealed, "It would be a great pity to have Detroit's two leading industries destroyed at one blow."[26]

Henry Ford himself was the symbol of his time. The Model-T wrecked rural America more surely than any devastation. Yet Ford spent many of his millions in re-creating that lost past in his Greenfield Village. He also revived the square dance and hillbilly music, while his automobiles were shaking to pieces the settled communities that had developed these rough arts.[27] Ford was a sort of Wild West Wind of Change, a destroyer and preserver. While his mind created the mass ways of a new civilization, his feet dragged in the folkways of the old customs of his childhood. Although he was the apostle of a new creed of business with the dictum that "anything which is economically right is also morally right," he could also be the prophet of nostalgia with advertisements which aimed to cure the depression of the thirties by asking Americans to return to their roots and "cultivate a plot of land" in the "good old pioneer way."[28] His coexistent mixture of invention and reaction made him the appropriate godhead of his days, capable of supporting mass production and prohibition at the same time, although they were natural enemies.

In 1900, there were some eight thousand horseless carriages on the American roads, which, in themselves, were little better than excuses for roads. Four years later, there were only 150 miles of paved highway in the United States, and 150,000 miles of surfaced track. The villages of America were connected by railroads, or else by dust and horses and buggies and bicycles. Thus the prohibitionists could dry up the country piecemeal, congregation by congregation, small area by small area. In places where the scarcity of news made all news welcome, and the lack of visitors made the itinerant clergyman an event, the dry control of the pulpits and the Chautauquas was all-important in bringing out the voters in the backcountry. Where culture was identified with the traveling tents of the Chautauqua shows, which brought their light orchestras and moral dramas and inspirational talks and dry lecturers to small towns that knew no better and sought the good, the prohibitionists were thus assured of steady and unfailing support. Even if the large and alien cities were growing in numbers and in evil, they were far away and unseen, dangerous rather than attractive. Those speakers who had seen them merely told of their depravity; there were few speakers to emphasize their virtues. The people of the country relied on their dominant faith to rule forever. They applauded such orators as the presidential candidate of the Prohibition party at the Wisconsin Chautauqua at Camp Cleghorn in 1911, when he declared, "No matter what may happen in spots in the United States, don't you people ever get alarmed, for in the long run the Anglo-Saxon is going to boss the job of running the United States of America."[29]

But the cars and the roads multiplied, and the confined audiences of the Chautauquas crumbled away. By 1916, there were more than 3,000,000 cars in the United States; by 1921, more than 9,000,000; by 1929, more than 23,000,000 cars, one for every five Americans. In 1930, the length of the surfaced roads was nearly 700,000 miles, of which 125,000 miles were paved highways. Tourism and the comforts of tourism — garages, filling stations, hotels, roadhouses, and snack bars — had created a new method of escape from the spying eyes of neighbors, and were permitting a New Freedom for the owners of cars that Woodrow Wilson had hardly envisaged.

The car developed into a symbol of success and prosperity, of liberation and power, to such an extent that it was the last luxury which the unemployed would relinquish. It became a necessity, for it conquered that space which kept Americans apart from each other. It even brought the family together in vacations and trips, although it also took children far away from home restraints. One Middletown mother confessed, "I never feel as close to my family as when we are all together in the car." And, above all, to an America whose gospel was work and self-denial for material rewards, the car represented the accrued benefits of toil and foregone pleasure. "It's prohibition that's done it," said an officer of the Middletown Trades Council; "drink money is going into cars."[30]

The car swept away many of the old sanctions of a closed village society. The repressive threats of nineteenth-century morality relied for a great part on the impossibility of escaping from the consequences or the place of misbehavior. The car and the contraceptive broke down many of the taboos and prohibitions of the time, to such an extent that a judge in a juvenile court referred to the automobile as "a house of prostitution on wheels."[31] Moreover, the anonymity of the new motor hotels and roadhouses, which supplied the liquor and jazz demanded by the drivers of the cars, gave a faceless freedom to the "easy riders" of the time. If speed was an intoxication in itself, liquor was sought to intoxicate the mind into more speed.

The very philosophy of Fordism, that of the assembly line and the standardized part and the five-dollar day, compelled workers and executives and their children to search madly for individuality at any price, at the wheel or in the speak-easy or on the bed. The warning of Billy Sunday, that no one could pray "Thy Kingdom come" and then look at God through the bottom of a beer mug, was meaningless to people who could not sit at a conveyor belt all day and then look at their own selves through the glass of the evangelical virtues. The new speed and spread of living brought by the mass-produced car was the necessary reward for the confined and mechanical labor put into the making of the mass-produced car. The modern factories made possible the escape of their toilers to the country, at the price of rural peace and the past.

The automobile became so much the representative of the new way of life that its use in nullifying national prohibition was inevitable. It was used to take buyers to the source of liquor, and liquor to prospective buyers. "Secondhand Fords are the bootlegger's chief deputies," wrote one social worker. Another lamented the widespread drinking of drivers with the dictum, "Fords have taken the place of the saloon."[32] Criminals penetrated the trucking companies and the Teamsters' Union, in order to acquire control of fleets of trucks to transport their supplies of bootleg from still to sale.[33] The armor-plated cars with windows of bullet-proof glass, the murders implicit in Hymie Weiss's phrase "to take for a ride," the sedans of tommy-gunners spraying the streets of gangland, all created a satanic mythology of the automobile that bid fair to rival the demonism of the saloon. The car was an instrument of death in the hands of crook and drunk, and prohibition was held to have spawned both of them. "Gasoline and alcohol will not mix," declared Judge Elliott, of Sioux Falls.[34] One of them had to be prohibited. And, although the abolition of the car itself was never

EASY RIDERS

seriously suggested, its misuse did add weight to the wet arguments for repeal, especially when several innocent drivers were shot down by prohibition agents on the watch for bootleggers. Indeed, the car was thought to be such a dangerous vehicle in prohibition days that the attorney general of Michigan had to forbid local drivers from putting on their windshield stickers which bore the American flag and the legend "Don't Shoot, I'm Not a Bootlegger."[35]

The second revolutionary carrier of change was the motion picture. In the beginning, it was welcomed by reformers and prohibitionists.* Such films as *The Saloon Dance* and *The Saloon-Keeper's Nightmare* in 1908 and *The Saloon Next Door* in 1910 preached dry propaganda. Reformers themselves introduced sex into the movies in an effort to warn audiences of the perils of the white-slave trade; but the popular success of *Traffic in Souls* in 1913 conjured up a host of imitations

---

* Only the Woman's Christian Temperance Union was always leery of the cinema. As early as 1906, it denounced the places where films were shown as "Five Cent Schools of Crime."

which were more concerned with giving their audiences a glimpse of vice than with teaching them how to avoid it.[36] Even so, the drys were quick to praise the twenty-one thousand picture houses which had been built by 1916. For these were substitutes for the saloon and kept drinkers out of the bar. The brewers were equally quick to denounce these competitors, both as false prophets and trade rivals. The wet *Mida's Criterion* complained, "Who has ever seen liquor portrayed in any but the most unfavorable light by the movies? The films accept every chance to link liquor with the drug habits. What makes the rural lover go wrong? Liquor, always liquor. And hooked up with liquor must be evil women. The movies have made a goat of liquor." And an investigator advised the Mayor of Cleveland that, although an occasional clergyman or educator criticized the movie theaters, "If you want to see the motion-picture business flayed alive and its skin hung up to dry, talk to a saloon-keeper or a pool-room operator or a prize-fight promoter or the manager of a burlesque show."[37] To the drys, the early motion pictures were a qualified good, and to the liquor trade, an unqualified evil.

By 1919, there was a growing movement among the drys to regulate and censor the motion pictures, although not to prohibit them. For the drys realized that they had done much to fill the gap of the closed saloons. One female dry even talked of the "divine right of the weary brain" to pleasure, and the necessary relaxation which the movie theaters provided through "the warmth, the low music, the soft light and the absence of the human voice." She thought that the movies were not a competition but a help to the home, for whole families could attend decent films there. The makers of films, however, were too concerned, as the brewers had been, with profits. If they did not clean up themselves, they would be cleaned up despite themselves.

> Close investigation has discovered that a large percentage of motion pictures are as harmful to the mind as alcohol is to the body. Many pictures are vulgar and have a tendency to lower public taste. Most pictures are melodramatic, stultifying and deadening all tender emotions and injecting into the mind scenes of crime and degradation, which tend to morbidity."[38]

The scandals of Hollywood in the early twenties, the divorce of Mary Pickford, the deaths of Virginia Rappe and William Deane Taylor and Olive Thomas, led to so much unfavorable publicity that the motion-picture industry intervened in the celluloid and private lives of the stars. The chairman of the Republican National Committee, Will H. Hays, who had conducted President Harding's successful campaign, was called in to become the moral censor of Hollywood, the official adviser against the bad taste that might lead to low profits. At first he was unsuccessful at stopping the deluge of daring movies which were assaulting the preconceptions of the small-town mind. The Middletown screens of 1925 sported a plethora of films about the gay and immoral doings of the imaginary upper crust of America. Such films were showing as *Alimony* — "brilliant men, beautiful jazz babies, champagne baths, midnight revels, petting parties in the purple dawn, all ending in one terrific smashing climax that makes you gasp"; *Flaming Youth* — "neckers, petters, white kisses, red kisses, pleasure-mad daughters, sensation-craving mothers, by an author who didn't dare sign his name; the truth bold, naked, sensational"; and other suggestive titles like *Married Flirts, Sinners in Silk, Women Who Give, The Price She Paid, Rouged Lips,* and *The Queen of Sin.*[39]* Although slow to realize the enormous effect that these visual examples would have on the manners and morals of the young, the protests of reformers and drys soon gathered momentum, and led to further regulation.

In 1933, the Motion Picture Research Council publicized the fact that nearly thirty million young people under the age of twenty-one visited the cinema each week. There they saw pictures, of which three-quarters dealt with crime, sex, and love. The films were concerned chiefly with the wealthy, and their violent and amoral lives. In only one-third of these pictures was there any effort by the hero or heroine to marry for love. Such revelations led to action by the Roman Catholic Church, which formed a Legion of Decency to boycott films that might harm its communicants, and the establishment in Hollywood of the "Breen Office" to ensure that the right always won on the screen, and that the law was always upheld.[40]

But in the same year that some prohibition of immorality in films was achieved in Hollywood, the prohibition of liquor was ended. More than any other mass medium, the movies had attacked the ideology of the drys and their primal faith that liquor was a sinful drink. A study in 1932 showed that films approved of drinking in a ratio of more than three to one.[41] Another study found that there was some reference to liquor in three films out of four. Moreover, while the hero drank in two out of five films and the heroine in one out of five, the villain swilled liquor in only one film out of ten.[42] There had been a sharp shift from the popular films of the boom, which still

---

* Similar lurid titles graced the stage of the time: *Young Blood, Sex, She Wouldn't Say No, Strictly Dishonorable, Bad Girl,* and *Greeks Had a Name For It.* Drinking was prevalent on stage throughout prohibition, although what was liquor to the audience was cold tea to the actors. There were even two moderate plays on the subject, *Speakeasy* and *Light Wines and Beer.*

preserved traces of the old rural morality, to the films of "realism" and violence, which were popular in the depression. A comparison of two successful pictures, one released at the peak of boom and one in the trough of slump, gives some idea of how films dealt with prohibition and reflected the changing attitudes of the time to that issue.

Lights of New York was the first all-talking motion picture. It was released in 1928. Its plot was simple. Two young men from Main Street are tricked by two city slickers into investing their all in a Broadway speak-easy, disguised as a barbershop. The Main Street hero meets his long-lost Main Street heroine, who is dancing in a night club. Both hate the wicked big-city life, which is shown in great detail; but they cannot return home to their small country town as failures. Eventually, the villainous owner of the night club murders a policeman over some cases of bootleg whisky, symbolically named Old Century. The villain tries to frame the hero with these cases of whisky and to have him "taken for a ride." He fails and is assassinated by his jealous mistress. The hero and heroine are suspected of the crime, but are saved by the confession of the murderess. The tough cop, spitting out a kindly thought from under his snap-brim hat, then delivers the moral from wicked New York to good Main Street: "If ye take my advice, ye'll get on the first train to the mountains an' the flowers an' the trees, an' leave the roarin' parties of the city to roar on without ye."

The film follows perfectly the pattern and assumptions of the old revival sermon. It makes out that cities are bad and that Main Street is good. It describes the life of sin in titillating detail, only to eschew the attraction of evil by making the lovers flee back to home, sweet home. It presumes that liquor was only drunk in the cities, and that prohibition was a joke there. City life is merely the distance from one speak-easy to another, or the interval between night clubs. Country life is the love of white-haired mothers and pure virgins, who completely trust their men. *Lights of New York* was a great success in America, since it provided an overdressed version of the same old hokum that had shocked and flattered the small town for a hundred years.

But the success of James Cagney in *The Public Enemy* provided a now type of screen hero and heroine for the hard-bitten audience of 1932. Mae West played in her first picture, *Night After Night*, with George Raft as the hero. He is also the owner of a speak-easy, but he is tough, brutal, a slum kid and a crook, lusting after the culture which he can never acquire. There is no pandering to rural virtue in dialogue or plot. When Raft asks one of his mistresses, "What's with you?" she replies, "Three cocktails." When one of Raft's clientele tells him that

From the Warner Brothers picture *Lights of New York*

NIGHT CLUB ENTERTAINMENT

she has just got her divorce and he replies that he never knew she was married, her answer is, "Joe, you've been watching me too closely." The once-rich society flapper, with whom Raft falls in love, is roughed up by him and told that she is just "another dame with a skirt on." The only difference between her and a cheap girl is how she manicures her nails. Raft's brutality is greeted by her adoring devotion. He then walks out to save his speak-easy from a hijacking attempt by a rival gang of crooks. The moral of the film seems to be that the crooks are loved by the cultured, and that the way to the rich and wenching life is the ownership of an illegal night club. No policeman appears in the piece at all, not even as comic relief. Vice is rewarded, and virtue ignored. Indeed, one line from Mae West summarizes the gospel of the whole film. In reply to a girl who admires her jewelry with the remark, "Goodness, what beautiful diamonds!" Mae West says, rolling up a flight of stairs with her inimitable shake, "Goodness had nothing to do with it, dearie."

The millions who liked and laughed at such films were not the millions who would vote against the repeal of prohibition. For better or for worse, the American films of the twenties had spread everywhere the desire to imitate the life of the rich, whether they were rich by inheritance or rich by lawless grabbing. And the life of the rich included liquor, its use and abuse. The usual drunkard on films, whether portrayed by Ben Turpin or Charlie Chaplin or W. C. Fields, was more a comedian than a menace to society. The usual hero, trapped into bootlegging by necessity, was less a crook than a creature of circumstance. And the criminal owners of speak-easies rose from the role of villain to displace the hero himself. In 1931, Alva Johnstone was to congratulate Al Capone ironically for carrying Broadway and Hollywood on his shoulders, and for solving the problems of the motion-picture industry. He had replaced sex with violence on the screen. "The movie massacres were like a breath of fresh air after all the impropriety and misconduct of the films."[43] Johnstone did not mention, however, that liquor played an integral part in portraying both sex and violence, and was glorified in the glorification of both. If the picture theaters were at first the rivals of the saloons, at the last they were the deluge of the drys.

The third carrier of change was the radio. The Census of 1930 reported that after less than a decade of the industry more than twelve million American families owned radios. By the end of 1933, there were seventeen million radios in the country. Two in every five villagers and one in every five farmers owned a set.[44] The ubiquitous voices of the air brought a standard pattern of culture to the land, based on the wish of the advertisers to please the greatest possible number and to offend the least. Thus, although praise of liquor was prohibited from the air, jokes at the expense of prohibition and the influence of city manners spread unchecked. Moreover, the political use of the radio by Franklin D. Roosevelt gave a great popular support to the economic methods which he advocated, such as repeal. The radio was yet another powerful instrument in bringing the city to the country.

The strength of the drys was based on the small town. Yet their control of methods of instruction and entertainment through churches and Chautauquas and isolation was broken down by the invasion of the automobiles and the movies and the radios. And this was no bad thing, even if some evils resulted from the new way of life, and even if national prohibition was destroyed in the process. As an analyst of the small town wrote in 1938:

> The people living in the little town have a richer life than their parents did. They can reach a motion-picture theater by a twenty-minute drive, they have radios, and they think nothing of jaunts to

Boston, New York or Canada that many of the old residents never made in an entire life-time. The point is not that life is better or worse. It is different. The town is no longer self-contained. Invention and change have let the inhabitants out, the outer world in.[45]

The changes of the new technology were irresistible. Isolation and ignorance became more difficult to conserve as communications became easier to develop. The psychology of prohibition in the small town was gradually replaced by a yearning for the life of the big city. Yet this metamorphosis of the country mind was not confined to the rural West and South. It was also evident in the urban literature of America, whose writers gave up their Jamaicas of Remembrance for an attack on abstinence.

CHAPTER 17

Jamaicas of Remembrance

Did it occur to you that personal liberty
Is liberty of the mind,
Rather than of the belly?

EDGAR LEE MASTERS

PROHIBITION produced no great literature. There was no *Uncle Tom's Cabin* of the dry cause, although the drys hoped in 1931 that Upton Sinclair's *The Wet Parade* might be this long-awaited work of art. It was not. Nothing replaced the most popular of all the temperance novels, T. S. Arthur's *Ten Nights in a Bar-Room*, written in 1854, and the play adapted from it, *The Drunkard*. Such different crusaders as Carry Nation and W. C. Fields played in *The Drunkard*, and it is the play with the longest consecutive run in the history of the world, over nineteen years without a break in the city of Los Angeles. In it and the novel, the classic conflict between good and evil, God and the saloon, pure small girls and unredeemed villains, is fought out to the last breath of sentiment and the last drop of innocent and guilty blood. The saloonkeeper, Simon Slade, gradually degenerates along with his inn, taking his family to perdition with him. The corrupter, Harvey Green, is the cause of ruin. "In what broad, black characters was the word TEMPTER written on his face! How was it possible for anyone to look thereon, and not read the warning inscription!" Only the drunken Joe Morgan is saved by the death of his little daughter, hit on the forehead by a beer mug in a saloon brawl. She dies, forgiving her father and making him swear to the pledge, for she is, as her mother says, "better fitted for heaven than for earth." Thus the good end chastened but happy, and the bad end chastized and unhappy, and the moral of the piece shines through any faults of characterization and style.[1]

The temporary alliance between the prohibition movement and the progressive movement led to some minor works by the social novelists of the time, Jack London and Upton Sinclair. London's autobiography of his drunkard's career, *John Barleycorn,* written in 1913, is as honest and moving a piece of work as he ever wrote. There is a terror of truth in his own knowledge of himself, a prophecy of his inexorable end through liquor and depression. The melancholia which drove him to drink drove him to that fatalism which made him write, "Suicide, quick or slow, a sudden spill or a gradual oozing away through the years, is the price John Barleycorn exacts. No friend of his ever escapes making the just, due payment."[2] The gift of alcohol was the dreadful "white logic." This revealed to the depressive drinker the veiled, bloody truths of existence and destroyed the illusions necessary for happy living, or living at all. London was a pessimist by nature, a believer in the tragic and fatal destiny of mankind. His dislike of liquor, his belief that it was a habit-forming poison which degenerated the race, his faith that women would preserve sinful men from their temptations — all these creeds turned *John Barleycorn* into marvelous dry propaganda. London's own tragic death made him appear the victim of the alcohol poison which he could not avoid.

When Upton Sinclair, dedicated to the same goals of his youth, wrote his indictment of liquor, *The Cup of Fury,* London's name led the list of those famous people known to Sinclair who had destroyed themselves by drink. O. Henry, Stephen Crane, Eugene Debs, Sinclair Lewis, Isadora Duncan, Sherwood Anderson, all figured in Upton Sinclair's appeal for prohibition.[3] But they were dead, while Sinclair lived on into a time when national prohibition was thirty years gone and gone for good.

Yet, although prohibition produced no great literature, the reaction to its morality and psychology produced much. The rigid tenets of the evangelical creed, which made inhibition and self-control the highest good, helped to cause a tension in some writers that made their creation possible. Mark Twain puts this conflict amusingly, although it gave him enough woe.

> Mine was a trained Presbyterian conscience and knew but the one duty — to hunt and harry its slave upon all pretexts and on all occasions, particularly when there was no sense nor reason in it. . . . In my early manhood and in middle life I used to vex myself with reforms every now and then. And I never had occasion to regret these divergencies for, whether the resulting deprivations were long or short, the rewarding pleasure which I got out of the vice when I returned to it always paid me for all that it cost.[4]

But if the revolts of a Twain against nineteenth-century morality were mild, those of an Emily Dickinson were more extreme. To her, the philosophy of restraint and inhibition was a crime. She was in rebellion against repression, in search of that liberty which America promised and American churches denied. In one charming poem, she spoke of this urge for an intoxication of the spirit.

> *A Drunkard cannot meet a Cork*
> *Without a Revery —*
> *And so encountering a Fly*
> *This January Day*
> *Jamaicas of Remembrance stir*
> *That send me reeling in —*
> *The moderate drinker of Delight*
> *Does not deserve the spring —*
> *Of juleps, part are in the Jug*
> *And more are in the joy —*
> *Your connoisseur in Liquors*
> *Consults the Bumble Bee —* [5]

With the muckraking novelists and social writers and poets, Theodore Dreiser, Frank Norris, Edgar Lee Masters, Carl Sandburg, and Sherwood Anderson, the revolt against the mentality of prohibition became more explicit. Their writings reflected a philosophy of pragmatism, an ethical relativism, a wish to see the world as it did, as it ate and drank and had sex. Although there was a sentimentalism born of a long literary tradition in the writings of these five men, their attack on the country morality of the time was new. Masters's sneer at dry motives was uncomfortably accurate in his *Spoon River Anthology*.

> *. . . Or do you think the poker room*
> *Of Johnnie Taylor, and Burchard's bar*
> *Had been closed up if the money lost*
> *And spent for beer had not been turned,*
> *By closing them, to Thomas Rhodes*
> *For larger sales of shoes and blankets,*
> *And children's cloaks and gold-oak cradles?*
> *Why, a moral truth is a hollow tooth*
> *Which must be propped with gold.*[6]

And Sherwood Anderson, who began the whole school of writing of the Lost Generation, was not kind in his picture of lusting ministers and drunken farmers in his *Winesburg, Ohio*.[7]

Denis Brogan has emphasized the importance of the wet and dry issue to American literature. It was, in Brogan's opinion, almost as devastating as the fight between the clericals and anticlericals in France. Indeed, it *was* a fight between clericals and anticlericals.

It mixed up Catholics, romantics, expatriates, libertarians, art-for-art's-sakers in a battle for free drinking, evolution, free thought, free love, Al Smith, Freud, Joyce, Karl Adam, Karl Marx, Russian movies, against traditionalists, Jew-baiters, Catholic-haters, political and social conservatives, moralists, legalists. Critics — or so-called critics — ceased to ask "What is he saying? How well does he say it?" and fell back on the simpler "Is he on our side?" It was possibly a greater crime in Stuart Sherman to defend prohibition than to be an academic critic and disciple of Paul Elmer More.[8]

On the wet side stood Hemingway, Dos Passos, Caldwell, Cabell, Cummings, Ring Lardner, Dorothy Parker, Scott Fitzgerald, Faulkner, and Thomas Wolfe. The critics aligned with them were Mencken, Van Wyck Brooks, Edmund Wilson, and Harold Stearns. Against them stood the last of the old muckrakers, Upton Sinclair, and the followers of the tradition of James and Howells, such as Edith Wharton, with their critical allies, More and Sherman, Irving Babbitt and William C. Brownell. Uneasily, in no man's land, stood Sinclair Lewis, with his savage eye and George F. Babbitt heart, and Willa Cather, whose "world broke in two in 1922 or thereabouts."[9]

Posterity has sanctioned the rebels and repeal, not the defenders and prohibition. Yet, the rebels at home suffered the same eclipse as the drys in the depression. *Vanity Fair* went into a common grave with the Eighteenth Amendment. Mencken could warn Paul Elmer More in 1922, "The Goths and the Huns are at the gate, and as they batter wildly they throw dead cats, perfumed lingerie, tracts against predestination, and the bound files of the *Nation,* the *Freeman* and the *New Republic* over the fence."[10] He could get hordes of young intellectuals to attack with the syringes of their contempt "the messianic delusion [which] is our national disease."[11] But the contempt of the twenties for reformers and their works — because all reform seemed to be garbed in the hypocritical shroud of prohibition — was superseded by the reforming drive of the thirties, when economic and social cure-alls pushed Mencken's diatribes into the dusty nostalgias of aging minds. The repeal of prohibition itself left the New Deal to promise new heavens on earth for those who looked for Messiahs. The preoccupation of the twenties with sex and liquor was displaced by a more basic search for food. For a rebellion against reform can only flourish on Easy Street.

But prohibition also sent the wet rebels abroad. They went to Paris and followed the creed of Hemingway's Lieutenant Frederick Henry, "I was not made to think. I was made to eat. My God, yes. Eat and drink and sleep with Catherine."[12] The trinity of food and sex and liquor, the directness of action and thought and word, which is the last refuge of sophistication, the search for the simple life and the American Adam, which had once been the mythological right of the frontiersman and the Indian — these were what the Lost Generation sought in the Select and the Ritz Bar. They sought an escape from that Puritan morality which they could never escape. In their flight, they created great works, which they thought sprang from nihilism and Dada, but which really sprang from their dream of the lost youth of a great nation, now corrupted in their minds by the materialism of easy money and the caricature of idiotic reforms. Yet, the expatriates, in their prohibition of the mentality of prohibition, did not give up the code of the drys. The drinking and the girls were taken less for themselves than for the cult of taking them. There was a sort of religious dedication to the Pamplona trail.[13] Liquor was drunk not only for enjoyment but as the liquid food of emancipation. For, as William Carlos Williams wrote, ". . . whisky was to the imagination of the Paris of that time like milk to a baby."[14] In this desperate reaction from prohibition, the Lost Generation prohibited itself from the need to understand complex humanity and its urgent problems. The escape from prohibition was the escape into egocentricity, and the blindness of the drys to anything but their own cause was matched by the blindness of the self-styled American expatriates to everything but the satisfaction of their own despair.

But some could neither fight at home nor flee abroad. Hard as they tried to escape from the social responsibilities of their time, their own lives involved them in the tragedies of a nation. Scott Fitzgerald was one of these. At first, he reflected current Princetonian manners in *This Side of Paradise,* and was surprised that the novel should become the pattern of two generations, first that of his own, and then that of his parents. The year of 1922 had been the peak of the younger generation. Although the Jazz Age went on afterwards,

> . . . it became less and less an affair of youth. The sequel was like a children's party taken over by the elders, leaving the children puzzled and rather neglected and rather taken aback. By 1923 their elders, tired of watching the carnival with ill-concealed envy, had discovered that young liquor will take the place of young blood, and with a whoop the orgy began.[15]

The writer from St. Paul, Minnesota, who had forged somewhat unconsciously the image of an era, was broken by that image, even as the image itself was broken by the Great Crash and the depression. Fitzgerald had seen the portents in the "widespread neurosis" which began in 1927. Contemporaries of his had begun to commit suicide. A speak-easy in Chicago killed one; a speak-easy in New York killed another. A maniac killed a third with an ax in a lunatic asylum, where they were being confined. The bloodiness of living was beating its way into the dream of boom, until, by 1931, the Jazz Age seemed as distant as the days before the First World War. "It was borrowed time anyhow — the whole upper tenth of a nation living with the insouciance of grand ducs and the casualness of chorus girls."[16]

The shock of consciousness was so great to Fitzgerald that he cracked up, and even forgot his lack of political commitment enough to flirt with the economic certainty of Marxism. He also kept to the bottle and the hard-drinking habits of prohibition; for, as George Bernard Shaw said of the Irishman, his imagination is such a torture that he cannot bear it without whisky.[17] Fitzgerald's prophecies and tragedies again ran neck and neck with the fact. In his finest novel, *The Great Gatsby*, the hero, Jay Gatsby, builds up a dream life of luxury on an estate at West Egg. The money of his fortune comes from crooked deals associated with prohibition.[18] The people who pass through the parties there are as temporary as the visitors to the speakeasies; Jay Gatsby's wealth and love of Daisy vanish like the boom. Only in the mind of the narrator from the Midwest is Gatsby remembered, hopelessly, lovingly. For Gatsby, like his America, remained true to the illusion of the rich and careless society which finally destroyed and ignored both him and his creator.

Another great writer who was damned by prohibition was Ring Lardner. He was also a victim to the heavy drinking of intellectuals during prohibition, when alcohol turned from being a mild aid to dining and conversation into almost a primary and constant necessity.[19] Lardner mocked at prohibition, but was drowned in a personal melancholy which drove him to the oblivion of bootleg liquor. He found in 1928 that prohibition had "sure been a godsend in a whole lot of ways." It had given lucrative employment to a great many men who did not have anything before except their courage. It had cemented the friendship between America and Canada. It had given women a new interest in life and something to talk about besides hair and children. And it had made the government appreciate the enormous extent of the coast line and the difficulty of defending it against invasion. Lardner concluded his remarks with an accurate forecast of his own and prohibition's future. "As far as it affecting the present and future consumption of alcohol is concerned, why a person that said that drinking in the U. S. was still in its infancy would be just about hitting the nail on the hammer."[20]

Indeed, as with any revolution, the ones who survived prohibition best were those who mocked it lightly and skirted it, those who sniped continually at human folly from the pages of the *New Yorker* and the tables of the Algonquin Hotel. Prohibition was neither to be attacked in a Mencken rage nor defied in a Fitzgerald "collegiate drunk.''[*] It should be defeated with mild quips, like those of Elmer Davis, who explained away the national tolerance of the Volstead Act by saying it made any place at all that contained liquor look like a wild café.[21] Prohibition was a tragedy only to alcoholics such as Dorothy Parker's *Big Blonde*, who regarded prohibition as "only a basis for jokes" until bootleg liquor made her sodden and suicidal.[22] It was also fatal to those who were trapped and killed by the excesses of the times, such as Scott Fitzgerald's friends and many thousands of the nameless murdered. The casual slaughter caused by prohibition was merely another sign of the contemporary carelessness of the wealthy and the creative, who would let society go hang as long as they did not have to be bored by the hanging. Occasionally, however, the killings of prohibition became too much for some of the sensitive, and provoked such bitter remarks as Ellen Glasgow's, "In the South we are substituting murder for a mint julep and calling it progress.''[23]

With the depression, the intellectuals forgot about the war between the wets and the drys, the clericals and the anticlericals, and turned to economics and welfare and social analyses. Sex and God and liquor were shoved to one side to make way for life and Marx and food. Federal writers' and artists' and theater projects employed those creators who could not make a living. The government intervened to feed those who had, less than a decade before, mocked at all government. The contempt of Stearns's thirty young intellectuals of 1922 for their crass mother-country was replaced by their content in 1938 for the efforts she was making to rescue herself and them. The prohibition mentality, which had seemed stupid when restricted to banning liquor in time of boom, seemed sensible enough when applied to personal sacrifice to save a nation's economy. When Stearns himself returned with other American exiles after his "thirteen years' French Sabbatical," it was to find a new hope in a new country, a new willingness to deny self for the good of everybody, "the communism beside which the shabby political doctrine of envy usually called by that name is as evanescent as steam — the communism of the spirit.''[24] Only with such a feeling, could personal prohibition have some meaning in the increased liberty of all.

The excesses of the intellectuals in the twenties were sometimes a match for the excesses of the wets and drys. The intellectuals gave up their duty to defend the cause of reason against the propaganda of prohibition. When such a good writer as Sinclair Lewis could have a

[*] Walter Winchell nastily defined a "collegiate drunk" as a state in which the drinker pretended to be completely drunk on two glasses of whisky.

great popular success with his travesty of a satire, *Elmer Gantry*, moderation was at a discount in America. When widespread applause could greet the remark that the center of American culture, New York, was an alien island off the eastern coast of the United States, rolling with wealth, bursting with pride, and scorning the Ten Commandments, reason was a drug on the market.[25] Indeed, the only reaction to such excesses and follies among intelligent people could be the despair of a Joseph Wood Krutch, who defined the "modern temper" as a disgust with all theories and philosophies, a sort of expectant hopelessness, a resignation with the human condition. "Ours is a lost cause and there is no place for us in the natural universe, but we are not, for all that, sorry to be human. We should rather die as men than live as animals."[26] Yet the prohibitionists refused to recognize that their cause, which was the cause of the human race, was lost. To the last, they insisted that prohibition made men live properly and alcohol made them die like animals.

CHAPTER 18

The Wet Counterattack

> Those who deliberately violate the law and disregard the Constitution because of their appetite for cocktails will some day face the situation where workingmen who hunger for bread will defy other laws as well as the Constitution and appropriate for themselves that which will satisfy their hunger. The slogan "To hell with the Constitution" is a boomerang.
>
> CHARLES STELZLE

THE FAILURE of the enforcement of national prohibition created great difficulties for the drys. Although they claimed that enforcement was improving each year, the progress was merely comparative, from the worst possible to the worse. The evils of prohibition, in turn, gave heart to the wets, whose contention that prohibition could not be enforced seemed to be true. Giant wet organizations, formed to fight the power of the Anti-Saloon League, seemed to spring up like genies from old bottles. For the first time, the dry pressure groups had a similar and challenging enemy to face.

The drys sought to draw attention to conspiracies abroad in order to explain the failure of prohibition at home. It was an old trick, recommended by Machiavelli. Congress itself, thankful to be spared the necessity of appropriating more money for home enforcement, spent the early days of prohibition trying to extend the provisions of the Volstead Act to the Philippines and to the American consular districts of China. It was part of a "fresh advance on a broad front west toward Asia."[1] The dry leaders said that the greater part of the liquor in the country came from foreign rumrunners and conspirators overseas, who were attacking the global prohibition revolution by trying to wreck it in the country of its birth. Roy Haynes, the Prohibition Commissioner, reported the meeting of an antiprohibition congress in Brussels, attended by representatives from Belgium, Canada, Spain, Finland, France, England, Denmark, Italy, Norway, Sweden, and Switzerland. There, "a world fight against prohibition was planned, with the United States as the center of the wet campaign." A certain

Count de Mun, of France, was placed at the head of an "international committee of defense to bring the dry people back into the wet fold."[2] With such delusions of international conspiracy, the drys explained their lack of success.

But, by 1926, prohibition was seen to be a failure at home and abroad by all except the drys. The New York *World* ran an article on the ebbing tide of prohibition. The article pointed out that Communist Russia had allowed the sale of vodka again after 1921. Almost all of the Canadian provinces had also dropped their dry laws. Turkey had established a state liquor monopoly in 1924, while referendums in Norway and Sweden had gone against total prohibition. England and France and Germany had loosened their liquor regulations. The article concluded, "The cause of temperance in many quarters of the globe exhibits a steady and hopeful progress that might well be envied by this Nation, in which fanatical legislation has done so much to destroy it."[3]

With the failure of the world prohibition revolution, the drys took refuge in isolationism. America was better than the rest of the world and should stay that way. But prohibition had the reverse effect on the wets, who became more international in their choice of liquor and holiday resorts and way of thinking. Indeed, the lapse of the Canadian provinces from prohibition to liquor sales was partly in answer to the enormous profits brought to Canada by smuggling and thirsty American tourists. More than a million American automobiles crossed yearly into Canada throughout the twenties. King George V of England, who thought American prohibition was an "outrage," was reported to be delighted by a contemporary rhyme:

> *Four and twenty Yankees,*
> *Feeling mighty dry,*
> *Took a trip to Canada*
> *And bought a case of rye.*
> *When the case was opened*
> *The Yanks began to sing —*
> *"To hell with the President!*
> *God save the King!"*[4]

Everywhere a contagion of foreign travel caught the imagination of the newly rich in America. They followed the advice of the song, "Way Down Yonder in the Cornfield":

> *Forty miles from whisky*
> *And sixty miles from gin,*
> *I'm leaving this damn country*
> *For to live a life of sin.*

The answer of the drys to drinking tourists was a recommendation by William Jennings Bryan that any American tourist seen drinking overseas should have his passport removed. With such suggestions of petty coercion, the great international crusade of the prohibitionists ended. And as their vast ambitions faded and the promised dry millennium failed to materialize, so their erstwhile supporters blamed them for being the deceivers of themselves and the whole nation. One by one, the five hundred thousand "opinion-makers," on whom the drys had relied to push through their reform, deserted the banner of the prohibitionists.

It was the loss of the support of the manufacturers, the middle classes, and the workingmen of America that doomed the drys. What had been sound eugenics and reform in 1910 was bad economics and fanaticism in 1930. Moreover, many of the more questionable policies of the League boomeranged against them. One was the use of smears in campaigns. When W. E. "Pussyfoot" Johnson confessed that he had had to lie and bribe and drink to put over national prohibition, telling enough falsehoods "to make Ananias ashamed of himself," he did not attract those men who believed in good government as well as the dry cause.[5] When Wheeler publicly praised the insertion of poison into industrial alcohol on the theory that those who drank it were committing deliberate suicide, he did not persuade others of the humanitarian aims of the League.[6] When Purley A. Baker advocated the use of economic boycott to drive wet businessmen to their knees, he could hardly be said to have the interests of industry at heart.[7] The truth was that the League was only concerned with the interests of the League, and it would use any methods to further its cause. Its good was prohibition, and its good was revolutionary in judging others and justifying itself by the sole touchstone of that good.

The League's techniques of lobbying might have been forgiven if the League, like the corporation lobbyists, had been discreet. But the dry leaders preferred to blazon abroad their cleverness, writing up their own smartness for the columns of the press. This helped their cause immediately, in the same way as terrorism immediately helps the cause of invasion by bringing about a universal panic. But, in the long run, this boasting damaged their cause irretrievably. For those who have been deceived into fear are unlikely to respect the employers of those deceits, once they have revealed themselves. When the League proclaimed itself in 1918 "the strongest political organization in the world," it remained powerful just as long as it persuaded others that it was the strongest. But the moment that the rival wet organizations appeared stronger than the League, the League was doubly lost. For boast of strength breeds real strength in opposition.

"Here's How!"

THE RESPECTABLE REPEALERS

Once the Eighteenth Amendment and the Volstead Act were accomplished facts, the drys had new foes. Those who wished to drink liquor by inclination rather than sell liquor by profession began to protest and organize themselves. The American Federation of Labor staged a spectacular rally in Washington, and its president Samuel Gompers warned the House Judiciary Committee that such oppressive legislation as the abolition of beer would lead to a rise of Bolshevism and radicalism in America.[8] An Association Opposed to National Prohibition, financed by hotel and real estate interests, asked all malcontent wets to wear a flower in their buttonholes on "Daisy Day."[9] And quietly in Washington, a Captain William H. Stayton formed the nucleus of the wet answer to the Anti-Saloon League, the Association Against the Prohibition Amendment. But these tiny beginnings of wet opposition were too late. By failing to organize an opposition outside the liquor trade, the wets chose to lose to the drys by default.[10]

The chief dry lobby and wet lobby, the Anti-Saloon League and the Association Against the Prohibition Amendment, were both investigated by the Senate, in 1926 and in 1930. The investigations merely showed how faithfully the organized drys and the organized wets imitated each other. Indeed, in the summary of his evidence before the Reed Committee in 1926, Wayne B. Wheeler admitted as much. He answered the charge that the League's political methods were unethical by saying falsely that they were the identical methods used by the liquor trade to control the politics of the nation for many years, and by saying truthfully that the Association Against the Prohibition Amendment had copied these methods to fight the League.[11]

The Association used precisely the same threats and organization at the grass roots as the League had. It supported all wets in elections, regardless of their party or their personal morality. It kept records of the votes of Congress on wet and dry measures, and circulated these records to its members. It subsidized research studies and put out propaganda to show the failure of prohibition. It encouraged the support of businessmen for economic reasons. It tried to place favorable articles in the newspapers and magazines. Indeed, in every political action, it was the Siamese twin of the Anti-Saloon League.

There was, however, one significant difference between the two, which the drys were quick to point out, since their mentality fed on theories of conspiracy and the machinations of Wall Street. While nine-tenths of the money donated to the League came through the churches from small contributors, three-quarters of the money given to the Association in 1929 came from the pockets of fifty-three millionaires.[12] The Association was definitely backed by the very wealthy, who hoped for relief from corporation and income taxes if a tax on liquor once again brought in money to the United States Treasury. The roll of contributors to the Association is a roll of the privileged, containing the names of three Du Pont brothers and John J. Raskob and Edward S. Harkness. It was unfortunate that the genuine interest of these men in personal liberty and repeal could be construed as an interest in the financial benefits which repeal might bring to them. The case against them was even more damning when the roll of the

Liberty League in the thirties revealed the same names that had backed the Association, the names of millionaires who opposed the taxes of New Deal economics in the name of personal liberty.

Nevertheless, support for the Association did not come directly from the liquor trade. Captain Stayton testified that a limit of one-twentieth of the total budget of the Association was allowed to be given by liquor interests. The rest was donated by other kinds of businessmen.[13] And this presented a new problem to the drys. They themselves had solicited the support of businessmen such as S. S. Kresge on the grounds that prohibition brought untold financial benefits to industry. Thus it was difficult for the League to resent an Association which sought the help of businessmen on the grounds of the economic benefits of repeal. Moreover, Pierre Du Pont, the head of the Association, had himself been a dry at the beginning of the twenties, and had only switched to the side of the wets when the economic benefits of prohibition appeared to be less than those of repeal.[14]

The decline of business support of the dry cause is reflected in the sorry tale of the League's finances which fell by one-fifth between 1920 and 1926 and by over one-half within the following six years. The final blow to the League was the defection of John D. Rockefeller, Jr., from the dry cause to the wet cause in 1932. Except for the faithful Kresge, who was too embarrassed financially to pay his pledged sums to the League, only Henry Ford was left among the billionaires to back prohibition with words rather than capital. He had written that if booze ever came back to the United States he was through with manufacturing. He was not interested in putting automobiles "into the hands of a generation soggy with drink."[15] Repeal came, but Ford went right on manufacturing.

Other wet organizations, staffed from the ranks of the respectable, were working for modification and repeal. A group like the Moderation League, formed in 1923, may have produced wrong statistics in proof of the failure of law enforcement, but its membership included such unimpeachable men as Elihu Root and Henry S. Pritchett, President of the Carnegie Foundation for the Advancement of Teaching. The increasing opposition by the lawyers of America to prohibition, which culminated in a two-thirds vote against the Eighteenth Amendment by the American Bar Association in 1930, could not be brushed aside by dry apologists as a demonstration of "the supercilious attitude of these great lawyers and their contempt for law."[16] Nor could the group of young repealers known as the Crusaders be wholly dismissed as a band of "young millionaires whose sense of social responsibility was perhaps not overwhelming, the sons of the munition manufacturers and Wall Street magnates," whose only object was "to help their fathers get rid of their income and corporation taxes."[17] Whatever the motives of these repeal groups and the Association Against the Prohibition Amendment, they were representative of the majority of Americans in their wish for repeal, as the testimony of the labor leaders before the Wickersham Commission demonstrated. They can only be called guilty of undue influence in their insistence on the unconditional surrender of the drys. Although both major parties agreed to provide against the return of the saloon in 1932, the influence of the wet lobbies upon Congress was so great that repeal was passed without any such safeguards. The victorious wets were no more ready to compromise than the victorious drys had been.

The intemperance of the winning wets was an exact replica of the excesses of the drys in their palmy days. If the Anti-Saloon League had accused the liquor trade of being more interested in profits than in the virtues of strong drink, so did the wets accuse the professional dry agitators of supporting their cause merely for their salaries. With Senator Reed, they denounced the League as a collection of Richmond Pearson Hobsons, "for God and morality at a price."[18] That this charge did not explain the labor of a Wheeler, who worked himself to death with assiduous devotion for a salary of $8000 a year, did not matter. The charge was made often enough to convince most people in a dollar-mad era that every reformer merely wished to feather his own nest and keep himself in a job. When Mayor Jimmy Walker characterized a reformer as a guy who floated through a sewer in a glass-bottomed boat, he was paying tribute to the rich who could afford the expense of glass boats as much as to fools who floated in such insane contraptions.

Even the attacks which the dry lobbies had made on the liquor lobby in Washington were now turned against them. Wayne Wheeler's claim that the Anti-Saloon League had spent $50,000,000 to put over prohibition made it appear the League had bought the Eighteenth Amendment.[19] The conspiracy theories which the drys had applied against the liquor trade were now leveled at themselves. They were the victims of their own victims. The wets hounded them continuously for lobbying and "government by propaganda."

In a popular series of articles in the Chicago *Tribune*, Arthur Sears Henning made an appeal to the conservative strongholds of prohibition sentiment by attacking the interlocking directorates of the dry lobbies, the pacifists, and the radicals at Washington. He denounced the "new lobbying" perfected by the church politicians, with its use of church voters, "canned" resolutions, tons of literature, chain letters, petitions, telegrams, "honorariums" to dry speakers, and "compensation" to favorable small-town newspaper editors. Moreover, he pointed to the misuse of free congressional mailing privileges by dry Representatives, who sent out their prohibitionist speeches from the *Congressional Record* to their constituents through the dry lobbies. The proliferation of executive secretaries and moral lobbies at Washington was a menace to fair government. The Anti-Saloon League was the most powerful lobby of all, "the mightiest engine of propaganda the world has ever beheld," and the lobby which spent the most money, about two million dollars a year.[20] There was, by this theory, a conspiracy of drys and money dedicated to reforming America by hook, crook, and Good Book.

Others took up the attack. Silas Bent, in *Strange Bedfellows*, said that the union of church and state had already come about. "The churches need no longer persuade; they need but issue a fiat to their servants in Congress, and the thing is done. They are becoming a little dizzy with their power. They realize that they have set up a political engine of infinite possibilities, and the effect upon the ministerial mind may possibly prove disastrous."[21] According to Bent, the power of the Federal Council of Churches had caused the abandonment of Secretary Wilbur's naval program, which was estimated to cost two billion dollars. The churches were making Congress adopt their policies of peace without defense and prohibition without the possibility of enforcement. Bent listed twenty-six religious or dry lobbies in Washington, which were spending some four million dollars a year on propaganda in Washington. The Methodist Board of Temperance, Prohibition and Public Morals claimed to influence the votes of four and a half million voters, the Anti-Saloon League the votes of twenty million voters. "It is enough to frighten any Congressmen — especially as the League has a card-index on each 'with special attention to misdemeanors.' "[22]

Similar attacks even reached Congress. Henry B. Joy sent to the Judiciary Committee of the House of Representatives evidence of the interlocking directorates of the Anti-Saloon League and the Federal Council of Churches. League leaders such as Bishops Nicholson and Cannon, and Cherrington and McBride, held powerful positions within the Council of the Churches. Joy reminded the Judiciary Committee that the duty of Congress was to the public and to the Constitution, "not to the Protestant Church hierarchy." The self-assumed claim of the Anti-Saloon League and of the Federal Council of Churches to represent twenty-five million communicants should be disrupted and exposed.[23]

The truth of these attacks did not matter so much as the fact that they were made and spread abroad. Although, in the short term, the attacks seemed to confirm the claim of the dry lobbies to huge influence and power, in the long run the dry committees suffered for their presumption. Once their methods and pretensions were exposed, their so-called followers refused to follow them. The revelation of the workings of the skeleton within the body of the evangelical churches led the flesh of the prohibition movement to desert the dry bone. The massive revolt of the South from prohibition in Congress was less a revolt from dry ideology than from ecclesiastical leadership. Moreover, the liberal element among the evangelical churches genuinely wished to concentrate on wider social problems than the narrow war against liquor. The Methodist Episcopal Church, South, went so far as to abolish its dry lobby after repeal, in the interests of general welfare as much as economy. For, as Bishop Mouzon said in an oblique assault on the head of the dry lobby, Bishop Cannon, "We used to have a Board of Temperance and Social Service. It paid mighty little attention to social service. Its attention was devoted principally to devising political methods to get rid of liquor."[24]

This perversion of some American churches into political action led many of their fervent believers to support repeal as a method of freeing their churches from pursuit of the false god of the dry lobbies. Their wish was to loosen what Congressman Boylan, of New York, called "the unholy alliance existing between many of the God-fearing people of this country and the bootleggers, hi-jackers, extortionists, and kidnapers."[25] Indeed, they would have supported the wet cause in larger numbers if the wet lobbies had not shown the same intolerance and fanaticism as the drys. Senator Glass actually accused the wet pressure groups in the Senate of "that sort of tyranny of spirit, that sort of mistaken feeling of domination, that almost literally destroyed the Anti-Saloon League, and wrought a damage to the churches and to religion that will not be repaired in the next half a century."[26]

But if their methods and their propaganda boomeranged against the dry lobbies, little hurt them more than the stand taken against them by their favorite ally, the women of America. Major Henry H. Curran, President of the Association Against the Prohibition Amendment, gave the wet women the credit for the sudden and melodramatic collapse of prohibition. He told Mencken that there was no way for a politician to avoid their cajoling. Congressmen could not refuse to see them, and began to fear their entreaties and power. When the wet Women's Organization numbered over a million members, "the great retreat began." Curran thought that the fight for repeal

> . . . offered the women their first chance to show that they could think for themselves in politics and, what is more, the first chance to prove that they had a very real power. The drys had been depicting all women as natural prohibitionists, which was just as offensive to

intelligent women as it would have been to intelligent men. So they leapt at the opportunity to give the dry evangelists a beating.[27]

In fact, the Woman's Christian Temperance Union and the National American Woman Suffrage Association had already shown the power of women in politics. Moreover, these groups had been led in their early days by women who had dedicated their whole lives to reform and had given up the pleasures of society. The wet women were, however, a different breed of reformer. Their organization was founded in 1929 by Mrs. Charles H. Sabin, the wife of the treasurer of the Association Against the Prohibition Amendment, and a leader of the smartest set in New York society.[28] Modeling her methods on those of her husband's organization, which was careful to choose a "man of reputation" to head each state group, Mrs. Sabin took her lieutenants from among her social equals, choosing women such as Mrs. August Belmont, Mrs. Pierre S. Du Pont, Mrs. Courtlandt Nicoll, Mrs. Archibald B. Roosevelt, and Mrs. Coffin Van Rennselaer.[29] This policy solved the problem of fund-raising and propaganda at one blow. Such fashionable matrons needed no salaries, had large incomes and little to do, and could command newspaper space by their actions and antics. Repeal became the smartest social movement ever put before American womanhood. An irresistible combination of snobbery and social betterment was offered to its adherents. To be one of the "Sabine Women" was a passport to social acceptance far more sure than was once rape by a Roman.

The vicious reaction of the embattled dry women to their new rivals showed how much they feared the appeal of the rich and the smart to their own sex. The Georgia Cyclone, Dr. Mary Armor, promised that, "as to Mrs. Sabin and her cocktail-drinking women, we will outlive them, out-fight them, out-love them, out-talk them, out-pray them and out-vote them."[30] A dry newspaper, the American Independent, said that "these wet women, though rich most of them are, are no more than the scum of the earth, parading around in skirts, and possibly late at night flirting with other women's husbands at drunken and fashionable resorts."[31] To the Prohibition party historian and leader, such females were "Bacchantian maidens, parching for wine — Wet women who, like the drunkards whom their program will produce, would take pennies off the eyes of the dead for the sake of legalizing booze."[32] But for Clarence True Wilson, they were merely contemptible, "The little group of wine-drinking society women who are uncomfortable under Prohibition."[33]

For the drys knew the enormous damage which the hordes of wet women did to their propaganda. Prohibition had been put through and was defended in terms of the necessary protection of the woman, the home, and the family. In 1920, every important organization of women, the Woman's Christian Temperance Union, the League of Women Voters, the Young Women's Christian Association, the Law Enforcement League, and the General Federation of Women's Clubs had endorsed prohibition. As long as the female sex kept a united front of organizations in favor of prohibition, no politician would dare perform an action which might seem to offend more than half of the electorate. Alfred E. Smith said, "When women entered the fight for repeal, sanity began to return to the country."[34] He could have added that sanity also began to return to Congress, once it realized that the militant wet females could vote as formidably as the militant drys. In the words of a Southern organizer of the wet women, "One bee is troublesome, yet not anything to bother about, but when a swarm gets after a man, he will take to the tall grass without arguing. So when the women get aroused and combine, the politicians capitulate."[35] Indeed they did, to what Mrs. Sabin called "the largest body of instructed, knowledgeable women ever let loose in a democracy."[36]

The dry organizations would never admit publicly that the wet opposition to them had changed its nature. To the end, they insisted that the wet pressure groups were financed in secret by the liquor trade. The large popular votes in favor of modification and repeal were caused by "political manipulation in connection with unparalleled vicious and insidious propaganda, backed by most powerful national and international financial interests."[37] Moreover, there was a complacency in the dry ranks about the inviolability of the Eighteenth Amendment as strong as the touching faith of the wets in 1918 that they could prevent the ratification of that amendment indefinitely. As the *National Advocate* noticed in October, 1930, there was an "astonishing indifference" among many of the friends of prohibition. Meanwhile, "the enemies of the amendment are organized and determined; they have unlimited financial resources, and they are led by a superb strategy. To counter all that the orators of the Anti-Saloon League close their eyes to the danger, and laughingly tell us that 'prohibition is here to stay.'"

While such assurances may have been necessary to keep up the good heart of the drys, they gulled the prohibitionists into a false security. Indeed, their self-confidence was contagious even to their enemies. Clarence Darrow wrote an article in *Vanity Fair* at the same time, pointing out that the Eighteenth Amendment "was not written to be repealed, but to make a change impossible." There was no hope, according to Darrow, of two-thirds of the Senate ever voting for repeal. Therefore, the only course of the wets was to annul the Volstead

Act by a simple majority in Congress and suffer the constitutional amendment forever.[38]

This feeling of inviolability and inherent fanaticism among the dry leaders prevented them from making terms with the wets while they still had the chance. A bloc of liberal dry leaders tried to persuade their standpat colleagues to back the resubmission of the Eighteenth Amendment; their reward would be safeguards from the wets against the return of the saloon. This plan, however, was opposed by F. Scott McBride and Arthur J. Barton and other militants. It came to nothing. And that, in the opinion of Colonel Patrick H. Callahan, an Irish Catholic dry, was the end of prohibition.

> After that it was every man for himself. The dry outfit was divided and full of dissension. What those fellows lack is the capacity to give and take. They have no sense of humor. The whole prohibition movement would have been better off if there had been more Irish in it. You can't do much with Puritans. They are too sure about everything.[39]

TURN LABOR, TURN CAPITAL

THE DRYS had the support of the overwhelming majority of employers and a small majority of labor leaders in the days before the Eighteenth Amendment. The actual workings of the prohibition law turned both of these groups against the drys. For the promise of the law was lost in the inadequacies of its practice.

The leaders of labor had supported, on the whole, the campaign against the saloons. But the answer to the heavy drinking of industrial workers was not to prohibit the saloons and the liquor trade by law but to provide the workers with acceptable substitutes. As Florence Kelley pointed out prophetically in 1923:

> Forbidding them beer, without affording an available substitute wherever they suffer from heat and heavy work, is merely tempting them to violate the Amendment. It is living in a fool's paradise to suppose that they will not violate it. They will also hate it. They will believe that they have been deprived, against their will, of beer which they have found refreshing and have been taught to regard as a food, and furnished instead with worthless stuff which they dislike. Their experience will, moreover, be incessantly so interpreted to them by the advocates of light wines and beer, within and without the ranks of organized labor.[40]

This was precisely what happened. The leaders of organized labor, who had supported both prohibition and beer, now came out openly for modification of the Volstead Act to permit the sale of beer and light wines. Samuel Gompers, the leader of the American Federation of Labor, had always taken a position in favor of beer. In 1922, the conference of the Federation passed a resolution supporting modification, and repeated the performance annually. By 1931, Labor's National Committee for Modification of the Volstead Act had been set up, and had decided that "Labor, above all, is the sufferer and victim when liberty is denied."[41] Moreover, many less abstract considerations had turned the leaders of labor from covert support of prohibition to open support of repeal.

The first was the failure of the unions in the twenties. Trade-union membership declined from more than five million members to less than three and a half million in the decade. The decline was due partly to prosperity, partly to the racketeering within the labor unions, partly to the "open shop" plans of the manufacturers, and partly to prohibition. For prohibition had strengthened the forces of corruption among employers and union leaders, had made the winning of strikes more difficult, and had blunted the edges of the class war. "Prohibition is making a capitalist of the worker," exulted John Cooper, of the Brotherhood of Locomotive Engineers, "creating a general ownership of the means of production and solving a strife that once seemed perpetual."[42] But not all labor leaders were so happy at the prospect of industrial peace. Watching the declining figures of their membership and fearing the competition of gangsters' and employers' unions, the labor leaders used prohibition as a means of whipping up class hatred again. They pointed out truthfully that prohibition was a rich man's law in fact, even if it applied equally to everybody in theory. They pointed out what even the wealthy Mrs. Sabin stressed, that the prohibition law was "the greatest piece of class legislation ever enacted in this country."[43]

This dangerous emphasis on the class aspects of the dry law was boosted by the wet press and the wealthy wet organizations. Cartoons and editorials lambasted the drys for their failure to enforce their law, thus creating one law for the rich, who could get decent drink, and another for the poor, who could not. It was useless for Ernest Cherrington to protest, "Before prohibition, industry was demanding total abstinence of the working men, while granting drinking privileges to the rich. There are some who would like to see that condition restored with its favored class."[44] The truth was that the rich drank openly and well under prohibition, while the poor were forced to drink badly. This increased the resentment of the poor against the rich. In vain, drys warned the well-to-do that their smartness in drinking was "the rankest stupidity, for as a class they would suffer most should the lawless get control and break up all law."[45] The rich went right on drinking, while the poor envied them and drank what they could.

"Beer's Bad for Our Workers"

Weed in N.Y.
Evening World

FISCAL YEAR

CHAR

The depression brought to a head the resentment of the workers and the fear of that resentment among their employers. According to Matthew Woll's accusation in 1931:

> Certain great employers supported prohibition so that the workers might be more efficient to produce, to produce, to produce. Well, we have produced and six million are unemployed. And prohibition has produced, too. It has produced the illicit still, the rumrunner, the speakeasy, the racketeer, graft, corruption, disrespect for law, crime.[46]

This lawlessness, spawned by prohibition, now threatened to spread with mass unemployment, and shake the roots of society. The same employers who had supported the Eighteenth Amendment a decade earlier to benefit themselves and their workers now advocated repeal to protect themselves from their workers. They hoped that legal beer would relieve some of the social tensions of the time and lessen class hatred. Indeed, they even seemed to confirm one of the theses of Engels, who made out that alcohol was a means of capitalist control as it made sodden the minds of the workers.

There were other reasons for the manufacturers to change over to the side of repeal. The first was that prohibition seemed to have lost them more than it had gained. The deficiency in government revenue from the liquor tax had been made up by a tax on the incomes of the wealthy and of corporations. The restoration of these incomes would be an incentive to business in the depression. Moreover, the labor unions still existed outside the saloons, and were strengthened when their members attended sober labor meetings. The failure of federal law enforcement showed that the private laws of the major companies against drinking by employees, which were widely used before prohibition, were sufficient to prevent industrial accidents; indeed, it was preferable for the workers, if drink they must, to drink good beer rather than bad hooch. Also, the increased consumer market promised by prohibition had not materialized. In fact, the profits of the liquor trade had been turned from the pockets of brewers and distillers to the pockets of criminals, who were making a nuisance of themselves by trying to muscle into legitimate industry. As a whole, prohibition now seemed to the manufacturers of America to be more trouble than it was worth.

Thus labor followed capital in accepting prohibition, and capital followed labor in accepting modification and repeal. The switchover of both employers and workers from the side of the drys to the side of the wets paralleled the switchover of the country. The change was mostly due to the economic propaganda of the time, and the fact that years of boom had changed to years of slump. It was strange, as Gilbert Seldes noticed, that the American people gave up the right to drink when they could most afford to drink, and clamored for its restoration when they did not even have the price of a bottle of good Burgundy.[47]

Resistance to the drys was contagious. Once their bandwagon to victory began to stall, the voices of the wets grew bolder. And once the wets had copied the methods of the Anti-Saloon League, they too had a club to brandish in the faces of members of Congress. Wet retribution at the polls could be even more damning for a politician than dry opposition. In wrecking the cause of moderation on dry Scylla, the politicians found themselves menaced by the equally fearsome wet Charybdis. It was in obedience to this new menace that they began to stand up against the Anti-Saloon League in Congress.

CHAPTER **19**

The Restive Congress

> Prohibition is not an issue in the Republican Party, and I
> don't believe it is in the Democratic Party.
> SENATOR SIMEON FESS, of Ohio, 1930

> Histhry always vindicates th' Dimmycrats, but niver in
> their lifetime. They see th' thruth first, but th' trouble is
> that nawthin' is iver officially thrue till a Raypublican sees it.
> FINLEY PETER DUNNE

THE FIRST major victory of the wets in Congress was won by Senator Reed, of Missouri, during the hearings of his subcommittee in
1926. He sent messengers to the Anti-Saloon League's headquarters at
Westerville, Ohio, and commandeered the files of the League. Photo-
graphic facsimiles of secret letters and papers were leaked to the press
to show up the dubious political methods of the League. Moreover,
Reed subpoenaed the failing Wheeler to testify before the subcommittee, and browbeat him badly. Yet Reed failed to prove that the League
had employed corrupt or unethical political methods. But he did
demonstrate that the League was vulnerable to a determined frontal
assault. The myth of the League's inviolability was never put together
again.

The first effects of Reed's bludgeonings were evident in the elections
of 1926. All lobbies and pressure groups walked warily. Although the
drys held their three-to-one majority in the House, they lost ground
slightly in the Senate. For the Democratic convention of 1924 had finally
identified the Northeastern section of the Democratic party with the
wet cause. Moreover, the wets had found a powerful leader in Alfred
E. Smith, four times governor of New York, and obvious presidential
timber for the 1928 election. Even Wheeler only claimed that 70 per
cent of the Democrats in the Senate supported him, a drop of 5 per
cent from the vote on the Eighteenth Amendment. Moreover, Wheeler
had supported the candidacy of Frank L. Smith in the senatorial race
in Illinois against an eminently respectable dry candidate. When Smith

was unseated for corruption, Wheeler suffered from his endorsement. His excuse for doing so was Machiavellian and suspect. He referred to a rule in an old Anti-Saloon League textbook which said that the League should support partially acceptable candidates whose election was certain, rather than entirely acceptable candidates whose election was impossible.[1]

Congress did little more for enforcement in 1927 and 1928 than it had done in previous years. While Coolidge kept cool, Congress blew cold on schemes for greater federal spending. A little under twelve million dollars a year was appropriated for the two years. One major prohibition measure was passed. The bill separated the Prohibition Bureau from the office of the Commissioner of Internal Revenue; furthermore, prohibition agents were at last brought under Civil Service rules, although no additional money was voted to carry out this purpose.[2] Ironically, although the bill was sponsored by Wheeler, its promulgation led to the dismissal of Roy A. Haynes from the Bureau and the end of Wheeler's influence over prohibition appointments.[3]

The debates on the bill showed how much the wet leaders of Congress had adopted the threats, slanders, and tactics of the drys. Senator Bruce turned Dr. Johnson's remark on Goldsmith, that he touched nothing he did not adorn, into the remark that prohibition touched nothing it did not defile. He accused Senator Smoot, of Utah, and the other drys of opposing the Civil Service rules in order to return to the old spoils system. He referred darkly to influences pushing the Senate on, which were "apparently stronger than the majority of the Members of this body." He then used a new wet weapon and an old dry weapon, when he said that he would keep the Association Against the Prohibition Amendment and other wet organizations informed about any Senator elected with wet support who dared to vote dry. The wets had been forced to adopt this policy in answer to those dry members of Congress who were "held to the severest accountability by such a system of drastic and all-pervading tyranny as was never known in the history of this Government." Bruce ended with a personal attack on the "third-sex" of "part preachers and part stump orators, part clergymen and part political intriguers and agitators, whose political instruments are scurrilous abuse, bulldozing, and the lavish use of money in political campaigns." Indeed, these were the very lessons which the drys had learned from the wets and the wets were relearning from the drys.

In particular, Bruce had singled out Wheeler for attack, as a "professional agitator and unofficial interloper." Senator Edwards, of New Jersey, followed with an assault on the Anti-Saloon League, with its "un-American, entirely selfish, bigoted, and intolerant appeals." As prejudiced as any dry reformer, Edwards found that prohibition and temperance were "as contrary and opposed as black and white." The bill itself was "a pork-barrel for the Wheelers, the McBrides, and the Wilsons," who, except for bootleggers and dive-keepers, were the only ones to reap a prohibition harvest. In view of these assaults, the sharp-tongued Senator from Missouri, James Reed, was remarkably mild. He merely bowed to Wheeler in mockery and termed him "his majesty."[4]

But the death of Wheeler's wife by fire in 1928, shortly followed by his own, removed him from the unkind tongues of all except those Anti-Saloon League leaders who spoke at his funeral. These other League leaders had always been jealous of Wheeler's personal power and prestige. The press had usually taken Wheeler's personal attitude to be the authoritative statement of the Anti-Saloon League. The other League leaders did not want such a situation to be repeated. They wished for all official statements of the League to be restricted to statements of the executive or legislative committees. Although Wheeler's policy of pressure politics was endorsed with the re-election of McBride as general superintendent of the League in 1928, a new educational campaign was launched under the leadership of McBride's rival, Ernest H. Cherrington. The League then agreed to bury its internal differences with the body of the dead Wheeler, and to unite in the campaign for a dry President in 1928.[5]

The congressional elections of 1928 were overshadowed by the bitterness of the presidential struggle between Hoover and Smith. For the first time, the leader of a major party was an avowed wet. Democrats, running for Congress on the Smith ticket, reaped the advantage of his attitude in the wet Northern cities and the disadvantage of his attitude in the dry rural areas. Although Smith split the Solid South, he also split the Republican North. If he lost more than 200 Southern counties, which had never voted Republican since the Civil War, he gained 122 Northern counties from the Grand Old Party.[6] Smith carried St. Paul, St. Louis, Cleveland, San Francisco, and Boston, and carried the ticket with him, on the whole. In Chicago, although Smith narrowly lost the city, he broke the complacent grip of the Republican machine there. Smith won new wet Democratic votes among those of German, Irish, and Slavic ancestry. He attracted many of the seventeen million new voters who had come of age in the previous eight years and who lived mainly in the large wet cities. Although the drys considered Herbert Hoover's plurality of more than six million votes to be an overwhelming referendum on the virtues of prohibition, Smith's defeat foreshadowed the defeat of the drys in four years' time. For he had identified repeal with the dominant group in the Democratic party, and he had swung behind that party the wet centers of population.

The vote in the House on the Jones Law shows the result of the election clearly. The law provided for the increase of penalties on first offenders against the Volstead Act. Although there was a classic debate in the Senate between Reed and Borah on the whole question of prohibition, nothing of importance was said in the House. The drys, however, seemed to gain their greatest congressional victory there by winning the roll call, 284 votes to 90. This was the lowest vote ever put together by the wets in the House on a major roll call. A comparison of the wet vote with the 128 votes which they mustered on the Eighteenth Amendment shows that the wets had lost 24 votes in West and South, but only 14 in the North. The North, which had provided little over half of the wet vote in 1917, now provided just under two-thirds. The strength of the wets was now concentrated in the Northern cities. A further analysis of the party vote on these two divisions shows that the Democratic party was split much more sharply between North and South on the issue of prohibition, while the Republican party had become more dry. Thus, although the drys had won their greatest victory in the House, the seeds of their defeat lay in that victory. Prohibition was at last identified with major party politics, for the wets had gained control of one of the two important parties. The defeat of the Republicans in a presidential election would now be considered a defeat of the drys, so long as the Northern wets controlled the Democrats. And the return of the Solid South to their Democratic allegiance could also mean their support of a wet policy.

The debate in the Senate on the Jones Law is one of the few living things in "that vast necropolis of buried oratory, the Congressional Record."[7] Reed was the most cutting and clever of the wets, Borah the most able and weighty of the drys. Such diverse Senators as Heflin and Brookhart joined in praising the debate as the best they ever heard. Reed first commented on the wetness of the Republican convention in Kansas City and of the Democratic convention in "dry" Houston, Texas. He had wanted to write a list of those who voted dry and drank wet in Congress; but, although he had done many wicked things in his life, he had never fallen yet to the level of a prohibition informer. He made a personal attack on Bishop Cannon, who had broken the Solid South against Al Smith. Cannon was one of America's "three popes."[8] Wayne B. Wheeler might be dead, "but his mantle has fallen upon the shoulders and his soul has entered the body of the Right Rev. Bishop Cannon. The philosophy of hate survives."

Reed found that the drys, in applying only the yardstick of voting on prohibition measures to their endorsed candidates, showed a lower

morality in their choice of officeholders than slum bosses. The fact
that the drys had given up the old style of temperance lectures showed
prohibition was doomed. It was making no new and passionate converts. "We have abandoned the Bible, the prayer book, and the temperance tract for the lash, the prison, the gun, and the bludgeon." Intolerance now ruled the land. "There is no knife so sharp as that held
in the hand of the bigot . . . no cruelty so relentless as the cruelty of
fanaticism." Christ had been crucified according to the forms of the
law. Joan of Arc had been so burned. Now the Jones Law sought to
persecute the modern defenders of freedom. Prohibition had filled the
land with spies, and the jails with 130,000 prisoners in two years. Did
this show the spirit of Christ at work in America?

As for the Volstead Act itself, which the Jones Law sought to supplement, it had been rightly vetoed by Woodrow Wilson for its idiocy.
The only people whom it helped were the farmers. The vineyards of
California were booming — wine-grapes had gone up from $20 a ton
to $175. As for cider, "they have now worked out a plan where one
can let his cider get hard, freeze it in a refrigerator, bore a hole in the
center where the alcohol is, and be drunk in five minutes. Compared
with that stuff old bourbon whisky was a mild tonic."* After a pause
for laughter, Reed continued, "Even from the silos, where nature
makes the stuff, the farm boy is drawing a supply."

Reed denounced the drys for failing in their purposes under prohibition:

> The bar is condensed into a gripsack. The sales are by the case
> instead of by the glass. The saloon is still here, and more people are
> engaged in the business than in pre-Volstead days. You did not exter-
> minate the brewery. You made millions of little breweries and in-
> stalled them in the homes of the people.

Worse that that, under prohibition, drug addiction had multiplied,
while American girls were guzzling liquor for the first time. Reed concluded with the observation of Montaigne that "it would be better for
us to have no laws at all than to have them in so prodigious numbers as
we have."

Reed's speech was so effective that Jones inserted an amendment
to his law pointing out that it was "the intent of Congress, that the
courts, in imposing sentence hereunder, should discriminate between
casual or slight violations and habitual sales of intoxicating liquors or
attempts to commercialize violations of the law." The increased penalties were now specifically aimed at large bootleggers, not at petty

* Senator Heflin later commented that one man had shushed another in the
gallery of the Senate during these remarks from Reed. The man's excuse had been
that he wanted to get the recipe.

offenders. And Senator Borah, of Idaho, rose to defend the laws of prohibition with all the reason at his command.

Borah reminded the Senate that the Eighteenth Amendment would stand in the Constitution "until the moral forces of the United States decide that something better is presented to control the liquor problem." The evils of prohibition were nothing compared with the evils of the saloons, even as the "pilfering thieves" of the Department of Prohibition were trivial in the light of the "saturnalia of corruption" in the high places of the government between 1921 and 1923. Borah disapproved of the philosophy of Mussolini, but he recommended his action of closing down 25,000 Italian saloons overnight by the stroke of a pen. America, however, was a democracy. The liquor traffic could not be ended so easily. "Possibly we can not prevent it entirely; possibly we can not ever prevent the use of alcoholic drinks altogether, but shall we continue the effort or shall we surrender in the fight?" Borah answered his own question by saying that, as long as the Eighteenth Amendment was in the Constitution, just so long would Congress be sworn to enforce it. Both he and Reed would "never see the day when the eighteenth amendment is out of the Constitution of the United States." That being so, Congress should co-operate, willy-nilly, in enforcing the law of the land.[9]

Whether Borah won his debate with Reed or not, the drys easily won the roll call, by 65 votes to 18. Although the wet vote in the Senate as in the House dropped from the total vote cast on the Eighteenth Amendment, a similar shift to a center of power based on the Northern Democrats is evident. While only 8 out of 20 wet votes came from the Northern Senators in 1917, 10 out of 18 did so in 1929. The North had become the rallying point of the wets. More and more, politicians had to be wet in the North to be elected at all.

Although these signs of the growing enmity of Congress to the dry lobbies were no bigger than a man's mouth or a minority vote, they were the beginnings of rebellion. And the dry majority in Congress continued their equivocal policy of speaking for prohibition and refusing to vote enough money to enforce it. The episode of the Bruce appropriation showed just how careful Congress was to keep bootleg liquor flowing. During the debate on an Appropriations Bill, the wet leader, Senator Bruce, of Maryland, suddenly offered an amendment which increased the appropriation of the Prohibition Bureau some twenty times. The new Prohibition Commissioner, Dr. James M. Doran, had asked for $300,000,000 a year to enforce the Volstead Act. Senator Bruce proposed to give it to him, on Ulysses Grant's principle that the only way to get rid of a bad law was to enforce it rigidly, rather than to let it fall into Grover Cleveland's "innocuous desuetude." This would compel the people to consider whether prohibition was a good or a bad thing, for they had never had prohibition. "The dry has the law, the wet has the liquor, and the prohibition agent has the boodle, and consequently more or less general contentment with the situation exists all ound." In answer to the gibe of Senator Caraway, of Arkansas, in the debate on the Jones Law, that those who said the law was unforceable were those who did not want it enforced, Bruce led those who wanted no dry law at all in an attempt to have it enforced and thus to end it. In a surprise roll call, which found wets and drys voting on the same side, the Bruce amendment for an increase of $256,000,000 to the appropriation of the Prohibition Bureau was passed.

But the dry lobbies, faced with this unwelcome gift, turned it down. They seemed to fear that large-scale enforcement would change their growing unpopularity into public disgust. Four days after the Bruce amendment was passed, it was eliminated from the Appropriations Bill.[10] A modest proposal by Senator Harris, of Georgia, to double the appropriation of the Prohibition Bureau to $25,000,000 was also turned down, since Secretary Mellon opposed the increase.

In the debate in the House, the wets also led the battle for an increase in the money spent on enforcement, while the drys opposed the increase. As La Guardia, of New York, said:

> It behooves the drys of the House to stand up courageously and demand the hundreds of millions of dollars it will require to enforce prohibition, and as they fail to do it, demonstrating the impossibility of enforcement, it is our right to seek through proper, constitutional, and legislative channels a change in the law.

The drys had no answer to La Guardia except the sneer of Crampton, of Michigan, that if states such as New York would only share the responsibility of enforcement with the federal government, the land would go dry without more federal spending. To this observation, La Guardia merely pointed to the lawlessness of Michigan, and said, "Let enforcement and prohibition, like charity, begin at home."[11] The final increase of the budget of the Prohibition Bureau was set at little more than a million dollars.

The dry majorities in Congress remained faithful to their policies of low budgets for prohibition enforcement. During the Hoover Administration, appropriations for the Prohibition Bureau averaged a little over fourteen million dollars a year, a mere annual increase of three million dollars over the sums spent by the purse-proud Coolidge Congresses. Only the President himself denied the policy of his do-little predecessors by election promise and executive practice. Originally, in his acceptance speech at Palo Alto after the Republican convention of 1928, Hoover had promised to set up a commission to investigate the problems of prohibition. Once in the White House, however, Hoover expanded the duties of the commission to include an examination of the whole field of law enforcement. This was a large undertaking. But, while the commission set about its tedious labors, the drys in Congress had a perfect excuse for doing next to nothing until the findings of the commission were made known.[12]

While the drys were waiting, the wets in Congress were not idle. In the second session of the Seventy-first Congress, more than sixty bills and resolutions were introduced to amend the prohibition laws. All died in Senate or House Committee, for these committees were strongholds of the drys. But when the preliminary findings of the Wickersham Commission were released on January 13, 1930, wet ribaldry in Congress rose to new heights. The commission recommended that the Prohibition Bureau be transferred to the Department of Justice; this should have been done ten years back. It advised the codification of prohibition laws over the last forty years and the strengthening of the padlock provisions of the Volstead Act; the laws should never have been so complex or so easily evaded. And worst of all, the commission recommended that "casual or slight violations" of the prohibition laws should be handled without trial by jury, to ease the congestion in the federal courts, many of which were four years behind schedule.

This last proposal brought wet shouts against tyranny to a crescendo. As Congressman Black, of New York, jeered, "the mountains labored and all they have brought forth is a ridiculous mess, a ridiculous legal mess. . . . How can you enforce a law that requires 50 per cent of the people to keep the other 50 per cent in jail all of the time?" Black could not resist a further jab at an unfortunate utterance on the subject of the Volstead Act by the favorite wet bogieman of the time. "The hereafter does not require its ministers to be sheriffs and policemen, and here we have Bishop Cannon the other day going a long, long way from the fundamental principles of Christianity in saying that he wanted to call out the army to wipe out the violators of this law." It was time for Congress to revolt with the people against clerical domination.[13] The Congress, however, ignored Black and passed another Prohibition Reorganization Act, at last transferring the Prohibition Bureau to the Department of Justice, although the Treasury kept control of industrial alcohol. As Major Henry Curran, of the Association Against the Prohibition Amendment, confessed, "There isn't a chance of Congress voting our way yet."[14]

In 1930, the state party conventions put the writing on the wall for the drys. Twenty-one state platforms in fourteen states demanded outright repeal of the Eighteenth Amendment. A repeal plank was adopted by the Democrats in all fourteen of these states, but only in seven by the Republicans. For the Grand Old Party had become, willy-nilly, identified as the party of the drys. It could not escape its record. Ohio leaders of the Anti-Saloon League had always preferred to work through the Republican party; even the Democratic Bishop Cannon had bolted to Hoover in 1928. The Republicans had been in power for nearly all of the time in which the Volstead Law had ruled in America. They were in charge of dry enforcement and pro-

THE LEANING TOWER SHOWS SIGNS OF COLLAPSE

hibition appointments. Thus the odium which prohibition brought to its supporters was also extended to the Grand Old Party.

In the congressional elections, the depression was largely ignored. Prohibition was the battleground — not economics.[15] Indeed, the only way that economics affected the situation was in the small fund at the disposal of the dry lobbies. The rich contributors to the dry cause could no longer afford to pay. The drys had a low campaign budget, while the wets had more and more money in their hands to secure repeal as a stimulant to the economy. The Democrats and the wets gained some notable victories. For the first time in more than a decade, the Democrats equaled the number of Republicans in the House and

Senate. Even though the drys managed to secure the defeat of one of their enemies, Thomas Heflin, of Alabama, the wet victories of Senator Buckley in the Anti-Saloon League stronghold of Ohio and of Senator Marcus Coolidge in Massachusetts showed that the wets were gaining significant strength in Congress for the first time in thirty years.

How much strength the wets actually gained was not evident immediately. Congress was careful to avoid any showdown on prohibition. Senate and House committees continued to kill bills before they reached a vote on the floor. Congress and the nation were waiting expectantly for the report of the Wickersham Commission.

CHAPTER 20

Dry President, Divided Commission

> "If eleven men for twenty months
> Write all they see and hear,
> Do you suppose," the Abstainer said,
> "That they can make it clear?"
> "I doubt it," said the Drinking Man,
> And wept into his beer.
>
> ANONYMOUS

WHEN HERBERT HOOVER accepted the Republican nomination for the presidency in 1928, he promised to appoint a commission to examine the workings of national prohibition. Once he was elected, he broadened the purpose of the promised commission. His Inaugural speech defined the duty of the commission as

> . . . a searching investigation of the whole structure of our Federal system of jurisprudence, to include the method of enforcement of the eighteenth amendment and the causes of abuse under it. Its purpose will be to make such recommendations for reorganization of the administration of Federal laws and court procedure as may be found desirable.[1]

The wet supporters of Hoover were disappointed by his modified proposal. It both lessened and increased the original purpose of the commission. The commission was limited to a consideration of the methods of enforcement. It was not allowed to say whether there should be a prohibition law at all; it had merely to discover how the workings of the law could be improved. Moreover, the commission was charged with examining the problems of all enforcement of the law, and this wide field might detract from the particular examination of prohibition. In addition, the opponents of prohibition did not class dry laws with other laws. They insisted that the drinker and the maker of drink could still be a law-abiding citizen. The defined purpose of the commission seemed to them to put consideration of the liquor question on the same level as consideration of murder and rape. The wet newspapers urged the commission to ignore all subjects other

361

than prohibition. "Not to do so," Frank Kent wrote, "would be to build on a false bottom."[2]

Hoover had great difficulty in staffing his commission. The members had to be chosen from the ranks of the moderates, who were more concerned with the question of good government than with the rights and wrongs of the prohibition problem. Thus the final choice of the eleven commissioners comprised people used to general problems of law and administration, although they had little actual knowledge of the particular problems of prohibition. The head of the commission, George W. Wickersham, had been Attorney General under President Taft; he was Hoover's fourth choice. The other ten included a former Secretary of War, a former state Chief Justice, a Circuit Judge, two District Judges, three practicing lawyers, the Dean of the Harvard Law School, and the President of Radcliffe. Hoover turned down the people recommended by the Anti-Saloon League and the Woman's Christian Temperance Union, and the commission refused to hear their spokesmen. Similarly, Hoover and the commission ignored the spokesmen of the extreme wets. Yet the commission, as a whole, was composed of safe conservative members, who could be expected to find in favor of the prohibition laws, if such findings were possible.*

While the commission collected evidence, Hoover, unlike the dry members of Congress, was not idle. He set about securing stricter enforcement of the dry law. The number of those jailed for liquor offenses rose steadily from 21,602 in the fiscal year of 1929 until it had more than doubled three years later.[3] The building of six new prisons was begun in order to accommodate the increased number of federal convicts. For Hoover wished his morality to be judged by his efficiency. He was concerned with the application of the laws rather than their validity. As he said to the Associated Press annual meeting in 1929, "If a law is wrong, its rigid enforcement is the surest guaranty of its repeal. If it is right, its enforcement is the quickest method of compelling respect for it."[4]

Hoover's exhortations to the populace to obey the laws of the land exceeded those of Harding and Coolidge in volume and moral fervor. In his Inaugural address, Hoover discovered the illuminating fact that "there would be little traffic in illegal liquor if only criminals patronized it . . . patronage from large numbers of law abiding citizens is supplying the rewards and stimulating crime."[5] At the initial meeting of the Wickersham Commission, he said, "A nation does not fail from

---

* Even the wet press approved of Hoover's choice of commissioners. The Boston *Transcript* found the commission full of "sturdy American brains." The New York *Times* had "nothing but praise," and the *Evening World* found it difficult to see how the commission could have been improved on.

"Don't Mind Me, Go Right On Working"

its growth of wealth or power. But no nation can for long survive the failure of its citizens to respect and obey the laws which they themselves make."[6] Nevertheless, Hoover appointed to his Cabinet six wets out of a total of ten men, according to the head of the Association Against the Prohibition Amendment. The two chiefs of the Treasury Department who were at first responsible for enforcement were both wet, Andrew Mellon and Ogden Mills. The Postmaster General was a wet machine politician. Hoover allayed the fears of the drys by asking his Cabinet to refrain from serving liquor in their own homes.[7]

In the meantime, the Wickersham Commission stuck to its task. The commissioners heard evidence for nineteen months, and spent half a million dollars. They found it impossible to restrict their investigation of prohibition to a mere examination of the problems of enforcement. Thus they decided

> . . . to go into the whole subject of enforcement of the Eighteenth Amendment and the National Prohibition Act; the present condition as to observance and enforcement of that Act and its causes; whether and how far the amendment in its present form is enforceable; whether it should be retained, or repealed, or revised, and a constructive program of improvement.[8]

This departure from their original purpose was to prove a great source of embarrassment to Hoover, who had tried to restrict the commissioners in such a way that he could adopt their recommendations without seeming to endorse or oppose national prohibition itself.

After a preliminary report, recommending minor changes, the Wickersham Commission came out with its final report. Two of the commissioners favored repeal, five wanted revision and government monopoly of the liquor traffic on the model of the Swedish system, two favored revision and further trial of the Eighteenth Amendment, and only two supported the *status quo*, with minor alterations. Only one of the commissioners directly opposed resubmission of the Eighteenth Amendment to the people. Yet ten out of the eleven commissioners signed a summary of the conclusions of the *Wickersham Report*, which stated that the commission as a whole opposed the repeal of the Eighteenth Amendment, the return of the legalized saloon in any form, the entry of the federal or state governments into the liquor business, and the modification of national prohibition to permit the sale of light wines and beer. The summary further stated that there was, as yet, no adequate observance or enforcement of the dry laws, since the means of enforcement were insufficient. There were other general recommendations for revision of the laws. These included abolition of the limitations on the prescriptions of medical liquor, repeal of the cider clause in the Volstead Act, strengthening of the regulations governing industrial alcohol and padlock injunctions, and quick trial of petty violators of the laws without benefit of jury. The summary concluded with the equivocal statement that there were "differences of view among the members of the commission as to certain of the conclusions stated," and that these differences were shown in the separate and individual reports of each commissioner.[9] The fact was not set down, however, that the individual reports made absolute nonsense of the so-called agreement of the commissioners in the summary. The divergent views of the commissioners individually and collectively can only be explained by their need to produce something definite after nineteen months of hard labor.

The method of release of the *Wickersham Report* to the press further darkened the obscure. Hoover first sent a message to Congress which said, "The commission, by a large majority, does not favor the repeal of the Eighteenth Amendment as a method of cure for the inherent abuses of the liquor traffic."[10] Hoover himself said that he agreed with the majority of the commissioners in wanting to keep the Eighteenth Amendment in its old form. He should have said that he agreed with the minority of the commissioners. For seven out of the eleven explicitly favored a change in the wording of the Eighteenth Amendment to allow the legal sale of some liquor. As Walter Lippmann commented:

> Everything possible was done officially to conceal this truth from the public generally, and from the rural voters in particular. It was cut out of the conclusions. It was suppressed in the official summary. It was ignored by the President. The official summary was so trickily devised that for nearly twenty-four hours it fooled every newspaper in America. . . . What was done was to evade a direct and explicit official confession that federal prohibition is a hopeless failure.

According to Lippmann, Hoover's repudiation of the real views of his commissioners put him straight in the camp of the nullificationists of the dry law, whom he continually denounced. For he could not enforce the dry law, and he refused to revise it. Therefore he must agree with the existing situation of widespread nullification in the United States.[11]

Once the full version of the *Wickersham Report* had reached the press, a howl of derision arose, which gave way to more sober comment. The New York *Herald Tribune* said that the general excellence of the report made all the more regrettable President Hoover's hasty and inexact comments upon it. The Norfolk *Virginian-Pilot* said that the report packed "the most damaging blow against constitutional prohibition that has been delivered." The San Francisco *Chronicle* found the report "a perfect picture of the public mind," for the confusion and conflicts of the commissioners over prohibition represented the confusion and conflicts of the country on the matter. The New York *Daily News* found one thing certain, that Hoover was drier than his picked crowd of intellectuals. The New Haven *Journal Courier* was profoundly disappointed that Hoover was "unable or unwilling to see this social tragedy in all of its dreadful aspects." Frank Kent, in the Baltimore *Sun*, confirmed this judgment, saying that any hope that President Hoover might "supply the leadership toward bettering the intolerable and disgusting condition prohibition has brought on the country — a condition vividly mirrored in the report — has no foundation." And the New York *Times* deplored the writing of "a dry caption on a wet article."

But the comments of the more responsible members of the press were nothing compared with the excuse which the *Wickersham Report* gave to the wits of the world of print. Howard Brubaker, in the *New Yorker* regretted the appearance of the report, for "from now on the people will have to do their own disagreeing on prohibition." Heywood Broun held that:

> Mr. Hoover stands revealed as the driest body this side of the Sahara. . . . He is for the Methodist Board of Morals lock, stock and bootlegger's barrel. . . . From now on he will campaign as a Republican only in name. He is endeavoring to put over a political merger. It is his apparent intention to fuse the Anti-Saloon League and the Republican Party, retaining the worst features of each.

Franklin P. Adams wrote a much-quoted poem in the New York *World,* called "The Wickersham Report":

> *Prohibition is an awful flop.*
> *We like it.*
> *It can't stop what it's meant to stop.*
> *We like it.*
> *It's left a trail of graft and slime,*
> *It don't prohibit worth a dime,*
> *It's filled our land with vice and crime,*
> *Nevertheless, we're for it.*[12]

The House of Representatives also had its fun with the report. As La Guardia pointed out, the Wickersham Commission itself was "not the child of those of us opposed to prohibition." It was "packed with drys." Yet only two of the commissioners favored no revision and no repeal of the Eighteenth Amendment and the Volstead Act, while the other nine disagreed, in one way or another. Boylan, of New York, joked that each individual commissioner understood the report, as did Chairman Wickersham and President Hoover, who had both said that the report was fully behind the Eighteenth Amendment. But there were at least eleven different ways of interpreting the report, and if two commissioners ever met with each other, they would never come to a mutual understanding of what they had done. Boylan suggested the appointment of a commission pledged that it "will not agree on anything. It must be understood before they are appointed that they must agree to disagree." Celler, of New York, termed the whole report the "Wicked-and-Sham" report, and asked why the commission could produce nothing better at the cost of half a million dollars.

The drys in the House were forced, like Blanton, of Texas, to find "a crumb of value for the people." He said that the commission as a whole did oppose the repeal of the Eighteenth Amendment, the return of the saloon, modification, and the entry of the government into the liquor trade. Moreover, the Eighteenth Amendment could never and would never be repealed. Finley, of Kentucky, congratulated La Guardia on his "undesirable eminence" as a wet leader, and was glad that he did not share it. The debate then degenerated to Celler quoting from a parody on the report printed in the New York *Evening Sun.* According to the parody, the commission had found that the country was divided into two parts — those who had a little still and those who still had a little. It had also found that corn sugar was the staff of life, with malt liquor a close second. Moreover, the report itself could be seized and searched, and no consistency would be found.[13]

The *Wickersham Report* did most damage to Hoover and the militant drys. Hoover now seemed to be more dry than the evidence of his own appointees warranted. And the militant drys, who had approved of the composition of the commission in the beginning, found it too late to attack its findings; Chairman Wickersham himself said that the report favored the wets rather than the drys.[14] Prohibition had been damned officially by a government commission appointed by a dry President. When Hoover stuck with the drys in his evaluation of the report of the commission, it was at the price of losing the support of moderates and of smirching his reputation for integrity and honesty.

The presentation and reception of the *Wickersham Report* was unfortunate. For it is a fascinating and fair document, if its summarized conclusions and Hoover's comments are ignored. It describes the unfortunate effects of an unpopular law on American society. It makes clear that, whatever the economic benefits of prohibition, dry enforcement is impossible outside a society rigidly bound by political and religious sanctions against alcohol, and by a police power intolerable in a democracy. It presents a fair view of the impossible burden of enforcement on weak federal institutions. It shows how the power of the states and of the people was still great enough to make any law of this nature unworkable, even if the federal government had wanted to make it work. In the commission's own words:

> There has been more sustained pressure to enforce this law than on the whole has been true of any other federal statute, although this pressure in the last four or five years has met with increasing resistance as the sentiment against prohibition has developed. No other federal law has had such elaborate state and federal enforcing machinery put behind it. That a main source of difficulty is in the attitude of at least a very large number of respectable citizens in all communities,

and of the majority of the citizens in most of our large cities and in several states, is made more clear when the enforcement of the National Prohibition Act is compared with the enforcement of the laws as to narcotics. There is an enormous margin of profit in breaking the latter. The means of detecting transportation are more easily evaded than in the case of liquor. Yet there are no difficulties in the case of narcotics beyond those involved in the nature of the traffic because the laws against them are supported everywhere by a general and determined public sentiment.[15]

In the absence of this sentiment, the prohibition of liquor in America was a dry dream.

CHAPTER **21**

The Fanaticism of Repeal

> All laws which can be violated without doing any one any injury are laughed at. Nay, so far are they from doing anything to control the desires and passions of men that, on the contrary, they direct and incite men's thoughts the more toward those very objects; for we always strive toward what is forbidden and desire the things we are not allowed to have. And men of leisure are never deficient in the ingenuity needed to enable them to outwit laws framed to regulate things which cannot be entirely forbidden. . . . He who tries to determine everything by law will foment crime rather than lessen it.
>
> SPINOZA

> Nothing is more attractive to the benevolent vanity of men than the notion that they can effect great improvement in society by the simple process of forbidding all wrong conduct, or conduct that they think is wrong, by law, and of enjoining all good conduct by the same means.
>
> JAMES COOLIDGE CARTER

> There is something sacred about big business. Anything which is economically right is morally right.
>
> HENRY FORD

MANY OF THE distinguished supporters of repeal were as fanatical as the drys. "My own feeling toward prohibition," said Dr. Nicholas Murray Butler, the President of Columbia University,

> . . . is exactly the feeling which my parents and my grandparents had toward slavery. I look upon the Volstead Act precisely as they looked upon the Fugitive Slave Law. Like Abraham Lincoln, I shall obey these laws so long as they remain on the statute book; but, like Abraham Lincoln, I shall not rest until they are repealed. The issue is one of plain, simple, unadorned morality.[1]

In such clear-cut terms, which smacked of the simple choices of a William Jennings Bryan, one of the leading educators of the nation announced his continuing opposition to prohibition. Other teachers of the young joined in the chorus, until even Abbott Lawrence Lowell, the President of Harvard University, added his moderate protest against prohibition: "It seems to have been an economic benefit not unmixed with a distinct moral detriment."[2] When such apostles of the law supported the repeal of one of the laws, the young in their charge could not be expected to obey what their teachers condemned.

But even worse for the dry cause than the distinguished advocates of repeal were the distinguished advocates of nullification of the law. According to Clarence Darrow, nullification of an unpopular law was an old national habit.[3] In the words of Walter Lippmann, it was "a normal and traditional American method of circumventing the inflexibility of the Constitution."[4] Even the President Emeritus of Yale University referred to nullification as a "safety valve which helps a self-governing community avoid the alternative between tyranny and revolution."[5] The plea of the drys for obedience to the Constitution, since the Eighteenth Amendment could never be repealed, was answered by the accusation of the wets that the drys had forced America into nullification by writing such an amendment into the Constitution. Indeed, the extreme wets urged every free-thinking American to drink until the drys had to capitulate. "Drink what you please, when you please," wrote Corey Ford. "Urge others to drink. Don't betray the bootleggers who are smuggling liquor for you. In every way possible flaunt your defiance of the Eighteenth Amendment. Render it inoperative; ignore it, abrogate it, wipe it out. While it stands there, let it be disobeyed."[6]

To such frank advocacy of counterrevolution by illegal means, the drys had no real answer except contempt. Senator Borah found nullification of the dry law "a slinking, silent, cowardly sapping of the very foundation of all order, all dignity, all government — the furtive, evasive betrayal of a nation."[7] Yet the militant wets saw nullification as the only course of action open to a brave man, the only "method of relief from oppression and corruption," the only way to get rid of "obsolete and unpopular laws."[8] In such an extreme situation, with neither drys nor wets yielding an inch of ground, only the compromisers and the law suffered. There could be, and was, no tenable middle ground in the battle.

A position of limited defeat could probably have been held until this day by the drys if they had supported the believers in modification. These men agreed with the dry premise that the Eighteenth Amendment could not be repealed and the wet premise that prohibition was impossible to enforce. Therefore, they suggested that the definition of the word "intoxicating" in the Eighteenth Amendment be modified to allow the sale of beer and light wines in those states which legalized that sale. Alfred E. Smith put forward this point of view in the campaign of 1928. His proposal was seriously discussed, as was another modification plan of 1930, the legalization of home-brew. But the dry leaders had been too long in the saddle to realize that they would have to shift their position to the center to save themselves from defeat. And the wets, watching their forces grow continually behind them, would not be satisfied after the major party conventions of 1932 with less than unconditional surrender, although their early campaign slogans had been modest enough — "Beer and Light Wines *Now,* but No Saloon *Ever.*"⁹

Many respectable educators and lawyers supported the doctrines of repeal and nullification to save, in their opinion, respect for the law. Yet the immediate effect of their actions was to increase the very spirit of lawlessness which afflicted the twenties. When such rocks of integrity as Dr. Nicholas Murray Butler spent much of their time in assaulting the dry laws, many violators felt themselves justified in their violation. For they were told often enough that widespread violation was the short cut to repeal. And their personal example of defiance of the law was passed on to their children and acquaintances. The extreme of the prohibition law encouraged an equally pernicious extreme of opposition. As Elihu Root wrote in 1930, "Compulsion through the law creates revulsion. You cannot make man just through the law, you cannot make man merciful through the law, you cannot make man affectionate through the law."¹⁰ But, apparently, the drys could make men excessive in their opposition to the law.

The wet propagandists also imitated the fanaticism of the drys. Prohibition was accused of four major economic crimes which had led to the Great Depression. The first was the destruction of the brewing and distilling industries; if these industries were restored, a million men would be put back to work. The second was the agricultural depression; if the supply of grain to the breweries were begun again, the farmers would benefit. The third was the large amount of government spending associated with enforcement of the prohibition law; repeal prohibition, and the federal government could cut its expenses. The fourth was the huge loss in federal revenue caused by the ending of the liquor tax; this tax had been made up in the twenties by a high income tax on the incomes of the wealthy; if the tax were restored, then the wealthy would get back their money and would invest it wisely, and the wheels of industry would begin turning again. When Bernard Baruch changed from support of the Eighteenth Amendment to support of repeal, he gave as three reasons for his metamorphosis that prohibition "encouraged disrespect for law, increased taxation, and transferred evils into homes."[11] Although his legal and moral reasons were admirable, his financial reason was the most urgent for rich supporters of repeal in the early years of the depression. For, throughout the twenties, the level of federal income had averaged three billion dollars a year, of which more than two-thirds came from taxes on incomes and corporations. The wealthy in America were paying three-quarters of a billion dollars a year on their private incomes. They were looking for some way to shed the load. Repeal of national prohibition seemed to be that way.

Indeed, if the tax situation of the wealthy is considered, national prohibition seems to have been an inefficient means of redistributing the wealth of America. The workingmen of America drank half their usual amount of liquor and saved one billion dollars a year. The middle classes drank the same amount of liquor and lost one billion dollars a year. The federal government lost something over half a billion dollars a year on liquor taxes, which it made up on income taxes from the rich and the corporations. Moreover, between one and two billion dollars were transferred from wealthy brewers and distillers to the *nouveaux riches* among the criminal classes, and from them to the underpaid judges and attorneys and policemen of the United States. Altogether, prohibition was a sort of irresponsible Robin Hood, stealing from the rich and giving to the poor. Only, unlike Robin Hood, prohibition was not thanked by the poor for its pains.

THE REVOLT OF CONGRESS

THE FIRST serious attack on prohibition after the *Wickersham Report* came from Congressman Lehlbach, of New Jersey, who introduced a resolution in the House calling for "naked repeal" of the Eighteenth Amendment. Lehlbach did not shilly-shally. He wanted two things made clear about the *Wickersham Report.* "The commission is practically unanimous that the Eighteenth Amendment is not observed and not enforced. A majority of the commission unequivocally state their belief that the Eighteenth Amendment can never be adequately enforced." Therefore, repeal was the only solution. With repeal, Congress should be given the power to aid the various states in enforcing their laws against the liquor traffic. In fact, Lehlbach wanted a return to the position in 1913, after the passage of the Webb-Kenyon Law. This was Woodrow Wilson's position before his death, and was the position later taken up by the sponsors of the Twenty-first Amendment. But the time for repeal had not come, and Lehlbach's resolution was killed in the House Committee on the Judiciary.[12]

The opening sessions of the Seventy-second Congress talked a great deal about prohibition during 1931, and did little. In that, they denied the example of the Wickersham Commission and showed an admirable consistency. They were, as usual, sitting on the fence, waiting for the results of the elections. The drys were obviously declining in power, the wets rising. It was not yet clear, however, that the wets would win in the presidential campaign. Congress did not want to jump into an apparent flood, only to break its ankle in hidden dry shallows. On the question of a popular referendum on prohibition, over one-third of House and Senate abstained from voting, although the drys only managed to defeat the measure in the Senate by three votes.

Nevertheless, the wets did force one showdown in the House. In La Guardia's words, the people had a right to know where the House stood on the issue of prohibition, "an opportunity heretofore denied them by their own Representatives."[13] On March 14, 1932, Congressman Beck, of Pennsylvania, and Linthicum, of Maryland, introduced a resolution to discharge the bill for repeal of the Eighteenth Amendment from further consideration by the House Committee on the Judiciary. Boylan, of New York, exulted in the growing power of the wets after twelve years of high taxation and bigotry. He was anxious to see such a splendid House returned in the elections; its return would depend in a large measure upon its vote on the present resolution. O'Connor, of New York, observed that only eighty-two members of the House had voted on the Eighteenth Amendment; a new body had since been elected. He was amused to see a complete volte-face in the attitude of the drys. He quoted Senators Sheppard and Jones and Bishop Cannon, who had pressed for the submission of national prohibition to the people in 1917 and now opposed a popular referendum. He was glad that the time had come to show who were the friends and foes of prohibition. He declaimed, " 'Tis the ides of March! Stand up and be counted!"

Indeed, the dry appeals of 1932 were the wet appeals of 1917. Where the wets had cried out for unity in time of war, the drys now cried out for unity in time of depression. Sumner, of Texas, spoke of the need for "a united people to deal with this terrible economic crisis of ours." He made the challenge to wet and dry: "Let us not turn aside from the challenge of the hour and divide our people." And he paralleled the complacency of the wets in 1917, that they could hold thirteen states indefinitely, by his assertion that the wets would never get two-thirds of Congress and three-quarters of the states to support them.

But Beck himself, in the last speech before the roll call, gave the most eloquent statement yet made in the House. He found it strange that the drys should maintain that the Constitution was unchangeable, when they themselves had written the Eighteenth Amendment into the Constitution and thus had destroyed the basic American principle of self-government. There was, in addition, no doubt that prohibition was an "experiment," and experiments should be voted upon frequently. He reminded the drys that "no such general revolt against the enforcement of a law has ever been known in our history." The amendment was passed in a "time of great hysteria" by Senates and legislatures not elected for that purpose. He quoted the Talmud and Aristotle to show that the prohibition law could never be enforced. As for the dry argument that unity was needed in time of depression, he said that depression demanded the repeal of prohibition "to clear the decks for other important public policies." Until prohibition was repealed, there would be "continued chaos in our national councils."[14]

The Beck-Linthicum resolution was defeated by 227 votes to 187. But the wets had made their best showing on a major vote since the Hobson resolution in 1914. In three years, they had doubled their vote in the House. A comparison of the vote with that on the Hobson resolution shows what had been prophesied in the vote on the Jones Law. The wets had gained support in the populous North and had lost it in the South. They had gained support in industrial states and had lost it in rural areas. The party conventions, however, would define the party line on prohibition, and the vote in the coming elections would be taken as a referendum on the issue, partially binding upon Congress.

The President, like Congress, was wary of prohibition. He was too clever a politician not to see that the wet tide was flooding in. He approached the Republican convention of 1932 with massive discretion. Many in New York suggested that the new bridge from Fort Tryon to the Palisades should be called the Hoover Bridge, since it was wet below and dry above and straddled the river with one foot on either side. This joke was at least more humorous than those which referred to the shack-towns outside Chicago as Hoovervilles and to newspapers stuffed inside trouserlegs to keep out the cold as Hoover Trousers. To one enemy, Hoover was the "Janus of America, with one wet face and one dry face, and neither face very handsome."[15] Ready to change his mind over prohibition, Hoover waited for the results of the Chicago convention.

Mencken noticed a vast change in the Republican delegates in 1932. They were aggressively wet. Never in his life had he been witness to "a more pervasive confidence, a showier or more bellicose cockiness."[16] This may have been partially due to the anger of the delegates in finding that racketeers had pushed up bootleg prices to double those of New York City. But the enthusiasm of the wets was also due to the bouquet of victory; more and more states were repealing their enforcement laws. The keynote speech at the convention incredibly made no mention of prohibition. The real battle for the plank took place before the Resolutions Committee in the parlor of the Congress Hotel. Bishop Cannon found himself treated with contempt. The two planks presented at the convention were not a wet and a dry plank, but a moist plank and a dripping one. The delegates, ignoring minor problems such as the worst depression in American history, fought cup and lip over the prohibition issue. The Hoover group secured only a three-fifths majority for their moist plank, which favored resubmission of the Eighteenth Amendment to the states if the federal government retained power to protect dry territory and to prevent the return of the saloon. The plank also declared with more hope than faith that prohibition was not "a partisan political question."[17]

But the drys themselves had made prohibition a partisan political question, by taking Hoover's victory in 1928 as a dry referendum. They had branded the Republican party as the party of prohibition. This charge appeared even more true when the Democrats adopted at their convention in 1932 a plank for the outright repeal of the Eighteenth Amendment. The Democrats had come out into the open as the party of the wets. By default, the Republicans were the party of the drys, even though their prohibition plank was, in Franklin D. Roosevelt's terms, "words upon words, evasions upon evasions, insincerity upon insincerity, a dense cloud of words."[18] This statement by Roosevelt, who seemed to many in 1932 the veritable apostle of repeal, would have also been a just description of his own past attitudes toward prohibition.

FRANKLIN DELANO ROOSEVELT: FROM CAUTION TO REPEAL

As AL SMITH exemplified the immigrant's view of prohibition, and Herbert Hoover the view of the native-born rural American, so Roosevelt had the attitude of the old American aristocrat towards the dry issue. The Roosevelt and the Delano families belonged to the squirearchy of upper New York State. They moved in an ordered and secure and polite society, undisturbed by the new rich and the new poor of the industrial cities. They believed in good manners rather than in rude honesty, in the compromises of well-bred tact rather than in the quarrels of opposed convictions. Roosevelt accepted the habits of his class unquestioningly throughout his life, even if he was thought to be a traitor to that class. He came into politics to heal, not to antagonize. He did not insist until he was powerful enough to command. He expected to govern all, not to lead a faction or a party. His equivocations on such subjects as prohibition were understandable in a man who thought that conversation on unpleasant matters was a sign, not of truth, but of boorishness.

Roosevelt preferred to try all things for all men, to apply "bold, persistent experimentation" to all problems and relationships in order that everyone might be a little gratified and served.[19] If this effort "above all, [to] try something" made Roosevelt seem slippery and evasive and weak to such commentators as Lippmann, yet it made him seem a good leader to the Brains Trust, who were to experiment under him. Raymond Moley wrote of Roosevelt just before his nomination in 1932:

> There is a lot of autointoxication of the intelligence that we shall have to watch. . . . But I believe that his complete freedom from dogmatism is a virtue at this stage of the game. He will stick to ideas after he has expressed them, I believe and hope. Heaven knows Hoover is full of information and dogmas but he has been imprisoned by his knowledge and God save us from four more years of that![20]

The instinctive quality which Roosevelt had, "a desire to please and an inborn intuition of what means would attain that end," made him not only a great democratic politician, receptive to the wants of the governed, but also a weathercock man, often uninsistent upon his own desires.[21]

Roosevelt even married into his own clique. He married his godfather's daughter, Eleanor Roosevelt. The godfather was a drunkard, who was loved by his daughter; in sorrow at his habits, she became a confirmed dry.[22] She married Franklin Roosevelt despite the disapproval of his formidable mother, Sara, who was also a dry. The teetotal tendencies of mother and wife often irked Franklin, although he could make political capital out of their known prohibitionist sympathies. He was a moderate drinker throughout his life, and even the passage of the Volstead Act did not make him dry. Rosenman's claim that Roosevelt drank only a "horse's neck" of ginger ale and lemon peel before repeal and beer after repeal is erroneous;[23] in fact, during the campaign summer of 1932, he often drove out to Rosenman's house at Wappingers Falls to drink cocktails there, since he was deprived of them in his own home.[24] Although no liquor was ever served officially in the Executive Mansion when Roosevelt was Governor of New York, he did serve cocktails after repeal in the White House.

Franklin Delano Roosevelt had "the best trade name in American political life."[25] He was inspired early with thoughts of a political career by the example of his distant cousin Theodore and by the lists of past Presidents in the family genealogies which his mother recited hour after hour. Although he was a traditional Democrat, there were certain similarities in his political career to that of the Republican Theodore. Both rose by holding positions in their state legislatures. Both were Assistant Secretaries of the Navy. Both were Governors of New York. Both ran as candidates for the vice presidency, although Franklin was unsuccessful. And both served more than one term as President of the United States. But their characters and policies were divergent. If Franklin tried to evade the issue of national prohibition by the same means as Theodore, by supporting local option and later state repeal, yet he used persuasion and silence rather than speeches about order and liberty to advertise his stand. If evidence of a wet majority in 1932 made Franklin declare for repeal in much the way that evidence of a dry majority had made Theodore declare for prohibition during the First World War, yet Franklin could claim reasonably that he had always been temperate in habits and speeches about drink. The evidence of Theodore's face and words made it difficult for him to pose as a moderate champion of the drys.

As state senator from upstate New York, Franklin Roosevelt was early dependent on rural votes, rural beliefs, and rural prejudices. In the elections and during his time in the Assembly, he attacked Tammany and machine politics, and voted puritan and progressive and dry, as a good farmer should. The fact that he was a Democrat was forgiven him in the country districts because he was connected with the great Republican, Theodore. His support of local option on the ticklish questions of prohibition and woman suffrage was acceptable in country and town alike as a reasonable method of sitting on the fence.

Roosevelt had already determined to rise to the presidency by means of the state governorship. Thus he had to placate the wets in New York City as well as the drys in Dutchess County. Unfortunately, he came under heavy pressure from the Anti-Saloon League while he was still dependent on the country vote for his seat in the Senate. In January, 1913, he unwillingly introduced a city option bill for the League against the opposition of Tammany. He was much more ready, however, to support the closing of the saloons in Highland Falls, the town adjoining West Point. He imitated Theodore Roosevelt in supporting prohibition where it aided military efficiency. In fact, he voted so regularly for dry measures that he was praised in an editorial of the *American Issue*.[26] The early dry record was used against him by the wets of both parties until he adopted the wet Democratic plank in 1932.

Roosevelt was made the Assistant Secretary of the Navy in the Wilson administration. He worked under Josephus Daniels and supported his measures for enforcing overt prohibition on the United

States fleet. Although the American Navy was distinguished as much by its drunkenness as for its bravery in the ports of Europe, its teetotalism on the high seas could not be questioned.

The nomination of Franklin D. Roosevelt as Vice President at the 1920 Democratic convention was due to his name rather than his national reputation. James M. Cox, the presidential candidate, was a wet from Ohio, the nominee of the party bosses. Roosevelt, throughout the convention, voted for Cox's dry opponent, McAdoo. But a man was needed to balance the ticket who was dry, Independent, identified with the Wilson administration, and likely to carry a valuable state. Roosevelt was available on all four counts. Boss Murphy backed him to get rid of a dangerous antagonist in state politics, the Westerners backed him as an opponent of Tammany, and the Southerners backed him for his supposed dry sympathies. There were no obvious opponents. The convention delegates were in a hurry to get home. The name of Roosevelt was thought to be a magic capable of gulling simple progressives into the belief that they were voting for Theodore.* Franklin Roosevelt was nominated by Alfred Smith, and was accepted by acclamation.

In the disastrous Democratic campaign of 1920, Roosevelt made valuable contacts among the leaders of the local state Democratic organizations, and created some good will for himself throughout the country. Reporters found him affable and charming, although he was widely suspected of weakness and lack of character.[27] These charges were harder to bring against him after his attack of infantile paralysis and his subsequent determined return to politics even though he was a permanent cripple. Roosevelt refused to recognize that he would never again be able to use his legs properly, and thus deceived himself into hope; it was "questionable whether he ever faced up completely to his condition."[28] This quality of self-deception was at once Roosevelt's greatest strength and weakness. It gave him the strength to overcome such crippling disabilities as poliomyelitis, and the weakness to evade a firm stand on such dangerous issues as prohibition.

For Roosevelt saw that, if prohibition were allowed to become a major issue, it would split the Democrats irreconcilably and prevent the party from concentrating on more important issues of economics and government. If party solidity was the aim of the good Democrat, he must equivocate over prohibition at the price of personal honesty. Thus Roosevelt spent some of his time recuperating from his disease in searching for an acceptable straddle for the liquor problem. In

---

* The wet Republican Chicago *Tribune* commented sourly on Franklin Roosevelt's nomination, "If he is Theodore Roosevelt, Elihu Root is Gene Debs, and Bryan is a brewer."

September, 1922, he advocated that a follower of his in Dutchess County should support a proposal for legalizing beer with a volume of up to 4 per cent of alcohol; but care should be taken about supporting light wines, which contained up to 15 per cent of alcohol. In 1923, Roosevelt saw William Jennings Bryan in Florida and suggested a national referendum on prohibition, saying that the drys would, of course, win easily. He wrote later to Bryan that New York State was not nearly as wet a state as some Democrats liked to make out — an oblique reference to Al Smith, the Governor of New York.[29]

However hard he tried, Roosevelt could not fail to take sides between Bryan and Smith. Although he warned Bryan that "hopeful idiots" among the wet Democrats were trying to arrange for the meeting of the party convention of 1924 in New York City in order to make the passage of a wet plank easier, he still nominated the wet Smith at the New York convention as the Happy Warrior. For Smith was the leader of the New York Democrats, and Roosevelt knew that he could not hope for a future in politics without some support from his home state. Both ambition and courtesy demanded that he should back Smith. Indeed, he had earlier commiserated with Smith over the repeal of the Mullan-Gage Law, and the difficult problem in which "this darned old liquor question" had placed the Governor of New York.[30] Roosevelt had pointed out the obvious, that repeal of the state enforcement law would hurt Smith nationally, although it would win him support in New York City and other large industrial centers. Roosevelt had suggested his usual subtle straddle, that Smith should veto the repeal bill on the grounds of moral obligation to support the Volstead Act and should then call a special session of the state legislature to pass another bill, which would effectively draw the teeth from all the penal provisions of the Mullan-Gage Law by requiring the law officers of the state to enforce the Volstead Act only when requested to do so by federal agents.

The antagonisms revealed between city and country Democrats in the convention of 1924 confirmed Roosevelt in his chosen role as peacemaker. Aided by his familiar and manager Louis Howe, he corresponded widely with all those who were powerful in the party organization, asking their views on how to strengthen the Democratic party. The answers demonstrated the deep divisions among the Democrats over the Ku Klux Klan and prohibition. Roosevelt's most useful role was obviously to be the doctor of the wounds of the party. He should try to concentrate the attention of the Democrats on the basic issues of prosperity and administration, even though prohibition had swelled out its monstrous importance until it overshadowed the minds of both parties and people in America.

In a state convention keynote speech for Smith in 1926, Roosevelt managed to talk so adroitly about prohibition that he was praised by his old dry Navy chief, Josephus Daniels. "I think you took only a light bath and came out in fine shape. From that speech nobody would call you an immersionist like Al Smith; they would rather think you took yours by sprinkling or pouring."[31] Although Smith was being equally cagey on the subject of prohibition before 1928, he was damned as a wet by his past. Roosevelt's straddle was far more effective and recommended him to the South and West as reasonably dry, even if he was not considered to be dedicated to the Eighteenth Amendment. Roosevelt confirmed this impression at a meeting of Democratic leaders in Washington at the beginning of 1927, when he urged them to issue a declaration of fundamental Democratic principles on Jefferson's birthday and to avoid such controversial issues as prohibition. There was even a movement by the Southern drys, led by Daniels and Carter Glass, to back Roosevelt against Smith in 1928. Louis Howe managed to quash this forlorn and damaging attempt at support. It could only precipitate a break with Smith and alienate the wet, industrial delegates, whom Roosevelt would need at succeeding conventions.

The best reason for Roosevelt's refusal to run in 1928 was that continuing prosperity had made it unlikely that any Democrat could oust the Republicans from control of the White House. Both Roosevelt and Howe knew this and concentrated on building up support for Roosevelt at the following convention. Al Smith's defeat in 1928 might make Roosevelt the most available candidate four years later. The example of William Jennings Bryan had taught the Democrats not to run losing horses two or three times. So Roosevelt demonstrated his faith in party unity by nominating Smith again at the national convention at Houston, and by suggesting that Cordell Hull, Roosevelt's new Southern supporter, should run as Vice President. Unfortunately, Hull's advisers tried to run him for the presidency, which made Smith favor the Arkansas Senator, Joseph Robinson, as his fellow candidate and sop to the South.

Roosevelt's influence helped to prevent the Smith supporters on the Resolutions Committee from writing a wet plank for the convention. He thought that Smith's repudiation of the dry compromise plank was ill-advised, and he strongly opposed Smith's choice of John J. Raskob as chairman of the Democratic National Committee. Raskob was a conservative and wealthy businessman, a Roman Catholic, and a wet; he emphasized the very issues which Roosevelt wanted ignored. If there was fundamental agreement between Republicans and Democrats on business matters, prohibition and religion would become disastrous major issues.[32] Roosevelt wrote to Daniels on July 20, 1928, that he was still doing his best to line up the campaign issues on something other than the wet and dry question, but that he was disturbed by events.[33] Yet he agreed to support Smith by running for Governor in New York State, although he was worried that prosperity might ensure both the election of Hoover and the Republican candidate for Governor of New York, Albert Ottinger.

While Smith lost his home state of New York to Hoover, Roosevelt narrowly won against Ottinger by twenty-five thousand votes. The religious prejudice, which had worked covertly against Smith, benefited Roosevelt, despite his pleas against any form of religious discrimination. For Roosevelt was an Episcopalian, while Ottinger was a Jew. Both candidates in New York played down the prohibition issue. Roosevelt did so because of his upstate support, Smith's wetness, and his own future national chances, while Ottinger concurred because of the wet New York City vote, Hoover's dryness, and the equivocal position upon prohibition of the Republican party in the state. In his twelve major campaign addresses, Roosevelt mentioned prohibition only twice. In upstate Utica, he declared that repeal of the Mullan-Gage Law had lessened graft without any effect on the efficiency of law enforcement against the bootleggers.[34] But in downstate Yonkers, Roosevelt misquoted Hoover's support of the "noble experiment" and identified himself with Governor Smith's stand against the Volstead Act. By a miracle of devious sincerity, Roosevelt said that both he and Smith demanded constructive action, which meant change from present conditions. Only Roosevelt carefully failed to state what specific change he and Smith desired.[35]

Roosevelt's victory and Smith's defeat put the new Governor in an embarrassing position. Smith would demand a say in the management of the state on the reasonable grounds of four terms' experience. If Roosevelt accepted the offer, he would appear to be Smith's figurehead. Therefore, he refused Smith's help and began the breach that presidential ambitions would make so bitter. For Roosevelt represented to Smith those very country, old-stock, mannered, Protestant people who had opposed the Roman Catholic city politician within the party and nation.

As Governor of New York, Roosevelt concentrated on an agricultural program to harden his upstate support; he also continued the type of progressive legislation which Smith had put through in his tenures of office. Roosevelt, however, did more than Smith by introducing relief measures against the effects of the depression. With these economic reforms, he sought to take the emphasis of his administration off prohibition. Yet, when he was called to the Governors' Conference at New London by Hoover on July 16, 1929, Roosevelt used prohibition to advertise himself. He said that the states were not doing enough to combat large-scale organized crime. There should be crime commissions in all states like the one in New York. This statement would have made no headlines, except that Roosevelt ended his plea by reading a letter from George W. Wickersham. This letter was Wickersham's first public statement since the session of his commission on law enforcement; it recommended that the states should give more help to the federal authorities in the enforcement of the Volstead Act. An immediate quarrel broke out among the dry and the wet governors; they voted, in the end, to shelve Wickersham's suggestion. Roosevelt cannily took no side in the debate.[36] He had secured publicity without committing himself.

Roosevelt continued to withstand pressure from both wets and drys to come out into the open about prohibition. When he was charged with lax enforcement of the federal laws in New York City, he quoted Police Commissioner Grover Whalen's figures, which proved that all but one in fifty prosecutions in the federal courts were initiated by the city police. When Walter Lippmann attacked him in the New York *World* for failing to support the states' rights solution to the prohibition problem, Roosevelt wrote in a hurt manner to a friend that it was the *World*

> . . . which literally drove Al Smith into sending that fool telegram after the Houston convention telling how wet he was. Al had every wet vote in the country but he needed a good many millions of the middle of the road votes to elect him President . . . the *World* did more harm to Al Smith's candidacy than all the Republican newspapers in the United States put together.[37]

But Roosevelt saw that the wets were gaining ground. He would not be able to straddle the prohibition issue during the gubernatorial campaign of 1930. Thus he thought it better to declare himself and appear honest than seem to be forced into wetness by his state party platform. He wrote, therefore, a public letter to Senator Robert Wagner, who had been elected temporary chairman of the Democratic state convention. Roosevelt said that he thought public opinion was overwhelmingly opposed to the Eighteenth Amendment. The amendment had not fostered temperance in the population but, to quote from a resolution of the American Legion, had "fostered excessive drinking of strong intoxicants," had "led to corruption and hypocrisy," had brought about "disregard for law and order," and had "flooded the country with untaxed and illicit liquor." Roosevelt stated that he personally shared this opinion. The principle of home rule over the liquor trade should be extended to states, cities, towns, and villages.

But each state should keep full control over the sale of liquor to prevent the return of the saloon.[38]

This letter was a calculated risk on Roosevelt's part. He hoped, by taking up a damp position, to appear as the friend of the moderate drys against the extreme wets. He succeeded. Of the letters that greeted his announcement, most were laudatory, although there were a few protests from the South. Even Raskob approved of Roosevelt's stand. Only five out of twenty-nine members of the Democratic National Committee who answered a circular from the New York *Times* opposed Roosevelt's solution to the prohibition problem.[39] Roosevelt, by returning to local option, had thrown back the responsibility of efficient enforcement onto each local community. A dry neighborhood could be dry; a wet one could be wet. Roosevelt was difficult to attack, since he had appealed to democracy as the answer to the problem of prohibition.

In the election for Governor, the Republican candidate, United States Attorney Charles Tuttle, came out for repeal of the Eighteenth Amendment and caused a landslide vote in favor of Roosevelt. He fell into the Democratic trap. The Roosevelt forces had arranged for an extreme wet plank to be written at the state convention so that Roosevelt himself could appear to be drier than his party, the last dike against the Democratic flood tide.[40] Tuttle, however, was responsible by his office for law enforcement in New York. His wet stand disgusted the dry upstate Republicans, who nominated a second candidate, a prohibitionist professor from Syracuse University. Roosevelt had great fun at the expense of his opponents, saying that the Republicans were trying to make their state party "an *amphibious ichthyosaurus* equally comfortable whether wet or dry, whether in the sea or on the land or up in the air."[41]

Roosevelt won New York by 725,000 votes, twice the majority Al Smith had ever polled. Roosevelt even carried upstate New York, the Republican stronghold. He immediately became front runner for the Democratic nomination for President in 1932. His policy on prohibition and economics seemed to be able to hold Democrats and win Republicans. Only blocking by Al Smith or sudden prosperity under Hoover appeared likely to keep Roosevelt from the White House.

But Roosevelt still had to walk delicately. He had to hold the Southern and Western Democrats behind him but avoid antagonizing Smith's city supporters enough to make them bolt in 1932. A split Democratic party would go down to certain defeat. Roosevelt saw himself as the great healer. He would use his personality like Warm Springs to relax the ills of his party. Thus, after his election in 1930, he was again silent on the subject of prohibition. Over and over again, he repeated that economics and depression were the big problems. He disliked the stupidity of such groups as the National Economic League, which decided in January, 1931, that prohibition was the major "paramount problem" of the United States; to them unemployment was far less important.[42] The Smith group in the Democratic National Committee agreed with this analysis. For Smith had become more and more a friend of big business and wanted to fight the Republicans on prohibition rather than depression, even if he split his own party behind him.

The quarrel between Roosevelt and Smith came into the open on the question of the Democratic party's stand on the Eighteenth Amendment. The supporters of Smith had kept their hold on the Democratic National Committee through John J. Raskob and Jouett Shouse. They hoped, by making prohibition a leading issue in the next convention, that a militant wet majority would block the Roosevelt bid to heal the party split by temporizing over the liquor problem, and would elect Smith as the obvious candidate of the wets.

In March, 1931, a combination of Roosevelt and the dry Southerners blocked a resolution by the Democratic National Committee to press for repeal of the Eighteenth Amendment. The price Roosevelt paid for this evasion was to allow for six years the Southern Democratic leaders of the houses of Congress to be the spokesmen of their party between elections, and thus to have a veto over national legislation. He also lost Smith's friendship. Smith thought Roosevelt was dodging on the subject of prohibition. He exploded to Clark Howell on December 2, 1931, "Why the hell don't he speak out – he has been more outspoken on the question than even I have been, and now ain't the time for trimming!" The time had come for a "showdown" against the iniquity of the Eighteenth Amendment; the Democrats should demand a referendum. Howell discreetly said that Roosevelt agreed with Smith's ideas.[43]

But Roosevelt evaded the prohibition issue more and more during the months before the presidential convention. Less forthright than Smith, he hedged on the ticklish subject, rather than being silent about it. His supporters on the Democratic Resolutions Committee were about to present a plank no wetter than the moist effort of the Republicans. Nevertheless, when Senator Barkley's keynote address demanding repeal of the Eighteenth Amendment was widely cheered by the convention delegates, Roosevelt withdrew by telephone his opposition to Smith's minority wet plank some fifteen minutes before Smith was due to present it from the convention floor.[44] Support of the Smith plank by most of the Roosevelt group on the National Committee except for Cordell Hull turned it into a majority plank at the last moment.[45] Smith was cheered tumultuously as he presented his wet plank. He attacked the moist minority plank of Cordell Hull and the hypocrisy of Herbert Hoover, who had sent for blotting paper and had dried up the report of the Wickersham Commission.

Roosevelt's political manager, Jim Farley, released the pledged Roosevelt delegates when the wet planks came up for the vote at the convention, knowing that the passage of the extreme wet plank would eliminate the best reason for nominating Smith or Governor Ritchie, of Maryland. With a repeal plank written into the party platform, Smith had little else to offer, while Roosevelt was offering panaceas for unemployment. Cordell Hull, presenting the minority damp plank, attacked Raskob for trying to emphasize prohibition and ignore depression after the Republican manner. In fact, if the Democrats imitated their opponents, it would be "a damnable outrage bordering on treason." Hull gave an indirect and moving defense of Roosevelt's political wisdom in seeking to bury the prohibition issue, while the delegates by a four-to-one majority whooped up Al Smith's personal honestly over repeal.[46] Even the Southern delegates mainly voted wet, with only Mississippi, Oklahoma, and Georgia holding firm for the drys.

The dry McAdoo, Smith's enemy, had his revenge as the spokesman for the California delegation that switched to Roosevelt and gave him the nomination. As Mencken wrote, eight years ago McAdoo had

> . . . led the hosts of the Invisible Empire against the Pope, the rum demon and all the other Beelzebubs of the Hookworm Belt. . . . The man who blocked him was Al Smith, and now he was paying Al back. If revenge is really sweet he was sucking a colossal sugar teat, but all the same there was a beery flavor about it that must have somewhat disquieted him.[4]

Roosevelt had made a virtue of necessity over prohibition. Committed by his party to outright repeal, he could forget his own equivocations on the issue in condemnation of Hoover's wobbling stand on the wobbling Republican plank. Once a decision was forced upon him, Roosevelt had the courage of his choice. For Roosevelt's way was that

> . . . of the common man as opposed to the intellectual and uncommon man. The common people understood Franklin Roosevelt and he understood them, largely . . . because their processes of looking at things and coming to conclusions were almost the same. This probably was why they trusted him even in situations where he took an action they didn't like.[48]

A majority of the common people may have been prepared to accept prohibition in time of war and boom, but not in time of depression. Roosevelt mirrored their feelings. If his evasive attitude toward prohibition before his election to the presidency in 1932 did not indicate his later strength in office, it is because the job of President gave the malleable Roosevelt the capacity to do the job well. For him, there was one way to power, the way of trimming; and another way in power, the way of power itself.

THE REPEAL ELECTION

THE MAJOR party conventions of 1932 showed how much the strength of the drys had suddenly collapsed. Mencken exulted, "Prohibition has suddenly fallen over like a house of cards. A year ago, even six months ago, the drys were still full of confidence, for they were sure that they had Lord Hoover in their cage. But he has broken out, slipped off his nose ring, and headed for the bad lands."[49] Walter Lippmann thought the conflict over the prohibition plank at both conventions reduced itself to the question of whether to be misleading or frank. Hoover was in control of the Grand Old Party, and Hoover wished to be misleading. He was thus regarded as a deserter by the drys, and by the wets as an unreliable convert. Yet Lippmann warned the wets that they were "certainly as fanatical and as ignorant and as intolerant as the drys ever were in the days when they were in the saddle."[50] But the moist Republican plank, which asked for resubmission of the Eighteenth Amendment to the states, was outbid by the Democratic plank, which demanded outright repeal. The wets backed Franklin Roosevelt, who promised them the most. And the drys were left in the sad position of choosing moderate wets against extreme wets. Will Rogers commented, "Both sides are wet and the poor old dry hasn't got a soul to vote for. He is Roosevelt's 'forgotten man.' "[51]

The drys had nowhere to go in 1932. Senator Borah rightly complained that the major parties had disenfranchised them.[52] But the fact was that the people were not interested in prohibition, except as an economic fallacy. The *Christian Century* wailed, "So far as the presidential campaign is concerned, the question of prohibition is a washed-out issue."[50] Although not a single church journal supported Roosevelt editorially, they also said little in praise of the moist Hoover. The reason for their offended silence was as blinkered as the reason for the Republican enthusiasm at the Chicago convention.

> How often did the reader of the church press in the depression start an editorial or article entitled "The Need of the Hour," "A Time

of Crisis," "The President Must Lead," "Moral Issues in the Election," "The Stakes in the Election," "It Is Time for the President to Act," only to discover that, far from dealing with the economic crisis, it was concerned with prohibition![54]

The landslide victory of Roosevelt showed the ineffectual quality of the church press. The preachers had shot their bolt against Al Smith in 1928. The virulence and unfairness of their attack upon him had lost them much of their former influence.

During the campaign of 1932, Hoover at last made what he thought was a definite statement upon prohibition. With unconscious humor, he said at Washington on August 11 that his conclusions on prohibition were "clear and need not be misunderstood." He then proceeded to obscure obscurity. He stated that he refused "on the one hand to return to the old saloon with its political and social corruption, or on the other to endure the bootlegger and the speakeasy with their abuses and crime." Either was intolerable. Resubmission to the states (which was a means of avoiding an outright declaration for repeal) was the answer. American statesmanship, exemplified by himself, was capable of working out such a solution and making it effective.[55]

But prohibition was no longer an important moral issue in a time of depression. Senator Moses might excuse the evasive Republican prohibition plank by saying that it must "appeal to that sweet reasonableness of the great majority of American people that always manifests itself, in the long run, whatever may be the bone of contention."[56] But the voters were only interested in the economic benefits which repeal might bring. And the Democrats shamelessly exploited the illusory prosperity which would result from the opening of the distilleries and the breweries, and the illusory relief which would be felt by the taxpayer. The Governor of Maryland, Albert Ritchie, claimed that the liquor trade would provide jobs for a million people.[57] Moreover, as Franklin Roosevelt himself charged, prohibition was diverting vast quantities of money into the hands of criminals and bootleggers, whose business "was in a real sense being supported by the government."[58] The dry crusade had become an economic whip for the Democrats to use in the flogging of the Republican party. The propaganda for Hoover and the prohibitionists in 1928, that they were the saviors of prosperity, branded them later as the traitors who had conspired to cause the depression.

In despair of both presidential candidates, the combined dry forces, which called themselves the National Prohibition Board of Strategy, declared war on both parties and decided to concentrate on holding Congress. Some dry leaders such as Daniel A. Poling did declare in desperation for Hoover.[59] But only a few. The disorganization of the drys was complete. The Woman's Christian Temperance Union recognized as much and decided to endorse neither candidate; it asked its members to vote according to conscience and appeal to the winner to enforce prohibition.[60] As Wheeler had said to Senator Reed, if the difference between the two candidates is "just a degree of wetness, you cannot get much moral enthusiasm up."[61]

The result of the election doomed the drys. The extreme candidate of the wets, Roosevelt, easily triumphed over the moist candidate, Hoover. The supporters of prohibition had called the previous election a referendum, and now the vote had gone against them. Although they rightly denied that prohibition was a major issue in the campaign, the very fact that it was an issue at all, and an economic issue, was fatal. For as a bootlegger had said at the Republican convention, the issue was now bread, not beer.[62] And if a party was returned to power with a mandate to put the nation back to work again, few would cavil at a measure designed to provide bread for millions through the manufacture of beer.

Herbert Hoover was defeated by the inadequacy of his moral and economic philosophy, as the prohibitionists were by theirs. Several decades of vindication by him and the drys have not whitened their sepulchers. Hoover believed in rugged individualism and free enterprise, as the advocates of abstinence believed in enforced teetotalism and lack of compromise. Hoover could not see that the nineteenth-century country morality which might suit the boom America of 1920 was a catastrophic basis on which to construct relief measures for the depression America of 1930. Equally, the drys could not accept the fact that the conditions caused by industrialism would never be fertile ground for those social restrictions which rural villages might welcome as safety precautions. Hoover, shifting about in the White House to save prosperity and party, was too narrow and too late to do so. The Anti-Saloon League was similarly too narrow and too late to concede enough to the supporters of temperance in 1932 to save the Eighteenth Amendment. Both the President and the drys worked long hours with convinced faith to rescue lost causes. Both failed.

Hoover claimed to be superman and myth, as the drys claimed to speak for majorities and God.

> The Herbert Hoover whom the people elected in 1928 never did exist in flesh. That Hoover was the embodiment of an idea, a legendary ideal, a portrait of intentions and not a picture of realities. That Hoover was the Great Humanitarian, the Great Engineer, the Great Secretary. The trinity was a creation of adulation, publicity, and vicarious materialization.[63]

The drys puffed themselves up as much as Hoover, and were as limited in fact. When Hoover, in 1930, accused the advocates of excessive appropriations of "playing politics with human misery," he had forgotten that he had played politics with the relief of human misery in war and with human prosperity in peace. The drys also forgot their exploitation of the psychology of war and of boom when they accused the wets of using the depression to secure repeal. The Anti-Saloon League linked the dry cause to Herbert Hoover and prosperity, and drowned with him in those chains.

THE TWENTY-FIRST AMENDMENT

ONCE THE depression had become too blatant to be ignored, the morality of prohibition seemed ridiculous. Hunger was more of a temperance teacher than any dry. Repeal became merely another method of fighting the slump. When the same Congress that had voted against the Beck-Linthicum resolution met again, it showed how much more it cared for the voice of the electorate than for its personal convictions. The drys were no longer so awesome. The popular vote had shown them powerless to prevent the elections of Democrats and wets. Thus the rump Congress merely did what its successors would have done, even if it contradicted all its previous professions by doing so. Both houses voted overwhelmingly for a Twenty-first Amendment to the Constitution to repeal the Eighteenth.

The drys tried to salvage what they could. On December 6, 1932, Senator Blaine, of Wisconsin, introduced a resolution which embodied the moist proposals of the Republican platform. He said that the political parties had finally resolved upon the question very definitely. Now was the time and now was the occasion to carry out that resolve which in his opinion reflected "the mature judgment of the people of the country." He opposed wet states interfering with dry states, or vice versa. Congress should prevent such interference and also, as both parties had pledged in their platforms, prevent the return of the saloon in any form. Otherwise, to paraphrase President Lincoln in saving the Union, it was his paramount object in this struggle to take prohibition out of the Constitution, either through state legislatures or through state conventions or even through plain congressional action.

But the wets were as pitiless in power as the drys had been. They would settle for nothing less than outright repeal of prohibition by the methods most favorable to them. They insisted on repeal by elected conventions. For, as Hastings, of Delaware, pointed out, "What they propose and what they hope to carry through is that the populace in the cities, most of which are wet, shall be arrayed against those in the country, most of whom are dry." The Census of 1930 had shown that more people now lived in the cities than in rural areas. By the convention method of repeal, the unfair representation of the country in the state legislatures would be discounted. For the delegates to the repeal conventions would be elected by straight numerical majorities.

The wets also insisted that nothing should be done to prevent the return of the saloon under another name. Walsh, of Massachusetts, read out an article which said that, even if the saloon was bad, the speak-easy was worse. The decision was not between saloon and no saloon but between saloon and speak-easy. For "the liquor evil is with us.- Prohibition has moved the saloons from the street corners into the speakeasies." The return of the saloon would be the lesser evil, for evil there had to be.[64]

This naked demand for the return of the saloon so horrified Glass, of Virginia, that he accused the wets of pride. He warned them that the return of the saloon would suit the drys best, for they could still inflame men's minds on that issue. And Capper, of Kansas, made a simple appeal from the last dry ditch. "All over the world a colossal struggle is going on between right and wrong. Crime has increased everywhere. As the population of the world is larger than ever before, I doubt if it has ever witnessed so gigantic a contest between good and evil as is now taking place." The propaganda of the wets was false. Repeal of prohibition would do nothing to help agriculture. The Senate must keep to the good side and preserve the Eighteenth Amendment.

The wets ignored the pleas of the drys. They listened to Tydings, of Maryland. He asked them, "Shall we be a bunch of hypocrites, lashed by the lash of the Anti-Saloon League, in the face of 13 years of dismal failure; or shall we honestly face these facts as they are now presented, and as everyone of us knows them? We have made a failure of this thing." The Senate agreed, and faced the facts. On February 16, 1933, they voted by 63 to 23 to submit the Twenty-first Amendment, which provided for the outright repeal of the Eighteenth, to state conventions for ratification. The only protection allowed to dry states by the Amendment was contained in the second section, which read: *"The transportation or importation into any State, Territory, or possession of the United States for delivery or use therein of intoxicating liquors, in violation of the laws thereof, is hereby prohibited."*[65]

The House debate on the measure on February 20 followed the pattern of the Senate. There were eloquent appeals from the extremists on both sides. For the wets, Celler, of New York, declaimed, "Let us flee from prohibition as one would from a foul dungeon, from a charnel house." For the drys, Blanton, of Texas, exhorted them to "Hold that Line!" Letters and telegrams were swamping him, urging him to fight the great fight to hold that line. It was La Guardia who pointed out gently that the line had been broken. The people and Congress were tired of prohibition. They had more important matters to debate. The wets had won. Nevertheless, "we are now too weary and too law-abiding to celebrate our victory. Congress will now be able to give its undivided attention to economic matters, less controversial but far more important." The division was taken. It gave the wets a victory by 289 votes to 121.[66]

An analysis of the votes on the roll calls in Senate and House show how the wets acquired their new majorities. The North even more preponderantly voted wet. The Midwest voted half wet and half dry, with many members voting wet from the industrial cities of Ohio and Indiana and from the farming lands of Wisconsin and Michigan and Minnesota. Kansas alone remained true to the dry cause, with no wet vote in twenty years. The Far West remained largely dry, although the wets picked up sporadic support there. But it was the heavy defection of the South to the wets that tipped the scales. From the Southern and border states, the wets had only gained 38 votes in the House on the Hobson resolution in 1914; on the question of the Twenty-first Amendment, they gained 104 votes. Only six Senators from these areas had voted against the Eighteenth Amendment; twenty voted in favor of the Twenty-first Amendment. The South had stopped whoring after the false gods of clerical politicians, and had returned to the fold of the Democratic party. So long as the Democratic President was a Protestant and a gentleman, the Solid South would follow his lead on prohibition and on economics. For the Democratic party was the party of the South, right or wrong, but always the party of the South.

In the interim period before the state conventions ratified the Twenty-first Amendment, President Roosevelt and Congress passed a bill allowing the sale of beer at 3.2 per cent of alcohol by volume or less. And the states themselves were quick to ratify the constitutional amendment. The drys at first were confident of holding at least thirteen states for the seven years allowed for ratification. But the apostasy of Southern states such as Alabama, Arkansas, and Texas by large majorities showed that the old arid areas had followed their members of Congress into the wet column. Even Bishop Cannon recognized a "mad stampede for repeal," although he salved dry pride by forecasting the return of national prohibition in the future.[67] On December 5, 1933, Utah became the thirty-sixth state to vote for the Twenty-first Amendment. In the capital of Maryland, a policeman immediately served formal notice on the State House bootlegger to stop his business.[68]

After some fourteen years of trial, national prohibition had been repealed. William Jennings Bryan, the greatest political champion of the drys, had been dead eight years. But Al Smith, the wet leader, was made president of the New York convention for repealing the Eighteenth Amendment. In his speech before the convention, Smith gave exactly the same reason for supporting the Twenty-first Amendment that Bryan had for the Eighteenth, that it was a vindication of the theory of democratic government. The wheel had turned full circle. The drys had once been radicals and democrats; they ended conservatives and autocrats. The wets had once been reactionaries and defenders of the Constitution; they ended as progressives and changers of the Constitution. Only Congress remained constant throughout national prohibition. It hated the nonsensical standards which the drys had inflicted upon politics, and did its best to ignore the matter.

Saloons were restored in 1933 under other names. They were called taverns, bars, cafés, clubs, and rests, but not saloons — except in the Far West, which stuck to the old name. State laws enforced certain regulations on the drinking places. In some states, customers had to be visible from the street. In others, since standing drinkers were supposed to consume double the amount of seated drinkers, the regulars at the bar were forced to squat on small steel toadstools. Swinging doors were no longer legal. Sometimes, only beer of 3.2 per cent of alcohol by volume could be served. Sometimes, saloons were entirely forbidden and retail liquor stores substituted. But, however it was, the bar and bartender, the liquor store dealer and his counter were again broadcast through the land. And they were regulated only as well as the government of each state would allow. The drys had the sole consolation of knowing they had made the word "saloon" an anathema and bad business, while they had failed to change the fact. As a dry pamphlet had warned before repeal, a rose by any other name was still a rose. For the saloon was "simply a place where men drank liquor and more liquor," whether they "painted it white, sold lilies at the door and had Uncle Sam for a bartender."[69]

THE IRRESPONSIBILITY OF THE WETS

WITH THE fanatics leading the drys to destruction, the wets paid them the compliment of imitating their fanaticism and winning the victory. The price of that victory was great — many of the five million alcoholics that now present the United States with one of its worst social problems. For the wet lobbies insisted on outright repeal rather than temperate and moderate repeal legislation. Even though their leaders claimed that "the repeal forces of the country have become the temperance forces of the country," they did not back up their words with acts.[70] It was the pressure of the wet lobbies on the Senate that caused the passage of the Twenty-first Amendment in its naked form, stripped of clauses requiring Congress to take concurrent action with the states to regulate the liquor trade and prevent the return of the saloon. Repeal was ratified haphazardly. The states were left high and wet, each to work out its own method of dealing with strong drink. There was no national monopoly set up to regulate the liquor business and to apply its profits to social welfare projects on the model of the Bratt system of Sweden or the Anderson plan in the *Wickersham Report*. The drink trade was returned to the hands of private interests, which once again sought to influence state legislatures and Congress, thus beginning again the sad cycle of liquor and politics and corruption.

The Association Against the Prohibition Amendment took the credit for the passing of the Twenty-first Amendment in its entirety; it had gained its victory "by bringing to bear every proper influence on Congress."[71] But it had also thrown away the only chance ever given to the federal government to take over a trade, whose misuse could bring great evil, in a year when the federal government could even have taken over the banking system of the country with popular approval. But, as Franklin Roosevelt was the savior of capitalism in the United States, so the Association Against the Prohibition Amendment was the savior of the private drink industry. Indeed, the chief members of the Association were such rock-ribbed conservatives that they refused to endorse Roosevelt against Hoover in 1932, although their constitution demanded that they back the wetter of the two candidates for President. Neither the Association, nor the Crusaders, nor the Voluntary Committee of Lawyers, nor the Hotel Men's Association would come out for Roosevelt, despite their dedication to repeal. Among the leading wet groups, only the Women's Organization for National Prohibition Reform endorsed Roosevelt. Even if the wet women leaders may have preferred Roosevelt as a product of fashionable New York society like themselves, they must be given the credit of being the only major wet organization to put repeal before Republicanism.[72]

With repeal, the fanaticism of the leading wets was turned against the economic and "socialist" measures of the New Deal, especially when it became clear that the drys would never succeed again in forcing through another constitutional amendment. But the fanaticism of the dry lobbies lingered on. Repeal for them was a setback necessary for prohibition's "permanent progress."[73] In January, 1933, they predicted that "within a year or two, the economic issue will have lost its importance and the wet and dry issue will have come to the fore again."[74] They took comfort in the fact that only a little more than one in five of the voting population had actually voted for repeal by state conventions. Among these voters, so the drys claimed, were many sincere prohibitionists who wanted to support Roosevelt's measures for economic recovery and clear the decks for a new counterattack on the evils of drink through a better-phrased constitutional amendment. In true millennial style, the *National Advocate* held out a hope of a glorious future to the prohibitionists. "There have ever been Gethsemanes, Calvaries, crosses and dark tombs. There have also ever been glorious resurrections, heavenly ascensions and a progressive kingdom of God."[75] National prohibition would come again, and would come to a nation prepared to enforce such a great reform properly and decently. For, in the words of Clinton N. Howard, America's one hope was "not in repeal, but in repentance; not in revenue, but in righteousness; not in returning to grog, but in returning to God."[76]

The wets, in their victory, were as arrogant as the drys had been. Like Wayne B. Wheeler, they were in the saddle and they drove through. Like the Anti-Saloon League, they gained support through false propaganda and plain lies. With the onset of the depression, they forgot their argument that prohibition had nothing to do with prosperity. They now said that, since the drys had claimed that prosperity was all their doing, then they were also responsible for the depression. This reasoning fitted in with the popular feeling against the false prophets of business and government, who had claimed too often that they had brought about good times to be able to disavow bad times. As Will Rogers commented sourly and truthfully in 1931:

> What does prohibition amount to, if your neighbors children are not eating? Its food, not drink is our problem now. We were so afraid the poor people might drink, now we fixed it so they can't eat. . . . The working classes didn't bring this on, it was the big boys that thought the financial drunk was going to last forever.[77]

With fourteen million unemployed, what worthy laborer without hire was going to believe the preacher who said that prohibition was the God-given remedy for keeping everyone in their jobs? When there was no work, what worker was going to credit the word of Ford that booze was bad for workers? After the slump, the images of preachers and businessmen as the voices of incontrovertible authority had cracked. Their pipings for teetotalism were jeered and ignored. The Anti-Saloon League and Wall Street had committed worse sins by more immoral methods than any occasional drunkard. All the dry horses and all the rich men could not put the shell of prohibition together again.

Yet the collapse of the drys along with the boom hardly excused the wets for misleading the United States over the economic reasons for repeal. The arguments of the Association Against the Prohibition Amendment were gravely misleading. Although jobs for some quarter of a million people were created directly by the return of the legal trade in liquor, and although some three-quarters of a million more men were benefited in the service trades connected with liquor, an equal number of bootleggers and alky cookers lost their jobs at the same time. Although bootlegging continued throughout the thirties because of unemployment and existing plant, it operated on a diminished scale.

Moreover, the farmers were not helped by repeal. Even if many farmers voted for repeal, thinking that "the opening up of the breweries and distilleries of the United States means prosperity for the farmer and the nation," only crops of barley, rye, and hops had an increased sale.[78] If anything, repeal hurt those farmers who made a profitable sideline out of moonshining, without doing anything to alleviate the distress caused by the slump in world food prices. When a national director of the Association Against the Prohibition Amendment assured farmers in North Dakota that prohibition had destroyed half of their resources, and that repeal would let them keep their money at home and sell their crops well and value their land at its true high value, he was guilty of the same biased exaggeration which the drys had shown in the Great War by promising the people victory over Germany as the return of prohibition.[79]

Repeal exposed yet another wet falsehood. The wets had accused prohibition of costing hundreds of million of dollars to enforce over the years. But the cost of enforcement of the liquor laws in the United States after the passage of the Twenty-first Amendment was hardly less than it had been before, since the volume of bootlegging was still large. In addition, a further disappointment was suffered by the wealthy backers of the wets, who had supposed that their taxes would be lowered after repeal. The huge spending of the New Deal Programs increased taxes on the wealthy, so that the opponents of prohibition became the opponents of the New Deal. For the taxes caused by the second were even greater than the taxes caused by the first. It was a sad May Day in 1936 for Al Smith, when his name was paraded around New York on a swastika, in company with the names of three other notorious and wealthy wets, Du Pont and Mellon and Hearst. The defenders of liberty against Hoover had become the defenders of reaction against Roosevelt, in the name of their morality and their taxes.

From the point of view of taxation, the prohibition crusade throughout had led to some strange situations. The fact that the Protestant churches had engaged in political activity during their fight for the

Eighteenth Amendment sparked off proposals that they should be taxed like other political organizations. The tax-exempt churches resisted this proposal with all their power, although they did not cease from political activity. The cities, too, had objected, in the days before the Eighteenth Amendment, that when the country districts of a state went dry the taxes levied in the wet cities of the state were used to enforce the very law which they opposed. The thing was ridiculous.

Yet the strangest situation of all had been rendered legal by a decision of the Supreme Court. The Court had ruled that the Bureau of Internal Revenue had the right to request income-tax returns from bootleggers. The Court saw no reason "why the fact that a business is unlawful should exempt it from paying the tax that if lawful it would have to pay." In the argument of the case, it was even suggested that bribes paid to government officials might be held deductible as business expenses.[80] To this day, the bootleggers of the last dry state in the Union, Mississippi, pay federal income tax and a state tax on their illegal profits.

PROFIT AND LOSS

The Eighteenth Amendment was voted in and voted out by Congress in unusual times. The war hysteria of 1917 was partly responsible for the large dry majorities in the Sixty-fifth Congress, the mentality of depression for the wet landslide in the Seventy-second. Both majorities were obtained by false economic promises, false appeals to patriotism, and false pleas for democracy. The Eighteenth Amendment was urged as a means of allowing the people to vote on the question of prohibition; the Twenty-first likewise. The Eighteenth Amendment was meant to put a sober America to work in winning the war; the Twenty-first to put a drinking America to work in defeating the depression. Both wet and dry oratory was equally misleading, from the cry of Congressman Hersey, of Maine, in 1917 to the chimera of Congressman Linthicum in 1932. Hersey had hoped that it would never be said of America that she sent her soldier boys to die to save democracy for the world, but herself she could not save.[81] Linthicum had said, "Pass this resolution, and depression will fade away like the mists before the noonday sun. The immorality of the country, racketeering, and bootlegging will be a thing of the past."[82] Prohibition did not save America, nor did repeal end immorality, racketeering, bootlegging, and the depression. The crime of Congress was in believing the panaceas of its members, when desperate times encouraged a belief in simple and fallacious and exaggerated remedies.

The economic claims of the wets were as biased and false as those of the drys. Neither the loss nor the gain of prohibition can be calculated in terms of dollars and cents. There can be no wholly reliable statistics of the volume and worth of the illegal liquor trade. Nor can there be any statistics of the exact value of prohibition in helping the United States to continue its period of prosperity throughout the twenties.

Some things are, however, sure. In strictly economic terms, prohibition helped the poorer people of America. The testimony of social workers is practically unanimous that during the first few years of the "experiment, noble in motive," the health and wealth of the workers of America increased and their drunkenness decreased. As one social worker wrote, "Formerly, drunkenness was taken for granted; now it is regarded as a problem." The price of this economic gain was the resentment of the poor against the "rich man's law" of prohibition, the murderous deaths of thousands of workers from foul bootleg concoctions, and the demoralization of their children by teaching them continual and open defiance of the law. "The illegal liquor traffic," as another social worker wrote, "appears to have a fascination for these youngsters whether they actually participate in it or not."[83]

It is also sure that prohibition did nothing to help the middle classes or the rich of America. In fact, they turned against it, except in those rural areas where the prohibitionists were still strong. The increase of the federal income tax and the abolition of the liquor tax made very seductive the wet argument that prohibition was costing the country two million dollars a day in taxes.[84] Even the industrialists of America, whose favorable statements were quoted by the drys in the thousands before the depression, deserted to the standard of the wets. The arguments for the increased productivity of a sober labor force lost their impact with the inefficient enforcement of the dry law and with the promised business benefits of repeal.

The failure of the drys, too, was also an economic one. At a critical moment in its career, the year of 1932, the Anti-Saloon League found itself short of funds. Its own bank in Westerville failed. As the *California Liberator* confessed, "The depression has hit the Anti-Saloon League just as it has hit every other agency. We must roll responsibility on the friends of prohibition as never before. Sacrificial service must be added to sacrificial giving."[85] But the friends of prohibition were hard hit too, and the siren song of wet propaganda was very appealing. Some lifelong drys voted wet in 1932 and 1933, in order to put an end to the depression through repeal, before regrouping their forces to fight for national prohibition once again. They had been convinced by the continuous wet campaign, now supported by the wealthy industrialists of America, as the drys had once been. This campaign aimed to lay every ill in the United States at the door of prohibition. A sympathetic member of Congress outlined the basic principle of the wets.

> Every time a crime is committed, they cry prohibition. Every time a girl or a boy goes wrong, they shout prohibition. Every time a policeman or politician is accused of corruption, they scream prohibition. As a result, they are gradually building up in the public mind the impression that prohibition is a major cause of all the sins of society.[86]

By 1932, this image was fixed in the popular mind. The people of America were persuaded that, with repeal, sin and depression would disappear from the land.

Of course, sin and depression remained in the land. Repeal did not solve the problems of America any more than prohibition had done. Thus, the drys accused the wets of having bought repeal by lies and millions of dollars. They had deluded the people into error. Yet, it was the dry James A. White who had invented the slogan, "No money is tainted if the Anti-Saloon League can get its hands on it."[87] It was the dry Wayne B. Wheeler who had calculated that the Eighteenth Amendment cost $50,000,000 to secure; another $15,000,000 was spent during the life of the amendment, making a total of $65,000,000; yet repeal had cost only $20,000,000.[88] It was the drys who invented the tactics of political pressure that the wets exploited so efficiently in their turn. It was the drys who claimed that prohibition would bring prosperity to American industry; the wets merely followed their example. Fanaticism bred fanaticism. The benificee was the liquor trade, which returned after repeal to the same position of power that it had held before prohibition. And Viscountess Astor, who said that the United States was wet when called dry and hoped that it would be dry when called wet, was disappointed.[89]

Three years after repeal, there appeared a good and detailed study of its consequences. The study found that women and the young drank much the same as in the prohibition era; businessmen drank less on week ends, and the poor and the respectable drank more. The opportunity for efficient regulation of the liquor traffic had been let slip at the end of repeal. Although this was partly due to the weakness of the drys after 1932 and to the strength of the fanatical wets, it was also due to the indifference of the American people.

> The general public, having, with a feeling of immense relief, voted for repeal, were singularly apathetic about the precise control methods which were then to be established. People had become tired of liquor as a topic of conversation, a topic which had claimed so much attention during prohibition, and were content to let the subject drop.[90]

In this lassitude about liquor laws, this infinite weariness about the evils or virtues of drink, the crazy quilt of American regulations for drinking was allowed to develop haphazardly, a tribute to the interaction between a powerful and dangerous drink trade, a preoccupied federal government, inadequate local administrations, and an indifferent people. If much of the present liquor problem in America is the price of dry laws, too hastily adopted and too hastily repealed, then the fault must be put to a national characteristic, an urge towards excess which has made this nation great in a small time, and has left little room for moderation.

The Blighted Roots

> The League was born of God, it has been led by Him, and we will fight on while He leads.
>
> F. Scott McBride

THE WETS were flabbergasted that repeal of prohibition came so suddenly and unexpectedly. Many of the leaders of the wets in 1931 did not expect repeal within ten years, if ever. Even after repeal, they feared that prohibition might return again. But, had they considered carefully, they would have seen that the return of prohibition was impossible. Many of its roots suffered from an enduring blight.

The tragedy of the prohibition movement was that it lost the support of moderates and liberals and became a revolutionary faction. The leadership of the movement, which included many intelligent reformers with wide social interests, such as Frances Willard and Jane Addams, Josephus Daniels, and Charles Stelzle, was taken over by extremists, who mistook the support of moderates against the saloon for their support in banning liquor altogether. The camp followers of prohibition always contained an extreme element, but the cause was not lost until the fanatics became the chieftains. The death of the supple Wayne B. Wheeler in 1928 left the image of the movement to farce and exaggeration, which the press exploited in the antics of Bishop James Cannon, Jr., Mabel Walker Willebrandt, and Ella A. Boole. Intelligent moderates, even though they might be personal teetotalers, turned against this dry caricature, which claimed to represent them. The leadership and membership of the drys were taken increasingly from lower social and economic groups.[1] The wealthy classes left the movement, including even the stern Rockefellers. Fanatics from the lower middle classes carried on the dry cause. Prohibition, which had always attracted bigots, ended by yielding to their domination.

Wheeler, although bitterly attacked during his lifetime, was respected for his genius at political manipulation. He was even liked by his political enemies. James M. Cox, who found Purley A. Baker, of the League, utterly without character and moved only by thought of self, revealed an unwilling admiration for Wheeler. He "would make any combination, would cohabit politically with the devil himself, to win."[2] Other wets paid tribute to Wheeler's likability and subtlety. Even Alfred E. Smith found that he had a "friendly personal attitude."[3] But once Wheeler was dead, Bishop Cannon took over the limelight with all of Wheeler's flair for personal publicity and little of his gift for political management. His trial before Congress and the council of the Southern Methodist Episcopal Church on charges of immorality, flour hoarding in the Great War, misuse of campaign funds, and speculation on the stock market did not help the dry cause, even though he was acquitted on all charges.

Some idea of the virulence stirred up against Cannon can be seen in the remarks of Senator Bruce, of Maryland, and Matthew Woll, of the American Federation of Labor. Bruce trumpeted:

> God forbid that any clergyman of this kind should ever come near me for the purpose of exercising any office that appertains to his profession. . . . Just as soon would I have a raven perched upon the head of my bed as to have such a clergyman approach me in my last agony. If he were to preach a funeral sermon over my corpse, I believe that like Lazarus, I would throw aside the cerements of the grave and come back to life in indignant resurrection.[4]

The fact that a bishop of the church refused to testify on certain matters before a congressional committee made him even more culpable. Matthew Woll told the Wickersham Commission that he did not know of any one who had done more damage than Cannon to respect for federal law, "because when we find a man in that position entering into the wet and dry controversy, and refusing to answer or challenging the authority of the Government to question him; if the church can defy the law and authorities, why can not everyone else?"[5] Indeed, Cannon became such a hated symbol of the League that Captain Stayton nominated him as the man most responsible for the repeal of the Eighteenth Amendment.[6]

By their refusal to compromise after their victory with the Eighteenth Amendment, the drys alienated the support of the psychologically tolerant, who had only supported them against the evils of the saloon and the trade in liquor, not against liquor itself. The definition in the Volstead Act that "intoxicating" meant one-half of 1 per cent of alcohol by volume, less than the alcoholic content of sauerkraut, was bad politics and bad psychology. Rollin Kirby's famous caricatures of the prohibitionist as a beak-nosed, top-hatted, etiolated, black string-bean, carrying an umbrella, seemed to be true, once the fanaticism of the victorious drys was revealed. The *Christian Century* itself admitted at the close of 1931 that the prohibitionists had "invited such a caricature and lent plausibility to it."[7]

Moreover, the wets were better at appealing to the temper of the times in the twenties. When the popular mood demanded laughter and Mayor Jimmy Walker and *What Price Glory?* in place of patriotism, the wet magazines such as the *Periscope* switched to mockery and good humor at the expense of their opponents. By these means, the wets won over to their side the psychologically tolerant and moderate, who were disgruntled more by the excesses of prohibition than they had been by the excesses of the saloon. The old-time liquor trade no longer seemed to be the vicious bloodsucker of the economy, the Shylock of society who gouged the wages from the honest workingman. It could complain, in all fairness, that it was the only business expropriated without compensation in a free capitalist country. Thus, when the depression came and wet propaganda claimed that repeal of the Eighteenth Amendment would put a million men back to work, restoration of a regulated liquor trade seemed economically and morally sound, just as its suppression had seemed so in time of war.

The wets won their eventual victory through injured innocence and sweet reason. They appealed both to the psychology of boom, when people wanted liquor to enjoy themselves, and slump, when they wanted liquor to forget themselves. Prosperity, as Frederick Lewis Allen pointed out, is more than an economic condition; it is a state of mind.[8] So is depression. Repeal came with startling suddenness because of the collapse of the national psychology along with the Stock Exchange. Conditions all over America paralleled those noticed by a Middletown businessman.

> I don't know whether it was the depression, but in the winter of '29-'30 and in '30-'31 things were roaring here. There was much drunkenness — people holding these bathtub gin parties. There was a great increase in women's drinking and drunkenness. And there was a lot of sleeping about by married people and a number of divorces resulted.

The same man noted that "drinking of the early-depression blatant sort" let up with repeal, although in the first days of repeal there were long lines standing at the store counters waiting to buy liquor.[9]

Freud put forward the hypothesis that many societies, like many people, might become neurotic under the pressures of civilization.[10] The demands of the ethical norms required by a social system create so many neuroses in so many individuals that the whole society may become neurotic. This hypothesis helps to explain the hysteria of the

LAW ENFORCEMENT

America of the jazz age and the prohibition era. The ethic of the time was in such discord with the fact that the conflict created in the individual made him prey to many disorders. The huge increase of the influence of psychoanalysis in the twenties points to a mass disturbance in the minds of Americans of the time. The crack-up in the life of F. Scott Fitzgerald, as he knew, was paralleled by the crack-up of his contemporaries, when the new gods of business failed and the old God was dead. The answer of the thirties should be a sober qualified happiness, not a forbidden spree. Liquor should be regulated and taxed, not totally banned and openly bootlegged.

Freud opposed prohibition because he knew that conflict between the individual and society was inevitable. There could be no dry millennium, however desirable it might appear to be. "It almost seems as if humanity could be most successfully united into one great whole if there were no need to trouble about the happiness of individuals."[11] But there is always need to trouble about the happiness of individuals. If any government tries to ban any particular form of happiness for any people, many will revolt in order to continue that habit of happiness. The old American belief in Adam, in a Garden of Eden on American soil, in the perfectability of the New World, in Rousseau's dangerous dictum that there is nothing bad that cannot be made good for something — such a dream of coerced paradise on earth is an illusion. For the only way to gain a paradise on earth is to persecute those who stand in the way of that paradise. The means of making a nation better than other nations often make it worse.

National prohibition is the reform which best demonstrated a curious ambivalence in the American character. There seemed to be a genuine desire for an ideal to be enacted into law, coupled with an equally genuine need to break that ideal law. As Rudyard Kipling wrote of the American, there was a "cynic devil in his blood . . . that bids him flout the Law he makes, that bids him make the Law he flouts."[12] It was as though America, conscious of the continual violence in her land, demanded stern regulation which she could not obey. Her urge to reform could only be allayed by the actual proof that reform did not work. The repeal of prohibition proved the truth of Mr. Dooley's remark, "What we call this here counthry iv ours pretinds to want to thry new experiments, but a sudden change gives it a chill. It's been to th' circus an' bought railroad tickets in a hurry so often that it thinks quick change is short change."[13] America may try many experiments, but it only tries failure once.

NEW EVIDENCE

THE OLD dry propaganda on medicine and venereal diseases, which had terrified voters into supporting the cause of prohibition, became increasingly ineffective. Indeed, the teaching of the drys seemed, in the light of new scientific research, as much of a caricature as their psychology. Their onetime standbys — the textbooks on hygiene, the doctrines of eugenics, the fear of syphilis, the rights of women, and the endorsement of the American Medical Association — were transmuted into weak or downright antagonistic elements in society.

Teachers' associations, which cared that children should be taught the truth, began to weed out dry horror propaganda from textbooks on hygiene. The percentage of space in these texts which was devoted to the topics of alcohol and tobacco declined to 2.7 in 1935 compared with 12.9 in 1910 and 13.4 in 1885.[14] The old texts

> . . . were literally "dripping wet" from alcohol and "reeked" with the odor of tobacco. On the title page, in the preface, the bulk of the introduction, a part of every chapter, one complete chapter, the glossary and index, the subject of alcohol and narcotics was presented prominently, seriously, diligently, and thoroughly with their morbid and demoralizing effects.[15]

Gradually, however, physiology and hygiene were no longer presented as subordinate branches of temperance teaching. The foundation of the Yale School of Alcohol Studies and the declining power of the Woman's Christian Temperance Union after repeal finally ensured a fair and reasonable treatment of the topics of alcohol and narcotics in most public schools. The Union, however, still sends its literature to many thousands of classrooms, telling of Mr. Intoxicants and Messrs. Pancreatic and Intestinal Juices, of Mrs. Gray Bunny and her six hoppy little teetotal bunnies, and of the victim of the nicotine weed who is a "cowardly worm twitching with dependence."

The supporters of eugenics did win some victories in the twenties. The immigration acts of 1921 and 1924, based on the false and racist findings of the Dillingham Commission and the Laughlin report, did restrict immigration into America in favor of the "Anglo-Saxon" peoples. But after the depression, economics took over from eugenics as the chief scientific interest of laymen. Moreover, racist assumptions were profoundly antagonistic to the philosophy of the New Deal. This philosophy assumed that men were equal and should be helped equally, whether they were "Anglo-Saxons," Balkan immigrants, or Negroes. People were ashamed of Madison Grant's praise of Nordic supermen and Lothrop Stoddard's fear of the "vast hordes of poor mongrelized creatures [from] the festering purlieus of Old World cities and the filthy villages of backward countrysides."[16] A feeling of equality comes more easily when the many are poor. The racist movements of the thirties such as the Silver Shirts seemed to be a threat to American institutions and democracy, not a defense of them. Although the extreme drys remained faithful to the last by commending the Nazi policy of the sterilization of the racially unfit and by praising Hitler as a "devoted teetotaler," few people listened to them any more.[17]

The drys lost another weapon when medical research increasingly confirmed the fact that alcohol did not attack the reproductive organs in human beings. Liquor in parents was not a menace to unborn children. A drunken mother could still have healthy babies. In addition, national prohibition did not reduce the number of feeble-minded children or the number of cases of venereal disease, which rose throughout the early twenties to an annual total of nearly half a million reported cases. Winfield Scott Hall, a devoted dry, was still lamenting after eight years of the dry reform, "Close to half our population are suffering in some degree — slightly or seriously — the ravage of that scourge which an outraged Mother Nature visits upon those who have broken her law of chastity."[18]

Indeed, prohibition did nothing directly to combat the huge amount of venereal diseases prevalent in the United States. After the moralistic efforts of the American Purity Alliance to fight the evil had culminated in its merger with the more scientific American Federation for Sex Hygiene in 1914, the war brought all the strength of patriotism to the reform. Venereal diseases were accused of being as secret, treacherous, and heartless as submarines. In 1918, the passage of the Chamberlain-Kahn bill in Congress set up a Division of Venereal Diseases in the United States Public Health Service, with an appropriation of more than four million dollars. By 1931, some 850 clinics had been founded, employing the Salvarsan and neo-Salvarsan remedies, which were far more effective than the old mercury cure. Although the Lynds discovered that Middletown doctors opposed the state clinics in order to keep the profits of curing venereal diseases to themselves, great progress was made in eliminating the evil during the twenties.

Eventually, venereal disease became such a problem in the depression that the American Institute of Public Opinion took a Gallup poll on the subject in 1935. The poll showed that a majority of the public wanted the topic discussed openly. The *Reader's Digest* published an article in July, 1936, "Why Don't We Stamp Out Syphilis?" This was followed by two popular books, *Shadow on the Land: Syphilis*, and the sensational *Ten Million Americans Have It*. The author of the first was Surgeon-General of the Public Health Services. He revealed that there were six million cases of syphilis in America. Every year, sixty thousand babies were born with congenital syphilis. Half of those who contracted the disease contracted it innocently.[19]

After these revelations, a full-scale campaign was launched against venereal diseases. After three centuries of misrepresentation, the illness was at last named and recognized. Indeed, the drys had helped by crusading against the menace in the first place. But prohibition was not the way to deal with syphilis. Penicillin was discovered, and the last great plague brought under control.

Perhaps nothing hit the ideology of the drys harder than the huge success of the Women's Organization for National Prohibition Reform, which boasted over a million members before it was disbanded with the repeal of prohibition. The first party which had asked for female suffrage in its platform, the Prohibition party, ended by being totally repudiated by many of the sex that it had sought to aid. Likewise, the leaders of the women's crusade had hoped to save America from male corruption and evil by the ballot. Their followers retorted by voting nine times out of ten in the same way as their husbands.

Dry propaganda depended on one premise, that good women did not enjoy drinking liquor. By definition, a woman was bad who did enjoy strong drink. This viewpoint made such drinking as there was among bourgeois city women in the nineteenth century a clandestine affair. Patent medicines were a great source of the supply of alcohol; when Lydia E. Pinkham's famous remedy for female ills was first analyzed, it was found to contain nearly one-fifth pure alcohol. Edward Bok, of the *Ladies Home Journal*, wrote to fifty members of the Woman's Christian Temperance Union and found that three out of four used patent medicines which had an alcoholic content of one-eighth to one-half pure spirits.[20] In fact, the general use of alcohol by women after the passing of prohibition seems to argue a surreptitious taste for liquor before. Although many women began their drinking in the speak-easies, some were merely doing openly what they had done before at home.

Drinking by women in industrial areas was always prevalent. A social worker who lived in the grim Lighthouse district of Philadelphia wrote of the era before prohibition:

> It is false to assume that women do not share the moral standards of their country, their class, and their neighborhood. The men drank at night and the women drank by day, gathering in this one's and that one's kitchen, supplied from the corner saloon where they carried their kettles. When too drunk to navigate thither themselves they sent the children as their messengers, who received their share on their return.[21]

Conditions did not improve during prohibition. Bootlegging became such a profitable sideline for housewives that great numbers took to the trade, both as manufacturers and carriers. Many speak-easies in New York were located in the front parlor of "first-floor flats," which still served as ordinary homes. Indeed, the widespread manufacture of home-brew during prohibition put children even more in contact with liquor than they had been during the days of the saloon.

Yet the drys ignored all evidence contrary to their creed, and insisted that only prostitutes and the selfish daughters of the rich drank illegally. The vast majority of the female race were virtuous. If only women were educated to see their own advantage, they would refuse to touch liquor. As late as 1929, Ella A. Boole admitted to only three sorts of women who opposed prohibition: those deceived by the wet newspapers, the "women of the underworld, with illiterate aliens from wine-growing countries, who cannot be counted upon for moral or patriotic issues," and a small, privileged class of self-centered women who held themselves above moral and civil law. Women as a whole were far too responsible to touch a drop of liquor, even if they were less clever than men.

> Men think logically, women biologically. The preservation of the race rests with the woman. Her instinct to protect the child leads her to deny herself privileges and liberties that injure the child. The woman's major reason for no repeal or modification of the Eighteenth Amendment is found in one word — "Children."[22]

The prohibitionists, by their preliminary backing of women's rights, found themselves burned by their own torch of freedom. The dry plea that the abolition of liquor would save the mother and the home became ridiculous when mothers sold liquor to provide an income for the home. With genetic and medical arguments against alcohol losing their vigor in the twenties, the drys could no longer scare the more sophisticated women into teetotalism for the sake of their babies. The connection between prostitution and the saloon no longer terrified a sex which now accompanied its menfolk into the speak-easy. In fact, prohibition did not reduce the number of whores in America; the number fell because of the very competition of the respectable women whom prohibition was designed to protect.* Efficient and popular methods of contraception allayed many of the sexual terrors of women, who had remained chaste less for fear of hell than for fear of pregnancy. The drys, by helping the emancipation of women, helped their own defeat. They had not foreseen that women, in demanding the rights of men, might also demand the right to drink, saying with Dorothy Parker that the Nineteenth Amendment came just too late to stop the Eighteenth.

But the unkindest cut of all to the drys came when the doctors of America reversed their position over the medicinal value of beverage alcohol. In 1921, after prohibition was safely part of the Constitution, the American Medical Association reconsidered its resolution declaring that liquor had no therapeutic value. Faced with attack from the spokesmen of the drys and with mounting opposition from the rank

---

* Because of the competition of enfranchised womanhood and the pressure of the Woman's Christian Temperance Union, only one official red-light district remained in the United States by 1925. That district was in Reno, Nevada.

RARE BEFORE PROHIBITION

COMMON DURING PROHIBITION

and file of American doctors, who were making a fortune in prescribing liquor for the ills of their patients, the leadership of the Association changed its mind. In 1921, the Council of the Association refused to confirm the resolution of 1917. In 1922, it adopted a report declaring that it was "unwise to attempt to determine moot scientific questions by resolution or by vote."[23] The report recommended that the Congress of the United States should take no action on the therapeutic value of alcohol. The doctors of America were, and should be, a law unto themselves on medical matters.

For the doctors had fallen out with the drys. In the first six months after the passing of the Volstead Act, more than 15,000 physicians and 57,000 druggists and drug manufacturers had applied for licenses to prescribe and sell intoxicating liquor.[24] The law-enforcement agencies of the government were insufficient to check the credentials of all the applicants. During this period, more than half a million doctors' prescriptions for whisky were issued in Chicago alone; the Treasury Department thought that over half of these prescriptions evaded the spirit or letter of the Volstead Act.[25] The notorious king of the bootleggers, George Remus, bought up chains of drugstores so that he could order truckloads of medicinal liquor and hijack his own drink on the road. The scandals about liquor, druggists, and doctors grew to such proportions that the prohibitionists had to proceed against their old supporters.

At the end of the Wilson administration, Attorney General Palmer had ruled that the Volstead Act placed no limit on the amount of beer and wine which doctors could prescribe to their patients. The drys, who still hoped in 1921 to banish all liquor from the United States, were angered by this ruling. They retaliated by forcing the Willis-Campbell Act through Congress, which had a dry majority in both houses. The Act forbade the prescription of beer as a medicine and limited the issuing of wine and hard liquor by doctors to one-half pint of alcohol for each patient every ten days. No doctor could issue more than one hundred prescriptions for liquor in ninety days unless some extraordinary reason made a larger amount necessary.[26]

The druggists and doctors of America called the act an attack on their professional integrity. It was also an attack on their profits. Since the Willis-Campbell Act remained on the statute books, the American Medical Association began to proceed against the prohibitionists. In addition to passing resolutions that alcohol might still be good for therapy, the Association polled nearly 54,000 doctors to discover how widespread the use of alcohol actually was in the field of medicine. It received 31,000 replies. Half of the doctors thought whisky was a necessary therapeutic agent, and one-quarter approved of the prescription of beer and wine. In addition, a quarter of the doctors said that they had seen cases of unnecessary suffering or death caused by bootleg liquor and the prohibition laws. Significantly, doctors in large cities were more in favor of alcohol than those in small towns and the countryside.

The physicians of America continued to prescribe strong drink for their patients throughout prohibition. In 1928, the Bureau of Prohibition reported that nearly seventy thousand doctors used alcohol prescription books, even if the amount of medical liquor was only a small proportion of the total liquor in circulation. During the fourteen years of prohibition, an annual average of ten million doctors' prescriptions for more than one million wine gallons of liquor soothed the ailments of sick Americans.[27] But the licensed pharmacists of America were being hard hit by the competition of the pirate drugstores, which were springing up all over the country and adding to the peculiarly American phenomenon of stores containing a soda fountain, a magazine stand, a counter for beauty products and biologicals, and an office for medical prescriptions all in one. Many of the new drugstores of the twenties took over the desirable corner sites of the old saloons and performed some of their functions. They provided a meeting place, partially satisfied the craving for social drinking with ice-cream sodas, and often sold illegal hair tonics to those with an urge for alcohol in any form.

Thus the prohibitionists alienated both the doctors and the pharmacists. The doctors were antagonized by the insistence of the drys that the prohibition laws could be enforced only when physicians submitted to regulation. The pharmacists were angered by the failure of the drys to enforce the laws and to eliminate the competition of drugstores which pretended to sell chemical products as a cover for selling alcohol. Long before 1933, both doctors and druggists realized that their efforts to gain a monopoly of beverage alcohol were unsuccessful. They welcomed repeal as a method of putting a moral front on their professions, discredited by the alcohol controversy. Moreover, new sources of income were appearing for the medical trade. Specialization, new hospitals, restricted entry into the profession at a time of expanding population, and laws putting many drugs under the power of a doctor's prescription, all forced medical fees upwards.[29] The pharmacists also benefited by the increasing dependence of Americans on pharmaceutical products. The trend has continued to the present day, when the drug manufacturers and doctors and pharmacists are among the most highly paid and privileged members of the community.

Thus the drys, in the years following the Eighteenth Amendment, were deserted by medical research, by textbooks on hygiene, and by the majority of women and doctors. The popular support of the dry cause dwindled throughout national prohibition and after repeal. The new society and morality of the urban twenties appeared to make prohibition and the ethics of the small town grotesque, antiquated, and downright disgusting. And when the slump came, rural discontent, which had provided much of the backing of prohibition, was swallowed up in the vast maw of urban discontent. When country and city alike were poor, prohibition seemed an idiotic hang-over from a lost past, something to be repealed and forgotten, a barrier equally in the way of New Deal economic reform and standpat defense of the liberties of the individual. The dry George Trimble wrote the epitaph of his whole cause from his grave in the cemetery of Spoon River.

> *For the radicals grew suspicious of me,*
> *And the conservatives were never sure of me —*
> *And here I lie, unwept of all.*[29]

Epilogue

I'd be afraid to enther upon a crusade against vice f'r fear I might prefer it to th' varchous life iv a rayspictable liquor dealer.

FINLEY PETER DUNNE

If you favor prohibition, you are a fanatic; if you don't, you are a criminal; and if you don't care either way, you haven't enough brains to form a conviction.

Portland (Maine) *Express*

IN THE BEGINNING was the farm, and the farm was God. This was the faith of the writers of the Constitution, of Thomas Jefferson, of Andrew Jackson. This was the cornerstone which the colonists used to build their free America, partly upon the earth and wholly within their minds. This was the good life which the pioneers sought along with their profits in the virgin lands; they would murder and dispossess the red Indians for such a good life. This was the myth which American preachers and politicians served with their lips during the nineteenth century, while the propagandists of Europe were turning from nostalgia for a rural golden age to euphoria about the urban age of steel. This was the creed that set piedmont against tidewater, West against East, debtor against Bank of America, Know-Nothing against learning, Populist against boss politics, country against city. This worship of a whitewashed past, this desperate clutch on a threatened present, this fear of a defeated future, made prohibition a crusade of the old Eden against the devils of the new Babylon. The Eighteenth Amendment was one of the last victories of the village pulpit against the factory proletariat, of the Corn Belt against the conveyor belt. When prohibition was finally repealed, a new civilization of national control and contact had taken over the local and distinct customs of general store and Main Street. In the end was the city, and the city was godless.

The wets and the cities showed the same arrogant righteousness in

413

victory that the drys and the country had done. When a wet in 1927 gibed that the Statue of Liberty was rightly represented as turning her back on America, he was speaking also for the drys and the villages of America after repeal. The conquest of the prohibitionists by the revived liquor trade was as merciless and unforgiving as their own conquest of the liquor trade had been. It was the tragedy of the drys that the revolution in technology and communications made impossible the dry law in the very decade in which it was passed. National prohibition came as soon as it could, but its coming was already too late. As de Tocqueville had noted in early America, it was not virtue which was great but temptation which was small. Temptation now flooded the land, and virtue was at the ebb.

The total failure of national prohibition, its passing into limbo as though it had never been, demands an answer to the question, Could it have been preserved? It could not, unless its supporters had been willing to compromise. But the reform was born in excess, and it perished by excess. If the leaders of the drys had accepted the plan of the winner of the Hearst Contest of 1929, which provided for the modification of the Volstead Act to allow the sale of light wines and beer, they might have satisfied labor and the majority of their countrymen to this day. But it was all or nothing for the drys, so that they ended with nothing.

The drys were fond of using the Biblical statement, "What is a man profited, if he shall gain the whole world, and lose his own soul?" Perhaps they should have heeded the statement themselves. If they had always concentrated on preaching the virtues of temperance and abstinence to men's souls, they would have preserved the high reputation of the Protestant churches in the United States and would have increased the considerable number of those religious people who were personally temperate. But they gave up their campaign of education for a campaign of political and legal coercion. They sought to gain the whole world by human laws. In the words of two of their leaders, "Both prohibition and anti-prohibition are like Bolshevism in that they are so aggressive that they must conquer the world or die in the world."[1] Obsessed by their impossible mission, the drys forgot their duty of mercy and charity towards society in the zealous pursuit of the drinking sinner. For the sake of fourteen years of the inefficient legal prohibition of the liquor trade in the United States, the dry movement passed from moderation to excess, and lost its own soul. For the enduring soul of man is a temperate thing.

Prohibition sought to regulate human morality and human habits. But the trouble with moral legislation is that it does not keep to the limits set by reasonable and respectable men. While there can be no theoretical limit to social laws against immorality, in practice their limit is set by the customs of the society which they are meant to regulate. When certain excessive laws become clubs or will-o'-the-wisps, instruments of real terror or invisible threat, the whole image of the law suffers. Too much enforcement of an unpopular law breeds resentment; too little breeds mockery. The only cure, then, for a law which no one wishes to obey is repeal or compulsion or re-education of the nation. If the law remains on the statute books, the resistance of the people will bring about resistance to other laws. Moral legislation should be limited in practice by the possible means of enforcement, for these means of enforcement are limited in turn by the laws which the respectable members of a society will agree to help enforce.

These limitations on the power of government presuppose the failure of prohibition in any democracy where the drinking of alcohol is a normal part of the life of many people. At the present time, India is also trying out "an experiment, noble in motive." Its chances of temporary success are better, although they are still unlikely to succeed in the long run. Prohibition can flourish only in those areas where there are strong religious and traditional sanctions against the use of liquor. The Hindu religion does possess these sanctions. But the inevitable industrial revolution which will overtake India, the massing of the peasants in the cities, the creation of an urban proletariat and middle class, and the breakdown of religious taboos will lead to a rise in the consumption of alcohol and the end of effective prohibition. At the best, prohibition can only work moderately well in rural and settled societies. It must fail in the crowd of the streets. For alcohol is easy to make and simple to sell and pleasant to consume, and few men will refuse so facile a method of escaping from the miseries of living.

The worst hang-over of prohibition in the United States has been the criminal control of large areas of American business and labor. After repeal, the infiltration of the bootlegging gangs into unions and gambling and extortion rackets increased steadily, as their state organizations centralized still further into national syndicates. The present division of America into four parts, each under a gang, sometimes a thousand strong, is the penultimate stage of the centralization of crime in America, which the profits of prohibition and modern communications have made possible. The Italian-Jewish syndicate of New York and Florida, the Cincinnati-Detroit-Canadian gambling group, the remnants of the Capone mob in Chicago, and the Chinese-American syndicate on the Pacific Coast are the heirs of prohibition days. So are the racketeering labor unions, whose integrity had hardly been penetrated before prohibition, but was dented during prohibition, and suffered badly after prohibition from gangsters seeking new sources of income.

The lessons of prohibition are plain. The fine frenzy of a minority, a long period of indoctrination, a powerful pressure group, and a state of national fear can cause the adoption of an ill-considered reform. But the success of an unpopular change is illusory, a mere string of words on a document. Enforcement is all. Moreover, the triumph of a moral cause often leads to the falling away of its followers. They think that the affair is finished. Once the Eighteenth Amendment was passed, the drys, in the accusation of Senator Barkley, of Kentucky, "celebrated throughout the country the death of John Barleycorn and baked their feet at a warm fire, retired to bed, and thanked the Almighty that it was all over."[2] In the struggle is the union. In the victory is the division. In the defeat is the end.

Acknowledgments

THREE MEN have encouraged me to begin, continue, and end this work. Their advice and corrections have been invaluable, although all errors in this book are my own. They have read parts of this work and have suggested new lines of inquiry. I am much indebted to Professors Denis Brogan, of Cambridge University, Oscar Handlin, of Harvard University, and Richard Hofstadter, of Columbia University.

I have also had helpful conversations with Professors John Blum, of Yale University, Peter Odegard, of the University of California at Berkeley, and Arthur Schlesinger, Jr., of Harvard University. In addition, my mother, my wife, and the editorial staff of the Atlantic Monthly Press have aided me vastly in the preparation of the final manuscript.

The work has been made possible by a research grant from the British Government, the generous provisions of a Harkness Fellowship of the Commonwealth Fund, and a research fellowship at Churchill College, Cambridge University. The staffs and resources of the Widener Library, Harvard University, the New York Public Library, the library of Columbia University, and the Pangloss Bookshop, Harvard Square, have also rendered me great service.

I am further indebted for permission to quote lengthy extracts from the following:

FUNK & WAGNALLS COMPANY for *Profit and Loss in Man* by A. Hopkins.
HARPER & BROTHERS for *Does Prohibition Work?* by M. Bruere.
HARPER & BROTHERS for *Dissertations by Mr. Dooley* by F. P. Dunne.
HARVARD UNIVERSITY PRESS for *The Letters of Theodore Roosevelt*, ed. by Elting Elmore Morison.
THE JOHNS HOPKINS PRESS for *A Carnival of Buncombe* by H. L. Mencken, ed. by Malcolm Moos.
HOUGHTON MIFFLIN COMPANY for *The Autobiography of Will Rogers*.
ALFRED A. KNOPF for *Prejudices: First, Second, Third, Fourth and Sixth Series* and *Making a President* by H. L. Mencken.
THE MACMILLAN COMPANY for *Men of Destiny* (1927) and *Interpretations 1931-32* (1932) by Walter Lippmann.

417

MRS. EDGAR LEE MASTERS for 19 lines from "Harry Carey Goodhue," 3 lines from "Jacob Godbey," 9 lines from "Sexsmith the Dentist," and 3 lines from "George Trimble" from *Spoon River Anthology* by Edgar Lee Masters, published by The Macmillan Company (1914, 1942).

CHARLES SCRIBNER'S SONS for *Mr. Dooley at His Best* by F. P. Dunne.

CHARLES P. TAFT for *The Life and Times of William Howard Taft* by H. Pringle.

Note on Bibliography

I HAVE not included a bibliography in this work, since all references in the text are fully documented in the footnotes. Although many unmentioned works have been consulted in the course of this study, their lack of importance and bias have warranted their exclusion. Contemporary writings on prohibition were interminable; I have mentioned in the footnotes most of those which seem to me to have some interest.

For those students of prohibition who wish to consult a proper bibliography, I recommend a report of a Special Advisory Committee of the Social Science Research Council, *Sources of Information Concerning the Operation of the Eighteenth Amendment* (New York, 1928); D. C. Nicholson and R. P. Graves, *Selective Bibliography on the Operation of the Eighteenth Amendment* (Bureau of Public Administration, Univ. of California, 1931). Also useful are the bibliographies contained in *The Standard Encyclopedia of the Alcohol Problem* (6 vols., Westerville, Ohio, 1925-1930); in L. Beman (ed.), *Prohibition of the Liquor Traffic* (New York, 1915) and *Prohibition, Modification of the Volstead Law* (New York, 1924); and in the six specialized Ph.D. theses, mentioned in the footnotes, by D. Heckman, G. Ostrander, J. Sellers, J. Timberlake, Jr., S. Unger, and D. Whitener. P. Odegard, *Pressure Politics* (New York, 1928) has an excellent bibliography on the Anti-Saloon League.

The findings of Herbert Hoover's National Commission on Law Observance and Enforcement, *Report on the Enforcement of the Prohibition Laws of the United States* (Summary and 5 vols., 71 Cong., 3 Sess., H.D. 722), are indispensable to all students of prohibition. The document is referred to as the *Wickersham Report* in the footnotes.

Notes

NOTES ON PREFACE

1. J. Daniels, *The End of Innocence* (Philadelphia, 1954), Preface.
2. W. Lippmann, *Men of Destiny* (New York, 1927), pp. 28-31.

NOTES ON CHAPTER ONE

1. Quoted in P. Johnstone, "Old Ideals Versus New Ideas in Farm Life," *Farmers in a Changing World* (U.S. Dept. of Agriculture Yearbook, Washington, D.C., 1940), p. 116. Johnstone's survey of the change in the life and attitudes of the American farmer is excellent. J. Kolb and E. Brunner's "Rural Life" in the Report of the President's Research Committee on Social Trends, *Recent Social Trends in the United States* (1-Vol. ed., New York, 1934) is good. A. Griswold, *Farming and Democracy* (New York, 1948), has a good chapter on Jefferson and agriculture, while the opening chapters of R. Hofstadter's *The Age of Reform* (New York, 1955) give a brilliant picture of the prejudices and politics of the Western farmer.
2. K. Marx, *The Communist Manifesto* (D. Ryazanoff, ed., London, 1930), p. 31.
3. H. Garland, *A Son of the Middle Border* (New York, 1917), pp. 129, 147.
4. *Ibid.*, p. 80.
5. E. Eggleston, *The Circuit Rider: A Tale of the Heroic Age* (New York, 1874), gives a stirring account of the trials and triumphs of the Western Methodist missionaries.
6. L. Atherton, in *Main Street on the Middle Border* (Univ. of Indiana, 1954), describes well the boomer psychology in small towns of the Midwest.
7. W. Cather, *O Pioneers!* (Boston, 1913), pp. 15-16.
8. W. Webb, *The Great Plains* (Boston, 1931), p. 502.
9. R. Hofstadter, *op. cit.*, pp. 70-81, has traced this theory of conspiracy through American rural reform movements.
10. The autobiographies of Sherwood Anderson, Edgar Lee Masters, Edgar Howe, and Hamlin Garland all give some idea of the drudgery of farm women. But James Agee and Walker Evans, in *Let Us Now Praise Famous Men* (Boston, 1941), give the most moving and poetical account of the terrible poverty and toil of women on poor farms.
11. B. Whitlock, *The Little Green Shutter* (New York, 1931), p. 11.
12. J. Cox, *Journey Through My Years* (New York, 1946), p. 9.
13. F. Franklin, *What Prohibition Has Done to America* (New York, 1922), p. 76.
14. H. Garland, *op. cit.*, p. 97.
15. *Sherwood Anderson's Memoirs* (New York, 1942), p. 23.
16. B. Whitlock, *op. cit.*, p. 39.
17. Quoted in J. Long, *Bryan: The Great Commoner* (New York, 1928), pp. 217-218. Bryan was speaking before the Democratic state convention of Nebraska.
18. *Official Report of the Proceedings of the Democratic National Convention, 1920*, p. 211.
19. In Erskine Caldwell's excellent series on American Folkways, H. Nixon's *Lower Piedmont Country* (New York, 1946) has a good chapter on "Ol' Corn Liquor" in Kentucky.

20. W. Sweet, *Revivalism in America* (New York, 1944), p. 118. This remark was the shocked comment of a Western missionary in 1826 in Ohio.
21. Quoted in L. Morris, *Not So Long Ago* (New York, 1949), p. 202.
22. See L. Atherton, *op. cit.*, p. 75.
23. Dr. and Mrs. W. Crafts, *Intoxicating Drinks and Drugs in All Lands and Times* (rev. ed., Washington, D.C., 1911), p. 15.
24. A. Hopkins, *Profit and Loss in Man* (New York, 1908), pp. 234-235.
25. W. Wilson to F. Cobb, editor of the New York *World*, April 1, 1917, quoted by R. Baker (ed.), *Woodrow Wilson: Life and Letters* (8 vols., New York, 1927-1939), VI, p. 506.
26. H. Mencken, *Americana, 1925* (New York, 1925), p. 211.
27. League for Public Discussion, *Debate on Prohibition* (New York, 1924), p. 38.
28. *Scientific Temperance Journal*, March, 1917.
29. H. Garland, *op. cit.*, p. 86.

NOTES ON CHAPTER TWO

1. See G. Allport, *The Nature of Prejudice* (Cambridge, Mass., 1954), pp. 174-175.
2. E. Cherrington, *History of the Anti-Saloon League* (Westerville, Ohio, 1913), pp. 76-77. He is commenting on the character of the leader of the League at that time, Purley A. Baker.
3. Quoted in S. Unger, *A History of the National Woman's Christian Temperance Union* (Ph.D., Ohio State Univ., 1933), p. 25. This is a good treatment of the subject.
4. A. Cullen in F. Tietsort (ed.), *Temperance — Or Prohibition?* (New York, 1929), p. 166.
5. *Ibid.*, pp. 251, 255.
6. S. Anderson, *Winesburg, Ohio* (New York, 1919), p. 55.
7. New York *Herald*, February 24, 1924.
8. E. Cherrington at San Francisco in 1930, quoted by Senator J. Reed, *The Rape of Temperance* (New York, 1930), p. 31.
9. S. Freud, *Civilization and Its Discontents* (New York, 1930), p. 31.
10. See H. Mowrer, "A Psychocultural Analysis of the Alcoholic," *American Sociological Review*, August, 1940. There is a good résumé in this article of the history of psychiatric interest in alcohol problems. Also see D. Gerard, "Intoxication and Addiction," *Quarterly Journal of Studies on Alcohol*, December, 1955. Both of these articles have been reprinted in R. McCarthy (ed.), *Drinking and Intoxication* (New Haven, Conn., 1959), an excellent collection of articles embodying the latest research on the question of alcohol. Especially brilliant is the article of A. Lee on "Techniques of Social Reform: an Analysis of the New Prohibition Drive."
    The centennial edition of the *National Temperance Almanac* in 1876 put the illogic of the dry position very succinctly:

> The first sin is in drinking the first glass. If the drunkard is a sinner — and the Bible plainly declares it — then he was a sinner when he took the first glass just as much as the thief or the murderer when he took the first step in the downward course. One glass has been known to produce drunkenness. It is continual sin from the first glass down to the drunkard's grave. No drunkard shall inherit the kingdom of God.

The *Almanac* also prints a charming verse of what the drys thought were the reasons of the drinker:

> If on my theme I rightly think,
> There are five reasons why men drink;
> Good wine, a friend, because I'm dry,

> *Or lest I should be by-and-by,*
> *Or any other reason why.*

11. J. Riley, Jr., and C. Marden, "The Social Pattern of Alcoholic Drinking," *Quarterly Journal of Studies on Alcohol,* September, 1947.
12. *Address of Colonel Henry Watterson at the Blue Grass Fair,* Lexington, Kentucky, August 12, 1907.
13. F. Tuohy, "Adventures of a British Investigator in 'Dry' New York," *Literary Digest,* January 17, 1920.
14. L. Beman (ed.), *Prohibition, Modification of the Volstead Law* (New York, 1924), p. 54.
15. W. Irwin, "More About 'Nigger Gin,' " *Collier's,* August 15, 1908.
16. *Cong. Record,* 63 Cong., 3 Sess., pp. 507, 605.
17. *Ibid.,* 63 Cong., 1 Sess., Appendix, p. 467.
18. Quoted in J. Sellers, *The Prohibition Movement in Alabama, 1702 to 1943* (Chapel Hill, N.C., 1943), p. 101.
19. See B. Washington, "Prohibition and the Negro," *Outlook,* March 14, 1908.
20. This aspect of prohibition in the South is dealt with by D. Whitener, *Prohibition in North Carolina, 1715-1945* (Chapel Hill, N.C., 1946), pp. 133-147. Both of these studies by Whitener and Sellers fill gaps in the study of prohibition in the South.
21. W. Cash, *The Mind of the South* (Anchor ed., New York, 1941), pp. 231-232. Cash's work is an intuitive tour de force on the motivations of the South.
22. Dr. and Mrs. W. Crafts, *World Book of Temperance* (Washington, D.C., 1909), pp. 57-58.
23. E. Cherrington, *The Evolution of Prohibition in America* (Westerville, Ohio, 1920), pp. 270-272.
24. Dr. and Mrs. W. Crafts, *Intoxicating Drinks and Drugs in All Lands and Times* (rev. ed., Washington, D.C., 1911), p. 15.
25. L. Banks, *The Lincoln-Lee Legion* (New York, 1903), p. 231.
26. Dr. and Mrs. W. Crafts, *Intoxicating Drinks,* etc., *op. cit.,* p. 27.
27. Quoted in W. Williams, *William Jennings Bryan: A Study in Political Vindication* (New York, 1923), p. 110.
28. *Proceedings of the Nineteenth National Convention of the Anti-Saloon League,* 1919, p. 35.
29. Dr. S. Hubbard, "Why Does Not Prohibition Prohibit?" *New York Medical Journal,* July 18, 1923.
30. A full account of the foundation and constitution of the World League Against Alcoholism may be found in E. Cherrington, *op. cit.,* pp. 365-374.
31. Pamphlet, Widener Library, Harvard. There is an extensive contemporary pamphlet collection catalogued under "PROHIBITION" in the library. Where possible, fuller information on pamphlet sources will be given.

NOTES ON CHAPTER THREE

1. M. Bruere, *Does Prohibition Work?* (New York, 1927), p. 280.
2. J. Thacher, *A Military Journal* (Boston, 1823), p. 154 *note,* quoted by J. Krout, *The Origins of Prohibition* (New York, 1925), p. 61. Krout's book is an excellent account of the early days of the temperance movement. Unfortunately, he ends with the passage of the Maine Law in 1851. His bibliography is good.
3. B. Rush, *An Inquiry into the Effects of Ardent Spirits on the Human Body and Mind* (Boston, 1811). The title was changed for the edition of 1811.
4. L. Beecher, *Six Sermons on the Nature, Occasions, Signs, Evils and Remedy of Intemperance* (Boston, 1827).
5. See W. Hawkins, *Life of John H. W. Hawkins* (Boston, 1859), and J. Gough, *Autobiography and Personal Recollections of John B. Gough* (Springfield, Mass., 1870) and *Platform Echoes* (London, 1885).

6. B. Whitlock, *The Little Green Shutter* (New York, 1931), pp. 21-22.

7. J. Krout, *op. cit.*, pp. 297-304.

8. Three devoted and misguided women processed scientific research for the dry cause: Mary H. Hunt (1830-1906), Cora F. Stoddard (1872-1936), and Emma L. Transeau (1857-1937). Mrs. Hunt filled the textbooks of the public schools with dry dogmas. On her death, her assistant Miss Stoddard became executive secretary of the Scientific Temperance Federation in 1906. During the next three decades, she and her devoted secretary, Miss Transeau, digested and abstracted suitable dry material in the *Scientific Temperance Journal*. Their glosses on the research of others were the basis of the medical authorities quoted by the prohibitionists.

9. *Permanent Temperance Documents, Seventh Report* (New York, 1852), p. 4.

10. There is a complete bibliography of the medical experiments, misused by the prohibitionists, under the heading of "Alcohol" in *The Standard Encyclopedia of the Alcohol Problem* (6 vols., Westerville, Ohio, 1925-1930), I, pp. 124-126.

11. L. Laitinen, "A Contribution to the Study of the Influence of Alcohol on the Degeneration of Human Offspring," *Proceedings of the Twelfth International Congress on Alcoholism, 1909*, pp. 263-270.

12. Elderton and Pearson, *A First Study of the Influence of Parental Alcoholism on the Physique and Ability of the Offspring* (London, 1910).

13. H. Emerson (ed.), *Alcohol and Man* (New York, 1932), p. 119. This book was the first good compendium of medical knowledge on the subject of alcohol, although the way had been prepared by the work of the Committee of Fifty, Dr. E. Starling, and Dr. R. Pearl. *The Christian Century*, December 7, 1932, commented that it was the task of all preachers and teachers to make the contents of the book known to schoolchildren and the common people as quickly as possible. Misrepresentation on the subject of alcohol declined after the publication of *Alcohol and Man*.

14. I. Fisher and E. Fisk, *How to Live* (18th ed., 6th ptg., New York, 1931), p. 79.

15. *Ibid.*, p. 80.

16. See C. Darrow and V. Yarros, *Prohibition Mania* (New York, 1927), pp. 135-146, for the controversy between wets and drys over experiments on animals.

17. A. Bluhm, "Zum Problem Alcohol und Nachkommenschaft," *Archiv für Rassen und Gesellschaftsbiologie* (München, 1930).

18. *Scientific Temperance Journal*, Summer, 1932.

19. *National Advocate*, October, 1931.

20. R. Park, *The Case for Alcohol* (London, 1909), quoted in *Five Feet of Information for Impartial Students of the Liquor Problem* (U.S. Brewers' Association, Chicago, 1910).

21. Interview with Professor Odegard, University of California at Berkeley.

22. P. Andreae, *The Prohibition Movement* (Chicago, 1915), p. 401.

23. H. Heinemann, *The Rule of "Not Too Much"* (Chicago, 1908), pp. 70-71.

24. E. Howe, *Plain People* (New York, 1929), p. 20.

25. There is a brilliant examination of the social and moral ideas in the McGuffey Readers in R. Mosier, *Making the American Mind* (New York, 1947). I have used his quotations on p. 118 from *McGuffey's Eclectic First Reader* (Cincinnati, 1836), p. 68.

26. M. Hunt, *An Epoch of the Nineteenth Century* (Boston, Mass., 1897), pp. 48-49.

27. See *The Standard Encyclopedia of the Alcohol Problem, op. cit.*, III, pp. 1269-1270, for this judgment and for the earlier quotation about "a whole Niagara of ballots."

28. *Report of 1887 to Woman's Christian Temperance Union* (pamphlet), Widener Library, Harvard.

29. J. Billings (ed.), *Physiological Aspects of the Liquor Problem* (2 vols., Boston,

1903), I, pp. 23, 30-33. The extracts are taken from *Brand's Physiology, Hygiene, Narcotics, No. 1 Series*, p. 19; *Authorized Physiological Series, No. 1*, p. 61; and *Brand's, No. 1, Good Health for Children Series*, p. 44 and p. 69.
30. *Ibid.*, p. 45.
31. *58 Cong., 2 Sess., S.D. 171*, p. 38.
32. Cited by S. Unger, *A History of the National Woman's Christian Temperance Union* (Ph.D., Ohio State Univ., 1933), p. 147.
33. T. Wolfe, *Look Homeward, Angel* (New York, 1929), p. 299.
34. Dr. J. Morel, "Prevention of Mental Diseases," *American Journal of Sociology*, July, 1899.
35. *Bulletin of the Chicago Department of Health*, 1916.
36. Quoted in *Scientific Temperance Journal*, Autumn, 1919.
37. There are three excellent books on these subjects: R. Hofstadter, *Social Darwinism in American Thought* (rev. ed., Boston, 1955); E. Goldman, *Rendezvous with Destiny* (rev. ed., New York, 1956); O. Handlin, *Race and Nationality in American Life* (Boston, 1957).
38. A. Siegfried, *America Comes of Age* (New York, 1927), p. 109.
39. C. Saleeby, *Parenthood and Race Culture* (London, 1910), p. 281. The American Library Association booklist of November, 1909, called the work, "The most valuable and scholarly work yet published on the theory and practice of eugenics. The first book to recommend to educated readers."
40. W. Stokes, *The Right to be Well-Born* (Lexington, Kentucky, 1917), pp. 137-141.
41. P. Odegard, *Pressure Politics* (New York, 1928), Appendix F, p. 274. Odegard's book is definitive on the workings and organization of the Anti-Saloon League.
42. R. Hobson, *The Great Destroyer* (Washington, D.C., 1911).
43. Emma L. Transeau in the *Scientific Temperance Journal*, December, 1913.
44. Pamphlet, Widener Library, Harvard.
45. *The Cyclopedia of Temperance, Prohibition and Public Morals* (ed. D. Pickett *et al.*, New York, 1917), p. 379.
46. E. Davis, *A Compendium of Temperance Truth* (Milwaukee, 1913), p. 82. Mrs. Davis was in charge of the Scientific Temperance Department of the Milwaukee Woman's Christian Temperance Union.
   Even toddlers in Sunday schools were not exempt from warnings about the connection of alcohol and venereal diseases. Mrs. Wilbur F. Crafts, in her "Blackboard Temperance Lessons," suggested that a Temperance Knight be drawn on the blackboard, armored with various protections against the assaults of King Alcohol. When referring to the piece of armor which covered the knight's private parts, the teacher was to say, "King Alcohol has killed off a lot of people by wounding them in the part of the body that I have covered with the waist piece."
47. *Proceedings of the Nineteenth National Convention of the Anti-Saloon League, 1919*, pp. 148-149.
48. J. Daniels, *The Navy and the Nation* (New York, 1919), p. 60.
49. Pamphlet, Widener Library, Harvard.
50. See H. Emerson (ed.), *op. cit.*, pp. 191-192.
51. *Proceedings of the Nineteenth National Convention of the Anti-Saloon League, 1919*, pp. 43-44.
52. W. Lippmann, *A Preface to Morals* (New York, 1929), pp. 286-287.
53. Quoted in O. Handlin, *op. cit.*, p. 153. Chapter Six of this excellent book, "The Horror," is very good on the bourgeois sexual mores of the nineteenth century. R. Burlingame, in *The American Conscience* (New York, 1957), points to the high birth rate, early marriages, and many brothels of the nineteenth century as proof that sexual repression did not flourish. He does not take into account the "double standard" between men and women, middle class and

proletariat. Nor does he consider the fears of pregnancy and venereal diseases, nor the real restrictions on sexual behavior caused by the prohibitions of fundamentalist religion.

54. *Cong. Record*, 63 Cong., 1 Sess., Appendix, p. 469.
55. H. Garland, *A Son of the Middle Border* (New York, 1917), p. 174.
56. C. Nation, *The Use and Need of the Life of Carry A. Nation* (rev. ed., Topeka, Kansas, 1908), pp. 54-55, 61, 66, 67, 75, 122, 143-144, 230.
57. W. Cash, *The Mind of the South* (Anchor ed., New York, 1941), p. 97. Cash is brilliant in his description of the sexual and racist fears of white Southerners.
58. R. Woods, *Substitutes for the Saloon* (rev. ed., Boston, 1919), Appendix III, p. 328. Woods was a social worker from the South End House in Boston, who turned his talents to the dry cause.
59. R. Hobson, *Alcohol and the Human Race* (New York, 1919), p. 115.
60. J. Addams, "A New Conscience and an Ancient Evil," *McClure's*, March, 1912.
61. J. London, *John Barleycorn* (New York, 1913), p. 336.
62. C. Stout, *The Eighteenth Amendment and the Part Played by Organized Medicine* (New York, 1921), p. 18. This little-known book, although biased by the fact that its author was a drug manufacturer, is the only work to examine the actions of the doctors over prohibition, and I am much in its debt.
63. S. Adams, "The Fraud Medicines Own Up," *Collier's*, January 20, 1912.
64. *Journal of the American Medical Association*, June 16, 1917.
65. *Cong. Record*, 65 Cong., 1 Sess., p. 5646.

NOTES ON CHAPTER FOUR

1. There is a detailed account of the connection between these churches and the dry cause in J. Timberlake, Jr., *Prohibition and the Progressive Movement, 1900-1919* (Ph.D., Harvard, 1957), pp. 88-128. By 1916, the Methodists were split into 17 bodies, the Baptists into 17 bodies, and the Presbyterians into 10 bodies. It is unfortunate that the Protestant churches seem to protest too much within themselves.
2. Quoted in H. Faulkner, *The Quest for Social Justice, 1898-1914* (New York, 1930), p. 224.
3. For all my information on the Anti-Saloon League, I have relied heavily on P. Odegard's history of the Anti-Saloon League, *Pressure Politics* (New York, 1928). It should be read by all those interested in prohibition. There is also a doctoral thesis on the subject by N. Dohn, *The History of the Anti-Saloon League* (Ohio State Univ., 1959). The thesis is disappointing, although full use has been made of the mass of material accumulated in the League's headquarters in Westerville, Ohio. The League is now called the Temperance League of America.
4. W. Anderson, *The Church in Action Against the Saloon* (rev. ed., Westerville, Ohio, 1910).
5. U. G. Humphreys, speaking at an Anti-Saloon League Superintendents' and Workers' Conference in 1909 [quoted in N. Dohn, *op. cit.*, p. 87].
6. Quoted in an anonymous article, "National Prohibition and the Church," *Unpopular Review*, IV, 1915.
7. *America*, March 6, 1915. For information about dry Catholics, see Sister J. Bland, *Hibernian Crusade: The Story of the Catholic Total Abstinence Union of America* (Washington, D.C., 1951). The Catholic temperance societies, which never numbered more than one Catholic out of two hundred in their ranks, began to react against the idea of prohibition after 1913, the very year that the Anti-Saloon League decided to press for total national prohibition. The Roman church genuinely feared that the drys might attack

the mass through the prohibition of sacramental wine. It also feared the connection of the drys with the anti-Catholic, nativist movements in the South and West. Moreover, Catholic priests had their greatest influence among the wet city populations, and they would jeopardize that influence by supporting prohibition. Finally, the faith itself had long supported temperance rather than prohibition. The great Cardinal Gibbons opposed even local option.

8.   C. Darrow and V. Yarros, *Prohibition Mania* (New York, 1927), p. 157.
9.   J. Erskine, *Prohibition and Christianity* (Indianapolis, 1927), p. 12.
10. See Dr. James Wallace, president of the Presbyterian Temperance Committee, Pamphlet, Widener Library, Harvard.
11. See E. Wasson, *Religion and Drink* (New York, 1914).
12. S. Freud, *Civilization and Its Discontents* (New York, 1930), p. 143.
13. *Cong. Record*, 63 Cong., 3 Sess., p. 557.
14. R. Calkins (ed.), *Substitutes for the Saloon* (Boston, 1901), p. 3, 124.
15. F. Laubach, "What the Church May Learn from the Saloon," *Survey*, September 27, 1913.
16. H. Roth, *Call It Sleep* (new ed., Paterson, N.J., 1960), p. 37.
17. R. Calkins, *op. cit.*, p. 61.
18. Jacob Riis, quoted in N. Hapgood and H. Moskowitz, *Up from the City Streets* (New York, 1927), p. 46.
19. C. Stelzle, *A Son of the Bowery* (New York, 1926), pp. 47-48.
20. A. Smith, *Up to Now: An Autobiography* (New York, 1929), pp. 31-33. Even after his defeat in 1928, Alfred E. Smith continued to praise Tammany as a good social influence.
21. See *Hearings before a Subcommittee of the Senate Committee on the Judiciary*, 65 Cong., 2 Sess., p. 83. Also see G. Turner, "Beer and the City Liquor Problem," *McClure's*, September, 1909.
22. M. Le Sueur, "Beer Town," *Life in the United States* (New York, 1933), p. 39. This collection of articles from *Scribner's Magazine* contains excellent first-hand accounts of life in America from the turn of the century. For the bad position of the saloonkeeper under the brewer, see A. Gleason, "The New York Saloon," *Collier's*, April 25, May 2, 1908.
23. P. Odegard, *op. cit.*, pp. 41, 57. His whole chapter, "From Conviction to Persuasion," is excellent on the use the drys made of the saloon as a symbol of horror.
24. G. Ade, *The Old-Time Saloon* (New York, 1931), pp. 28-31.
25. P. Odegard, *op. cit.*, p. 249.
26. G. Ade, *op. cit.*, p. 8.
27. See G. Howard, "Alcohol and Crime," *American Journal of Sociology*, July, 1918.
28. W. Irwin, "The American Saloon," *Collier's*, February 29, 1908.
29. T. Wolfe, *Look Homeward, Angel* (New York, 1929), p. 300.
30. E. Cherrington, *The Evolution of Prohibition in America* (Westerville, Ohio, 1920), p. 374.
31. *Scientific Temperance Journal*, June, 1916.
32. R. Calkins (ed.), *Substitutes for the Saloon* (rev. ed., Boston, 1919), Preface.
33. Quoted in *ibid.*, Preface.
34. W. Burke, "The Anti-Saloon League as a Political Force," *Annals of the American Academy*, November, 1908, p. 29.

NOTES ON CHAPTER FIVE

1.   Quoted in D. Leigh Colvin, *Prohibition in the United States* (New York, 1926), p. 75. Colvin's book is an excellent history of the first fifty years of the Prohibition party and brings out very well its quarrels with the Anti-Saloon League, although its writer is firmly committed to the ideology of the party.

2. Quoted in A. Hopkins, *Profit and Loss in Man* (New York, 1908), pp. 298-299.

3. *Keynote Address of Clinton N. Howard at the Prohibition Party National Convention*, Atlantic City, New Jersey, July 10, 1912. Pamphlet, Widener Library, Harvard.

4. D. Leigh Colvin, *op. cit.*, pp. 384-387.

5. This was the phrase of Clinton N. Howard. The party, in the *American Prohibition Yearbook, 1916*, p. 110, also denounced the League's "good man" theory in no uncertain terms:

> The teaching of this false and pernicious theory has done more to keep the political power of the [liquor] traffic intact, more to delay the coming of real prohibition, than all the machinations of the Lorimers, Cannons, Penroses and Bartholds, in and out of Congress, and more than all the millions of corruption money spent by the liquor interests. [The four names are those of notorious city bosses of the time.]

6. Quoted in N. Dohn, *The History of the Anti-Saloon League* (Ohio State Univ., 1959), p. 133. From the *American Issue* (Maryland ed.), February 26, 1910.

7. *The Anti-Saloon League Catechism* (Westerville, Ohio, 1910).

8. *Proceedings of the Fifteenth International Congress Against Alcoholism, 1921*, p. 101.

9. *The Standard Encyclopedia of the Alcohol Problem* (Westerville, Ohio, 1930), VI, p. 2909.

10. See *Proceedings of the Fifteenth National Convention of the Anti-Saloon League, 1913*, pp. 25-29.

11. H. Chalfant, *These Agitators and Their Idea* (Nashville, Tenn., 1931), pp. 219, 222.

12. *Wickersham Report*, IV, p. 784.

13. The vote on the county option bill in the state legislature of 1908 shows the bipartisan support of those legislators who backed League measures. Voting for the bill were 80 Republicans, 75 Democrats, and 3 Independents.

14. P. Odegard, *Pressure Politics* (New York, 1928), p. 97.

15. Quoted in N. Dohn, *op. cit.*, p. 118, from the *American Issue*, October 13, 1905.

16. P. Odegard, *op. cit.*, pp. 9-10.

17. Office of the Executive Committee of the Coalition of Ohio Dry Republicans, 1917, Pamphlet, Oberlin College Library, Ohio.

18. Letter of Harry M. Daugherty to Charles Reid, June 18, 1917.

19. Quoted in H. Chalfant, *op. cit.*, p. 284.

20. *Proceedings of the Nineteenth National Convention of the Anti-Saloon League, 1919*, p. 34.

21. The statement is that of a dry observer of the Women's Crusade of 1873 against the saloons in Ohio. R. Hofstadter, *The Age of Reform* (New York, 1955), p. 20, points out the odd combination of love and hatred in American reform movements.

22. H. Commager (ed.), *Selected Writings of William Dean Howells* (New York, 1950), p. 800.

23. G. Ostrander, *The Prohibition Movement in California, 1848-1933* (Ph.D., Univ. of California, 1957), p. 17. Ostrander's thesis is the best regional study of the prohibition movement. It is particularly good on the connection between the rural reform movements and the prohibitionists.

24. M. Coolidge, *Why Women Are So* (New York, 1912), p. 39.

25. *Ibid.*, p. 249.

26. *Ibid.*, p. 267. Small boys shamed the few women who dared to wear "bloomers" with the chant:

> *Gibbery, gibbery gab, the women had a confab*
> *And demanded the rights to wear the tights,*
> *Gibbery, gibbery gab.*

27. Quoted in S. Unger, *A History of the National Woman's Christian Temperance Union* (Ph.D., Ohio State Univ., 1933), pp. 263-264. Unger is excellent on the subject of Frances Willard's "Do Everything" policy, and her ousting of the antisuffragette, Mrs. Wittenmyer, from control of the Woman's Christian Temperance Union in 1879. There is a good biography of Frances Willard, pointing out her wide reform interests and the subsequent narrowing of the aims of the Union, by M. Earhart, *Frances Willard: From Prayers to Politics* (Univ. of Chicago, 1944).
28. G. Ostrander, *op. cit.*, p. 102.
29. Quoted in J. Higham, *Strangers in the Land* (Rutgers Univ., 1955), p. 41. Higham's book is a classic on the reception of immigrants in the United States.
30. C. Russell, *Obstructions in the Way of Justice* (National American Woman Suffrage Assoc., New York, 1908).
31. *North American Review*, October 5, 1906.
32. L. Banks, *The Saloon-Keeper's Ledger* (New York, 1895), p. 98.
33. L. Banks, *Ammunition for Final Drive on Booze* (New York, 1917), p. 251.
34. *Report of the Wisconsin Vice Committee* (Madison, Wisc., 1914), p. 98.
35. See J. Timberlake, Jr., *Prohibition and the Progressive Movement, 1900-1919* (Harvard, 1957), pp. 330-334. This thesis stresses the similar views held by those American-born, middle-class Protestants who supported both the drys and the progressives; but it wrongly discounts the importance of the conflict of city and country in the progressive movement.
36. I. Irwin, *The Story of the Woman's Party* (New York, 1921), p. 178, quoting the *Suffragist*, November 11, 1916.
37. W. White, "Who Killed Cock Robin?" *Collier's*, December 16, 1916.
38. H. Chalfant, *op. cit.*, p. 128.
39. *Proceedings of the Citizenship Conference on October 14, 1923*, Washington, D.C., p. 115.
40. L. Banks, *Ammunition for Final Drive on Booze* (New York, 1917), p. 384.
41. Quoted in R. Vecoli, "Sterilization: A Progressive Measure?" *Wisconsin Magazine of History*, Spring, 1960. This is an excellent study on the close connection between the eugenicists and the progressives in Wisconsin.
42. See H. Loughlin (ed.), *Eugenical Sterilization in the United States* (Chicago, 1922), p. 322. This is a fascinating compilation of the sterilization laws and hopes of the eugenicists. A reading of the *Scientific Temperance Journal* during these years reveals further close connections between the prohibition and the eugenics movements. An article in November, 1916, summarizes well the attraction which eugenics held for contemporary reformers.

> From beginning to end the whole eugenic program is one of education. Every element in it, knowledge of hereditary laws, segregation of the unfit, restriction of immigration, prevention of dangerous racial admixture, the abolition of customs and opportunities that lead to poison habits, improvement of environment, provision for proper social opportunities, the avoidance of social disease and social immorality, and pride in family stock are all important parts in a great educational effort that is as much a call to patriotism as is the call to relief work or to military preparedness.

43. E. Masters, *Spoon River Anthology* (new ed., New York, 1917), p. 12.
44. Quoted in D. Whitener, *Prohibition in North Carolina, 1715-1945* (Chapel Hill, N.C., 1943), p. 156.

45. Quoted in *The Cyclopedia of Temperance, Prohibition, and Public Morals* (ed. D. Pickett *et al.*, New York, 1917), p. 220.
46. G. Ostrander, *op. cit.*, p. 112.
47. H. Fosdick, "The Prohibition Question," *Sermon Delivered at the Park Avenue Baptist Church, New York, October 14, 1928*.
48. S. Unger, *op. cit.*, p. 207.
49. C. Aked, "Man and His Neighbor," *Appleton's*, July, 1908 [quoted in J. Timberlake, Jr., *op. cit.*, p. 146]. Timberlake is particularly good on the labor movement, and its relationships with the churches and employers.
50. C. Reitell, "Men, Machinery and Alcoholic Drink," *Annals of the American Academy*, September, 1923, p. 109.
51. D. Sharp, "A Chain in Alcohol," *Century*, January, 1926.
52. D. Leigh Colvin, *op. cit.*, pp. 52-53.
53. A. Hopkins, *op. cit.*, p. 31.
54. Quoted in D. Pickett, "Prohibition and Economic Change," *Annals of the American Academy*, September, 1932, p. 102.
55. J. Koren, *Economic Aspects of the Liquor Problem* (Boston, 1899), p. 21.
56. R. Bagnell, *Economic and Moral Aspects of the Liquor Business* (Ph.D., Columbia, 1911), p. 14.
57. S. Crowther, *Prohibition and Prosperity* (New York, 1930), p. 47.
58. Quoted in W. Stayton, "Our Experiment in National Prohibition," *Annals of the American Academy*, September, 1923, p. 31.
59. *Proceedings of the Thirteenth National Convention of the Anti-Saloon League, 1909*, p. 46.
60. *The National Temperance Almanac, 1876*, p. 17.
61. C. Wood (ed.), "A Criticism of National Prohibition" (A.A.P.A., Washington, D.C., 1926), p. 44.
62. Dr. I. Goldstein, *Address to the First National Conference of Labor's National Committee for Modification of the Volstead Act*, Philadelphia, April 27-28, 1931.
63. *Seamen's Journal*, August 13, 1913, quoted in J. Timberlake, Jr., *op. cit.*, p. 236.
64. *The Saloon vs. the Labor Union*, Address by the Reverend Father Cassidy, Fall River, Mass., November 26, 1911.
65. C. Stelzle, *A Son of the Bowery* (New York, 1926), p. 116. Stelzle was both a dry and a Socialist. He wanted efficient prohibition because it would cause "social unrest" and the rise of socialism in America.
66. W. Rauschenbusch, *Christianizing the Social Order* (New York, 1912), p. 456.
67. Mrs. R. Robbins, *Address to the Citizenship Conference*, Washington, D.C., October 13-15, 1923.
68. F. Kelley, "Laborers in Heat and in Heavy Industries," *Annals of the American Academy*, September, 1923, p. 178.
69. W. Anderson, "Prohibition — Anderson Answers," *Forum*, July, 1919.

NOTES ON CHAPTER SIX

1. H. Mencken, *Prejudices: Second Series* (New York, 1920), pp. 214-215.
2. For an adequate history of lobbying in America, see K. Schriftgiesser, *The Lobbyists* (Boston, 1951).
3. M. Hunt, *An Epoch in the Nineteenth Century* (Boston, Mass., 1897), p. 8.
4. *Ibid.*, p. 12. The account is written by Mrs. Mary Lowe Dickinson.
5. T. Wolfe, *Look Homeward, Angel* (New York, 1929), p. 300.
6. W. and M. Bryan, *The Memoirs of William Jennings Bryan* (Chicago, 1925), p. 291.
7. *Proceedings of the Fifteenth International Congress Against Alcohol, 1920*, p. 123.
8. Under the leadership of Frances Willard, the Woman's Christian Tem-

perance Union gave up its initial nonpartisan policy and endorsed the Prohibition party.

9. E. Cherrington, *History of the Anti-Saloon League* (Westerville, Ohio, 1913), pp. 59-61. A full account of the League's organization and methods of pressure politics will be found in P. Odegard, *Pressure Politics* (New York, 1928), pp. 1-126. It is interesting that both the Ku Klux Klan and the chief wet organization, the Association Against the Prohibition Amendment, also circulated among their members before each election lists of candidates who were, in the Klan's words, "favorable," "neutral," or "unfavorable" to their respective causes.

10. J. Pollard, *The Road to Repeal* (New York, 1932), p. 107.

11. Washington *Times*, December 17, 1917.

12. New York *Times*, March 29, 1926.

13. *Proceedings of the Nineteenth National Convention of the Anti-Saloon League, 1919*, p. 101. Mrs. Tilton, who once worked for the Boston Associated Charities, was a link between the drys and the social workers of America.

14. *Address to the United States Brewers' Association*, Atlantic City, N.J., October 3, 1913.

15. G. Ostrander, *The Prohibition Movement in California, 1843-1933* (Ph.D. Univ. of California, 1957), p. 140. Ostrander is particularly good on the split among the liquor interests in California.

16. P. Odegard, *op. cit.*, pp. 73-75.

17. S. Unger, *A History of the National Woman's Christian Temperance Union* (Ph.D., Ohio State Univ., 1933), p. 96.

18. See the list of "Heralds of Abstinence and Prohibition" in Dr. and Mrs. W. Crafts, *World Book of Temperance* (Washington, D.C., 1911).

19. H. Asbury, *The Great Illusion* (New York, 1951), p. 111. Asbury calls his book an "Informal History of Prohibition." It does present an enticing and chronological array of facts without much interpretation. It is particularly good on descriptive color passages, such as the events on January 16, 1920, when prohibition was passed, and on the changes in New York night life under prohibition. Asbury has also written informal and dramatic histories of Chicago, *Gem of the Prairies* (New York, 1940), and of San Francisco, *The Barbary Coast* (New York, 1933). These two books give a robust picture of vice in the days of the saloons.

20. B. Whitlock, *The Little Green Shutter* (New York, 1931), p. 39.

21. By Hugh d'Arcy. There is a charming collection of saloon songs edited by Frank Shay and illustrated by John Held, Jr., *My Pious Friends and Drunken Companions* (New York, 1927). It is dedicated to the wet proposition, "All Americans are two or three drinks below normal."

22. *The Cyclopedia of Temperance, Prohibition and Public Morals* (ed. D. Pickett *et al.*, New York, 1917), p. 264.

23. C. Sandburg, *Abraham Lincoln: The Prairie Years* (2 vols., New York, 1926), I, p. 272. This matter is also discussed in P. Odegard, *op. cit.*, pp. 60-62.

24. Pamphlet, Widener Library, Harvard.

25. *The Worldwide Prohibition Program, Plans Inaugurated by the Conference of the Anti-Saloon League of America* (Columbus, Ohio, November 19-22, 1918).

26. *Scientific Temperance Journal*, Spring, 1919.

27. M. Sullivan, *Our Times* (6 vols., New York, 1926-1935), V, p. 578. Sullivan's volumes are an invaluable guide to the period from 1900 to 1925.

28. Quoted in *ibid.*, p. 580.

29. *Journal of the American Medical Association*, June 16, 1917.

30. J. Daniels, *The Wilson Era: Years of War and After, 1917-1923* (Chapel Hill, N.C., 1946), p. 196.

31. G. Ostrander, *op. cit.*, p. 142.
32. New York *Times*, July 8, October 14, 1917.
33. O. Pilat and J. Ranson, *Sodom by the Sea* (New York, 1941), pp. 115-116.
34. New York *Times*, December 22, 27, 30, 1917.
35. Quoted in R. Gabriel, *The Course of American Democratic Thought* (New York, 1940), p. 369.
36. H. Laswell, *Propaganda Technique in the World War* (London, 1938), p. 96.
37. Newton D. Baker, quoted in M. Sullivan, *op. cit.*, V, p. 423.
38. The New York *Times*, June 18, 1917, reporting the baccalaureate address of Dr. W. Faunce at Brown University. The academic world was so patriotic that even William Howard Taft, no friend of prohibition at the time, appealed to the Yale Class Committee of '71 to have "dry" reunions in the interest of food preservation during the war.
39. H. Mencken, *Prejudices: Fourth Series* (New York, 1924), pp. 162-163.
40. John Lord O'Brian, Assistant to the Attorney General in espionage cases, quoted by Z. Chafee, Jr., in his classic *Free Speech in the United States* (Harvard, 1948), p. 64. There is a definitive work on this hysteria after the war, R. Murray, *Red Scare* (Univ. of Minnesota, 1955).
41. There is a definitive thesis on the German-American Alliance by C. Child, *The German-Americans in Politics, 1914-1917* (Ph.D., Univ. of Wisconsin, 1939). I am indebted to this for my judgment of the Alliance, and for my quotations from its speakers.
42. *Ibid.*, p. 111.
43. See *Hearings Before a Subcommittee of the Senate Committee on the Judiciary*, 65 Cong., 2 Sess., S. 3529, I, p. 309.
44. *Hearings Before a Subcommittee of the Senate Committee on the Judiciary*, 65 Cong., 2 Sess., S.R. 307, I, p. 3.
45. H. Mencken, *op. cit.*, p. 163.
46. M. Warren, *Everybody's*, November, 1917.
47. R. Hutton, Wisconsin Superintendent of the Anti-Saloon League, in *Anti-Saloon League Yearbook, 1918*.
48. *The White Book on Prohibition* (Boston, 1918), pp. 68-69.
49. *National Bulletin*, August, 1917.
50. *North American Review*, June, 1917.
51. Quoted in *U.S. Brewers' Association Yearbook, 1918*.
52. W. Faulkner, *Soldier's Pay* (New York, 1926), pp. 198-199.
53. H. Asbury, *op. cit.*, p. 136, also takes up this point of view.
54. *Cong. Record*, 65 Cong., 2 Sess., pp. 429-451.
55. Quoted in J. Reed, *The Rape of Temperance* (New York, 1931), p. 116.
56. *Worldwide Prohibition Program, op. cit.*
57. Quoted in W. Leuchtenburg's brilliant *The Perils of Prosperity, 1914-1932* (Univ. of Chicago, 1958), p. 76.
58. *Proceedings of the Nineteenth National Convention of the Anti-Saloon League, 1919*, p. 82.
59. *Ibid.*, p. 137.
60. *Cong. Record*, 66 Cong., 1 Sess., p. 7627.
61. New York *Herald*, June 14, 1919.
62. Wayne B. Wheeler in the New York *Times*, March 29, 1926.
63. N. Best, *Yes, "It's the Law" and It's a Good Law* (New York, 1926), pp. 62-63.
64. G. Chesterton, *What I Saw in America* (New York, 1922), p. 151.

NOTES ON CHAPTER SEVEN

1. In the preface to his *Memoirs*, Bryan wrote proudly that he

   . . . was born a member of the greatest of all the races — the Caucasian Race, and had mingled in [his] veins the blood of English,

Irish, and Scotch. One has only to consider the limitations upon one's opportunities imposed by race to understand the incalculable benefit of having the way opened between the child and the stars.

Two of his most popular later lectures were called "America's Mission" and "The White Man's Burden."

2. W. and M. Bryan, *The Memoirs of William Jennings Bryan* (Philadelphia, 1925), p. 294.
3. M. Werner, *Bryan* (New York, 1929), p. 18.
4. C. Darrow, *The Story of My Life* (New York, 1932), pp. 90, 91.
5. W. and M. Bryan, *op. cit.*, p. 290.
6. J. Long, *Bryan: The Great Commoner* (New York, 1928), pp. 221-222.
7. *The Letters of Theodore Roosevelt* (E. Morison, ed., 8 vols., Harvard, 1951-1954), VII, p. 724.
8. W. and M. Bryan, *op. cit.*, pp. 288, 294. Bryan himself complained sadly to Wayne B. Wheeler that he had lost political influence by accepting money from the Anti-Saloon League.
9. F. Iglehart, *King Alcohol Dethroned* (New York, 1917), pp. 303-305. Bryan was speaking at a dinner in his honor at the Hotel La Fayette, Washington, on December 6, 1916.
10. M. Werner, *op. cit.*, p. 261.
11. *Ibid.*, p. 254.
12. The message was signed by the leading six in the Anti-Saloon League: Purley A. Baker, James Cannon, Jr., A. J. Barton, Edwin C. Dinwiddie, Wayne B. Wheeler, and Ernest C. Cherrington. It finished with the rousing paragraph:

> Generations yet unborn will rise up to call you blessed. Women and children without number who have had to sit in sackcloth and ashes, robbed of their right and despoiled of their best treasures by the greedy, conscienceless, lecherous traffic in strong drink, will not cease to thank God that He sent you to help proclaim the day of their deliverance.

13. V. and O. Case, *We Called It Culture* (New York, 1948), pp. 84-110. Bryan's gestures during his lectures were so spectacular that a silent film promoter, George R. Dalton, negotiated with the Great Commoner to make a film from his prohibition lectures called *Throughout the Ages*. Bryan was to denounce the portrayals of various historical, Oriental and European drinking orgies, and also to get the picture distributed by the churches, the Anti-Saloon League, and the W.C.T.U. Dalton ended by suing Bryan for breach of contract.
14. W. and M. Bryan, *op. cit.*, p. 295.
15. The Ku Klux Klan unkindly burned a fiery cross at Dayton, Ohio, upon the news of Bryan's death. The inscription on the cross read: IN MEMORY OF WILLIAM JENNINGS BRYAN, THE GREATEST KLANSMAN OF OUR TIME, THIS CROSS IS BURNED; HE STOOD AT ARMAGEDDON AND BATTLED FOR THE LORD.

It is doubtful that Bryan was a member of the Klan, although he wanted the Klan's support in his campaign to be elected as a Senator for Florida in 1926.
16. Reprinted in the Boston *Herald*, July 29, 1925.
17. *Catholic Total Abstinence Union of America: Souvenir of the 35th Annual Convention* (Wilkes-Barre, Pa., 1905), p. 42.
18. *Series I, Vol. 3, of Library of Congress microfilm of Theodore Roosevelt's letters*, pp. 236-244.
19. *The Letters of Theodore Roosevelt, op. cit.*, VII, p. 773.
20. December 13, 1917. The letter is reproduced between pages 44 and 45 of Deets Pickett, *The Wooden Horse, or America Menaced by a Prus-*

sianized Trade (New York, 1918). The letter was used by the prohibitionists in 1917 as evidence for their Christmas Day denunciation of the widespread drunken immorality in Pershing's army. Theodore Roosevelt immediately denied that he had alleged any such thing.

21. *The Letters of Theodore Roosevelt, op. cit.*, VI, p. 1131.
22. *The Cyclopedia of Temperance, Prohibition and Public Morals* (D. Pickett, ed., New York, 1917), p. 341.
23. *The Letters of Theodore Roosevelt, op. cit.*, VIII, p. 930 (my italics).
24. J. Leary, Jr., *Talks with T. R.* (Boston, 1920), pp. 22-24. On pp. 291-295, Leary claims that Roosevelt was not a supporter of the Eighteenth Amendment *in private*. He is reported to have said that prohibition was bound to leave unrest; tenement dwellers had nothing to take the saloon's place. It was already bad form to drink in the middle of the day and to drink heavily if one was a politician; the opposite had been true in Roosevelt's youth. Close to a majority of Tammany was now teetotal. This was not a matter of morals, but of efficiency. Drinking declined as soon as it was recognized as an economic factor. But its decline was hard on the social side of life. A "dry" dinner was apt to be a sad sort of affair; dining would become a lost art.

    According to Leary, Roosevelt placed the responsibility for prohibition squarely on the shoulders of the liquor dealers, good and bad. The good liquor dealer did not line up with the progressives to stamp out the bad, and thus suffered the same fate.

25. J. Bishop, *Theodore Roosevelt and His Time* (2 vols., New York, 1920), II, p. 453.
26. *Cong. Record,* 65 Cong., 1 Sess., p. 2209.
27. *The Letters of Theodore Roosevelt, op. cit.*, V, p. 699.
28. Letter to H. E. Hinshaw, July 11, 1908, quoted in H. Pringle, *The Life and Times of William Howard Taft* (2 vols., New York, 1939), I, p. 375.
29. Letter to C. N. Prouty, April 2, 1914, *Ibid.*, II, p. 862.
30. Letter to Cooper Lyon, May 17, 1915, *Ibid.*, II, p. 862.
31. *U.S. Brewers' Association Yearbook,* 1919.
32. H. Pringle, *op. cit.*, II, p. 982.
33. M. Pusey, *Charles Evans Hughes* (2 vols., New York, 1951), I, p. 339.
34. See 226 U.S. 192 (1912). A full account of the case is given in W. Ransom: *Charles E. Hughes: The Statesman as Shown in the Opinions of the Jurist* (New York, 1916), pp. 122-126.
35. M. Pusey, *op. cit.*, I, p. 386.
36. See 253 U.S. 350 (1919).
37. H. Pringle, *op. cit.*, II, p. 983.
38. M. Pusey, *op. cit.*, II, pp. 575-578.
39. *Ibid.*, II, pp. 649-650.
40. *Woodrow Wilson: Life and Letters* (R. Baker, ed., 8 vols., New York, 1927-1939), I, p. 61.
41. E. McAdoo, *The Woodrow Wilsons* (New York, 1937), p. 131.
42. *Woodrow Wilson: Life and Letters, op. cit.*, III, pp. 63-64.
43. *Cong. Record,* 63 Cong., 3 Sess., p. 1690.
44. A. Link, *Wilson: The Road to the White House* (Princeton, 1947), p. 389 note.
45. A. Link, *Wilson: The New Freedom* (Princeton, 1956), pp. 259-260.
46. This was the estimate of Professor Alonzo Taylor, mentioned by C. Darrow and V. Yarros, *Prohibition Mania* (New York, 1927), p. 28.
47. J. Tumulty, *Woodrow Wilson as I Know Him* (New York, 1921), p. 418.
48. *Ibid.*, p. 421. The plank is supposed to have read:

    We recognize that the American saloon is opposed to all social, moral, and economic order, and we pledge ourselves to its absolute elimination by the passage of such laws as will finally and effectually exterminate it. But we favor the repeal of the Volstead Act and the substitution for it of a law permitting the manufacture and sale of light wines and beer.

49. W. McAdoo, *Crowded Years* (Boston, 1931), pp. 388-389.
50. P. McKown, *Certain Important Domestic Policies of Woodrow Wilson* (Univ. of Pennsylvania, 1932), pp. 18-19.
51. In his *Making Woodrow Wilson President* (New York, 1921), p. 208, William F. McCombs gives an uncorroborated but interesting early description of Wilson's Messianic rigidity. McCombs had gone to Wilson to collect his reward after the successful election campaign of 1912. The new President turned to his former political manager and said, "Before we proceed, I wish it clearly understood that I owe you nothing. . . . Whether you did little or much, remember that God *ordained that I should be the next President of the United States.* Neither you nor any other mortal or mortals could have prevented that!"

NOTES ON CHAPTER EIGHT

1. *Proceedings of the Ninth Brewers' Congress, 1869*, p. 13.
2. H. Asbury, *The Great Illusion* (New York, 1951), pp. 105-106.
3. S. Unger, *A History of the National Woman's Christian Temperance Union* (Ph.D., Ohio State Univ., 1933), p. 63.
4. F. Dunne, *Dissertations by Mr. Dooley* (New York, 1906), p. 277.
5. *Cong. Record*, 66 Cong., 1 Sess., p. 4909. There are good descriptions of the political corruption engineered by the liquor trade in P. Odegard, *Pressure Politics* (New York, 1928), pp. 244-266; F. Dobyns, *The Amazing Story of Repeal* (New York, 1940), pp. 213-245; and D. Leigh Colvin, *Prohibition in the United States* (New York, 1926). The last two books must be partially discounted, since they show bias towards the dry cause.
6. There is a full and detailed account of the pressure of the Anti-Saloon League on Congress in P. Odegard, *op. cit.*, pp. 127-180.
7. *Cong. Record*, 62 Cong., 3 Sess., p. 761.
8. *Ibid.*, p. 2836.
9. G. Muller, *National Liquor Dealers' Journal*, April 2, 1913.
10. Clark Distilling Co. v. Western Maryland R. Co., 242 U.S. 311 (1917).
11. *Cong. Record*, 63 Cong., 3 Sess., pp. 498-616.
12. Quoted in P. Odegard, *op. cit.*, p. 158.
13. The drys passed the third law, which dried up the Army and Navy, by tacking a clause onto the Selective Service Draft Act.
14. See W. Graham, "After National Prohibition — What?" *North American Review*, April, 1917.
15. *Woodrow Wilson: Life and Letters* (R. Baker, ed., 8 vols., New York, 1927-1939), VII, pp. 137-138.
16. Quoted in J. Steuart, *Wayne Wheeler, Dry Boss* (New York, 1928), pp. 106-107.
17. J. Tumulty, *Woodrow Wilson as I Know Him* (New York, 1921), p. 413.
18. *Cong. Record*, 65 Cong., 1 Sess., p. 2171. Prohibition was also extended to Hawaii during the war.
19. P. Odegard, *op. cit.*, p. 171.
20. I. Fisher, *Prohibition at Its Worst* (rev. ed., New York, 1927), pp. 12-13. Fisher was in a position to know about the backstage negotiations at this time, since he was serving at Washington on the Council of National Defense.
21. New York *Times*, March 31, 1926.
22. *Cong. Record*, 65 Cong., 1 Sess., p. 5648.

23. Like Harding and Borah, who protested over the constitutionality of the time-limit clause to the Eighteenth Amendment, Norris voted for the amendment after speaking against it.
24. *Cong. Record*, 65 Cong., 1 Sess., pp. 5548-5560, 5585-5627, 5636-5667.
25. *Cong. Record*, 65 Cong., 2 Sess., pp. 422-470.
26. C. Merz, *The Dry Decade* (New York, 1931), p. 76. Merz's book is the only good general account of prohibition. It is based largely on newspaper files. Unfortunately, it was published before the release of the *Wickersham Report*, although Walter Lippmann considered it better than the report, praising it for its "mastery of material, intellectual candor and restrained brilliance of statement."
27. *Cong. Record*, 65 Cong., 2 Sess., p. 458.
28. C. Merz, *op. cit.*, p. 71.
29. For instance, over the question of ratification of prohibition in the New York state assembly, one voter in rural Putnam County had as much representation as four voters in Rochester, five in Syracuse, and seven in parts of Manhattan.
30. C. Merz, *op. cit.*, Appendix D, pp. 315-316.
31. Quoted in F. Dobyns, *op. cit.*, p. 253. Dobyns gives a full-scale assault on the Eighteenth Amendment from the point of view of a fanatical dry.
32. See 253 U.S. 350 (1920).
33. *Cong. Record*, 65 Cong., 2 Sess., pp. 463-464.
34. H. Phillips, in the New York *Evening Sun*, March 12, 1930.
35. In his autobiography, *Bishop Cannon's Own Story* (R. Watson, ed., Duke Univ., 1955), p. 289, Cannon says that Wheeler was the principal author of the Volstead Act. This is also confirmed in J. Steuart, *op. cit.*, pp. 149-152.
36. Although the Anti-Saloon League exerted itself in 1920 to save Volstead's seat, it was unable to win the election for him in 1922. The wets and moderates hated him too much. He was unseated after twenty successive years in Congress, and became legal adviser to the chief of the North Western Dry Enforcement District.
37. The full text of the message is contained in *The Standard Encyclopedia of the Alcohol Problem* (Westerville, Ohio, 1930), VI, p. 2782.
38. For the full text of the Volstead Act, see *U.S. Statutes*, Vol. 41, Pt. 1, pp. 305-322.
39. *Cong. Record*, 66 Cong., 1 Sess., pp. 2869, 2894.
40. *Ibid.*, p. 2956.

NOTES ON CHAPTER NINE

1. *Independent*, January 17, 1920.
2. *Outlook*, January 28, 1920.
3. L. Graves, "Getting the Stuff in Carolina," *New Republic*, May 26, 1920.
4. Porter Emerson Browne, "My Country, 'Tis of Everybody Else," *McClure's*, February, 1920.
5. S. Leacock, *The Truth About Prohibition from the Viewpoint of an Eminent Professor*, Pamphlet, Widener Library, Harvard.
6. D. Roper, *Independent*, January 31, 1920.
7. *Nation*, February 7, 1920.
8. Quoted in H. Asbury, *The Great Illusion* (New York, 1951), p. 142. Asbury's colorpiece on the first days of prohibition is excellent.
9. L. Graves, *op. cit.*
10. V. and R. Cornell, "It's All Moonshine!" *Collier's*, January 17, 1920.
11. *Nation*, March 13, 1920.
12. H. Asbury, *op. cit.*, p. 145.
13. New York *Times*, February 20, 1920.
14. See C. Merz, *The Dry Decade* (New York, 1931), pp. 59-61.

15. Letter of S. J. Beck, *Nation*, March 6, 1920.
16. Dr. La Place, *Proceedings of the Fifteenth International Congress Against Alcoholism*, 1920, p. 114.

NOTES ON CHAPTER TEN

1. Quoted in H. McBain, *Prohibition, Legal and Illegal* (New York, 1928), p. 166.
2. *The Cyclopedia of Temperance, Prohibition and Public Morals* (ed. D. Pickett, New York, 1917), pp. 247-248.
3. B. Hall, *Thrift* (Chicago, 1916), Pamphlet, Widener Library, Harvard.
4. H. Adams, *The Education of Henry Adams* (Modern Lib. ed., 1931), p. 335.
5. J. Reed, "The Pestilence of Fanaticism," *American Mercury*, May, 1925. See also J. Mayer, *The Regulation of Commercialized Vice* (New York, 1922).
6. C. Towns, "The Injury of Tobacco," *Century*, March, 1912.
7. Quoted in Dr. and Mrs. W. Crafts, *Intoxicating Drinks and Drugs in All Lands and Times* (rev. ed., Washington, D.C., 1911), p. 267.
8. M. Sullivan, *Our Times* (6 vols., New York, 1926-1935), V, p. 589.
9. Quoted in R. Miller, *American Protestantism and Social Issues, 1919-1939* (Univ. of N.C., 1958), p. 19.
10. For these three quotations on jazz, I am indebted to two brilliant articles by N. Leonard, Jr., entitled "The Opposition to 'Jazz' in the United States, 1918-1929," *Jazz Monthly*, June, July, 1058.
11. New York *World*, December 11, 1913.
12. C. Wilson, "Call Out the Marines," *Collier's*, July 13, 1929.
13. Bishop J. Cannon, Jr., *Hearings before a Subcommittee of the Senate Committee on the Judiciary*, 69 Cong., 1 Sess., p. 1057.
14. J. Koren, *Alcohol and Society* (New York, 1916), pp. 206, 242.
15. F. Cockrell, "Blunders that Outlawed the Liquor Traffic," *Current History*, October, 1930.
16. J. Chapman, "Drink, and the Tyranny of Dogma," *Outlook*, January 16, 1924.
17. *Wickersham Report*, Summary, p. 33.
18. *Ibid.*, II, p. 132.
19. *Ibid.*, Summary, p. 11.
20. *Ibid.*, Summary, pp. 16-17. And *Statistics Concerning Intoxicating Liquors* (U.S. Treasury Dept., Washington, D.C., 1933), p. 97.
21. R. Haynes, *Prohibition Inside Out* (New York, 1923), p. 44.
22. *Wickersham Report*, Summary, p. 17.
23. I. Reeves, *Ol' Rum River* (Chicago, 1931), p. 33.
24. S. Walker, *The Night Club Era* (New York, 1933), p. 76.
25. Quoted in C. Merz, *The Dry Decade* (New York, 1931), p. 123.
26. *Cong. Record*, 67 Cong., 4 Sess., p. 1512.
27. R. Smith, "Politics and Prohibition Enforcement," *Independent*, October 3, 1925.
28. C. Mills, "Where the Booze Begins," *Collier's*, October 15, 1927.
29. M. Willebrandt, *Inside of Prohibition* (Indianapolis, 1929), pp. 113-114.
30. *Wickersham Report*, II, p. 202. The turnover in the higher administrative posts of the Prohibition Bureau averaged 25 per cent a year for the first ten years of prohibition. A peak of 66 per cent was reached in 1922, and the lowest point was 11 per cent in 1925.
31. Quoted in *Periscope*, November, 1929.
32. *Wickersham Report*, II, pp. 162-163.
33. R. Haynes, *op. cit.*, p. 156.
34. *Reforming America with a Shotgun* (A.A.P.A., Washington, D.C., 1929).
35. J. Addams, "Prohibition and Chicago," *Survey Graphic*, October, 1929.

36. Woodcock even had to issue an exoneration of the Bureau and a plea to the citizens of America called "The Value of Law Observance" (Washington, D.C., 1930).

37. Quoted in *Reforming America with a Shotgun, op. cit.*

38. *Cong. Record,* 70 Cong., 1 Sess., p. 2155.

39. *Wickersham Report,* Summary, p. 45.

40. The figures are taken from *Statistics Concerning Intoxicating Liquors, op. cit.,* pp. 95-97. The quotation comes from *The Memoirs of Herbert Hoover* (3 vols., London, 1952), II, p. 276. The comparative figures for the number of jail sentences for prohibition offenders favor the figure for 1932, for suspended and paroled and probated sentences were included by the authorities in this total, and not in the total for 1927.

41. S. Walker, *op. cit.,* p. 159.

42. *Cong. Record,* 66 Cong., 1 Sess., p. 2875.

43. See F. Dobyns, *The Amazing Story of Repeal* (New York, 1940), pp. 284-298.

44. J. Steuart, *Wayne Wheeler, Dry Boss* (New York, 1928), p. 152.

45. C. Merz, *op. cit.,* pp. 201-205. Merz is particularly good on the failure of the states to co-operate with the federal government in enforcing the dry laws.

46. New York *Times,* January 29, 1928.

47. H. Wilson, *Dry Laws and Wet Politicians* (Stoughton, Mass., 1922), *passim.*

48. I. Reeves, *op. cit.,* Introduction.

49. New York *Times,* September 13, 1925.

50. T. Walnut, "The Human Element in Prohibition Enforcement," *Annals of the American Academy,* September, 1923, pp. 201-207.

51. W. Wheeler, "Are the Wets Hypocrites in Their Plea for State Rights?" *Current History,* October, 1926.

52. *Wickersham Report,* IV, pp. 75, 123, 151, 179, 665, 768, 936.

53. *Ibid.,* III, p. 12.

54. See C. Merz, *op. cit.,* pp. 267-274; H. McBain, *op. cit.,* pp. 60-76; H. Johnston, *What Rights Are Left?* (New York, 1930), pp. 34-43.

55. For a full survey of the referendums on prohibition, see C. Robinson, *Straw Votes* (Columbia Univ., 1932), Appendix B.

56. *Wickersham Report,* Summary, p. 43.

57. In Scripps-Howard chain, December 4, 1929.

58. J. Brebner, *North Atlantic Triangle* (New Haven, 1945), pp. 293-294.

59. R. Haynes, *op. cit.,* p. 87.

60. *Wickersham Report,* V, pp. 383-387.

61. *Hearings before a Subcommittee of the Senate Committee on the Judiciary,* 69 Cong., 1 Sess., pp. 91-92.

62. *The Balance of International Payments of the United States in 1924* (Dept. of Commerce, Washington, D.C., 1925). These figures are at a minimum. The *Wickersham Report,* I, p. 132, gives a further estimate for smuggled liquor of some five million gallons for 1929-1930.

63. Imports of spirits into the Bahamas had a value of more than $3,000,000 in 1922; their value had been $20,000 in 1918. Between 1925 and 1929, imports of whisky from Canada to the British West Indies more than doubled and to St. Pierre and Miquelon increased about four times. Roy Haynes credited prohibition with paying off the long-standing public debt of the off-shore islands.

64. A. Moray, *The Diary of a Rum-Runner* (London, 1929).

65. See J. Barbican, *The Confessions of a Rum-Runner* (London, 1927); F. Van de Water, *The Real McCoy* (New York, 1931); and R. Carse, *Rum Row* (New York, 1959).

66. H. Van Loon, "Heroes All," *Forum,* January, 1925.

67. *Hearings before a Subcommittee of the Senate Committee on the Judiciary,* 69 Cong., 1 Sess., p. 68.
68. *Ibid.,* p. 182.
69. *Wickersham Report,* Summary, p. 28.
70. *Ibid.,* p. 27.
71. Some idea of the prevalence of industrial alcohol in the early days of prohibition is given by a report of a Philadelphia analyst in 1922, who discovered that 94 out of 98 samples of current bootleg liquor contained denatured alcohol.
72. New York *World,* August 9 to 16, 1926. The series of articles was written by Robert Barry.
73. New York *Times,* December 30, 1926.
74. Dr. Leon Walters, in the New York *Times,* January 5, 1927.
75. H. Wilson, *op. cit.,* p. 129.
76. Dr. James Doran, in the New York *Times,* January 18, 1930. The Bureau's estimate of diverted industrial alcohol at this time was put at the low figure of 9,000,000 gallons a year.
77. *Wickersham Report,* I, p. 132.
78. *Ibid.,* IV, p. 411.
79. *Ibid.,* Summary, pp. 29-30.
80. C. Warburton, "Prohibition and Economic Welfare," *Annals of the American Academy,* September, 1932, p. 90.
81. R. Haynes, *op. cit.,* pp. 276-277.
82. M. Willebrandt, *op. cit.,* p. 90.
83. C. Merz, *op. cit.,* p. 119.
84. John Judge, Jr., *Noble Experiments* (New York, 1930). The recipe of Senator Reed for pumpkin gin was "simple and interesting." A ripe pumpkin was plugged, and the seeds removed. It was then packed with sugar, the plug reinserted, and sealed with paraffin. In thirty days, both the sugar and meat of the pumpkin were transformed into high-powered gin. As for applejack, all that was necessary was to buy apple juice, let it ferment, freeze it, and pour off the unfrozen alcohol from the center. Reed was not a friend of the drys.
85. *The Penalty of Law Obedience,* Pamphlet, Widener Library, Harvard.
86. See H. Feldman, *Prohibition. Its Economic and Industrial Aspects* (New York, 1927), p. 66.
87. *Wickersham Report,* I, p. 121.
88. *Ibid.,* I, p. 134.
89. *Ibid.,* I, p. 132.
90. C. Warburton, *op. cit.,* p. 90.
91. Compare G. Ostrander, *The Prohibition Movement in California, 1848-1933* (Ph.D., Univ. of California, 1957), pp. 177-181.
92. Colonel L. Brown, quoted in C. Darrow and V. Yarros, *Prohibition Mania* (New York, 1927), p. 150. But, as Peter Odegard told me, the California grape growers resented prohibition by the time of the thirties and the depression. The overproduction of grapes, which prohibition encouraged, and the uncertainty of the market led to great ills in the California grape industry. The growers preferred the steady market given by legal wine drinking.
93. *Wickersham Report,* I, p. 132.
94. C. Warburton, *op. cit.,* p. 90.
95. R. Haynes, *op. cit.,* p. 107.
96. *Wickersham Report,* IV, p. 1103.
97. Interview with Miss Justo, June 20, 1960.
98. *Hearings before a Subcommittee of the Senate Committee on the Judiciary,* 69 Cong., 1 Sess., pp. 57-58.
99. A bill for deporting alien violators of the Volstead Act passed the House

of Representatives by a vote of 222 to 73, in 1922. This vicious measure was killed by Senate indifference.

100. *Wickersham Report,* Summary, p. 33. For the ubiquity of home-brewing, see also J. Flynn, "Home, Sweet Home-Brew," *Collier's,* September 1, 1928.

101. J. Reed, *op. cit.,* p. 135.

102. D. Cassidy, " 'Moonshine' on the Mississippi," *New Republic,* May 15, 1929.

103. *Wickersham Report,* III, pp. 78-79.

104. F. Brown, "Prohibition and Mental Hygiene," *Annals of the American Academy,* September, 1932, p. 67.

105. C. Norris, "Our Essay in Extermination," *North American Review,* December, 1928.

106. W. Shepherd, "Kansas, By Ginger!" *Collier's,* July 26, 1930.

107. Quoted in *Periscope,* May, 1930.

108. *Hearings before a Subcommittee of the Senate Committee on the Judiciary,* 69 Cong., 1 Sess., pp. 96-97.

109. M. Willebrandt, *op. cit.,* p. 209.

110. *Ibid.,* p. 200.

111. *Wickersham Report,* II, pp. 167, 176-177, 178.

112. New York *Times,* January 17, 1925.

113. H. Mencken, *Americana, 1925* (New York, 1925), pp. 257-258.

114. G. Ostrander, *op. cit.,* p. 173.

115. New York *Evening Post,* April 18, 1929.

116. *Hearings before a Subcommittee of the Senate Committee on the Judiciary,* 69 Cong., 1 Sess., p. 57.

117. *Prohibition Enforcement* (A.A.P.A., Washington, D.C., 1930), p. 20.

118. *Statistics Concerning Intoxicating Liquors, op. cit.,* p. 97.

119. Fourteen new judgeships were created in 1922. Congress thought that this creation would set a maximum to the number of judges needed in the United States; but the pressure of prohibition cases made them increase the number of judges still more. Yet, by the time of repeal, there were still too few judges to do the work required by the prohibition laws.

120. *Statistics Concerning Intoxicating Liquors, op. cit.,* p. 97.

121. *Wickersham Report,* Summary, pp. 56, 57.

122. *Ibid.,* p. 58. In 1930, the next largest classes of long-term federal prisoners were provided by violators of the Narcotics Acts (22 per cent of the total), and of the National Motor Vehicle Theft, or Dyer, Act (13.2 per cent of the total).

123. H. Hoover, *Memoirs, op. cit.,* II, p. 267.

124. *Wickersham Report,* III, pp. 350-351.

125. H. McBain, *op. cit.,* p. 61. I have relied heavily on McBain's excellent critique of the effect of prohibition on the law of America. Also useful is a contemporary legal guide for wets, H. Johnston, *What Rights Are Left?* (New York, 1930).

126. See 267 U.S. 132 (1924).

127. De Pater v. United States, 34 Fed. (2nd) 275. The Circuit Court of Appeals for the Fourth Circuit decided to follow the reasoning of the Supreme Court in the case of United States v. Berkeness, 275 U.S. 149 (1927), that Congress in the Volstead Act had made "a general policy to protect the home against intrusion through the use of search warrants."

128. *Padlock Procedure* (U.S. Treasury Dept., Washington, D.C., 1930), p. 5.

129. H. McBain, *op. cit.,* p. 125.

130. See 254 U.S. 88 (1920); 272 U.S. 321 (1926).

131. See 267 U.S. 188 (1924).

132. See 260 U.S. 377 (1922).

133. See 273 U.S. 1 (1926), and cases quoted in H. McBain, *op. cit.*

134. See 277 U.S. 438 (1927). I am also indebted to P. Freund, "Mr. Justice

Brandeis," in *Mr. Justice* (Durham and Kurland, eds., Univ. of Chicago, 1956).

135. Captain Stayton to Senator Goff. *Hearings before a Subcommittee of the Senate Committee on the Judiciary,* 69 Cong., 1 Sess., I, p. 1491. To distinguish this committee, which investigated the senatorial elections of 1926, from that which investigated prohibition in 1926, it will hereafter be called the "Reed Committee."
136. Quoted by P. Jessup, *Elihu Root* (2 vols., New York, 1938), II, p. 476.
137. W. Lippmann, *Interpretations, 1931-1932* (New York, 1932), p. 317.

NOTES ON CHAPTER ELEVEN

1. H. Ellis, *The Criminal* (New York, 1895), p. 97. A favorite statement of Lombroso for the drys was his dictum:

   Alcohol, then, is a cause of crime, first, because many commit crime in order to obtain drink; further, men sometimes seek in drink the courage necessary to commit crime, or as an excuse for their misdeeds; again, because it is by the aid of drink that young men are drawn into crime; and because the drink shop is the place for the meeting of accomplices, where they not only plan their crimes but also squander their gains.

2. J. Landesco, "Prohibition and Crime," *Annals of the American Academy,* September, 1932, p. 125.
3. *Wickersham Report,* IV, p. 372.
4. J. Landesco, *op. cit.,* p. 125. Landesco points out that the rise of the monopolistic gang leader can be seen in the life history of one Chicago mobster, Mont Tennes, who began by owning one gambling saloon and ended by taking a cut from all gambling through his ownership of the wires for communicating gambling news.
5. See H. Gosnell, *Machine Politics* (Univ. of Chicago, 1937), pp. 42-44.
6. J. Landesco, "Organized Crime in Chicago," *Illinois Crime Survey* (Chicago, 1929), Part 3.
7. L. Adamic, *Dynamite* (New York, 1931), pp. 347-353.
8. There is a good analysis of the private armies of America in J. Shalloo, *Private Police* (Ph.D., Univ. of Philadelphia, 1933).
9. New York *Times,* May 3, 1928.
10. There are good accounts of the Ford Service's connection with the prohibition racketeers in L. Morris, *Not So Long Ago* (New York, 1949), and K. Sward, *The Legend of Henry Ford* (New York, 1948).
11. L. Velie, *Labor, U.S.A.* (New York, 1959), p. 180.
12. E. Lavine, *Gimme* (New York, 1931), p. 126.
13. *Wickersham Report,* III, p. 166.
14. G. Hostetter, quoted in *ibid.,* IV, pp. 328-329.
15. *Ibid.,* IV, pp. 330-331. The whole section on Illinois in the *Wickersham Report* is an extraordinary and fascinating document on prohibition and crime.
16. J. Landesco, "Prohibition and Crime," *op. cit.,* p. 124.
17. J. Landesco to James O'Donnell Bennett, *Wickersham Report,* IV, p. 410.
18. See Supplement, "The Prisoner's Antecedents," to *Prisoners, 1923: Crime Conditions in the United States as Reflected in Census Statistics of Imprisoned Offenders* (Washington, D.C., 1926), p. 67. Crime was more prevalent in urban than rural areas. The statistics showed that 25.1 people in each 100,000 were committed to jail in the cities, only 7.6 in the country. These figures did seem to prove certain dry arguments about the wickedness of the cities.

19. C. Wright Mills, *The Power Elite* (New York, 1956), p. 82.
20. A. Lindesmith, "Organized Crime," *Annals of the American Academy*, September, 1941.
21. *Wickersham Report*, III, p. 156.
22. New York *Times*, May 10, 1931.
23. S. Strunsky, *The Living Tradition* (New York, 1939), p. 52.
24. *Wickersham Report*, IV, p. 415.
25. Quoted in L. Greene, *The Era of Wonderful Nonsense* (Indianapolis, 1939), pp. 250-253. The interview with Capone was conducted by Mrs. Eleanor Patterson, the editor of the Washington *Herald*.
26. New York *Times*, December 28, 1919.
27. *Ibid.*, June 14, 1931.
28. *New Republic*, October 28, 1931.
29. *Illinois Crime Survey, op. cit.*, p. 1083.
30. Senator Edwards, *Plain Talk*, December, 1927.
31. *Wickersham Report*, IV, p. 370.
32. New York *Times*, April 5, 1929.
33. S. Walker, *The Night Club Era* (New York, 1933), p. 213.
34. M. Tillitt, *The Price of Prohibition* (New York, 1932), p. 12.
35. See M. Bruere, *Does Prohibition Work?* (New York, 1927), pp. 285-291, for a description of the "first-floor flats" of New York.
36. J. London, *John Barleycorn* (New York, 1913), p. 101.
37. New York *World*, March 31, 1930.
38. *Proceedings of the Twenty-second National Convention of the Anti-Saloon League, 1925.*
39. Proprietor, "Running a Speakeasy," *New Freeman*, June 11, 1930.
40. Quoted in *Periscope*, February, 1931.
41. T. Veblen, *The Theory of the Leisure Class* (Modern Lib., New York, 1934), p. 70.
42. *Wickersham Report*, III, pp. 111, 125.
43. *Ibid.*, p. 161.
44. R. Lusk, "The Drinking Habit," *Annals of the American Academy*, September, 1932, pp. 48-49.
45. F. Dunne, *Mr. Dooley at His Best* (New York, 1938), p. 259.
46. M. Bruere, *op. cit.*, pp. 171-172.
47. E. Wilson, "The Lexicon of Prohibition," *The American Earthquake* (New York, 1958), pp. 89-91.
48. C. Warburton, "Prohibition and Economic Welfare," *Annals of the American Academy*, September, 1932, pp. 89-97.
49. G. Ade, *The Old-Time Saloon* (New York, 1931), p. 56.
50. See H. Keyserling, *America Set Free* (London, 1930), p. 426. Keyserling also noted that in the Bible the third curse recorded is attached to the first prohibitionist, Ham, the son of Noah.
51. G. Nathan, *Land of the Pilgrim's Pride* (New York, 1927), pp. 6-7.
52. F. Scott Fitzgerald, *The Last Tycoon* (New York, 1941), p. 75.
53. S. Lewis, *Babbitt* (New York, 1922), p. 215.
54. M. Bruere, *op. cit.*, p. 63.
55. J. Freeman, *If Not the Saloon — What?* (New York, 1903), p. 11.
56. *Cong. Record*, 70 Cong., 2 Sess., p. 3728.
57. See M. Bruere, *op. cit.*, p. 61.
58. See R. McCarthy (ed.), *Drinking and Intoxication* (New Haven, Conn., 1959), pp. 205-230.
59. W. Wheeler, "Is There Prohibition?" *North American Review*, September, 1925.
60. For the necessity of the speak-easy to the middle classes, see R. and H. Lynd, *Middletown in Transition* (New York, 1937), pp. 276-277. This book was the successor of the path-breaking *Middletown* (New York, 1929), which

examines the habits and customs of the town of Muncie, Indiana. It set a standard for subsequent sociological research, and is the best survey of the changes in American town life between 1890 and 1925. When the book was published, it met with praise from the *Catholic World* as well as the *Christian Century*, and did much to destroy the hocus-pocus about the virtue of the Midwest. Stuart Chase, in the New York *Herald Tribune* of February 3, 1929, called the work a "priceless document," since for the first time anthropology had "swung its searchlight upon white Christian Nordics, carrying on their mores and taboos in the middle of the grain culture belt of the greatest Republic ever heard of." Meanwhile, R. L. Duffus commented in the New York *Times* of January 20, "Those who cling to their childish illusions about their native land will wish that the Lynds had scrutinized the Patagonians instead."

61. See H. Stearns, *America — A Re-appraisal* (New York, 1937), p. 71. Stearns, who edited a notorious attack on American civilization in 1922, returned to praise his country in a similar volume, which appeared in 1938. He shared in the assumptions of those American intellectuals who saw few virtues in the vulgarity of prosperity, and many in the poverty of depression.

62. F. Dunne, *op. cit.*, p. 261.

63. J. Riley and C. Marden, "The Social Pattern of Alcoholic Drinking," *Quarterly Journal of Studies on Alcohol*, September, 1947, p. 272.

NOTES ON CHAPTER TWELVE

1. *Annual Report of the A.A.P.A.*, 1928.

2. There is an excellent thesis by D. Heckman, *Prohibition Passes: The Story of the Association Against the Prohibition Amendment* (Ph.D., Ohio State Univ., 1939). He deals fully with the propaganda techniques and organization of the Association.

3. J. Spender, *Through English Eyes* (New York, 1928), p. 155.

4. R. Binkley, *Responsible Drinking* (New York, 1930), p. 4.

5. D. Leigh Colvin, *Prohibition in the United States* (New York, 1926), p. 435.

6. J. Clark, Jr., "The Prohibition Cycle," *North American Review*, May, 1933.

7. H. McBain, *Prohibition, Legal and Illegal* (New York, 1928), p. 15.

8. R. Haynes, *Prohibition Inside Out* (New York, 1923), p. 304.

9. Colonel Dan Morgan Smith, *Proceedings of the Nineteenth National Convention of the Anti-Saloon League*, 1919, p. 98.

10. Statement of January, 1919, quoted in *Anti-Saloon League Yearbook*, 1922.

11. F. Franklin, *What Prohibition Has Done to America* (New York, 1922), p. 120.

12. C. Darrow in answer to the Rev. John H. Holmes, *Debate on Prohibition* (New York, 1924), p. 8.

13. U.S. District Attorney Hayward, New York *Times*, December 26, 1922.

14. H. Warner, *Prohibition: An Adventure in Freedom* (Westerville, Ohio, 1928), p. 142.

15. *Ibid.*, p. 145.

16. M. Hughes, *The Logic of Prohibition* (Pasadena, Calif., 1915), p. 57.

17. W. Anderson, "Prohibition — Anderson Answers," *Forum*, July, 1919.

18. P. Andreae, *The Prohibition Movement* (Chicago, 1915), p. 419.

19. H. Mencken, "Dithyrambs on Alcohol," Pamphlet, Widener Library, Harvard.

20. *Anti-Saloon League Yearbook*, 1922.

21. *Wickersham Report*, III, p. 310.

22. *Ibid.*, III, p. 270.

23. R. Haynes, *op. cit.*, p. 166.

24. *Wickersham Report*, V, p. 60.

25. *Ibid.*, III, p. 16, 55, 97.

26. F. Dunne, *Mr. Dooley at His Best* (New York, 1938), p. 261.
27. Quoted in H. Barnes, *Prohibition Versus Civilization* (New York, 1932), p. 68.
28. R. Haynes, *op. cit.,* pp. 291, 294.
29. S. Strauss, "Things Are in the Saddle," *Atlantic Monthly,* November, 1924.
30. See the Introduction by the editor of *Ladies Home Journal* to S. Crowther, *Prohibition and Prosperity* (New York, 1930). See also the estimates of I. Fisher, *Prohibition at Its Worst* and *Prohibition Still at Its Worst* (Alcohol Information Committee, New York, 1926, 1928). Fisher's estimates of the annual saving of prohibition are set at the ludicrous figure of six billion dollars a year, a total of sixty billion dollars in the decade. His strange calculations were attacked by the even stranger calculations of C. Darrow and V. Yarros, *Prohibition Mania* (New York, 1927). Yet such was the fear of economists at venturing their reputations on the quicksands of the dry and wet economic war of propaganda that Fisher could find no professional economist to deny the benefits of prohibition (*American Economic Review,* March, 1927).
31. Quoted in H. Miller, "An Economist Looks at Prohibition," *Town and Gown,* October, 1930. See also *Anti-Saloon League Yearbook,* 1931, and W. MacLeod, "Great Britain's Attitude on the Drink Problem," *Current History,* August, 1930.
32. R. Scott, "Prohibition as Seen by a Business Man," *North American Review,* September, 1925.
33. W. Williams, "Worker's Speakeasy," *Survey Graphic,* February 1, 1931.
34. *Recent Economic Changes* (Washington, D.C., 1930).
35. See *Does Prohibition Pay?* (A.A.P.A., Washington, D.C., 1930). This estimate is more moderate than the exaggerated figures of M. Tillitt, *The Price of Prohibition* (New York, 1932), who calculated that the annual bootleg liquor bill during the years after 1922 was 2½ times that of the average years between 1914 and 1916. Tillitt also charged prohibition with the deaths of 70,000 men from bad alcohol. He was more concerned with sensation than accuracy in these particular estimates.
36. C. Warburton, *The Economic Results of Prohibition* (Ph.D., Columbia, 1932), pp. 260-263.
37. G. Seldes, *The Years of the Locust* (Boston, 1933), p. 213. For an extreme dry view of the wickedness of the wet economic propaganda campaign, see F. Dobyns, *The Amazing Story of Repeal* (New York, 1940), pp. 375-396; and E. Gordon, *The Wrecking of the Eighteenth Amendment* (Francestown, N.H., 1943).

NOTES ON CHAPTER THIRTEEN

1. *Selected letters of William Allen White, 1899-1943* (W. Johnson, ed., New York, 1947), p. 260.
2. A. Longworth, *Crowded Hours* (New York, 1933), p. 325.
3. H. Mencken, *A Carnival of Buncombe* (M. Moos, ed., John Hopkins, Baltimore, 1956), pp. 18, 35.
4. *The Autobiography of William Allen White* (New York, 1946), p. 616.
5. S. Adams, *Incredible Era* (Boston, 1939), p. 297. This story was also heard from a different source by Will Irwin.
6. *He Was "Just Folks"* (C. Asher, ed., Chicago, 1923).
7. S. Adams, *op. cit.,* p. 8.
8. *Ibid.,* p. 72.
9. J. Steuart, *Wayne Wheeler, Dry Boss* (New York, 1928), p. 161.
10. See W. White, *Masks in a Pageant* (New York, 1928), p. 402.
11. *New York Times,* July 8, 1920.
12. H. Mencken, *A Carnival of Buncombe, op. cit.,* p. 39.
13. *New York Times,* June 6, 17, 1920.
14. J. Steuart, *op. cit.,* p. 163.

15. New York *Times,* October 14, 1920.
16. New York *Times,* September 27, 1920.
17. J. Cox, *Journey Through My Years* (New York, 1946), p. 334.
18. A. Longworth, *op. cit.,* p. 324.
19. New York *Times,* July 5, 1922.
20. *Message to Congress,* December 8, 1922.
21. S. Adams, *op. cit.,* p. 372.
22. New York *Times,* May 17, 1923.
23. Letter of June 11, 1923.
24. *Speeches and Addresses of Warren G. Harding, President of the United States: Delivered during the Course of his Tour from Washington, D.C., to Alaska and Return to San Francisco, June 20 to August 2, 1923* (Washington, D.C., 1923), p. 107.
25. C. Coolidge, *The Autobiography of Calvin Coolidge* (New York, 1929), p. 20.
26. *Ibid.,* p. 235.
27. *Ibid.,* p. 173.
28. C. Fuess, *Calvin Coolidge: The Man from Vermont* (Boston, 1940), p. 105.
29. D. Gilfond, *The Rise of Saint Calvin* (New York, 1932), p. 29.
30. Coolidge says of Crane, in his *Autobiography,* p. 114, "He confirmed my opinion as to the value of a silence which avoids creating a situation where one would otherwise not exist, and the bad taste and the danger of arousing animosities and advertising an opponent by making any attack on him."
31. R. Woods, *The Preparation of Calvin Coolidge* (Boston, 1924), p. 121.
32. W. White, *A Puritan in Babylon* (New York, 1938), p. 151. William Allen White wrote this second biography of Coolidge to correct the eulogies of his first, inaccurate biography, written in 1925.
33. J. Steuart, *op. cit.,* p. 162.
34. New York *Times,* October 21, 1923.
35. *Message to Congress,* December 6, 1923.
36. *Estimate of Appropriations for the Fiscal Year Ended June 30, 1924,* p. 669.
37. A. Longworth, *op. cit.,* p. 325.
38. W. White, *Calvin Coolidge: The Man Who Is President* (New York, 1925), p. 156.
39. *Selected Letters of William Allen White, 1899-1943, op. cit.,* p. 263.
40. H. Mencken, *A Carnival of Buncombe, op. cit.,* p. 104.
41. J. Steuart, *op. cit.,* pp. 225-226. And T. Huntley, *The Life of John W. Davis* (New York, 1924), Appendix A, p. 293.
42. R. Leiter, *John W. Davis and his Campaign of Futility* (Ph.D., Harvard, 1958), p. 75, note.
43. B. La Follette, *Robert M. La Follette* (2 vols., New York, 1953), I, pp. 17-19.
44. *Ibid.,* II, p. 1119. This letter was written on August 11, 1924, and is in the La Follette Papers. It is interesting that there is no mention of La Follette's position on prohibition, either in his official *Autobiography,* published in 1913, or in the statement of his political philosophy, published in 1920. He was as discreet on the subject as his political contemporaries.
45. W. Lippmann, *Men of Destiny* (New York, 1927), pp. 13-14.
46. Coolidge, however, was never stupid enough to state flatly that "the chief business of the American people is business" without some qualification. This remark appeared in a speech of his to the American Society of Newspaper Editors in Washington on January 17, 1924. It was widely quoted out of context, in order to make Coolidge a prophet rather than an excuse for his times. In context the remark merely prefaces a paragraph which states that the accumulation of wealth is only a means to better living and better education. Coolidge included hopefully, "So long as wealth is made the means and not the end, we need not greatly fear it. And there was never a time when wealth was so generally regarded as a means, or so little regarded as an end, as today."

47. William Allen White, in his *A Puritan in Babylon,* credits the stories of Coolidge's disappointment in pages 401 to 404. He believes Irwin H. Hoover's story of that disappointment. Ike Hoover was head usher of the White House for many years, although he did not like Coolidge. His *Forty-two Years in the White House* (Boston, 1934) is an interesting, although unreliable, account of the private lives of many Presidents. For Coolidge's own version, see his C. Coolidge, *op. cit.,* p. 240.

NOTES ON CHAPTER FOURTEEN

1. J. Cannon, *Bishop Cannon's Own Story* (Duke Univ., 1955), p. 297.
2. *Ibid.,* p. 298.
3. H. Mencken, *Making a President* (New York, 1932), p. 6.
4. *Ibid.,* pp. 8, 82.
5. F. Kent, *The Democratic Party* (New York, 1928), p. 440.
6. Letter to Wayne B. Wheeler, quoted in J. Steuart, *Wayne Wheeler, Dry Boss* (New York, 1928), p. 159.
7. J. Cannon, *op. cit.,* p. 298.
8. New York *Times,* November 1, 1924.
9. J. Cannon, *op. cit.,* pp. 333-335. Cannon contradicts Wheeler's biographer, J. Steuart, who maintains wrongly that Wheeler was dictator to both the Democratic and the Republican conventions in 1924.
10. *Cong. Record,* 69 Cong., 2 Sess., p. 5298.
11. I. Oakley, "The Prohibition Law and the Political Machine," *Annals of the American Academy,* September, 1923, p. 174.
12. *Cong. Record,* 66 Cong., 1 Sess., p. 7627.
13. *Cong. Record,* 66 Cong., 2 Sess., p. 5655. Letter of Wayne B. Wheeler to Senator Sheppard, dated April 3, 1920.
14. New York *Times,* February 13, 1921.
15. C. Merz, *The Dry Decade* (New York, 1931), p. 83. There is a good description by Merz of these halcyon days for Congress, pp. 75-100.
16. Letter of H. W. Marsh, secretary of the National Civil Service Reform League, to Dr. W. W. Keen, of Philadelphia, March 24, 1928.
17. See *Current History,* December, 1923.
18. *Cong. Record,* 69 Cong., 2 Sess., p. 4527.
19. J. Cannon, *op. cit.,* p. 305. Bishop Cannon was jealous of Wheeler's reputation between 1919 and 1928.
20. J. Steuart, *op. cit.,* pp. 194-196.
21. U.S. Bureau of the Census, *Statistical Abstract of the United States, 1960* (Washington, D.C., 1960), p. 5.
22. C. Merz, *op. cit.,* p. 206.
23. *Cong. Record,* 68 Cong., 1 Sess., p. 3237.
24. New York *Times,* November 7, 1924.
25. J. Steuart, *op. cit.,* p. 226.
26. *Hearings before a Subcommittee of the Senate Committee on the Judiciary,* 69 Cong., 1 Sess., p. 868.
27. J. Steuart, *op. cit.,* p. 234.
28. New York *Times,* April 27, 1926.
29. Mrs. D. Leigh Colvin, New York *Times,* September 12, 1929. Mrs. Colvin was president of the New York State Woman's Christian Temperance Union, and later became head of the national organization.
30. Clinton N. Howard corrected this figure in the New York *Herald Tribune,* February 19, 1929. He discovered 342 speak-easies in Washington, 39 on Pennsylvania Avenue, and 46 on Northwest Ninth Street.
31. *Cong. Record,* 70 Cong., 2 Sess., pp. 155-157.
32. M. Willebrandt, *Inside of Prohibition* (Indianapolis, 1929), pp. 143-147.
33. New York *Times,* May 14, 1924.

34. *Wickersham Report*, V, p. 162.
35. M. Willebrandt, *op. cit.*, pp. 147-149.
36. The Anti-Saloon League was alleged to have a similar report for similar purposes of pressure.
37. *Outlook*, May 28, 1930.
38. *Reed Committee*, I, p. 563.
39. *Ibid.*, I, p. 705. Pittsburgh had been plagued by an efficient Prohibition Commissioner, who had persecuted the speak-easies there. Just before the elections, he was transferred to Philadelphia to persecute the liquor interests behind Vare. A Pittsburgh reporter testified that the speak-easy operators behind Pepper generally said, "The election is on, and it is all right now."
40. *Ibid.*, I, pp. 826-828.
41. *Ibid.*, I, p. 1244.
42. Chicago *Tribune*, October 1, 1926.
43. *Reed Committee*, III, p. 2013.
44. *Ibid.*, I, p. 1067.
45. C. Wooddy, *The Case of Frank L. Smith* (Univ. of Chicago, 1931), pp. 224-225.
46. *Reed Committee*, IV, p. 2403.
47. *Wickersham Report*, III, p. 156.
48. *Reed Committee*, II, p. 1883.
49. *Ibid.*, III, p. 2028.
50. *Ibid.*, III, p. 2042.
51. E. Lavine, *Gimme* (New York, 1931), p. 180.

NOTES ON CHAPTER FIFTEEN

1. W. Lippmann, *Men of Destiny* (New York, 1927), p. 68.
2. E. Ross, *Sin and Society* (Boston, 1907), p. 153.
3. There is a good discussion of this change in E. Goldman, *Rendezvous With Destiny* (rev. ed., New York, 1956), pp. 220-247.
4. C. Walsh, *Feminism* (New York, 1917), pp. 139-140.
5. I. Tarbell, "Ladies at the Bar," *Liberty*, July 26, 1930.
6. *Wickersham Report*, I, p. 324.
7. Mrs. Anna Petit, San Francisco *Examiner*, October 15, 1929.
8. G. Norris, *Fighting Liberal* (New York, 1925), p. 406.
9. There is no good history of the Ku Klux Klan, although G. Myers, *History of Bigotry in the United States* (New York, 1943), is interesting. J. Mecklin, *The Ku Klux Klan* (New York, 1924), makes clear the importance of the movement at the time.
10. R. Hofstadter, *The Age of Reform* (New York, 1955), pp. 291-295, points out the tragic quality in the Klan's resistance to the new morality in America.
11. W. Cash, *The Mind of the South* (Anchor ed., New York, 1941), p. 314. And A. Rutledge, "Prohibition and the Negro," *Outlook*, May 28, 1930.
12. H. Fosdick, "Will Science Displace God?" *Harper's*, August, 1926. C. Luther Fry's chapter "Changes in Religious Organizations" in the Report of the President's Research Committee on Social Trends, *Recent Social Trends in the United States* (New York, 1934), pp. 1009-1060, is extremely valuable on the changes in the Protestant churches between 1900 and 1930.
13. R. Haynes, *Prohibition Inside Out* (New York, 1923), p. 210. See also *Hearings before the Select Committee on Investigation of the Bureau of Internal Revenue*, 68 Cong., 2 Sess., p. 2184.
14. *Research Bulletin Number 5*, "The Prohibition Situation" (Dept. of Research and Education, Federal Council of Churches of Christ in America, New York, 1925), pp. 50-51.
15. W. McLoughlin, Jr., has written a brilliant biography of Billy Sunday, *Billy Sunday Was His Real Name* (Univ. of Chicago, 1955). At the height of his

influence between 1896 and 1918, Sunday's career and sermons represented perfectly the myth and words which the American middle classes wished to hear. They wanted to hear a famous farm boy denounce the saloon and foreigners and Huns and Reds in the picturesque language of the evangelical gutter. They wanted to see the living proof of the American success story, a sort of Reverend Horatio Alger. The fact that Billy Sunday transferred his evangelical efforts after the Great War from the Midwest and the fringes of New York to the fertile and reactionary field of the South shows how the fundamentalist and Manichaean audience to which he appealed had become concentrated below the Potomac.

16. *Periscope,* October, 1925.
17. The Church Temperance Society went so far as to relinquish its affiliations with the Anti-Saloon League after this incident. Its director, Dr. Empringham, once a national vice president of the League, polled three thousand Episcopalian clergymen on the subject of prohibition. It was the first large poll taken from the ranks of the clergy. Seven out of ten clergymen said that prohibition was a failure in their localities and wanted modification of the Volstead Act; one-half wanted outright repeal of the Eighteenth Amendment. Since this poll received wide publicity, it did further damage to the image of the united dry Protestant churches, an image carefully created by the Anti-Saloon League. The only reply of Wayne B. Wheeler to the results of the poll was a sneer at the whole Episcopalian Church:

> It has done practically nothing in comparison with other churches, to help eliminate the liquor traffic. This is true with reference to many other evils also. The purpose of Christianity and the Church is to destroy the works of evil and darkness. A beautiful form of church service, without works, counts for but little.

18. J. Cannon, *Bishop Cannon's Own Story* (Duke Univ., 1955), p. 357.
19. *Hearings before a Subcommittee of the Senate Committee on the Judiciary,* 68 Cong., 1 Sess., p. 1626.
20. *The Memoirs of Herbert Hoover* (3 vols., London, 1952), I, pp. 2-7. Hoover found the nineteenth-century families so self-reliant that they were "their own lawyers, labor leaders, engineers, doctors, tailors, dressmakers and beauty parlor artists." Unfortunately, they did not have time for much more than the necessities of life and religion. Ellis Parker Butler commented sourly on the culture of Iowa:

> *Three million yearly for manure,*
> *But not one cent for literature.*

21. *Ibid.,* I, p. 102.
22. See J. Hamill, *The Strange Career of Mr. Hoover under Two Flags* (New York, 1931), and C. Wood, *Herbert Clark Hoover — An American Tragedy* (New York, 1932). Although Hoover admits in his *Memoirs* that one of the reasons for his defeat was the Great Depression, he wrote that the main cause for Roosevelt's victory was the campaign of attack on himself launched by the publicity manager of the Democratic National Committee, and the smear books of Hamill and his like. The truth of the matter was that Hoover had had so much publicity as the author of prosperity that he could only expect vicious personal attacks upon himself as the speculator of depression.
23. Address at Philadelphia, Pennsylvania, October 27, 1928. This remark of Hoover's was also used in his favor by wet Republican newspapers in Northern cities.
24. Remark of S. Parker Gilbert, quoted in O. Villard, *Prophets, True and False* (New York, 1928), p. 24.
25. *Ibid.,* p. 25.
26. W. Rogers, *The Autobiography of Will Rogers* (Boston, 1949), p. 158.

27. E. Davis, "Hoover the Medicine Man," *Forum*, October, 1930.
28. N. Hapgood and H. Moskowitz, *Up from the City Streets* (New York, 1927), p. 94.
29. H. Pringle, *Alfred E. Smith: A Critical Study* (New York, 1927), p. 320.
30. A. Smith, *Up To Now: An Autobiography* (New York, 1929), pp. 114, 286-287.
31. Address at Milwaukee, Wisconsin, September 29, 1928, reprinted in his *Campaign Addresses* (Democratic National Committee, Washington, D.C., 1928), p. 117.
32. See H. Moskowitz, *Alfred E. Smith* (New York, 1924), pp. 248-258.
33. A. Smith, *op. cit.*, p. 287.
34. *Ibid.*, p. 163.
35. H. Moskowitz, *op. cit.*, p. 245. Smith suggested that the Republicans should run the local Anti-Saloon League leader, William H. Anderson, for Governor in 1920. Anderson was later sent to prison for forgery on a trumped-up charge. Jimmy Walker, the future Mayor of New York and at this time a leading Tammany orator, denounced Anderson as the "most drunken man in the State, drunk with the power that he exercises over the Republican Party."
36. Address at Chicago, Illinois, October 19, 1928.
37. F. Kent, *Political Behavior* (New York, 1928), p. 277, gives an interesting discussion of the usefulness of the separate ballot system to Smith.
38. A good critique of Smith's position on the repeal of the Mullan-Gage Law will be found in H. Pringle, *op. cit.*, pp. 327-332.
39. H. Moskowitz, *op. cit.*, p. 261.
40. William Allen White, with his usual felicity of phrase, writes brilliantly on this subject in *Masks in a Pageant* (New York, 1928), pp. 471-473. His charitable judgment of Smith in this book was denied by his partisan action in the election of 1928, when he accused Smith at Olathe, Kansas, on July 12, of voting against bills which sought to curb gambling, prostitution, and saloons in New York. Rebuked severely by Walter Lippmann among others, White withdrew the first two charges. But the damage was already done. The slanders against Smith were increased in the West and South. Bishop James Cannon, Jr., quotes White's accusation without mentioning his recantation in *Bishop Cannon's Own Story, op. cit.*, p. 445.
41. See C. Marshall, *Governor Smith's American Catholicism* (New York, 1928). The full text of Smith's reply is printed in *Progressive Democracy: Addresses and State Papers of Alfred E. Smith* (New York, 1928), pp. 254-269.
42. Smith's daughter, Emily Smith Warner, in her *The Happy Warrior* (with H. Daniel, New York, 1956), p. 185, tells of Judge Proskauer repeating the opinion of Cardinal Hayes on Smith's reply — "it was both good Catholicism and good Americanism." President Kennedy took up much the same position in 1960.
43. H. Mencken, *A Carnival of Buncombe* (H. Moos, ed., Johns Hopkins, Baltimore, 1956), p. 143.
44. Chicago *Tribune*, July 12, 1927.
45. J. Steuart, *Wayne Wheeler, Dry Boss* (New York, 1928), pp. 286-287.
46. J. Cannon, *op. cit.*, p. 396.
47. *The Memoirs of Herbert Hoover, op. cit.*, II, p. 202.
48. See R. Smith and N. Beasley, in their *Carter Glass: A Biography* (New York, 1939), pp. 282-283. Even Senator Glass, of Virginia, who loyally supported Smith in 1928, was shocked that Smith should "slap his platform in the face." Glass complained sadly that "nothing was left for us but to come home and appeal to the South for party regularity."
49. R. Peel and T. Donnelly, *The 1928 Campaign* (New York, 1931), p. 33.
50. V. Dabney, *Dry Messiah: The Life of Bishop Cannon* (New York, 1949), p. 178.

51. O. Villard, *op. cit.*, p. 7. This "reliable" story was frequently used against Smith since it came from the pro-Smith *Nation*. It was one of the minor factors in his defeat.
52. *Current History*, December, 1928.
53. J. Cannon, *op. cit.*, p. 399.
54. The dry head of the Baltimore *Sun's* Washington Bureau wrote from Asheville that four-fifths of the delegates freely admitted in private that they were mainly opposing Smith for his religion. [See V. Dabney, *op. cit.*, p. 180.]
55. O. White, "Workers in the Vineyard." *Collier's*, October 6, 1928.
56. R. Peel and T. Donnelly, *op. cit.*, p. 63.
57. H. Mencken, *A Carnival of Buncombe, op. cit.*, p. 192.
58. The most recent and exhaustive study of the roles of prohibition and religion in the 1928 election can be found in Robert M. Miller's painstaking *American Protestantism and Social Issues* (Univ. of North Carolina, 1958), pp. 48-62. While I agree with Mr. Miller's conclusions, "that the Klan did not play a crucial role in the election; that clergymen did not force their congregations into the anti-Smith camp; that prohibition was not a straw man; and that not all of the religious arguments are on the level of sheer bigotry," I disagree with his implications that the Klan did not represent an important part of Al Smith's opposition, that clergymen did not lead many votes against him, that prohibition was not the mark of much religious bigotry or that many clergymen did not display that same bigotry. R. Hofstadter, in "Could a Protestant Have Beaten Hoover in 1928?" *Reporter*, March 17, 1960, gives a judicious summary of the problem.
59. Address at Oklahoma City, September 20, 1928.
60. Address at New York City, November 3, 1928.
61. *Selected Letters of William Allen White, 1899-1943* (W. Johnson, ed., New York, 1947), p. 287.
62. Address at Omaha, September 18, 1928.
63. Address at Milwaukee, Wisconsin, September 29, 1928.
64. Address at Nashville, Tennessee, October 12, 1928.
65. Address at Chicago, Illinois, October 19, 1928.
66. Address at Philadelphia, Pennsylvania, October 27, 1928.
67. Address at Baltimore, Maryland, October 29, 1928.
68. Quoted in *Program of the Sixth Commonwealth Conference on the Political Issues of 1928* (Univ. of Iowa, May 15, 1928), p. 67.
69. New York *Times*, October 27, 29, 1928.
70. *Ibid.*, July 25, October 31, 1928.
71. *Ibid.*, September 28, 1928.
72. H. Mencken, *A Carnival of Buncombe, op. cit.*, p. 205.
73. A. Smith, *Up To Now, op. cit.*, pp. 407-408.
74. New York *Times*, October 13, November 5, 1928.
75. *Ibid.*, November 8, 20, 1928. By some alchemy, Dr. Butler calculated that 21,000,000 wet votes had been cast in the election.
76. *Anti-Saloon League Yearbook*, 1928.
77. New York *Times*, November 10, 16, 1928.
78. F. Ray, *White House Blues* (New York, 1932), pp. 36-37.
79. K. Hubbard, *Abe Martin's Town Pump* (New York, 1929), p. 45.
80. W. Rogers, *The Autobiography of Will Rogers, op. cit.*, p. 204.
81. W. Lippmann, *Men of Destiny, op. cit.*, p. 8.

NOTES ON CHAPTER SIXTEEN

1. G. Whidden, "Our Arid Press," *New Freeman*, September 10, 1930.
2. See Report of the President's Research Committee on Social Trends, *Recent Social Trends in the United States* (New York, 1934), pp. 423-427.
3. *Proceedings of the Twelfth Annual Convention of the Anti-Saloon League, 1907*, p. 45.

4. See results of a poll summarized in *Anti-Saloon League Yearbook*, 1912.
5. C. Stelzle, *A Son of the Bowery* (New York, 1926), pp. 272-273.
6. See W. Irwin, "Tainted News Methods of the Liquor Interests," *Collier's*, March 13, 1909.
7. See *Hearings before a Subcommittee of the Senate Committee on the Judiciary*, 71 Cong., 2 Sess., p. 4236.
8. Survey of the Methodist Board of Temperance, Prohibition, and Public Morals, cited in D. Heckman, *Prohibition Passes: The Story of the Association Against the Prohibition Amendment* (Ph.D., Ohio State Univ., 1939), p. 88.
9. See *American Magazine*, January, 1917; *McClure's*, April, 1917; *Leslie's*, November 27, 1920; *The Vanity Fair Book, 1930-1931* (New York, 1931).
10. Howard Brubaker in *New Yorker*, quoted in *Periscope*, September, 1929.
11. See E. Emery and H. Smith, *The Press and America* (New York, 1954), pp. 624-626. This is an excellent and concise history.
12. Quoted in L. Greene, *The Era of Wonderful Nonsense* (Indianapolis, 1939), p. 69. This book contains a fair selection of the more sensational journalistic ballyhoos of the twenties. See also, I. Leighton ed., *The Aspirin Age* (New York, 1949); F. Allen, *Only Yesterday* (New York, 1931); J. Morris, *What a Year!* (New York, 1956); L. Snyder and R. Morris eds., *A Treasury of Great Reporting* (New York, 1949); and M. Barrett, *The Jazz Age* (New York, 1959), whose selection of photographs gives a remarkable picture of the time.
13. M. Willebrandt, *Inside of Prohibition* (Indianapolis, 1929), p. 271.
14. *Recent Social Trends in the United States, op. cit.*, p. 537. And see map on page 453, which defines the metropolitan areas of the United States in terms of the circulation of the major city newspapers.
15. C. Robinson, *Straw Votes* (Columbia Univ., 1932), pp. 146-171. Robinson finds fault with the sampling, the bias towards male and wet voters, and the refusal of the drys to co-operate in such polls. He suggests corrections by comparison with the state referenda on prohibition, with the estimates of editors of daily newspapers in 1931, and with the vote on the Beck-Linthicum resolution (which did *not*, however, reflect accurately the will of the constituents of the members of the House). Yet, in the final analysis, even if the findings of the *Digest* were biased in favor of repeal, the fact that they were widely believed to be accurate was a telling blow at the drys.
16. Quoted in V. Dabney, *Dry Messiah: The Life of Bishop Cannon* (New York, 1949), p. 299.
17. *Wickersham Report*, IV, p. 379.
18. *Ibid.*, IV, pp. 349-419.
19. *The Memoirs of Herbert Hoover* (3 vols., London, 1952), II, p. 277.
20. S. Walker, *The Night Club Era* (New York, 1933), p. 107. Walker's description of night-life and crime and café society in New York during prohibition is an excellent piece of reporting.
21. This is the opinion of H. Asbury in his article on these two men in *The Aspirin Age, op. cit.*, p. 40.
22. New York *Times*, July 15 to August 26, 1923; *ibid.*, March 28 to April 4, 1926; *ibid.*, August 5 to 25, 1929.
23. H. Mencken, *Prejudices: Sixth Series* (New York, 1927), p. 23.
24. Quoted in *Periscope*, February, 1930.
25. R. Binkley, *Responsible Drinking* (New York, 1930), p. 159.
26. Quoted in *Periscope*, October, 1929.
27. L. Morris, *Not So Long Ago* (New York, 1949), p. 373. Morris wrote an excellent and witty account of the origins and effects of the trinity of the communications revolution — the motion pictures, the car, and the radio.
28. Quoted in K. Sward, *The Legend of Henry Ford* (New York, 1948), p. 229.
29. Eugene W. Chafin on August 13, 1911, Pamphlet, Widener Library, Harvard.

30. R. and H. Lynd, *Middletown* (New York, 1929), pp. 256 note, 257.
31. *Ibid.*, p. 114.
32. M. Bruere, *Does Prohibition Work?* (New York, 1927), pp. 109, 160.
33. The sharp comment of John Judge, Jr., was, "If prohibition is repealed, Ford is going to quit making cars. If it isn't, Mack is going to make bigger trucks."
34. M. Bruere, *op. cit.*, p. 302.
35. Milwaukee *Journal*, August 3, 1929.
36. L. Morris, *op. cit.*, p. 114.
37. Both of these extracts are quoted in *The Cyclopedia of Temperance, Prohibition and Public Morals* (ed. D. Pickett, New York, 1917), pp. 284-285.
38. A. Woodward, *Substitutes for the Saloon* (rev. ed., Boston, 1919), pp. 358-367, Appendix D.
39. R. and H. Lynd, *op. cit.*, p. 266.
40. There was censorship both in Hollywood and in certain states, such as Kansas, Maryland, New York, Ohio, Pennsylvania, and Virginia. Also some cities had their boards of censors, particularly Boston and Chicago. This form of local censorship was upheld by the Supreme Court as late as January, 1961, by a 5 to 4 decision. The Hollywood "production code" forbade the triumph of crime or the attack on "correct" standards of life. Mencken had a good time listing the words banned in Hollywood scripts, such as *broad, bum, chippy, cocotte, courtesan, eunuch, fairy* (in the sense of homosexual), *floozy, harlot, bit, mamma, huzzy, madam* (in the sense of brothel-keeper), *nance, pansy, sex, slut, trollop, tart, wench,* and *whore*.
41. *Recent Social Trends in the United States, op. cit.*, p. 427.
42. E. Dale, *The Content of Motion Pictures* (New York, 1935), p. 168.
43. *The Vanity Fair Book, 1930-1931* (New York, 1931), p. 89.
44. D. Heckman, *op. cit.*, p. 107.
45. R. L. Duffus in H. Stearns (ed.), *America Now: An Inquiry into Civilization in the United States* (New York, 1938), p. 389.

NOTES ON CHAPTER SEVENTEEN

1. T. Arthur, *Ten Nights in a Bar-Room* (Philadelphia, 1854), pp. 40, 73.
2. J. London, *John Barleycorn* (New York, 1913), p. 15.
3. U. Sinclair, *The Cup of Fury* (London, 1957). Some idea of Sinclair's loss of proportion in later years can be seen in his theory that alcohol is one of the means through which communism rules and subverts. This was exactly Engels's theory about the connection between alcohol and capitalism.
4. *Mark Twain's Autobiography* (C. Neider, ed., New York, 1959), pp. 41, 44.
5. *The Complete Poems of Emily Dickinson* (T. Johnson, ed., Boston, 1960), p. 669.
6. E. Masters, *Spoon River Anthology* (new ed., New York, 1917), p. 68.
7. Edmund Wilson, in his *American Earthquake,* points out the huge debt of American writers to Anderson and quotes Saroyan's remark, "We are all his collaborators."
8. D. Brogan, *American Themes* (London, 1948), p. 192.
9. Quoted by W. Leuchtenburg, *The Perils of Prosperity, 1914-1932* (Univ. of Chicago, 1958), p. 273.
10. H. Mencken, *Prejudices: Third Series* (New York, 1922), p. 176.
11. H. Mencken, *Prejudices: First Series* (New York, 1919), p. 16.
12. E. Hemingway, *A Farewell to Arms* (Modern Lib., New York, 1932), p. 249.
13. There are brilliant chapters by John W. Aldridge in his *After the Lost Generation* (New York, 1951) on the effect the cult of Hemingway had on his American contemporaries. Malcolm Cowley also deals with this well in his *Exile's Return.*
14. *Selected Letters of William Carlos Williams* (J. Thirlwall, ed., New York, 1957).

15. F. Scott Fitzgerald, *The Crack-Up* (E. Wilson ed., New York, 1945), p. 15.
16. *Ibid.*, p. 21.
17. Quoted in E. Wilson, *The Shores of Light* (New York, 1952), p. 31. Wilson's literary chronicle of the twenties and the thirties is acute and informative, particularly on Scott Fitzgerald, who called Wilson his literary conscience.
18. J. Dos Passos in his *Manhattan Transfer* also took up the theme of rags to riches through quick bootlegging fortunes.
19. See F. Hoffman, *The Twenties* (New York, 1955), p. 18. Hoffman's book is a definitive text on the American writers of the decade. He is particularly good on Mencken.
20. R. Lardner, *The Love Nest and Other Stories* (London, 1928), p. 246. Although Wilson and Fitzgerald always championed Lardner, it is only recently that he has been given a critical resurrection.
21. Quoted in F. Hoffman, *op. cit.*, p. 323.
22. D. Parker, *Laments for the Living* (London, 1930), p. 164.
23. Quoted in *Periscope*, October, 1929.
24. H. Stearns (ed.), *America Now* (New York, 1938), Preface.
25. Quoted in C. Merz, *The Great American Band-Wagon: A Study of Exaggerations* (New York, 1928), p. 233.
26. J. Krutch, *Our Modern Temper* (New York, 1929), p. 249.

NOTES ON CHAPTER EIGHTEEN

1. C. Merz, *The Dry Decade* (New York, 1931), p. 81.
2. R. Haynes, *Prohibition Inside Out* (New York, 1923), p. 178.
3. Quoted in C. Darrow and V. Yarros, *Prohibition Mania* (New York, 1927), p. 195.
4. Quoted Congressman Upshaw, *Cong. Record*, 67 Cong., 4 Sess., p. 1513.
5. See *Hearst's International Cosmopolitan*, May, 1926. Johnson had a remarkable career somewhat similar to Theodore Roosevelt's as a lawman in the Badlands. He was commissioned by the federal government to enforce prohibition on the Indian territories, which later became the state of Oklahoma. He was a propagandist for the League and later became a living martyr, when he lost an eye to a stone flung by a London mob. Ernest Cherrington wrote him a letter of appreciation. The letter stated that the great service which both of Johnson's eyes had rendered to the dry cause was not to be compared with the remarkable service which he had rendered in the loss of one of them. A contemporary slogan ran, "Pussyfoot's Eye Will Make England Dry." It did not. Johnson did, however, take the credit for bringing prohibition to Ceylon. His nickname of "Pussyfoot" was a tribute to his devious methods. It was tragic for the sincere members of the League that it did not disown him after his damaging revelations.
6. *New York Times*, December 30, 1926.
7. In 1912, Purley A. Baker put out an economic manifesto. It ran:

> Temperance people must learn to quit spending their money where it is used against their principles. When the Christian Women, who do most of the buying, withdraw their support from business men who espouse the saloon and give their support to business men who oppose the saloon, there will soon be no saloon-supporting business men. This battle is not a rose-water conflict. It is war — continued, relentless war. The rule of successful warfare is to cut off the enemy's supplies and at every point reduce his fighting force to a minimum.

The use of the economic boycott in the ultra-capitalist world of 1912 provoked much the same reactions as the use of "sit-in" tactics by Negroes in the segregated lunch counters of the South. The *National Bulletin* of the National Wholesale Liquor Dealers' Association of America denounced

Baker's words in March, 1912, as a "law breaking manifesto." The *Bulletin* continued, "That the Anti-Saloon League and its bosses hold themselves above all the laws of God and man in their methods of warfare has long been known to those who oppose them."

8. New York *Times,* June 15, July 4, 1919.
9. *Ibid.,* January 31, June 23, 1919. The Association claimed to be interested in personal liberty rather than the bad effect which prohibition would have on the profits of the hotel business.
10. C. Merz, *op. cit.,* p. 212.
11. J. Steuart, *Wayne Wheeler, Dry Boss* (New York, 1928), p. 271.
12. P. Odegard, *Pressure Politics* (New York, 1928), p. 190. And *Hearings before a Subcommittee of the Senate Committee on the Judiciary,* 71 Cong., 2 Sess., III, p. 3895. F. Dobyns, in his *The Amazing Story of Repeal* (New York, 1940), carries this theory of a conspiracy of millionaires and liquor traders to overturn the Eighteenth Amendment beyond the limits of credibility.
13. *Reed Committee,* I, p. 1250.
14. F. Dobyns, *op. cit.,* pp. 17-18.
15. *Pictorial Review,* September, 1929.
16. F. Dobyns, *op. cit.,* p. 86.
17. *Ibid.,* p. 102.
18. *Reed Committee,* I, p. 824.
19. New York *Times,* March 29, 1926.
20. Chicago *Tribune,* July 10, 11, 12, 1927. Perhaps the ultimate point in this method of influence was reached by an advertisement carried in the *New Republic,* January 16, 1961, which ran: "Let us MAKE YOUR OPINIONS COUNT. Let us SEND THEM TO EVERY CONGRESSMAN. Let us do this for 33 cents a month."
21. S. Bent, *Strange Bedfellows* (New York, 1928), p. 52.
22. *Ibid.,* p. 59.
23. Letter of Henry B. Joy to Hon. George S. Graham, April, 1930. Pamphlet, Widener Library, Harvard.
24. Quoted in V. Dabney, *Dry Messiah: The Life of Bishop Cannon* (New York, 1949), p. 322.
25. *Cong. Record,* 72 Cong., 1 Sess., p. 6001.
26. *Ibid.,* 72 Cong., 2 Sess., p. 4221.
27. Baltimore *Evening Sun,* June 29, 1932.
28. The chronicler of the Women's Organization for National Prohibition Reform, Grace C. Root, wrote of Mrs. Charles H. Sabin that her mind had "an instinct for the jugular." Her history of the organization, *Women and Repeal* (New York, 1934), reveals exactly the hectic, inaccurate, moneyed aura that surrounded the workings of the group.
29. *Reed Committee,* I, p. 1238. In many ways, Mrs. Sabin's organization was an offshoot of the Association Against the Prohibition Amendment. It adopted the same policy of outright repeal as its male predecessor. The only known disagreement between the two was in the presidential election of 1932.
30. New York *Tribune,* June 18, 1930.
31. Quoted in G. Root, *op. cit.,* p. 110.
32. New York *Times,* May 23, 1932.
33. New York *American,* May 30, 1929.
34. A. Smith, "On the Way to Repeal," *New Outlook,* August, 1933.
35. Quoted in G. Root, *op. cit.,* p. 159.
36. *Ibid.,* p. 127.
37. E. Cherrington, *Anti-Saloon League Yearbook,* 1932-1933.
38. *The Vanity Fair Book, 1930-1931* (New York, 1931), p. 5.
39. H. Mencken, *Making a President* (New York, 1932), pp. 118-124. Mencken said that Colonel Callahan, of Kentucky, was the last survivor of the bloc

of Irish Catholic Prohibitionists, "which at its peak consists of no less then eight or nine members, lay and clerical, and some say even ten."

40. F. Kelley, "Laborers in Heat and in Heavy Industries," *Annals of the American Academy*, September, 1923, p. 178.
41. See *Proceedings of the First National Conference of Labor's National Committee for Modification of the Volstead Act*, 1931.
42. J. Cooper, "Prohibition from the Workingman's Standpoint," *North American Review*, September, 1925.
43. See Note 41, *op. cit.*
44. *Answers to Favorite "Wet" Arguments* (2nd ed., Westerville, Ohio, 1929). Many industries, particularly among the railroad and motor industries, forbade their workers to drink, even before prohibition. A typical poster in a plant read: YOU CAN'T DRINK AND MAKE GOOD. In contrast, however, some mining companies kept towns like Butte, Montana, wide open throughout prohibition, in order to keep their workers penniless, and prevent their escape to better jobs in other towns.
45. N. Spangler, General Manager of the Jackson Iron and Steel Company, quoted by F. Tompkins in "Prohibition," *Annals of the American Academy*, September, 1923, p. 19.
46. See Note 41, *op. cit.* By the end of prohibition, as the *Wickersham Report* showed, scarcely a labor leader could be found to say a word in favor of the Eighteenth Amendment and the Volstead Act.
47. G. Seldes, *The Years of the Locust* (Boston, 1933), p. 214.

NOTES ON CHAPTER NINETEEN

1. J. Steuart, *Wayne Wheeler, Dry Boss* (New York, 1928), pp. 276-277.
2. Senator Blease scoffed at the Republican government's use of Civil Service rules. He instanced the Republican appointments of postmasters in South Carolina. According to him, the Republicans paid no more attention to the rules than "a blind mule would pay to a blind bridle."
3. Senator Edwards saw a hidden motive in the bill.

> The real purpose is to create some 10 or 12 new jobs for Wayne B. Wheeler, who is now engaged in rounding up dry delegates for Mr. Coolidge in the 1928 convention. Wheeler needs this additional patronage to strengthen his fast-weakening hold on "dry America." . . . There is a gentleman in the Prohibition Unit now, a Mr. Roy Haynes, a protégé of the old, discredited Daugherty crowd, who wants one of these jobs. He, too, has been active in the prohibition lobby which has infested the Capitol Building day after day.

In fact, Edwards, Wheeler, and Haynes all underestimated the resourcefulness of Andrew Mellon, who used the Reorganization Bill to exclude the influence of the Anti-Saloon League from the Prohibition Bureau.

4. *Cong. Record*, 69 Cong., 2 Sess., pp. 3676, 4527, 4984, 5297-5299, 5331-5343.
5. "The New Policy of the Anti-Saloon League," *Literary Digest*, January 7, 1928.
6. S. Lubell, *The Future of the American Politics* (London, 1952), p. 35.
7. Congressman Beck, of Pennsylvania, delivered this remark in the House debate on the report of the Wickersham Commission.
8. Carter Glass, of Virginia, first termed Cannon thus in the campaign of 1928.
9. *Cong. Record*, 70 Cong., 2 Sess., pp. 3638-3653.
10. *Cong. Record*, 70 Cong., 2 Sess., pp. 518, 716-725. In the debate, the dry Senator Caraway delivered another tart remark. The election of 1928 had proved to him that a majority of Americans supported prohibition, but whether for themselves or for their neighbors he could not say.

11. *Ibid.*, p. 5184.
12. There is an excellent description of Congress and prohibition at that time in H. Warren, *Herbert Hoover and the Great Depression* (New York, 1959), pp. 209-223.
13. *Cong. Record,* 71 Cong., 2 Sess., p. 1668.
14. *Hearings before a Subcommittee of the Senate Committee on the Judiciary,* 71 Cong., 2 Sess., p. 3889.
15. See H. Warren, *op. cit.*, pp. 126-127.

NOTES ON CHAPTER TWENTY

1. *The State Papers and Other Public Writings of Herbert Hoover* (W. Myers, ed., 2 vols., New York, 1934), I, p. 6.
2. ˉ Baltimore *Sun,* quoted *Periscope,* July, 1929.
3. W. Myers and W. Newton, *The Hoover Administration* (New York, 1936), p. 537.
4. *Ibid.*, p. 384.
5. *The State Papers and Other Public Writings of Herbert Hoover, op. cit.*, I, p. 5.
6. R. Wilbur and A. Hyde, *The Hoover Policies* (New York, 1937), p. 552.
7. F. Dobyns, *The Amazing Story of Repeal* (New York, 1940), p. 350. Pearson and Allen, and Alice Roosevelt Longworth confirm the wetness of Washington under the Hoover regime. Although Senator Howell, of Nebraska, introduced a bill to dry up the District of Columbia in the Seventy-first Congress, it somehow failed to pass the Senate, being talked out by Senator Ashurst, of Arizona. (*Cong. Record,* 71 Cong., 3 Sess., pp. 2966-2971, 3158-3160.)
8. *Wickersham Report,* Summary, p. 1.
9. *Ibid.*, pp. 83-84.
10. *Message to Congress,* January 20, 1931.
11. W. Lippmann, "The Great Wickersham Mystery," *Vanity Fair,* April, 1931. Hoover, in the retrospect of his *Memoirs* (3 vols., London, 1952), II, pp. 277-278, claims that his message to Congress was a reproduction of the views of the Wickersham Commission. He says that the commissioners were put in an impossible position by the open nullification of the dry law in America, and that this nullification accounted partly "for their indirect damnation of the law and, at the same time, their recommendation against repeal." He adds that he did not believe that a majority of Americans supported repeal until the winter of 1932.
12. For these comments, see *Periscope,* February, March, 1931.
13. *Cong. Record,* 71 Cong., 3 Sess., pp. 2888-2889, 2909-2913. The parody was written by H. I. Phillips.
14. New York *Times,* March 13, 1931.
15. *Wickersham Report,* Summary, pp. 79-80.

NOTES ON CHAPTER TWENTY-ONE

1. Address at the Annual Dinner of the Missouri Society, April 29, 1924.
2. A. Lowell, "Reconstruction and Prohibition," *Atlantic Monthly,* February, 1929.
3. C. Darrow and V. Yarros, *Prohibition Mania* (New York, 1927), p. 181.
4. W. Lippmann, "Our Predicament Under the Eighteenth Amendment," *Harper's,* December, 1926.
5. A. Hadley, "Law Making and Law Enforcement," *Harper's,* November, 1925.
6. *Vanity Fair,* May, 1930.
7. Quoted in C. Merz, *The Dry Decade* (New York, 1931), p. 292.
8. C. Darrow, quoted in H. Barnes, *Prohibition Versus Civilization* (New York, 1932), p. 119.

9. D. Heckman, *Prohibition Passes: The Story of the Association Against the Prohibition Amendment* (Ph.D., Ohio State Univ., 1939), p. 74, quotes this slogan of the A.A.P.A.
10. P. Jessup, *Elihu Root* (2 vols., New York, 1938), II, p. 476.
11. Quoted in M. Tillitt, *The Price of Prohibition* (New York, 1932), p. 149.
12. *Cong. Record,* 71 Cong., 3 Sess., p. 3693.
13. *Cong. Record,* 72 Cong., 1 Sess., p. 6002.
14. *Ibid.,* pp. 6000-6004.
15. C. Wood, *Herbert Clark Hoover — An American Tragedy* (New York, 1932), p. 315.
16. H. Mencken, *Making a President* (New York, 1932), p. 35. Mencken was as blind to the depression as the Republicans were. He thought their convention was the worst, the stupidest, and the most dishonest he had. ever seen. The only thing that gave it any intellectual dignity was "its frank recognition of the overmastering importance of prohibition as an issue. It has not wasted any time gabbling about the world courts, farmers' relief, and other such banshees, but has given over its whole time and thought to the one great question of questions." Mencken was always more concerned that everyone should have the right of getting drink than the right of getting jobs or food. The depression and repeal made him rapidly lose influence.
17. In his *Memoirs,* III, p. 319, Hoover claims that he approved of only the main idea of the Republican plank, that of resubmission to the states. The drys wrote the preamble and the wets wrote the conclusion. He was distressed by the straddle. If this is true, why did Hoover not denounce the plank as Al Smith denounced his party plank on prohibition in 1928?
18. Speech at Sea Girt, New Jersey, August 27, 1932.
19. Address at Oglethorpe University, May 22, 1932, from *The Public Papers and Addresses of Franklin D. Roosevelt* (S. Rosenman, ed., 13 vols., New York, 1938-1950), I, p. 646.
20. R. Moley, *After Seven Years* (New York, 1939).
21. F. Freidel, *Franklin D. Roosevelt: The Apprenticeship* (Boston, 1952), p. 23. Freidel's three volumes on Roosevelt are definitive and excellent.
22. *Ibid.,* p. 67.
23. S. Rosenman, *Working with Roosevelt* (London, 1952), p. 47.
24. F. Freidel, *Franklin D. Roosevelt: The Triumph* (Boston, 1956), p. 142, *note.*
25. S. Rosenman, *op. cit.,* p. 27.
26. "An Advocate of Christian Patriotism," *American Issue,* March, 1913.
27. Henry F. Pringle commented later on Roosevelt in the campaign of 1920 that he could not recall whether Roosevelt had said anything worth saying or whether anyone had listened. Roosevelt had seemed to be a pleasing personality, thirty-eight years old, of strong physique, without discernible enemies, and perfectly contented in his obscure role. (*The Nation,* April 27, 1932.)
28. F. Freidel, *Franklin D. Roosevelt: The Ordeal* (Boston, 1954), p. 103.
29. *Ibid.,* p. 161.
30. *Ibid.,* p. 162.
31. J. Burns, *Roosevelt: The Lion and the Fox* (New York, 1956), p. 98.
32. F. Freidel, *Franklin D. Roosevelt: The Ordeal, op. cit.,* p. 227.
33. *Ibid.,* p. 247.
34. *The Public Papers and Addresses of Franklin D. Roosevelt, op. cit.,* I, pp. 51-53.
35. *Ibid.,* p. 71.
36. *Ibid.,* pp. 367-376. Also F. Freidel, *Franklin D. Roosevelt: The Triumph, op. cit.,* pp. 74-75.
37. Letter to Professor James C. Bonbright, *The Roosevelt Letters* (E. Roosevelt, ed., 3 vols., London, 1952), III, pp. 52-53.
38. *The Public Papers and Addresses of Franklin D. Roosevelt,* I, pp. 320-321.

39. New York *Times*, September 11, 1930. See also F. Freidel, *Franklin D. Roosevelt: The Triumph, op. cit.*, pp. 141-146.
40. H. Gosnell, *Champion Campaigner: Franklin D. Roosevelt* (New York, 1952), p. 98.
41. F. Freidel, *Franklin D. Roosevelt: The Triumph, op. cit.*, p. 161.
42. D. Wecter, *The Age of the Great Depression, 1929-1941* (New York, 1948), p. 71.
43. *The Roosevelt Letters, op. cit.*, III, pp. 75-76.
44. E. Warner, *The Happy Warrior* (with H. Daniel, New York, 1956), pp. 257-258.
45. James Farley, in *Jim Farley's Story* (New York, 1948), p. 18, says that "Cordell Hull, *against our advice*, spoke for the milder proposal." (*my italics*)
46. *The Memoirs of Cordell Hull* (2 vols., London, 1948) I, p. 152.
47. H. Mencken, *Making a President, op. cit.*, p. 163.
48. F. Perkins, *The Roosevelt I Knew* (New York, 1946), pp. 125-126.
49. H. Mencken, *Making a President, op. cit.*, p. 65.
50. W. Lippmann, *Interpretations, 1931-1932* (New York, 1932), pp. 284-298.
51. *The Autobiography of Will Rogers* (Boston, 1949), p. 288.
52. New York *Times*, September 22, 1932.
53. *Christian Century*, September 21, 1932.
54. R. Miller, *American Protestantism and Social Issues, 1919-1939* (Univ. of N.C., 1958), p. 120.
55. See *The State Papers and Other Public Writings of Herbert Hoover* (W. Myers, ed., 2 vols., New York, 1934), II, pp. 261-263; and *The Hoover Policies* (New York, 1937), pp. 555-556.
56. *The Literary Digest Political Cyclopedia* (E. Thwing, ed., New York, 1932), p. 267.
57. *Ibid.*, p. 278.
58. Speech at Sea Girt, New Jersey, August 27, 1932.
59. New York *Times*, September 28, 1932.
60. *Ibid.*, November 4, 1932.
61. *Reed Committee*, I, p. 826.
62. New York *Times*, June 16, 1932.
63. H. Warren, *Herbert Hoover and the Great Depression* (New York, 1959), pp. 298-299. The contradictions and inadequacy of Hoover's philosophy are beautifully expressed in his *American Individualism* (New York, 1932), and in his Address at King's Mountain, on October 7, 1930 (*The State Papers of Herbert Hoover, op. cit.*, I, p. 395-401). Perhaps R. Moley's judgment of Hoover gives the best sentence on his achievement: "Hoover, *in the abundant resources of his own conscience*, can know that he will live as the greatest Republican of his own generation." (*my italics*)
64. From *Liberty*, January 21, 1933.
65. *Cong. Record*, 72 Cong., 2 Sess., pp. 4005, 4142-4177, 4220-4231. The full wording of the Twenty-first Amendment reads:

    SECTION 1. The eighteenth article of amendment to the Constitution of the United States is hereby repealed.
    SECTION 2. The transportation or importation into any State, Territory, or possession of the United States for delivery or use therein of intoxicating liquors, in violation of the laws thereof, is hereby prohibited.
    SECTION 3. This article shall be inoperative unless it shall have been ratified as an amendment to the Constitution by conventions in the several States, as provided in the Constitution, within seven years from the date of the submission hereof to the States by the Congress.

66. *Ibid.*, pp. 4514-4517.

67. V. Dabney, *Dry Messiah: The Life of Bishop Cannon* (New York, 1949), p. 316.
68. *Ibid.*, p. 317.
69. National Reform League (1930), Pamphlet, Widener Library, Harvard.
70. *Statement of Pierre S. du Pont at the Annual Dinner of the Association Against the Prohibition Amendment*, December 6, 1932.
71. Jouett Shouse, in the *Annual Report of the Association Against the Prohibition Amendment, 1933.*
72. Mrs. Sabin's endorsement of Franklin D. Roosevelt for his unequivocal stand on prohibition led to bitter recriminations within her Women's Organization, to the resignation of 150 old members and to the accession of 137,000 new members. Mrs. Douglas Robinson put the point of view of the objectors succinctly in the New York *Herald Tribune*, July 17, 1932. She said that Mrs. Sabin and her supporters had laid themselves "open to the criticism, long pre-empted by the drys, of being fanatical." She also felt that these women had repudiated the spirit of their own slogan, "Patriotism before Party," by adding another clause, "Repeal before Patriotism." To Republicans such as Mrs. Robinson, Herbert Hoover was the only man capable of curing the economic ills of America. The answer of those wet Republicans who backed Roosevelt's stand on prohibition was put by the Republican Congresswoman from California, Mrs. Florence Kahn. "Public questions of great moment, on which the stability of our Government depends, are pressing for solution. But around them all we find contained the long tentacles of this octupus — Prohibition." According to Mrs. Kahn, repeal was the first and necessary step in ending the depression.
73. *National Advocate*, December, 1932.
74. *Ibid.*, January, 1933.
75. *Ibid.*, January, 1933.
76. *Ibid.*, February, 1934.
77. *The Autobiography of Will Rogers, op. cit.*, p. 255.
78. From the letter of a North Dakota farmer to the Hearst Temperance Contest Committee in *Temperance — or Prohibition* (New York, 1929), p. 176. E. Kirkpatrick and E. Tough, in their judicious article, "Prohibition and Agriculture," *Annals of the American Academy*, September, 1933, pp. 113-119, warned that repeal of the Eighteenth Amendment "would have little noticeable effect on the amounts or prices of crops produced." But their warning was too late. It would, doubtless, have been ignored by farmers, who believed the insistent propaganda of the wets.
79. Statement of Pierce Blewett, quoted D. Heckman, *op. cit.*, p. 191.
80. See 274 U.S. 259 (1926). See also H. Johnston, *What Rights Are Left?* (New York, 1930), pp. 84-90.
81. *Cong. Record*, 65 Cong., 2 Sess., p. 443.
82. *Cong. Record*, 72 Cong., 1 Sess., p. 6000.
83. *Wickersham Report*, I, p. 311, 325.
84. *Report of the Association Against the Prohibition Amendment, 1933.*
85. Quoted in G. Ostander, *The Prohibition Movement in California, 1848-1933.*
86. P. Odegard, *The American Mind* (Columbia, 1930), p. 180.
87. Quoted A. Lee, "The New Prohibition Drive," in R. McCarthy, ed., *Drinking and Intoxication* (New Haven, Conn., 1959), p. 418.
88. D. Heckman, *op. cit.*, p. 381.
89. New York *Times*, December 15, 1932.
90. L. Harrison and E. Laine, *After Repeal: A Study of Liquor Control Administration* (New York, 1936), p. 3.

NOTES ON CHAPTER TWENTY-TWO

1. See J. Gusfield, "Social Structure and Moral Reform: A Study of the

Woman's Christian Temperance Union," *American Journal of Sociology,* November, 1955.

2. J. Cox, *Journey Through My Years* (New York, 1946), p. 179.
3. A. Smith, *Up To Now* (New York, 1929), p. 286.
4. Quoted in V. Dabney *Dry Messiah: The Life of Bishop Cannon* (New York, 1949), p. 326.
5. *Wickersham Report,* III, p. 156.
6. V. Dabney, *op. cit.,* p. 318.
7. *Christian Century,* December 15, 1931.
8. F. Allen, *Only Yesterday* (New York, 1931), p. 338.
9. R. and H. Lynd, *Middletown in Transition* (New York, 1937), pp. 172, 272. The Lynds unaccountably omitted a study of prohibition from their *Middletown.*

    The most rapid increase in the divorce rate in American history up to that time took place during national prohibition. For every hundred marriages performed, the following was the divorce rate:

1887	5.5	1916	10.6
1896	6.8	1922	13.1
1906	8.2	1931	17.3

10. S. Freud, *Civilization and Its Discontents* (New York, 1930), p. 141.
11. *Ibid.,* p. 135.
12. *Rudyard Kipling's Verse* (incl. ed., New York, 1924), p. 211.
13. F. Dunne, *Dissertations by Mr. Dooley* (New York, 1906), p. 271.
14. A. Roe, "A Survey of Alcohol Education in the United States," *Quarterly Journal of Alcohol Studies,* March, 1943.
15. R. Tompkins, "Fifty Years in the Teaching of Physiology and Hygiene in the Elementary Schools" (Master's Thesis, Temple Univ., 1935), quoted in A. Roe, *op. cit.*
16. When M. Grant's *The Passing of the Great Race* (New York, 1916) was published, even the *Annals of the American Academy* endorsed its racist assumptions with few reservations, saying that "the volume should be studied by all who are interested in the future of our own country and in democracy at large." The *Atheneum's* verdict was mystified and wrong:

    > We had thought that this species of race ecstacy, this enthusiasm for laying stress on the racial basis of European history, with which the name of Houston Stewart Chamberlain is associated, was going out of fashion, even in Germany. But that a writer in democratic America should give currency to these doctrines is passing strange.

    The book sold widely and was taken very seriously in America, even in academic circles. Ellsworth Huntington, in the *Yale Review* of April, 1917, wrote:

    > The whole lesson of biology is that America is seriously endangering her future by making fetishes of equality, democracy, and universal education. They are of great value, but only when they have good hereditary material upon which to work. The books of Morgan, Conklin, and Grant all show that we must drastically revise our immigration policy and must strive even more diligently to perpetuate the rapidly diminishing type of strong-willed idealists who have been the country's chief leaders.

    The quotation comes from L. Stoddard, *Re-forging America* (New York, 1927), p. 156. Stoddard's books, *The Rising Tide of Color Against White World-Supremacy* (New York, 1920) and *The Revolt Against Civilization: the Menace of the Underman* (New York, 1922), sold even more widely than Grant's, although some reviewers took them to pieces. Franz Boas called the first "vicious propaganda" and the *Nation* and *Atheneum* called the second a "farrago of scientific half-truths and journalistic nightmare," and made the sad comment that "it is a symptom of the times that Mr. Stoddard is taken seriously." It was, indeed.

17. *Scientific Temperance Journal,* Winter, 1939-1940.
18. *National Advocate,* January, 1927.
19. T. Parran, *Shadow on the Land: Syphilis* (New York, 1937).
20. E. Bok, "The 'Patent Medicine' Curse" and "A Few Words to the W.C.T.U.," *Ladies Home Journal,* May, September, 1904.
21. Mrs. Robert Bradford, quoted in M. Bruere, *Does Prohibition Work?* (New York, 1927), p. 237.
22. E. Boole, *Give Prohibition Its Chance* (New York, 1929), p. 120.
23. *Journal of the American Medical Association,* June 3, 1922.
24. New York *Times,* July 4, 1920.
25. C. Stout, *The Eighteenth Amendment and the Part Played by Organized Medicine* (New York, 1921), p. 48.
26. *U.S. Statutes,* Vol. 42, Pt. I, pp. 222-224.
27. *Statistics Concerning Intoxicating Liquors, 1933, op. cit.,* p. 10.
28. See H. Cabot, *The Doctor's Bill* (New York, 1935) and H. Moore, "Health and Medical Practice," *Recent Social Trends in the United States* (New York, 1934), pp. 1061-1113, for the changes in medical practice between 1890 and 1930.
29. E. Masters, *Spoon River Anthology* (new ed., New York, 1917), p. 49.

NOTES ON EPILOGUE

1. C. Wilson and D. Pickett, *The Case For Prohibition* (New York, 1923), p. 258.
2. *Cong. Record,* 70 Cong., 2 Sess., p. 3731.

Index

Prohibition Bureau (*Cont.*)
357; transferred to Justice Department, 358
Prohibition enforcement: in the states, 192-197; weak links in chain of, 209-211. *See also* Prohibition Bureau
Prohibition Inside Out, 258
Prohibition laws, pre-Civil War, 4
Prohibition party, founding of, 30, 46, 83; candidates in presidential election, 84; influence upon elections of 1884 and 1888, 84; and the Anti-Saloon League, 85-87; decline of, 87; endorses female suffrage, 93, 94; economics of, 101-103, 249-251
Prohibition Reorganization Act, 358
Prohibitionists: techniques and methods of, 39-42; scare tactics of, 45, 46-50, 51; caricatured, 401-402
Propaganda, 106, 127-128; prohibitionist, 106-111, 113-114; counter, of brewers and distillers, 111-112, 114-115, 120, 121; and authority taken out of context, 114; wet versus dry, 242-251; dry, failure of, 404-412. *See also* Press, popular
Proskauer, Judge Joseph H. 298
Prosperity, backwoods, 289
Prostitution, 78, 408
Protection money, 233
Publicity, unfavorable to motion-picture industry, 320
Pure Food and Drug Bill, 201
Purple Gang, 222

QUIN, REPRESENTATIVE PERCY E. (Miss.), 29

RACKETS, 225-229, 415. *See also* Gangsters
Radicalism in early West, 14
Radio, 324
Raft, George, 322-323
Raids on speak-easies, 232
Randall, Representative Charles H. (Calif.), 118
Rappe, Virginia, 320
Raskob, John J., 338, 380, 383, 384, 385
Rauschenbusch, Walter, 105
Ray, Felix, 304
Reader's Digest, 406

Recent Economic Changes, 250
Red Scare of 1919, 126-127, 174
Reed, Senator James A. (Mo.): circulates recipes for pumpkin gin and applejack, 204; on brewing and winemaking as domestic arts, 207; appointed to Senate Committee on the Judiciary, 277; heads Senate investigatory subcommittee, 279; denounces League, 340; wins first major victory for wets in Congress, 350; heads wet faction in Congress, 350, 353-354
Reed Bone-dry Amendment, 148, 156
Reed Committee, 224, 279-284, 338
Reform: trinity of, 91-92; crusades, 180-182
Reform League. *See* National Civil Service Reform League
Religion: in the early West, 13; fundamentalist, in the South, 31-32; makes prohibitionist stand seemingly untenable, 69-70; as campaign issue (1928), 299, 301-304
Remus, George, 185n.; 410
Remus mob, 222
Reno, Nev., red-light district in, 408n.
Repeal: as smart social movement, 343; demanded by state platforms (1930), 358; becomes political issue, 358-359; increasing support for, 369-372; resolution introduced in House, 372-373; as election issue, 386-389; amendment, 389-392; wet falsehoods exposed by, 394-395, 398; consequences of, 398; cost of, 398; psychological appeal of movement for 402
Republican convention of 1932, 374-375
Republican party, platform of 1888, 84
Review of Reviews, 309
Revolution: agrarian, 10-11; American, 10, 37
Rhode Island, 18th Amendment challenged by, 143
Ritchie, Governor Albert C. (Md.), 196, 385, 387
Roads, American, 316-317
Robbins, Representative Edward E. (Pa.), 161
Robbins, Raymond, 138
Roberts, Justice Owen J., 145

About the author

Andrew Sinclair is one of the most brilliant graduates of Eton and Cambridge University in recent years. He began his study of prohibition under Denis Brogan at Cambridge, then continued his research and writing in the United States with the historians Oscar Handlin, of Harvard, and Richard Hofstadter, of Columbia. During the two years he spent in this country he traveled extensively, interviewing and gathering material.

Mr. Sinclair, who is also a novelist, is married and lives in Soho Square, London. He is at present a Research Fellow of Churchill College, Cambridge.

HARPER COLOPHON BOOKS